THE PARIS REVIEW
ANTHOLOGY

THE PARIS REVIEW
ANTHOLOGY

Edited by GEORGE PLIMPTON

W · W · NORTON & COMPANY · NEW YORK · LONDON

The text of this book is composed in Avanta, with
display type set in Bernhard Modern Roman.
Composition and Manufacturing by The Haddon Craftsmen Inc.
Book design by Antonina Krass.

First Edition

Library of Congress Cataloging-in-Publication Data
The Paris Review Anthology / edited by George Plimpton.
p.   cm.
1. Literature, Modern—20th century.   2. Literature, Modern—20th
century—History and criticism.   3. Paris Review.   I. Plimpton,
George.   II. Paris Review.
PN6014.P23   1990
808.8′004—dc20   89-35274

ISBN 0-393-02769-4

W. W. Norton & Company, Inc., 500 Fifth Avenue, New York, N. Y. 10110
W. W. Norton & Company Ltd., 37 Great Russell Street, London WC1B 3NU
1 2 3 4 5 6 7 8 9 0

For Peter Matthiessen, Harold L. Humes, William Pène du Bois, Thomas H. Guinzburg, Donald Hall, and John Train, who started the enterprise, and for the long list of dedicated editors who succeeded them.

The editor also wishes to thank a number of the *Paris Review* editors for their assistance in putting together this anthology: these include Antonio Weiss, Beth Drenning, Elizabeth Gaffney, Elizabeth Seay, James Windolf, Susannah Hunnewell, and Wahn Yoon; also from W. W. Norton, Ed Barber and Juli Goldfein.

CONTENTS

8   *Contents*

NONFICTION

PART TWO: 1960–1966

FICTION

POETRY

NONFICTION

PART THREE: 1967–1973

FICTION

POETRY

Nonfiction

PART FOUR: 1974–1980

Fiction

POETRY

NONFICTION

PART FIVE: 1981–1987

FICTION

Poetry

NONFICTION

ART

INTRODUCTION

To select an anthology's worth from a literary magazine in operation since 1953 is not a comfortable task. Over four hundred fiction entries and a thousand-odd poems have appeared in the pages of the *Paris Review* over the years, so that representation on merit alone—at least in this editor's opinion—would result in an anthology weighing in the neighborhood of fifty pounds!

A number of determinations seemed called for. The poetry editors (who had full powers in their department) were asked to pick, within limits, what they felt was most representative of their respective tenures. As for fiction, the choices focused on shorter works to allow more variety and a greater number of selections. Omitted were a number of stories and poems which have been widely published in other anthologies and collections. Excerpts from novels subsequently published were passed up unless from the earliest stages of a work-in-progress.

The anthology is divided into five sections, each representing seven years of the magazine's history. The number is quite arbitrary, vaguely linked to the fact that there have been five poetry editors, each on the job until the familiar seven-year itch got to them and they moved on to something else. These editors, Donald Hall, X. J. Kennedy, Tom Clark, Michael Benedikt, and Jonathan Galassi, have contributed introductions to each respective poetry section with a few words about their choices. To lead off each section of the anthology, the undersigned has written some words to describe the progress of the magazine through the years.

To begin with, the *Paris Review* was founded in Paris in 1953 by Peter Matthiessen (subsequently the author of *At Play in the Fields of the Lord* and *The Snow Leopard,* among many other books) and Harold L. Humes *(The Underground City; Men Die).* Studying at Cambridge at the time, I was asked if I would become the editor-in-chief. Other pivotal editors in its earliest days were John Train, the managing editor, William Pène du Bois, the art editor, and Tom Guinzburg, later publisher of the Viking Press, who oversaw operations in New York City.

Paris in the fifties was a provident place to start a magazine. The city was inexpensive. For a dollar, if one looked, a dinner could be had of *bifteck, pommes frites,* and a glass or two of wine. A room in a pension on the Left Bank, with a big armoire in which to store one's belongings, could be rented for fifteen dollars a month. As a consequence, along with the lure of the city itself, a relatively large corps of writers and artists from abroad were on hand. With expenses so low and with such a flux of aspiring writers and artists it was not surprising that a number of literary magazines sprung up. Chief among these were Sindbad Vail's *Points* ("A Magazine for the Young Writer") and *Merlin,* whose editors included Alex Trocchi, Austryn Wainhouse, Patrick Bowles, Richard Seaver, and Christopher Logue. They met in the back of a garage where the magazine had its "offices." The contents of *Merlin* were much closer to the *engagé* French counterparts such as *Les Temps Modernes*—an amalgam of existentialism, avant-garde, and politically and socially oriented essays and fiction. It published (very much like its literary forebears of the Twenties) pungent and all-encompassing manifestoes: "*Merlin* will hit at all clots of rigid categories in criticism and life, and all that is unintelligibly partisan." Sindbad Vail, on the other hand, was more interested in what his magazine pronounced on its cover—a magazine for young writers. He looked askance at the work of anyone over twenty-five. He came from an appropriate enough literary background: his father, Laurence Vail, had been one of the sixteen to sign the surrealist proclamation which appeared in *transition* and ended with the famous line, "the plain reader be damned."

It seemed essential to start off a magazine—especially in Paris—with pronouncements and aims of this sort. The manifesto of another literary magazine I happened upon—*The Phoenix* (Henry Miller was the European editor)—proclaimed that "as soon as *The Phoenix* has brought together a group of us—no matter how small—we shall go off to Mexico or South America and take up the life-mode which the Aztecs and Incas let fall."

Nothing of this sort crossed the minds of the editors of the *Paris Review* as they sat in the cafés and decided what direction their magazine would take. Their eventual course was disarmingly simple: the main idea was to devote the magazine largely to creative work and put the critical material (which tended to be the main fare in the literary magazines of the time) in the back of the book. If any concessions to critical evaluations were to be made, the editors, rather than relying on a third party for an essay or critique, would go to the authors themselves (when possible) to try to get *them* to talk about their work. This led to a regular feature in the magazine: its interviews with famous authors on their craft.

It was determined that the magazine would never cultivate any "isms." In the twenties, Margaret Anderson, the editor of the *Little Magazine,* counted up the number of "isms" that her magazine had supported and it came to twenty-three. Obviously a number of "schools" would appear in the *Paris Review* over the years, but none of these would be supported editorially as a matter of magazine policy.

As for the subscribers' opinions, these were never a matter of concern. The editors adhered to the distinguished if somewhat time-worn dictate (which was also Margaret Anderson's) that the *Paris Review* would make no compromise with public taste.

The editors also decided to emphasize the appearance of the magazine with colorful covers and art portfolios within. The stories in early issues were illustrated (in 1954 Andy Warhol did a drawing of the front of a truck for a Mac Hyman story entitled *The Hundredth Centennial*) in an attempt to brighten up the pages and make the *Review* look less like a law school journal.

In Paris at the time, William Styron *(Lie Down in Darkness, The Confessions of Nat Turner, Sophie's Choice)* set down these principles in a preface which was to introduce the first issue. John Train, the managing editor, who was a comparative literature major at college, felt that Styron had relegated the essay and criticism to an excessively low status. He wrote Styron a letter about this, which explains why the *Paris Review* preface appears as Styron's reply in the form of a "Letter to an Editor."

The printing of the magazine in its earliest numbers was done in a gloomy plant on the Rue Sablière. A single light bulb hung over an ancient flatbed printing press that looked like a steam locomotive lying on its side. Proofreading the big sheets that exuded from between the roller-wheels of this vast Brobdingnagian structure was never easy in the dim light of the composing room, and no one seemed good at it anyway. An advertisement for the Alliance Française announced that it was the "oldest and last expensive" language school in Paris, which of course—as was pointed out by the horrified advertisers—was supposed to read "the *least* expensive . . ."

The first issue of the *Paris Review* featured only three poets—Donald Hall, the first poetry editor, Robert Bly, and George Steiner, the well-known critic who in those days signed his work with the initial F. before the George. Peter Matthiessen, the fiction editor in the first years of the

Review, selected four stories: by Terry Southern, Eugene Walter, Anton Blondin, a young French writer, and one of his own. The nonfiction included a gloomy piece by Henri de Montherlant on the paupers' common grave in the Pantin cemetery outside Paris, translated by Matthiessen (whose wife translated the Blondin story), who used a pseudonym in his contributor's notes so it wouldn't appear as though the magazine was a one-man (and wife) effort. The other major piece of nonfiction was an interview with E. M. Forster on the craft of writing. There were a number of illustrations, including a full-page view looking down on the bones of the common grave.

The cover design by comparison was cheerful and proclamatory. A trumpeter astride a winged horse, it was drawn by William Pène du Bois from "La Renommée" by Coysevox in the Tuileries Gardens. The names of the contributors ran down the left-hand side of the cover. The price in francs, dollars, and shillings was shown across the base: the cost of the *Paris Review* in 1953 was seventy-five cents.

In the upper left-hand corner of the cover perched the *Paris Review* "bird." Also designed by William Pène du Bois, it was an American eagle shown carrying a pen and, for the French connection, wearing a Phrygian hat, the *bonnet rouge* worn by the French revolutionists of the 18th century. The bird stayed up in its corner for seven years until the artist Larry Rivers utilized the entire cover space for his design of a winged helmet; the bird, to the regret of some, vanished, never to appear again, at least on the magazine's cover. It did put in an appearance at the New York World's Fair (1964–65) on a pair of metal pennants that hung from the crosstrees of the center pole of the *Paris Review* booth ("The Smallest Pavilion at the Fair") until the flags blew down in a summer storm.

Starting with its first issue, the *Paris Review* has hoped over the years to introduce readers to writers of promise. Literary magazines tend to take an obsessive pride in authors it "discovers," whose first work appears in its pages. The *Paris Review* has been no exception. Its editors drop names: Philip Roth, Evan S. Connell, Mary Lee Settle, Mona Simpson, T. Coraghessan Boyle, Joy Williams, Edward Hoagland, Robert Shacochis, Alan Gurganus, Jay McInerney, Charlie Smith, Rick Bass, the first translations of Italo Calvino, Samuel Beckett's French novels, a host of poets . . . Perhaps in deference to Philip Roth's comment that he was "discovered" by an obstetrician in Hoboken, New Jersey, it would be best to say that the "earliest" efforts of a large number of poets and writers have appeared in the pages of the *Review*.

There have been lapses. We had a chance to publish Edward Albee's early playlet *The Sandbox*. My suggestion that the character of the grandmother might be toned down a bit so miffed the author that he had it withdrawn. He said about the play later (indeed, in a *Paris Review* interview): "I'm terribly fond of *The Sandbox.* I think it's an absolutely beautiful, lovely, perfect play!"

Cynthia Ozick sent in a number of stories which were returned. Certainly a mistake by one of the editors was sending back the Pension Grillparzer section from *The World According to Garp,* an almost perfect story, on the grounds that it was too "derivative of Thomas Pynchon." A copy of the editor's rejection letter was posted for awhile in the *Review* office as a caveat to manuscript readers. Heaven knows how many other submissions were missed! While I was interviewing the Pulitzer–prize winning author of *Ironweed,* William Kennedy, for the craft of writing series, he told me that *he* had received a number of rejection slips from the *Paris Review.*

Nonetheless, enough important work has been accepted to provide an anthology of consequence. The proof follows. It would seem appropriate enough to start things off with William Styron's "Letter to an Editor" which set forth our aims so many springs ago.

—G.P.

Part One

1953–1959

Letter to an Editor

Dear—:

The preface which you all wanted me to write, and which I wanted to write, and finally wrote, came back to me from Paris today so marvelously changed and re-worded that it seemed hardly mine. Actually, you know, it shouldn't be mine. Prefaces are usually communal enterprises and they have a stern dull quality of group effort about them—of Manifesto, Proclamation of Aims, of "Where We Stand"—of editors huddled together in the smoke-laden, red-eyed hours of early morning, pruning and balancing syntax, juggling terms and, because each editor is an individual with different ideas, often compromising away all those careless personal words that make an individualistic statement exciting, or at least interesting. Prefaces, I'll admit, are a bore and consequently, more often than not, go unread. The one I sent you, so balanced and well-mannered and so dull—I could hardly read it myself when I finished it—when it came back to me with your emendations and corrections I couldn't read it at all. This, I realize, is the fault of neither or none of us; it's inevitable that what Truth I mumble to you at Lipp's over a beer, or that Ideal we are perfectly agreed upon at the casual hour of 2 A.M. becomes powerfully open to criticism as soon as it's cast in a printed form which, like a piece of sculpture, allows us to walk all around that Truth or Ideal and examine it front, side, and behind, and for minutes on end. Everyone starts hacking off an arm, a leg, an ear—and you end up with a lump. At any rate, I'd like to go over briefly a few of the things you questioned; we'll still no doubt disagree, but that's probably for the better. There are magazines, you know, where a questioning word amounts to dishonesty, and disagreement means defection.

First, I said, "Literarily speaking, we live in what has been described as the Age of Criticism. Full of articles on Kafka and James, on Melville, or whatever writer is in momentary ascendancy; laden with terms like

"architectonic," "Zeitgeist," and "dichotomous," the literary magazines seem today on the verge of doing away with literature, not with any
philistine bludgeon but by smothering it under the weight of learned
chatter." (Perfect beginning for a preface, you may note; regard the arch
rhythms, the way it fairly looks down the nose at the reader.)

All right, then I said, "There is little wonder" (always a nice oblique
phrase to use in a preface) "that, faced with Oedipus and Myth in
Charlotte Brontë, with meter in Pope and darkness in Dante, we put
aside our current quarterly with its two short poems, its one intellectual-
ized short story, in deference to *Life*, which brings us at least "The Old
Man and the Sea." This, of course, as you remember, was only by way of
getting to the first brave part of the Manifesto: that the *Paris Review*
would strive to give predominant space to the fiction and poetry of both
established and new writers, rather than to people who use words like
Zeitgeist. Now in rebuttal, one of you has written that it is not always
editorial policy that brings such a disproportion of critical manuscripts
across the editors' desks, pointing out that "in our schools and colleges
all the emphasis is on analysis and organization of ideas, not creation."
The result is that we have critics, not creators, and you go on to suggest
that, since this is the natural state of things, we should not be too
haughty in stating our intention of having more fiction and poetry in the
Paris Review.

To this I can only say: *d'accord*. Let's by all means leave out the lordly
tone and merely say: dear reader, the *Paris Review hopes* to emphasize
creative work—fiction and poetry—not to the exclusion of criticism, but
with the aim in mind of merely removing criticism from the dominating
place it holds in most literary magazines and putting it pretty much
where it belongs, i.e., somewhere near the back of the book. O.K? But as
for *Zeitgeist*, which you accuse me of denouncing unnecessarily, I still
don't like it, perhaps because, complying with the traditional explanation of intolerance, I am ignorant of what it means. I hope one of you
will help me out.

Among the other points I tried to make was one which involved the
Paris Review having no axe to grind. In this we're pretty much in agree-
ment, I believe, although one of you mentioned the fact that in the first
number of *The Exile* there were "powerful blasts" by Pound, among
others, which added considerably to the interest of the magazine. True,
perhaps. But is it because we're sissies that we plan to beat no drum for
anything; is it only because we're wan imitations of our predecessors—
those who came out bravely for anything they felt deeply enough was
worth coming out bravely for? I don't think so. I think that if we have no
axes to grind, no drums to beat, it's because it seems to us—for the

moment, at least—that the axes have all been ground, the drumheads burst with beating. This attitude does not necessarily make us—as some of the Older Boys have called us—the Silent Generation (the fact of the *Paris Review* belies that), or the Scared Generation, either, content to lie around in one palsied, unprotesting mass. It's not so much a matter of protest now, but of waiting; perhaps, if we have to be categorized at all, we might be called the Waiting Generation—people who feel and write and observe, and wait and wait and wait. And go on writing. I think the *Paris Review* should welcome these people into its pages—the good writers and good poets, the non-drumbeaters and non-axe-grinders. So long as they're good.

Finally, and along these lines, I was taken pretty much to task by one of you for making the perhaps too general statement that there are signs in the air that this generation can and will produce literature equal to that of any in the past. Well, I suppose that is another ringing Assertion, but it's a writer's statement, almost necessarily, and not a critic's. A critic nowadays will set up straw-men, saying that Mailer had Ahab in mind when he created Sergeant Croft, that Jim Jones thought of Hamlet when he came up with his bedevilled Private Prewitt, stating further, however, that neither of these young men have created figures worthy of Melville or Shakespeare; they do this, or they leap to the opposite pole and cry out that no one writing today even *tries* to create figures of the tragic stature of Lear. For a writer, God forbid either course. I still maintain that the times get precisely the literature that they deserve, and that if the writing of this period is gloomy the gloom is not so much inherent in the literature as in the times. The writer's duty is to keep on writing, creating memorable Pvt. Prewitts and Sgt. Crofts, and to hell with Ahab. Perhaps the critics are right: this generation may not produce literature equal to that of any past generation—who cares? The writer will be dead before anyone can judge him—but he *must* go on writing, reflecting disorder, defeat, despair, should that be all he sees at the moment, but ever searching for the elusive love, joy, and hope— qualities which, as in the act of life itself, are best when they have to be struggled for, and are not commonly come by with much ease, either by a critic's formula or by a critic's yearning. If he does not think one way or another, that he can create literature worthy of himself and of his place, at this particular moment in history, in his society, then he'd better pawn his Underwood, or become a critic.

Ever faithfully yours,

—BILL STYRON

FICTION

SAMUEL BECKETT

Extract from Molloy: Stones

There are people the sea doesn't suit, they prefer the mountains or the plain. Personally, I feel no worse there than anywhere else. Much of my life has ebbed away before this shivering expanse, to the sound of waves in storm and calm, and the claws of the surf. Before, no, more than before, one with, spread on the sand, or in a cave. In the sand I was in my element, letting it trickle between my fingers, scooping holes that a moment later filled in or that filled themselves in, casting it in the air by handfuls, rolling in it. And in the cave, lit by the beacons at night, I knew what to do to be no worse than anywhere else. And that my land went no further, in one direction at least, did not displease me. And to feel there was one direction at least in which I could go no further, without first wetting myself, then drowning myself, was a blessing. For I have always said, First learn to walk, then you can take swimming lessons. But don't imagine my region ended at the coast, that would be a grave mistake. For it was this sea too, its reefs and distant islands, and its hidden depths. And I too once went forth on it, in a sort of oarless skiff, but I paddled with an old bit of driftwood. And I sometimes wonder if I ever came back, from that voyage. For I see myself putting to sea, and the long hours without landfall, I do not see the return, the tossing on the breakers, and I do not hear the frail keel grating on the shore. I took advantage of being at the seaside to lay in a store of sucking stones. Yes, on this occasion I laid in a considerable store. I distributed them equally among my four pockets and sucked them turn and turn about. This raised a problem which I first solved in the following way. I had say sixteen stones, four in each of my four pockets, these being the two pockets of my trousers and the two pockets of my greatcoat. Taking a stone from the right pocket of my greatcoat, and putting it in my mouth, I replaced it in the right pocket of my greatcoat by a stone from the right pocket of my trousers, which I replaced by a stone from the left pocket of my trousers, which I replaced by a stone from the left pocket of my greatcoat, which I replaced by the stone which was in my mouth, as soon as I had finished sucking it. In this way there were always four stones in each of my four pockets, but not quite the same stones. And when the desire to suck took hold of me again, I drew again on the right pocket of my greatcoat, certain of not taking the same stone as the last time. And while I sucked it I rearranged the other stones in the way I have just described. And so on. But this solution did not satisfy me fully. For it did not escape me that, by an extraordinary hazard, the four stones circulating thus might always be the same four. In which case, far from sucking the sixteen stones turn and turn about, I was really only sucking four, always the same, turn and turn about. But I shook them well in my pockets, before I began to suck, and again, while I sucked, before transferring them, in the hope of obtaining a more general circulation of the stones from pocket to pocket. But this was only a makeshift that could not content a man like me. So I began to look for something else. And the first thing I hit upon was that I might do better to transfer the stones four by four, instead of one by one, that is to say, during the sucking, to take the three stones remaining in the right pocket of my greatcoat and replace them by the four in the right pocket of my trousers, and these by the four in the left pocket of my trousers, and these by the four in the left pocket of my greatcoat, and finally these by the three from the right pocket of my greatcoat, plus the one, as soon as I had finished sucking it, which was in my mouth. Yes, it seemed to me at first that by so doing I would arrive at a better result. But on further reflection I had to change my mind, and confess that the circulation of the stones four by four came to exactly the same thing as their circulation one by one. For if I was certain of finding each time, in the right pocket of my greatcoat, four stones totally different from their immediate predecessors, the possibility nevertheless remained of my always chancing on the same stone, within each group of four, and consequently of my sucking, not the sixteen turn and turn about as I wished, but in fact four only, always the same, turn and turn about. So I had to seek elsewhere than in the mode of circulation. For no matter how I caused the stones to circulate, I always ran the same risk. It was obvious that by increasing the number of my pockets I was bound to increase my chances of enjoying my stones in the way I planned, that is to say one after the other until their number was exhausted. Had I had eight pockets, for example, instead of the four I did have, then even the most diabolical hazard could not have prevented me from sucking at least eight of my sixteen stones, turn and turn about. The fact of the matter is I should have needed sixteen pockets for all my anxiety to be dispelled. And for a long time I could see no other conclusion but this, that short of having sixteen pockets, each with its stone, I could never reach the goal I had set myself, short of an extraordinary hazard. And if at a pinch I could double the number of my pockets, were it only by dividing each pocket in two, with the help of a few safety-pins let us say, to quadruple them seemed to be more than I could manage. And I didn't feel inclined to take all that trouble for a half-measure. For I was beginning to lose all sense of measure, after all this wrestling and wrangling, and to say, It's either all or nothing. And if I was tempted for an instant to establish a more equitable proportion between my stones and my pockets, by reducing the former to the number of the latter, it was only for an instant. For it would have been an admission of defeat. And sitting on the shore, before the sea, the sixteen stones spread out before my eyes, I gazed at them in anger and perplexity. For just as I had difficulty in sitting on a chair, or in an armchair, because of my stiff leg you understand, so I had none in sitting on the ground, because of my stiff leg and my stiffening leg, for it was about this time that my good leg, good in the sense that it was not stiff, began to stiffen. It needed a prop under the ham you understand, and even under the whole length of the leg, the prop of the earth. And while I gazed thus at my stones, brooding on endless martingales all equally defective, and crushing handfuls of sand, so that the sand ran through my fingers, and fell back on the strand, yes, while I held thus in suspense my mind and a part of my body, one day suddenly it dawned on the former, dimly, that I might perhaps achieve my purpose without increasing the number of my pockets, or reducing the number of stones, but simply by sacrificing the principle of trim. The meaning of this illumination, which suddenly began to sing within me, like a verse of Isaiah, or of Jeremiah, I did not penetrate at once, and notably the word trim, which I had never met with, long remained obscure. Finally I seemed to grasp that this word trim could not mean anything else, anything better, than the distribution of the sixteen stones in four groups of four, one group in each pocket, and that it was my refusal to consider any distribution other than this that had vitiated my calculations until then and rendered the problem literally insoluble. And it was on the basis of this interpretation, whether right or wrong, that I finally reached a solution, inelegant assuredly, but sound, sound. Now I am willing to believe, indeed I firmly believe, that other solutions to this problem might have been found, and indeed may still be found, no less sound, but much more elegant, than the one I shall now describe, if I can. And I believe too that had I been a little more insistent, a little more resistent, I could have found them myself. But I was tired, tired and I contented myself ingloriously with the first solution that was a solution, to this problem. But not to go over the heartbreaking stages through which I passed before I came to it, here it is, in all its hideousness. It was merely (merely!) a matter of putting for example, to begin with, six stones in the right pocket of my greatcoat, or supply-pocket, five in the right pocket of my trousers, and five in the left pocket of my trousers, that makes the lot, twice five ten plus six, and none, for none remained, in the left pocket of my greatcoat, which for the time being remained empty, empty of stones that is, for its usual contents remained, as well as occasional objects. For where do you think I hid my vegetable knife, my silver, my horn and the other things, that I have not yet named, perhaps shall never name. Good. Now I can begin sucking. Watch me closely. I take a stone from the right pocket of my greatcoat, suck it, stop sucking it, put it in the left pocket of my greatcoat, the one empty (of stones). I take a second stone from the right pocket of my greatcoat, suck it, put it in the left pocket of my greatcoat. And so on until the right pocket of my greatcoat is empty (apart from its usual and occasional contents) and the six stones I have just sucked, one after the other, are all in the left pocket of my greatcoat. Pausing then, and concentrating, so as not to make a balls of it, I transfer to the right pocket of my greatcoat, in which there are no stones left, the five stones in the right pocket of my trousers, which I replace by the five stones in the left pocket of my trousers, which I replace by the six stones in the left pocket of my greatcoat. At this stage then the left pocket of my greatcoat is again empty of stones, while the right pocket of my greatcoat is again supplied, and in the right way, that is to say with other stones than those I have just sucked. These other stones I then begin to suck, one after the other, and to transfer as I go along to the left pocket of my greatcoat, being absolutely certain, as far as one can be in an affair of this kind, that I do not suck the same stones as a moment before, but others. And when the right pocket of my greatcoat is again empty (of stones), and the five I have just sucked are all in the left pocket of my greatcoat, then I proceed to the same redistribution as a moment before, or a

similar redistribution, that is to say I transfer to the right pocket of
my greatcoat, now again available, the five stones in the right pocket
of my trousers, which I replace by the six stones in the left
pocket of my trousers, which I replace by the five stones in the
left pocket of my greatcoat. And there I am ready to begin again. Do
I have to go on? No, for it is clear that after the next series, of sucks and
transfers, I shall be back where I started, that is to say with the first six
stones back in the supply pocket, the next five in the right pocket of my
stinking old trousers and finally the last five in left pocket of same, and
my sixteen stones will have been sucked once at least in impeccable
succession, not one sucked twice, not one left unsucked. It is true that
the next time I could scarcely hope to suck my stones in the same order
as the first time and that the first, seventh and twelfth for example of the
first cycle might very well be the sixth, eleventh and sixteenth respectively of the second, assuming the worst came to the worst. But that was
a drawback I could not avoid. And if in the cycles taken together utter
confusion was bound to reign, at least within each cycle taken separately
I could be easy in my mind, at least as easy as one can be, in a proceeding
of this kind. For each cycle to be identical, as to the succession of stones
in my mouth, and God knows I had set my heart on it, the only means
were numbered stones or sixteen pockets. And rather than make twelve
more pockets or number my stones, I preferred to make the best of the
comparative peace of mind I enjoyed within each cycle taken separately.
For it was not enough to number the stones, but I would have had to
remember, every time I put a stone in my mouth, the number I needed
and look for it in my pocket. Which would have spoilt the taste of stones
for me, in a very short time. For I would never have been sure of not
making a mistake, unless of course I had kept a kind of register, in which
to tick off the stones one by one, as I sucked them. And of this I believed
myself incapable. No, the only perfect solution would have been the
sixteen pockets, symmetrically disposed, each one with its stone. Then I
would have needed neither to number nor to think, but merely, as I
sucked a given stone, to move on the fifteen others, each to the next
pocket, a delicate business admittedly, but within my power, and to call
always on the same pocket when I felt like sucking. This would have
freed me from all anxiety, not only within each cycle taken separately,
but also for the sum of all cycles, though they went on forever. But
however imperfect my own solution was, I was pleased at having found it
all alone, yes, quite pleased. And if it was perhaps less sound than I had
thought in the first flush of discovery, its inelegance never diminished.
And it was above all inelegant in this, to my mind, that the uneven
distribution was painful to me, bodily. It is true that a kind of equilib-

rium was reached, at a given moment, in the early stages of each cycle, namely after the third suck and before the fourth, but it did not last long, and the rest of the time I felt the weight of the stones dragging me now to one side, now to the other. So it was something more than a principle I abandoned, when I abandoned the equal distribution, it was a bodily need. But to suck the stones in the way I have described, not haphazard, but with method, was also I think a bodily need. Here then were two incompatible bodily needs, at loggerheads. Such things happen. But deep down I didn't give a tinker's curse about being off balance, dragged to the right hand and the left, backwards and forwards. And deep down it was all the same to me whether I sucked a different stone each time or always the same stone, until the end of time. For they all tasted exactly the same. And if I had collected sixteen, it was not in order to ballast myself in such and such a way, or to suck them turn about, but simply to have a little store so as never to be without. But deep down I didn't give a fiddler's curse about being without, when they were all gone they would be all gone, I wouldn't be any the worse off, or hardly any. And the solution to which I rallied in the end was to throw them all away but one, which I kept now in one pocket, now in another, and which of course I soon lost, or threw away, or gave away, or swallowed. It was a wild part of the coast. I don't remember having been seriously molested. The black speck I was, in the great pale stretch of sand, who could wish it harm? Some came near, to see what it was, whether it wasn't something of value from a wreck, washed up by the storm. But when they saw the jetsam was alive, decently if wretchedly clothed, they turned away. Old women and young ones, yes, too, come to gather wood, came and stared, in the early days. But they were always the same and it was in vain I moved from one place to another, in the end they all knew what I was and kept their distance. I think one of them one day, detaching herself from her companions, came and offered me something to eat and that I looked at her in silence, until she went away. Yes, it seems to me some such incident occurred about this time. But perhaps I am thinking of another stay, at an earlier time, for this will be my last, my last but one, there is never a last, by the sea. However that may be I see a woman coming towards me and stopping from time to time to look back at her companions. Huddled together like sheep they watch her recede, urging her on, and laughing no doubt, I seem to hear laughter, far away. Then it is her back I see, as she goes back, now it is towards me she looks back, but without stopping. But perhaps I am merging two times in one, and two women, one coming towards me, shyly, urged on by the cries and laughter of her companions, and the other going away from me, un-hesitatingly. For those who came towards me I saw coming from afar, most of the time, that is one of the advantages of the seaside. Black specks in the distance I saw them coming, I could follow all their antics, saying, It's getting smaller, or, It's getting bigger and bigger. Yes, to be taken unawares was so to speak impossible, for I turned often towards the land too. Let me tell you something, my sight was better at the seaside! Yes, raking far and wide over these vast flats, where nothing lay, nothing stood, my good eye saw more clearly and there were even days when the bad one too had to look away. And not only did I see more clearly, but I had less difficulty in saddling with a name the rare things I saw. These are some of the advantages and disadvantages of the seaside. Or perhaps it was I who was changing, why not? And in the morning, in my cave, and even sometimes at night, when the storm rages, I felt reasonably immune from the elements and mankind. But there too there is a price to pay. In your box, in your caves, there too there is a price to pay. And which you pay willingly, for a time, but which you cannot go on paying forever. For you cannot go on buying the same thing forever, with your little pittance. And unfortunately there are other needs than that of rotting in peace, it's not the word, I mean of course my mother whose image, blunted for some time past, was beginning now to harrow me. So I went back inland, for my town was not strictly speaking on the sea, whatever may have been said to the contrary. And to get to it you had to go inland, I at least knew of no other road. For between my town and the sea there was a kind of swamp which, as far back as I can remember, and some of my memories have their roots deep in the immediate past, there was always talk of draining, by means of canals I suppose, or of transforming into a vast port and docks, or into a city on piles for the workers, in a word of redeeming somehow or other. And with the same stone they would have killed the scandal, at the gates of their metropolis, of a stinking steaming swamp in which an incalculable number of human lives were yearly engulfed, the statistics escape me for the moment and doubtless always will, so complete is my lack of interest in this aspect of the question. It is true they actually began work and that work is still going on in certain areas in the teeth of adversity, setbacks, epidemics and the apathy of the Public Works Department, far from me to deny it. But from this to proclaiming that the sea came lapping at the ramparts of my town, there was a far cry. And I for my part will never lend myself to such a perversion (of the truth), until such time as I am forced to or find it convenient. And I knew this swamp a little, having risked my life in it, cautiously, on several occasions, at a period of my life richer in illusions than the one I am trying to patch together here, I mean richer in certain illusions, in others poorer. So there was no way of coming at my town directly, by sea, but you had to disembark well to the north or the south and take to the highways, just imagine that, for they had never heard of Watt, just imagine that too. And now my progress, slow and painful at all times, was more so than ever, because of my short stiff leg, the same which I thought had long been as stiff as a leg could be, but damn the bit of it, for it was growing stiffer than ever, a thing I would not have thought possible, and at the same time shorter every day, but above all because of the other leg, supple hitherto and now growing rapidly stiff in its turn but not yet shortening, unhappily. For when the two legs shorten at the same time, and at the same speed, then all is not lost, no. But when one shortens, and the other not, then you begin to be worried. Oh not that I was exactly worried, but it was a nuisance, yes, a nuisance. For I didn't know which foot to land on, when I came down. Let us try and get this dilemma clear. Follow me carefully. The stiff leg hurt me, admittedly, I mean the old stiff leg, and it was the other which I normally used as a pivot, or prop. But now this latter, as a result of its stiffening I suppose, and the ensuing shock to nerves and sinews, was beginning to hurt me even more than the other. What a story, God send I don't make a balls of it. For the old pain, do you follow me, I had got used to it, in a way, yes, in a kind of way. Whereas to the new pain, though of the same family exactly, I had not yet had time to adjust myself. Nor should it be forgotten that having one bad leg plus another more or less good, I was able to nurse the former, and reduce its suffer-ings to the minimum, to the maximum by using the former exclusively, with the help of my crutches. But I no longer had this resource! For I no longer had one bad leg plus another more or less good, but now both were equally bad. And the worse, to my mind, was that which till now had been good, at least relatively good, and whose change for the worse I had not yet schooled myself to endure. So in a way, if you like, I still had one bad leg and one good, or rather less bad, with this difference how-ever, that the less bad now was the less good of heretofore. It was there-fore on the old bad leg that I often longed to lean, between one crutch-stroke and the next. For while still extremely sensitive, yet it was less so than the other, or it was equally so, if you like, but it did not seem so to me, because of its seniority. But I couldn't! What? Lean on it. For it was shortening, don't forget, whereas the other, though stiffening, was not yet shortening, or so far behind its fellow, that to all intents and pur-poses, intents and purposes I'm lost, who cares. If I could even have bent it, at the knee, or even at the hip, I could have made it seem as short as the other, long enough to land on the true short one, before taking off again. But I couldn't. What? Bend it. For how could I bend it, when it was stiff? I was therefore compelled to work the same old leg as hereto-fore, in spite of its having become, on the sensory level at least, the worse of the two and the more in need of nursing. Sometimes to be sure, when I was lucky enough to chance on a road conveniently cambered, or by taking advantage of a not too deep ditch or any other breach of surface, I managed to lengthen my short leg, for a short time. But it had done no work for so long that it did not know how to go about it. And I think a pile of dishes would have better supported me than it, which had so well supported me, when I was a tiny tot. And another factor of disequilibrium was here involved, I mean when I thus made the best of the lie of the land, I mean my crutches, which I would have needed one short and one long if I was to remain vertical. No? I don't know. In any case the ways I went were for the most part little forest paths, that's understandable, where differences of level, though abounding, were too confused and too erratic to be of any help to me. But did it make such a difference after all, as far as the pain was concerned, whether my leg was free to rest or whether it had to work? I think not. For the suffering of the leg at rest was constant and monotonous. Whereas the leg condemned to the increase of pain inflicted by work knew the decrease of pain bestowed by work suspended, the space of an instant. But I am human, I think, and my progress suffered, from this state of affairs, and from the slow and painful progress it had always been, whatever may have been said to the contrary, was changed, saving your presence, to a veritable calvary, without limit to its stations or hope of crucifixion, though I say it myself, and no Simon, and reduced me to frequent halts. Yes, my progress reduced me to stopping more and more often, it was the only way to progress, to stop. And though it is no part of my tottering intentions to treat here in full, as they deserve, these brief moments of the immemorial expiation, I shall nevertheless deal with them briefly, out of the goodness of my heart, so that my story, so clear till now, may not end in darkness, the darkness of these towering forests, these giant leaves where I hobble, listen, fall, rise, listen and hobble on, wondering sometimes, need I say, if I shall ever see again the hated light, at least unloved, stretched palely between the last boles, and my mother, to settle matters, and if I would not do better, at least just as well, to hang myself from a bough, with a liane.

—Translated by Patrick Bowles in collaboration with the author

ITALO CALVINO

Last Comes the Raven

The stream was a net of limpid, delicate ripples, with the water running through the mesh. From time to time, like a fluttering of silver wings, the dorsum of a trout flashed on the surface, the fish at once plunging zigzag down into the water.

—Full of trout, one of the men said.

—If we toss a grenade in, they'll all come floating to the top, bellies up, said the other; he detached a grenade from his belt and started to unscrew the baseplate.

Then the boy, who had stood aside looking on, walked over, a mountain youth with an apple-look to his face. —Let me have it, he said, taking the rifle from one of the men. —What does he want to do? the man said, intending to re-claim the rifle. But the boy was levelling it at the water, in search of a target, it seemed. "If you shoot, you'll only scare the fish away," the man started to say, but did not have time. A trout had surfaced, flashing, and the boy had pumped a bullet into it as though having anticipated the fish's exact point of appearance. Now, with its white underside exposed, the trout floated lifeless on the surface. —Cripes, the men said. The boy reloaded the rifle and swung it around. The air was crisp and tensed: one could distinguish the pine needles on the opposite bank and the knitted texture of the stream. A ripple broke the surface: another trout. He fired: now it floated dead. The men glanced briefly at the fish, briefly at the boy. —He shoots well, they said.

The boy swung the barrel again, into the air. It was curious, to think of it, that they were encompassed by air, actually cut off from other things by meters of air. But when the boy aimed the rifle, the air then became an invisible straight line stretching from the muzzle to the thing . . . to the hawk, for instance, floating above on wings that seemed scarcely to move. As he pressed the trigger, the air continued crystalline and clear as ever, but at the upper end of the line the kestrel folded its wings, then dropped like a stone. The open breech emitted a fine smell of powder.

He asked for more cartridges. The number of men watching had now swelled behind him on the bank of the stream. The cones at the top of the pine trees on the other bank—why were they visible and withal out of reach? Why that empty span between him and them? Why were the cones, although a part of him, in the chamber of his eye—why were they *there,* so distant? And yet if he aimed the rifle that empty span was clearly a deception: he touched the trigger and at that instant a cone, severed at the stem, fell. The feeling was one of caressive emptiness: the emptiness of the rifle bore which extended off into the air and was occupied by the shot, straight to the pine cone, the squirrel, the white stone, the flowering poppy. —He doesn't miss a one, the men said, and no one had the audacity to laugh.

—Come, come along with us, the leader said. —You give me the rifle then, the boy returned. —All right. Certainly.

So he went.

He left with a haversack filled with apples and two rounds of cheese. His village was a patch of slate, straw, and cattle muck in the valley bottom. And going away was wonderful, for at every turn there was something new to be seen, trees with cones, birds flitting among the branches, lichen-encrusted rocks, everything in the shaft of the false distances, of the distances occupied by gunshot that gulped up the air between. But he wasn't to shoot, they told him: those were places to be passed in silence, and the cartridges were for fighting. But at a certain point a leveret, frightened by the footsteps, scampered across the trail, amid shouts and the bustle of the men. It was just about to vanish into the brake when the boy stopped it with a shot. —A good shot, the leader himself conceded,—but this is not a pleasure hunt. You're not to shoot again, even if you see a pheasant.

But scarcely an hour had elapsed before there were more shots from the column.

—It's the boy again! the leader stormed, going forward to overtake him.

The boy grinned with his rosy and white apple-face.

—Partridges, he said, displaying them. They had burst up from a hedge.

—Partridges, crickets or whatever else, I gave you fair warning. Now let me have the rifle. And if you make me lose my temper once more, back to the village you go.

The boy sulked a little; it was no fun to be hiking without a rifle, but as long as he remained with them he might hope to have it again.

In the night they bedded down in the chalet of herdsmen. The boy awakened immediately the sky grew light, while the others still slept. He took their finest rifle and loaded his haversack with cartridges and went out. The air was timorous and crisp, as one may discover it in the early morning. Not far from the house stood a mulberry tree. It was the hour in which jays were arriving. There, he saw one! He fired, ran to pick it up, and stuffed it into his haversack. Without moving from where the jay had fallen, he looked about for another target. A dormouse! Startled by the first shot, it was scurrying toward safety in the crown of a chestnut tree. Dead, it was simply a large mouse with a grey tail that shed shocks of fur at touch. From beneath the chestnut tree he sighted, in a field off below him, a mushroom, red with white prickles and poisonous. He crumbled it with a shot, then went to see if really he had got it. What fun it was, going from one target to another like that: one might in time go all the way round the world! He spied a large snail on a rock; he sighted on its shell, and going over to it noticed nothing but the shattered rock and a spot of iridescent spittle. Thus did he wander from the chalet, down through unfamiliar fields.

From the stone he saw a lizard on a wall, from the wall a puddle and a frog, from the puddle a signboard on the zigzagging road, and beneath it: beneath it men in uniform advancing on him with arms at the ready. When the boy came forth with his rifle, smiling, his face rosy and white like an apple, they shouted, raising their guns. But the boy had already seen and fired at one of the gold buttons on the chest of one of them. He heard the man scream and then bullets, in a hail and single shots, whistling over his head: he had already flattened to the ground behind a pile of rocks on the hem of the road, in a dead angle. The rock pile was long and he could move about; and he was able to peep out from unexpected points, see the flash of the soldiers' musketry, the grey and gloss of their uniforms, and fire at a chevron, at an insigne. Then quickly scramble along the ground to fire from a new position.

Then he heard a burst of fire behind him, raking over his head into the ranks of the soldiers: his companions had appeared on the rescue with machine guns. —If the boy hadn't awakened us with his firing . . . they were saying.

Covered by his companions, the boy was better able to see. Suddenly a bullet grazed his cheek. He turned: a soldier had got to the road above him. He threw himself into the drainage ditch, gaining shelter again, at the same time firing; the bullet, though failing to hit the soldier, glanced off his riflestock. Now, from the sounds that he heard, he could tell that his adversary's rifle had jammed; the soldier flung it to the ground. Then the boy rose up. The soldier had taken to his heels and the boy fired at him, popping an epaulette into the air.

The boy gave chase. The soldier dashed into the woods, at first vanishing but presently reappearing within range. The boy burned a crease in the dome of the soldier's helmet, next shot off a belt loop. One after the other, they had meanwhile come into a dale, to which they were both of them strangers, and where the din of the battle was no longer heard. In time, the soldier found himself without any more trees before him, instead a glade overgrown with knotted thicket clumps. And the boy was himself about to come out of the woods.

In the middle of the clearing stood a large rock. The soldier barely made it, jumping behind and doubling up with his head between his knees. There, for the time being, he felt, he was out of danger: he had some grenades with him, and the boy would have to maintain a respectful distance; he could do no more than keep him pinned down with his rifle, insuring that he did not escape. Certainly, had it been possible for him simply to dive into the thickets, he would be safe, able then to slide down the heavily bearded slope. But there was that open tract to cross. How long would the boy wait? And would he continue to keep his rifle trained on him? The soldier decided to try an experiment: he put his helmet on his bayonet and stuck it out from behind the rock. There was a shot and the helmet, pierced through, bowled along the ground.

The soldier kept his wits; doubtless, aiming at the rock and the area around it was quite easy, but the soldier would not get hit if he was nimble enough. Just then a bird raced overhead, a hoopoe perhaps. One shot and it fell. The soldier wiped sweat from around his neck. Another bird, a missel thrush, went over: it fell too. The soldier swallowed. This was very likely a flyway; for other birds continued to go over, all of them different, and as the boy fired, they fell. A thought came to the soldier: "If he's watching birds, then he can't be watching me. Just as he fires I'll jump for the bushes." But it might be well to test his plan first. He picked up his helmet and placed it back on the tip of his bayonet. Two birds flew over this time: snipes. Waiting, the soldier regretted wasting so fine an occasion on the test. The boy fired at one of the snipes; the soldier raised his helmet. A second shot rang out and he saw the helmet leap into the air. The soldier's mouth tasted of lead; he had no sooner noticed this than the second bird fell. He must not lose his head: behind the rock with his grenades, he was safe. And why then, even though hidden, couldn't he try to get the boy with a grenade? He lay on his back and, caring not to be seen, stretched back his arm, primed his strength, and pitched the grenade. A good throw; it would go some distance; but describing only half of a parabola, still in mid-air, it was exploded by a rifle blast. The soldier flattened himself against the ground to escape the shrapnel.

When next the soldier raised himself the raven had come.

He saw, circling lazily above him, a bird, a raven perhaps. The boy would certainly shoot it down. But no shot followed. Was the raven perhaps too high? And yet he had brought down higher and swifter birds than that. Finally, he fired: now it would drop. No. Unperturbed, it continued to soar in the sky, slowly, round and round. A pine cone toppled from a near-by tree. Had he taken to shooting at pine cones? One by one, as he hit them, the cones fell, striking with a dry crunch. At each report the soldier glanced up at the raven: was it falling? Not yet. Lower and lower, the black bird continued to circle overhead. Could it be, really, that the boy didn't see it? Or perhaps the raven didn't exist at all, was only a hallucination. But perhaps—perhaps a man near death sees all the birds fly over . . . and when he sees the raven it means that the hour has come. In any case, he must tell the boy, who went on shooting at mere pine cones.

The soldier rose to his feet and pointed up at the black bird:

—There's the raven! he shouted in his own language. The bullet struck him through the heart of the spread eagle embroidered on his jacket.

The raven came down slowly, wheeling.

—Translated by Ben Johnson

EVAN S. CONNELL

The Beau Monde of Mrs. Bridge

PARKING

The black Lincoln that Mr. Bridge gave her on her 47th birthday was a size too long and she drove it as cautiously as she might have driven a locomotive. People were always blowing their horns at her or turning their heads to stare when they went by. The Lincoln was set to idle too slowly and in consequence the engine sometimes died when she pulled up at an intersection, but as her husband never used the Lincoln and she herself assumed it was just one of those things about automobiles, the idling speed was never adjusted. Often she would delay a line of cars while she pressed the starter button either too long or not long enough. Knowing she was not expert she was always quite apologetic when something unfortunate happened, and did her best to keep out of everyone's way. She changed into second gear at the beginning of any hill and let herself down the far side much more slowly than necessary.

Usually she parked in a downtown garage where Mr. Bridge rented a stall for her. She had only to honk at the enormous doors, which would then trundle open, and coast on inside where an attendant would greet her by name, help her out, and then park the formidable machine. But in the country club district she parked on the street, and if there were diagonal stripes she did very well, but if parking was parallel she had trouble judging her distance from the curb and would have to get out and walk around to look, then get back in and try again. The Lincoln's seat was so soft and Mrs. Bridge so short that she had to sit very erect in order to see what was happening ahead of her. She drove with arms thrust forward and gloved hands tightly on the large wheel, her feet just able to depress the pedals all the way. She never had serious accidents but was often seen here and there being talked to by patrolmen. These patrolmen never did anything partly because they saw immediately that it would not do to arrest her, and partly because they could tell she was trying to do everything the way it should be done.

When parking on the street it embarrassed her to have people watch, yet there always seemed to be someone at the bus stop or lounging in a doorway with nothing to do but stare while she struggled with the wheel and started jerkily backward. Sometimes, however, there would be a nice man who, seeing her difficulty, would come around and tip his hat and ask if he might help.

"Would you, please?" she would ask in relief, and after he opened the door she would get out and stand on the curb while he put the car in place. It was a problem to know whether he expected a tip or not. She knew that people who stood around on the streets were in need of money, still she did not want to offend anyone. Sometimes she would hesitantly ask, sometimes not, and whether the man would accept a twenty-five-cent piece or no, she would smile brightly up at him, saying, "Thank you so much," and having locked the Lincoln's doors she would be off to the shops.

MINISTER'S BOOK

If Mrs. Bridge bought a book it was almost always one of three things: a best seller she had heard of or seen advertised in all the stores, a self-improvement book, or a book by a Kansas City author no matter what it was about. These latter were infrequent, but now and again someone would explode on the midst of Kansas City with a Civil War history or something about old Westport Landing. Then, too, there were slender volumes of verse and essays usually printed by local publishing houses, and it was one of these that lay about the living room longer than any other book with the exception of an extremely old two-volume set of *The Brothers Karamazov* in goldpainted leather which nobody in the house had ever read and which had been purchased from an antique dealer by Mr. Bridge's brother. This set rested gravely on the mantelpiece between a pair of bronze Indian chief heads—the only gift from cousin Lulubelle Watts that Mrs. Bridge had ever been able to use—and was dusted once a week by Hazel with a peacock feather duster.

The volume that ran second to *The Brothers Karamazov* was a collection of thoughts by the local minister, Dr. Foster, a short and congenial and even jovial man with a big, handsome head capped with soft golden white hair that he allowed to grow long and which he brushed toward the top of his head to give himself another inch or so. He had written these essays over a period of several years with the idea of putting them into book form, and from time to time would allude to them, laughingly, as his memoirs. Then people would exclaim that he surely mustn't keep them to himself until he died, at which Dr. Foster, touching the speaker's arm, would laugh heartily and say, "We'll think it over, we'll think it over," and clear his throat.

At last, when he had been preaching in Kansas City for 17 years and his name was recognized, and he was always mentioned in *The Tattler* and sometimes in the city paper, a small publishing firm took these essays which he had quietly submitted to them several times before. The book came out in a black cover with a dignified grey-and-purple dust jacket which showed him smiling pensively out of his study window at dusk, hands clasped behind his back and one foot slightly forward.

The first essay began: 'I am now seated at my desk, the desk that has been a source of comfort and inspiration to me these many years. I see that night is falling, the shadows creeping gently across my small but (to my eyes) lovely garden, and at such times as this I often reflect on the state of Mankind.'

Mrs. Bridge read Dr. Foster's book, which he had autographed for her, and was amazed to find that he was such a reflective man, and so sensitive to the sunrise which she discovered he often got up to watch. She underlined several passages in the book that seemed to have particular meaning for her, and when it was done she was able to discuss it with her friends, who were all reading it, and she recommended it strongly to Grace Barron who at last consented to read a few pages.

With ugly, negative books about war and communists and perversion and everything else constantly flooding the counters this book came to her like an olive branch. It assured her that life was worth living after all, that she had not and was not doing anything wrong, and that people needed her. So, in the shadow of Dostoievsky, the pleasant meditations of Dr. Foster lay in various positions about the living room.

MAID FROM MADRAS

The Bridges gave a cocktail party not because they wanted to have cocktails with a mob of people, but because it was about time for them to be giving a party. Altogether more than eighty people stood and wandered about the home which stood on a hillside and was in the style of a Loire valley chateau. Grace and Virgil Barron were there, Madge and Russ Arlen, the Heywood Duncans, Wilhelm and Susan Van Metre looking out of place, Lois and Stuart Montgomery, the Beckerle sisters in ancient beaded gowns and looking as though they had not an instant forgotten the day when Mrs. Bridge had entertained them in anklets, Noel Johnson huge and by himself because she was in bed suffering from exhaustion, Mabel Ehe trying to start serious discussions, Dr. and Mrs. Batchelor whose Austrian refugee guests were now domestics in Los Angeles, and even Dr. Foster, smiling tolerantly, appeared for a whisky sour and a cigarette while gently chiding several of the men about Sunday golf. There was also an auto salesman named Beachy Marsh who had arrived early in a double-breasted pin-stripe business suit instead of a tuxedo, and being embarrassed about his mistake did everything he could think of to be amusing. He was not a close friend but it had been necessary to invite him along with several others.

Mrs. Bridge rustled about the brilliantly lighted home checking steadily to see that everything was as it should be. She glanced into the bathrooms every few minutes and found that the guest towels, which resembled pastel handkerchiefs, were still immaculately overlapping one another on the rack—at evening's end only three had been disturbed—and she entered the kitchen once to recommend that the extra servant girl, hired to assist Hazel, pin shut the gap in the breast of her starched uniform.

Through the silver candelabra and miniature turkey sandwiches Mrs. Bridge went graciously smiling and chatting a moment with everyone, quietly opening windows to let out the smoke, removing wet glasses from mahogany table tops, slipping away now and then to empty the onyx ashtrays she had bought and distributed throughout the house.

Beachy Marsh got drunk. He slapped people on the shoulder, told jokes, laughed loudly, and also went around emptying the ashtrays of their magenta-colored stubs, all the while attempting to control the tips of his shirt collar which had become damp from perspiration and were rolling up into the air like horns. Following Mrs. Bridge halfway up the carpeted stairs he said hopefully, "There was a young maid from Madras, who had a magnificent ass; not rounded and pink, as you probably think—it was grey, had long ears, and ate grass."

"Oh, my word!" replied Mrs. Bridge, looking over her shoulder with a polite smile but continuing up the stairs, while the auto salesman plucked miserably at his collar.

LAUNDRESS IN THE REAR

Every Wednesday the laundress came, and as the bus line was several blocks distant from the Bridge home someone would almost always meet her bus in the morning. For years the laundress had been an affable old negress named Beulah Mae who was full of nutshell wisdom and who wore a red bandanna and a dress that resembled a dyed hospital gown. Mrs. Bridge was very fond of Beulah Mae, speaking of her as 'a nice old soul' and frequently giving her a little extra money or an evening dress that had begun to look dated, or perhaps some raffle tickets that she was always obliged to buy from girl scouts and various charities. But there came a day when Beulah Mae had had enough of laundering, extra gifts or no, and without saying a word to any of her clients she boarded a bus for California to live out her life on the seashore. For several weeks Mrs. Bridge was without a laundress and was obliged to take the work to an establishment, but at last she got someone else, an extremely large and doleful Swedish woman who said during the interview in the kitchen that her name was Ingrid and that for 18 years she had been a masseuse and liked it much better.

When Mrs. Bridge arrived at the bus line the first morning Ingrid saluted her mournfully and got laboriously into the front seat. This was not the custom, but such a thing was difficult to explain because Mrs. Bridge did not like to hurt anyone's feelings by making them feel inferior, so she said nothing about it and hoped that by next week some other laundress in the neighborhood would have told Ingrid.

But the next week she again got in front, and again Mrs. Bridge pretended everything was all right. However on the third morning while they were riding up Ward Parkway toward the house Mrs. Bridge said, "I was so attached to Beulah Mae. She used to have the biggest old time riding in the back seat."

Ingrid turned a massive yellow head to look stonily at Mrs. Bridge. As they were easing into the driveway she spoke: "So you want I should sit in the back."

"Oh, Gracious! I didn't mean that," Mrs. Bridge answered, smiling up at Ingrid. "You're perfectly welcome to sit right here if you like."

Ingrid said no more about the matter and next week with the same majestic melancholy rode in the rear.

FRAYED CUFFS

Ordinarily Mrs. Bridge examined the laundry but when she had shopping to do, or a meeting, the job fell to Hazel who never paid much attention to such things as missing buttons or loose elastic. Thus it was that Mrs. Bridge discovered Douglas wearing a shirt with cuffs that were noticeably frayed.

"For Heaven's sake!" she exclaimed, taking hold of his sleeve. "Has a dog been chewing on it?"

He looked down at the threads as though he had never before seen them.

"Surely you don't intend to *wear* that shirt?"

"It looks perfectly okay to me," said Douglas.

"Just look at those cuffs! Anyone would think we're on our way to the poorhouse."

"So is it a disgrace to be poor?"

"*No!*" she cried. "But we're *not* poor!"

EQUALITY

Mrs. Bridge approved of equality. On certain occasions when she saw in the newspapers or heard over the radio that labor unions had won another victory she would think: 'Good for them!' And, as the segregational policies of the various states became more and more subject to criticism by civic groups as well as by the federal government, she would feel that it was about time, and she would try to understand how discrimination could persist. However strongly she felt about this she was careful about what she said because she was aware that everything she had was hers through the efforts of one person: her husband. Mr. Bridge was of the opinion that people were not equal. In his decisive manner of speaking, annoyed that she should even puzzle over such a thing, he said, "You take all the people on earth and divide up everything, and in six months everybody would have just about what they have now. What Abraham Lincoln meant was equal rights, not equal capacity."

This always seemed exactly what she was trying to point out to him, that many people did not have equal rights, but after a few minutes of discussion she would be overwhelmed by a sense of inadequacy and would begin to get confused, at which he would stare at her for a moment as though she were something in a glass box and then resume whatever he had been doing.

She invariably introduced herself to members of minority groups at whatever gathering she found herself associating with them.

"I'm India Bridge," she would say in a friendly manner, and would wish it were possible to invite the people into her home. And when, among neighborhood friends she had known for a long time and who offered no unusual ideas, the increased means of certain classes were discussed, she would say, "Isn't it nice that they can have television and automobiles and everything."

In a northern town a negro couple opened a grocery store in a white neighborhood; that night the windows were smashed and the store set afire. Newspapers published photographs of the ruined property, of two smirking policemen, and of the negro couple who had lost their entire savings. Mrs. Bridge read this story while having breakfast by herself several hours after her husband had left for work. She studied the miserable faces of the young negro and his wife. Across the newspaper the morning sun slanted warm and cheerful, in the kitchen Hazel sang hymns while peeling apples for a pie, all the earth as seen from her window seemed content, yet such things still came to pass. In her breakfast nook, a slice of buttered toast in hand, Mrs. Bridge felt a terrible desire. She would press these unfortunate people to her breast and tell them that she, too, knew what it meant to be hurt but that everything would turn out all right.

GLOVES

She had always done a reasonable amount of charity work along with her friends, particularly at a little store on 9th street where second-hand clothing that had been collected in drives was distributed. In this store were two rooms, in the front one a row of card tables placed together, behind which stood the charity workers who were to assist people seeking something to wear, and in the back room were several more card tables and collapsible wooden chairs where Mrs. Bridge and her fellow workers ate their lunch or relaxed when not on duty in front.

She often went down with Madge Arlen. One week they would drive to their work in the Arlen's Chrysler, the next week in Mrs. Bridge's Lincoln, and when this was the case Mrs. Bridge always drew up before the garage where her parking stall was rented. She honked, or beckoned if someone happened to be in sight, and shortly one of the attendants whose name was George would come out buttoning up his jacket and he would ride in the rear seat to the clothing store. There he would jump out and open the door for Mrs. Bridge and after that drive the Lincoln back to the garage because she did not like it left on the street in such a neighborhood.

"Can you come by for us around six, or six-fifteen-ish, George?" she would ask.

He always answered that he would be glad to, touched the visor of his cap, and drove away.

"He seems so nice," said Mrs. Arlen as the two of them walked into their store.

"Oh, he is!" Mrs. Bridge agreed. "He's one of the nicest garage men I've ever had."

"How long have you been parking there?"

"Quite some time. We used to park at that awful place on Walnut."

"The one with the popcorn machine? Lord, isn't that the limit?"

"No, not that place. The one with the Italians. You know how my husband is about Italians. Well, that just seemed to be headquarters for them. They came in there to eat their sandwiches and listen to some opera broadcast from New York. It was just impossible. So finally Walter said, 'I'm going to change garages.' So we did."

They walked past the row of card tables piled high with soiled and sour unwashed clothing and continued into the back room where they found some early arrivals having coffee and eclairs. Mrs. Bridge and Mrs. Arlen hung up their coats and also had coffee, and then prepared for work. The reform school had sent down some boys to assist and they were put to work untying the latest sacks of used clothing and dumping them out.

By two o'clock everything was ready for the day's distribution. The doors were unlocked and the first of the poor entered and approached the counter behind which stood Mrs. Bridge and two others with encouraging smiles, all three of them wearing gloves.

ROBBERY AT HEYWOOD DUNCANS

The Bridges were almost robbed while attending a cocktail party at the Heywood Duncans'. Shortly after ten o'clock, just as she was taking an anchovy cracker from the buffet table, four men appeared in the doorway with revolvers and wearing plastic noses attached to horn-rimmed glasses for disguise. One of them said, "All right, everybody. This is a stick-up!" Another of the men—Mrs. Bridge afterwards described him to the police as not having worn a necktie—got up on the piano bench and from there stepped up on top of the piano itself where he pointed his gun at different people. At first everybody thought it was a joke, but it wasn't because the robbers made them all line up facing the wall with their hands above their heads. One of them ran upstairs and came down with his arms full of fur coats and purses while two others started around the room pulling billfolds out of the men's pockets and drawing rings from the ladies' fingers. Before they had gotten to either Mr. or Mrs. Bridge, who were lined up between Dr. Foster and the Arlens, something frightened them and the one standing on the piano called out in an ugly voice, "Who's got the keys to that blue Cadillac out front?"

At this Mrs. Ralph Porter screamed, "Don't you tell him, Ralph!"

But the bandits took Mr. Porter's keys anyway and after telling them all not to move for thirty minutes they ran out the porch door.

It was written up on the front page of the newspaper, with pictures on page eight, including a close-up of the scratched piano. Mrs. Bridge, reading the story in the breakfast room next morning after her husband had gone to work, was surprised to learn that Stuart Montgomery had been carrying just $2.14 and that Mrs. Noel Johnson's ring had been zircon.

FOLLOW ME HOME

How the scare actually started no one knew, although several women, one of whom was a fairly close friend of Madge Arlen, claimed they knew the name of someone who had been assaulted not far from Ward Parkway. Some thought it had happened near the Plaza, others thought farther south, but they were generally agreed that it had happened late at night. The story was that a certain lady of a well-known family had been driving home alone and when she had slowed down for an intersection a man had leaped up from behind some shrubbery and had wrenched open the door. Whether the attack had been consummated or not the story did not say, the important part was that there had been a man and he had leaped up and wrenched open the door. There was nothing in the paper about it, nor in *The Tattler* which did not print anything unpleasant, and the date of the assault could not be determined for some reason, only that it had been on a dark night not too long ago.

When this story had gotten about none of the matrons wished to drive anywhere alone after sundown. As it so happened they were often obliged to go to a cocktail party or a dinner by themselves because their husbands were working late at the office, but they went full of anxiety, with the car doors locked. It also became customary for the husband-host to get his automobile out of the garage at the end of an evening and then to follow the unescorted matrons back to their homes. Thus there could be seen processions of cars driving cautiously and rather like funerals across the boulevards of the country club residential district.

So Mrs. Bridge came home on those evenings when her husband did not get back from the office in time, or when he was too tired and preferred to lie in bed reading vacation advertisements. At her driveway the procession would halt, engines idling, while she drove into the garage and came back out along the driveway so as to be constantly visible, and entered by the front door. Having unlocked it she would step inside, switch on the hall lights, and call to her husband, "I'm home!" Then, after he had made a noise of some kind in reply, she would flicker the lights a few times to show the friends waiting outside that she was safe, after which they would all drive off into the night.

NEVER SPEAK TO STRANGE MEN

On a downtown street just outside a department store a man said something to her. She ignored him. But at that moment the crowd closed them in together.

"How do you do?" he said, smiling and touching his hat.

She saw that he was a man of about fifty with silvery hair and rather satanic ears.

His face became red and he laughed awkwardly. "I'm Gladys Schmidt's husband."

"Oh, for Heaven's sake!" Mrs. Bridge exclaimed. "I didn't recognize you."

CONRAD

While idly dusting the bookcase one morning she paused to read the titles and saw an old red-gold volume of Conrad that had stood untouched for years. She could not think how it happened to be there. Taking it down she looked at the flyleaf and found: *Ex Libris* Thomas Bridge.

She remembered then that they had inherited some books and charts upon the death of her husband's brother, an odd man who had married a night club entertainer and later died of a heart attack in Mexico.

Having nothing to do that morning she began to turn the brittle, yellowed pages and slowly became fascinated. After standing beside the bookcase for about ten minutes she wandered, still reading, into the living room where she sat down and did not look up from the book until Hazel came in to announce lunch. In the midst of one of the stories she came upon a passage that had once been underlined, apparently by Tom Bridge, which remarked that some people go skimming over the years of existence to sink gently into a placid grave, ignorant of life to the last, without ever having been made to see all it may contain. She brooded over this fragment even while reading further, and finally turned back to it again, and was staring at the carpet with a bemused expression when Hazel entered.

Mrs. Bridge put the book on the mantel for she intended to read more of this perceptive man, but during the afternoon Hazel automatically put Conrad back on the shelf and Mrs. Bridge did not think of him again.

VOTING

She had never gone into politics the way some women did who were able to speak with masculine inflections about such affairs as farm surplus and foreign subsidies. She always listened attentively when these things came up at luncheons or circle meetings; she felt her lack of knowledge and wanted to know more, and did intend to buckle down to some serious studying. But so many things kept popping up that it was difficult to get started, and then too she did not know exactly how one began to learn. At times she would start to question her husband but he refused to say much to her, and so she would not press the matter because after all there was not much she herself could accomplish.

This was how she defended herself to Mabel Ehe after having incautiously let slip the information that her husband told her what to vote for.

Mabel Ehe was flat as an adolescent but much more sinewy. Her figure was like a bud that had never managed to open. She wore tweed coats and cropped hair and frequently stood with hands thrust deep into her side pockets as if she were a man. She spoke short positive sentences, sometimes throwing back her head to laugh with a sound that reminded people of a dry reed splintering. She had many bitter observations in regard to capitalism, relating stories she had heard from unquestionable sources about women dying in childbirth because they could not afford the high cost of proper hospitalization or even the cost of insurance plans.

"If I ever have a child—" she was fond of beginning, and would then tear into medical fees.

She demanded of Mrs. Bridge: "Don't you have a mind of your own? Great Scott, woman, you're an adult. Speak out! We've been emancipated." Ominously she began rocking back and forth from her heels to her toes, hands clasped behind her back while she frowned at the carpet of the Auxiliary clubhouse.

"You're right," Mrs. Bridge apologized, discreetly avoiding the smoke Mabel Ehe blew into the space between them. "It's just so hard to know *what* to think. There's so much scandal and fraud, and I suppose the papers only print what they want us to know." She hesitated, then, "How do you make up *your* mind?"

Mabel Ehe removed the cigarette holder from her small cool lips. She considered the ceiling and then the carpet, as though debating on how to answer such a naïve question, and finally suggested that Mrs. Bridge might begin to grasp the fundamentals by a deliberate reading of certain books, which she jotted down on the margin of a tally card. Mrs. Bridge had not heard of any of these books except one and this was because its author was being investigated, but she decided to read it anyway.

There was a waiting list for it at the public library but she got it at a rental library and settled down to go through it with the deliberation that Mabel Ehe had advised. The author's name was Zokoloff, which certainly sounded threatening, and to be sure the first chapter was about bribery in the circuit courts. When Mrs. Bridge had gotten far enough along that she felt capable of speaking about it she left it quite boldly on the hall table, however Mr. Bridge did not even notice it until the third evening. He thinned his nostrils, read the first paragraph, grunted once, and dropped it back onto the hall table. This was disappointing. In fact, now that there was no danger involved, she had trouble finishing the book. She thought it would be better in a magazine digest, but at last she did get through and returned it to the rental library, saying to the owner, "I can't honestly say I agree with it all but he's certainly well informed."

Certain arguments of Zokoloff remained with her and she found that the longer she thought about them the more penetrating and logical they became; surely it *was* time, as he insisted, for a change in government. She decided to vote liberal at the next election, and as time for it approached she became filled with such enthusiasm and anxiety that she wanted very much to discuss government with her husband. She began to feel confident that she could persuade him to change his vote also. It was all so clear to her, there was really no mystery to politics. However when she challenged him to discussion he did not seem especially interested, in fact he did not answer. He was watching a television acrobat stand on his thumb in a bottle and only glanced across at her for an instant with an annoyed expression. She let it go until the following evening when television was over, and this time, he looked at her curiously, quite intently, as if probing her mind, and then all at once he snorted.

She really intended to force a discussion on election eve. She was going to quote from the book of Zokoloff. But he came home so late, so tired, that she had not the heart to upset him. She concluded it would be best to let him vote as he always had, and she would do as she herself wished, still upon getting to the polls, which were conveniently located in the country club shopping district, she became doubtful and a little uneasy. And when the moment finally came she pulled the lever recording her wish for the world to remain as it was.

PHILIP ROTH

The Conversion of the Jews

"You're a real one for opening your mouth in the first place," Itzie said. "What do you open your mouth all the time for?"

"I didn't bring it up, Itz, I didn't," Ozzie said.

"What do you care about Jesus Christ for anyway?"

"I didn't bring up Jesus Christ. He did. I didn't even know what he was talking about. Jesus is historical, he kept saying. Jesus is historical." Ozzie mimicked the monumental voice of Rabbi Binder.

"Jesus was a person that lived like you and me," Ozzie continued. "That's what Binder said—"

"Yea? . . . So what! What do I give two cents whether he lived or not. And what do you gotta open your mouth!" Itzie Lieberman favored closed-mouthedness, especially when it came to Ozzie Freedman's questions. Mrs. Freedman had to see Rabbi Binder twice before about Ozzie's questions and this Wednesday at four-thirty would be the third time. Itzie preferred to keep *his* mother in the kitchen; he settled for behind-the-back subtleties such as gestures, faces, snarls and other less delicate barnyard noises.

"He was a real person, Jesus, but he wasn't like God, and we don't believe he is God." Slowly, Ozzie was explaining Rabbi Binder's position to Itzie, who had been absent from Hebrew School the previous afternoon.

"The Catholics," Itzie said helpfully, "they believe in Jesus Christ, that he's God." Itzie Lieberman used "the Catholics" in its broadest sense—to include the Protestants.

Ozzie received Itzie's remark with a tiny head bob, as though it were a footnote, and went on. "His mother was Mary, and his father probably was Joseph," Ozzie said. "But the New Testament says his real father was God."

"His *real* father?"

"Yea," Ozzie said, "that's the big thing, his father's supposed to be God."

"Bull."

"That's what Rabbi Binder says, that it's impossible—"

"Sure it's impossible. That stuff's all bull. To have a baby you gotta get laid," Itzie theologized. "Mary hadda get laid."

"That's what Binder says: 'The only way a woman can have a baby is to have intercourse with a man.' "

"He said *that,* Ozz?" For a moment it appeared that Itzie had put the theological question aside. "He said that, intercourse?" A little curled smile shaped itself in the lower half of Itzie's face like a pink mustache. "What you guys do, Ozz, you laugh or something?"

"I raised my hand."

"Yea? Whatja say?"

"That's when I asked the question."

Itzie's face lit up like a firefly's behind. "Whatja ask about—intercourse?"

"No, I asked the question about God, how if He could create the heaven and earth in six days, and make all the animals and the fish and the light in six days—the light especially, that's what always gets me, that He could make the light. Making fish and animals, that's pretty good—"

"That's damn good." Itzie's appreciation was honest but unimaginative: it was as though God had just pitched a one-hitter.

"But making light . . . I mean when you think about it, it's really something," Ozzie said. "Anyway, I asked Binder if He could make all that in six days, and He could *pick* the six days He wanted right out of nowhere, why couldn't He let a woman have a baby without having intercourse."

"You said intercourse, Ozz, to Binder?"

"Yea."

"Right in class?"

"Yea."

Itzie smacked the side of his head.

"I mean, no kidding around," Ozzie said, "that'd really be nothing. After all that other stuff, that'd practically be nothing."

Itzie considered a moment. "What'd Binder say?"

"He started all over again explaining how Jesus was historical and how he lived like you and me but he wasn't God. So I said I under*stood* that. What I wanted to know was different."

What Ozzie wanted to know was always different. The first time he had wanted to know how Rabbi Binder could call the Jews "The Chosen People" if the Declaration of Independence claimed all men to be created equal. Rabbi Binder tried to distinguish for him between political equality and spiritual legitimacy, but what Ozzie wanted to know, he insisted vehemently, was different. That was the first time his mother had to come.

Then there was the plane crash. Fifty-eight people had been killed in a plane crash at La Guardia, and in studying a casualty list in the newspaper his mother had discovered among the list of those dead eight Jewish names (his grandmother had nine but she counted Miller as a Jewish name); because of the eight she said the plane crash was "a tragedy." During free-discussion time on Wednesday Ozzie had brought to Rabbi Binder's attention this matter of "some of his relations" always picking out the Jewish names. Rabbi Binder had begun to explain cultural unity and some other things when Ozzie stood up at his seat and said that what he wanted to know was different. Rabbi Binder insisted that he sit down and it was then that Ozzie shouted that he wished all fifty-eight were Jews. That was the second time his mother came.

"And he kept explaining about Jesus being historical, and so I kept asking him. No kidding, Itz, he was trying to make me look stupid."

"So what he finally do?"

"Finally he starts screaming that I was deliberately simple-minded and a wise-guy, and that my mother had to come, and this was the last time. And that I'd never get bar-mitzvahed if he could help it. Then, Itz, then he starts talking in that voice like a statue, real slow and deep, and he says that I better think over what I said about the Lord. He told me to go to his office and think it over." Ozzie leaned his body towards Itzie. "Itz, I thought it over for a solid hour, and now I'm convinced God could do it."

Ozzie had planned to confess his latest transgression to his mother as soon as she came home from work. But it was a Friday night in November and already dark, and when Mrs. Freedman came through the door, she tossed off her coat, kissed Ozzie quickly on the face, and went to the kitchen table to light the three yellow candles, two for the Sabbath and one for Ozzie's father.

When his mother lit candles she would move her arms slowly towards her, dragging them through the air, as though persuading people whose minds were half made up. And her eyes would get glassy with tears. Even when his father was alive Ozzie remembered that her eyes had gotten glassy, so it didn't have anything to do with his dying. It had something to do with lighting the candles.

As she touched the flaming match to the unlit wick of a Sabbath candle, the phone rang, and Ozzie, standing only a foot from it, plucked it off the receiver and held it muffled to his chest. When his mother lit candles Ozzie felt there should be no noise; even breathing, if you could manage it, should be softened. Ozzie pressed the phone to his breast and watched his mother dragging whatever she was dragging, and he felt his own eyes get glassy. His mother was a round, tired, grayhaired penguin of a woman whose gray skin had begun to feel the tug of gravity and the weight of her own history. Even when she was dressed up she didn't look like a chosen person. But when she lit candles she looked like something better; like a woman who knew momentarily that God could do anything.

After a few mysterious minutes she was finished. Ozzie hung up the phone and walked to the kitchen table where she was beginning to lay the two places for the four-course Sabbath meal. He told her that she would have to see Rabbi Binder next Wednesday at four-thirty, and then he told her why. For the first time in their life together she hit Ozzie across the face with her hand.

All through the chopped liver and chicken soup part of the dinner Ozzie cried; he didn't have any appetite for the rest.

On Wednesday in the largest of the three basement classrooms of the synagogue, Rabbi Marvin Binder, a tall, handsome, broad-shouldered man of thirty with thick strong-fibered black hair, removed his watch from his pocket and saw that it was four o'clock. At the rear of the room Yakov Blotnik, the seventy-one year old custodian, slowly polished the large window, mumbling to himself, unaware that it was four o'clock or six o'clock, Monday or Wednesday. To most of the students Yakov Blotnik's mumbling, along with his brown curly beard, scythe-nose, and two heel-trailing black cats, made of him an object of wonder, a foreigner, a relic towards whom they were alternately fearful and disrespectful. To Ozzie the mumbling had always seemed a monotonous, curious prayer; what made it curious was that old Blotnik had been mumbling so steadily for so many years Ozzie suspected he had memorized the prayers and forgotten all about God.

"It is now free-discussion time," Rabbi Binder said. "Feel free to talk about any Jewish matter at all—religion, family, politics, sports—"

There was silence. It was a gusty, clouded November afternoon and it did not seem as though there ever was or could be a thing called baseball. So nobody this week said a word about that hero from the past, Hank Greenberg—which limited free-discussion considerably.

And the soul-battering Ozzie Freedman had just received from Rabbi

Binder had imposed its limitation. When it was Ozzie's turn to read aloud from the Hebrew book the rabbi had asked him petulantly why he didn't read more rapidly. He was showing no progress. Ozzie said he could read faster but that if he did he was sure not to understand what he was reading. Nevertheless, at the rabbi's repeated suggestion Ozzie tried, and showed a great talent, but in the midst of a long passage he stopped short and said he didn't understand a word he was reading, and started in again at a drag-footed pace. Then came the soul-battering.

Consequently when free-discussion time rolled around none of the students felt too free. The rabbi's invitation was answered only by the mumbling of feeble old Blotnik.

"Isn't there anything at all you would like to discuss?" Rabbi Binder asked again, looking at his watch. "No questions or comments?"

There was a small grumble from the third row. The rabbi requested that Ozzie rise and give the rest of the class the advantage of his thought.

Ozzie rose. "I forget it now," he said and sat down in his place.

Rabbi Binder advanced a seat towards Ozzie and poised himself on the edge of the desk. It was Itzie's desk and the rabbi's frame only a dagger's-length away from his face snapped him to sitting attention.

"Stand up again, Oscar," Rabbi Binder said calmly, "and try to assemble your thoughts."

Ozzie stood up. All his classmates turned in their seats and watched as he gave an unconvincing scratch to his forehead. "I can't assemble any," he announced, and plunked himself down.

"Stand up!" Rabbi Binder advanced from Itzie's desk to the one directly in front of Ozzie; when the rabbinical back was turned Itzie gave it five-fingers off the tip of his nose, causing a small titter in the room. Rabbi Binder was too absorbed in squelching Ozzie's nonsense once and for all to bother with titters. "Stand up, Oscar. What's your question about?"

Ozzie pulled a word out of the air. It was the handiest word. "Religion."

"Oh, now you remember?"

"Yes."

"What is it?"

Trapped, Ozzie blurted the first thing that came to him. "Why can't He make anything He wants to make!"

As Rabbi Binder prepared an answer, a final answer, Itzie, ten feet behind him, raised one finger on his left hand, gestured it meaningfully towards the rabbi's back, and brought the house down.

Binder twisted quickly to see what had happened and in the midst of the commotion Ozzie shouted into the rabbi's back what he couldn't have shouted to his face. It was a loud, toneless sound that had the timbre of something stored inside for about six days.

"You don't know! You don't know anything about God!"

The rabbi spun back towards Ozzie. "What?"

"You don't know—you don't—"

"Apologize, Oscar, apologize!" It was a threat.

"You don't—"

Like a snake's tongue, Rabbi Binder's hand flicked out at Ozzie's cheek. Perhaps it had only been meant to clamp the boy's mouth shut, but Ozzie ducked and the palm caught him squarely on the nose.

The blood came in a short, red spurt on to Ozzie's shirt front.

The next moment was all confusion. Ozzie screamed, "You bastard, you bastard!" and broke for the classroom door. Rabbi Binder lurched a step backwards, as though his own blood had started flowing, violently in the opposite direction, then gave a clumsy lurch forward and bolted out the door after Ozzie. The class followed after the rabbi's huge blue-suited back, and before old Blotnik could turn from his window, the room was empty and everyone was headed full speed up the three flights leading to the roof.

If one should compare the light of day to the life of man: sunrise to birth; sunset—the dropping down over the edge—to death; then as Ozzie Freedman wiggled through the trap door of the synagogue roof— his feet kicking backwards bronco-style at Rabbi Binder's outstretched arms—at that moment the day was fifty years old. As a rule, fifty or fifty-five reflects accurately the age of late afternoons in November, for it is in that month, during those hours, that one's awareness of light seems no longer a matter of seeing, but of hearing: light begins clicking away. In fact, as Ozzie locked shut the trapdoor in the rabbi's face, the sharp click of the bolt into the lock might momentarily have been mistaken for the sound of the vast gray light that had just throbbed through the sky.

With all his weight Ozzie kneeled on the locked door; any instant he was certain that Rabbi Binder's shoulder would fling it open, splintering the wood into shrapnel and catapulting his body into the sky. But the door did not move and below him he heard only the rumble of feet, first loud then dim, like thunder rolling away.

A question shot through his brain. "Can this be *me?*" For a thirteen year old who had just labeled his religious leader a bastard, twice, it was not an improper question. Louder and louder the question came to him—"Is it me? It is me?"—until he discovered himself no longer kneeling, but racing crazily towards the edge of the roof, his eyes crying, his throat screaming, and his arms flying every which way as though not his own.

"Is it me? Is it me Me ME ME ME! It has to be me—but is it!"

It is the question a thief must ask himself the night he jimmies open his first window, and it is said to be the question with which bridegrooms quiz themselves before the altar.

In the few wild seconds it took Ozzie's body to propel him to the edge of the roof, his self-examination began to grow fuzzy. Gazing down at the street, he became confused as to the problem beneath the question: was it, is-it-me-who-called-Binder-a-Bastard? or, is-it-me-prancing-around-on-the-roof? However, the scene below settled all, for there is an instant in any action when whether it is you or somebody else is academic. The thief crams the money in his pockets and scoots out the window. The bridegroom signs the hotel register for two. And the boy on the roof finds a streetful of people gaping at him, necks stretched backwards, faces up, as though he were the ceiling of the Hayden Planetarium. Suddenly you know it's you.

"Oscar! Oscar Freedman!" A voice rose from the center of the crowd, a voice that, could it have been seen, would have looked like the writing on scroll. "Oscar Freedman, get down from there. Immediately!" Rabbi Binder was pointing one arm stiffly up at him; and at the end of that arm, one finger aimed menacingly. It was the attitude of a dictator, but one—the eyes confessed all—whose personal valet had spit neatly in his face.

Ozzie didn't answer. Only for a blink's length did he look towards Rabbi Binder. Instead his eyes began to fit together the world beneath him, to sort out people from places, friends from enemies, participants from spectators. In little jagged star-like clusters his friends stood around Rabbi Binder, who was still pointing. The topmost point on a star compounded not of angels but of five adolescent boys was Itzie. What a world it was, with those stars below, Rabbi Binder below . . . Ozzie, who a moment earlier hadn't been able to control his own body, started to feel the meaning of the word control: he felt Peace and he felt Power.

"Oscar Freedman, I'll give you three to come down."

Few dictators give their subjects three to do anything; but, as always, Rabbi Binder only looked dictatorial.

"Are you ready, Oscar?"

Ozzie nodded his head yes, although he had no intention in the world—the lower one or the celestial one he'd just entered—of coming down even if Rabbi Binder should give him a million.

"All right then," said Rabbi Binder. He ran a hand through his black Samson hair as though it were the gesture prescribed for uttering the first digit. Then, with his other hand cutting a circle out of the small piece of sky around him, he spoke. "One!"

There was no thunder. On the contrary, at that moment, as though "one" was the cue for which he had been waiting, the world's least thunderous person appeared on the synagogue steps. He did not so much come out the synagogue door as lean out, onto the darkening air. He clutched at the doorknob with one hand and looked up at the roof.

"Oy!"

Yakov Blotnik's old mind hobbled slowly, as if on crutches, and though he couldn't decide precisely what the boy was doing on the roof, he knew it wasn't good—that is, it wasn't-good-for-the-Jews. For Yakov Blotnik life had fractionated itself simply: things were either good-for-the-Jews or no-good-for-the-Jews.

He smacked his free hand to his in-sucked cheek, gently. "Oy, Gut!" And then quickly as he could he jacked down his head and surveyed the street. There was Rabbi Binder (like a man at an auction with only three dollars in his pocket, he had just delivered a shaky "Two!"); there were the students, and that was all. So far it-wasn't-so-bad-for-the-Jews. But the boy had to come down immediately, before anybody saw. The problem: how to get the boy off the roof?

Anybody who has ever had a cat on the roof knows how to get him down. You call the fire department. Or first you call the operator and you ask her for the fire department. And the next thing there is a great jamming of brakes and clanging of bells and shouting of instructions. And then the cat is off the roof. You do the same thing to get a boy off the roof.

That is, you do the same thing if you are Yakov Blotnik and you once had a cat.

It took a short while for the engines, all four of them, to arrive. As it turned out Rabbi Binder had four times given Ozzie the count of three; had he not decided to stop, by the time the engines roared up he would have given him three one hundred and seven times.

The big hook-and-ladder was still swinging around the corner when one of the firemen leaped from it, plunged headlong towards the yellow fire hydrant in front of the synagogue, and with a huge wrench began unscrewing the top nozzle. Rabbi Binder raced over to him and pulled at his shoulder.

"There's no fire . . ."

The fireman mumbled something sounding like "Screw, buddy," back over his shoulder to him and, heatedly, continued working at the nozzle.

"But there's no fire, there's no fire . . ." Binder shouted. When the fireman mumbled again, the rabbi grasped his face with both his hands and pointed it up at the roof.

To Ozzie it looked as though Rabbi Binder was trying to tug the fireman's head out of his body, like a cork from a bottle. He had to giggle at the picture they made: it was a family portrait—rabbi in black skull-cap, fireman in red firehat, and the little yellow hydrant squatting beside like a kid brother, bareheaded. From the edge of the roof Ozzie waved at the portrait, a one-handed, flapping, mocking wave; in doing it his right foot slipped from under him. Rabbi Binder covered his eyes with his hands.

Firemen work fast. Before Ozzie had even regained his balance, a big, round, yellowed net was being held on the synagogue lawn. The firemen who held it looked up at Ozzie with stern, feelingless faces.

One of the firemen turned his head towards Rabbi Binder. "What, is the kid nuts or something?"

Rabbi Binder unpeeled his hands from his eyes, slowly, painfully, as if they were tape. Then he checked: nothing on the sidewalk, no dents in the net.

"Is he gonna jump, or what?" the fireman shouted.

In a voice not at all like a statue, Rabbi Binder finally answered. "Yes, yes, I think so . . . He's been threatening to . . ."

Threatening to? Why, the reason he was on the roof, Ozzie remembered, was to get away; he hadn't even thought about jumping. He had just run to get away, and the truth was that he hadn't really headed for the roof as much as he'd been chased there.

"What's his name, the kid?"

"Freedman," Rabbi Binder answered. "Oscar Freedman."

The fireman looked up at Ozzie. "What is it with you, Oscar? You gonna jump, or what?"

Ozzie did not answer. Frankly, the question had just arisen.

"Look, Oscar, if you're gonna jump, jump—and if you're not gonna jump, don't jump. But don't waste our time, willya?"

Ozzie looked at the fireman and then at Rabbi Binder. He wanted to see Rabbi Binder cover his eyes one more time.

"I'm going to jump."

And then he scampered around the edge of the roof to the corner, where there was no net below, and he flapped his arms at his sides, swishing the air and smacking his palms to his trousers on the downbeat; he began screaming like some kind of engine, "Wheeeee . . . wheeeeee," and leaning way out over the edge with the upper half of his body. The firemen whipped around to cover the ground with the net. Rabbi Binder mumbled a few words to Somebody and covered his eyes. Everything happened quickly, jerkily, as in a silent movie. The crowd, which had arrived with the fire-engines, gave out a long, Fourth-of-July fireworks, oooh-aahhh. In the excitement no one had paid the crowd much heed, except, of course, Yakov Blotnik, who swung from the doorknob counting heads. "Fier und tsvansik . . . finf und tsvantsik . . . Oy, Gut!" It wasn't like this with the cat.

Rabbi Binder peeked through his fingers, checked the sidewalk and net. Empty. But there was Ozzie racing to the other corner of the roof. The firemen raced with him but were unable to keep up. Whenever Ozzie wanted to he might jump and splatter himself upon the sidewalk, and by the time the firemen scooted to the spot all they could do with their net would be to cover the mess.

"Wheeeee . . . wheeeee . . ."

"Hey, Oscar," the winded fireman yelled, "what the hell is this, a game or something?"

"Wheeeee . . . wheeeee . . ."

"Hey, Oscar—"

But he was off now to the other corner, flapping his wings fiercely. Rabbi Binder couldn't take it any longer—the fire engines from nowhere, the screaming suicidal boy, the net. He fell to his knees exhausted, and with his hands curled together in front of his chest like a little dome, he pleaded, "Oscar, stop it, Oscar. Don't jump, Oscar. Please come down . . . Please don't jump."

And further back in the crowd a single voice, a single young voice, shouted a long word to the boy on the roof.

"Jump!"

It was Itzie. Ozzie momentarily stopped flapping.

"Go ahead, Ozz—jump!" Itzie broke off his point of the star and courageously, with the inspiration not of a wise-guy but of a disciple, stood alone. "Jump, Ozz, jump!"

Still on his knees, his hands still curled, Rabbi Binder twisted his body back. He looked at Itzie, then, agonizingly, back up to Ozzie.

"Oscar, DON'T JUMP! PLEASE, DON'T JUMP . . . please please . . ."

"Jump!" This time it wasn't Itzie but another point of the star. By the time Mrs. Freedman arrived to keep her four-thirty appointment with Rabbi Binder, the whole little upside down heaven was shouting and pleading for Ozzie to jump, and Rabbi Binder no longer was pleading with him not to jump, but was crying into the dome of his hands.

Understandably Mrs. Freedman couldn't figure out what her son was doing on the roof. So she asked.

"Ozzie, my Ozzie, what are you doing? My Ozzie, what is it?"

Ozzie stopped wheeeeeing and slowed his arms down to a cruising flap, the kind birds use in soft winds, but he did not answer. He stood against the low, clouded, darkening sky—light was clicking down more swiftly now, as on a small gear—flapping softly and gazing down at the small bundle of a woman who was his mother.

"What are you doing, Ozzie?" She turned toward the kneeling Rabbi Binder and rushed so close that only a paper-thickness of dusk lay between her stomach and his shoulders.

"What is my baby doing?"

Rabbi Binder gaped up at her but he too was mute. All that moved was the dome of his hands; it shook back and forth like a weak pulse.

"Rabbi, get him down! He'll kill himself. Get him down, my only baby . . ."

"I can't," Rabbi Binder said, "I can't . . ." and he turned his handsome head toward the crowd of boys behind him.

"It's them. Listen to them."

And for the first time Mrs. Freedman saw the crowd of boys and she heard what they were yelling.

"He's doing it for them. He won't listen to me. It's them." Rabbi Binder spoke like one in a trance.

"For them?"

"Yes."

"Why for them?"

"They want him to . . ."

Mrs. Freedman raised her two arms upward as though she were conducting the sky. "For them he's doing it!" And then in a gesture older than pyramids, older than prophets and floods, her arms came slapping down to her sides. "A martyr I have. Look!" She tilted her head to the roof. Ozzie was still flapping softly. "My martyr."

"Oscar, come down, *please,*" Rabbi Binder groaned.

In a startlingly even voice Mrs. Freedman called to the boy on the roof. "Ozzie, come down, Ozzie. Don't be a martyr, my baby."

Like a litany, Rabbi Binder repeated her words. "Don't be a martyr, my baby. Don't be a martyr."

"Gawhead, Ozz—*be* a Martin!" It was Itzie. "Be a Martin, be a Martin," and all the voices joined in singing for Martindom. "Be a Martin, be a Martin . . ."

Somehow when you're on a roof the darker it gets the less you can hear. All Ozzie knew was that two groups wanted two new things: his friends were spirited and musical about what they wanted; his mother and the rabbi were even-toned, chanting, about what they didn't want. The rabbi's voice was without tears now and so was his mother's.

The big net stared up at Ozzie like a sightless eye. The big, clouded sky pushed down. From beneath it looked like a gray corrugated board. Suddenly, looking up into that unsympathetic sky, Ozzie realized all the strangeness of what these people, his friends, were asking: they wanted him to jump, to kill himself; they were singing about it now—it made them that happy. And there was an even greater strangeness: Rabbi Binder was on his knees, trembling. If there was a question to be asked now it was not, "Is it me?" but rather, "Is it us?" . . . is it us?"

Being on the roof, it turned out, was a serious thing. If he jumped would the singing become dancing? Would it? What would jumping stop? Yearningly, Ozzie wished he could rip open the sky, plunge his hands through, and pull out the sun; and on the sun, like a coin, would be stamped JUMP or DONT JUMP.

Ozzie's knees rocked and sagged a little under him as though they were setting him for a dive. His arms tightened, stiffened, froze, from shoulders to fingernails. He felt as if each part of his body were going to vote as to whether he should kill himself or not—and each part as though it were independent of *him*.

The light took a long, loud, unexpected click down and the new darkness quickly, like a gag, hushed the friends singing for this and the mother and rabbi chanting for that.

Ozzie stopped counting votes, and in a curiously high voice, like one who wasn't prepared for speech, he spoke.

"Mamma?"

"Yes, Oscar."

"Mamma, get down on your knees, like Rabbi Binder."

"Oscar—"

"Get down on your knees," he said, "or I'll jump."

Ozzie heard a whimper, then a quick rustling, and when he looked down where his mother had stood he saw the top of a head and beneath that a circle of dress. She was kneeling beside Rabbi Binder.

He spoke again. "Everybody kneel." There was the sound of everybody kneeling.

Ozzie looked around. With one hand he pointed toward the synagogue entrance. "Make *him* kneel."

There was a noise, not of kneeling, but of body-and-cloth stretching. Ozzie could hear Rabbi Binder saying in a gruff whisper, ". . . or he'll *kill* himself," and when next he looked there was Yakov Blotnik off the doorknob and for the first time in his life upon his knees in the Gentile posture of prayer.

As for the firemen—it is not as difficult as one might imagine to hold a net taut while you are kneeling.

Ozzie looked around again; and then, still in the voice high as a young girl's, he called to Rabbi Binder.

"Rabbi?"

"Yes, Oscar."

"Rabbi Binder, do you believe in God?"

"Yes."

"Do you believe God can do Anything?" Ozzie leaned his head out into the darkness. "Anything?"

"Oscar, I think—"

"Tell me you believe God can do Anything."

There was a second's hesitation. Then:

"God can do Anything."

"Tell me you believe God can make a child without intercourse."

"He can."

"Tell me!"

"God," Rabbi Binder admitted, "can make a child without intercourse."

"Mamma, you tell me."

"God can make a child without intercourse," his mother said.

"Make *him* tell me." There was no doubt who *him* was.

In a few moments Ozzie heard an old comical voice say something to the increasing darkness about God.

Next, Ozzie made everybody say it. And then he made them all say they believed in Jesus Christ—first one at a time, then all together.

When the catechizing was through it was the beginning of evening. From the street it sounded as if someone on the roof might have sighed.

"Ozzie?" A woman's voice dared to speak. "You'll come down now?"

There was no answer, but the woman waited, and when a voice finally did speak it was thin and crying, and exhausted as that of an old man who has just finished pulling the bells.

"Mamma, don't you see—you shouldn't hit me. He shouldn't hit me. You shouldn't hit me about God, Mamma. You should never hit anybody about God—"

"Ozzie, please come down now."

"Promise me, Mamma, promise me you'll never hit anybody about God."

He had asked only his mother, but for some reason everyone kneeling in the street promised he would never hit anybody about God.

Once again there was silence.

"I can come down now, Mamma," the boy on the roof finally said. He turned his head both ways as though checking the traffic lights. "Now I can come down . . ."

And he did, right into the center of the yellow net that glowed in the evening's edge like an overgrown halo.

TERRY SOUTHERN

The Sun and the Still-Born Stars

Sid Peckham and his wife were coast farmers and Sid was a veteran of World War II. They were eking out the narrowest sort of existence on a little plot of ground just east of Corpus Christi, about an eighth of a mile from the Gulf.

The cost of their farm was two hundred dollars. For one reason or another Sid had not been able to get a G.I. loan to buy the land outright, but he and Sarah had scraped together enough money for the down payment. Now, to meet the quarterly installments of twenty-five dollars, they depended entirely upon what could be raised there and sold for the vegetable markets of Corpus Christi, namely soft melons and squash.

Sid and Sarah were of a line of unimaginative, one-acre farmers who very often had not owned the land they worked, and whose life's spring was less connected to the proverbial love of the land than twisted somehow around a vague acceptance of work, God's will and the hopeless, unsurprising emptiness of life. The only book in their little house was the Bible, which they never read.

For a time, before the war, they had lived on the even smaller farm of Sarah's father, sharing a little room in the back and working most of the day in the melon patch. Then Sid was gone, in the Army, for three years.

They had one letter from France, but for all it said of what was happening it could have been written from Fly, two miles away, or even from his own family's place across the road.

> Dear Sari
>
> They told us all to write. Hope you are all well. I am fine. The place here and the food is all right. Rain yesterday here, and today. I hope you and the family are all right.
>
> God keep you.
>
> Sid Peckham

In other respects, the letter was an epitome of their relationship. Speech between them was empty and hushed.

Only sometimes now Sid spoke of the *films* he had seen in the Army. Then he was more expressive than at any other time.

"That one were right good," he would say, "I seen it on the boat."

Sarah would listen. They had never gone to see films before. But since the war, every Saturday they walked the two miles into Fly for the new movie. The movie in Fly played once on Saturday night and once again on Tuesday afternoon. Sid and Sarah went to the Saturday night showing, and they always left the house well before sundown in order to get good seats. All the seats were the same price, fifteen cents. They saw comedies and mysteries, westerns, dramas, and classic histories, one a week for seven years.

In the darkened cinema their faces were like a single wooden mask. Sometimes Sarah had difficulty in grasping the mood of a film at all. Then she would try to take her cue from Sid, leaning out to turn and peer at his face. But it never told her anything, and as soon as he noticed he would push her away again back down into her own seat.

Only, if Sid had seen the film before, Sarah might watch him from the side, how he covered his mouth and clucked from time to time, nodding his head at the screen. The way this happened though, it never failed to strike Sarah as being different from what was happening at the same instant on the screen. And Sarah's brow would sometimes go all dark furrowed, and she might draw her stiff fingers back and forth over the palm of her hand.

Later in the moonlight, on the narrow dirt road as they walked back to their place, Sarah would walk a little behind Sid and stare at the back of his head. Or else she might shoot a furtive, intent look at him from the side.

"Nice film weren't it, Sid?"

"It weren't a bad film," Sid would say, and after a moment, "I seen it before now. I seen it in *Englelan.*"

Sid Peckham had picked up one or two expressions in England. One of them was "piping" for hot, or more often to augment hotness. Only he had distorted it to "piper," so that now they sometimes referred to the coffee of a morning as being "piper hot." Or if Sarah simply asked, "How does this soup taste to you, Sid?" Sid might say, "It's a right good soup, it's piper hot."

But somewhere behind this, the mask of each expressed life, deep under the dead wooden simplicity of their ever separate, unspoken awareness, little things were crawling alive, breeding and taking on great, secret shape.

During the day their labor was equally divided, until at last one Friday when Sarah was in the sixth month of her first pregnancy, it fell upon Sid to do most of the work in the patch. For her part, Sarah wondered if now, with the coming expense of the child, they would continue to go into Fly on Saturday for the movie. For they had never, above the quarterly payments on the land, had money to spare at the time the payments were made. And moreover, with Sid working the patch alone, it was difficult to see how they would meet the next payment at all.

Saturday, and Sarah awoke from a dreamless sleep, in a summer darkness long before dawn. At waking, this darkness was pure, and except for the night wind, perfectly still. She sought, but no notion of time could form in her mind, and she knew as soon that beneath the swift softness of the wind the night was alive with sound.

She was very still, her head straight against the flat cotton mattress. And as out from the ceiling center, where the untrained vision lay, the room grew, like an image on a screen, slowly down around her to a vague, somehow familiar definition, she knew that he was awake too, and she touched his shoulder.

"What's that noise, Sid?"

"It's somethin' in the patch," he said without moving.

A dry electric rustling filled the room. They lay still for another moment as the rustling stopped, then started up again, and Sid got stiffly out of bed and went to the window.

"What is it?" asked Sarah. Sitting up now she could see Sid looking steadily out the window, but from the side, with his back almost flat against the wall. Then he was all crouched down, so that his eyes seemed at the level of the sill, peering out across the patch.

Sarah left the bed and knelt beside him. At the window the sounds were not the same as before. There was a scratching, a dry tinsel sound. Leaf against leaf, and leaf against vine. And these were of the night, but in the heart of the patch where the dark form lay moving, just there, were the different sounds, the heavy, wetmouth breaking of melons, and the sound of breathing. And while the rustling of the leaf and vine stopped, the breathing went on. Yet somehow heard by Sarah as indistinct so that she shook her head and turned it first this way and then that, out against the night and at last even to peer into Sid's face.

"Where, Sid?" she asked, "what is it?" because she saw that his eyes stared straight unblinking into the dark.

"It's an animal I reckon," said Sid. He stood up slowly and took his clothes off the chair. "I reckon it's a hog."

Sarah stayed hunched at the sill, looking out the window and back at Sid as he put on his clothes.

"It's bigger than a hog." she said.

"I know it," said Sid.

In the room she saw his back as he left the door, and at once out the window how he appeared at the corner of the house, a shadow in the darkness, creeping along the fence of the patch. Opposite the window he stopped, crouched peering out over the patch. And where the heavier shadow lay, there was nothing now except the still night, and the breathing.

Then Sarah saw Sid rise, holding a large white rock. And she put out her hand, for in this light she saw him as though a film of oil lay stretched across the window. But in a sudden bound he was over the fence, throwing the stone and rushing ahead, as to Sarah at the window the two sounds were joined in a loud tearing sound of the breaking leaf and vine. And as quickly the single shape was split, formed and reformed, and was lost twisting down through the darkness.

She stayed at the window while the sounds broke away, dying across the patch, down toward the sea. Then she went to bed.

Sometime after sunrise she awoke again, and was still alone in the room. When she was up and dressed, she made the bed and began to sweep the floor; but once, near the window, she stopped and stood there, staring out over the land. Across the piece of yard to the fence, over the patch, and beyond the field, lay the dim sea, rising back high against the morning, and nothing stirred, but the brilliant shooting patterns of the sun, moving out across the land.

Sarah fixed the breakfast and Sid had not returned. Then she went out into the patch and chopped weeds until she was sick. She was lying on the bed when Sid came in at almost noon. His clothes were wet and torn; there were short deep cuts on his face.

"What is it, Sid?"

For a moment he stood motionless in the doorway.

"It was a hog," he said then, "a sea-hog."

Sarah waited.

"I druv it back into the water," said Sid. And he took off his clothes and lay down.

In the late afternoon he awoke and got up hurriedly. Out in the patch he worked in a frenzy for two hours. Then he sat down on the back steps.

In the kitchen, mending the torn clothes, Sarah saw his head turned away from the setting sun, and always south to the sea.

After supper they went straight to bed and Sarah didn't wake until light. He was gone.

She got up and dressed. Instead of fixing the breakfast, she took the hoe from the back steps and went to work in the patch. By mid-morning she could no longer feel her arms and shoulders. She tried to straighten up and something moved through her back like a burning coal.

She sat on the steps with her face in her arms. Much later, she got up, and under the hot sun walked down through the patch and the field toward the sea. Above the throbbing heat of noon she could hear ahead the constant play of the surf, and something more when she began to climb the dunes. But when she reached the top of the dune and looked down onto the vast mirrored surf below, she saw that he stood alone, in apparent dead fatigue, and Sarah could only follow the dull sweep of his eyes on the retreating darkness in the water.

She lay on the dune for a while after Sid left the beach, plodding past her, back up across the field toward the patch and the house.

When Sarah reached the house, Sid was asleep. He slept into the afternoon, then he went out into the patch with his hoe. She saw as he passed how his mouth was fixed straight, like the breaking length of a black string. After an hour, he was sitting on the back steps.

From her chair at the kitchen table Sarah watched Sid with his pocket-knife whittle off the handle of the hoe. He spent the rest of the afternoon there on the steps, sharpening the end of the hoe handle with his knife, so that finally what was left of the hoe was a sharp-pointed, hardwood spear about three feet long. Then he went to bed.

And Sarah followed. She lay in bed, her eyes opened, turning ever again from where the ceiling spread above them like a veil to Sid's face and back, and back again. Night. Night and the image of night.

She did not awake until late.

The land on the Gulf between Corpus Christi and Fly is a flat burning waste, with only the most gradual rise of dune above the surf.

At the still blaze of noon, there is a wildness here in the heat and light, and atop the dunes the air is overhung with a sound like water beating against some distant cliff but this is the sound of the sun, which strikes and rises from the dead sand in black lined waves.

As Sarah climbed, crawling, she stopped, feeling the rise of sound and light, turned herself, her eyes, straight into the panic sun, and she slowly stood, her eyes strained to blackness. But then she was there, on the crest of the highest dune where she dropped to her knees at the sight of the endless sea stretched shorewise in an explosion of light. And below, deep in the burning surf, Sid Peckham fought for his life.

Sarah lay on the dune, half dazed by the flat crystal brilliance of the scene below as the two bodies heaved and pitched together in some heavy soundless purpose. Now one, now the other in ascendancy, they fell and rose, threshing, their rage a slowly desperate waltz.

Here from high atop the dune, she heard the muted scream and saw the lunge in the surf below, how the two fell grappling beneath the water, then rose wavering, fixed in heavy changing arcs of strength, leaning now toward the sea, now toward the land, but always flat under the burning sun. They gave no quarter except to fatigue till one beating arc wavered and fell, in favor of sea or shore.

And then to Sarah the battle seemed locked like a poised weight, and she sprang up from the dune and rushed down to the sea. The hardwood spear stood jutting aslant from the sand below the surf, and as the girl threw herself between them she wrenched the spear from the sand, and turning its point from shore to sea and back, and back again, all her knowing was struck dim by the terrible flux of weight, balance, and change, her eyes blind to the tearing sun. Great cloud head image on the silver screen, the approach and retreat, *approach and retreat,* the growing approach, approach, approach, flat huge swelling on the silver screen, uncontained growing, swelling, swelling swelling swelling to a scream.

"Stop."

Lilt. And the white surf around them feathered out all rose and pink, their motion faded to an end as gradual and even as the close of slow music.

For a long while Sarah stood in the surf seeing only where the water broke silver and red around the upright spear. Then she drew out the spear and facing the sea, she felt the tremor beneath her feet as the weight was dragged away along the sand, under the water. And she was alone.

Back at the house she worked in the patch until night, then she went to bed. Before dawn she awoke, while the moon was still high and there was no sound except the stirring of the night wind. But beyond the patch and past the field, from down at the sea, she could hear something like the surf on rock cliffs, and above this, the listening that came up through the night.

She got out of bed and dressed, walked through the kitchen and out the door. Near the back steps, struck straight in the ground was the hoe handle that had been fashioned into a spear. Sarah would know as she passed, from the way the shadow fell under the moon, just how early or late the morning was.

She crossed the patch and was into the field before she could remember and touch the pocket of her thin dress. There were two coins there: a nickel and a quarter. She stiffened a little and stood still, holding the coins in her hand. A small cloud passed under the moon, and for an instant on the left the dirt road to Fly was only a twisting shadow. Then the cloud was gone. The road to Fly was clear. And as she moved to the point beyond, where the road met the field, she knew that it was all right too, the man who sold the tickets would give her the change himself.

POETRY

Introduction

Donald Hall was the *Paris Review*'s first poetry editor. A Harvard graduate, an editor of the *Advocate* there, I knew him as a fellow classmate in 1950, the first year of Archibald MacLeish's famous English S course. In 1952 Hall was studying at Christ Church, Oxford at about the time the magazine was first being discussed in Paris. In the spring of 1952 I looked him up when I was visiting Oxford with the King's College, Cambridge tennis team. We had a great number of drinks in a place called, as I remember, White's. A figure of considerable reputation at Oxford, Hall had won the Newdigate Prize for Poetry. Over drinks he agreed to become the poetry editor of the magazine and the prize-winning poem, appropriately enough entitled "Exile," was published in the first edition.

Hall went on to become by far the most prolific of the *Paris Review* editors. He once told me that he was too scared to count all the books and tracts he was responsible for—understandable because they include biographies, juveniles, textbooks, poetry and essay volumes, editions, anthologies, and one encyclopedia. A part-time participatory journalist, he went through spring training with the Pittsburgh Pirates—so heavily bearded that he looked like a member of a House of David team—and wrote about it in *Playing Around*. Among his collected poems are *Kicking the Leaves* (1978), *Happy Man* (1986), and *The One Day* for which he won the National Book Critics Circle Award (1988). He reports that his friends say that he gets better as he approaches senility. Here is what he remembers about his earlier years with the *Review.*

—G.P.

*   *   *

Early on we decided that we had a purpose: we would represent a generation of writers. When you are in your early twenties nothing seems so important as your own generation. There is nothing about which you have such clear and distinct ideas, and therefore nothing about which you are more likely to mistake yourself. Of course it is your duty to impose your mistakes on others, not to mention your brighter moments. Thus I put forward the poetry of Robert Bly and Adrienne Rich; when I became aware of Louis Simpson, James Wright, W. D. Snodgrass, and W. S. Merwin, I recruited them for the *Paris Review.* Because I began editing for this magazine while I studied in England, I brought Geoffrey Hill and Thom Gunn to the magazine early; later Ted Hughes, Donald Davie, Philip Larkin, and Charles Tomlinson. If I feel pride in these accomplishments, it follows as the night the day that I feel shame for my omissions and rejections. I rejected Frank O'Hara and Allen Ginsberg when I should have known better. At the time, Allen wrote George claiming that I would not recognize a poem if it buggered me in broad daylight. Much as I regret my error, I am pleased that I called forth this visionary moment from Allen; of course, we collapsed into friendship in our moderate middle age.

Not that everything was smooth, editing for the *Paris Review.* George complained on occasion that I chose *endless* poems about animals, alternating them with poems that lamented the loss of Christian faith; George made it clear that he was not personally opposed to animals, only to a magazine that smelled like a zoo; George allowed as how Alfred, Lord Tennyson and Matthew Arnold had perhaps exhausted the poetic possibilities of the subsiding sea of faith.

My own problems with the magazine were minor: lost manuscripts, threats of murder, lost issues, overstock, fecklessness breeding like smallpox in the Paris office. I remember a poet in Philadelphia who, asked to wait year after year because of tardy issues, revised his poem semiannually, sending me new versions which I dutifully forwarded to Paris—he always promising never to touch it again; I always promising that the issue would arrive on our shores a week from Tuesday. Finally, after seven years, we printed his poem in the version he had originally submitted.

—Donald Hall

ROBERT BLY

Two Choral Stanzas

I

The dove returns; it found no resting place;
It was in flight all night above the shaken seas;
Beneath ark eaves
The dove shall magnify the tiger's bed;
Give the dove peace;
The split-tail swallows leave the sill at dawn,
At dusk blue swallows shall return.
On the third day the crow shall fly;
The crow, the crow, the spider-coloured crow,
The crow shall find new mud to walk upon.

II

And as we spoke the Nicene Creed we were called out
To fight the barn afire
And here the summer's corn is born again
In reformation into air,
The children cry and call
And throw their snowballs in the fire; the barleys burn;
The walls are folding; burning rust and gold
The loft hangs fire in air; the straw and chaff
Burn black the timid dampness of the night
And churn the ancient wall-stones to a dust.

PHILIP BOOTH

Seadog and Seal

In hill fire Fall
come home from sea,
I climb the shoal
sea-edge to lie
ledged in the sun:
warm and dry
on my rock, vain
as a sunning seal,
I am his twin;
but he slides away
in the tidal run
while I lie high
aground, a hull
stranded free
of the ebbtide pull.

No bell-toll roll
calls me to sea,
wheeled cry of gull
or mackerel sky;
no man in Maine
has strength to ply
the offshore seine
my shipmates haul:
fathoms green
as a mermaid's eye
weight the brine
where their bones lie.
And I, I fill
my dogwatch day
with sail to furl.

Only the seal
in his tide-rip play
will sight that hull,
ship lost at sea

in a seaweed glen.
Diving free
and seaward as men
go down, O seal
once my twin,
what vanity
lies under the sun!
under curved cry
of gull, bell-toll,
where over me
the green hills roll.

JAMES DICKEY

Mindoro, 1944

Above the dog-eye-colored land
And town of San José
Of hot dog-fur and tin,
Six boys have slung a coffin by the ropes,
And they and all of it are growing in-
ward, in the motion of the sun
Unbearably shimmering to uncoil.
Many have been killed, and they are lying down.
Light falls, man falls: together.
Sun rises from earth alone.

The bottled brightness of heat
Holds queerly a spade's scratched flame.
There is a log, a trembling barge
In air, and it is hard to hollow or to load.
Its wood-grain sews a sheet among their hands.
Each equal eye is in the mighty head
Of military gold. Behind their wheels
The trucks are lifting roads from where they lie.

Wheel falls, man falls: together.
Dust rises from earth alone.

In the balance walking breathless in their palms
He must not seem to move or be aware.
He leans, he feels he leans
Slowly from fist to fist again around.
He does not know how much or where
He swings, nor yet how much
Of him is stalled between, afloat inside
The muscles of their arms. He feels it shake.
He feels it pant, a pack of dogs, with life.
Beast falls, man falls: together.
Birth rises from earth alone.

He strains to remember when.
May it be now he rises from this place
Like flame along the hair of burning string,
Inwinding, as he glows among his knots,
Six tall sway-headed forms? And this be his?
'Who, among you come, has not yet seen
Mutilation in full flight slain?'
He asks. Truthfully they are still.
Truth falls, man falls: together.
Thought rises from earth alone.

He is! He is outside!
He glitters sandily all about the spade!
He dances like dust in the pit
In all their good arms at once!
Blind as he is, as a ball of paper on fire,
He knows he must do nothing with the world!
Nothing! And see it blazing, there! He cries,
And laughs in it. He clings with their hands to the ropes.
His heart stops all around him, in the sun.
He picks up everything and loves.
Sun falls, man falls: together.
Light rises from earth alone.

DAVID FERRY

On the Way to the Island

After we fled away from the shuddering dock,
The sea upheld us, would not let us go
Nor drown us, and we danced all night in the dark,
Till we woke to discover the deck was made of glass,
All glass, and, leaning together, we lovers looked down,
Say a hundred miles, say a million years, and there
Were the fish, huge, gaping, graceless, flashing
Their innocent frightening scales in the dark!

My lady wears brilliants in her hair, and the sun
Makes their fakery sparkle, so beautiful
Is she my lady, so pitiful is she,
Her white arms so naked after those scales,
Her coquetry pretty after those monsters,
Beginning her history there in the deep dark.
My lady, I love you because of the dark
Over which your glass slippers so ignorantly danced!

ALLEN GROSSMAN

Holy Ghost Hospital

How all things shatter, fall away, and break.
In this time of my great happiness I pass
And repass the gates of the Holy Ghost
Where all men die,
And the bridegroom comes to remember loneliness.
Around the stony saints the old men crawl,
Around and around, and all roads lead to the wall.

The street beyond is all stuffed up with toys,
Where children die, fair girls and boys,
In their narrow cribs devoured by serpents.
A dying widow combs thick yellow hair
And scatters bread crumbs from a kitchen crock.
I see the white birds in her back-street flock.
"Boidy, boidy, boidy, remember me."
This world is like a stone stuck in my shoe.
I shall die here in my loneliness, I too.
A squirrel above my head devours the bread,
And all the birds go hungry. Listen,
We are all related to the dead.
There is more sorrow now abroad
Than tears can signify,
More fear than fears can warn. Husband and priest,
Conspire with me
Against the dark-hearted sea.
No god could be well pleased with Cambridge Street.
At day's end what could descend but dust and darkness
On this hanging tree,
On my love and me.

THOM GUNN

The Wound

The huge wound in my head began to heal
About the beginning of the seventh week.
Its valleys darkened, its villages became still:
For joy I did not move and dared not speak,
Not doctors would cure it, but time, its patient skill.

And constantly my mind returned to Troy.
After I sailed the seas I fought in turn
On both sides, sharing even Helen's joy

Of place and growing up—to see Troy burn—
As Neoptolemus, that stubborn boy.

I lay and rested as prescription said.
Manœuvered with the Greeks, or sallied out
Each day with Hector. Finally my bed
Became Achilles' tent, to which the lout
Thersites came reporting numbers dead.

I was my self: subject to no man's breath:
My own commander was my enemy.
And while my belt hung up, sword in the sheath,
Thersites shambled in and breathlessly
Cackled about my friend Patroclus' death.

I called for armour, rose, and did not reel.
But, when I thought, rage at his noble pain
Flew to my head, and turning I could feel
My wound break open wide. Over again
I had to let those storm-lit valleys heal.

GEOFFREY HILL

Genesis

I

Against the burly air I strode
Crying the miracles of God.

And first I brought the sea to bear
Upon the dead weight of the land;
And the waves flourished at my prayer,
The rivers spawned their sand.

And where the streams were salt and full
The tough pig-headed salmon strove,
Ramming the ebb, in the tide's pull,
To reach the steady hills above.

II

The second day I stood and saw
The osprey plunge with triggered claw,
Feathering blood along the shore,
To lay the living sinew bare.

And the third day I cried: 'Beware
The soft-voiced owl, the ferret's smile,
The hawk's deliberate stoop in air,
Cold eyes, and bodies hooped in steel,
Forever bent upon the kill.'

III

And I renounced, on the fourth day,
This fierce and unregenerate clay,
Building as a huge myth for man
The watery Leviathan,

And made the long-winged albatross
Scour the ashes of the sea
Where Capricorn and Zero cross,
A brooding immortality—
Such as the charmed phoenix has
In the unwithering tree.

IV

The phoenix burns as cold as frost;
And, like a legendary ghost,
The phantom-bird goes wild and lost,
Upon a pointless ocean tossed.

So, the fifth day, I turned again
To flesh and blood and the blood's pain.

v

On the sixth day, as I rode
In haste about the works of God,
With spurs I plucked the horse's blood.

By blood we live, the hot, the cold,
To ravage and redeem the world:
There is no bloodless myth will hold.

And by Christ's blood are men made free
Though in close shrouds their bodies lie
Under the rough pelt of the sea;

Though Earth has rolled beneath her weight
The bones that cannot bear the light.

RICHARD HOWARD

On Tour

It is the movement that disturbs the line,
    Thickening the form,
    Turning into warm
Compression what had once been cold and fine.

Seen from down here, if only we remained,
    These hills are high:
    Driving on, the sky
Imposes, and no longer can be trained

By any structure of the seeming ground.
    Landscape, I discover,
    As the car gains over
Something that changes from a little mound

To monstrous eminence before your eyes,
　　Landscape can flaunt, can
　　Fail like the heart of man:
And when you see the difference in size

Of cliffs we once considered at the bright
　　Grass along their peak
　　And then saw from the bleak
Extremity of sand below, the sight

Gives more than pause—alas, it gives the slow
　　Ruin of our hopes
　　Fed upon the slopes
From where we've been to where we want to go.

TED HUGHES

Crow Hill

The farms are stinking craters in
Sheer sides under the sodden moors;
When it is not wind it is rain,
Neither of which will stop at doors:
One will damp beds and the other shake
Dreams beneath sleep it cannot break.

Between the weather and the rock
Farmers make a little heat;
Cows that sway a bony back,
Pigs upon delicate feet
Hold off the sky, trample the strength
That shall level these hills at length.

Buttoned from the blowing mist
Walk the ridges of ruined stone;

What humbles these hills has raised
The arrogance of blood and bone,
And thrown the hawk upon the wind,
And lit the fox in the dripping ground.

DONALD JUSTICE

Sestina

I woke by first light in a wood
Right in the shadow of a hill
And saw about me in a circle
Many I knew, the dear faces
Of some I recognized as friends.
I knew that I had lost my way.

I asked if any knew the way.
They stared at me like blocks of wood.
They turned their backs on me, those friends,
And struggled up the stubborn hill
Along that road which makes a circle.
No longer could I see their faces.

But there were trees with human faces.
Afraid, I ran a little way
But must have wandered in a circle.
I had not left that human wood;
I was no farther up the hill.
And all the while I heard my friends

Discussing me, but not like friends.
Through gaps in trees I glimpsed their faces.
(The trees grow crooked on that hill.)
Now all at once I saw the way:
Above a clearing in the wood
A lone bird wheeling in a circle

And in that shadowed space the circle
Of those I thought of still as friends.
I drew near, calling, and the wood
Rang and they turned their deaf faces
This way and that, but not my way.
I stood alone upon the hill.

And it grew dark. Behind the hill
The sun slid down, a fiery circle;
Screeching, the bird flew on her way.
It was too dark to see my friends.
But then I saw them, and their faces
Were leaning above me like a wood.

Around me they circle on the hill.
But what is wrong with my friends' faces?
Why have they changed that way to wood?

X. J. KENNEDY

In a Prominent Bar in Secaucus One Day

> *With thanks to Claire McAllister for*
> *pointing out that these words may be sung*
> *to the tunes of 'The Old Orange Flute' and*
> *'Sweet Betsy from Pike.'*

In a prominent bar in Secaucus one day
Rose a lady in skunk with a topheavy sway,
Raised a knobby red finger—all turned from their beer—
While with eyes bright as snowcrust she sang high and clear:

'Now who of you'd think from an eyeful of me
That I once was a princess, and proud as could be?—
Oh I'd never sit down by a tumbledown drunk
If it wasn't my dears, for the high cost of junk.

'All the gents used to swear that the white of my calf
Beat the down of the swan by a length and a half—
In the kerchief of linen I caught to my nose
Ah, there never fell snot, but a little gold rose.

'I had seven gold teeth and a toothpick of gold,
My Virginia cheroot was a leaf of it rolled,
And I'd light it each time with a hundred in cash—
Why the bums used to fight if I flicked them an ash.

'In a car like the Roxy I'd roll to the track,
A steel-guitar trio, a bar in the back,
And the wheels made no noise, they turned over so fast—
It would take you ten minutes to see me go past.

'When the horses bowed down to me that I might choose
I bet on them all, for I hated to lose—
Now I'm saddled each night for my butter and eggs
And the broken threads race down the backs of my legs.

'Let you hold in mind, girls, that your beauty must pass
Like a lovely white clover that rusts with its grass—
Keep your bottoms off barstools and marry you young
Or you'll end—an old barrel with many a bung.

'For when time takes you out for a spin in his car
You'll be hard-pressed to stop him from going too far
And be left by the roadside, for all your good deeds,
Two toadstools for tits and a face full of weeds.'

All the house raised a cheer, but the man at the bar
Made a phonecall and up pulled a red patrol car
And she blew us a kiss as they copped her away
From that prominent bar in Secaucus, N.J.

PHILIP LARKIN

Referred Back

That was a pretty one, I heard you call
From the unsatisfactory hall
To the unsatisfactory room where I
Played record after record, idly,
Wasting my time at home, that you
Looked so much forward to.

Oliver's *Riverside Blues*, it was. And now
I shall, I suppose, always remember how
The flock of notes those antique negroes blew
Out of Chicago air into
A huge remembering pre-electric horn
The year after I was born
Three decades later made this sudden bridge
From your unsatisfactory age
To my unsatisfactory prime.

Truly, though our element is time,
We are not suited to the long perspectives
Open at each instant of our lives.
They link us to our losses: worse,
They show us what we have as it once was,
Blindingly undiminished; just as though
By acting differently we could have kept it so.

John Logan

The Mallard's Going

At the end of October a mallard
came down
         to the lake's edge
         and at a gesture
of the air
         without a look or rush
or noise of ritual
without great earth shift
               left

us; and pulled in waterbright folds
behind him
         the last lengths of our year
while willows dropped their paper
tears and a swan's head moved
round
     as thin as snow
     upon the turned
             wind.

W. S. Merwin

SOW

There is an archipelago rising
Out of the green waters that, rippling
And swaying, are the oak tree's shadow
In the afternoon wood. A shoal of small islands
Lying sheltered, close off-shore to leeward

Of the one largest whose great coast looms there
White in the shifting dimness like
Chalk downs seen from far out through the dawn
Mist, or the clouded moon full-swollen:
The old sow asleep with her litter. When
The wind blows there is no white water
Spills seetheing in over the outer reefs, though the sound
Of the sea's edge plays all about there,
But only from the tree-top the leaves' long sighing
In the waving boughs lends to the silent
Rocking shadow the rustling water-words
That slide through the shallows of that island sleep;
And no tide-race pulls and rips in the dark
Narrows breathing between them, but so gently
Does the eddying darkness slip and brush
In all their harbours, flooding and slumbering
Deep in their valleys, and over their
Dim hills drifting without splash or sound
But itself altering to all their contours,
That if one stood and watched one could not tell
Whether indeed they were honest islands,
Firm above the sea's surface, or a mirage,
Or a range sunk long ago whose white ghost
Only now had risen there through the deluding
Waters of afternoon. She is known, waking
For one fierce as foul, who can strike panic in
And put to flight whatever intruder,
Who treads unharmed on the adder, and will
Kill a grown man for the joy of it
With crushing and cruel mangling, or with
Weight worse than the nightmare's, will lie
On her own offspring at an ungainly whim
Or to hear the snap of many bones. But beyond this,
Of what she is in the waters of shadow,
Of those islands riding the green deep, such
Tales are told as would make one believe
That no man had ever visited them
And returned. For though it is said
That the worst of fates would be to founder
Near those shores and be cast up there,
They are flattered in fancy with fruit trees
And the abodes of saints; past coy rhymes

Cajoling the lesser coasts, are courted
In fables, called fair in fair tales
Where mariners, caught, cozened to swine-shapes,
Sink under shadows; until it would seem
As though they who spoke placated thereby
Some foul inevitability besetting
Voyagers, thus making desperate
Shift to show its hideous countenance
Both to itself and to them as a thing
Benign; or as though their breath, playing
In story over those coasts had come
To recognize itself as such a water
And shadow as white shores rose from
Upon whose fierce sleep it must break.

ROBERT MEZEY

In the Environs of the Funeral Home

In the environs of the funeral home
The smell of death was absent. All I knew
Were flowers rioting and odors blown
Tangible as a blossom into the face,
To be inhaled and hushed—and where they grew
Smothered the nostrils in the pungent grass.

Hyacinths of innocence and yellow-hammers
That beat the air at dawn, at dusk, to metal
Immortality, that flush where a bee clamors
For wine, are blooms of another color. See
How the flush fades as it descends the petal,
How deep the insect drinks, how quietly.

The point of this is a bitter paradox:
That violets flying a silver and gold elation,

And flapping ruffles of the white lilacs,
Shaking the air to tempt the golden bee,
Stiffen at the moment of consummation,
Swayed with guilt and weight of the bee's body.

These flowers, when cut and used, will remain ruddy,
As though made deathless in the very way
Their cutter kept the hue in the human body
That they were cut to celebrate and mourn.
The coffin has sprouted in dark mahogany
Out of them—edged, and shining like a thorn.

CHRISTOPHER MIDDLETON

News from Norwood

Professor Palamedes darts down Westow Street.
Nothing explains how he avoids
Colliding with mutton, plastics, pianos.
Professor Palamedes, darting down Westow Street,
Tunnels through petrol fumes and tundra;
Rhomboid oysterbeds under his rubbers,
Sparrows and sandwiches scatter before him.

Where is he going, Professor Palamedes?
It's well past three. What has he forgotten?
What can he have forgotten, Professor Palamedes,
Who stood with Agur by Solomon's elbow,
Who flogged the sea, full of nymphs and sheep,
Whom meat moods or helpful harmonies do not perplex?

Let us say he is going toward the stranger.
Again: he is going toward the stranger.
No matter who. The stranger. Who showed his face.

Who showed his face over Solomon's shoulder;
Who saw at Salamis, as planks buckled and the nymphs
Cheered, how sheep just went on cropping grass,
Side by side, to a tinkling of bells.

VASSAR MILLER

Love Song for the Future

To our ruined vineyards come,
Little foxes, for your share
Of our blighted grapes, the tomb
Readied for our common lair
Ants, we open you the cupboard;
Flee no more the heavy hand
Harmless as a vacant scabbard
Since our homes like yours are sand.

Catamounts so often hunted,
Wend your ways through town or city,
Since both you and we are haunted
By the Weird Ones with no pity.
Deer and bear we used to stalk,
We would spend our dying pains
Nestling you with mouse and hawk
Near our warmth until it wanes.

Weave across our faces, spiders,
Webwork fragile as a flower;
Welcome, serpents, subtle gliders,
For your position fails in power.
Loathed no longer, learn your worth,
Toad and lizard, snail and eel—
Remnants of a living earth
Cancelled by a world of steel,

Whose miasmic glitter dances
Over beast's and man's sick daze
While our eyes which scorned St. Francis
Watch Isaiah's vision craze:
Ox and lion mingling breath
Eat the straw of doom; in tether
To the selfsame stake of death
Wolf and lamb lie down together.

LOUIS SIMPSON

The Battle

Helmet and rifle, pack and overcoat,
Marched through a forest. Somewhere up ahead
Guns thudded. Like the circle of a throat
The night on every side was turning red.

They halted and they dug. They sank like moles
Into the clammy earth between the trees,
And slept. The sentries, standing in their holes,
Felt the first snow. Their feet began to freeze.

At dawn the first shell landed with a crack.
Then shells and bullets swept the icy woods.
This lasted many days. The snow turned black.
The corpses stiffened in their scarlet hoods.

Most clearly of that battle I remember
The tiredness of eyes, how hands looked thin
Around a cigarette, and the bright ember
Would pulse with all the life there was within.

W. D. SNODGRASS

The Campus on the Hill

Up the reputable walks of old established trees
They stalk, children of the *nouveaux riches;* chimes
Of the tall Clock Tower drench their heads in blessing:
"I don't wanna play at your house;
I don't like you any more."
My house stands opposite, on the other hill,
Among meadows, with the orchard fences down and falling;
Deer come almost to the door.
You cannot see it, even in this clearest morning.
White birds band in the air between
Over the garbage landfill and those homes thereto adjacent,
Hovering slowly, turning, settling down
Like the flakes sifting imperceptibly onto the little town
In a waterball of glass.
Yet, this morning, beyond this quiet scene,
The floating birds, the backyards of the poor,
Beyond the shopping plaza, the dead canal, the hillside lying
                                        tilted in the air,

Tomorrow has broken out today:
Riot in Algeria, in Cyprus, in Alabama;
Aged in wrong, the empires are declining,
And China gathers, soundlessly, like evidence.
What shall I say to the young on such a morning?—
Mind is the one salvation?—also, grammar?—
No, my little ones lean not toward revolt. They
Are the Whites, the vaguely furiously driven, who resist
Their souls with such passivity
As would make Quakers swear. All day, dear Lord, all day
They wear their godhead lightly.
They look out from their hill and say,
To themselves, "We have nowhere to go but down;
The great destination is to stay."
Surely the nations will be reasonable;
They look at the world—don't they?—the world's way?
The clock just now has nothing more to say.

WILLIAM STAFFORD

What God Used for Eyes Before We Came

At night sometimes the big fog roams in tall
from the coast and away tall on the mountain road
it stands without moving while cars wander along
in the canyons they make with their lights maintaining the worth

of local things. Along the continent shelf and back
far for searching the light engages the stone.

The brain blurring to know wanders that road,
goes the way Jesus came, irresistible,
calm over irrelevant history
toward a continent wall that moth rays touch—
our land backed by being old at night, lying deep,
the gray air holding ruin rock at Hovenweep.

GEORGE STEINER

A Samurai Who Tried to Kill All the Roosters in Japan

He: Deep in the cockerel's golden heart
      I loosed my bolt.
      The clarion-bird lies mute
      under a fitful sky.

      I shot the bell-ringer
      with rusted Colt. Now you and I
      forever lip to lip may lie
      and time must part.

She: Clock's chariot is a juggernaut,
        beneath its blade
        both days and works are naught.
        New cocks will sing
        incessant dawn,
        and changes ring
        across cathedral lawn,

        until both shaft and bullet strike
        your marksmanship and my affright.

CHARLES TOMLINSON

Distinctions

The seascape shifts

Between the minutest interstices of time
Blue is blue.

A pine-branch
Tugs at the eye: the eye
Returns to grey-blue, blue-black or indigo
Or it returns, simply,
To blue-after-the-pine-branch.

Here, there is no question of aberrations
Into pinks, golds or mauves:
This is the variation Pater indicated
But failed to prove.

Art exists at a remove
Evocation, at two,
Discusses a blue that someone
Heard someone talking about.

JAMES WRIGHT

Lying in a Hammock at a Friend's Farm in Pine Island, Minnesota

Over my head, I see the bronze butterfly,
Asleep on the black trunk,
Blowing like a leaf in green shadow.
Down the ravine behind Duffy's empty house,
The cowbells follow one another
Into the distances of the afternoon.
To my right,
In a field of sunlight between two pines,
The droppings of last year's horses
Blaze up into golden stones.
I lean back, as the evening darkens and comes on.
A chicken-hawk floats over, looking for home.
I have wasted my life.

To a Friend Condemned to Prison

Long I have seen those eyes,
Alert, astonished, bright,
Turn softly and survey
The girl in the falling light,
Or see down lucid skies
Soft bodies shift away.

Now, in the peopled dark,
Where hands make love to stone,
The shimmering vision falls,
The flesh lies down alone.
Only the mind hangs stark
Above the curving walls.

Hold to the mind, and die!—
Is all I say or know.

Yet you, embracing grief,
Father its children now
Forgiving, proud, you lie
With murderer, pervert, thief:

Nothing to do but keep
The body beaten down,
The clothing clean and frayed.
Nothing to do but drown
The blood in its own sleep,
And bid the heart lie dead.

NONFICTION

Introduction

A magazine starting out in Paris almost invariably has a café associated
with it (one's rooms tended to be too small to have gatherings of more
than three or four without people sitting on the floor). The *Paris Review*
had two—its earliest discussions in a Montparnasse bar called the Chap-
lain. A smoke-filled place in which William Styron said you could write
your name in the cigarette haze with your finger, it had a grand piano,
actually in tune, on which music students would play with varied skills.
Talks about the magazine went on with Scriabin études playing in the
background.

Later the *Review* people moved to the Café de Tournon. It was
around the corner from their small office in Les Éditions de la Table
Ronde, a publishing subsidiary of the house of Plon, a solemn, conservative, very austere publishing concern in a great enclosed courtyard at 8
rue Garancière opposite the walls of the Garde Republicaine.

Every evening at six the concierge locked the door from Les Editions
de la Table Ronde to the courtyard. Keys were not entrusted to *Review*
personnel, so the procedure for editors working late was to leave by the
windows—hanging from the sill by the fingertips and then dropping into
the Rue Garancière below. It was a jarring descent, especially for the
shorter members of the staff. On occasion, this exodus—which must

have looked like the flight of second-story men surprised in mid-job—coincided with the return of the mounted Garde Republicaine from an official function—often the ceremonial arrival of a head of state at the Elysée Palace. As they turned into their quarters across the street, their horses' hooves clattering on the cobblestones, they would glance haughtily from under the brims of their plumed helmets at the editors . . . as if a descent of cat burglars, their legs flailing briefly as they dropped from the facade of Editions Plon, was beneath their dignity to do anything about.

The Café de Tournon was not only the hangout of convenience for the *Review* people, who would drop down from the office window after dusk to meet there for a drink, but it was removed from St. Germain-des-Près, where the tourists sat in the cafés and craned their necks looking for Jean-Paul Sartre and Simone de Beauvoir, and from Montparnasse, where the older tourists sat in the Dôme or the Rotonde and chatted about *that* generation. Thus it had a comfortable, private, and rather drowsy ambiance of its own. Regulars did not talk about the Café de Tournon too much . . . for fear it would be overrun and "spoiled." Those who went there had an almost proprietary attitude about it.

Eugene Walter, who was an associate editor of the *Review*, wrote a sketch about the Café de Tournon:

"Everybody turned up sooner or later. The very pretty, very witty Francine du Plessix; the minxy bright-eyed Bee Dabney, who drew wonderful cats and monkeys. The English poet Christopher Logue. He liked so much to propagate the idea that he was a somewhat shady character; he told wondrous wild tales to further the effect. I like his work very much. The *Paris Review* published a fine suite of poems in which precious stones speak in the first person; I still get a tingle on a line from "Diamonds": "Brighter than a thicket of drawn knives, I . . ." When Christopher's mother visited Paris, he tried to keep her under wraps, finally brought her to the Tournon. Everybody thought she'd be, at the least, a red-haired Polish gypsy, or a Tunisian midwife, but she was a pink-cheeked little English lady with a silk print dress and a cameo.

"How many books were written in or around the Tournon? Who knows? I must say, I remember one day looking up from my Dubonnet and there were about ten people busy writing, staring into spaces, sipping endless black coffees or aperitifs. Some might have been doing accounts or lessons, who knows, but among those I saw scribbling on one occasion or another were William Gardner Smith, Austryn Wainhouse, Max Steele, Evan Connell, Jr., Mary Lee Settle, Sissel Lange-Nielsen, Nanos Valaoritis, Daphne Athas, Jean Garrigue. All these and more, sometimes only jotting notes or reading proofs—or writing letters, for the post office was just at the corner. The place was a beehive. Jane Lougee, publisher of the literary review, *Merlin*, sometimes brought her Siamese cat when she came for a Pernod with the *Merlin* editor, Alexander Trocchi, or the gifted and intelligent Richard Seaver. Mary Louise Wainhouse was studying Russian and often gossiped with the Finnish art historian, Renata Fitzthum-Eckstadt. Stravinsky turned up a couple of times; so did Clara Malraux and Jean Duvignaud.

"M. Alézard, the proprietor, opened the place in the morning, with Arnauld, the red setter, zanier than most of his ilk. Later, Mme. Alézard would turn up. They made excellent fried or scrambled eggs on a hot plate not much bigger than a silver dollar. The coffee was superior: perhaps that is why it became a literary café. There was a whole bevy of completely delightful Brazilians who frequented the place, because of the coffee. They were very skitty, chattery, often sang. I loved them. One day the Brazilian currency was devalued and one by one they vanished. I still miss them. A delightful creature from Madeira, Celestino Mendès-Sargo, amused us mightily with a song in Portuguese about Jupiter and the Muses: "The only way to live, ladies, is to try everything. . . ."

"Gurney Campbell, author (with Daphne Athas of the *Observer* prize play, *Sit on the Earth*), was already outlining her trilogy of plays about Gandhi. The Dutch photographers, Otto van Noppen and Dominic Beretty, were part of all this, as well as Robert Silvers, who had just finished his military service and been sent to me by Cecil Hemley, the publisher-poet. Robert began to help in the *Paris Review* office. Edith Schor knew all the words and the music of *La Carmagnole*, the dance steps too, and we'd sing and dance it in a circle, lally gagging back to the Tournon after the play-readings. A catchy tune. Once a policeman cautioned against singing it publicly; another time we got a bucket of water on our heads. It was a people's song during the French Revolution and is still frowned upon in the 6th and 7th *arrondissements:*

> *Ah, we'll see it yet,*
> *We'll see it yet:*
> *We'll hang the high-born from the lampposts!*
> *Dance, dance the Carmagnole!*

"Well, never a dull moment. The Communist bookshop on Rue Racine was blown up. A famous old restaurant closed and the cellar was found to be full of cat bones. Rabbit had been a great *specialité* on the menu. An eccentric Austrian committed suicide in the hotel where Catherine Morison lived with her grandmother's fans. The Café de Tournon buzzed and tingled day and night . . . gossip à gogo. . . .

"The biggest Percheron horses I ever saw or imagined came in mid-morning to bring the beer. The wine came in a tank-truck; a hose was inserted into a hole in the sidewalk opening into the cellar of the cafe. I used to time how long it took to fill the daily-depleted wine reservoir. One Monday morning, 23 minutes. The boy from the bakery brought paper sacks of hot croissants, but the long French loaves were stuck unwrapped into his bicycle basket. So much for finicky modern hygiene: the horses, the flies . . . but nobody ever died in the café, as far as I know. The poet and cinéast James Broughton was usually among the last few who closed the café at night. John Train would zoom up on a motorbike; zoom off, return, zoom again. About 2 A.M. the weary waiter, Charles, would start sweeping up cigarette butts, paper, etc., making cheerful insults about "these Bohemians." The image of him at work seemed downright emblematic, like Father Time himself sweeping away. Ho-hum, another day, another decade. Oh well, it was all immensely young and stimulating and fun and now seems beyond belief innocent and productive, in this establishment which was literary salon, permanent editorial board meeting, message center, short-order eatery, debating club, study hall. Four literary reviews in English, one in French; who knows how many books and other works springing forth from this noisy, smokey, clattery, raunchy, beat-up café?"

The piece that follows was published in the sixth number of the *Review*. A reminiscence by Nathan Asch, it describes the famous Dôme, a 1920's counterpart of a cafe like the Tournon. The account had been recommended by Malcolm Cowley. The nonfiction pieces—at least in the early issues—seemed always to have a Paris background. That is true not only of the Asch piece but of the nonfiction material which follows: a portrait of the young Australian, Vali, who was a familiar figure on the nighttime streets of the Left Bank in the 1950's.

—G.P.

NATHAN ASCH

The Nineteen-Twenties: An Interior

The Café du Dôme de Montparnasse was exactly like that; no American who was trying to be a writer in Paris in the 1920s could fail to recognize the truth of Nathan Asch's picture. Asch himself belonged to a somewhat later group than mine; he was one of the young men, mostly Midwesterners—though he was an exception, having been born in Poland and educated at Syracuse University—who gathered round that remarkable magazine edited by Ford Madox Ford, the Transatlantic Review. *Later he wrote a number of novels, beginning with* The Office, *that were well received by the critics and had a larger sale in Germany than in the United States; the Germans before Hitler thought that he was a better novelist than his father, Sholem Asch. The Second World War put a temporary stop to his career as a writer. Though overage he enlisted in the Air Force, and though assigned to Public Relations, he flew several combat missions over Germany; he wrote some wonderful letters about his experiences, but didn't publish a word. That was a grave tactical error. When he got home and started writing again, he found that editors and publishers had forgotten his name, and his postwar work—which includes three novels and many stories—has largely remained in manuscript. Some of this unpublished work is extremely good, though it isn't fashionable. This picture of a day at the Dôme is a section of a novel,* Paris Was Home. *Hemingway, who might or might not be recognized as one of the characters in the section, read the novel and had some objections not connected with his own appearance or nonappearance in it. But he also said, ". . . when Nathan writes about the Dôme at the end and when life was exciting and truly remembered because he was fighting then to be a writer . . . it is absolutely first rate." It is.*

—Malcolm Cowley

On the corner made by the boulevards Montparnasse and Raspail and the rue Delambre, across the street from the large and garish Café de la Rotonde, during those earlier days, was the then smaller place called the Café du Dôme. The Rotonde had new soft benches and polished tables. On the walls it had paintings of nudes, and still-lives of fruit and flowers, and landscapes of Brittany and the south of France. It had a fancy, spacious washroom with a woman in charge. The Dôme was smoke-stained and gloomy, and beyond the bar the seating part was circular and on different levels, so that if you were looking for somebody, you went up steps and around, glancing at both sides—in the daytime so little light came through that you almost had to lean over a table, peering, to recognize someone—and then down the steps and you were back at the bar. The toilet was down a deep stairs, and at the bottom there were two doors. The Men's part was a narrow square where above a hole in the floor stood out two raised foot soles. You carefully stepped on those, twisted around, let your pants down. For toilet paper you used cut-out leaves of the city directory.

The Dôme used to open at five-thirty in the morning. The bakery truck came, and a tray of crescent rolls was set on the counter, to surprise one with still-warmth when one took one to dip into the coffee. Outside in the street light stood a row of all night taxis, their meters covered, and inside, the chauffeurs fortified themselves for the ride home. Their voices were night-air-laden, and when an early worker came in to call out in a just-waked-up voice, "Good day," they slowly turned their heads and did not answer. Beer pipes were being iced, racks of wine brought up, red wine and white wine and mineral water set for quick use under the counter. Even at this early hour some had a shot of wine mixed with mineral water for their breakfast. If it was his early shift, César came in, in a worn black suit, stiff shirt and stained derby hat, stood at the counter for his coffee like anybody else, lifted the glass with shaking fingers and sipped carefully; then without his hat and jacket, polished bald head reflecting the light, and his stiff shirt but a dickey, went inside to sweep and mop. A party of all-night revelers arrived, filled the Dôme with un-morning-like laughter, called for drinks. When the angry César brought them, they did not drink, but their voices becoming languid and forced, ordered breakfast instead, did not eat it, sat in more silence, aware of César's exasperated banging around them, tired in the midst of the brisk morning. The dawn was greying the street outside, dimming the lights inside. The taxis had gone. At the counter stood clerks from neighborhood stores, concierges from nearby buildings, railroad men from the Montparnasse station, postmen, housewives, models, hardly dressed, hardly awake. A meticulously dressed gentleman arrived, sat down with his back toward the window, placed his folded newspaper at the exact center of the table, waited while César tied on an apron, put on a very worn black jacket; and a napkin on his arm, shuffled to the counter to push through the crowd, brought the coffee pot and the pitcher of hot milk. The gentleman took a pince-nez out of a case in his breast pocket, set the case beside the saucer and picked up the paper. He unfolded it, and began reading the top column on the left. The crowd thinned out at the counter; inside, people began arriving for breakfast or for the day. They drank their coffee quickly, hardly looking at the front page of their newspaper, calling for César to come take their money, or left the sum plus the copper tip and walked out. Or they dawdled picking out their place, trying to picture the day's coming scene from the seat, and sat down at first stiff and strange, as if they were moving to a spot that would take living in and breaking in, without calling for César, anxious that he should not come quickly, so that the few things that would happen through a day of sitting would each have a significance. When finally César stood in front of them, they not only asked for coffee, but also for writing materials, or a knife from the kitchen to cut the pages of a book they had brought. If the one glass of coffee this morning would be the only thing they would order through the day, or if they did not even have the necessary change to pay for it and had rehearsed how they would act with César—desperately hoping that this morning he was on the early shift—they made a ceremony of ordering the coffee. They put a sickly grimace on their face and said nothing so that César would be forced to ask how they felt, to which they would reply that they felt badly, they had spent a miserable night—of course César could suggest a quarter of a bottle of mineral water, and when he felt malicious, he did—so that César would say sympathetically, "What I think you need is a little black coffee," and would go off for the glass and the coffee pot. They waited for a business-bound gentleman to leave his newspaper behind him, or they opened the ink-stained writing book, took out the ragged blotter, the three sheets of paper, the two envelopes, unscrewed the ink bottle, dipped the rusty pen and began, staring off into space. When a friend came who they knew was as broke as they were, they pushed their chair a little to the side so that he could sit down, and helped him by setting the empty coffee glass between the two of them so that César would not know who had been having the coffee and would not dare interrupt the excited discussion they were having. But if the friend was getting an allowance from home, maybe had received a check yesterday and had not blown it all on the big party last night, they rose from the chair as soon as he entered the café, and leaned forward over the table, their hand stretched out, so that he would be forced to come toward them, to be grasped by the hand and be pulled sitting down, be helped with suggestions for breakfast, such as the shirred eggs in a sizzling pan the Dôme kitchen cooked so well. The inside corner tables against which no one bumped passing, and from which one could observe the street door and at least two levels of the café, were taken in the morning and remained taken through the day, the evening and the early night. The empty coffee glasses gathered dead cigarette butts. Here a sheet of paper had been torn nervously in half, then half again and again into tiny bits, which scattered on the floor, on the clothing, on the table and into the glass, and there at a spotless table sat a figure immovable through the

breakfast hour, who was still there at noon during the apéritif hour, and
after lunch, and at the second apéritif hour before dinner, and for liqueurs after dinner, and through the long evening, in the same position,
mummy-like, oblivious of the passing scene. But mostly each new arrival
in the café changed the mood of the place. When the outside door
squeaked open, and one glimpsed movement between a column and an
edge of the protruding wall, one had time to build up expectantly an
image before the person circled the café and came to the level where one
was sitting. The texture of the clothes had looked unfamiliar, but more,
the very movement of the fragment of the figure one had seen, the step
forward, had seemed strange and exciting and new. It was an art dealer,
he was bored with the pot-boiling painters he was pushing, he wanted
someone young and vigorous, a talent he could really back. Of course his
conditions would be strange. He would say, "My boy, you've got something, which will take years of developing, but on which I'll take a
chance. I'll get you a studio and canvas and paints and food, and I realize
that even an artist must have relaxation, so I will provide you with a little
friend, a serious young married woman, who is crazy about painters, but
who has a jealous husband, so she will not be able to waste too much of
your time. But no more café life for you, no more weeks wasted becaus
you feel you must do the female figure now, and do not have the money
for a model." It was a business man in Paris from South Africa, from the
States, who had made millions in steel, and who was now seeking an
interest for his remaining years, who with his keen mind would realize
the validity of this plastic form, this solidity, this purpose, and who
would propose beginning an art collection using one's work, the very root
of the theory, as a nucleus. It was a publisher who was looking for young
talent. It was an orchestra conductor on a search for fresh scores. It was
someone anonymous who after a long talk would shake hands upon
departure, leaving in the palm of one's hand a crumpled thousand-franc
note. Or perhaps only order one another coffee. When the new arrival
finally reached where one sat, he proved to be one of the regulars wearing
a new pair of pants. But hope had been stirred, the heart had been lifted,
the door of the Dôme was still open, maybe the angel would still come.
How some of the regulars existed no one but themselves knew. Where
did the Mad Roumanian come from? No one knew whether he was a
Roumanian, since no one had ever talked to him, but that was what he
was called. He arrived every morning on a bicycle which he chained to a
tree outside of the Dôme, and stiffly walked in, one of his baggy pant legs
tied with a clip, making him look like half of a zouave, in a short black
pelérine, buttons fastened with silk frogs, and a high fur collar. He made
the round of the Dôme, turning like a soldier, his eyes left and right,

quickly glancing at an occupant of a table, and when he saw it was a woman, bowing and removing his hat. But he kept his hat on and his pelérine buttoned when he sat down and ordered one quarter liter of beer, which was cheaper even than one coffee, remaining thereafter, while the white rim on the beer in front of him expired, absolutely motionless, to the point of not blinking his eyelids. What did the husband do of the woman with the elephantine legs and the little nervous pop-eyed dogs? He was always well-dressed, with white piping on his waistcoat and a flower in his buttonhole, and he loved his wife and her dogs, letting her use him as another cane as slowly she made her way into the Dôme, pushed a chair out for her and eased her into it; then picked up the dogs one by one, setting each on the palm of his hand as if to emphasize his tininess and lifted him to slide him off on the table. The dogs stood on the bright surface, trembling, almost caving in on their pencil-thin legs, while he nuzzled and kissed them, happy if from nearby tables there came gestures of astonishment. Occasionally he carried the dogs outside of the Dôme where he sat them under a tree and watched lovingly while they did their miniature duties, and at one in the afternoon and at eight in the evening he and his wife of the monstrous legs slowly moved toward the Montparnasse station and the Lavenue restaurant for their meals, the dogs stepping daintily before them. But when did he have time to go to a bank? How did he ever get that wife of his up a few stairs? Toward eleven o'clock the manager of the Dôme came in. His wife, who was cashier, was already sitting silently over the cash box, and as she took his hat her large diamond ring flashed from above. The manager said a few words soundlessly to her, clasped his hands back of him, and turned to survey his café. He smelled fresh and looked spotlessly clean, and he balanced himself on the balls of his feet. When he became aware of the man with the wife and the dogs, his eyes shone, his mouth opened, he moved, his hands unclasping themselves. The man rose and took the manager's outstretched hands and shook them. Still holding hands, they sat down, the man whispering into the manager's ear, the manager listening and nodding, after which he rose and again gazed around, his eyes lighting on another table, toward which he again excitedly moved, his hand out. He thus made the round of the café, but he did not shake everybody's hand, although one never knew whether one was being ignored, because sometimes one could not manage to get into the manager's line of vision. The Dôme began filling up for the apéritif hour. On the tables stood buckets of ice and soda siphons. The waiters went with trays laden with saucers, stemmed glasses and bottles of fruit and herb wine. Now the solitary characters at the strategic tables had as their neighbors local businessmen, painters who had given up the lean struggle and made up with the world and were paid off with studios and models and not only rich lunches but even with glasses of pungent appetite-provoking wine, idlers nursing their hangovers with mineral water, tourists agape at this artists' café. The talk that arose was in many languages. An English girl was loudly enumerating the many different kinds of potables she consumed the night before with anesthetic results so that who had taken her to her hotel room and had undressed her and put her to bed, and whether he had profited by her unconscious state, would forever be a mystery to her. An American in a Basque shirt and beret, his feet in Catalan rope sandals reposing on another chair—the unseemliness of the position infuriating César—was explaining the French romantic poets to a young Frenchman, who wore a starched collar and had a pimply face. A Dutch art dealer rose to greet his lunch guest who was a sculptor and a Russian Jew, who had lost an eye in the Foreign Legion and was now a French citizen. A couple were quarreling either in Danish or Norwegian. The manager stood at the door and greeted the more substantial clients. For those who arrived who to him were most substantial, he would try to find a table. When the only table even partially vacant had at it one of the penurious regulars, the manager would bow slightly to him and mumble something that might have been an apology and a request for room, to which the regular would return a short, stiff bow, and then look away and above him, and the party would settle down, the lady in the chair with the back to the wall, next to him, the men each nodding to him who appeared not to see them, the manager pulling over a necessary chair from another table. The regular would bring his empty glass to the very corner of the table, almost touching him, and would thus stick out, a proud dry island, oblivious of the waves of effusion that lapped around him, each escort urging on the lady and each other the most elaborate concoctions, cassis wine mixed with vermouth, and lightened with seltzer, or dark bitter picon sweetened with grenadine. The Dôme was not a restaurant, but one could order for lunch the one dish that had been prepared in the kitchen for the staff. César liked to become a restaurant waiter for a change, and it was with a flourish that he cleared the glasses off, leaving only the piled-up saucers, and of course the single glass and saucer of the regular who picked his up himself and miserably held it and set it down again upon the white paper tablecloth César spread out and set with salt cellar, pepper grinder and bread. With the arrival of the daily dish, perhaps boiled beef sprinkled with rock salt, and served with a large mealy potato, the agonizingly slow ceremony of the meal would begin, heard and smelled rather than seen by the rigidly-aloof figure at the corner of the table. The faint grunt of pleasure, the click of silverware handled, the clank of it on the plate, the squeal of it holding and cutting, the unheard moment of lifting to the mouth, the sound of mastication, the smacking of the lips, the plop of the cork from the bottle, the gasp of drinking, were combined with the rising steam from the meat and the potato, the odor of cheese and fruit, the fumes of wine, and the deeper intermingling fumes of coffee, brandy and cigar, and torturingly slowed down by table talk and the digesting belch. The drooling, starving regular still held his head high and waited for the never coming addition of the saucers and settlement of the bill, the lunchers' departure, the removal of the breadcrumb-scattered, food and wine-stained tablecloth, during which he again held close to him that glass and saucer of his, and the final return into that emptiness in which he would sit and wait for he knew not what, unseeing. The Dôme was now almost deserted, the manager and his wife had their lunch at one table, and the waiters and the bar-help at another. A few people would return for coffee, but during the early part of the afternoon the place took on a somnolent aspect. Occasionally a stranger from another part of Paris ventured inside its gloom, found seated here and there badly and sometimes strangely dressed figures, would judge this another home of frustration and failure, and would depart for the brighter Rotonde across the street, or for another café of more elegance and verve perhaps across the river. But here was not only time wasted and work abandoned and careers given up. At these tables also breath-taking ideas came, the jagged flash was followed by the blinding brilliance of illumination, the sudden harmony and balance of comprehension, the clear detail of pattern, the rounding out of form. Here sometimes answers did follow questions, and hard certainty came after months of doubt. From neighborhood hotel rooms and studios there did occasionally stagger in men to dissolve the bitter realization of absolute failure in alcohol, to droop daily over mounting piles of saucers, and eventually to disappear. But also from the same hotels and nearby studios came books and plays and stories and paintings and sculptures and musical scores that were to be published, produced, shown and played throughout the world, and the creators of them came to the Dôme to think of them. It was time for César, if he was on the early shift, to make his collections. Other waiters simply figured the totals owed them by passing with their successors at the station from table to table and adding up the pink-edged one-franc-seventy-five coffee saucers and the blue-edged four-franc brandy saucers, lifting them slightly and dropping them, so that the china rang warningly of the eventual settlement. They then received from their successors the sum and went off their shift. But César's relation with his clients was a personal one. He had been at the Dôme since long before the first war when the place had been a small meeting place of taxi chauffeurs.

He had watched the artists move down to the Montparnasse district from the Butte on Montmartre, the foreigners come from the Latin Quarter. The legend that he owned three apartment houses and was in on the syndicate with the manager to build a magnificent café down the street that would outshine the Rotonde was on a par with the legend that he would be a rich man if he could collect the money owed to him. The truth was that off duty he was a pot-bellied shabby little old man, while at the Dôme he had the dignity and knew it, and was a good waiter, even if rather old. He said his adieux from table to table, the palm of his hand resting lightly and remindingly on the saucers, and one paid him as an aside, talking of something else. At some tables he did not touch the saucers, and some he passed by entirely. In a minute he would again be wearing his old derby hat and his outer coat and standing at the bar for the final coffee, and he was tired and a little sad. However, if this was his day of late shift, he was rested, his face fresh and pink, his bald head shining, and he went from table to table, greeting his clients, happy. Toward four o'clock the whores began coming in. When it was raining, some who were strange to the place wandered in hopelessly, to be off the street, and made one round of the tables, stepping stiffly, bag held tightly under the elbow, head bent in a single oblique look, so that the eyes moving with the body would pass the eyes at the tables below, meeting them for an instant of sharp provocation. They then sat down at the table near the door and watched the outside downpour. The whores who were regulars used the Dôme as their home. They sauntered in smilingly, some finished with their shopping, some back from an exercising walk, or after an early afternoon of puttering around the room in their hotel. They greeted César, waved at acquaintances, set themselves in their usual places with a grateful sigh. They ordered coffee, they examined their purchases and showed them around. They called to one another, inquired as to each other's health and state of mind, glancing around their section of the café for likely prospects, but off-handedly, as if this was not their main purpose in being at the Dôme. Indeed sometimes it wasn't, for the time being one was not a whore. One had met the requirements of a sculptor and was now spending the days on a stand naked except for a sheet that was wetted down to simulate draperies. Or, after a night together, one had found herself enthusiastic about a medical student; luckily he was receiving an allowance, one could move in with him, and cook soup on his stove. One had just found a beef bone and some leeks, one was now waiting to go home with him. "Sorry, monsieur, I'm not in the business (using the English word) for the moment." Sometimes a whore brought a pet into the café, a cross-eyed Siamese cat, whose bluish fur she irritatingly fondled, or a tiny chameleon she placed on her neck where it stayed motionless trying to change to the color of her skin. But mostly, after the small flurry of their entrance, the whores relaxed into waiting. They drank their coffee, smoked their cigarettes, lifted their eyes expectantly at the sight or sound of the outer door opening, waiting for the entrant to reach their part of the café, watched if he would sit down back of a table, lift his face toward the approaching waiter, and then look around him, so that the eyes for the first time would meet. Some of them would begin flirting, eyes crinkling, the corners of the mouth raising themselves progressively higher, until the whole face invitingly smiled. Some after the first glance, did not look again at the man until the waiter said the gentleman asked permission to offer a drink, or the man rose to approach, bent over with a bow, and asked if he might sit down. Sometimes the woman and the man aware of her proximity would sit for a long time side by side, she studiously looking everywhere but at him, he glancing more and more inquiringly at her, wondering whether the offer of a cigarette or a drink or a remark about the weather or a general off-hand observation about the Dôme, "Don't you think the Quarter is becoming ruined?" or "I find this café has a particular ambiance" would provide the conversation wedge. The before-dinner crowd began to appear, and now the Dôme would remain full until late in the evening. On clear days the painters stayed in the studios until they could use up the last bits of light, but during rainy, murky weather they might come down to sketch at the Dôme. There would be an interesting position of the arms and shoulders in a figure slouching in the corner and an effort made quickly to remember it on paper before the figure lost its spontaneity by freezing, so that a page in the sketchbook would be turned over and another position, of a head lost deeply in a newspaper, noted down. Many of the workers in the studios and rooms now said their first word for the day. Tired of pumping, or wrestling with themselves, and of the closeness of their rooms, of the unshaved indefiniteness of a long questing day, they shaved closely, booted themselves tightly, dressed carefully and appeared at the Dôme to rest. They acted formally, with a flourish of manners, rose when a friend approached them, shook hands with him effusively; when two French painters met, they greeted each other with deference, called each other "Master." When a very great man appeared at the Dôme he received what was almost a court reception. Even while his party still approached outside on the terrace, a stir went through inside, the news united the tables. The manager who had never read a book or looked at a picture in his life sprang to the door; from her cash box above, his wife flashed her diamond and smiled. The great figure, deep in a coat and heavy muffler, was escorted to a table quickly cleared, was seated at a chair pushed out, slightly away from it, his hat shapeless on his head, his gnarled hands resting on a cane. The café craned its neck, even those who did not consider him a great man at all, but an already rotting corpse, a notorious potboiler, who perhaps had shown promise in his youth, but had outlived both, having sold out for this kind of adulation; even they were uneasy in the presence of world fame. The tone of their voices as they tried to ignore it was strident, strained. Others wanted to know the reason for the stir, who on earth was that? At the table of honor the great man did not look up as he shook hands, as he nodded at something that was whispered to him. The group sitting around him were wreathed in vicarious modesty, in smiles. Then a slight figure among them provoked a deeper stir. Was that she? the fragile wraith with the velvet ribbon around her neck and the girlish curls? princess, countess, wife of the banker, peasant girl? the one of the elopements, suicides, convents? of the sufferings trumpeted and the celebrated anguish? was that the Muse really in her wasted flesh? My God, how old she was! Fascinated they stared at the two skeletons of an immortal love. Somebody murmured, "His work has survived just about as well as she." Irritated and provoked by this devotion to a memory, by worship of tears shed in a never-to-be-recaptured past, a group of obscure youths were giving birth to a new art movement. In Paris from the French provinces, from New Jersey, from a canton in Switzerland, from a small Polish town, their minds limber and their elbows restless, they eagerly tore through words and their meanings. They pointed their fingers insolently, they spoke loudly. They wanted to know what was true, what survived. Had that woman, for years moaned about, survived? Either in her present decaying physical state? or in the form, so sickening that it could no longer be borne today, presented to the world by her lover? The answer was obvious. In life as well as in art, in dreams as well as in reality, nothing survived. Nothing, rien, niente, garnichts, nic and nichevo. The truth was nothing, reality was nothing. God and the world of the spirit and the world of hard demonstrated fact, all were nothing. That was fine. Let's celebrate the Nothing. Let's write about the Nothing, paint the Nothing, play the Nothing on a clarinet. Let's publish a manifesto, and proclaim that in the beginning there was nothing, and that it had stretched through duration to end finally and irrevocably in nothing. They began to plan a demonstration at a forthcoming performance at the Paris Opéra which they would break up by rising in their seats and making insignificant noises, they started working on a magazine which would have a blank colorless cover, and they tried to decide whether the inside pages too would be blank, or whether they would be filled with meaningless single letters of various printer's types, or unconnected words. Through the teeming, undistinguishable, many-lingual noise that permeated the Dôme there came clearly and distinctly, "Theo was a pig last night. He made pipi in his bed." A woman painter and her girl friend, in blue tailored suits, bouttonnières in their lapels and upturned feathered hats, their hair cut alike, both looking alike, except that the woman was bony and old and her girl was beautiful and slim, sat with their eyes fixed on the wall above the crowd. Across from them a young man stared at the girl, tried by sheer concentration to move her eyes on him, succeeded finally and found that her gaze was unseeing, as if asleep-eyes-open, as if through film. An American with bleached blond hair cut the atmosphere with his proudly aquiline profile. Others exhibited a fantastically figured scarf, or a monocle held in a disdainful face. Some appeared day after day, at the same table and with the same companions, arranged themselves in their chairs, César brought them beer or coffee, and they sat, finding neither pleasure in talking among themselves nor in looking around them. Some of them had piled on the table that-day-received home newspapers which they did not tear open, or held cigarettes in their mouth which they did not light. Nor did they seem lost in thought, but rather inert, at the Dôme as they might be walking in the street or asleep in bed. The foreign correspondents, French newspaper men, art and literary critics, aesthetes, painters, sculptors, composers, writers of novels, short stories and historical essays, politicians and would-be statesmen, conspirators and plotters, spies and adventurers, and the neophytes and students of these pursuits and arts, and their counterparts in lies, charlatans, petty and elaborate crooks, remittance men, hangers-on, parasites, male, female, homosexual, those still in school and those already retired, together with the idlers, lookers-on and tourists, all together with their wives, lovers, mistresses and whores, congregated here and drank sherry, port, madeira, dry and sweet vermouth, sparkling wine, brandy straight and with water, coffee with hot milk and without it, beer light and dark, mineral water. They chatted, gossiped, argued and discussed, or silently waited, looked around at the door or stared at the crowd, or were stared at by it. They thought of dinner at Foyot's restaurant near the Senate building, to begin with grey caviar or belon oysters, with natural still champagne. Or they wondered whether to eat their radishes and veal cutlets at Baty's on the corner, where tablecloths were not clean, or whether to go further up the boulevard to where the tableclothes were cleaner. Some decided that if their friend didn't appear, the six francs still in their pocket would buy them a horsemeat steak and four cigarettes in the near-by dairy. Some still stiffly sat, that morning's empty glass eternally before them. They went off with the friend who had arrived, their places quickly taken, returned an hour later filled with meat and wine, eyes shining-dull, looking around the Dôme for vacated chairs, sank in them, waited for the friend to order filtered coffee. Imperceptibly the evening at the Dôme began. The whores who had managed a dinner invitation had taken stock of their new conquests, had decided whether upon return to the Dôme they would excuse themselves to run down to the ladies' room, to reappear as strangers, their faces only a short time before so interested now unrecognizably blank, to saunter past the abandoned dinner partner to a single vacant chair, or whether to spend this part of the evening laughing and talking with him, or to listen soberly to the story of his troubles and his life, or if he had struck a tender chord in them to begin to tell him their story. Now in the mellow off-guard after-dinner time was the moment to ask for the favor, try to borrow the money, begin to whisper insinuatingly, with a growing intensity. Now faces were watched for expressions as they listened, as the lips moved, as the heart rose, as the urge grew greater. The smallest, the slightest nod would lighten everything. The heart would grow easier, the lowering atmosphere of the Dôme would become intimate, easily the words would come, "César, a brandy." But if the attentive brows of the face so near would fold closer, and after an instant of unbelievable waiting, the head would start not nodding but negatively shaking from side to side. . . . There lay a pit and a darkness. It was impossible, unthinkable. One's tightness could not become tighter, nor one's heart a heavier ball, with hopelessness more hopeless still, with no balm possible, with no money even to escape in a drink. The murmur of the lips became more persuasive, the eyes watched desperately, darting from brow to lips, to the coming movement of the head for indication of the forming decision within. There was a fear in the Dôme of failure, loneliness, of the coming night, of the threatening tomorrow. What if no man could be attracted? what if the door would be locked? what if the letter didn't come? or if it came, the answer would be a No? How long could one continue searching, waiting, with turbulence inside, and nervousness shaking the fingers, and an indifferent objective world without? The Dôme was full of troubles, each one's seeming the worst possible, least capable of any possible solution. This young American, the most promising of an outstanding class at a famous university, with the appearance of whose first book American letters were pronounced to have reached self-sufficient stature, and whose second book so eagerly awaited had been announced for publication at a date postponed again and again, sat bent over this thirtieth glass of sherry that day. The palm of his hand shielded the sight of it from him, as if he didn't want to realize that he had been trying to stay in his room that day and the preceding days and weeks and months, so that he could try to think and try to get to work, but was being constantly driven by a void, an urge, a thirst, a call-it-what-you-will, to the point where now waking in the morning he could not even open his eyes until he crawled out of bed and somehow dressed—a desperate superstition prevented him from keeping a bottle in the same room with the typewriter—so that he could feel his way down the stairs and outside and to the Dôme for his first looking-at-the-world drink of sherry that day. This Danish couple, Paris correspondents for a Copenhagen paper, who for the past forty years had sat so across from each other and watched the other's beloved face, had now come upon their periodic crisis, wracking their heads for the subject of their weekly Paris letter, he thinking that she looked much too shabby to cover the fashion openings, and she waiting for the frightened look of his eyes distended with the coming of his evening migraine headache. At this loose hour, the evening beginning to swing toward the long day's end, terrible decisions were made, and inevitable ones postponed. Conversations were started, assertions made, taken up, agreed to with reservations or quietly denied, or jumped on, contradicted with vehemence and fire, with a banging of the fist that shook the saucers on the table, that made neighbors turn around and stare. The mild haze that had begun to envelop and calm the screaming mind with the first drink before dinner, had filled and thickened through the wines and food, and now with the warming sips of brandy had permeated the mind with a beatific fog. A party had started, friends long separated, now pounding each other's back, were together again. "Cognac?" "Whiskey" "No, let's have champagne." "Let's have a magnum." From behind the intervening wall in the center, from two levels away, the manager, who did not speak a word of the language spoken, had already heard. He took a large shining metal bucket off the shelf near where his wife sat—who had already written down an imposing figure in the ledger sheet under César's name—handed it to the bar man back of the counter who was breaking up pieces of ice, while another bar man lifted the trapdoor in the floor to disappear and reappear with the enormous bottle to be set carefully in the bucket and surrounded with ice half-filled with water, the manager gave the neck of the bottle a preliminary twirl, and it was borne away, head covered with a napkin, and held high so that it could be seen by everybody, so that everybody could anticipate, while the bottle was cooling, the celebrating pop. Other parties were making up, to shock with their casual dress and language the diplomatic set dancing decorously across the river at My Sister's Garden, to mix with the house girls and the tourists in the great dives of the rue Fontaine, to listen to Bricktop sing American songs, to look at bare flesh whining and importuning in the brothels of the rue Bondel. Their places were taken by

those from the other side of the river who came to see the artists. At one
table, where the drinking had begun before dinner and dinner itself had
been missed, the saucers had been rising higher and higher, had become
four, then five, then six stacks, and César had been forced to bring
another table for nothing but the saucers, and the drinkers were self-
consciously glancing from time to time at the proof of their prowess on
the other table, and wanted to raise their eyes to the other people in the
café, to see the effect on them, and half did not dare to and half did not
deign to, and they turned a vacuous drunken grin on their faces, and
called for César to bring them more drinks. While the starving ones still
starved and the snobbish ones still showed their profiles, acting as if they
were where they did not want to be, and the arguments continued, and
the love-making and love-catching went on, both spurious and real. It
was ten o'clock, eleven o'clock, eleven-thirty, time to go to bed, to be
ready to wake up with a clear head tomorrow. Between a table of drinkers at which a loud argument was going on and a table of tourists who
were staring open-mouthed at them, at a little round table, with only a
cigarette-littered saucer from a glass of beer, his arms folded on the table,
his head on his arms, a man raucously snored. César shook him, but
succeeded only in changing the tone of the snore. A gap of empty chairs
showed itself now at the Dôme. For the last time the lonely derelicts
found themselves alone at the tables. They stayed in their spots for
another moment, as if unable to unhinge themselves, then began to add
up the coppers and the nickels, blanching at the thought that they might
be short. Once again César passed them, bearing for somebody's supper
the dish the kitchen served at all hours, garnished sauerkraut, or a deep
dish of mussels cooked in their own juice. The manager was ready to go
home, waited for his wife to turn the ledger over to one of the bar-men.
César leaned on one of the empty tables to take the weight off his feet;
he was sorry this was his day of late shift, he was carefully watching the
colossal party with the extra table for nothing but saucers. The counter
was crowded again with railroad men, taxi chauffeurs, neighborhood
concierges in for nightcap, street whores off the sidewalk for a moment.
The café part appeared stale and gloomy. The members of the fabulous
party seemed to have lost heart; when one of them suggested snails on
the rue de la Gaité, none agreed. They were only held together by the
legend each one of them was tiredly making up, of the number of individual drinks, incredible total number of saucers, unheard of amount of
francs. Each one was also counting the amount of actual francs he had in
his pocket to help in the settlement, and was considering the resultant
other pressing settlements postponed. After all, one had to leave, move
through the dark streets, stand waiting at the locked door for the open-

ing buzz, begin climbing up stairs that were lighted up for exactly one minute. Why didn't one leave? Cesar shuffled to the innermost empty part of the café and began piling chairs up on the tables, exposing a floor littered with torn paper, cigarette butts, burnt matchsticks, breadcrumbs under a place where somebody had eaten. As the time to close up approached, César left half-awake islands of the people who remained. They watched him, thinking, "Just another drink, another moment." He was coming nearer and nearer to them, making their island smaller and smaller. Soon he would snatch the glasses from their table, stack up the saucers and wipe up underneath, and not lay down the saucers again, but hold them and wait, angry and mumbling. The Dôme used to close at two o'clock.

GEORGE PLIMPTON

Vali

The girl in the photograph (next page) and whose drawings follow is Vali Myers. In Paris, where she lives, she goes under other names: bartenders in the little *boîtes* where she dances call her *le chat;* concierges refer to her as *la bête;* she is also called variously *l'enfant du feu* for her flaming copper-red almost orange hair, and *la morte vive* for her corpse-white face and heavy eye-shadow—a cosmetic oddity which started an *existentialiste* fashion that enjoyed a minor vogue a few years ago. She is Australian by birth. Her father is a sailor and her mother a violinist in the Sydney Symphony Orchestra. Vali came to France just after the war. Still under twenty she became at once the symbol and plaything of the restless, confused, vice-enthralled, demi-monde that populated certain of the cafés and *boîtes* of the Left Bank—La Petite Source, Le Mabillon, Le Café Metro, La Chope Gauloise, Le Monaco.

She is the subject of a book entitled *Love on the Left Bank* (published by André Deutsch) which describes the 'hipster' group which frequented these cafés. The book includes a mawkish and unfortunate text, but amazing photographs—graphic studies of Vali and her friends, young faces, always sad, drug-haunted, and topped with ferocious crops

of hair. The majority of the photographs are group portraits crowded with faces, but rarely faces of animation—each subject apart from the other so that often the collection seems a study of asylum inmates.

Prominent throughout the book are the photographs of Vali—close-ups of her extraordinary face, a phantom-face that befits the Paris backgrounds of the night-time empty streets, the crumbling and leaning buildings of the Latin Quarter, and the dark and smoke-laden *boîtes* where Vali danced in a tight ring of spectators to the rhythm of African bush songs.

Her dancing is remarkable—a sinuous shuffling, bent-kneed, her shoulders and hands moving at trembling speed to the drumbeats. She wears blue jeans, a man's shirt pulled in at the waist by a wide black belt, and worn red ballet slippers that she often kicks off to dance in flat-splayed barefeet. Her audience, almost always men, stare at her rather than watch, and it is curious that their feet never tap to the splurge of African music, nor do hands or fingers tap out the time—an absorption on the part of her spectators that is solely visual. A friend explains it as follows: "I watched her dance and I never heard the music. I said to her 'Man, how can you dance like that? You must be a missing link.' And that was it. Like I guess Kiki of Montparnasse was for those people in the twenties, Vali was the same for us. You saw in her the personalization of something torn and loose and deep-down primitive in all of us—and, man, you could see it moving right around in front of you in ballet slippers and a man's shirt."

Vali never danced in a professional stage show. She preferred the tiny square-footage cleared for her in little clubs such as l'Escale on the Rue Monsieur-le-Prince, or the Rose Rouge; on Saturday she would invariably turn up at the vast ballroom of the Bal Nègre on the Rue Blomet— there to dance hour after hour with the Senegalese, dancers from the Cameroons, from Martinique.

Occasionally, someone impressionable and rich enough would slip her a few hundred francs. But Vali, in her early days in Paris, lived on practically nothing. Her few belongings were scattered throughout the Quarter in cafés, chambres de bonnes, in studios where she would sometimes sit for an artist. She carried her prize possessions with her in a wire carrying-case shaped like a bird-cage. In it she had a bandana, her eye make-up and face powder, a volume of poetry by Thomas Chatterton, her art materials, and a curious piece of fur shaped like a miniature fox with two bead eyes embedded at one end: a keepsake she refers to as 'the feeley' and which she talks to from time to time, and often dusts, heavily, with face powder.

Cosmetics constitute an important part of Vali's life. It takes her over an hour to make herself up in the morning. First she slaps her face, lips included, pure-white with face powder; then with infinite care she paints an inch-wide circle of black eye-shadow around her eyes. The preparation she uses is called kohl—a combination of oil and a black dust from India. "In the East, you know," she says, "they use this eye stuff to keep out evil. The flies won't cross the black. It might look strange to people, but the Gods in Tibet are ugly too and they keep away the bad things."

After Vali has put on her face she runs her hands through a twisted and unruly growth of orange hair that reaches her waist and she is ready for the day.

The aspect she presents to the outside world is naturally a most striking one; Vali can recall a number of instances when people have suddenly come upon her around a corner and have screamed. Most women are appalled by her. The writer Gabriel Pommerand points out in an essay on Vali that "women can only regard her aspect with contempt since she disobeys every last law of conventional beauty." Some women, though, particularly from the world of fashion, are charmed by her manner and personality. They give her bolts of material out of which she makes floor-length house-robes. The reaction of men is completely human. They enjoy watching her dance; many have fallen in love with her; many are amused by her company in the sense that one might enjoy being accompanied, as Pommerand writes, by "a cheetah on a leash."

Communicating with Vali is not easy. Vali's discernment of the world around her is on the simplest plane of sensory perception. Asked where she comes from in Australia she will not reply with the name of a town, or geographical location, or distances in miles, but will say, "Behind me is the lagoon . . . you can smell it . . . and beyond it the sea which you can't see but you can hear it no matter where you go in the bush . . . the bush is crazy . . . a tree here and a tree there . . . in each tree a kookaburra, a bird what laughs like a crazy jackass . . . and he goes into the grass . . . flies up again and takes the snake and whacks the head against a branch . . . whck . . . whck . . . whck"—this in the cockney-like Australian accent, the voice thin and slow, interspersed with the 'hipster' language she has picked up in the Paris cafés.

Vali has almost no general knowledge. Her interests are particular and esoteric. She knows the works of Edward Fitzgerald, Edith Sitwell, reads Emily Bronte every day, and is copying out the works of Yeats and one day will have his collected works in her childish round hand. She is devoted to the Irish poets—impressed by them, among other reasons, because she mistakenly believes them all to have died at a very early age. Almost any artist who has died young interests Vali. The great literary figure in her life, for example, is the eighteenth-century English poet

Thomas Chatterton. On her bedside table she keeps a postcard repro-
duction of the poet's death painted by Henry Wallis—the original hangs
in the Pre-Raphaelite section of London's Tate Gallery—showing the
poet, his hair as red as Vali's and almost as abundant, collapsed across a
bed from a fatal dose of arsenic taken just before his eighteenth birthday.

Chatterton is not a well-known poet; but his failure, his precocity, his
misery, the romantic turn to his verse, his suicide—all of it has had a
combustive effect on Vali. She herself had plans to do away with herself
on her twenty-third birthday. Her closest friends were invited to watch,
to sit at the foot of her bed while she lay on it with her 'feeley' tucked in
beside her, and, unaware of the legal consequences that would befall her
audience as accessories before and to the fact, she was to swallow arsenic
while they watched.

Two years ago Vali renounced some of her strange urges, married a
young Austrian architect, and gave up her café-wanderings for a tiny
room in a hotel on the rue des Canettes near St. Germain-des-Prés—a
hotel run by a woman called Celeste who is said to have been Proust's
housekeeper. Celeste, bizarre enough herself, is one of the few women
who appreciate Vali. "Ah!" she says, "You are going up to see the
strange one, my favorite jewel."

With marriage Vali's life has changed. Though she continues to paint
up her face and still dances—to the music of a single cracked record
played on an ancient wind-up victrola—she rarely leaves her room for
her old haunts. She refers to her past as 'that old time of the cafés,' 'that
weird time,' and speaks of having escaped what was a 'little like a battlefield.' She is happy in marriage and with the boxed-in security of a little
room which is lighted dully by electricity and smells strongly of Egyptian
incense. She has cut herself off from the outside world. The single window facing on the street is shielded by heavy curtains which have
scarcely been opened since Vali and her husband moved in. Vali has
seen little sunlight in two years. She hates the sunlight and in her early
days in Paris when circumstances drove her on occasion into the daytime
streets she hugged the buildings, keeping to the shadows, and across
open streets she would run—her arm thrown up to shield her face from
the sun. The night-time, and the moon, she loves, and never leaves the
hotel until long after dusk—usually at midnight, to forage with her
husband in the streets and gutters for tinsel paper on bon-bon and cigarette packages. The two use the tinsel paper to make tiny and wispish
mobiles which are so delicate that suspended from the ceiling in that
airless room they can shudder and revolve in the force of a laugh.

Tinsel paper has also been used in the careful construction of minus-
cule replicas of human figures which stand on the bedside table. They

are of Vali herself, her husband, the 'feeley', and a few of their belong-ings—a bed, Vali's red ballet shoes. When the two go on a trip, this family is packed carefully in a little box and goes along with them. In the manner of the pagan image-worshippers Vali takes almost a manic care of these tiny figures—their welfare closely and mystically identified with her own.

Almost all the artifacts in the room have an equivalently mystical identification. And the same can be said of Vali's drawings. She speaks of them as manifestations of an urge for peace and security. She draws mainly self-portraits—Beardsley-like reflections of herself, usually lying in a death-stiff attitude on a bed; she is asleep (or dead), composed, guarded by owls and five-petaled flowers which are among the devices she considers good luck. Five is her 'protective number'; she insisted on room *15* in the hotel (room *5* was permanently occupied by another resident), and has tattooed on her foot a flower with five petals which she did herself with a needle and colored inks. "I need my owls and my flowers," she says, "to keep away the bad things. I am very naughty."

The drawings sometimes take Vali as many as two years to complete. In her early days she worked on them at the café tables, eyes smarting in the smoke as she touched an English-made fine-nibbed pen across the paper "like a fly"—each touch made with the care of a Persian miniature painter with his brush of a cat tail hair.

Once completed, Vali refuses to sell her drawings. It is not a matter of the time she has expended on them, but simply that her identification with each is such that a sale would destroy a prop she needs to support her bizarre existence. The drawings are, in effect, preservatives of life according to the extraordinary and lonely canon which she has created for herself.

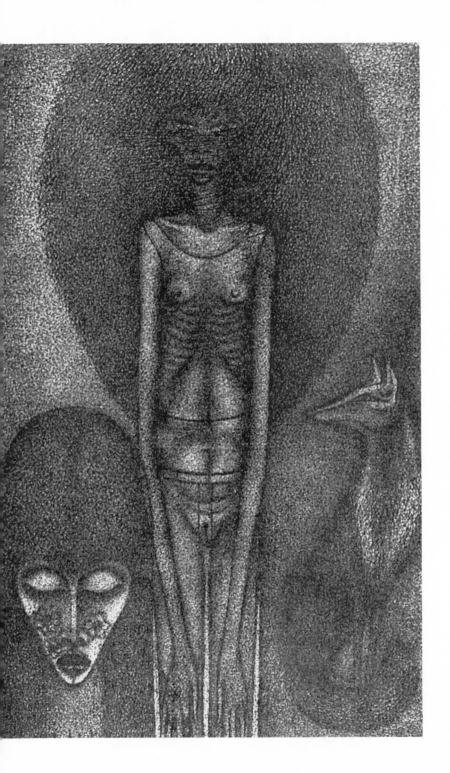

With only darkness for a lover   London . 54

PART TWO

1960–1966

Introduction

What Malcolm Cowley described as unique about the *Paris Review* in the history of literary publications was that it was willing to use commercial devices in promoting itself. He referred to the practice as "enterprise in the service of art." From the magazine's beginnings, portions of the editors' energies were devoted to getting it subscribed to, and distributed as widely as possible. Posters were pasted up on Paris walls by flying squads supplied with paste and brushes; for years the tatters of a *Paris Review* affiche remained affixed to the ceiling of the lavatory in the Café du Dôme. The grandest (and most foolish) of these enterprises was the so-called "Booth" which was introduced at the New York World's Fair in 1964. It stood outside the Pavillion of Paris on the Avenue Harry S Truman down from the Astral Fountain and the "Vatican" where the *Pietà* was on display. The booth was designed by the magazine art editor, William Pène du Bois—a charming mushroomlike structure with a movable roof that was winched up along a center flagpole. It was built in Katonah, New York, at no great expense, by a firm of swimming pool specialists. It was occasionally referred to as the "smallest pavillion at the Fair." It was made of wood, only ten by ten. But the booth had great style. There was a metal flagpole at each point of the roof, which was octagonal. The sides of the booth were decorated with blowups from pages of the *Paris Review*—both artwork and text—a chunk of Céline, Hemingway, Frost, a line or two from an interview with Evelyn Waugh:

> Interviewer: *What about Ronald Firbank?*
> Waugh: *I enjoyed him very much when I was young. I cannot read him now.*
> Interviewer: *Why?*
> Waugh: *I think there would be something wrong with an elderly man who would enjoy Firbank.*

Passersby would circle the booth, reading it. The salespeople in the booth were as decorative as the booth itself—a series of very young, pretty girls, a few of them French, all of whom were in love with the managing editor of the magazine at the time, Peter Ardery. In the booth they usually worked in pairs. They would arrive early in the morning, crawl on hands and knees into the booth from the little side-panel, crank up the roof, and set up the counters for the day's work; at closing time the roof would be cranked down and the girls would emerge like hedgehogs from a burrow onto the Avenue Harry S Truman. Most people walking by took the structure to be an information booth. On a weekend day, a thick ring of people would cluster around it, the ones in the back rising up on their toes and shouting over the heads of the others to get directions to the "Vatican."

On sale was the *Paris Review* as well as the other literary magazines. It was a brave display—not unlike what is in the window of the Gotham Book Mart on 47th Street, except not as dusty. A feather-mop duster was kept in the booth, and sometimes a brisk wind swept down the Avenue Harry S Truman and riffled the pages of the magazines.

The booth was open for the last five weeks of the Fair's 1964 season—by the end of which time the total gross sales had amounted to $379.70. The best day brought in thirty dollars, the worst—a rainy Tuesday—a few cents more than a dollar.

While a more prudent organization might have foregone the second year of the Fair, the *Paris Review* decided that an intensification of effort might bring better results. The booth was expanded into a complex by adding three bookstalls, modeled after those on the quais along the Seine. Enrique Castro-Cid, the Chilean sculptor, was persuaded to build a four-foot tall weatherproof robot which was to stand in front of the booth and do something to attract attention. No one actually saw what it looked like or indeed what it was programmed to do. There was word that it looked like a giant erect green grasshopper; within was a voice box which was to produce a sound or a sentence to alarm passersby and make them stare at it—at which point the grasshopper would wave an antennalike arm at the booth. This was conjecture, because Castro-Cid became entranced with the sculpture and as it slowly took form in his studio, he decided not to risk it on the Avenue Harry S Truman.

Nonetheless, in its second year of operation things went much more briskly. The booth sold French magazines such as *Elle,* records, books, little French flags on black wooden stands, French cigarettes, posters, Charles de Gaulle face-masks, tinny Eiffel Towers and Statues of Liberty, some fitted out with red light bulbs, just a tremendous glut of doodads and gimmickry. And in there somewhere, just a pie-slice of them now on the counter, were the literary magazines—*Hudson, Sewanee, Partisan,* the less-known affairs of the heart, and the *Paris Review,* along with *Paris Review* T-shirts and sweat shirts. The big sellers were shopping bags and French cigarettes. One of the booth girls thought that the de Gaulle face-masks might catch on. So she wore one. What a sight it was to approach along the Avenue Harry S Truman and see a Charles de Gaulle (sometimes a pair of them if she had a friend working with her) peering out of the shadows of the booth! One day she saw someone coming down the avenue whom she recognized as a close relative—an aunt maybe, or a cousin. She had the option of calling out through the mouth of the de Gaulle mask, "Hi, Aunt Genevieve," or whomever. But she didn't. She just let that person cruise on by—past that strange little complex with all those crazy things for sale.

One of the more ambitious money-raising projects was a succession of "Revels." These were fund-raising benefits held in New York, dances mostly, of which the first three were held in the Village Gate in Greenwich Village, one in a vast honeycombed West Side discotheque named the Cheetah, one in an abandoned church amongst a grove of trees on Welfare Island in the East River—this in 1969 before Welfare became Roosevelt and the island was attached to Manhattan by a tramway—and the last one on a decrepit sidewheeler steamer moored at the South Street Seaport. The Revels were memorable affairs, with so much effort spent by staff members that often the fund-raising aspects of the events were forgotten.

What many people remembered about the Revels was the use of mixed-media devices—especially films, which were shown simultaneously on a multitude of screens. These were artfully spliced from reels of 16mm stock purchased at cut-rate out of 42nd Street camera-shop bins—many of them old Pathé newsreels so that the revelers would look up to see on the great screens hung around the halls, or, in the case of the island Revel, set among the trees, a curious variety of image . . . a Ping-Pong match, a chimpanzee on a bicycle, the slow, writhing collapse of the suspension bridge at Yakima, Washington, a zoot-suit fashion show, a sequence of a monster grasshopper attacking a Quonset hut from a science-fiction film, a Krazy Kat cartoon, a series of rocket failures at Cape Canaveral in which the missiles would bestir themselves briefly and then sit back down on their columns of flame and disappear in gigantic explosions . . . all of these activities going on concurrently and silently, the projector beams crisscrossing, the screens in a constant movement of image. This kind of visual decoration was very much of an innovation then. Sometimes the big reels were run backwards: a rocket would mend itself and sit back down on its column of billowing flame and extinguish it; a Ping-Pong match lost very little in reverse, and the giant grasshopper, retreating awkwardly from his victims, took on a poignant helter-skelter demeanor.

The effort put into the Revels was at once an advantage and a detriment to the success of the affairs: people bought tickets and came, but the expense of making the occasions memorable often cut sharply into the receipts. At the Welfare Island Revel, for example, two rented pianos were placed out in a glade of shade trees. The evening was cool, the weather threatening. Very few discovered the pianos. James Blake, the ex-convict writer who had written an extraordinary prison chronicle for the magazine entitled "The Joint," played one of the pianos at two in the morning . . . a slow barrel-house . . . a few people standing to listen in the light of hurricane lamps hung from the trees, with the great skyline of midtown Manhattan behind them through the leaves, and the faint hum of traffic coming across the water from the East River Drive. A couple of hours later a rain shower swept through and ruined both pianos. Almost all the profits from the Revel were paid to the piano rental company . . . indeed the total realized from that Revel, to which almost a thousand people came, was about fourteen dollars.

—G.P.

FICTION

Jorge Luis Borges

Funes the Memorious

I remember him (I have no right to utter this sacred verb, only one man
on earth had that right and he is dead) with a dark passion flower in his
hand, seeing it as no one has ever seen it, though he might look at it from
the twilight of dawn till that of evening, a whole lifetime. I remember
him, with his face taciturn and Indian-like and singularly *remote*, behind
the cigarette. I remember (I think) his angular, leather-braiding hands. I
remember near those hands a maté gourd bearing the Uruguayan coat of
arms; I remember a yellow screen with a vague lake landscape in the
window of his house. I clearly remember his voice: the slow, resentful,
nasal voice of the old-time dweller of the suburbs, without the Italian
sibilants we have today. I never saw him more than three times; the last
was in 1887 . . . I find it very satisfactory that all those who knew him
should write about him; my testimony will perhaps be the shortest and
no doubt the poorest, but not the most impartial in the volume you will
edit. My deplorable status as an Argentine will prevent me from indulging in a dithyramb, an obligatory genre in Uruguay whenever the subject
is an Uruguayan. *Highbrow, city slicker, dude:* Funes never spoke these
injurious words, but I am sufficiently certain I represented for him those

misfortunes. Pedro Leandro Ipuche has written that Funes was a precursor of the supermen, "a vernacular and rustic Zarathustra"; I shall not debate the point, but one should not forget that he was also a kid from Fray Bentos, with certain incurable limitations.

My first memory of Funes is very perspicuous. I can see him on an afternoon in March or February of the year 1884. My father, that year, had taken me to spend the summer in Fray Bentos. I was returning from the San Francisco ranch with my cousin Bernardo Haedo. We were singing as we rode along and being on horseback was not the only circumstance determining my happiness. After a sultry day, an enormous slate-colored storm had hidden the sky. It was urged on by southern wind, the trees were already going wild; I was afraid (I was hopeful) that the elemental rain would take us by surprise in the open. We were running a kind of race with the storm. We entered an alleyway that sank down between two very high brick sidewalks. It had suddenly got dark; I heard some rapid and almost secret footsteps up above; I raised my eyes and saw a boy running along the narrow and broken path as if it were a narrow and broken wall. I remember his baggy gaucho trousers, his rope-soled shoes. I remember the cigarette in his hard face, against the now limitless storm cloud. Bernardo cried to him unexpectedly: "What time is it, Ireneo?" Without consulting the sky, without stopping, he replied: "It's four minutes to eight, young Bernardo Juan Francisco." His voice was shrill, mocking.

I am so unperceptive that the dialogue I have just related would not have attracted my attention had it not been stressed by my cousin, who (I believe) was prompted by a certain local pride and the desire to show that he was indifferent to the other's tripartite reply.

He told me the fellow in the alleyway was one Ireneo Funes, known for certain peculiarities such as avoiding contact with people and always knowing what time it was, like a clock. He added that he was the son of the ironing woman in town, María Clementina Funes, and that some people said his father was a doctor at the meat packers, an Englishman by the name of O'Connor, and others that he was a horse tamer or scout from the Salto district. He lived with his mother, around the corner from the Laureles house.

During the years eighty-five and eighty-six we spent the summer in Montevideo. In eighty-seven I returned to Fray Bentos. I asked, as was natural, about all my acquaintances and, finally, about the "chronometrical" Funes. I was told he had been thrown by a half-tamed horse on the San Francisco ranch and was left hopelessly paralyzed. I remember the sensation of uneasy magic the news produced in me: the only time I had seen him, we were returning from San Francisco on horseback and he was running along a high place; this fact, told me by my cousin Bernardo, had much of the quality of a dream made up of previous elements. I was told he never moved from his cot, with his eyes fixed on the fig tree in the back or on a spider web. In the afternoons, he would let himself be brought out to the window. He carried his pride to the point of acting as if the blow that had felled him were beneficial . . . Twice I saw him behind the iron grating of the the window, which harshly emphasized his condition as a perpetual prisoner: once, motionless, with his eyes closed; another time, again motionless, absorbed in the contemplation of a fragrant sprig of santonica.

Not without a certain vaingloriousness, I had begun at that time my methodical study of Latin. My valise contained the *De viris illustribus* of Lhomond, Quicherat's *Thesaurus*, the commentaries of Julius Caesar and an odd volume of Pliny's *Naturalis historia*, which then exceeded (and still exceeds) my moderate virtues as a Latinist. Everything becomes public in a small town; Ireneo, in his house on the outskirts, did not take long to learn of the arrival of these anomalous books. He sent me a flowery and ceremonious letter in which he recalled our encounter, unfortunately brief, "on the seventh day of February of the year 1884," praised the glorious services my uncle Gregorio Haedo, deceased that same year, "had rendered to our two nations in the valiant battle of Ituzaingó" and requested the loan of any one of my volumes, accompanied by a dictionary "for the proper intelligence of the original text, for I am as yet ignorant of Latin." He promised to return them to me in good condition, almost immediately. His handwriting was perfect, very sharply outlined; his orthography, of the type favored by Andrés Bello: *i* for *y*, *j* for *g*. At first I naturally feared a joke. My cousins assured me that was not the case, that these were peculiarities of Ireneo. I did not know whether to attribute to insolence, ignorance or stupidity the idea that the arduous Latin tongue should require no other instrument than a dictionary; to disillusion him fully, I sent him the *Gradus ad Parnassum* of Quicherat and the work by Pliny.

On the fourteenth of February, I received a telegram from Buenos Aires saying I should return immediately, because my father was "not at all well." May God forgive me; the prestige of being the recipient of an urgent telegram, the desire to communicate to all Fray Bentos the contradiction between the negative form of the message and the peremptory adverb, the temptation to dramatize my suffering, affecting a virile stoicism, perhaps distracted me from all possibility of real sorrow. When I packed my valise, I noticed the *Gradus* and the first volume of the *Naturalis historia* were missing. The *Saturn* was sailing the next day, in the morning; that night, after supper, I headed towards Funes' house. I was astonished to find the evening no less oppressive than the day had been.

At the respectable little house, Funes' mother opened the door for me.

She told me Ireneo was in the back room and I should not be surprised to find him in the dark, because he knew how to pass the idle hours without lighting the candle. I crossed the tile patio, the little passageway; I reached the second patio. There was a grape arbor; the darkness seemed complete to me. I suddenly heard Ireneo's high-pitched, mocking voice. His voice was speaking in Latin; his voice (which came from the darkness) was articulating with morose delight a speech or prayer or incantation. The Roman syllables resounded in the earthen patio; my fear took them to be indecipherable, interminable; afterwards, in the enormous dialogue of that night, I learned they formed the first paragraph of the twenty-fourth chapter of the seventh book of the *Naturalis historia.* The subject of that chapter is memory; the last words were *ut nihil non iisdem verbis redderetur auditum.*

Without the slightest change of voice, Ireneo told me to come in. He was on his cot, smoking. It seems to me I did not see his face until dawn; I believe I recall the intermittent glow of his cigarette. The room smelled vaguely of dampness. I sat down; I repeated the story about the telegram and my father's illness.

I now arrive at the most difficult point in my story. This story (it is well the reader know it by now) has no other plot than that dialogue which took place half a century ago. I shall not try to reproduce the words, which are now irrecoverable. I prefer to summarize with veracity the many things Ireneo told me. The indirect style is remote and weak; I know I am sacrificing the efficacy of my narrative; my readers should imagine for themselves the hesitant periods which overwhelmed me that night.

Ireneo began by enumerating, in Latin and in Spanish, the cases of prodigious memory recorded in the *Naturalis historia:* Cyrus, king of the Persians, who could call every soldier in his armies by name; Mithridates Eupator, who administered the law in the twenty-two languages of his empire; Simonides, inventor of the science of mnemonics; Metrodorus, who practiced the art of faithfully repeating what he had heard only once. In obvious good faith, Ireneo was amazed that such cases be considered amazing. He told me that before that rainy afternoon when the blue-gray horse threw him, he had been what all humans are: blind, deaf, addlebrained, absent-minded. (I tried to remind him of his exact perception of time, his memory for proper names; he paid no attention to me.) For nineteen years he had lived as one in a dream: he looked without seeing, listened without hearing, forgetting everything, almost everything. When he fell, he became unconscious; when he came out, the present was almost intolerable in its richness and sharpness, as were his most distant and trivial memories. Somewhat later he learned that he was paralyzed. The fact scarcely interested him. He reasoned (he felt) that his immobility was a minimum price to pay. Now his perception and his memory were infallible.

We, at one glance, can perceive three glasses on a table; Funes, all the leaves and tendrils and fruit that make up a grape vine. He knew by heart the forms of the southern clouds at dawn on the 30th of April, 1882, and could compare them in his memory with the mottled streaks on a book in Spanish binding he had only seen once and with the outlines of the foam raised by an oar in the Río Negro the night before the Quebracho uprising. These memories were not simple ones; each visual image was linked to muscular sensations, thermal sensations, etc. He could reconstruct all his dreams, all his half-dreams. Two or three times he had reconstructed a whole day; he never hesitated, but each reconstruction had required a whole day. He told me: "I alone have more memories than all mankind has probably had since the world has been the world." And again: "My dreams are like you people's waking hours." And again, toward dawn: "My memory, sir, is like a garbage heap." A circle drawn on a blackboard, a right triangle, a lozenge—all these are forms we can fully and intuitively grasp; Ireneo could do the same with the stormy mane of a pony, with a herd of cattle on a hill, with the changing fire and its innumerable ashes, with the many faces of a dead man throughout a long wake. I don't know how many stars he could see in the sky.

These things he told me; neither then nor later have I ever placed them in doubt. In those days there were no cinemas or phonographs; nevertheless, it is odd and even incredible that no one ever performed an experiment with Funes. The truth is that we live out our lives putting off all that can be put off; perhaps we all know deep down that we are immortal and that sooner or later all men will do and know all things.

Out of the darkness, Funes' voice went on talking to me.

He told me that in 1886 he had invented an original system of numbering and that in a very few days he had gone beyond the twenty-four-thousand mark. He had not written it down, since anything he thought of once would never be lost to him. His first stimulus was, I think, his discomfort at the fact that the famous thirty-three gauchos of Uruguayan history should require two signs and two words, in place of a single word and a single sign. He then applied this absurd principle to the other numbers. In place of seven thousand thirteen, he would say (for example) *Máximo Pérez;* in place of seven thousand fourteen, *The*

Railroad; other numbers were *Luis Melián Lafinur, Olimar, Sulphur, the reins, the whale, the gas, the caldron, Napoleon, Augustín de Vedia.* In place of five hundred, he would say *nine.* Each word had a particular sign, a kind of mark; the last in the series were very complicated . . . I tried to explain to him that this rhapsody of incoherent terms was precisely the opposite of a system of numbers. I told him that saying 365 meant saying three hundreds, six tens, five ones, an analysis which is not found in the "numbers" *The Negro Timoteo* or *meat blanket.* Funes did not understand me or refused to understand me.

Locke, in the seventeenth century, postulated (and rejected) an impossible language in which each individual thing, each stone, each bird and each branch, would have its own name; Funes once projected an analogous language, but discarded it because it seemed too general to him, too ambiguous. In fact, Funes once remembered not only every leaf of every tree of every wood, but also every one of the times he had perceived or imagined it. He decided to reduce each of his past days to some seventy thousand memories, which would then be defined by means of ciphers. He was dissuaded from this by two considerations: his awareness that the task was interminable, his awareness that it was useless. He thought that by the hour of his death he would not even have finished classifying all the memories of his childhood.

The two projects I have indicated (an infinite vocabulary for the natural series of numbers, a useless mental catalogue of all the images of his memory) are senseless, but they betray a certain stammering grandeur. They permit us to glimpse or infer the nature of Funes' vertiginous world. He was, let us not forget, almost incapable of ideas of a general, Platonic sort. Not only was it difficult for him to comprehend that the generic symbol *dog* embraces so many unlike individuals of diverse size and form; it bothered him that the dog at three fourteen (seen from the side) should have the same name as the dog at three fifteen (seen from the front). His own face in the mirror, his own hands, surprised him every time he saw them. Swift relates that the emperor of Lilliput could discern the movement of the minute hand; Funes could continuously discern the tranquil advances of corruption, of decay, of fatigue. He could note the progress of death, of dampness. He was the solitary and lucid spectator of a multiform, instantaneous and almost intolerably precise world. Babylon, London and New York have overwhelmed with their ferocious splendor the imaginations of men; no one, in their populous towers or their urgent avenues, has felt the heat and pressure of a reality as indefatigable as that which day and night converged upon the hapless Ireneo, in his poor South American suburb. It was very difficult for him to sleep. To sleep is to turn one's mind from the world; Funes, lying on his back on his cot in the shadows, could imagine every crevice and every molding in the sharply defined houses surrounding him. (I repeat that the least important of his memories was more minute and more vivid than our perception of physical pleasure or physical torment.) Towards the east, along a stretch not yet divided into blocks, there were new houses, unknown to Funes. He imagined them to be black, compact, made of homogeneous darkness; in that direction he would turn his face in order to sleep. He would also imagine himself at the bottom of the river, rocked and annihilated by the current.

With no effort, he had learned English, French, Portuguese and Latin. I suspect, however, that he was not very capable of thought. To think is to forget differences, generalize, make abstractions. In the teeming world of Funes, there were only details, almost immediate in their presence.

The wary light of dawn entered the earthen patio.

Then I saw the face belonging to the voice that had spoken all night long. Ireneo was nineteen years old; he had been born in 1868; he seemed to me as monumental as bronze, more ancient than Egypt, older than the prophecies and the pyramids. I thought that each of my words (that each of my movements) would persist in his implacable memory; I was benumbed by the fear of multiplying useless gestures.

Ireneo Funes died in 1889, of congestion of the lungs.

—Translated by James E. Irby

STANLEY ELKIN

The Guest

On Sunday Bertie walked into an apartment building in St. Louis, a city where, in the past, he had changed trains, waited for buses, or thought about Klaff, and where, more recently, truckers dropped him, or traveling salesmen stopped their Pontiacs downtown just long enough for him to reach into the back seat for his trumpetcase and get out. In the hallway he stood before the brass, mailboxed wall seeking the name of his friend, his friends' friend really, and his friends' friend's wife. The girl had danced with him at parties in the college town, and one night—he imagined he must have been particularly pathetic, engagingly pathetic—she had kissed him. The man, of course, patronized him, asked him questions that would have been more vicious had they been less naïve. He remembered he rather enjoyed making his long, patient answers. Condescension always brought the truth out of him. It was more appealing than indifference anyway, and more necessary to him now. He supposed he didn't care for either of them, but he couldn't go further. He had to rest or he would die.

He found the name on the mailbox—Mr. and Mrs. Stephen Feldman—the girl's identity, as he might have guessed, swallowed up in the husband's. It was no way to treat women, he thought gallantly.

He started up the stairs. Turning the corner at the second landing he saw a man, moving cautiously downward, burdened by boxes and suitcases and loose bags. Only when they were on a level with each other did Bertie, through a momentary clearing in the boxes, recognize Stephen Feldman.

"Old man, old man," Bertie said.

"Just a minute," Feldman said, forcing a package aside with his chin. Bertie stood, half a staircase above him, leaning against the wall. He grinned in the shadows, conscious of his ridiculous fedora, his eye patch rakishly black against the soft whiteness of his face. Black-suited, tiny, white-fleshed, he posed above Feldman, dapper as a scholarly waiter in a restaurant. He waited until he was recognized.

"Bertie? Bertie? Let me get rid of this stuff. Give me a hand, will you?" Feldman said.

"Sure," Bertie said. "It's on my family crest. One hand washing the other. Here, wait a minute." He passed Feldman on the stairs and held the door for him. He followed him outside.

"Take the key from my pocket, Bertie, and open the trunk. It's the blue convertible."

Bertie put his hand in Feldman's pocket. "You've got nice thighs," he said. To irritate Feldman he pretended to try to force the house key into the trunk lock. Feldman stood impatiently behind him, balancing his heavy burdens. "I've been to Dallas, lived in a palace," Bertie said over his shoulder. "There's this great Eskimo who blows down there. Would you believe he's cut the best side ever recorded of 'Mood Indigo?'" Bertie shook the key ring as if it were a castanet.

Feldman dumped his load on the hood of the car and took the keys from Bertie. He opened the trunk and started to throw things into it. "Going somewhere?" Bertie asked.

"Vacation," Feldman said.

"Oh," Bertie said.

Feldman looked toward the apartment house. "I've got to go up for another suitcase, Bertie."

"Sure," Bertie said.

He went up the stairs behind Feldman. About halfway up he stopped to catch his breath. Feldman watched him curiously. He pounded his chest with his tiny fist and grinned weakly. *"Mea culpa,"* he said. "Mea booze. Mea sluts. Mea pot. Me-o-mea."

"Come on," Feldman said.

They went inside and Bertie heard a toilet flushing. Through a hall, through an open door, he saw Norma, Feldman's wife, staring absently into the bowl. "If she moves them now you won't have to stop at God knows what kind of place along the road," Bertie said brightly.

Norma lifted a big suitcase easily in her big hands and came into the living room. She stopped when she saw Bertie. "Bertie! Stephen, it's Bertie."

"We bumped into each other in the hall," Stephen said.

Bertie watched the two of them look at each other.

"You sure picked a time to come visiting, Bertie," Feldman said.

"We're leaving on our vacation, Bertie," Norma said.

"We're going up to New England for a couple of weeks," Feldman told him.

"We can chat for a little with Bertie, can't we Stephen, before we go?"

"Of course," Feldman said. He sat down and pulled the suitcase next to him.

"It's very lovely in New England." Bertie sat down and crossed his legs. "I don't get up there very regularly. Not my territory. I've found that when a man makes it in the Ivy League he tends to forget about old Bertie," he said sadly.

"What are you doing in St. Louis, Bertie?" Feldman's wife asked him.

"It's my mid-western swing," Bertie said. "I've been down south on the southern sponge. Opened up a whole new territory down there." He heard himself cackle.

"Who did you see, Bertie?" Norma asked him.

"You wouldn't know her. A cousin of Klaff's."

"Were you living with her?" Feldman asked.

Bertie shook his finger at him. The Feldmans stared glumly at each other. Stephen rubbed the plastic suitcase handle. In a moment, Bertie thought, he would probably say, "Gosh, Bertie, you should have written. You should have let us know." He should have written! Did the Fuller

Brush man write? Who would be home? Who wouldn't be on vacation? They were commandos, the Fuller Brush man and he. He was tired, sick. He couldn't move on today. Would they kill him because of their lousy vacation?

Meanwhile the Feldmans weren't saying anything. They stared at each other openly, their large eyes in their large heads on their large necks largely. He thought he could wait them out. It was what he *should* do. It should have been the easiest thing in the world—to wait out the Feldmans, to stare them down. Who was he kidding? It wasn't his forte. He had no forte. *That* was his forte. He could already hear himself begin to speak.

"Sure," he said. "I almost married that girl. Klaff's lady cousin. The first thing she ever said to me was 'Bertie, they never build drug stores in the middle of the block. Always on corners.' It was the truth. Well, I thought, this was the woman for me. One time she came out of the ladies' john of a Greyhound bus station and she said, 'Bertie, have you ever noticed how public toilets often smell like bubble gum?' That's what it was like all the time. She had all these institutional insights. I was sure we could make it together. It didn't work out." He sighed.

Feldman stared at him but Norma was beginning to soften, Bertie thought. He wondered randomly what she would be like in bed. He looked coolly at her long legs, her wide shoulders. Like Klaff's cousin. Institutional.

"Bertie, how are your eyes now?" she asked.

"Oh," he said, "still seeing double." He smiled. "Two for one. It's all right when there's something to look at. Other times I use the patch."

Norma seemed sad.

"I have fun with it," he said. "It doesn't make any difference which eye I cover. I'm ambidextrous." He pulled the black elastic band from his forehead. Instantly there were two large Stephens, two large Normas. The four Feldmans like a troupe of Jewish acrobats. He felt surrounded. In the two living rooms his four hands fumbled with the two patches. He felt sick to his stomach. He closed one eye and hastily replaced the patch. "I shouldn't try that on an empty stomach," he said.

Feldman watched him narrowly. "Gee, Bertie," he said finally, "maybe we could drop you someplace."

It was out of the question. He couldn't get into a car again. "Do you go through Minneapolis, Minnesota?" he asked indifferently.

Feldman looked confused and Bertie liked him for a moment. "We were going to catch the Turnpike up around Chicago, Bertie."

"Oh, Chicago," Bertie said. "I can't go back to Chicago yet."

Feldman nodded.

"Don't you know anybody else in St. Louis?" Norma asked.

"Klaff used to live across the river, but he's gone," Bertie said.

"Look, Bertie . . ." Feldman said.

"I'm fagged," Bertie said helplessly, "locked out."

"Bertie," Feldman said, "do you need any money? I could let you have twenty dollars."

Bertie put his hand out mechanically.

"This is stupid," Norma said suddenly. "Stay *here*."

"Oh, well—"

"No, I mean it. Stay *here*. We'll be gone for two weeks. What difference does it make?"

Feldman looked at his wife for a moment and shrugged. "Sure," he said, "there's no reason you couldn't stay here. As a matter of fact you'd be doing us a favor. I forgot to cancel the newspaper, the milk. You'd keep the burglars off. They don't bother a place if it looks lived in." He put twenty dollars on the coffee table. "There might be something you need," he explained.

Bertie looked carefully at them both. They seemed to mean it. Feldman and his wife grinned at him steadily, relieved at how easily they had come off. He enjoyed the idea himself. At last he had a real patron, a real matron. "O.K.," he said.

"Then it's settled," Feldman said, rising.

"It's all right?" Bertie said.

"Certainly it's all right," Feldman said. "What harm could you do?"

"I'm harmless," Bertie said.

Feldman picked up the suitcase and led his wife toward the door. "Have a good time," Bertie said, following them. "I'll watch things for you. Rrgghh! Rrrgghhhfff!"

Feldman waved back at him as he went down the stairs. "Hey," Bertie called, leaning over the banister, "did I tell you about that crazy Klaff? You know what nutty Klaff did out at U.C.L.A.? He became a second-story man." They were already down the stairs.

Bertie went back into the house. Closing the door he pressed his back against it and turned his head slowly across his left shoulder. He imagined himself photographed from underneath. "Odd man in," he said. In a moment he bounded off the door and into the center of the living room. "I'll bet there's a lease," he thought. "I'll bet there's a regular lease that goes with this place." He considered this for a moment with an awed respect. He couldn't remember ever having been in a place where the tenants actually had to sign a lease. He walked into the dining room and turned on the chandelier lights. "Sure there's a lease," Bertie said. He hugged himself. "How the fallen are mighty," he said.

He remembered his need to rest. In the living room he lay down on the couch without taking off his shoes. He sat up and pulled them off but when he lay down again he was uneasy. He had gotten out of the habit, living the way he did, of sleeping without shoes. In his friends' leaseless basements the nights were cold and he wore them for warmth. He put the shoes on again, but found he wasn't tired anymore. It was a fact that dependence gave him energy. He was never so alert as when people did him favors. It was having to be on your own that made you tired.

"Certainly," Bertie said to the committee, "it's a scientific fact. We've suspected it for years, but until our researchers divided up the town of Bloomington, Indiana, we had no proof. What our people found in that community was that the orphans and bastards were all the time sleepy and run down, but that the housewives and folks on relief were wide awake, alert, raring to go. It's remarkable. We can't positively state the link yet, but we're fairly certain that it's something to do with dependency in league perhaps with a particularly virulent form of—ahem—gratitude. Ahem. Ahem."

As he lectured the committee he wandered around the apartment, touring from right to left. He crossed from the living room into the dining room and turned right into the kitchen and then right again into the small room Feldman used for his study. "Here's where all the magic happens," Bertie said, glancing at the contour chair near Feldman's desk. He went back into the kitchen. "Here's where all the magic happens," he said, looking at Norma's electric stove. He stepped into the dining room and continued on, passing Norma's paintings, of picturesque little side streets in Mexico, of picturesque little side streets in Italy, of picturesque little side streets in Puerto Rico, until he came to a door that led to the back sun parlor. He went through it and found himself in a room with an easel, with paints in sexy little tubes, with brushes, with palettes and turpentine and rags. "Here's where all the magic happens," Bertie said and walked around the room to another door. He opened it and was in the Feldmans' master bedroom. He looked at the bed. "Here's where all the magic happens," he said. Through a door at the other end of the room was another small hall. On the right was the toilet. He went in and flushed it. It was one of those toilets with instantly renewable tanks. He flushed it again. And again. "The only kind to have," he said out of the side of his mouth, imagining a rental agent. "I mean it's like this. Supposing the missus has diarrhea or something. You don't want to have to wait until the tank fills up. Or suppose you're sick. Or suppose you're giving a party and it's mixed company. Well it's just corny to whistle to cover the noise, you know what I mean? 'Sjust corny. On the other hand you flush it once, suppose you're not through, then what happens? There's the damn noise after the water goes down. What have you accomplished? This way"—he reached across and jiggled the little lever and then did it a second time, a third, a fourth—"you never have any embarrassing interim, what we in the trade call 'flush lag.' "

He came out of the bathroom and at the other end of the hall found another bedroom, smaller than the first. It was the guest bedroom and Bertie knew at once that he would never sleep in it, that he would sleep in the Feldmans' big bed.

"Nice place you got here," he said when he had finished the tour.

"Dooing de woh eet ees all I tink of, what I fahting foe," the man from the Underground said. "Here ees eet fahrproof, air-condition and safe from Nazis."

"Stay out of Volkswagens, kid," Bertie said.

Bertie went back into the living room. He wanted some music but it was a cardinal principle with him never to blow alone. He would drink alone, take drugs alone, but somehow the depths of depravity were for him represented by having to play jazz alone. He had a vision of himself in a cheap hotel room sitting on the edge of an iron bedstead. Crumpled packages of cigarettes were scattered throughout the room. Bottles of gin were on top of the Gideon Bible, the Western Union blanks. His trumpet was in his lap. "Perfect," Bertie said. "Norma Feldman could come in and paint it in a picture." Bertie shuddered.

The phonograph was in the hall between the dining and living rooms. It was a big thing, with the AM and the FM and the short wave and the place where you plugged in the color television when it was perfected. He found records in Feldman's little room and went through them rapidly. "Ah mad Jamahl for Christ's sake." He took the record out of its sleeve and broke it across his knee. He stood up slowly and kicked the fragments of the broken recording into a neat pile.

He turned around and scooped up as many of Feldman's recordings as he could carry and brought them to the machine. He piled them on indiscriminately and listened with visible, professional discomfort. He listened to *The New World Symphony,* to Beethoven's *Fifth,* to *My Fair Lady,* The Kingston Trio. The more he listened the more he began to dislike the Feldmans. When he could stand it no longer he tore the playing arm viciously away from the record and looked around him. He saw the Feldmans' bookcase.

"I'll read," he said.

He took down the Marquis de Sade and Henry Miller and Ronald Firbank and turned the pages desultorily. Nothing happened. He tried reading aloud in front of a mirror. He went back to the bookcase and looked for *The Egg and I* and *Please Don't Eat the Daisies.* The prose of a certain kind of bright housewife always made Bertie erotic but the Feldmans owned neither book. He browsed Rachel Carson's *Silent Spring* with only mild lasciviousness.

He went into their bedroom and opened the closet. He found a pair of Norma's shoes and put them on. Although he was no fetishist he had often promised himself that if he ever had the opportunity he would see what it was like. He walked around the apartment in Norma's high heels. All that happened was that he got a pain in his calves.

In the kitchen he looked into the refrigerator. There were some frozen mixed vegetables in the freezer compartment.

"I'll starve first," Bertie said.

He found a Billie Holliday record and put it on the phonograph. He hoped that Klaff out in Los Angeles was at this moment being beaten with rubber hoses by the police. He looked up at the kitchen clock. "Nine," he said. "Only seven in L.A. They probably don't start beating them up until later."

"Talk Klaff," he snarled, "or we'll drag you into the Blood Room."

"Flake off, copper," Klaff said.

"That's enough of that, Klaff. Take that and that and that."

"Bird lives," Bertie screamed suddenly, invoking the dead Charlie Parker. It was his code cry.

"Mama may have," Billie Holliday wailed, "Papa may have, But God Bless the child who's got his own, who—oo—zz—"

"Who—oo—zz," Bertie wailed.

"Got his own," Billie said.

"I'll tell him when he comes in, William," Bertie said.

Bertie waited respectfully until Billie was finished and turned off the music.

He wondered why so many people felt that Norman Mailer was the greatest living American novelist.

He sat down on the Feldmans' coffee table and marveled at his being alone in so big and well furnished an apartment. The Feldmans were probably the most substantial people he knew. Feldman was the only one from the old crowd who might make it, he guessed. Of course he was Jewish and that helped. Some Jews swung pretty good but he always suspected that in the end they would hold out on you. But then who wouldn't, Bertie wondered. Kamikaze pilots, maybe. Anyway this was Bertie's special form of anti-semitism and he cherished it. Melvin Gimpel, for example, his old roommate. Every time Melvin tried to kill himself by sticking his head in the oven he left the kitchen window open. Bertie laughed, remembering the time he had found Gimpel on his knees with his head on the oven door, oddly like the witch in Hansel and Gretel. Bertie closed the window and shook Gimpel awake.

"Mel," he yelled, slapping him and laughing. "Mel."

"Bertie, go away. Leave me alone, I want to kill myself."

"Thank God," Bertie said. "Thank God I'm in time. When I found that window closed I thought it was all over."

"What, the window was closed? My God, was the window closed?"

"Melvin Gimpel is so simple
Thinks his nipple is a pimple," Bertie recited.

Bertie hugged his knees, and then, again, felt a wave of the nauseous sickness he had experienced that morning. "It's foreshadowing. One day as I am shoveling my walk I will collapse and die."

When the nausea left him he thought again about his situation. It was odd, he thought, being alone in so big a place. He had friends everywhere and made his way from place to place like an old time slave on the Underground Railway. For all the pathos of the figure he knew he deliberately cut, there were always people to do him favors, give him money, beer, drugs, to nurse him back to his normal state of semi-invalidism, girls to kiss him in the comforting way he liked. This was probably the first time he had been alone in months. He felt like a dog whose master has gone away for the weekend. Just then he heard some people coming up the stairs and he growled experimentally. He went down on his hands and knees and scampered to the door, scratching it with his nails. "Rrrgghhf," he barked. "Rrgghhfff!" He heard whoever it was fumbling to open a door on the floor below him. He smiled. "Good dog," he said. "Good dog, goodog, gudug, gudugguduggudug."

He whined. He missed his master. A tear formed in the corner of his left eye. He crawled to a full-length mirror in the bathroom. "Ahh," he said. "Ahh." Seeing the patch across his eye he had an inspiration. "Here, Patch," he called. "Come on, Patch."

He romped after his own voice.

He moved beside Norma Feldman's easel in the sun parlor. He lowered his body carefully, pushing himself slightly backwards with his arms. He yawned. He touched his chest to the wooden floor. He wagged his tail and then let himself fall heavily on one side. He pulled his legs up under him and fell asleep.

When he awoke he was hungry. He went into the kitchen but he knew nothing about cooking. He fingered the twenty dollars in his pocket that Feldman had given him. He could order out. The light in the hall where the phone and phone books were was not good, so he tore "Restaurants" from the Yellow Pages and brought the sheets with him into the living room. Only two places delivered after one A.M. It was already one-thirty. He dialed the number of a pizza place closest to him. It was busy so he dialed the other number.

"Pal, bring over a big one, half shrimp, half mushroom. And two six-packs." He gave the address. The man explained that the truck had just gone out and that he shouldn't expect delivery for at least another hour and a half.

"Put it in a cab," Bertie said. "While Bird lives Bertie spends."

He took out another dozen or so records and piled them on the machine. He sat down on the couch and drummed his trumpetcase with his fingers. He opened the case and fit the mouthpiece to the body of the horn. He put the trumpet to his lips and experienced the unpleasant shock of cold metal he always felt. He still thought it strange that men could mouth metal this way, ludicrous that his own official attitude should be a kiss. He blew a few bars in accompaniment to the record and put the trumpet back in the case. He felt in the side pockets of the trumpetcase and took out two pair of dirty underwear, some handkerchiefs and three pair of socks. He unrolled one of the pairs of socks and saw with pleasure that the drug was still there. He took out the bottle of carbon tetrachloride. This was what he cleaned his instrument with. It was what he would use to kill himself when he had finally made the decision.

He held the bottle to the light. "If nothing turns up," he said, "I'll drink this. And to hell with the kitchen window."

The cab driver brought the pizza and Bertie gave him the twenty dollars.

"I can't change that," the driver said.

"Did I ask you to change it?" Bertie said.

"That's twenty bucks there."

"Bird lives. Easy come, easy go go go," Bertie said.

The driver started to thank him.

"Go." He closed the door.

He spread Norma Feldman's largest tablecloth over the dining room table and then he took some china and some sterling from the big breakfront and laid several place settings. He found champagne glasses.

Unwrapping the pizza, he carefully plucked all the mushrooms from it ("American mushrooms," he said. "Very square. No visions.") and laid them in a neat pile on the white linen. ("Many mushloom," he said. "Mushloom crowd.") He poured some beer into a champagne glass.

He rose slowly from his chair.

"Gentlemen," he said, "to the absent Klaff. May the police in Los Angeles, California beat his lousy ass off." He drank all the beer in one gulp and tossed the glass behind him over his shoulder. He heard the glass shatter and then a soft sizzling sound. He turned around and saw that he had gotten one of Norma's paintings right in a picturesque side street. Beer dripped ignobly down a donkey's leg. "Goddamn," Bertie said appreciatively, "*action* painting."

He ate perhaps a quarter of the pizza and got up from the table, wiping the corner of his lips with a big linen napkin.

"Gentlemen," he said, "I propose that the ladies retire to the bedroom while we men enjoy our cigars and port and some good talk."

"I propose that we men retire to the bedroom and enjoy the ladies," he said in Gimpel's voice.

"Here, here," he said in Klaff's voice. "Here, here. Good talk. Good talk."

"If you will follow me, gentlemen," he said in his own voice. He began to walk around the apartment. "I have been often asked the story of my life. These requests usually follow a personal favor someone has done me, a supper shared, a bed made available, a ride in one of the several directions. Indeed, I have become a sort of troubadour who does not sing so much as whine for his supper. Most of you—"

"Whine is very good with supper," Gimpel said.

"Gimpel, my dear, why don't you run into the kitchen and play?" Bertie said coolly. "Many of you may know the humble beginnings, the sordid details, the dark Freudian patterns, and those of you who are my friends—"

Klaff belched.

"Those of you who are my *friends*, who do not run off to mix it up with the criminal element in the Far West, have often wondered what will ultimately happen to me, to 'Poor Bertie' as I am known in the trade."

Bertie unbuttoned his shirt and let it fall to the floor. He looked defenceless in his undershirt, his skin pale as something seen in moonlight.

"Why, you wonder, doesn't he do something about himself, pull himself up by his bootstraps? Why, for example, doesn't he get his eyes fixed? Well, I've tried."

He kicked off his shoes.

"You have all admired my bushy moustache. Do you remember that time two years ago I dropped out of sight for four months? Well let me tell you what happened that time."

He took off his black pants.

"I had been staying with Royal Randle, the distinguished philologist and drunk. You will recall that Royal with Klaff and Myers and Gimpel

and myself once constituted a quintet known familiarly as 'The Irrespon-
sibles.' " Bertie sighed. "You remember the promises: 'It won't make
any difference, Bertie. It won't make any difference, Klaff. It won't make
any difference, fellas.' He married the girl in the Muu Muu."

He was naked now except for his socks. He shivered once and folded
his arms across his chest.

"Do you know why the girl in the Muu Muu married Randle?" He
paused dramatically. *"To get at me, that's why.* The others she didn't
care about. She knew even before I did what they were like. Even what
Klaff was like. She knew they were corrupt, that they had it in them to
sell me out, to settle down—that all anyone had to do was wave their
deaths in front of them and they'd come running, that reason and fucking money and getting it steady would win again. But in me she recognized the real enemy, the last of the go-to-hell-god-damn-its. Maybe the
first.

"They even took me with them on their honeymoon. At the time I
thought it was a triumph for dependency, but it was just a trick, that's all
that was. The minute they were married this girl in the Muu Muu was
after Randle to do something about Bertie. And it wasn't 'Poor' Bertie
this time. It was she who got me the appointment with the Mayor. Do
you know what His Honor said to me? 'Shave your moustache and I'll
give you a job clerking in one of my supermarkets.' Christ, friends, do
you know I *did* it? Well, I'm not made of stone. They had taken me on
their honeymoon for God's sake."

Bertie paused.

"I worked in that supermarket *for three hours.* Clean shaved. My
moustache sacrificed as an earnest to the Mayor. Well I'm telling you
you don't know what square *is* till you've worked in a supermarket for
three hours. They pipe in Mantovani. *Mantovani!* I cleared out for four
months to raise my bushy moustache again and to forget. What you see
now isn't the original, you understand. It's all second growth, and believe
me it's not the same."

Bertie drew aside the shower curtain and stepped into the tub. He
paused with his hand on "Hot."

"But I tell you this, friends, I tell you this. That I would rather be a
moustached bum than a clean-shaved clerk. I'll work. Sure I will. When
they pay anarchists. When they subsidize the hip. When they give
grants to throw bombs. When they shell out for gainsaying."

He pulled the curtain and turned on the faucet and the rush of water
was like applause.

After his shower Bertie went into the second bedroom and carefully
removed the spread from the cot. Then he punched the pillow and

mussed the bed. "Very clever," he said. "It wouldn't do to let them think I *never* slept here." He had once realized with sudden clarity that he would never, so long as he lived, make a bed.

He went then into the other bedroom and ripped the spread from the big double bed. For some time, in fact since he had first seen it, Bertie had been thinking about this bed. It was the biggest bed he would ever sleep in. (He thought invariably in such terms. One cigarette in a pack would suddenly become distinguished in his mind as the best, or the worst, he would smoke that day. A homely act, such as tying his shoe-laces, if it had occurred with unusual case, would be remembered forever. This lent to his vision an oblique sadness, conscious as he was that he was forever encountering experiences which would never come his way again.)

He slipped his naked body between the sheets and had no sooner made himself comfortable than he became conscious of the phonograph, still playing in the little hall. He couldn't hear it very well. He thought about turning up the volume but he had read somewhere about neighbors. He got out of bed and went to the phonograph. He moved the heavy machine through the living room, pushing it with difficulty over the seamed, bare wooden floor, trailing deep scratches. "Remember not to walk barefoot over there," he thought. At one point one of the legs caught in a loop of the Feldmans' shag rug and Bertie strained to free it, finally breaking the thick thread and producing an interesting pucker along one end of the rug, not unlike the pucker in raised theatrical curtains. At last he maneuvered the machine into the hall just outside the bedroom. He plugged it in. He went back for the Billie Holliday recording he had heard earlier and put it on the phonograph. By lifting the arm that held and steadied the records on the spindle and pulling it back, he fixed it so the record would play all night.

He got back into the bed.

"Ah," he said, "the *sanctum sanctorum.*" He rolled over and over from one side of the bed to the other. He tucked his knees into his chest and went under the covers. "It makes you feel kind of small and insignificant," he said.

"Ladies and Gentlemen, this is Graham Macnamee speaking to you from the Cave of the Winds. I have made my way into the heart of this darkness to find my friend, Poor Bertie, who, as you know, entered the bed eight weeks ago. Bertie is with me now, and while there isn't enough light for me to be able to see his condition, his voice may tell us something about his physical state. Bertie, just what *is* the official record?"

"Well, Graham, some couples have been known to stick it out for seventy-five years. Of course your average is much less than that, but still—"

"Seventy-five years."

"Seventy-five, yes sir. It's amazing, isn't it, Graham, when you come to think? All that time in one bed."

"It certainly is," Graham Macnamee said. "Do you think you'll be able to go the distance, Bert?"

"Who, me? No, no. A lot of folks have misunderstood my purpose in coming here. I'm rather glad you've given me the opportunity to clear that up. Actually my work here is scientific. This isn't a stunt or anything like that. I'm here to learn."

"Can you tell us about it, Bert?"

"Graham, it's been a fascinating experience if you know what I mean, but frankly there are many things we still don't understand. I don't know why they do it. All that licit love, that regularity. Take the case of Stephen and Norma, for example. And incidentally, you don't want to overlook the significance of that name 'Norma.' Norma/Normal, you see?"

"Say, I never thought of that."

"Well, I'm trained to think like that, Graham. In my work you have to."

"Say," Graham Macnamee said.

"Sure. Well the thing is this, buddy, when I first came into this bed I felt the aura, know what I mean, the *power.* I think it's built into the mattress or something."

"Say."

"Shut your face, Graham, and let me speak, will you please? Well, anyway, you feel surrounded. Respectable. Love is made here, of course, but it's not love as we know it. There are things that must remain mysteries until we have more facts. I mean Graham, checks could be cashed in this bed, for Christ's sake, credit cards honored. It's ideal for family reunions and high teas. Graham, it's the kind of place you wouldn't be ashamed to take your mother."

"Go to sleep, Bert," Graham Macnamee said.

"Say," Bertie said.

Between the third and fourth day of his stay in the Feldmans' apartment Bertie became restless. He had not been outside the house since the Sunday he had come, even to bring in the papers Feldman had told him about. (Indeed, it was by counting the papers that he knew how long he had been there, though he couldn't be sure since he didn't know whether the Feldmans had taken the Sunday paper with them.) He could see them on the back porch through the window of Norma's sun parlor. With the bottles of milk they made a strange little pile. He was not after all a caretaker. He was a guest. Feldman could bring in his own papers, drink his own damn milk. For the same reasons he had determined not even to answer the phone when it rang.

One evening he tried to call Klaff at the Los Angeles County Jail, but the desk sergeant wouldn't get him. He wouldn't even take a message.

Although he had not been outside since Sunday, Bertie had only a vague desire to go out. He weighed this against his real need to rest and his genuine pleasure in being alone in so big an apartment. Like the man in the joke who does not leave his Miami hotel room because it is costing him thirty-five dollars a day, Bertie decided he had better remain inside.

With no money left he was reduced to eating the dry, cold remainder of the pizza, dividing it mathematically into a week's provisions like someone on a raft. (Bertie actually fancied himself, not on a raft perhaps, but set alone and drifting in, say, the *Queen Mary.*) To supplement this he opened some cans of soup he found in the pantry and drank the contents straight, without first heating it or even adding water.

Steadily he drank away at the Feldmans' not really large stock of liquor. The twelve cans of beer, of course, had been devoured by the second morning.

After the second full day in the apartment his voices began to desert him. It was only with difficulty that he could manage his imitations, and only for short lengths of time. The glorious discussions that had gone on long into the night were now out of the question. He found he could not do Gimpel's voice any more and even Klaff's was increasingly difficult and largely confined to his low, caressing obscenities. Mostly he talked with himself, although it was a real strain to keep up his end of the conversation and it always made him cry when he said how pathetic he was and asked himself where do you go from here. "Oh to be like Bird," he thought. "Not to have to be a bum. To ask, as it were, no quarter."

At various times during the day he would call out, "Bird lives," in seeming stunning triumph. But he didn't believe it.

He watched a lot of television. ("I'm getting ammunition," he said. "It's scientific.")

And twice a day he masturbated in the Feldmans' bed.

He settled gradually, then, into restlessness. He knew, of course, that he had it always in his power to bring himself back up to the heights he had known in those wonderful first two days. He was satisfied, however, not to use this power, and thought of himself as a kind of soldier, alone, in a foxhole, in enemy territory, at night, at a bad time in the war, with one bullet in his pistol. Oddly he derived more pride (and comfort, and a queer security) from this single bullet than others might from whole cases of ammunition. It was his *strategic* bullet, the one he would use to get the big one, turn the tide, make the difference. The Feldmans would be away two weeks. He would not waste his ammunition. Just as he divided the stale pizza, cherishing each piece as much for the satisfaction he took from possessing it during a time of emergency as for any sustenance it offered, so he enjoyed his knowledge that at any time he could recoup his vanishing spirits. He shared with the squares ("Use their own weapons to beat them, Bertie.") a special pride in adversity, in having to do without, in having to expose whatever was left of his character to the narrower straits. It was strange, Bertie thought seriously, it was the paradox of the world and an institutional insight that might have come right out of the mouth of that slut in Dallas, but the most peculiar aspect of the squares wasn't their lack of imagination or their bland bad taste, but their ability, like the wildest fanatics, like the furthest out of the furthest out, to cling to the illogical, finally untenable notion that they must *have* and *have* in order to live, at the same time that they realized that it was better not to have. What seemed so grand to Bertie, who admired all impossible positions, was that they believed both things with equal intensity, never suspecting for a moment any inconsistency. And here was Bertie, Bertie thought, here was Bertie, inside their capitol, on the slopes of their mountains, on their smooth shores, who believed neither of these propositions, who believed in not having and in not suffering too, who yet realized the very same pleasure they would in having and not using.

It was the strangest thing that would ever happen to him, he thought.

"Are you listening, Klaff, you second-story fink?" Bertie yelled. "Do you see how your old pal is developing what is called character?"

And so, master of himself for once, he resolved (feeling what someone taking a vow feels) not to use the last of his drugs until the strategic moment of strategic truth.

That was Wednesday evening. By Thursday morning he had decided to break his resolution. He had not yielded to temptation, had not lain fitfully awake all night (indeed, his resolution had given him the serenity to sleep well) in the sweaty throes of withdrawal. There had been no argument or rationalization, nor had he decided that he had reached his limit or that this was the strategic moment he had been waiting for. He yielded as he always yielded, spontaneously, suddenly, unexpectedly, as the result neither of whim nor calculation. His important decisions were almost always reached without his knowledge and Bertie was often as surprised as the next one to see what he was going to do, to see, indeed, that he was already doing it. (Once someone had asked him whether he believed in Free Will and Bertie, after considering this for a moment as it applied to himself, had answered, "Free? Hell, it's positively *loose.*")

Having discovered his new intention Bertie was eager to realize it. As often as he had taken drugs (he never called it anything but drugs, never used the cute or obscene names, never even said "dope"; to him it was always "drugs," medicine for his spirit), they were still a major treat for him. ("It's a rich man's game," he had once told Klaff, and then he had leaned back philosophically. "You know, Klaff, it's a good thing I'm poor. When I think of the snobbish ennui of your wealthy junkies, I realize that they don't know how to appreciate their blessings. God keep me humble, Klaff. Abstinence makes the heart grow fonder, a truer word was never spoken.") Nor did a drug ever lose its potency for him. If he graduated from one to another it was not in order to recover some fading jolt, but to experience a new and different one. He held in contempt all those who professed disenchantment with the drugs they had been raised on and frequently went back to rediscover the old pleasures of marijuana, as a sentimental father might chew some of his boy's bubble gum. "Loyalty, Gimpel," he exclaimed, "loyalty, do you know what *that* is?"

He would and did try anything, though currently his favorite was mescaline for the visions it induced. Despite what he considered his eclectic tastes in these things, however, there were one or two things he would not do. He never introduced any drug by hypodermic needle. This he found disgusting and, frankly, painful. (He often said he could stand anything but pain and was very proud of his clear, unpunctured skin. "Not a mark on me," he would say, waving his arms like a professional boxer.) The other thing he would not do was take his drugs in the presence of other users for he found the company of addicts offensive. He was not above what he called "seductions," however. A seduction for him was to find some girl and talk her into letting him share his drugs with her. Usually it ended in their lying naked in a bed together, both of them serene, absent of all desire and what Bertie called "unclean thoughts."

"You know," he would say to the girl beside him, "I think that if all the world's leaders would take drugs and lie down on the bed naked like this without any unclean thoughts, that the cause of world peace would be helped immeasurably. What do you think?"

"I think so too," she would say.

Once he knew he was going to take the drug Bertie made his preparations. He went first to his trumpetcase and took out the last small packet of powder. He opened it carefully, first closing all the windows so that no sudden draft could blow any of it away. This had once happened to a friend of his and Bertie had never forgotten the warning.

"I am not one on whom a lesson is lost," Bertie said.

"You're o.k., Bertie," a Voice said. "Go, save France."

He laid it on the Feldmans' coffee table and carefully spread the paper, exactly like the paper wrapper around a stick of chewing gum, looking almost lustfully at the soft, flat layer of ground white powder. He held out his hand to see how steady it was and although he was not really shaky he did not trust himself to lift the paper from the table. He brought a water tumbler from the Feldmans' kitchen and gently placed it upside down on top of the powder. He was not yet ready to take it. Bertie was a man who postponed his pleasures as long as he possibly could. He let candy dissolve in his mouth and played with the threads on his tangerine before eating the fruit. It was a weakness in his character perhaps, but he laid it lovingly at the feet of his poverty.

He decided to wait until sundown to take the drug, reasoning that when it wore off it would be early next morning and he would be ready for bed. Sleep was one of his pleasures, too, and he approved of regularity in small things, taking a real pride in being able to keep hours. To pass the time until sundown he looked for something to do. He found some tools and busied himself by taking Norma's steam iron apart. There was still time left and he took a canvas and painted a picture. Because he did not know how to draw he simply covered the canvas first with one color and then with another, applying layer after layer of the paint thickly. Each block of color he made somewhat smaller than the last so that the finished painting portrayed successive jagged margins of color. He stepped back and considered his work seriously.

"Well it has texture, Bertie," Hans Hofmann said.

"Bertie," the Voice said suddenly, "I don't like to interrupt when you're working, but it's sundown."

"So it is," he said, looking up.

He went back into the living room and removed the tumbler. Taking up the paper in his fingers and creasing it as if he were a cowboy rolling a cigarette, Bertie tilted his head far back and inhaled the powder deeply. This part was always uncomfortable for him.

"Ooo," he said, "the bubbles." He stuffed the last few grains up his nose with his fingers. "Waste not, want not," he said.

Bertie sat down to wait. After half an hour in which nothing happened he became uneasy. "It's been cut," he said. "Sure, depend upon friends to do you favors." He was referring to the fact that the drug had been a going-away present from friends in Oklahoma City. He decided to give it fifteen more minutes. "Nothing," he said at last, disappointed. "Nothing."

The powder, as it always did, left his throat scratchy, and there was a bitter taste in his mouth. His soft palate prickled. He seized the water tumbler from the coffee table and walked angrily into the kitchen. He ran the cold water. He gargled and spit in the sink. In a few minutes the bitter taste and the prickly sensation had subsided and he felt about as he had before he had taken the drug. He was conscious however of a peculiar smell, unpleasant, unfamiliar, nothing like the odor of rotting flowers he associated with the use of drugs. He opened a window and leaning out, breathed the fresh air. As soon as he came away from the window, however, the odor was overpowering. He went to see if he could smell it in the other rooms. When he had made his tour he realized that the stench *must* be coming from the kitchen. Holding his breath he came back to see if he could locate its source. The kitchen was almost as Norma had left it. Bertie, of course, had done no cooking and although there were some empty soup and beer cans in the sink he knew *they* couldn't be causing the odor. He shrugged. Then he noticed the partially closed door to Stephen's study.

"Of course," he said. "Whatever it is must be in there." He pushed the door open. In the middle of the floor were two blackish mounds that looked like dark sawdust. Bertie stepped back in surprise.

"Camel shit," he said. "My God, how did *that* get in here?" He went closer to investigate. "That's what it is all right." He had never seen it before but a friend had and had described it to him. This stuff fitted the description perfectly. He considered what to do.

"I can't leave it there," he said. He found a dustpan and a broom and propping the pan against the leg of Stephen's chair he began to sweep the stuff up. He was surprised at how remarkably gummy it seemed. When he finished he washed the spot on the floor with a foaming detergent and stepped gingerly to the back door. He lifted the lid of the garbage can and shoved the broom and the contents of the dustpan and the dustpan itself into the can.

He went into the bathroom and washed his hands.

In the living room he saw the Chinaman.

"Jesus," Bertie said breathlessly.

The Chinaman lowered his eyes in a shy, almost demure smile. He said nothing, but motioned Bertie to sit in the chair across from him. Bertie, too frightened to disobey, sat down.

He waited for the Chinaman to tell him what he wanted. When after an hour (Bertie heard the chime clock strike nine times and then ten times) the Chinaman still had not said anything, he began to feel a little calmer. "Maybe he was just tired," Bertie thought, "and came in to rest." He realized that perhaps he and the Chinaman had more in common than had at first appeared. He looked at the fellow in this new light and saw that he had been foolish to fear him. The Chinaman was small, smaller even than Bertie. In fact he was only two feet tall. Perhaps what made him seem larger was the fact that he was wrapped in wide, voluminous white silk robes. Bertie stared at the robes, fascinated by the delicate filigree trim up and down their length. To see this closer he stood up and walked tentatively toward the Chinaman. The Chinaman gazed steadily frontwards and Bertie, seeing no threat, continued toward him.

He leaned down over the Chinaman and grasping the delicate lacework between forefinger and thumb gently drew it toward his eye. "May I!?" Bertie said. "I know a good deal about this sort of thing."

The Chinaman lowered his eyes.

Bertie examined the weird symbols and designs and, although he did not understand them, recognized at once their cabalistic origin.

"Magnificent," Bertie said at last. "My God, the man-hours that must have gone into this. *The sheer craftsmanship!* That's really a terrific robe you've got there."

The Chinaman lowered his eyes still further.

Bertie sat down in his chair again. He heard the clock strike eleven and he smiled at the Chinaman. He was trying to be sympathetic, patient. He knew the fellow had his reasons for coming and that in due time they would be revealed, but he couldn't help being a little annoyed. First the failure of the drug and then the camel shit on the floor and now this. However, he remained very polite.

There was nothing else to do so Bertie concentrated on the Chinaman's face.

Then a strange thing happened.

He became aware, as he scrutinized the face, of some things he hadn't noticed before. First he realized that it was the oldest face he had ever seen. He knew that this face was old enough to have looked on Buddha's. It was only *faintly* yellow, really, and he understood with a sweeping insight that originally it must have been white, as it was largely still, a striking, flat white, naked as a sheet, bright as teeth, that its yellowness was the yellowness of fantastic age, of pages in ancient books. As soon as he perceived this he understood the origin and mystery of the races. All men had at first been white; their different tints were only the shades of their different wisdoms. "Of course," he thought. "Of course. It's beautiful. Beautiful."

The second thing he noticed was that the face seemed extraordinarily wise. The longer he stared at it the wiser it seemed. Clearly this was the wisest Chinaman, and thus the wisest man, in the history of the world. Now he was impatient for the Chinaman to speak, to tell him his secrets, but Bertie also understood that so long as he was impatient the Chinaman would *not* speak, that he must become serene, as serene as the

Chinaman himself, or the Chinaman would go away. As this occurred to him the Chinaman smiled and Bertie knew he had been right.

Bertie was aware that if he just sat there, deliberately trying to become serene, nothing would happen. He decided that the best way to become serene was to ignore the Chinaman, to go on about his business as if the Chinaman weren't even there.

He stood up. "Am I getting warm?" Bertie asked.

The Chinaman lowered his eyes and smiled.

"Well, then," Bertie said, rubbing his hands, "let's see."

He went into the kitchen to see if there was anything he could do there to make him serene.

He washed out the empty cans of soup.

He strolled into the bedroom and made the bed. This took him an hour. (He heard the clock strike twelve and then one.)

He took a record off the machine and, starting from the center hole and working to the outer edge, counted all the ridges. (This took him fourteen seconds and he was pleased at how quickly and efficiently he worked.)

He found a suitcase in one of the closets and packed all of Norma's underwear into it.

He got a pail of water and some soap and washed all the walls in the small bedroom.

It was in the dining room, however, that he finally achieved serenity. He studied Norma's pictures of side streets throughout the world and with sudden insight understood what was wrong with them. He took some tubes of white paint and with a brush worked over the figures, painting back into the flesh all their original whiteness. He made the Mexicans white, the Negroes, feeling as he worked an immense satisfaction, the satisfaction not of the creator, nor even of the reformer, but of the restorer.

Swelling with serenity he went back into the living room and sat down in his chair.

For the first time the Chinaman met Bertie's gaze directly, and Bertie realized that something important was going to happen.

The Chinaman slowly, very slowly, began to open his mouth. Bertie watched the slow parting of the Chinaman's thin lips, the gleaming teeth, white and bright as fence pickets. Gradually the rest of the room darkened and the thinly padded chair on which Bertie sat grew incredibly soft. Bertie knew they had been transported somehow, that they were now in a sort of theater. The Chinaman was seated on a kind of raised platform. Meanwhile the mouth continued to open, slowly as an ancient drawbridge. Tiny as the Chinaman was the mouth seemed enormous. Bertie gazed into it, seeing nothing. At last, deep back in the mouth, Bertie saw a brief flashing, as of a small crystal on a dark rock suddenly illuminated by the sun. In a moment he saw it again, brighter now, longer sustained. Soon it was so bright that Bertie had to force himself to look at it. Then the mouth went black. Before he could protest the brightness was overwhelming again and he saw a cascade of what seemed like diamonds tumble out of the Chinaman's mouth. It was the Chinaman's tongue.

The tongue, twisting, turning over and over like magicians' silks pulled endlessly from a tube, continued to pour from the Chinaman's mouth.

Bertie saw that it had the same whiteness as the rest of his face and was studded with bright, beautiful jewels. On the tongue, long now as an unfurled scroll, were black, thick Chinese characters. It was the secret of life, the world, the universe. Bertie could barely see for the tears of gratitude in his eyes. Desperately he wiped the tears away with his fist. He looked back at the tongue and stared at the strange words, realizing that he could not read Chinese. He was sobbing helplessly now but he knew there was not much time. The presence of the Chinaman gave him courage and strength and he *forced* himself to read the Chinese. As he concentrated it became easier, the characters somehow re-forming, translating themselves into a sort of decipherable Chinesey script, like the words "Chop Suey" on the neon sign outside a Chinese restaurant. Bertie was breathless from his effort and the stunning glory of what was being revealed to him. Frequently he had to pause, punctuating his experience with queer little squeals.

"Oh," he said. "Oh. Oh."

Then it was over.

He was exhausted but his knowledge glowed in him like fire. "So *that's* it," was all he could say. "So *that's* it. So *that's* it."

Bertie saw that he was no longer in the theater. The Chinaman was gone and Bertie was back in the Feldmans' living room. He struggled for control of himself. He knew it was urgent that he tell someone what had happened to him. Desperately he pulled open his trumpetcase. Inside he had pasted sheets with the names, addresses and phone numbers of all his friends.

"Damn Klaff," he said angrily. "Damn second-story Klaff in his lousy jail."

He spotted Gimpel's name and the phone number of his boarding house in Cincinnati. He tore the sheet from where it was pasted inside the lid and rushed to the phone. He placed the call. "Life and death," he screamed at Gimpel's bewildered landlady, "life and death."

When Gimpel came to the phone Bertie began to tell him, coherently, but with obvious excitement, all that had happened. Gimpel was as excited as himself.

"Then the Chinaman opened his mouth and this tongue with writing on it came out."

"Yeah!" Gimpel said. "Yeah? Yeah?"

"Only it was in Chinese," Bertie shouted.

"Chinese," Gimpel said.

"But I could read it, Gimpel! *I could read it!*"

"I didn't know you could read Chinese," Gimpel said.

"It was the meaning of life."

"Yeah?" Gimpel said. "Yeah? What'd it say? What'd it say?"

"What?" Bertie said.

"What'd it say? What'd the Chink's tongue say was the meaning of life?"

"I forget," Bertie said and hung up.

He slept until two the next afternoon and when he awoke he felt as if he had been beaten up. His tongue was something that did not quite fit in his mouth, and throughout his body he experienced a looseness of the bones, as though his skeleton were a mobile put together by an amateur. He groaned dispiritedly, his eyes still closed. He knew he had to get up out of the bed and take a shower and shave and dress, that only by making extravagant demands on it would his body give him any service at all. "You *will* make the Death March," he warned it ruthlessly.

He opened his eyes and what he saw disgusted him and turned his stomach. His eye patch had come off during the night and now there were two of everything. He saw one eye patch on one pillow and another eye patch on another pillow. Hastily he grabbed for it but he had chosen the wrong pillow. He reached for the other eye patch and the other pillow but somehow he had put out one of his illusory hands. It did not occur to him to shut one eye. At last, by covering all visible space, real or illusory, with all visible fingers, real or illusory—like one dragging a river—he recovered the patch and pulled it quickly over one of his heads.

He stood stunned in his hot shower and then shaved, cutting his neck badly. He dressed. "Whan 'e iz through his toilette, *Monsieur* will see how much better 'e feel," his valet said.

He doubted it and didn't answer.

In the dining room he tried not to look at Norma's paintings but could not help noticing that many of her sunny side streets had, overnight, become partial snow scenes. He had done that, he remembered, though he could not recall now exactly why. It seemed to have something to do with a great anthropological discovery he had made the night before.

He finished the last of the pizza, gagging on it briefly.

Considering the anguish of his body it suddenly occurred to him that perhaps he was hooked. This momentarily appealed to his sense of the dramatic, but then he realized that it would be a terrible thing to have happen to him. He could not afford to be hooked and he knew with a sense of calm sadness that his character could no more sustain the responsibility of a steady drug habit than it could sustain the responsibility of any other kind of pattern.

"Oh what a miserable bastard I am," he said.

In near panic he considered leaving the Feldmans' apartment immediately but he knew that he was in no condition to travel.

"You wouldn't get to the corner," he said.

He felt massively sorry for himself. The more he considered it the more certain it appeared that he was hooked. It was terrible. Where would he get the money to buy the drugs? What would they do to his already depleted physical resources?

"Oh what a miserable bastard I am," he said again.

To steady himself he took a bottle of Scotch from the shelf in the pantry where Feldman kept it. Bertie did not like hard liquor. Though he drank a lot, it was beer he drank, or, when he could get them, the sweeter cordials. Scotch and bourbon had always seemed vaguely square to him. But he had already finished the few liqueurs that Feldman had, and now nothing was left but Scotch. He poured himself an enormous drink.

Sipping it calmed him (though his body still ached) and he considered what to do. If he *was* hooked the first thing was to tell his friends. Telling his friends his latest failure was something Bertie regarded as a sort of responsibility. Thus his rare letters to them usually brought Bertie's intimates—he laughed at the word—nothing but bad news. He would write that a mistress had given him up, and, with his talent for mimicry, set down her last long disappointed speech to him, in which she exposed in angry, honest language the hollowness of his character, his infinite weakness as a man, his vileness. When briefly he had turned to homosexuality to provide himself with funds, the first thing he did was write his friends about it. Or he wrote of being fired from bands when it was discovered how bad a trumpeter he really was. He spared neither himself nor his friends in his passionate self-denunciations.

Almost automatically, then, he went into Feldman's study and began to write to all the people he could think of. As he wrote he pulled heavily at the whiskey remaining in the bottle.

At first the letters were long, detailed accounts of symptoms and failures and dashed hopes, but as evening came on and he grew inarticulate he realized it was more important—and, indeed, added to the pathos of his situation—for him just to get the facts to them.

"Dear Klaff," he wrote at last, "I am hooked. I am at the bottom, Klaff. I don't know what to do." Or "Dear Randle, I'm hooked. Tell your wife. I honestly don't know where to turn."

And "Dear Myers, how are your wife and kids? Poor Bertie is hooked. He is thinking of suicide."

That one day he would have to kill himself he had known for a long time. It would happen, and even in the way he had imagined. One day he would simply drink the bottle of carbon tetrachloride. But he had been in no hurry. Now it seemed like something he might have to do before he had meant to, and, oddly, what he resented most was the idea of having to change his plans.

He imagined what people would say.

"I let him down, Klaff," Randle said.

"Everybody let him down," Klaff said.

"Everybody let him down," Bertie said. "Everybody let him down."

Weeping, he took a last drink from Feldman's bottle and stumbled into the living room where he passed out on the couch.

That night Bertie was awakened by a flashlight shining in his eyes. Bertie threw one arm across his face defensively and struggled to sit up. So clumsy were his efforts that whoever was holding the flashlight started to laugh.

"Stop that," Bertie said indignantly, and thought, "I have never been so indignant in the face of danger."

"You said they were out of town," a voice said. The voice did not come from behind the flashlight and Bertie wondered how many there might be.

"Jesus, I thought so. Nobody's answered the phone for days. I never seen a guy so plastered. He stinks."

"Kill him," the first voice said.

Bertie stopped struggling to get up.

"Kill him," the voice repeated.

"What is this?" Bertie said thickly. "What is this?"

"Come on, he's so drunk he's harmless," the second voice said.

"Kill him," the first voice said again.

"You kill him," the second voice said.

The first voice giggled.

They were playing with him, Bertie knew. Nobody who did not know him could want him dead.

"Turn on the lights," Bertie said.

"Screw that," the second voice said. "You just sit here in the dark, sonny, and you won't get hurt."

"We're wasting time," the first voice said.

A beam from a second flashlight suddenly intersected the beam from the first.

"Say," Bertie said nervously, "it looks like the opening of a supermarket."

Bertie could hear them working in the dark, moving boxes, pulling drawers.

"Are you folks Negroes?" Bertie called. No one answered him. "I mean I dig Negroes, man—*men*. Miles. Jay Jay. Bird lives." Bertie heard a closet door open.

"You *are* robbing the place, right? I mean you're actually *stealing*, aren't you? This isn't just a social call. Maybe you know my friend Klaff?"

The men came back into the living room. From the sound of his footsteps Bertie knew one of them was carrying something heavy.

"I've got the T.V.," the first voice said.

"There are some valuable paintings in the dining room," Bertie said.

"Go see," the first voice said.

One of Norma's pictures suddenly popped out of the darkness as the man's light shone on it.

"Crap," the second voice said.

"You guys can't be all bad," Bertie said.

"Any furs?" It was a third voice and it startled Bertie. Someone flashed a light in Bertie's face. "Hey you," the voice repeated, "does your wife have any furs?"

"Wait a minute," Bertie said as though it were a fine point they must be made to understand, "you've got it wrong. This isn't *my* place. I'm just taking care of it while my friends are gone." The man laughed.

Now all three flashlights were playing over the apartment. Bertie hoped a beam might illuminate one of the intruders but this never happened. Then he realized he didn't want it to happen, that he was safe as long as he didn't see any of them. Suddenly a light caught one of the men behind the ear. "Watch that light. Watch that light," Bertie called out involuntarily.

"I found a trumpet," the second voice said.

"Hey, that's mine," Bertie said angrily. Without thinking he got up and grabbed for the trumpet. In the dark he was able to get his fingers around one of the pistons, but the man snatched it away from him easily. Another man pushed Bertie back down on the couch.

"Could you leave the carbon tetrachloride?" Bertie asked miserably.

In another ten minutes they were ready to go.

"Shouldn't we do something about the clown?" the third voice said.

"Nah," the second voice said.

They went out the front door.

Bertie sat in the darkness. "I'm drunk," he said after a while. "I'm hooked and drunk. It never happened. It's still the visions. The apartment is a vision. The darkness is. Everything."

In a few minutes he got up and wearily turned on the lights.

"Magicians," Bertie thought, seeing even in a first glance all they had taken. Lamps were gone, drapes. He walked through the apartment. The T.V. was gone. Suits were missing from the closets. Feldman's typewriter was gone. The champagne glasses. The silver. His trumpet was gone.

Bertie wept. He thought of phoning the police but then wondered what he could tell them. They had been in the apartment twenty minutes and he hadn't even gotten a look at their faces.

Then he shuddered, realizing the danger he had been in. "Thieves," he said. "Killers." But even as he said it he knew it was an exaggeration. He personally had never been in any danger. He had the fool's ancient protection, his old immunity against consequence.

He wondered what he could say to the Feldmans. They would be furious. Then, as he thought about it, he realized that this, too, was an exaggeration. They would not be furious. Like the thieves they would make allowances for him, as people always made allowances for him. They would forgive him and possibly even try to give him something toward the loss of his trumpet.

Bertie began to grow angry. They had no right to patronize him like that. If he was a clown it was because he had chosen to be. It was a way of life. Why couldn't they respect it? He should have been hit over the head like other men. How dare they forgive him? For a moment it was impossible for him to distinguish between the thieves and the Feldmans.

Then he had his idea. As soon as he thought of it he knew it would work. He looked around the apartment to see what he could take. There was some costume jewelry the thieves had thrown on the bed. Bertie scooped it up and stuffed it into his pockets.

He looked at the apartment one more time and then got the hell out of there. "Bird lives," he sang to himself as he raced down the stairs. "He lives and lives."

It was wonderful. How they would marvel. He couldn't get away with it. Even the Far West wasn't far enough. How they hounded you if you took something from them! He would be back, no question, and they would send him to jail, but first there would be the confrontation, maybe even in the apartment itself, Bertie in handcuffs, and the Feldmans staring at him, not understanding and angry at last, and something in their eyes like fear.

LEONARD MICHAELS

City Boy

"Phillip," she said, "this is crazy."

I didn't agree or disagree. She wanted some answer. I bit her neck.
She kissed my ear. It was nearly three in the morning. We had just
returned. The apartment was dark and quiet. We were on the living
room floor and she repeated, "Phillip, this is crazy." Her crinoline broke
under us like cinders. Furniture loomed all around in the darkness—
settee, chairs, a table with a lamp. Pictures were cloudy blotches drifting
above. But no lights, no things to look at, no eyes in her head. She was
underneath me and warm. The rug was warm, soft as mud, deep. Her
crinoline cracked like sticks. Our naked bellies clapped together. Air
fired out like farts. I took it as applause. The chairs smirked and spit
between their feet. The chandelier clicked giddy teeth. The clock ticked
as if to split its glass. "Phillip," she said, "this is crazy." A little voice
against the grain and power. Not enough to stop me. Yet once I had
been a man of feeling. We went to concerts, walked in the park, trembled in the maid's room. Now in the foyer, a flash of hair and claws. We
stumbled to the living room floor. She said, "Phillip, this is crazy." Then
silence, except in my head where a conference table was set up, ashtrays
scattered about. Priests, ministers and rabbis were rushing to take seats. I
wanted their opinion, but came. They vanished. A voice lingered, faintly
crying, "You could mess up the rug, Phillip, break something . . ." Her
fingers pinched my back like ants. I expected a remark to kill good death.
She said nothing. The breath in her nostrils whipped mucus. It cracked
in my ears like flags. I dreamed we were in her mother's Cadillac, trailing
flags. I heard her voice before I heard the words. "Phillip, this is crazy.
My parents are in the next room." Her cheek jerked against mine, her
breasts were knuckles in my nipples. I burned. Good death was killed. I
burned with hate. A rabbi shook his finger, "You shouldn't hate." I lifted
on my elbows, sneering in pain. She wrenched her hips, tightened muscles in belly and neck. She said, "Move." It was imperative to move. Her
parents were thirty feet away. Down the hall between Utrillos and Vlamincks, through the door, flick the light and I'd see them. Maybe like us,
Mr. Cohen adrift on the missus. Hair sifted down my cheek. "Let's go to
the maid's room," she whispered. I was reassured. She tried to move. I
kissed her mouth. Her crinoline smashed like sugar. Pig that I was, I
couldn't move. The clock ticked hysterically. Ticks piled up like insects.

Muscles lapsed in her thighs. Her fingers scratched on my neck as if looking for buttons. She slept. I sprawled like a bludgeoned pig, eyes open, loose lips. I flopped into sleep, in her, in the rug, in our scattered clothes.

Dawn hadn't shown between the slats in the blinds. Her breathing hissed in my ear. I wanted to sleep more, but needed a cigarette. I thought of the cold avenue, the lonely subway ride. Where could I buy a newspaper, a cup of coffee? This was crazy, dangerous, a waste of time. The maid might arrive, her parents might wake. I had to get started. My hand pushed along the rug to find my shirt, touched a brass lion's paw, then a lamp cord.

A naked heel bumped wood.

She woke, her nails in my neck. "Phillip, did you hear?" I whispered, "Quiet." My eyes rolled like Milton's. Furniture loomed, whirled. "Dear God," I prayed, "save my ass." The steps ceased. Neither of us breathed. The clock ticked. She trembled. I pressed my cheek against her mouth to keep her from talking. We heard pajamas rustle, phlegmy breathing, fingernails scratching hair. A voice, "Veronica, don't you think it's time you sent Phillip home?"

A murmur of assent started in her throat, swept to my cheek, fell back drowned like a child in a well. Mr. Cohen had spoken. He stood ten inches from our legs. Maybe less. It was impossible to tell. His fingernails grated through hair. His voice hung in the dark with the quintessential question. Mr. Cohen, scratching his crotch, stood now as never in the light. Considerable. No tool of his wife, whose energy in business kept him eating, sleeping, overlooking the park. Pinochle change in his pocket four nights a week. But were they his words? Or was he the oracle of Mrs. Cohen, lying sleepless, irritated, waiting for him to get me out? I didn't breathe. I didn't move. If he had come on his own he would leave without an answer. His eyes weren't adjusted to the dark. He couldn't see. We lay at his feet like worms. He scratched, made smacking noises with his mouth.

The question of authority is always with us. Who is responsible for the triggers pulled, buttons pressed, the gas, the fire? Doubt banged my brain. My heart lay in the fist of intellect, which squeezed out feeling like piss out of kidneys. Mrs. Cohen's voice demolished doubt, feeling, intellect. It ripped from the bedroom.

"For God's sake, Morris, don't be banal. Tell the schmuck to go home and keep his own parents awake all night, if he has any."

Veronica's tears slipped down my cheeks. Mr. Cohen sighed, shuffled, made a strong voice. "Veronica, tell Phillip . . ." His foot came down on my ass. He drove me into his daughter. I drove her into his rug.

"I don't believe it," he said.

He walked like an antelope, lifting hoof from knee, but stepped down hard. Sensitive to the danger of movement, yet finally impulsive, flinging his pot at the earth in order to cross it. His foot brought me his weight and character, a hundred fifty-five pounds of stomping *schlemiel,* in a mode of apprehension so primal we must share it with bugs. Let armies stomp me to insensate pulp—I'll yell "Cohen" when he arrives.

Veronica squealed, had a contraction, fluttered, gagged a shriek, squeezed, and up like a frog out of the hand of a child I stood spread-legged, bolt naked, great with eyes. Mr. Cohen's face was eyes in my eyes. A secret sharer. We faced each other like men accidentally met in hell. He retreated flapping, moaning, "I will not believe it one bit."

Veronica said, "Daddy?"

"Who else you no good bum?"

The rug raced. I smacked against blinds, glass broke and I whirled. Veronica said, "Phillip," and I went off in streaks, a sparrow in the room, here, there, early American, baroque and rococo. Veronica wailed, "Phillip." Mr. Cohen screamed, "I'll kill him." I stopped at the door, seized the knob. Mrs. Cohen yelled from the bedroom, "Morris, did something break? Answer me."

"I'll kill that bastid."

"Morris, if something broke you'll rot for a month."

"Mother, stop it," said Veronica. "Phillip, come back."

The door slammed. I was outside, naked as a wolf.

I needed poise. Without poise the street was impossible. Blood shot to my brain, thought blossomed. I'd walk on my hands. Beards were fashionable. I kicked up my feet, kicked the elevator button, faced the door and waited. I bent one elbow like a knee. The posture of a clothes model, easy, poised. Blood coiled down to my brain, weeds bourgeoned. I had made a bad impression. There was no other way to see it. But all right. We needed a new beginning. Everyone does. Yet how few of us know when it arrives. Mr. Cohen had never spoken to me before; this was a breakthrough. There had been a false element in our relationship. It was wiped out. I wouldn't kid myself with the idea that he had nothing to say. I'd had enough of his silent treatment. It was worth being naked to see how mercilessly I could think. I had his number. Mrs. Cohen's, too. I was learning every second. I was a city boy. No innocent shitkicker from Jersey. I was the A train, the Fifth Avenue bus. I could be a cop. My name was Phillip, my style New York City. I poked the elevator button with my toe. It rang in the lobby, waking Ludwig. He'd come for me, rotten with sleep. Not the first time. He always took me down, walked me through the lobby and let me out on the avenue. Wires began tugging him up the shaft. I moved back, conscious of my genitals hanging upside down. Absurd consideration; we were both men one way or another. There were social distinctions enforced by his uniform, but they would vanish at the sight of me. "The unaccommodated thing itself." Off ye lendings!" The greatest play is about a naked man. A picture of Lear came to me, naked, racing through the wheat. I could be cool. I thought of Ludwig's uniform, hat, whipcord collar. It signified his authority. Perhaps he would be annoyed, in his authority, by the sight of me naked. Few people woke him at such hours. Worse, I never tipped him. Could I have been so indifferent month after month? In a crisis you discover everything. Then it's too late. Know yourself, indeed. You need a crisis every day. I refused to think about it. I sent my mind after objects. It returned with the chairs, settee, table and chandelier. Where were my clothes? I sent it along the rug. It found buttons, eagles stamped in brass. I recognized them as the buttons on Ludwig's coat. Eagles, beaks like knives, shrieking for tips. Fuck'm, I thought. Who's Ludwig? A big coat, a whistle, white gloves and a General MacArthur hat. I could understand him completely. He couldn't begin to understand me. A naked man is mysterious. But aside from that, what did he know? I dated Veronica Cohen and went home late. Did he know I was out of work? That I lived in a slum downtown? Of course not.

Possibly under his hat was a filthy mind. He imagined Veronica and I might be having sexual intercourse. He resented it. Not that he hoped for the privilege himself, in his coat and soldier hat, but he had a proprietary interest in the building and its residents. I came from another world. *The* other world against which Ludwig defended the residents. Wasn't I like a burglar sneaking out late, making him my accomplice? I undermined his authority, his dedication. He despised me. It was obvious. But no one thinks such thoughts. It made me laugh to think them. My genitals jumped. The elevator door slid open. He didn't say a word. I padded inside like a seal. The door slid shut. Instantly, I was ashamed of myself, thinking as I had about him. I had no right. A better man than I. His profile was an etching by Dürer. Good peasant stock. How had he fallen to such work? Existence precedes essence. At the controls, silent, enduring, he gave me strength for the street. Perhaps the sun would be up, birds in the air. The door slid open. Ludwig walked ahead of me through the lobby. He needed new heels. The door of the lobby was half a ton of glass, encased in iron vines and leaves. Not too much for Ludwig. He turned, looked down into my eyes. I watched his lips move.

"I vun say sumding. Yur bisniss vot you do. Bud vy you mek her miserable? Nod led her slip. She has beks unter her eyes."

Ludwig had feelings. They spoke to mine. Beneath the uniform, a man. Essence precedes existence. Even rotten with sleep, thick, dry bags under his eyes, he saw, he sympathized. The discretion demanded by his job forbade anything tangible, a sweater, a hat. "Ludwig," I whispered, "you're all right." It didn't matter if he heard me. He knew I said something. He knew it was something nice. He grinned, tugged the door open with both hands. I slapped out onto the avenue. I saw no one, dropped to my feet and glanced back through the door. Perhaps for the last time. I lingered, indulged a little melancholy. Ludwig walked to a couch in the rear of the lobby. He took off his coat, rolled it into a pillow and lay down. I had never stayed to see him do that before, but always rushed off to the subway. As if I were indifferent to the life of the building. Indeed, like a burglar. I seized the valuables and fled to the subway. I stayed another moment, watching good Ludwig, so I could hate myself. He assumed the modest, saintly posture of sleep. One leg here, the other there. His good head on his coat. A big arm across his stomach, the hand between his hips. He made a fist and punched up and down.

I went down the avenue, staying close to the buildings. Later I would work up a philosophy. Now I wanted to sleep, forget. I hadn't the energy for moral complexities: Ludwig cross-eyed, thumping his pelvis in such a nice lobby. Mirrors, glazed pots, rubber plants ten feet high. As if he were generating all of it. As if it were part of his job. I hurried. The buildings were on my left, the park on my right. There were doormen in all the buildings; God knows what was in the park. No cars were moving. No people in sight. Streetlights glowed in a receding sweep down to Fifty-ninth Street and beyond. A wind pressed my face like Mr. Cohen's breath. Such hatred. Imponderable under any circumstances, a father cursing his daughter. Why? A fright in the dark? Freud said things about fathers and daughters. It was too obvious, too hideous. I shuddered and went more quickly. I began to run. In a few minutes I was at the spit-mottled steps of the subway. I had hoped for vomit. Spit is no challenge for bare feet. Still, I wouldn't complain. It was sufficiently disgusting to make me live in spirit. I went down the steps flatfooted, stamping, elevated by each declension. I was a city boy, no mincing creep from the sticks.

A Negro man sat in the change booth. He wore glasses, a white shirt, black knit tie and a silver tie clip. I saw a mole on his right cheek. His hair had spots of grey, as if strewn with ashes. He was reading a newspaper. He didn't hear me approach, didn't see my eyes take him in, figure him out. Shirt, glasses, tie—I knew how to address him. I coughed. He looked up.

"Sir, I don't have any money. Please let me through the turnstile. I come this way every week and will certainly pay you the next time."

He merely looked at me. Then his eyes flashed like fangs. Instinctively, I guessed what he felt. He didn't owe favors to a white man. He didn't have to bring his allegiance to the transit authority into question for my sake.

"Hey, man, you naked?"

"Yes."

"Step back a little."

I stepped back.

"You're naked."

I nodded.

"Get your naked ass the hell out of here."

"Sir," I said, "I know these are difficult times, but can't we be reasonable? I know that . . ."

"Scat, mother, go home."

I crouched as if to dash through the turnstile. He crouched, too. It proved he would come after me. I shrugged, turned back toward the steps. The city was infinite. There were many other subways. But why had he become so angry? Did he think I was a bigot? Maybe I was running around naked to get him upset. His anger was incomprehensible otherwise. It made me feel like a bigot. First a burglar, then a bigot. I needed a cigarette. I could hardly breathe. Air was too good for me. At the top of the steps, staring down, stood Veronica. She had my clothes.

"Poor, poor," she said.

I said nothing. I snatched my underpants and put them on. She had my cigarettes ready. I tried to light one, but the match failed. I threw down the cigarette and the matchbook. She retrieved them as I dressed. She lit the cigarette for me and held my elbow to help me keep my balance. I finished dressing, took the cigarette. We walked back toward her building. The words "thank you" sat in my brain like driven spikes. She nibbled her lip.

"How are things at home?" My voice was casual and morose, as if no answer could matter.

"All right," she said, her voice the same as mine. She took her tone from me. I liked that sometimes, sometimes not. Now I didn't like it. I discovered I was angry. Until she said that I had no idea I was angry. I flicked the cigarette into the gutter and suddenly I knew why. I didn't love her. The cigarette sizzled in the gutter. Like truth. I didn't love her. Black hair, green eyes, I didn't love her. Slender legs. I didn't. Last night I had looked at her and said to myself, "I hate communism." Now I wanted to step on her head. Nothing less than that would do. If it was a perverted thought, then it was a perverted thought. I wasn't afraid to admit it to myself.

"All right? Really? Is that true?"

Blah, blah, blah. Who asked those questions? A zombie; not Phillip of the foyer and rug. He died in flight. I was sorry, sincerely sorry, but with clothes on my back I knew certain feelings would not survive humiliation. It was so clear it was thrilling. Perhaps she felt it, too. In any case she would have to accept it. The nature of the times. We are historical creatures. Veronica and I were finished. Before we reached her door I would say deadly words. They'd come in a natural way, kill her a little. Veronica, let me step on your head or we're through. Maybe we're through, anyway. It would deepen her looks, give philosophy to what was only charming in her face. The dawn was here. A new day. Cruel, but change is cruel. I could bear it. Love is infinite and one. Women are not. Neither are men. The human condition. Nearly unbearable.

"No, it's not true," she said.

"What's not?"

"Things aren't all right at home."

I nodded intelligently, sighed, "Of course not. Tell me the truth, please. I don't want to hear anything else."

"Daddy had a heart attack."

"Oh God," I yelled. "Oh God, no."

I seized her hand, dropped it. She let it fall. I seized it again. No use. I let it fall. She let it drift between us. We stared at one another. She said, "What were you going to say? I can tell you were going to say something."

I stared, said nothing.

"Don't feel guilty, Phillip. Let's just go back to the apartment and have some coffee."

"What can I say?"

"Don't say anything. He's in the hospital and my mother is there. Let's just go upstairs and not say anything."

"Not say anything. Like moral imbeciles go slurp coffee and not say anything? What are we, nihilists or something? Assassins? Monsters?"

"Phillip, there's no one in the apartment. I'll make us coffee and eggs . . ."

"How about a roast beef? Got a roast beef in the freezer?"

"Phillip, he's *my* father."

We were at the door. I rattled. I was in a trance. This was life. Death!

"Indeed, your father. I'll accept that. I can do no less."

"Phillip, shut up. Ludwig."

The door opened. I nodded to Ludwig. What did he know about life and death? Give him a uniform and a quiet lobby—that's life and death. In the elevator he took the controls. "Always got a hand on the controls, eh Ludwig?"

Veronica smiled in a feeble, grateful way. She liked to see me get along with the help. Ludwig said, "Dots right."

"Ludwig has been our doorman for years, Phillip. Ever since I was a little girl."

"Wow," I said.

"Dots right."

The door slid open. Veronica said, "Thank you, Ludwig." I said, "Thank you, Ludwig."

"Vulcum."

"Vulcum? You mean, 'welcome'? Hey, Ludwig, how long you been in this country?"

Veronica was driving her key into the door.

"How come you never learned to talk American, baby?"

"Phillip, come here."

"I'm saying something to Ludwig."

"Come here right now."

"I have to go, Ludwig."

"Vulcum."

She went directly to the bathroom. I waited in the hallway between Vlamincks and Utrillos. The Utrillos were pale and flat. The Vlamincks were thick, twisted and red. Raw meat on one wall, dry stone on the other. Mrs. Cohen had an eye for contrasts. I heard Veronica sob. She ran water in the sink, sobbed, sat down, peed. She saw me looking and kicked the door shut.

"At a time like this . . ."

"I don't like you looking."

"Then why did you leave the door open? You obviously don't know your own mind."

"Go away, Phillip. Wait in the living room."

"Just tell me why you left the door open."

"Phillip, you're going to drive me nuts. Go away. I can't do a damn thing if I know you're standing there."

The living room made me feel better. The settee, the chandelier full of teeth and the rug were company. Mr. Cohen was everywhere, a simple, diffuse presence. He jingled change in his pocket, looked out the window and was happy he could see the park. He took a little antelope step and tears came into my eyes. I sat among his mourners. A rabbi droned platitudes: Mr. Cohen was generous, kind, beloved by his wife and daughter. "How much did he weigh?" I shouted. The phone rang.

Veronica came running down the hall. I went and stood at her side when she picked up the phone. I stood dumb, stiff as a hatrack. She was whimpering, "Yes, yes . . ." I nodded my head yes, yes, thinking it was better than no, no. She put the phone down.

"It was my mother. Daddy's all right. Mother is staying with him in his room at the hospital and they'll come home together tomorrow."

Her eyes looked at mine. At them as if they were as flat and opaque as hers. I said in a slow, stupid voice, "You're allowed to do that? Stay overnight in a hospital with a patient? Sleep in his room?" She continued looking at my eyes. I shrugged, looked down. She took my shirt front in a fist like a bite. She whispered. I said, "What?" She whispered again, "Fuck me." The clock ticked like crickets. The Vlamincks spilled blood. We sank into the rug as if it were quicksand.

POETRY

Introduction

Donald Hall picked the next two poetry editors—X. J. Kennedy, who had the most abbreviated of the tenures (1961–1964), and Tom Clark who then held the position until 1973. Kennedy was a graduate student at the University of Michigan where Hall was teaching as an assistant professor. Occasionally, Kennedy saw him around the campus. He has always felt that Hall had asked a number of his closer poet friends about the job before propositioning him and was quite relieved when Kennedy replied eagerly, "Yes! Yes!"

Kennedy enjoyed his duties (especially corresponding with fellow poets) but then found that his job as an instructor of composition at the University of North Carolina at Greensboro, raising a young family, and having to deal with the contents of the crates of poems sent down from New York was simply too taxing. "The magazine was not coming out very regularly then," he has recalled. "My correspondence began to be largely with angry poets wondering when their work was going to appear."

Since then Kennedy has published a half-dozen collections of poetry. In 1985 he won the Los Angeles Times Book Award for *Crossties*. He has written a number of successful children's books, including one called *Ghastlies, Goops, and Pincushions*.

—G.P.

*   *   *

In a memorable covering letter of the time, an aspiring contributor imagined that I'd be reading her poems over a glass of absinthe in the Deux Magots, at the right hand of Sartre himself. In reality, life wasn't that way at all. I was holed up in a Greensboro, N.C. tenement, teaching four sections of freshman English at the Woman's College, and the *Paris Review*'s poetry operation had to share a bedroom with a new baby, diapers, and a changing table. At least half my time as poetry editor was spent in shooing into print the manuscripts that Donald Hall had previously accepted. At the same time, I had to keep the magazine's Paris editor, Patrick Bowles, from slipping in poems by his spaced-out friends. He snuck just one past me—I first read it in print, and for weeks thereafter had a severe problem with the bottle.

A historian once charged that in my brief reign as poetry czar I printed only stuff by curmudgeonly formalists. In truth, the magazine in those early sixties was printing Creeley, Levertov, Bly, Ezra Pound, and less famous revolutionaries. Those were Hall acquisitions, but like him I took the best poems that came in, whatever their shape or kind. Some were early works of writers who went on to become better known: Philip Levine, Anne Stevenson, Fred Chappell, Ian Hamilton, and the Ulster bard James Simmons. Issue 31, the tenth anniversary number, boasted a sheaf of new work by people who had helped Hall build the magazine's name for poetry: Bly, Simpson, Rich, Justice, Merwin, James Wright, Hill, Tomlinson, and others—a brawling variety.

—X.J. Kennedy

JAMES CAMP

Brief History of the Confederate Aristocracy

Too many domes of colored ass
Stained the white radiance.

FRED CHAPPELL

Tiros II

From where I watched, the shiny satellite
Almost occluded summer Sirius.
I might have sworn they'd touch and set the night
Afire, transforming to a furious
Match. They did not. The new light went on by,
Like a silver zipper zipping up the sky.

This is how we will climb the stars, they say
And I perfectly agree. Some blinking
Bullet shot past the moon, shot past day
And night, will flounder on through the winking
System, a man aboard—not you or I,
Of course, but some young sir who likes to fly.

For all I know, there are animals, birds,
Bats, plants, and men out there; perhaps, far back,
A titanic spacefish, too huge for words,
Which gobbles up the worlds, a shape of black.
Its length is measurable in light-years:
It has five tails and thirteen pairs of ears.

And this is not some queer extreme we think
Of, idling, but iron fact. For space is real
And near and cold and black as India ink,
And frightening as falling down a well.
Those stubborn codes the stars are sending—why
Not assess some newer history?

HENRI COULETTE

The Blue-Eyed Precinct Worker

Liberal, blue-eyed, shivering, trying not
to look like a bill
collector or detective,
I move through the slums in a drizzle—
the slums of Pasadena, where—nutmeg, bronze,
and purple—the Negroes live.

They look out and laugh—Mrs. Bessie Simpson,
Miss Delilah Jones,
the eleven Tollivers.
They are extras in a bad movie
starring no one they have ever seen before,
no one that they care to know.

I am like a man rich in the currency
of a lost kingdom,
for this both is and is not
what I sought. Somewhere, a screen door bangs
and bangs, but in the half-light I can't see where,
or give the sound direction.

A black and white sausage of a mongrel bitch
follows me, sniffing;
her obscene stump of a tail
motionless. We go, the two of us,
to the muddy edge of the dark arroyo.
The street light blooms overhead;

Our shadows burst forth, monstrous and alien.
There, on the far rim,
are the houses of the rich.
It is the dinner hour, and they eat
prime rib of unicorn or breast of phoenix.
It is another precinct.

Oddly enough, I am consoled by the thought
of the delicate
small animals that move down

through the arroyo: white coyote,
masked coon, and the plumed skunk. Come, Citizen Dog,
we have chosen the short straw.

DONALD HALL

Sleeping

The avenue rises toward a city of white marble.
I am not meeting anyone. The capitol is empty.
I enter the dome of sleep.
. . .
I was lying on the sofa to rest, to sleep
a few minutes, perhaps.
I felt my body sag into the hole of sleep.
All at once I was awake and frightened.
My own death was drifting near me
in the middle of life. The strong body
blurred and diminished into the dark waters.
The flesh floated away.
. . .
The shadow is a tight passage
that no one will be spared
who goes down
to the deep well.
In sleep, something remembers.
Three times since I woke
from the first sleep,
it has drunk that water.
Awake, it is still sleeping.

JOHN HEATH-STUBBS

The Peacock and the Snake

"It was your fault! It was your fault!" cried the Peacock.
"And it was yours too," whispered the Snake.

"It was lust! It was lust!" shouted the Peacock.
"Yes, and pride, and vanity"—so the Snake.

"I loved him! I loved him!" shrieked the Peacock.
"And she was sweet, sweet," hissed the Snake.

"I look at my feet and I scream"—the Peacock.
"And I have no feet"—the Snake.

"It was your fault!" "Yours also, perhaps?"—thus the
                                    Peacock-Angel
And the diabolical Snake, down in the filthiest pothole,

Where they exist, reproached each other,
Timeless in their torment. But somewhere

Within the innocent jungle the peacock (which is a bird)
Displays beneath the bough a fragment of God's splendour;

And the coiled snake (which is a reptile)
Deployed upon the ground a portion of His subtlety.

GEOFFREY HILL

A Prayer to the Sun

(I.M. MIGUEL HERNANDEZ)

(1)
Darkness
above all things
the Sun
makes
rise

(2)
Vultures
salute their meat
at noon
(Hell is
silent)

(3)
Blind Sun
our ravager
bless us
so that
we sleep.

(Miguel Hernandez, poet of the Spanish Civil War, died in prison in 1942)

DONALD JUSTICE

Last Days of Prospero

Some change in the wording of the charm,
Some slight reshuffling of negative
And verb, perhaps—that should suffice.
So, so. Meanwhile he paced the strand,

Debating, as old men will, with himself
Or the waves, though, as it was, the sea
Seemed only to go on washing and washing
Itself, as if to be clean of something.

BERNARD KEITH

Essay on Meter

The delicate foot of
Phoebe Isolde Farmer
taps measures acceptable to, among others, the
★★★ Poetry Journal and the
University of ★★★ ★★★ Review and to
her brother, a minister, who is paying
for the printing of a small
volume—while he should be
praying, "Lord, grant her
wings."

PHILIP LEVINE

The Turning

Unknown faces in the street
and winter coming on. I
stand in the last moments of
the city, no more a child,
only a man—one who has
looked upon his own nakedness
without shame and in defeat
has seen nothing to bless.
Touched once, like a plum, I turned
rotten in the meat, or like
the plum blossom I never
saw, hard at the edges, burned
at the first entrance of life,
and so endured, unreckoned,
untaken, with nothing to give.
The first Jew was God; the second
denied him; I am alive.

GEORGE MACBETH

Eating Ice-Cream with a Girl

I lift my cone to hers
As if drinking a toast.

Her pink tongue, like a cat's,
Darts out, licks,
Lingering on the cream.

Smiling a little, I watch
Her cross her legs, concerned
Only with what she eats.

Her teeth caress the crisp
Wafer: I bite,
Eager with appetite.

Thirst-quenching, cooled,
Slowly, water-ice drips.
Gulping, I finish mine

And lick my fingertips.
Nibbling, she makes hers last.

W. S. MERWIN

Marica Lart

Now
We do not even know
What to wish for you

Oh sleep rocked
In an empty hand.

Robert Pack

Birthday

Lighthouse. Sand shadows. Burn of brandy.
A candlestick, black,
She sent with no note for his birthday.

Upside-down, the flame flares
On the dark curve of his glass.
What thought, he forgets what thought it was

That made him laugh. Nesting cries
Sharpen grey cliffs, grey weather.
Shall he return, weary buoy bell?

Surf against the shore
Bridles, neighing like horses
What his plumbed eyes tell.

Adrienne Rich

End of an Era

This morning, flakes of sun
peel down to the last snowholds,
the barbed-wire leavings of a war
lost, won, in these dead-end alleys.
Stale as a written-out journalist,
I start to sort my gear.
Nothing is happening. City, dumb
as a pack of thumbed cards, you
once had snap and glare

and secret life; now, trembling
under my five grey senses' weight,
you fall and flatten
queasily on the table.

Baudelaire, I think of you! Nothing changes,
rude and self-absorbed the current
dashes past, asking nothing, poetry
extends its unsought amnesty,
autumn saws the great grove down.
Some voices, though, shake in the air like heat.
I see myself hardened against queer sights:
myself, perhaps, the queerest,
man running wild
in his selfmade wilderness.
Everyone greets me; all are nonchalant.
We have so much
in common: even squalor.
I walk into my house and see
tourists fingering this and that.
My mirrors, my portfolios
don't suit their style.

Still, those few friends,
living and dead,
with whom things aren't too easy . . .
Certain old woods are sawdust,
from now on have to be described?
Nothing changes. The bones of the mammoths
are still in the earth.

JAMES SIMMONS

Me and the World

Walking the streets of the city, sitting in a bar,
Sometimes I take delight in the things I see;
Sometimes I hardly notice what things are:
They are the same—delight depends on me.

Today the tram's lurch and slide, footsteps,
The noise of birds are all clear and dear to me.
My hand at rest on the heavy, shining wood
Of the bar counter seems good, and the amber pint
And the floor and the faces and shapes of men
And sunlight falling there, and the taste of beer
And the feel of smoke in my lungs, and small things—
Shreds of tobacco and pieces of orange peel—
Are all lovely, and I see them clearly—
Perhaps that's all things need. I feel
My stump of pencil is worn down with poems
And I am being worn and shaped by the rubbing of life
As a shell is by the sea—as sensibly.

Outside the crippled houses respond
To the continual miracle of sun and dust.
Roofs, railings and the time of year
Walk beautifully together because they must,
And rare colours, blended by hard wear,
On cheap cottons of city children
Invite not pity but the satisfaction of love.
The rare ointment of formal praise
Is suddenly useful on such wedding days.
Useful to me—these things can't hear my praise
And for other people today was like other days.
I have felt what we used to call God's Glory
As clearly as music or drink or a funny story.
Why did I feel it? Will it come back to me?
What was it that I saw in what I see?

LOUIS SIMPSON

Lines Written Near San Francisco

1

I wake and feel the city trembling.
Yes, there is something unsettled in the air
And the earth is uncertain.

And so it was for the tenor Caruso.
He couldn't sleep—you know how the ovation
Rings in your ears, and you re-sing your part.

And then the ceiling trembled
And the floor moved. He ran into the street.
Never had Naples given him such a reception!

The air was darker than Vesuvius.
"O mamma mia,"
He cried, "I've lost my voice!"

At that moment the hideous voice of Culture,
Hysterical woman, thrashing her arms and legs,
Shrieked from the ruins.

At that moment everyone became a performer.
Otello and Don Giovanni
And Figaro strode on the midmost stage.

In the high windows of a burning castle
Lucia raved. Black horses
Plunged through fire, dragging the wild bells.

The curtains were wrapped in smoke. Tin swords
Were melting; masks and ruffs
Burned—and the costumes of the peasants' chorus.

Night fell. The white moon rose
And sank in the Pacific. The tremors
Passed under the waves. And Death rested.

2.

Now, as we stand idle
Watching the silent, bowler-hatted man,
The engineer, who writes in the smoking field;

Now as he hands the paper to a boy,
Who takes it and runs to a group of waiting men,
And they disperse and move toward their wagons,

Mules bray and the wagons move—
Wait! Before you start—
(Already the wheels are rattling on the stones)

Say, did your fathers cross the dry Sierras
To build another London?
Do Americans always have to be second-rate?

Wait! For there are spirits
In the earth itself, or the air, or sea.
Where are the aboriginal American devils?

Cloud shadows, pine shadows
Falling across the bright Pacific bay—
(Already they have nailed rough boards together.)

Wait only for the wind
That rustles in the eucalyptus tree.
Wait only for the light

That trembles on the petals of a rose.
(The mortar sets—the Banks are the first to rise)
Wait for a rose, and you may wait forever.

The silent man mops his head and drinks
Cold lemonade. San Francisco
Is a city second only to Paris.

3.

Every night, at the end of America,
We taste our wine, looking at the Pacific.
How sad it is, the end of America!

While we were waiting for the land,
They'd finished it—with gas drums
On the hilltops, cheap housing in the valleys,

Where lives are mean and wretched.
But the Banks thrive, and the realtors
Rejoice—they have their America.

Still, there is something unsettled in the air.
Out there on the Pacific
There's no America but the Marines.

Whitman was wrong about the People,
But right about himself. The land is within.
At the end of the open road we come to ourselves.

Though mad Columbus follows the sun
Into the sea, we cannot follow.
We must remain, to serve the returning sun,

And to set tables for death.
For we are the colonists of Death—
Not, as some think, of the English.

And are preparing thrones for him to sit,
Poems to read, and beds
In which it may please him to rest.

This is the land
The pioneers looked for, shading their eyes
Against the sun—the world of flowers and dreams.

ANNE STEVENSON

Television

Hug me, mother of noise,
Find me a hiding place.
I am afraid of my voice.
I do not like my face.

NONFICTION

Louis-Ferdinand Céline

*J. Darribehaude is a French film director and televi-
sion producer whose interest in Céline's work was
rewarded when Céline first became his friend and
then accorded him the interviews here printed in English translation for the first time. When considering
a screen version of* Journey to the End of Night, *he
called on Céline with a tape-recorder and asked him
to suggest ideas for the script. Céline, who had long
envisaged such a film, responded with an unusually
complete impromptu monologue which amounted to
a working draft for a film scenario.*

Well, here you are. July '14. We're in the Avenue du Bois. And here
we have three somewhat nervy Parisiennes. Ladies of the time—time
of Gyp. So then, for God's sake, we hear what they're saying. And
along the Avenue du Bois, along the *alléc cavalière* goes a general, his
aide de camp bringing up the rear, on horseback, of course, on
horseback. So the first of the ladies, for God's sake, "O I say, it's General de Boisrobert, did you see?" "Yes, I saw." "He greeted me, didn't
he?" "Yes, yes, he greeted you. I didn't notice him. I'm really not interested, you know." "But the *aide de camp,* it's little Boilepère, O he
was there yesterday, he's impossible, don't show you've seen anything,

don't look, don't look. He was telling us all about the big exercises at Mourmelon, you know! O, he said, it means war, I'll be leaving, I'm going . . . He's impossible, isn't he, with his war . . ."
Then you hear music in the distance, ringing, warlike music.
"D'you think so, really?"
"O yes, darling, they're impossible, with this war of theirs. These military parades in the evenings, what d'you think they look like? It's ludicrous, it's comic opera. Last time at Longchamps I saw all those soldiers with stewpots on their heads, sort of helmets, you'd never believe it, it's so ugly, that's what they call war, making themselves look ugly. It's ridiculous, in my opinion, quite ridiculous. Yes yes yes, ridiculous. O do look, there's the attaché, the Spanish Embassy. He's talking war too, darling, it's quite appalling, O really I'm quite tired of it, we'd do far better to go on a shoot and kill pheasants. Wars nowadays are ridiculous, for heavens' sake, it's unthinkable, one just can't believe in them any more. They sing those stupid songs, no really, like Maurice Chevalier, actually he's rather funny, he makes everyone laugh."
So there you are, yes, that's all.
"O, I'd far rather talk about the flower carnival, yes, the flower carnival, it was so pretty, so lovely everywhere. But now they're going off to war, so stupid, isn't it, it's quite impossible, it can't last."
Good, O.K., we've got a curtain-raiser there, we're in the war. Good. At that point you can move into Paris and show a bus, there are plenty of striking shots, a bus going down towards the *Carrefour Drouot,* at one point the bus breaks into a gallop, that's a funny sight to see, the three-horse Madeleine-Bastille bus, yes, get that shot there. Good, right. At that point you go out into the countryside. Take the landscapes in *Journey.* You're going to have to read *Journey* again—what a bore for you. You'll have to find things in *Journey* that still exist. The Passage Choiseul, you're sure to be able to take that. And there'll be Epinay, the climb up to Epinay, that'll still be there for you. Suresnes, you can take that too, though it's not the same as it was . . . And you can take the Tuileries, and the Square Louvois, the little street, you ought to get a look at that, see what fits in with your ideas.
Then there's mobilization. All right. At that point you begin the *Journey.* This is where the heroes of *Journey* go off to war—part of the big picture. You'll need a pile of dough for that . . .
Then the end.
I'm giving you a dreamy passage here, then maybe you can show a bit of the Meuse countryside, that's where I began in the war, by the way, a bit of Flanders, good, fine, you just need to look at it, it's very evocative, and then very softly you begin to let the rumbling of the guns rise up.

What you knew the war by, what the people of '14 knew it by, was the gunfire, from both sides. It was a rolling BLOM BELOLOM BELOM, it was a mill, grinding our epoch down. That's to say, you had the line of fire there in front of you, that was where you were going to be written off, it was where they all died. Yes and what you were supposed to do was climb up there with your bayonet. But for the most part it meant shooting and flames. First shooting, then burning. Villages burning, everything burning. First shooting, then butchery.

Show that as best you may, it's your problem, work it out. I'm relying on little Descaves, there. You need music to go with the sound of the guns. Sinister kind of music, kind of deep Wagnerian music, he can get it out of the music libraries. Music that fits everything. Very few speeches. Very few words. Even for the big scene, even for the three hundred million. Gunfire. BELOMBELOLOM BOM, *tactactac.* Machine-guns—they had them already. From the North Sea to Switzerland there was a four-hundred-and-fifty kilometre strip which never stopped chewing up men from one end to the other. Yes, O yes, whenever a guy got there he said, so this is where it happens, this is where the chopper is, eh. That was where we all slaughtered each other. No dreaming there! One million seven hundred thousand died just there. More than a few. With retreats, advances, retreats, louder and louder BOBOOMS, big guns, little guns, not many planes, no, you can show a plane vaguely, but they weren't much, no, what scared us was the gunfire, pure and simple. The Germans had big guns and they were a big surprise, for the French army, 105's, we didn't have any. O.K. And bicycles which you bent in half and folded up.

So to end your story, the *Journey*, see, it ends, well, it ends as best it can, eh, but still, there is one end, a conclusion, a signature after the *Journey*, a really lifelike one. The book ends in philosophical language, the book does, but not the film. Here's how it is for the film. This was one way I saw the end, like this: there's an old fellow—I think of him as Simon—who looks after the cemetery, the military cemetery. Well, he's old now, he's seventy, he's worn out. And the director of the military cemetery, the curator, he's a young man and he's let him know it's time he retired. Ah, he says, by all means, I'd like nothing better, can't get about any more. Because you see, they've built him a little hut, not far from Verdun, you know, a hut, so this hut, this kind of Nissen hut, he's turned it into a little café-bar at the same time, and he's got a gramophone, but really, a period gramophone, yes! So in this bar, he serves people drinks and he talks, you know, he tells his story, tells it to lots of people, and you see the bar, and people coming in, many people used to come, they don't come any more, to visit the graves of their dear departed, but after all those tombs of the dear departed he feels pretty old, eh, and it's a lot of trouble getting there, so much trouble he doesn't go any more, himself, because he says, I'm too old, I can't, I can't move. Walk three kilometres over those furrows, too much bloody trouble, it is, impossible, I'd come back dead, I would, I'm worn out, worn out, I am. And he has an opportunity to say that because the director of the cemetery has found someone to take his place. And who is this someone who'll take his place? I'll tell you. It's . . . they're Armenians. A family of Armenians. There's a father, a mother, and five little children. And what are they doing there? Well, they'd gone to Africa, like all Armenians, and they'd been kicked out of it, and someone told them they could go and hide up North, they'd find a cemetery and a fellow just on the point of quitting and they could take his place. And oh, he says, that's fine, because the kids are sick, Africa's too hot for them anyway. So Simon takes them in. The cemetery-keeper. He has his peaked cap on and all. Well, he says, you'll be taking my place. You'll be none too warm, though. If you want to make a bit of a fire, there's wood for the fetching, though the wood fire's just an old stove for his pot, and he says, me, I can't last any longer, because of all this running around. There used to be the Americans, in the old days. There still are the Americans, too, down under there, you'll see, you'll find them . . . well, I'll show you the gate where they come in, it's not far, hardly a kilometre, but I can't do it any more—because he limps too, you see, he limps too—I'm wounded, I am, disabled eighty per cent after '14, it makes a difference! I'll be going to live with my sister. A fine bitch of a woman she was. Lives at Asnières! Dirty slut, she is! She says I've got to go, she says I've got to but I don't know that I'll get on with her, haven't seen her for thirty years now, I haven't, dirty slut she was, must be more of a slut than ever by now. She's married, she says they've a room, maybe, I don't know what I'll do there, still, can't stay here, can I, can't do the job, I can't do it. There aren't many doing it nowadays, two or three of them still come, there used to be plenty, they used to come in droves, in the old days, in memory of them all, the French and the English, there are all kinds buried down there, but you'll see, like they told me, oh, put the crosses right, yes, some have fallen down, of course they have, time does its work, crosses won't stay up for ever, so I put the crosses right as best I could for a long time, but I don't go any more now, no, no, I can't, I have to lie down afterwards, you see, I can't, and lying down here wouldn't be any pleasure, and I've no one with me, so the visitors come and as it happens one good woman, an American, a very old American woman and she says, "I want to see my old friend John Brown, my dear uncle that died, don't you have him there?" "O," he says, "it's all in the registers, wait a moment, I'll go and have a look, yes, I'll show you the register, there," and he shows her the register and says, "I kept it well, you see, there, can't say I didn't do that, eh, now let's see, Brown, Brown, Brown. Oh, yes, yes, yes, yes, yes. Well, you know, it's down in the *Fauvettes* cemetery, down there, lady, hard to find, it is. No, no, please, him over there, with his wife and children, very interesting, the grounds are, they'll put it all in order for you; and I can't, you see, I can't, I've told you I can't, it's no use, madam, and believe me if you try going over there, eh, eh, let me tell you, finding where he is, he's there all right, in my register, but it's a long while since I went to look at it, the American one, it's a long way, two and a half kilometres at least, no, no, let them do it, they'll do it. I can serve you what there is, though, granadilla juice, lemon. Oh, you'd like a cup of coffee, oh, to be sure, we couldn't say no to a cup of coffee, I'll make you a cup of coffee.

And he makes her a cup of coffee, d'you follow, he's got a nose for a wealthy dame. Well, he says, you see, my sister, over in Asnières, here's the coffee, a little coffee? Do you know, that reminds me, I'm not so sure she knows how to make it. A trollop, she is, I say it myself. Eh, I don't know what I'll do, I don't, still, have to go, really have to go. So there it is. Yes. I'm going. Yes, I'm really going, I'm going to leave you with them. Don't be frightened, now! (the others are beginning to look scared). Oh, it's none too warm here, but just you put some wood on and it warms up, that's no trouble. Oh, you'll see, it's no joke, here. What about a bit of music. Ah, it was a good one, that gramophone there was, a fine one, ah yes, one from the old days, it was, it was a . . . and he gets out a wind-up thing and they play the old-time records, but really the old-time, eh—*Viens Poupoule! Ma Tonkinoise!*—there you are, you see, it's better with that on, isn't it, you can play it all summer long, you can, that'll bring them in again, once they've swabbed the place down a bit, just needs doing, eh? Well, madam, going back, are you? Going to Paris, are you? You've got a car? Well, now, I must say, that'd be a help, that would, fancy that, eh, going back in a car . . .

—Translated from the French by Patrick Bowles

PART THREE

1967–1973

Introduction

On occasion, "Notices" appeared in the magazine. They ranged in topics from the fortunes of a horse named The Paris Review (which raced under the colors of the Greentree Stables) to stirring pleas for financial support. Here is one which appeared in 1976 about an oddity of the *Paris Review*—its vast masthead—which may also give a suggestion of the nature and spirit of the enterprise.

NOTICE

Not long ago the managing editor of this magazine asked, "Who *are* all these people?" She was referring to those listed on the masthead of the *Paris Review*—which is indeed a solid bloc of names, as if a page torn from the telephone directory had somehow settled into place on the printing press. The list runs from the top of the page to the bottom. The managing editor has been with the magazine for over four years. She remarked, "There are almost sixty names here. I hardly know any. What do they do?"

An inspection revealed that her mathematics were indeed correct, and that in truth some of those listed had not communicated with the magazine for many years. Their subscriptions had elapsed and it was thought that perhaps one or two had died. A pruning process seemed called for. . . .

Within a day or so of the publication of the "streamlined" masthead the following communication, excerpts from which appear below, was received from one of the expunged:

> *Dear George,*
> *. . . . It has come to pass that, without my even "resigning," I am no longer an Advisory Editor of the* Paris Review. *John Phillips graces the masthead no more, and the chagrin of it is devastating.*
> *I first felt the sting a couple of weekends ago when my 14-year-old*

son James came home from Andover, where everybody reads the Review. *"Hey," he told me, "I thought you said you were supposed to be an Advisory Editor of the* Paris Review. *Well, you're not." Before I could remonstrate he showed me the latest issue, where from all that proliferation of friends and helpers past and present this one was absent.*

Absent also, as my shamefaced researches have revealed, are the names of that capital chap, physician, and raconteur, Jonathan Miller, and of Ben Johnson—I don't doubt also a swell fellow but whom, like so many of my quondam merry colleagues on that crowded page, I have not had the pleasure of meeting. . . . The Johnson-Miller-Phillips line has been cast into the hopper of oblivion.

Was it something I said, George? What could I have done? I fear your answer will be quite simply, "nothing." Johnson, Miller, and I have done, literally, nothing. Nothing either to subvert or to assist the publication which for years had flattered us with honorific titles. That being so, I don't dispute the justice of our being cast out. And yet I can only wonder how much more than nothing is expected of an Advisory Editor? . . .

The letter was signed, *"Your crestfallen, John P. Marquand."*

Marquand's letter (his *nom de plume* is John Phillips) was not the only stirring of reaction . . . proving that if nothing else the masthead is apparently read with great care. These offices, dismayed, rushed to make amends. Marquand was written a letter which began, "Rarely, indeed since Jason pleaded with Medea for the lives of their children, has there been such a moving message as yours. . . ." He was informed, along with the others, that the Johnson-Miller-Phillips trio had been plucked out of the "hopper of oblivion" and reinstated . . . which indeed can be checked by an inspection of the masthead of this present issue (unless that heavily-read page has been torn out by an over-eager reader).

How odd, upon recollection, to have considered dispensing with this valuable trio. Ben Johnson, though this magazine has not heard from him in fifteen years, was responsible for the first publication in English of a number of Italian writers, among them Dino Buzzati and Italo Calvino. John Phillips, the aggrieved letter-writer, not only contributed some of his own work ("The Engines of Hygeia" and "Bleat Blodgette") but found us the unpublished Malcolm Lowry manuscript entitled *Lunar Caustic* about the author's incarceration in the mental ward at Bellevue. Jonathan Miller put together an extraordinary photographic essay of an autopsy which remained unprinted since the magazine could never discover the identity of the gent on the slab in order to ask (if somewhat hesitatingly) the nearest of kin for permission to publish.

These offices should have known better than to tamper with the masthead. In the earliest days of the magazine Harold L. Humes, one of the founders and who was expected to function as its first managing editor, took to reading *Huckleberry Finn* on the steppes of La Rotonde in Montparnasse and working on his estimable first novel, *Underground City*, instead of performing his duties . . . and was thus peremptorily lowered down the masthead to the position of Advertising and Circulation Manager. This uncalled for debasement came to his attention when the shipment of the first issue of the magazine arrived in New York from France. Humes took action, not by writing an aggrieved letter à Marquand, but by going down to the wharves with a rubber stamp made up with his name and an exalted title; he got into the shipping crates where he began stamping the masthead page in red ink, half a thousand or so copies, until his arm got tired.

Since that time it has always been a principle of the *Paris Review* that recognition of effort on its behalf, however slight, can only be acknowledged (since financial remuneration is limited) by being added to the masthead. In an Index published this year a total of 188 names of "merry colleagues" were listed as having helped the magazine at some stage in its life.

Many papers and magazines refuse to recognize the labors of their minions, much less the guiding spirits. *The New Yorker* lists only seven names, Mr. William Shawn, its editor, not among them. The *New York Times* has fifteen. Others do better. *The New York Review of Books* lists twenty-three, *Harper's* twenty-four, and *Playboy* (circulation 6,000,000) has an eighty-three name masthead. Of our brethren, *Partisan* lists forty-five; *Antaeus,* twenty; The *Hudson Review,* thirteen; *Transatlantic Review,* nine; *Ploughshares,* five; and the *Unmuzzled Ox* only four.

With its sixty, the *Paris Review* is high on the counts of both commercial and literary magazines . . . twenty-five ahead of *The New Republic,* twenty-nine in front of *The Atlantic Monthly,* ten over *Esquire,* twenty-seven over the *Saturday Review,* and seven atop the *National Lampoon.* The champion of all is *Rolling Stone* with 119—certainly a target to shoot at if we can survive over the coming years . . . which might be easier if we could only get all our masthead people to subscribe!

—G.P.

FICTION

GEORGES PEREC

Between Sleep and Waking

I

At first the darkness sometimes forms the vague outline of an ace of
spades: from a point in front of you two lines recede, diverge and, after
tracing a vast curve, turn back towards you.

Later it becomes an ocean, a black sea over which you sail, as if your
nose were the point or rather the stem of a gigantic steamship. Everything is black. No night, no darkness, the entire world is black, intrinsi-
cally black as on a photographic negative, and the only whiteness, or
perhaps grayness, is in the surge your passage raises on each side of your
nose, along your eyes, which are perhaps the sides of the ship, where
formerly the ace of spades had figured as if in mere prelude to this wake,
the whitish, undulating trail that you cut in front of you as you glide over
the black water. The water encompasses you on all sides, a black, motionless sea, extraordinarily smooth, lacking even phosphorescence, and
yet you feel that you could detect every detail, the slightest cloud if there
were a sky, the merest shoal if there were an horizon. But there is only
sea, and you are all stem cutting without effort, sound, or tremor the
deep white tracks of your way, like a share ploughing up a field.

Soon, however, someplace overhead, as if an inset, as if a screen appeared and a motion picture negative were projected on it, there is the same ship only now seen from above, in its entirety, and as for you, you are on the deck leaning over the railing or rather the gunnel, in a somewhat romantic attitude. For a long time the double image remains absolutely precise; and indeed if there is any one thing that irritates, that bothers you, it's that you can no longer manage to tell whether first of all you are the stem all by itself, raising white waves as it glides over the sea, and subsequently, almost simultaneously, some such thing as the consciousness of being this stem, which is to say the entire ship overhead on which you are the motionless passenger who is leaning from the deck in a slightly romantic attitude; or whether, on the contrary, there is first of all the entire ship gliding over the black sea with you, its only passenger, leaning against the gangway, and then a single detail inordinately magnified of this ship, the stem that divides the billows and raises on either side two waves—dense, white, but perhaps too definite in their contours to be really waves, they are more undulations, effects of drapery, with something about them rather stately, almost slowed down.

For a long time the two ships—the part and the whole, your stem nose and your steamship body—sail in consort without giving you any chance to dissociate them: you are at once the stem and the ship and yourself on the ship. Then a first contradiction occurs, but it is perhaps only an optical illusion ascribable to differences of scale and perspective: it appears to you that the ship is moving slowly, more and more slowly, perhaps a little as if you saw it from a greater and greater distance, from higher and higher up; and yet you, leaning on the gunnel, do not grow any smaller at all, you still remain as visible as ever; and as far as the stem is concerned, it moves faster and faster, it is no longer gliding but shoots over the water, like a motorboat or even an outboard, no longer an ocean liner at all.

At this point, and here things become much worse, as if you knew, perhaps by experience, that what is in the process of taking shape is the beginning of the end, since you will never be able to stand the intensity of what is foreshadowed for more than a few moments, for more than a few seconds, even though nothing as yet has been revealed except, perhaps, a premonitory sign at the most, a token whose meaning was not even certain, and whose elucidation you await in the vain hope that everything will stay blurred for as long as possible, because you know already that the moment of awakening is about to lay hold of you, it's precisely your impatience that has brought it on and every effort you make to delay it only speeds its onset;—at this point, as it does every time, there emerges, not slowly enough, the feeling at once thrilling and dismal, wonderful and heartbreaking, from the start too precise and becoming very soon an almost painful throb: the absurd certainty—or, instead, not yet quite absurd but sure to become absurd—that this is a true memory, exact in every detail: the sea was black, the ship made slow headway through the narrow channel, projecting sheaves of white foam along its sides, you were leaning over the railing of the promenade deck in the slightly romantic attitude adopted by all passengers looking at sea gulls while they take the air; you experienced the same feeling that you now experience, and nevertheless you experience no feeling now other than the perilous, the ever more perilous one of knowing that such a memory is at once impossible and ineradicable.

Later, much later—you may have woken up several times, dozed back to sleep several times, you have turned on your right side, on your left side, you have lain on your back, lain face down, perhaps you have even turned on the light, perhaps smoked a cigarette—later, much later, sleep becomes a target, no, it's rather you who become sleep's target. It's a widening, intermittent focus. In front of you, or more exactly in front of your eyes, sometimes a little to the left, sometimes a little to the right, never at the center, a myriad of little white dots gradually draw together, finally assuming some cat-like shape, the profile of a panther's head, which moves forward, grows larger as it bares two sharp fangs, then disappears, giving way to a luminous spot that broadens, turns into a rhombus, a star, and swoops down on you, missing you at the last second as it goes by on your right. The phenomenon recurs several times at regular intervals—nothing at first, then faintly luminous dots, a panther's head in outline, filled out, growing larger, roaring, baring two sharp fangs; afterwards a ball of light that heads towards you, just misses you, passing so close that you almost thought you had touched, felt, and heard it; then again nothing, for a long time—white dots, the panther's head, the star that swells and brushes against you.

Then, for a long time, nothing; or else, sometimes, later, somewhere, something like a white sun exploding . . .

II

The meeting of eye and pillow gives birth to a mountain, a fairly gentle slope forming a quarter circle (or more precisely the lesser arc of a circle) that stands out in the foreground, darker than the remaining space. This mountain isn't interesting; it's normal. For the time being your mind is absorbed by a task that you must perform but that you are unable to define exactly; it seems to be the sort of task that is scarcely important in itself and that perhaps is only the pretext, the opportunity, of making sure you know the rules: you imagine, for example, and this is immediately confirmed, that the task consists of sliding your thumb or even your whole hand onto the pillow. But is doing this really your concern? Don't your years of service, your position in the hierarchy, exempt you from this chore? This question is plainly much more important than the task itself, and there is nothing to help you solve it, you didn't think that so much later you would have to account for things in this way. Besides, on further reflection you realize that the problem is still more complicated: it isn't a matter of knowing whether or not you should slide your thumb in a manner befitting your rank, your duties, your seniority, but rather of this: sooner or later, in any event, you will have to slide your thumb up, but on top of the pillow if you have sufficient seniority, underneath if you haven't, and of course you have no notion of your seniority, which seems considerable but perhaps not considerable enough. Perhaps they have even picked a moment to ask you precisely this question when no one, not even the most upright of judges, would be able unquestioningly to assert that you have or have not got sufficient seniority?

The question could also be asked about your feet or thighs. It in fact means nothing: the real problem is one of contacts. There are theoretically two kinds of contact: between your body and the sheets, as in the case of your left thigh, your right foot, your right forearm, part of your belly—a contact that is fusion, osmosis, liquefaction; and between your body and itself, where flesh meets flesh, where the left foot is crossed over the right foot, where the knees meet, where your elbow ventures against your stomach—these contacts being sharp, hot or cold, or hot and cold. Obviously it's possible with hardly any risk to reverse the whole operation and assert that, on the contrary, the left foot is under the right foot, the right thigh under the left thigh.

What is most clear in all this is that obviously you are not lying down, either on your right side or on your left side, legs slightly bent, arms embracing the pillow, but that you are hanging head downwards like a hibernating bat or, more, like an overripe pear on a pear tree: which means that at any moment you may fall, something that in fact strikes you as not particularly bothersome, since your head is perfectly shielded by the pillow; but you are duty bound to escape this danger, even if it is minute. But if you review the means at your command, it does not take you long to realize that the situation is more serious than you first reckoned, if only in that loss of horizontality is rarely conducive to sleep. Therefore you must make up your mind to fall, even though you foresee that this will scarcely be enjoyable (one never knows when the fall will end) but above all you don't know how to go about falling, it's only when you aren't thinking about it that you start to fall, and how can you not think about it since it so happens you *are* thinking about it? It's something no one has ever seriously faced and that nevertheless is of some consequence: there ought to be texts on the subject, authoritative texts that would enable one to deal with these situations, far commoner than is generally believed.

Three quarters of your body have taken refuge in your head. Your heart has settled in your eyebrow, where it has made itself perfectly at home, pulsating like a thing alive, with, at the most, a very slightly exaggerated acceleration. You are obliged to perform a roll call of your body, to verify the wholeness of your limbs, your organs, your entrails, your mucous membranes. You would certainly like to rid your head of all these lumps that encumber and weigh it down, and at the same time you are pleased at having saved as much as you could, for everything else is lost, you have no more feet, no more hands; your calf has quite melted away.

All this is more and more complicated. First you would have to remove your elbow, and in the space thus vacated you could place at least part of your belly, continuing in this manner until you were more or less reconstituted. But it's frightfully difficult: some parts are missing, of others there are two, others have swollen to inordinate size, others put forward utterly insane territorial claims. Your elbow is more elbow than ever (you had forgotten that anything could be so thoroughly elbow), a nail has replaced your hand. And of course it's always at that very moment that the tormentors decide to intervene. One sticks a blackboard eraser in your mouth, another stuffs cotton in your ears; several pit sawyers have started working in your sinuses; a pyromaniac sets fire to your stomach, sadistic tailors squeeze your feet, cram too small a hat on your head, force you into too tight a coat and use a necktie to strangle you; a chimney sweep and his accomplice have let a knotted rope into your windpipe which, in spite of their praiseworthy efforts, they are unable to extract.

They are there nearly every time. You know them well. It's almost reassuring. If they're around, sleep isn't far away. They will make you suffer a little, then get fed up and leave you in peace. They hurt you, it's true, but you keep towards your pain—as towards all the other feelings you discern, all the thoughts crossing your mind, all the impressions you receive—an attitude of complete detachment. Without astonishment you see yourself astonished, without surprise surprised, without pain assaulted by the tormentors. You wait for them to calm down. You relinquish to them every organ they want. From afar you see them wrangling over your belly, your nose, your throat, your feet.

But often—so often—this is the ultimate trap. The worst then comes to pass, emerging slowly, imperceptibly. At first everything is calm—too calm; normal—too normal. Everything seems set never to move again. But after that you are aware, you begin to be aware, with a certainty more and more relentless, that you have lost your body—no, rather you see it, not far away from you, but you will never be one with it again.

You are no more than an eye. A huge, steady eye that sees everything, your limp body as well as yourself, the beholder beheld, as if it had turned completely round in its socket and without uttering a word was gazing on you, your inside, your dark, empty, sea-green, startled, helpless inside. It looks at you and pins you down. You will never stop seeing yourself. You are unable to do anything, you are unable to escape yourself, you are unable to escape your gaze, you will never be able to: even if you managed to fall asleep so deeply that no shock, no summons, no searing pain could wake you up, there would still be this eye, your eye, which will never shut, which will never fall asleep. You see yourself, you see yourself seeing yourself, you watch yourself watching yourself. Even if you woke up, your vision would abide, identical, unchangeable. Even if you managed to accumulate thousands, or thousands of thousands of eyelids, there would still be, behind them, this eye to see you. You are not asleep, but sleep will not return again. You are not awake and you will never wake up again. You are not dead, and not even death could bring you deliverance.

—Translated from the French by Harry Mathews

MORDECAI RICHLER

A Liberal Education

Joyce phoned him at the office. Before she could get a word out, he said, "If you ask me, almost all of Doug's problems can be traced to that bloody school."

"Would you rather that he was educated as you were?"

Mortimer had been to Upper Canada College. "I don't see why not."

"Full of repressions and establishment lies."

Establishment. Camp. WASP. She had all the bloody modish words. "Well I—"

"We'll discuss it later. Just please please don't be late for the rehearsal."

Mortimer had only been invited to the rehearsal for the Christmas play because he was in publishing and Dr. Booker, the founder, wanted Oriole to do a book about Beatrice Webb House. Drama was taught at the school by a Miss Lilian Tanner, who had formerly been with Joan Littlewood's bouncy group. A tall, willowy young lady, Miss Tanner wore her long black hair loose, a CND button riding her scrappy bosom. She assured Mortimer he was a most welcome visitor to her modest little workshop. Mortimer curled into a seat in the rear of the auditorium, trying to appear as unobtrusive as possible. He was only half-attentive to begin with, reconciled to an afternoon of tedium larded with cuteness.

"We have a visitor this afternoon, class," Miss Tanner began sweetly, "Mr. Mortimer Griffin of Oriole Press."

Curly-haired heads, gorgeous pig-tailed heads, whipped around; everybody giggly.

"Now all together, class . . ."

"GOOD AFTERNOON, MR. GRIFFIN."

Mortimer waved, unaccountably elated.

"Settle down now," Miss Tanner demanded, rapping her ruler against the desk. "Settle down, I said."

The class came to order.

"Now this play that we are going to perform for the Christmas concert was written by . . . class?"

"A marquis!"

"Bang on!" Miss Tanner smiled, flushed with old-fashioned pride in her charges, and then she pointed her ruler at a rosy-cheeked boy. "What's a marquis, Tony?"

"What hangs outside the Royal Court Theatre."

"No, no, darling."

There were titters all around. Mortimer laughed himself, covering his mouth with his hand.

"That's a marquee. This is a marquis. A—"

A little girl bobbed up, waving her arms. Golden head, red ribbons.

"A French nobleman!"

"Righty-ho! And what do we know about him . . . class?"

A boy began to jump up and down. Miss Tanner pointed her ruler at him.

"They put him in prison."

"Yes. Anybody know why?"

Everybody began to call out at once.

"Order! Order!" Miss Tanner demanded. "Whatever will Mr. Griffin think of us?"

Giggles again.

"You have a go, Harriet. Why was the marquis put in prison?"

"Because he was absolutely super."

"Mmm . . ."

"And such a truth-teller."

"Yes. Any other reasons . . . Gerald?"

"Because the puritans were scared of him."

"Correct. And what else do we know about the marquis?"

"Me, me!"

"No, me, Miss. Please!"

"Eeney-meeney-miney-mo," Miss Tanner said, waving her ruler, "catch a bigot by the toe . . . Frances!"

"That he was the freest spirit what ever lived."

"*Who* ever lived. Who, dear. And who said that?"

"Apollinaire."

"Jolly good. Anything else . . . Doug?"

"Um, he cut through the banality of everyday life."

"Indeed he did. And who said that?"

"Jean Genet."

"No."

"Hugh Hefner," another voice cried.

"Dear me, that's not even warm."

"Simone de Beauvoir."

"Right. And who is she?"

"A writer."

"Good. Very good. Anybody know anything else about the marquis?"

"He was in the Bastille and then in another place called Charenton."

"Yes. All together, class . . . Charenton."

"CHARENTON."

"Anything else?"

Frances jumped up again. "I know. Please, Miss Tanner. Please, me."

"Go ahead, darling."

"He had a very, very, very big member."

"Yes indeed. And—"

But now Frances' elder brother, Jimmy, leaped to his feet, interrupting. "Like Mummy's new friend," he said.

Shrieks. Laughter. Miss Tanner's face reddened, for the first time she stamped her foot. "Now I don't like that, Jimmy. I don't like that one bit."

"Sorry, Miss Tanner."

"That's tittle-tattle, isn't it?"

"Yes, Miss Tanner."

"We mustn't tittle-tattle on one another here."

" . . . sorry . . ."

"And now," Miss Tanner said, stepping up to the blackboard, "can anyone give me another word for member?"

"COCK," came a little girl's shout, and Miss Tanner wrote it down.

"Beezer."

"PWICK."

"Male organ."

"PENIS."

"Hard-on."

Miss Tanner looked dubious. She frowned. "Not always," she said, and she didn't write it down.

"FUCKING-MACHINE."

"*Putz.*"

"You're being sectarian again, Monty," Miss Tanner said, somewhat irritated.

"Joy-stick."

A pause.

"Anybody else?" Miss Tanner asked.

"Hot rod."

"Mmm. Dodgey," Miss Tanner said, but she wrote it down on the blackboard, adding a question mark. "Anybody else?"

"Yes," a squeaky voice cried, now that her back was turned.

"Teakettle."

Miss Tanner whirled around, outraged. "*Who said that?*" she demanded.

Silence.

"Well, I never. I want to know who said that. *Immediately.*"

No answer.

"Very well, then. No rehearsal," she said, sitting down and tapping her foot. "We are simply going to sit here and sit here and sit here until who ever said that owns up."

Nothing.

"I'm sorry about this fuck-up, Mr. Griffin. It's most embarrassing."

Mortimer shrugged.

"I'm waiting, class."

Finally a fat squinting boy came tearfully to his feet. "It was me, Miss Tanner," he said in a small voice. "I said teakettle."

"Would you be good enough to tell us why, Reggie?"

" . . . when my nanny . . . I mean my little brother's nanny, um, takes us, ah, out . . ."

"Speak up, please."

"When my nanny takes me, um, us . . . to Fortnum's for tea, well before I sit down she always asks us do we, do . . ." Reggie's head hung low; he paused, swallowing his tears, ". . . do I have to water my teakettle."

"Well. Well, well. I see," Miss Tanner said severely. "Class, can anyone tell me what Reggie's nanny is?"

"A prude!"

"Repressed!"

"Victorian!"

"All together now."

"REGGIE'S NANNY IS A DRY CUNT!"

"She is against . . . class?"

"Life-force."

"And?"

"Pleasure!"

"RIGHT. *And truth-sayers.* Remember that. Because it's sexually repressed bitches like Reggie's nanny who put truthsayers like the marquis in prison."

The class was enormously impressed.

"May I sit down now?" Reggie asked.

"Sit down, what?"

"Sit down, please, Miss Tanner?"

"Yes, Reggie. You may sit down."

At which point Mortimer slipped out of the rear exit of the auditorium, without waiting to see a run-through of the play, without even finding out what play they were doing.

"Excuse me, beg your pardon," Mortimer muttered, leading Joyce and Agnes Laura Ryerson to their seats in the Beatrice Webb auditorium, which was gaily tricked out with reams of colored ribbons, balloons, and mistletoe for the Christmas play. A rosy-cheeked boy skipped across the stage waving a placard which read: PHILOSOPHY IN THE BEDROOM. He was followed by a giggly, plump ten-year-old girl with another placard: DIALOGUE THE FOURTH.

Mortimer focused on the stage, where four nude ten-year-olds (two boys, two girls) were frolicking on an enormous bed. The effect was comic, making Mortimer recall an old *Saturday Evening Post* cover by Norman Rockwell which had a freckled little girl sitting at her mother's dressing table, the gap between her teeth showing as she puckered her lips to try on her mother's lipstick.

The boy playing Dolmance said, "I see but one way to terminate this ridiculous ceremony: look here, Chevalier, we are educating this pretty girl, we are teaching her all a little girl of her age should know and, the better to instruct her, we join—we join—we join—"

"Some practice to theory," the prompter hissed.

"—some practice to theory. She must have a tableau dressed for her: it must feature a prick—"

"Louder, please," a parent behind Mortimer called out.

"—a prick discharging, that's where presently we are; would you like to serve as a model?"

The Chevalier de Mirvel, played by a big black West Indian boy whom the audience desperately wanted to do well, responded, biting back his laughter, "Surely, the proposal is too flattering to refuse, and Mademoiselle has the charms that will quickly guarantee the desired lesson's effects."

Madame de Saint-Ange, a gawky child, all ribs and knees it seemed, squealed, "Then let's go on: to work!"

Which was when they fell to wrestling on the bed, the Chevalier de Mirvel, to judge by his laughter, being the most ticklish of the four.

"Oh, indeed," Eugenie hollered, " 'tis too much, you abuse my inexperience to such a degree . . ."

The West Indian boy kissed Eugenie.

"Smack, smack," Dolmance called out, for Miss Tanner had encouraged them to improvise.

"Here comes the mushy stuff," Madame de Saint-Ange pitched in, alienating herself from her part. She was, after all, only playing Madame de Saint-Ange. For real, as Miss Tanner had explained, she was Judy Faversham.

"Oh, God!" the West Indian boy hollered. "What fresh, what sweet attractions!"

Agnes Laura Ryerson's face went the color of ashes. Behind Mortimer, a man demanded gruffly of his wife, "When does Gerald come on stage?"

"Quiet, James."

Yet another father voiced his displeasure. "There aren't enough parts."

"It's a classic, Cyril."

"All the same, it's a school play. There should be more parts. It's jolly unfair to the other children."

Mortimer's attention was gripped by the free-for-all on stage. Puzzling over the nude, goose-pimply children entwined on the bed, he wondered, the Chevalier de Mirvel aside, which leg, what ribcage, belonged to whom. Dolmance squealed: "I have seen girls younger than this sustain still more massy pricks: with courage and patience life's greatest obstacles are surmounted—"

"Here come the clichés," the man behind Mortimer said, groaning.

"—'Tis madness to think one must have a child deflowered by only very small pricks. I hold the contrary view, that a virgin should be delivered to none but the vastest engines to be had . . ."

Suddenly the stage lights dimmed and the bed was abandoned to the Chevalier de Mirvel and Eugenie. Secondary lights brightened and behind the free-floating gauze that formed the rear bedroom wall there magically loomed the boys and girls of the second form, Doug's form, cupids as it were, humming a nervy, bouncy tune and carrying flickering, star-shaped lights. There was enthusiastic applause and only one harsh cry of "Derivative!" from the man behind Mortimer, as the kids filed onstage and formed a circle round the bed, where the Chevalier de Mirvel and Eugenie still tussled. Then, taking the audience completely by surprise, a fairy godmother, wearing a tall pointed hat, all sparkly and wound round and round in shimmering blue chiffon, was suspended in mid-air over the bed. The fairy godmother was none other than Mr. Yasha Krashinsky, who taught Expressive Movement at Beatrice Webb House.

Deafening applause greeted the rotund, dangling Yasha Krashinsky, a touching measure of support, as it was widely known that he had soon to appear at Old Bailey, charged with importuning outside Covent Garden. While the second form choir hummed, Yasha Krashinsky chanted: "Le Chevalier de Mirvel is wilting. Our fair Eugenie is fading fast. They will only make it, grownups, if you believe in the cure-all powers of the orgasm. Grownups, do you believe in the orgasm?"

"Yes!"

The pitch of the humming heightened. Yasha Krashinsky chanted: "The young virgin and her lover cannot hear you. Louder, grownups. Do you believe in the orgasm?"

"YES! YES! YES!"

Blackness on stage. The throbbing of drums. Squeals from the bed. One of the boys from the second form choir took a step forward, raised his arms aloft, and shouted: "Hip! Hip!"

"HURRAH!" returned the choir.

"Hip! Hip!"

"HURRAH!"

A spotlight picked out the fairy godmother, Yasha Krashinsky, as he was lowered with a clunk onstage, and poured a flask of red paint into a bucket.

"EUGENIE IS A WOMAN NOW," the choir sang to the tune of "Pomp and Circumstance." "EUGENIE IS A WOMAN NOW."

Once the play was done, the children skipped off to the dining hall, where choc-ices, a conjurer, and a Popeye cartoon show awaited them. The adults remained in the auditorium, where they were served *vin rosé* and cheese squares. Dr. Booker, Yasha Krashinsky, and finally Miss Lilian Tanner mounted the stage to shouts of bravo, and the meeting was called to order. Mortimer was immensely encouraged to discover that he was not alone in being rather put off by the Beatrice Webb House production of *Philosophy in the Bedroom.* He was in a minority, a reactionary minority, but he was not alone. As the meeting progressed beyond niceties, Mortimer was heartened to see other parents come to the boil. The play was not the issue. It was, however, symptomatic of what some parents felt had come to ail the school.

Francis Wharton, the enlightened TV producer, began by saying he had always voted socialist; he deplored censorship in any shape or form, on either side of the so-called Iron Curtain; Victorian double standards were anathema to him; but all the same he thought it a bit much that just because his thirteen-year-old daughter was the only girl in the fifth form to stop at petting—

"Shame," somebody called out.

—*heavy petting*—

The objector shrugged, unimpressed.

—was no reason for her to come home with a scarlet T for Tease painted on her bosom.

This brought Lady Gillian Horsham, the Oxfam organizer, to her feet. Lady Horsham wished for more colored neighbors in Lowndes Square. She had, she said, found the play on the twee side here and there, but, on balance, most imaginative.

"Yes, yes," Dr. Booker interrupted bitingly, "but?"

Lady Horsham explained that her daughter, also in the fifth form, but not so cripplingly inhibited as the previous speaker's child—

"Hear! Hear!"

—had already been to the London Clinic to be fitted with a diaphragm.

"That's the stuff!"

"Good girl!"

But, she continued, but, wasn't it all rather premature? Not, mind you, that she was a prude. But, as they were all socialists, it seemed to her irresponsible that while their sisters in Africa and India were in such desperate need of diaphragms—

"Not germane," somebody hollered.

Yes, it was germane, Lady Horsham continued. But look at it another way, if you must. Parents were already overburdened with spiraling fees, the cost of summer and winter uniforms, hockey sticks, cricket bats, and whatnot. Was it fair that they should now also have to fork out for new diaphragms each term as, let's face it, these were growing girls? Couldn't the girls of the fifth form, without psychological damage—

"Your question, please?"

—without risk, practice *coitus interruptus?*

"Spoil-sport!"

"Reactionary!"

Dr. Booker beamed at his people, gesturing for silence. "If I may make a positive point, there is no reason why the tuck shop co-op, which already sells uniforms the girls have outgrown to younger students, could not also dispose of diaphragms that have begun to pinch, *so long as the transaction was not tarnished by the profit motive.*"

Next to speak up, Tony Latham, the outspoken Labour backbencher, explained that while it certainly did not trouble him personally that his boy masturbated daily, immediately following the Little Fibber Bra commercials on ITV, it was quite another matter when his parents, up from the country, were visiting. Latham's parents, it was necessary to understand, were the product of a more inhibited, censorious age: it distressed them, rather, to see their only grandchild playing with himself on the carpet, while they were taking tea.

"Your question, Mr. Latham?"

Could it be put to Yasha Krashinsky, overworked as he is, that he keep the boys for five minutes after Expressive Movement class, and have them masturbate before they come home?

"But I do," Yasha put in touchily. "I do, my dear chap."

Other, more uncompromisingly radical parents now demanded their say. There could be no backsliding at Beatrice Webb House. "You begin," a lady said, "by forbidding masturbation in certain rooms or outside prescribed hours and next thing you know the children, our children, are driven back into locked toilets to seek their pleasure, and still worse have developed a sense of guilt about auto-stimulation."

"Or," another mother said, looking directly at Lady Horsham, "you allow one greedy-guts in the fourth form to hold on to her precious little hymen and next thing out goes fucking in the afternoon."

Some compromises were grudgingly agreed to. Diaphragms, for instance, would be made optional until a girl reached the sixth form. On the other hand, Dr. Booker absolutely refused to stream girls into classes of those who did and those who didn't. It would be heartless, he said feelingly, to stamp a girl of twelve frigid for the rest of her life. Some, if not all, late developers might grow up to surpass seemingly more avid girls in sexual appetite.

There followed a long and heated discussion on the play, its larger meanings within meanings, and then a debate on Beatrice Webb House finances, co-op shares, and needs and plans for the future. Dr. Booker received a standing ovation at the end.

JAMES SALTER

Am Strande von Tanger

Barcelona at dawn. The hotels are dark. All the great avenues are pointing to the sea.

The city is empty. Nico is asleep. She is bound by twisted sheets, by her long hair, by a naked arm which falls from beneath her pillow. She lies still, she does not even breathe.

In a cage outlined beneath a square of silk that is indigo blue and black, her bird sleeps, Kalil. The cage is in an empty fireplace which has been scrubbed clean. There are flowers beside it and a bowl of fruit. Kalil is asleep, his head beneath the softness of a wing.

Malcolm is asleep. His steel-rimmed glasses which he does not need—there is no prescription in them—lie open on the table. He sleeps on his back and his nose rides the dream world like a keel. This nose, his mother's nose or at least a replica of his mother's, is like a theatrical device, a strange decoration that has been pasted on his face. It is the first thing one notices about him. It is the first thing one likes. The nose in a sense is a mark of commitment to life. It is a large nose which cannot be hidden. In addition, his teeth are bad.

At the very top of the four stone spires which Gaudi left unfinished the light has just begun to bring forth gold inscriptions too pale to read. There is no sun. There is only a white silence. Sunday morning, the early morning of Spain. A mist covers all of the hills which surround the city. The stores are closed.

Nico has come out on the terrace after her bath. The towel is wrapped around her, water still glistens on her skin.

"It's cloudy," she says. "It's not a good day for the sea."

Malcolm looks up.

"It may clear," he says.

Morning. Villa-Lobos is playing on the phonograph. The cage is on a stool in the doorway. Malcolm lies in a canvas chair eating an orange. He is in love with the city. He has a deep attachment to it based in part on a story by Paul Morand and also on an incident which occurred in Barcelona years before: one evening in the twilight Antonio Gaudi, mysterious, fragile, even saintlike, the city's great architect, was hit by a streetcar as he walked to church. He was very old, white beard, white hair, dressed in the simplest of clothes. No one recognized him. He lay in the street without even a cab to drive him to the hospital. Finally he was taken to the charity ward. He died the day Malcolm was born.

The apartment is on Avenida General Mitre and her tailor, as Nico calls him, is near Gaudi's cathedral at the other end of town. That's a working-class neighborhood, there's a faint smell of garbage. The site is surrounded by walls. There are quatrefoils printed in the sidewalk. Soaring above everything, the spires. *Sanctus, sanctus,* they cry. They are hollow. The cathedral was never completed, its doors lead both ways into open air. Malcolm has walked, in the calm Barcelona evening, around this empty monument many times. He has stuffed peseta notes, virtually worthless, into the slot marked: DONATIONS TO CONTINUE THE WORK. It seems on the other side they are simply falling to the ground or, he listens closely, a priest wearing glasses locks them in a wooden box.

Malcolm believes in Malraux and Max Weber: art is the real history of nations. In the details of his person there is evidence of a process not fully complete. It is the making of a man into a true instrument. He is preparing for the arrival of that great artist he one day expects to be, an artist in the truly modern sense which is to say without accomplishments but with the conviction of genius. An artist freed from the demands of craft, an artist of concepts, generosity, his work is the creation of the legend of himself. So long as he is provided with even a single follower he can believe in the sanctity of this design.

He is happy here. He likes the wide, tree-cool avenues, the restaurants, the long evenings. He is deep in the currents of a slow, connubial life.

Nico comes onto the terrace wearing a wheat-colored sweater.

"Would you like a coffee?" she says. "Do you want me to go down for one?"

He thinks for a moment.

"Yes," he says.

"How do you like it?"

"*Solo,*" he says.

"Black."

She likes to do this. The building has a small elevator which rises slowly. When it arrives she steps in and closes the doors carefully behind her. Then, just as slowly, she descends, floor after floor, as if they were decades. She thinks about Malcolm. She thinks about her father and his second wife. She is probably more intelligent than Malcolm, she decides. She is certainly stronger-willed. He, however, is better-looking in a strange way. She has a wide, senseless mouth. He is generous. She knows she is a little dry. She passes the second floor. She looks at herself in the mirror. Of course, one doesn't discover these things right away. It's like a play, it unfolds slowly, scene by scene, the reality of another person changes. Anyway, pure intelligence is not that important. It's an abstract quality. It does not include that cruel, intuitive knowledge of how the new life, a life her father would never understand, should be lived. Malcolm has that.

At ten-thirty, the phone rings. She answers and talks in German, lying on the couch. After it is finished Malcolm calls to her, "Who was that?"

"Do you want to go to the beach?"

"Yes."

"Inge is coming in about an hour," Nico says.

He has heard about her and is curious. Besides, she has a car. The morning, obedient to his desires, has begun to change. There is some early traffic on the avenue beneath. The sun breaks through for a moment, disappears, breaks through again. Far off, beyond his thoughts, the four spires are passing between shadow and glory. In intervals of sunlight the letters on high reveal themselves: *Hosanna.*

Smiling, at noon, Inge arrives. She is in a camel skirt and a blouse with the top buttons undone. She's a bit heavy for the skirt which is very short. Nico introduces them.

"Why didn't you call last night?" Inge asks.

"We were going to call but it got so late. We didn't have dinner till eleven," Nico explains. "I was sure you'd be out."

No. She was waiting at home all night for her boyfriend to call, Inge says. She is fanning herself with a postcard from Madrid. Nico has gone into the bedroom.

"They're such bastards," Inge says. Her voice is raised to carry. "He was supposed to call at eight. He didn't call me until ten. He didn't have time to talk. He was going to call back in a little while. Well, he never called. I finally fell asleep."

Nico puts on a pale grey skirt with many small pleats and a lemon pullover. She looks at the back of herself in the mirror. Her arms are bare. Inge is talking from the front room.

"They don't know how to behave, that's the trouble. They don't have any idea. They go to the Polo Club, that's the only thing they know."

She begins to talk to Malcolm.

"When you go to bed with someone it should be nice afterwards, you should treat each other decently. Not here. They have no respect for a woman."

She has green eyes and white, even teeth. He is thinking of what it would be like to have such a mouth. Her father is supposed to be a surgeon. In Hamburg. Nico says it isn't true.

"They are children here," Inge says. "In Germany, now, you have a little respect. A man doesn't treat you like that, he knows what to do."

"Nico," he calls.

She comes in brushing her hair.

"I am frightening him," Inge explains. "Do you know what I finally did? I called at five in the morning. I said, why didn't you call? I don't know, he said—I could tell he was asleep—what time is it? Five o'clock, I said. Are you angry with me? A little, he said. Good, because I am angry with you. Bang, I hung up."

Nico is closing the doors to the terrace and bringing the cage inside.

"It's warm," Malcolm says, "leave him there. He needs the sunlight."

She looks in at the bird.

"I don't think he's well," she says.

"He's all right."

"The other one died last week," she explains to Inge. "Suddenly. He wasn't even sick."

She closes one door and leaves the other open. The bird sits in the now brilliant sunshine, feathered, serene.

"I don't think they can live alone," she says.

"He's fine," Malcolm assures her. "Look at him."

The sun makes his colors very bright. He sits on the uppermost perch. His eyes have perfect, round lids. He blinks.

The elevator is still at their floor. Inge enters first. Malcolm pulls the narrow doors to. It's like shutting a small cabinet. Faces close together they start down. Malcolm is looking at Inge. She has her own thoughts.

They stop for another coffee at the little bar downstairs. He holds the door open for them to go in. No one is there—a single man reading the newspaper.

"I think I'm going to call him again," Inge says.

"Ask him why he woke you up at five in the morning," Malcolm says. She laughs.

"Yes," she says. "That's marvelous. That's what I'm going to do."

The telephone is at the far end of the marble counter, but Nico is talking to him and he cannot hear.

"Aren't you interested?" he asks.

"No," she says.

Inge's car is a blue Volkswagen, the blue of certain airmail envelopes. One fender is dented in.

"You haven't seen my car," she says. "What do you think? Did I get a good bargain? I don't know anything about cars. This is my first. I bought it from someone I know, a painter, but it was in an accident. The motor is scorched.

"I know how to drive," she says. "It's better if someone sits next to me, though. Can you drive?"

"Of course," he says.

He gets behind the wheel and starts the engine. Nico is sitting in the back.

"How does it feel to you?" Inge says.

"I'll tell you in a minute."

Although it's only a year old, the car has a certain shabbiness. The material on the ceiling is faded. Even the steering wheel seems abused. After they have driven a few blocks, Malcolm says, "It seems all right."

"Yes?"

"The brakes are a little weak."

"They are?"

"I think they need new linings."

"I just had it greased," she says.

Malcolm looks at her. She is quite serious.

"Turn left here," she says.

She directs him through the city. There is a little traffic now but he seldom stops. Many intersections in Barcelona are widened out in the shape of an octagon. There are only a few red lights. They drive through vast neighborhoods of old apartments, past factories, the first vacant fields at the edge of town. Inge turns in her seat to look back to Nico.

"I'm sick of this place," she says. "I want to go to Rome."

They are passing the airport. The road to the sea is crowded. All the scattered traffic of the city has funneled onto it, buses, trucks, innumerable small cars.

"They don't even know how to drive," Inge says. "What are they doing? Can't you pass?

"Oh, come on," she says. She reaches across him to blow the horn.

"No use doing that," Malcolm says.

Inge blows it again.

"They can't move."

"Oh, they make me furious," she cries.

Two children in the car ahead have turned around. Their faces are pale and reflective in the small rear window.

"Have you been to Sitges?" Inge says.

"Cadaques."

"Ah," she says. "Yes. Beautiful. There you have to know someone with a villa."

The sun is white. The land lies beneath it the color of straw. The road runs parallel to the coast past cheap bathing beaches, campgrounds, houses, hotels. Between the road and the sea is the railroad with small tunnels built beneath it for bathers to reach the water. After a while this begins to disappear. They drive along almost deserted stretches.

"In Sitges," Inge says, "are all the blonde girls of Europe. Sweden, Germany, Holland. You'll see."

Malcolm watches the road.

"The brown eyes of the Spaniards are irresistible to them," she says.

She reaches across him to blow the horn.

"Look at them! Look at them crawling along!"

"They come here full of hopes," Inge says. "They save their money, they buy little bathing suits you could put in a spoon, and what happens? They get loved for one night, perhaps, that's all. The Spanish don't know how to treat women."

Nico is silent in the back. On her face is the calm expression which means she is bored.

"They know nothing," Inge says.

Sitges is a little town with damp hotels, the green shutters, the dying grass of a beach resort. There are cars parked everywhere. The streets are lined with them. Finally they find a place two blocks from the sea.

"Be sure it's locked," Inge says.

"Nobody's going to steal it," Malcolm tells her.

"Now you don't think it's so nice," she says.

They walk along the pavement, the surface of which seems to have buckled in the heat. All around are the flat, undecorated facades of houses built too close together. Despite the cars, the town is strangely vacant. It's two o'clock. Everyone is at lunch.

Malcolm has a pair of shorts made from rough cotton, the blue glazed cotton of the Tauregs. They have a little belt, slim as a finger, which goes only halfway around. He feels powerful as he puts them on. He has a runner's body, a body without flaws, the body of a martyr in a Flemish painting. One can see vessels laid like cord beneath the surface of his limbs. The cabins have a concrete back wall and hemp underfoot. His clothes hang shapeless from a peg. He steps into the corridor. The women are still undressing, he does not know behind which door. There is a small mirror hung from a nail. He smooths his hair and waits. Outside is the sun.

The sea begins with a sloping course of pebbles sharp as nails. Malcolm goes in first. Nico follows without a word. The water is cool. He feels it climb his legs, touch the edge of his suit and then with a swell— he tries to leap high enough—embrace him. He dives. He comes up smiling. The taste of salt is on his lips. Nico has dived, too. She emerges close by, softly, and draws her wetted hair behind her with one hand. She stands with her eyes half-closed, not knowing exactly where she is. He slips an arm around her waist. She smiles. She possesses a certain, sure instinct of when she is most beautiful. For a moment they are in serene dependence. He lifts her in his arms and carries her, helped by the sea, toward the deep. Her head rests on his shoulder. Inge lies on the beach in her bikini reading *Stern*.

"What's wrong with Inge?" he says.

"Everything."

"No, doesn't she want to come in?"

"She's having her period," Nico says.

They lie down beside her on separate towels. She is, Malcolm notices, very brown. Nico can never get that way no matter how long she stays outside. It is almost a kind of stubbornness as if he, himself, were offering her the sun and she would not accept.

She got this tan in a single day, Inge tells them. A single day! It seems unbelievable. She looks at her arms and legs as if confirming it. Yes, it's true. Naked on the rocks at Cadaques. She looks down at her stomach and in doing so induces it to reveal several plump, girlish rolls.

"You're getting fat," Nico says.

Inge laughs. "They are my savings," she says.

They seem like that, like belts, like part of some costume she is wearing. When she lies back, they are gone. Her limbs are clean. Her stomach, like the rest of her, is covered with a faint, golden down. Two Spanish youths are strolling past along the sea.

She is talking to the sky. If she goes to America, she recites, is it worthwhile to bring her car? After all, she got it at a very good price, she could probably sell it if she didn't want to keep it and make some money.

"America is full of Volkswagens," Malcolm says.

"Yes?"

"It's filled with German cars, everyone has one."

"They must like them," she decides. "The Mercedes is a good car."

"Greatly admired," Malcolm says.

"That's the car I would like. I would like a couple of them. When I have money, that will be my hobby," she says. "I'd like to live in Tangier."

"Quite a beach there."

"Yes? I will be black as an Arab."

"Better wear your suit," Malcolm says.

Inge smiles.

Nico seems asleep. They lie there silent, their feet pointed to the sun. The strength of it has gone. There are only passing moments of warmth when the wind dies all the way and the sun is flat upon them, weak but flooding. An hour of melancholy is approaching, the hour when everything is ended.

At six o'clock Nico sits up. She is cold.

"Come," Inge says, "we'll go for a walk up the beach."

She insists on it. The sun has not set. She becomes very playful.

"Come," she says, "it's the good section, all the big villas are there. We'll walk along and make the old men happy."

"I don't want to make anyone happy," Nico says, hugging her arms.

"It isn't so easy," Inge assures her.

Nico goes along sullenly. She is holding her elbows. The wind is from the shore. There are little waves now which seem to break in silence. The sound they make is soft, as if forgotten. Nico is wearing a grey tank suit with an open back, and while Inge plays before the houses of the rich, she looks at the sand.

Inge goes into the sea. Come, she says, it's warm. She is laughing and happy, her gaiety is stronger than the hour, stronger than the cold. Malcolm walks slowly in behind her. The water *is* warm. It seems purer as well. And it is empty, as far in each direction as one can see. They are bathing in it alone. The waves swell and lift them gently. The water runs over them, laving the soul.

At the entrance to the cabins the young Spanish boys stand around waiting for a glimpse if the shower door is opened too soon. They wear blue woolen trunks. Also black. Their feet appear to have very long toes. There is only one shower and in it a single, whitened tap. The water is cold. Inge goes first. Her suit appears, one small piece and then the other, draped over the top of the door. Malcolm waits. He can hear the soft slap and passage of her hands, the sudden shattering of the water on concrete when she moves aside. The boys at the door exalt him. He glances out. They are talking in low voices. They reach out to tease each other, to make an appearance of play.

The streets of Sitges have changed. An hour has struck which announces evening, and everywhere there are strolling crowds. It's difficult to stay together. Malcolm has an arm around each of them. They drift to his touch like horses. Inge smiles. People will think the three of them do it together, she says.

They stop at a café. It isn't a good one, Inge complains.

"It's the best," Nico says simply. It is one of her qualities that she can tell at a glance, wherever she goes, which is the right place, the right restaurant, hotel.

"No," Inge insists.

Nico seems not to care. They wander on separated now, and Malcolm whispers, "What is she looking for?"

"Don't you know?" Nico says.

"You see these boys?" Inge says. They are seated in another place, a bar. All around them, tanned limbs, hair faded from the long, baking afternoons, young men sit with the sweet stare of indolence.

"They have no money," she says. "None of them could take you to dinner. Not one of them. They have nothing. This is Spain," she says.

Nico chooses the place for dinner. She has become a lesser person during the day. The presence of this friend, this girl she casually shared a life with during the days they both were struggling to find themselves in the city, before she knew anybody or even the names of streets, when she was so sick that they wrote out a cable to her father together—they had no telephone—this sudden revelation of Inge seems to have deprived the past of decency. All at once she is pierced by a certainty that Malcolm feels contempt for her. Her confidence, without which she is nothing, has gone. The tablecloth seems white and dazzling. It seems to be illuminating the three of them with remorseless light. The knives and forks are laid out as if for surgery. The plates lie cold. She is not hungry but she doesn't dare refuse to eat. Inge is talking about her boyfriend.

"He is terrible," she says, "he is heartless. But I understand him. I know what he wants. Anyway, a woman can't hope to be everything to a man. It isn't natural. A man needs a number of women."

"You're crazy," Nico says flatly.

"It's true."

The statement is all that was needed to demoralize her. Malcolm is inspecting the strap of his watch. It seems to Nico he is permitting all this. He is stupid, she thinks. This girl is from a low background and he finds that interesting. She thinks because they go to bed with her they will marry her. Of course not. Never. Nothing, Nico thinks, could be farther from the truth, though even as she thinks she knows she may be wrong.

They go to Chez Swann for a coffee. Nico sits apart. She is tired, she says. She curls up on one of the couches and goes to sleep. She is exhausted. The evening has become quite cool.

A voice awakens her, music, a marvelous voice amid occasional phrases of the guitar. Nico hears it in her sleep and sits up. Malcolm and Inge are talking. The song is like something long-awaited, something she has been searching for. She reaches over and touches his arm.

"Listen," she says.

"What?"

"Listen," she says, "it's Maria Pradera."

"Maria Pradera?"

"The words are beautiful," Nico says.

Simple phrases. She repeats them, as if they were litany. Mysterious repetitions: dark-haired mother . . . dark-haired child. The eloquence of the poor, worn smooth and pure as a stone.

Malcolm listens patiently but he hears nothing. She can see it: he has changed, he has been poisoned while she slept with stories of a hideous Spain fed bit by bit until now they are drifting through his veins, a Spain devised by a woman who knows she can never be more than part of what a man needs. Inge is calm. She believes in herself. She believes in her right to exist, to command.

The road is dark. They have opened the roof to the night, a night so dense with stars that they seem to be pouring into the car. Nico, in the back, feels frightened. Inge is talking. She reaches over to blow the horn at cars which are going too slow. Malcolm laughs at it. There are private rooms in Barcelona where, with her lover, Inge spent winter afternoons before a warm, crackling fire. There are houses where they made love on blankets of fur. Of course, he was nice then. She had visions of the Polo Club, of dinner parties in the best houses.

The streets of the city are almost deserted. It is nearly midnight,

Sunday midnight. The day in the sun has wearied them, the sea has drained them of strength. They drive to General Mitre and say good night through the windows of the car. The elevator rises very slowly. They are hung with silence. They look at the floor like gamblers who have lost.

The apartment is dark. Nico turns on a light and then vanishes. Malcolm washes his hands. He dries them. The rooms seem very still. He begins to walk through them slowly and finds her, as if she had fallen, on her knees in the doorway to the terrace.

Malcolm looks at the cage. Kalil has fallen to the floor.

"Give him a little brandy on the corner of a handkerchief," he says.

She has opened the cage door.

"He's dead," she says.

"Let me see."

He is stiff. The small feet are curled and dry as twigs. He seems lighter somehow. The breath has left his feathers. A heart no bigger than an orange seed has ceased to beat. The cage sits empty in the cold doorway. There seems nothing to say. Malcolm closes the door.

Later, in bed, he listens to her sobs. He tries to comfort her but he cannot. Her back is turned to him. She will not answer.

She has small breasts and large nipples. Also, as she herself says, a rather large behind. Her father has three secretaries. Hamburg is close to the sea.

POETRY

Introduction

Tom Clark, the second of Donald Hall's recommendations for poetry editor (he had taken Hall's course in Yeats and Joyce at Michigan), was studying at Caius College, Cambridge on a Fulbright Scholarship when he was offered the job of poetry editor. From his predecessor, X. J. Kennedy, he inherited a file of "a hundred accepted poems from every English professor in America." The home office decided he could return these with a short, if profound, letter of apology, along with the excuse that a change of editors meant a change in the principles of selection. According to Clark "Two of the professors wrote me threatening letters."

Clark, allied with the so-called 10th Street poets, edited the poetry from the East Village until 1968. Married that year (at his wedding the poets David Shapiro, Dick Gallup, and Larry Fagin, all of whose poems he published in the magazine, performed the musical number "I Love You Truly"), he immediately moved to California, a move precipitated by a burglary and trashing of his apartment that took place during the wedding.

During the end of his tenure Clark became bored with his usual criteria for selection, and by his own admission began to accept poems coming in over the transom by poets who had never been published before or would be subsequently. In Clark's words he "wished to open it up a little." There was a certain amount of grumbling in the home office at publishing these curious things, but never any real pressure applied to make Clark abandon his methods of selection.

His own work is varied and prolix. His published volumes of poetry include *Fractured Karma, Disordered Ideas,* and *Easter Sunday.* He has written biographies of Jack Kerouac and Damon Runyan. His novels include *The Exile of Céline.* He has written extensively on the subject of baseball—in fiction, fact, and poetry.

—G.P.

* * *

I first met George Plimpton in Cambridge in September or October of 1963, in company with my friend, former teacher, and predecessor as poetry editor, Don Hall, and the late writer-thinker and "teleguided" genius Harold "Doc" Humes—all early shaping hands in the magazine. George took us to see E. M. Forster in his rooms at King's College, overlooking the Great Lawn and College Chapel. Forster—or "Morgan," as George, a former student at King's, amazingly got away with calling him—showed us recent European translations of his works, and even ran through his latest Yugoslavian royalty figures for our benefit. This visit to the great novelist's private chambers sticks in my mind because the only time I ever went back was also *Paris Review*–related. A few years later I was interviewing Allen Ginsberg in Cambridge for the magazine's "Art of Poetry" series. Allen demanded that we make a pilgrimage to Forster, whom, I guess, he considered the top literary honcho in town—sort of a "Take me to your leader" kind of thing. I was horrified at this request, because Allen was already in his finger-cymbals and deep-breathing phase, had a prophet's beard, had just been thrown out of Czechoslovakia by the secret police, and was, in my book, just *way* too all-around outrageous to be walking in on E. M. Forster. We went around to the venerable storyteller's rooms, but (to my great relief) he wasn't in. Allen did leave a cheery note for him, decorated with exploding sunflowers, third eyes, peace symbols, and skull-and-crossbones. I've always wondered what E. M. Forster made of that note.

Soon enough I became somewhat weird myself, and so (George being very tolerant) did the *Paris Review* poetry section. At the time, I considered the prevailing academic poetry of America, which had previously dominated the section, pretty dreary stuff. In its place I installed new poems that were more to my own taste, bringing into the magazine, over the early and middle years of the sixties, several groups of writers never before seen in the magazine, or, for that matter, anywhere else in the polite and elevated atmosphere of midcentury mainstream literary publications. In forcing this mutation upon the magazine's poetry section I was, of course, not picking writers out of thin air. They'd been around, some of them for quite a while. In came the so-called "Objectivist" poets: Lorine Niedecker, Louis Zukofsky, George Oppen, Carl Rakosi— all of whom seemed like news at the time, though some were nearly E. M. Forster's age. In came the "Black Mountain" writers: Charles Olson, Ed Dorn, John Wieners, Joel Oppenheimer (Robert Creeley, too, but he'd already had two poems in Issue 29); the New York poets: Edwin Denby, James Schuyler, John Ashbery, Frank O'Hara, Leroi Jones (Amiri Baraka), Barbara Guest, Kenneth Koch; the Beats and "San Francisco Renaissance" poets: Ginsberg, Gary Snyder, Robert Duncan, Philip Whalen, Joanne Kyger, Michael McClure. Used to being left out, it took some of these writers a little time to cotton to being let in, but before long the magazine was lucky enough to be getting from most of them not only new work, but in many cases the very best work they were doing—or had ever done.

The time I'm talking about was a very active and fertile one in American poetry. The poets named above were not only producing excellent work of their own but seeding a new poetic generation. Inspired by them, and by the socio-psychic electricity of the times, younger writers like Ed Sanders, Ted Berrigan, Ron Padgett, Anne Waldman, Dick Gallup, Aram Saroyan, Jim Carroll, Bill Berkson, Lewis MacAdams, John Giorno, and Clark Coolidge came forward to more or less take over the poetry section by 1970. During 1970–1974 I tried to open up the magazine to some interesting "unknowns" who would, I hoped, not only show the democratic diversity of talent that had arrived on the scene, but would give some hint as to what direction all that energy was going to take.

—Tom Clark

JOHN ASHBERY

The Bungalows

Impatient as we were for all of them to join us,
The land had not yet risen into view: gulls had swept the gray steel
    towers away
So that it profited less to go searching, away over the humming earth

Than to stay in immediate relation to these other things—boxes, store
    parts, whatever you call them—
Whose installedness was the price of further revolutions, so you knew
    this combat was the last.
And still the relationship waxed, billowed like scenery on the breeze.

They are the same aren't they,
The presumed landscape and the dream of home
Because the people are all homesick today or desperately sleeping,
Trying to remember how those rectangular shapes
Became so extraneous and so near
To create a foreground of quiet knowledge
In which youth had grown old, chanting and singing wise hymns that
Will sign for old age
And so lift up the past to be persuaded, and be put down again.

The warning is nothing more than an aspirate "h";
The problem is sketched completely, like fireworks mounted on poles:
Complexion of evening, the accurate voices of the others.
During Coca Cola lessons it becomes patent
Of noise on the left, and we had so skipped a stage that
The great wave of the past, compounded in derision,
Submerged idea and non-dreamer alike
In falsetto starlight like "purity"
Of design that had been the first danger sign
To wash the sticky, icky stuff down the drain—pfui!
How does it feel to be outside and inside at the same time,
The delicious feeling of the air contradicting and secretly abetting
The interior warmth? But the land curdles the dismay in which it's
    written
Bearing to a final point of folly and doom
The wisdom of these generations.
Look at what you've done to the landscape—
The ice-cube, the olive—
There is a perfect tri-city mesh of things
Extending all the way along the river on both sides
With the end left for thoughts on construction
That are always turning to alps and thresholds
Above the tide of others, feeding a European moss rose without glory.

We shall very soon have the pleasure of recording
A period of unanimous tergiversation in this respect

And to make that pleasure the greater, it is worth while
At the risk of tedious iteration, to put first upon record a final protest:
Rather decaying art, genius, inspiration to hold to
An impossible "calque" of reality, than
"The new school of the trivial, rising up on the field of battle,
Something of sludge and leaf-mold," and life
Goes trickling out through the holes, like water through a sieve,
All in one direction.

You who were directionless, and thought it would solve everything if
     you found one,
What do you make of this? Just because a thing is immortal
Is that any reason to worship it? Death, after all, is immortal.
But you have gone into your houses and shut the doors, meaning
There can be no further discussion.
And the river pursues its lonely course
With the sky and the trees cast up from the landscape
For green brings unhappiness—*le vert porte malheur.*
"The chartreuse mountain on the absinthe plain
Makes the strong man's tears tumble down like rain."

All this came to pass eons ago.
Your program worked out perfectly. You even avoided
The monotony of perfection by leaving in certain flaws:
A backward way of becoming, a forced handshake,
An absent-minded smile, though in fact nothing was left to chance.
Each detail was startlingly clear, as though seen through a magnifying
     glass,
Or would have been to an ideal observer, namely yourself—
For only you could watch yourself so patiently from afar
The way God watches a sinner on the path to redemption,
Sometimes disappearing into valleys, but always *on the way,*
For it all builds up into something, meaningless or meaningful
As architecture, because planned and then abandoned when
     completed,
To live afterwards, in sunlight and shadow, a certain amount of years.
Who cares about what was there before? There is no going back,
For standing still means death, and life is moving on,
Moving on towards death. But sometimes standing still is also life.

TED BERRIGAN

The Fiend

Red-faced and romping in the wind
I too am reading the technical journals, but
Keeping Christmas-safe each city block
With tail-pin. My angels are losing patience,
Never win. Except at night. Then
I would like a silken thread
Tied round the solid blooming winter.
Trees stand stark-naked guarding bridal paths;
The cooling wind keeps blowing, and
There is a faint chance in geometric boxes!
It doesn't matter, though, to show he is
Your champion. Days are nursed on science fiction
And you tremble at the boots upon the earth
As my strength and I walk out and look for you.

RICHARD BRAUTIGAN

The San Francisco Weather Report

Gee, You're so Beautiful That It's Starting to Rain

Oh, Marcia,
I Want your long blonde beauty
to be taught in high school,
so kids will learn that God
lives like music in the skin
and sounds like a sunshine harpsichord.
I want high school report cards
    to look like this:

Playing with Gentle Glass Things
   A

Computer Magic
   A

Writing Letters to Those You Love
   A

Finding out about Fish
   A

Marcia's Long Blonde Beauty
   A+!

JIM CARROLL

Heroin

Sat for three days in a white room
a tiny truck of white flowers
was driving through the empty window
to warn off your neighbors
and their miniature flashlights.

by afternoon
across the lake
a blind sportsman had lost his canoe.
He swam,
by evening
toward the paper cup
of my hand.

At dawn,
clever housewives tow my Dutch kitchen
across the lawn.

and in the mail a tiny circus
filled with ponies
had arrived.

You,
a woman with feathers
have come so often lately
under my rubber veranda,
that I'm tearing apart all those tactless warnings
embroidered across your forehead.

Marc,
I'm beginning to see those sounds
that I never even thought
I would hear.

Over there a door is knocking
for example
with someone you hate.
and here I beg another to possess somehow
the warmth of these wooden eyes

so beside me
a lightbulb is revolving
wall to wall,
a reminder of the great sun
which had otherwise completely collapsed
down to the sore toe of the white universe.

its chalky light
rings
like a garden of tiny vegetables
to gather the quiet of these wet feelings
together

once again

like the sound of a watch
on your cold white wrist
which is reaching for a particular moment
to reoccur . . .

which is here . . . now.

Tom Clark

Superballs

You approach me carrying a book
The instructions you read carry me back beyond birth
To childhood and a courtyard bouncing a ball
The town is silent there is only one recreation
It's throwing the ball against the wall and waiting
To see if it returns
One day
The wall reverses
The ball bounces the other way
Across this barrier into the future
Where it begets occupations names
This is known as the human heart a muscle
A woman adopts it it enters her chest
She falls from a train
The woman rebounds 500 miles back to her childhood
The heart falls from her clothing you retrieve it
Turn it over in your hand the trademark
Gives the name of a noted maker of balls

Elastic flexible yes but this is awful
You say
Her body is limp not plastic
Your heart is missing from it
You replace your heart in your breast and go on your way

CLARK COOLIDGE

Bee Elk

arch film duds
"Cheever" can aiming laps
dorm sieve

nor black   tugs toward colog
alight paramecium bloom ice
chigger geer dads
          block

but a prime buds
Keds nor slam up labs
sham a shatter
        puree

tins
    clock sauna
Coit ether

till sit mid sides
sign laughter
      Anthracite

    tea lure

ROBERT CREELEY

The Finger

Either in or out of
the mind, a conception
overrides it. *So that*
that time I was a stranger,

bearded, with clothes that were
old and torn. I was told,
it was known to me, my
fate would be timeless. Again

and again I was to
get it right, the story I
myself knew only the way of,
but the purpose if it

had one, was not mine.
The quiet shatter of the light,
the image folded into
endlessly opening patterns—

had they faced me into
the light so that my
eye was blinded? At moments
I knew they had gone but

searched for her face, the pureness
of its beauty, the endlessly sensual—
but no sense as that now reports it.
Rather, she was beauty, that
Aphrodite I had known of,
and caught sight of as *maid*—
a girlish openness—or known
as a woman turned from the light.

I knew, however, the other,
perhaps even more. She was there

in the room's corner, as she would be,
bent by a wind it seemed

would never stop blowing,
braced like a seabird,
with those endlessly clear grey eyes.
Name her, Athena—what name.

The osprey, the sea, the waves.
To go on telling the story,
to go on though no one hears it,
to the end of my days?

Mercury, Hermes, in dark glasses.
Talk to him—but as if
one talked to the telephone,
telling it to please listen—

is that right, have I said it—
and the reflecting face echoes
some cast of words in mind's eye
attention a whip of surmise.

And the power to tell
is glory. One unto one
unto one. And though all
mistake it, it is one.

I saw the stones thrown
at her. I felt a radiance transform
my hands and my face.
I blessed her, I was one.

Are there other times?
Is she that woman,
or this one. Am I the man—
and what transforms.

Sit by the fire.
I'll dance a jig I learned
long before we were born
for you and you only then.

I was not to go
as if to somewhere,
was not in the mind
as thinking knows it,

but danced in a jigging
intensive circle
before the fire and its heat
and that woman lounging.

How had she turned herself?
She was largely warm—
flesh heavy—and smiled
in some deepening knowledge

There are charms.
The pedlar and the small dog
following and the whistled,
insistent song.

I had the pack,
the tattered clothing,
was neither a man nor not one,
all that—

and who was she
with the fire behind her,
in the mess of that place,
the dust, the scattered pieces,

her skin so warm,
so massive, so stolid in her
smiling the charm did not
move her but rather

kept her half-sleepy attention,
yawning, indulging the manny
who jiggled a world before her
made of his mind.

She was young,
she was old,

she was small.
She was tall with

extraordinary grace. Her face
was all distance, her eyes
the depth of all one had thought of
again and again and again.

To approach, to hold her,
was not possible
She laughed and turned
and the heavy folds of cloth

parted. The nakedness
burned. Her heavy breath
her ugliness, her lust—
but her laughing, her low

chuckling laugh, the way
she moved her hand to the
naked breast, then to
her belly, her hand with its fingers.

Then *shone*—
and whatever is said
in the world, or forgotten,
or not said, makes a form.

The choice is simply,
I will—as mind is a finger,
pointing, as wonder
a place to be.

Listen to me, let
me touch you
there. You are young again,
and you are looking at me.

Was there ever
such foolishness more
than what thinks it knows
and cannot see, was there ever

more? Was the truth
behind us, or before?
Was it one
or two, and who was I?

She was laughing, she was
laughing at me
and I danced, and
I danced.

Lovely, lovely woman, let
me sing, *one to*
one to one, and let
me follow.

EDWIN DENBY

Sonnet

Roar drowns the reproach, facing him
Quite near, subway platform, she heeds
Head tossing slow like a pony's
In the wrong, the pinto I rode
A boy of twelve, that lovely head
Quarrels I believed riders win
White-haired pass these lovers in luck
Hurry to ballet, its invention
Where there's no quarrel, but there's fate
A scream unhurried of music's choice
And we recognize the games played
In heaven, foreknowing they cease
The move, the pitch arrive, turn to air
Here, as if love said forever

EDWARD DORN

The Poet Lets His Tongue Hang Down

A one-question interview from Bean News

I would enquire of you
The Slinger leaning forward askt
One of the 4 Great Questions
Least troubling my mind since my arrival:

WHO ARE THE BARBARIANS?

As if in a space elapsed
between our sighting then hearing a jet
The Poet grew pale
and his blaring transistor fell
from his Ivory Fingers
    four of whom
    jumped off at the knuckles
    and ran off with all his rings
    and straightway sent notes
    to the six who stayed
    expressing contempt and dismay
And the temperature fell in his veins
and his mouth weakened
and grew slack
and his left eye left the track
and wandered about the landscape
unlocused and his tongue
fell out over his chin
and his nose migrated
even as Gondwana too gorged
on the immensities of time to be observed
so that its movement is proven
by the striations of its slippage
as they are the scars of the Earth
And his ears floated upward
as if Helium was all they heard
and his feet came off and sped over the horizon
leaving even the wings of his ankles

and his shoes filled with dust
an instant ghost town complete
with banging shutters and peeling posters
of those of us wanted, dead or alive
Then his hair blew away
in a dust bowl condition
   like in the Grapes of Wrath
   and things what they were
   all the people of his barren scalp
   packed up and found their way to California
   around the craters of this once rich terrain,
And his brain snapped shut like a greasy spoon
when the last customer has et his chops
   then gone out the door wiping his chin
   with one hand while the other buys "The Times"
   which he reads standing on the corner
   toothpick in his mouth "Rams clobber Lions" in his eye
   and turns the pages to the comics where Rex Morgan
   is performing and can't be reached
   as his hand comes up from scratching his ass
   to catch the pages in the Michigan Winde
But the poet's Head was during this lapse
busy with alterations
and when the job was done
the bang of hammers
the whine of bandsaws gone
And all the baffling pulled off
his Head was a pyramid
the minimum solid

   And one of his eyes came home
trying to look like the trip had been a bore
when signs to the contrary were all over the floor
and he smiled
But the Eye on top of his pyramid
would say no more

Robert Duncan

Lammas Dream Poem

This is what comes of a Lammas Eve, tho I did not think of that at all this year until I had awakened at two in the night with the lines "My mother would be a falconress, And I a falcon at her wrist" being repeated insistently in my mind. I got up and took my notebook into the kitchen, for it would not let go. And when I wrote down the hour and date, I saw it was Lammas. "August 1, 1964," I wrote: "Lammas tide, 2 A.M." Then I remembered that George Stanley had told me that Saturn, my birth-planet, was particularly brilliant in the sky. "But that's between one-thirty and two in the morning," he said, "long after you are asleep."

There is a curious misplacement upward in the dream poem, for the bell which is actually attacht to a falcon's leg by a bewit just above the jess, in the dream becomes a set of bells sewn round the hood, a ringing of sound in the poet-bird's thought.

My mother would be a falconress,
and I, her gay falcon treading her wrist,
would fly to bring back
from the blue of the sky to her, bleeding, a prize,
where I dream in my little hood with many bells
jangling when I'd turn my head.

My mother would be a falconress,
and she sends me as far as her will goes.
She lets me ride to the end of her curb
where I fall back in anguish.
I dread that she will cast me away,
for I fall, I mis-take, I fail in her mission.

She would bring down the little birds.
And I would bring down the little birds.
When will she let me bring down the little birds?
pierced from their flight with their necks broken,
their heads like flowers limp from the stem?

I tread my mother's wrist and would draw blood.
Behind the little hood my eyes are hooded.

I have gone back into my hooded silence,
talking to myself and dropping off to sleep.

For she has muffled my dreams in the hood she has made me,
sewn round with bells, jangling when I move.
She uses a barb that brings me to cower.
She sends me abroad to try my wings
and I come back to her. I would bring down
the little birds to her
I may not tear into, I must bring back perfectly.

I tear at her wrist with my beak to draw blood,
and her eye holds me, anguisht, terrifying.
She draws a limit to my flight.
Never beyond my sight, she says.
She trains me to fetch and to limit myself in fetching.
She rewards me with meat for my dinner
but I must never eat what she sends me to bring her.

Yet it would have been beautiful, if she would have carried me,
always, in a little hood with the bells ringing,
at her wrist, and her riding
to the great falcon hunt, and me
flying up to the curb of my heart from her heart
to bring down the skylark from the blue to her feet,
straining, and then released for the flight.

My mother would be a falconress
and I her gerfalcon, raised at her will,
from her wrist sent flying, as if I were her own
pride, as if her pride
knew no limits, as if her mind
sought in my flight beyond the horizon.

Ah, but high, high in the air I flew.
And far, far beyond the curb of her will,
were the blue hills where the falcons nest,
and then I saw west to the dying sun,
It seemed my human soul went down in flames.

I tore at her wrist, at the hold she had for me,
until the blood ran hot and I heard her cry out,
far, far beyond the curb of her will

to horizons of stars beyond the ringing hills of the world where the
    falcons nest
I saw, and I tore at her wrist with my savage beak.
I flew, as if sight flew from the anguish in her eye beyond her sight,
sent from my striking loose, from the cruel strike at her wrist,
striking out from the blood to be free of her.

My mother would be a falconress,
and even now, years after this,
when the wounds I left her had surely heald,
and the woman is dead,
her fierce eyes closed, and if her heart
were broken, it is stilld;
I would be a falcon and go free.
I tread her wrist and wear the hood,
talking to myself, and would draw blood.

ALLEN GINSBERG

City Midnight Junk Strains

for Frank O'Hara

Switch on lights yellow as the sun
                       in the bedroom . . .
The gaudy poet dead   Frank O'Hara's bones
                       under squares of grass
An emptiness at 8 PM in the Cedar Bar
        Throngs of drunken
           guys talking about paint
      & lofts, and Pennsylvania youth.
           Klein attacked by his heart
& chattering Frank
        stopped forever—
Faithful drunken adorers, mourn.
          The busfare's a nickel more
           past his old apartment on 9th Street by the park.
Delicate Peter loved his praise,

I wait for the things he says
                about me—
Did he think me an Angel
as angel I am still talking into earth's microphone
                    willy nilly
        —to come back as words ghostly hued
                    by early death
    but written so bodied
            mature in another decade.
Chatty prophet
        of yr own loves, personal
        memory feeling fellow
    Poet of building-glass
I see you walking as you said with your tie
flopped over your shoulder   in the wind down 5th Avenue
            under the handsome breasted workmen
                on their scaffolds ascending Time
                    & washing the windows of Life
    —off to a date with Martinis & a blond
                beloved poet far from home
                    —with thee and Thy sacred Metropolis
        in the enormous bliss   of a long afternoon
        where death is the shadow
                cast by Rockefeller Center
                    over your intimate street.
Who were you, black suited, hurrying to meet,
        Unsatisfied one?
                Unmistakable,
                    Darling date
for the charming solitary/ young poet with a big cock
            who could fuck you all night long
                    till you never came,
        trying your torture on his/ obliging fond body
        eager to satisfy god's whim that made you
                Innocent, as you are.
I tried/ your boys and found them ready
        sweet and amiable
            collected gentlemen
                with large sofa apartments
lonesome to please   for pure language;
and you mixed with money
                because you knew language enough to be rich
                    If you wanted your walls to be empty—

deep philosophical terms for Edwin Denby serious as Herbert Read
with silvery hair   announcing   your dead gift
to the crowd   whose greatest op art   frisson
was the new sculpture   your big blue wounded body
            made in the Universe
      when you went away   to Fire Island for the weekend
tipsy with a crowd of decade-olden friends
Peter stares out the window   at the robbers
      distracted   in Amphetamine
and I stare into my head   & look for your/ broken roman nose
            your wet mouth-smell of martinis
                  & a big artistic tipsy kiss.
40's only half a life   to have filled
            with so many fine parties and evenings'
            interesting drinks together with one
                  faded friend or new
                  understanding social cat
I want to be there in your garden party in the clouds
            all of us naked
strumming our harps and reading each other   new poetry
            in the boring celestial
                  friendship Committee Museum.
You're in a bad mood?
            Take an Asprin.
            In the dumps?
                  I'm falling asleep
                        safe in your thoughtful arms.
Someone uncontrolled by History would have to own Heaven,
                  on earth as it is.
I hope you satisfied your childhood love
Your puberty fantasy   your sailor punishment on your knees
                        your mouth-suck
Elegant insistency
                  on the honking self-prophetic Personal
                  as Curator of funny emotions to the mob,
Trembling one, whenever possible.   I see New York thru your eyes
            and hear of one funeral a year nowadays
                  From Billie Holliday's time
            appreciated more and more
      a common ear
                  for our deep gossip.

                                          —*July 29, 1966*

LEROI JONES (AMIRI BARAKA)

Tele/vision

In the beginning of my love wild hearts and trees. Greenness. The waves
at the end of the street. Dynamite proposals. To be a man,
or a white thing crawling through nuns' dreams. In
the beginning of my heart we walked and rode
motorcycles into each other, killing each other,
fucked japs, in the beginning, and were sammy davis
for allen ginsberg's frank sinatra. the beginning,
of the alien. of the path back to my self. the cold
illinois skeletons of doestoevsky. in the track crossing,
in the movie feeling (that's saturday evening culture
for the blind). I hurt myself. I struck and stabbed
and wounded my own gentle flesh. I began. This sliding
talking pictures of old relatives sudden heroes who were
dead spitos of the winded-up-leroy heading down belmont avenue
thinking he was grey. James Edward's nose was too ugly hunched open
like that. And the other dude, the doctor, calling him dirty names
invisible kike of the mind. In the beginning I was not born but plotted.
They came north to make me. Brain sparks and the cold cinder wheel.
Sharpened. Remembering. African dances for tarzan, until the jungle
     pots
boil darkness and the hot sun fashions it into black heroes. Run out of
the south, from falling down wells, from cursing in my sleep, and the
     dead
fall through the space "of all endeavour." Bullshit, I limped along with
the rest of the niggers, and was beautiful then to invisible greys. They
found me, found each at the end of the long slaughter house. Who will
     save
the jesusnigger? Who will come back smiling and licking him silent
     knowledge.
Who will be the final coming attraction and beautiful character actor of
my bonafide creation? The me's of it. The strong I's. Yell. They.
     CRAAAAAA
AYYYYYYYYYYYYYYYYVE to good faith blessing. Ahhh. The
     nature.
The smell. I am whole.

I am whole.

KENNETH KOCH

The Interpretation of Dreams

I

You are my Sweetheart
Sang the tin can
I was sitting on a truck
As it rolled along
You are my Truck
Sang my Sweetheart
Somehow it was menacing
An ominous song
I hardly knew what to say I went into the truck
It was amazing
That autumn afternoon, when every affection came unsought
As from an unstoppered lute and a glass of campari
Was downed from a shimmering glass and quickly as if nothing
Could harm the eternal beaver any more. But a policeman of high
    reflection
Suddenly stood up for the traffic crossings' protection
And were we sad, lost in thought at our newfound abortionlessness
In stages, because of a green kerchief stuck in your pocket
As one asks What's the difference between that and a handkerchief?
    and
Between each stop and its parenthesis? Let's assume we have too much
And pound on the marble table top. It has always gone best that way
Yet you're thinking (I think) "Yet the hand falls off
And the streets of Paris will continue to go every which way.
No, in spite of your palaver
And a summertime gift for describing the rose
You will have to take me into another valley
Where reality is not affliction." Or if you did not think that all at once
Toward that our thoughts have been gathering. Whose omnibus is that
    parked outside the S. S. Rose
With a Himalayan flagboy in the window of the car
Scratching his initials A.H., A.H., as the winter evening dies
And turns into a springtime fogbound morning? I was sleeping in the
    hay

When we awoke. One could just barely make out the sky. A truck
    raced past.
Then I realized where we were. It was potato season. And, Spiff! this
    season was to be our last
Before we dangled before tomatoes, hard red ones and yellow yummy
Tomatoes and huge hard pink ones which were brighter than the nose
Of Snow White in Walt Disney's fiction. I am going into slaveland
To help these tomatoes get free, but they come thumping
After. "Wait for us! Wait! You will see! It is impossible to serve us
    unless we are there!"
And the tomatoes turned into apples. I was wide awake. The cook said,
    "You are my Sweetheart."
And a band played "The Abortion of the Sleeper may be the Swan
    Song of the Sheep-Man's Heart."

2

Into this valley my sweetheart came
The tomatoes were hard as her nose
She was available exactly
Five minutes every afternoon
Then she took Snow White
Into the kidney parlor
She said "Snow White, be an actress!"
And Snow White implored the yellow movies
To be more reasonable about Al Capp
"He's a swell guy"
We know we know
But he's not purple anymore
A large picture flew through the sky
My Sweetheart put on it
"I am the Capostranni of the Rose"
And William Butler Yeats died
When Auden wrote the poem
About the deftness of the steamship
Plying through the harbor
Is my Sweetheart's nose.

3

Meanwhile Snow White and her boyfriend
Have gone up into the mountains.
It is amazing what they will do for a game of bingo!

No! That is not what they are doing. Look!
They are making love! I didn't know that was allowed in the movies
In this country! But that must be what they are doing!
She is lying beneath him and every time his body rose
I saw her fingerprints gripping the dust like the U.S.S. Idaho
In an old story. Do you know the one of the Frightening Fidget?
Well, in this one old Doctor Barnose
Is riding along through Italy on a great white highway
Made of marshmallows, when some greensuited policemen come out
And make him stop to show his passport, which he had had made out
     of clothes
As a modern novelty, but they threw him in the purple prison,
Where like an Italianate tirade of grapejuice something exists to this
     day
Numbered among the aquanauts who saved this country
From being bombed by the submarines which I purchased you for my
     birthday
In one of my most powerful moods, on the Pomeranian coast.

                              4

The gasoline must come to a halt, as the great apple shipments have
     done.

The true Advisor to the lesser party will not permit the Eczema to come
Into the park of Dutiful Silence. This is an Order imposed by Law.

The Marlene Dietrich suitcases are not to be opened
Except by the pink hands of the Prelate in charge of the bombing.
(Cardinal Spellman, I am dreaming of you! I am seeing your plumpness
     insulted by bombs!
And then I am seeing the grass-green acne of the trends.)
In charge of fishes Israel is put; in charge of Packaging, Summer.
(I am sorry, Winslow Homer, that you did not get this job,
And you, yearning seminarians of our Hungarian Pall Mall,
But it is a direct icing I get, and not a "forwarded," from the Divine.)

And now I think it is time to cut out Music.

                              5

The musicians are viciously bald. They will not listen to the music
Whether it is good or bad. They say, "Oklahoma has taken the best
     music.

And then Snow White. We have nothing left."
They laugh, the musicians, at their own sorrow.
But at least the music has stopped.
I hated the music, it was always resounding in the ears
Like a broken fiddle. I am glad you have imposed on them to stop.
It was of their own free will, like the other decisions
They have made, like which fish to have on Wednesday
And how to catch mackerel without a rod. I am tired now of "not
    hearing" the music
In such a lively way. Can we go down to the harbor?
In the harbor everything was a bad job.
The courts were out of work and the community centers were filled
    with people
Eating pastry-cakes shaped like sheets of music. "All those good pies," I
    said,
"Being wasted like a nuthouse." And I run rampant.
I rock around smashing everything I could find.
They had destroyed my darling and I was going to ruin them as well.
Then struck the clock. It was the time of the oyster and the octopus.
I walked out of the fishstore with a prayer.
The universe was ringing with a song.

6

Snow White had brought the music back.

7

The yoyo capitalists are filled
By the pastry which tyrants heat
On Mediterranean ovens.
You now feel that you will never understand;
But it is about to open, becoming easy
As one may say "Ah!" at the sight of a pink island
Or a tremendous pink apple which is of a different kind
From every other apple one has ever tasted
And as Snow White
Who had an island pedigree in black and white
Came ravished when in colors.

A new hydrofoil has started
To invent the sea. And when the sea comes in
The birthday poem is finished and a nude start begins

On some fantastic island—"Fantastic island?" I'll never question you
    any more.
But sexuality is not all, even though it is beautiful
As Moravian gusts. One also needs a spellbinding heart
And a lethal spelling book, which gives the Seminole report.

"I'm in love with apples,"
The old seminarian says.
But the young Arethusa knows better:
"Alpheus is in love with me."

8

Oh American homerun hitter! your balls! your balls!
They are sailing over our trees
And when they land
We feel we pick up a killer
Oh American homerun hitter
Dressed in white tie and tails!

And you smote your guitar
Good cousin Jute with a loud report.
"This is America! This is the Capitalist country
Where witnesses write on the trees
And black meets white
In a catapult, blast, and explosion. It is not Nude Island."
"So what?" said the caterpillar, and
"So what?" whispered the trees. From every direction the
    "so-whatters" came running
To compel him to retain his distance.
The porkchop and the shark said
"If you come too close to us, we die.
Remember the speech of the living.
And welcome back to Thorax Island."

Then a picture of Snow White completely blocked out the sky.

9

And I was with you again
But we were going in different directions.
We met and started to go in the same direction.
Then once more our paths crossed and we met again

Under the believable blue of a traffic light where we had first met
The village coconut who had forbidden our meetings
But now we meet all the time.
"You go this way and I'll go that,
And when we head back we will meet
And declare our love."

This is the foundation of the emotions.
The sky is our parade ground and our glove.
The fish in the bay are the slaves of their time and not of art
But somehow our emotions can become their emotions.
This is the beginning of Realism. This is the end of the ideal.
This is the degree of front and back.

LORINE NIEDECKER

Who Was Mary Shelley

Who was Mary Shelley?
What was her name
before she married?

She eloped with Shelley,
she rode a donkey
till the donkey had to be carried.

Mary was Frankenstein's creator
his yellow eye
before her husband was to drown.

Created Frankenstein nights
after Byron, Shelley
talked the candle down.

Who was Mary Shelley?
She read Latin, Greek, Italian.
She bore a child

who died
and yet another child
who died.

FRANK O'HARA

A True Account of Talking to the Sun at Fire Island

The Sun woke me this morning loud
and clear, saying "Hey! I've been
trying to wake you up for fifteen
minutes. Don't be so rude, you are
only the second poet I've ever chosen
to speak to personally
                              so why
aren't you more attentive? If I could
burn you through the window I would
to wake you up. I can't hang around
here all day."
                         "Sorry, Sun, I stayed
up late last night talking to Hal."

"When I woke up Mayakovsky he was
a lot more prompt" the Sun said
petulantly. "Most people are up
already waiting to see if I'm going
to put in an appearance."
                                    I tried
to apologize "I missed you yesterday."
"That's better" he said "I didn't

know you'd come out. You may be
wondering why I've come so close?"
"Yes" I said beginning to feel hot
wondering if maybe he wasn't burning me
anyway.
       "Frankly I wanted to tell you
I like your poetry. I see a lot
on my rounds and you're okay. You may
not be the greatest thing on earth, but
you're different. Now, I've heard some
say you're crazy, they being excessively
calm themselves to my mind, and other
crazy poets think you're a boring
reactionary. Not me.
                    Just keep on
like I do and pay no attention. You'll
find that people always will complain
about the atmosphere, either too hot
or too cold too bright or too dark, days
too short or too long.
                    If you don't appear
at all one day they think you're lazy
or dead. Just keep right on, I like it.

And don't worry about your lineage
poetic or natural. The Sun shines on
the jungle, you know, on the tundra
the sea, the ghetto. Whatever you were
I knew it and saw you moving. I was waiting
for you to get to work.
                    And now that you
are making your own days, so to speak,
even if no one reads you but me
you won't be depressed. Not
everyone can look up, even at me. It
hurts their eyes."
                    "Oh Sun, I'm so grateful to you!"

"Thanks and remember I'm watching. It's
easier for me to speak to you out
here. I don't have to slide down

between buildings to get your ear.
I know you love Manhattan, but
you ought to look up more often.
                                    And
always embrace things, people earth
sky stars, as I do, freely and with
the appropriate sense of space. That
is your inclination, known in the heavens
and you should follow it to hell, if
necessary, which I doubt.
                              Maybe we'll
speak again in Africa, of which I too
am especially fond. Go back to sleep now
Frank, and I may leave a tiny poem
in that brain of yours as a farewell."

"Sun, don't go!" I was awake
at last. "No, go I must, they're calling
me."
        "Who are they?"
                              Rising he said "Some
day you'll know. They're calling to you
too." Darkly he rose, and then I slept.

CHARLES OLSON

Maximus from Dogtown-II

the Sea—turn yr Back on
the Sea, go inland, to
Dogtown: the Harbor

the shore the City
are now
shitty, as the Nation

is—the World
tomorrow unless
the Princes

of the Husting the sons
who refused to be Denied
the Demon (if Medea

kills herself—Medea
is a Phoenician
wench, also Daughter

of the Terror) as J-son
Johnson Hines
son Hines

sight Charles
John Hines
Ol'
      son

the Atlantic
Mediterranean
Black Sea time

is done in done for gone
Jack Hammond
put a stop to

surface underwater galaxy
time: there is no sky
space or sea left

earth is interesting
ice is interesting
stone is interesting

flowers are
         Carbon
Carbon is
Carboniferous
Pennsylvania

Age
under
Dogtown
the stone

the watered
rock Carbon
flowers, rills

Aquarian Time
after fish
—fish was

Christ o Christ pick the seeds
out of yr teeth—how handsome
the dead dog lies! (horror X

the Migma is where
Seeds Christ was supposed to pick out
:Wyngacrshock hoik Grape Vine HOYK the Dutch

& the Norse
and Algonquins:
He-with-the-House-on-his-Head

she-who-Lusted After-the
Snake-in-the-Pond
Dogtown berries smell

as The-Grub-Eaten-Fish-Take-The-Smell-Out-Of-The
Air   a   e   r the Ta of
Dogtown (the Ta metarsia

is the Angel Matter
not to come until (rill!
3000; we will carry water

up the hill the Water the Water to
make the Flower hot—Jack
& Jill will

up Dogtown hill on top one day the
Vertical American thing will
show from Heaven the ladder

come down to the Earth
of Us All, the Many who
know
     there is One!
     One Mother
     One Son

One Daughter
and Each the Father
of Him-Her-Self:

the Genetic
is Ma the Morphic
is Pa the City is Mother

     Polis, the Child-Made-Man-Woman is

(Mary's Son
Elizabeth's
Man) MONOGENE:
          in COLLAGEN
the monogene,   in Kollagen

               LEAP onto
               the LAND, the AQUARIAN
               TIME
the greater the water you add
the greater the decomposition
so long as the agent is protein
the carbon of four is the corners

in stately motion to sing in high bitch voice the fables
of wood and stone and man and woman loved

and loving in the snow
and sun
          the weather

on Dogtown
is protogonic but the other side of heaven
is Ocean

filled in the flower the weather
on Dogtown the other side of heaven
is Ocean

Dogtown the *under*
vault heaven
is Carbon Ocean   Dogtown the *under*
is Annisquam   vault—the 'mother'
                         rock: the Diamond (Coal) the Pennsylvanian

                                        Age   the soft
                                              (Coal) LOVE

Age the soft (Coal love
hung-up burning
under the City: bituminous

Heart to be turned to Black
Stone   the Black Chrysanthemum
is the Throne of Creation   Ocean

                is the Black Gold Flower

Ron Padgett

Big Bluejay Composition

Compositions in harmony

the sunlight rods over the Commuter's Spa

                bluejay

                                        oh

I don't want to go in and watch Gene Tierney on tv moonlight

when   the shadow of a doubt

        tiptoes down the hall

                crumpled tossed in wastebasket

Rainbow Colored Pencils made by Eberhard Faber maker of Mongols

ie Children of Paradise

                gray line wiggle

    a large permanent flinch

  just under the skin then

She turned to me   in the flying starlight

in the   in the

  tiny as a (there are no straight lines in a curve) breeze

breeze curving

     moonlight

       when the m-moon shines
       over the cow's shit

                bzzzzzzzzz

              bzzzz

the square of the sum
    of two .flashing. numbers   from the now on bzzz

suddenly the onions replaced the onusphere

    —to leon the counterpoint—   and Tommie Vardeman
    stuck his

head out the door a very old auto racer

gray wearing glasses

bluejay

sweet as stops

I catch my breath   I cry (cont. p. 42)

of planetary music

heard in trance

well the figurine of the bluejay

1/2 in the dimensional side of God

the earth is still———

. . . stars . . . stars . . .

God is in a trance, now's the time to compose a few
immortal lines

re's the immortal paper?

e immortal brain?   star

we go trot

trot-trot

past the abattoir

sliding 1968 sliding
_____

under the beauty of

broken thunder

he goes over center

k-boom   softness is northern
              alert

                    alarming

the north,

le même nord où la mission Albert agonise maintenant parmi
    les cristaux

that is the wild blue yonder

screwed onto a bolt from the blue

                    magnetic,

the pursuit of Hedonism emerges boink from unwrinkled
    clouds

while . . . trumpets . . . Haloed, long pause

          from across the ocean long pause

              came gunshot

a piece of rain fell and hit the horizon

              Slowly I turned . . .

behind us loomed the awesome figure of the gigantic baked enamel ape,
which Professor Morrison had, with fanatical patience, constructed over
the years.

                              A bluejay

Tennessee raised in the dark

to the highest power

                    Tennessee is the n it made

I have spoken

— — — —

I am speaking

like a sunset going down

behind

the rising dawn

to ♪ ot   mother,

Remember me   in your semi-conscious prayers   hit the
brakes

when the dew is glistening on the bluejay

and I go walkie to nightmare school

and the refinery is blasting away

Process and Reality   on this damp, foolish evening

bl   here

the future
casts a pall bearer on the present—in the future the present
will be

a thing of the past   losing altitude

You shake

No

your head No

the smell of coffee on a morning the smell of hot coffee on a

winter's morning

the table is set in the breakfast room frost on the windows
sunlight

              lock into which Mr. Morrison is inserting his key
floods the hardware store ∧ the black and white cereal box the
      porcelain

the fresh peaches the milk +

Now our mighty battleships will steam the bounding main

                    people jetting along

a symphony of tweets

                          the light of the Eternal Flame
                          clearly visible

from where you sit

in those great, golden heights   no doggie
                                     in the neighborhood

    all the doggies have gone off to war to be male nurses

the moonlight on the earthquake

        into which many doggies fell

      plunged fiery and screaming

                                        in their machines

          . . .

gravely   the Statue of Liberty

turned and faced the nation, finally!

a medium-sized flesh-colored male sexual organ extending

from its inner ear,

"The period in history termed Modern is now over" it said

                                        –CLICK–

the bluejay fluttered on its shoulder

"Y-you'd b-b-better b-b-believe it!" it cried wildly

CARL RAKOSI

The Founding of New Hampshire

A slender plank above a waterhole,
planted on end to meet my wants,
I hear its whisper in the stock.
It does not sway a hair's breadth.
Another stake driven in and well shaved
points against the light from the layout,
                              poor pointing.
The maple fits upon the joist like a flower,
                              a picked beam,

a great wood to plane and saw.
I tell my wife the walls are up,
the strips nailed at snug right angles,
              the floors are oiled.
The Yankee poles are almost columns.

Braced against a gloomy magnitude,
I loiter civil on my soles and buffeted,
killing time in these traditions.
Are the woodsmells getting sweeter,
or the broker working at my back,
so that all the concord in my timber
can not warm this house.

ED SANDERS

The leaves of heaven
are ever greene,
& the leaves of the
soul are Sere
& cold

I have failed
my mother
& she has
failed me

Everything about
a human
is doomed
his life, his
things, his
hope, his
work—

The pallbearer
barfs on the
diaper

The phantoms,
The phantoms,
what to do
about the
phantoms?

kiss a hot
wet lightbulb

ARAM SAROYAN

a man stands
on his
head one
minute—

then he
sit
down all
different

JAMES SCHUYLER

Buried at Springs

There is a hornet in the room
and one of us will have to go
out the window into the late
August mid-afternoon sun. I
won. There is a certain challenge
in being humane to hornets
but not much. A launch draws
two lines of wake behind it
on the bay like a delta
with a melted base. Sandy
billows, or so they look,
of feathery ripe heads of grass,
an acid-yellow kind of
goldenrod glowing or glowering
in shade. Rocks with rags
of shadow, washed dust clouts
that will never bleach.

It is not like this at all.
The rapid running of the
lapping water, a hollow knock
of someone shipping oars,
it's eleven years since
Frank sat at this desk and
saw and heard it all:
the incessant water the
immutable crickets only
not the same: new needles
on the spruce, new seaweed
on the lowtide rocks,
other grass and other water
even the great gold lichen
on a granite boulder
even the boulder quite
literally is not the same

II

A day, subtle and suppressed
in mounds of juniper enfolding
scratchy pockets of shadow
while bigness—rocks, trees, a stump—
stand shadowless in an overcast
of ripe grass. There is nothing
but shadiness, like the boggy depths
of a stand of spruce, its resonance
just the thin scream
of mosquitoes ascending.
Boats are light lumps on the bay
stretching past erased islands
to ocean and the terrible tumble,
and London ("rain persisting")
and Paris ("changing to rain").
Delicate day, setting the bright
of a young spruce against the cold
of an old one hung with unripe cones
each exuding at its tip
gum, pungent, clear as a tear,
a day stained and fractured
as the quartz in ribbons in the rocks

of a dulled and distant point,
a day like a gull passing
slowly flapping its wings
in a kind of lope, a day without
breeze enough to shake loose
the last fireweed flowers,
a faintly clammy day, like wet silk,
stained by one dead branch
the harsh russet of dried blood.

GARY SNYDER

Hop, Skip, & Jump

for Jim and Annie Hatch

    the curvd lines toe-drawn, round cornerd squares
bulge out doubles from its single pillar line, like,
Venus of the Stone Age.
she takes stone,
with a white quartz band for her lagger.
                        she
   takes a brown-stained salt sticky cigarette
                butt.
he takes a mussel shell. he takes a clamshell. she takes
a stick.
he is tiny, with a flying run & leap
shaggy blond—misses all the markers,
               tumbles from one foot.
           they are dousing
a girl in a bikini down the beach
          first with cold seawater
        then with wine.
  double-leg single-leg stork stalk turn

on the end-square—hop, fork, hop, scoop the marker,
  we have all trippt and fallen.
   surf rough and full of kelp,
  all the ages—
draw a line on another stretch of sand—
      and—
       everybody try
to do the hop, skip, and jump.

          4. X. 1964—Muir Beach

LORENZO THOMAS

Displacement

I

To a lotus beaming in the grime

Behind the house,

The light is very clear

The parasol is painted

We moving
Guy at the
Wheel sd
"I see
They got it
Finished" But
Nothing is
Finished.

Every day someone returns
To the field

Before his wanting becomes a rainbow
He must pause.

The waters rise up
In a dull sheaf

As if miracles were due

But it is only
The harvest;
Only the buffalo's bulk
In the water,
The new figure of Buddha beside the road
Between Phu Xuan and Tan Thuan Dong
Shivering in the cold
Flood of vast brown sky

II

Wish you were heir
To more naturalness
Than simple lust
For daily bread and restaurants
Where the waiters
Still speak French

Wish you could hear more
In the dark

More than crickets
Your grandfather's cough
Or the songs of
The little fishes

Listen. This is modern times all over the world

Go sit under a tree.

Who studies the physics
Of nonentities?

A facsimile becoming a disguise

Who is not supposed to be reading
This postcard

I am pleased to surprise the people
Any afternoon
And those who do not
Care to understand
That I know. You know.

Everywhere it is the same thing
Only different.
High officials
Flash by
Hostaged in their
Entourage.

She told me I'm glad
We are not important
We can go walk around
And sit in cheap
Cafés by the road

Saigon, VNCH 1971

ANNE WALDMAN

Warming Up

to Kenneth Koch

It's so cold in here I can't do anything

All night on the phone talking to cold people
who remind you how cold you are

It's pretty boring

But then freezing brings us all together

Like the death of someone you know and love
or the almost death

depending how it looks to you

Pretty convincing!

when someone's holding a gun to your forehead

That's certainly not boring

In fact, it might even stir you to action!

I think I'll just stay frozen a while until this moment passes.

There, it's gone.

But it's still pretty cold in here

I've even turned on the oven

Some people I know don't even have an oven

Think of that!

Some people don't even have heat

Like dead people.

We get heat sometimes when the landlady's cold,
which doesn't seem to be right now, 1 A.M.

Maybe she's dead!

I think I'll give her a call.

No, I don't think I will.

I'll just sit here and think about California, or Rome
or some other pretty hot places I've been.

New York City can get pretty hot, come to think of it

So hot sometimes you're wishing for winter

And here it is!

JOHN WIENERS

The Spoiled Son

I have built a world for myself
slowly, and without design
of flowers and paintings from other times,

Out of buttons and gold frames,
smiling faces of poets.
I have ignored the coughs of my parents

from darkened rooms; and within
I have erected structures that withstand time.
I walk there in frozen sunlight.

Arrange books and hold conversations with angels.
I tempt young men
and plan festivities far overseas.

I hear doors open and close;
I do not go near them
but wait for the world to disclose

New arrangements, new order of flowers,
new mail to open. My sister hears
the conversations I hold and walks away

with the moon in her arms. I do not trail after
but accept the footstep on the stair,
the whisper in the dark,

the new arriving of innumerable cracklings in the night.

NONFICTION

Introduction

A series that was in the *Paris Review* from the start were interviews with famous writers on their craft. One of the early ideas was that, while it would be difficult to elicit original material from established authors—the magazine could hardly afford to pay for their work—it might be possible to get them to talk about writing in an interview. Their names would appear on the cover. That would help sales and subscriptions. Furthermore, in an Age of Criticism when so many magazines were devoted to explanations and exegesis of contemporary texts, the notion was to skip the indirect approach and seek out the authors in person to see what *they* had to say.

The magazine was fortunate that during its planning stages in 1952 I was studying at King's College, Cambridge where a great literary person-age resided—E. M. Forster, "Morgan" as everyone, both students and faculty, called him—a somewhat rumpled, shy personage who lived in rooms overlooking the Great Lawn of the college and was then consid-ered the greatest living novelist in the English language (*Passage to India, Howard's End,* and so forth) though in fact he had not published a novel since 1924. At the time he was working on an opera with Benja-min Britten *(Billy Budd)* and he would ask undergraduates, "What . . . um . . . do you know about writing operas?"

That was very much in the tradition of the college—that intellectual curiosity was shared among those within its walls, whatever their reputation or age. Typically, Forster took an interest in the *Paris Review*. He was told of the plans to limit criticism in the magazine, and if a contemporary author was to be the subject, the hope was to interview him first-hand rather than relying on an interpretive study. In fact, would Forster agree to be the first interviewee?

He agreed and the interview, which was conducted by P. N. Furbank and F. J. H. Haskell, one writing down the answers in pencil while the other concentrated on the questions (tape recorders were still a few years away), was a feature in the first issue of the *Paris Review*. In it Forster talked about the problems that made it difficult for him to write fiction, namely what he called "fiction technicalities." The form of the interview established that of subsequent interviews—conducted with over one hundred and fifty novelists, poets, essayists, and biographers to date—many of these compiled in eight volumes entitled *Writers at Work*.

The length of the interviews increased over the years as the series grew in prominence and writers found it a distinguished forum in which to talk about themselves and their work. E. M. Forster's interview was twelve pages in length; Elie Wiesel, the Nobel Prize winner, had valuable things to say for forty-six pages. James Laughlin, the publisher of *New Directions*, became so involved in his interview that it spilled over into the following issue.

The range of topics in the interviews is wide—everything from what kind of instrument the author uses to write with (the prototypical *Paris Review* question) to far weightier subjects such as the moral responsibility of the literary community.

Many of the interviews have been published in book form in a series entitled *Writers at Work*. Eight volumes have appeared. A kind of compendium has been planned entitled *The Writer's Chapbook*. Its purpose is to focus on subject rather than author—namely, a reorganization under various headings (Plot, Character, Working Habits, Writers' Block, and so forth). Readers will be saved the effort of pushing their way through a hundred-odd numbers of the magazine to find out what authors had to say about a particular issue.

The topic ("Portraits") picked for the following excerpts is more general than most in the *Chapbook*. Often those being interviewed produced short and lively descriptions of their contemporaries; these seemed more appropriate for this anthology.

—G.P.

Portraits

MAXWELL BODENHEIM

He was a fascinating talker, in spite of the stammer, and he knew everybody. He was a great friend of Bill Williams. You must have heard the story of his broken arm? He called up Williams at Rutherford and said, "I've broken my arm. Can I come and stay with you till it heals?" Bill said, "Certainly." About a month or two went by and Max did nothing about having the cast examined or changed, so finally Bill insisted on looking at it and discovered that there had never been any broken arm.

—Conrad Aiken

BRENDAN BEHAN

Behan always wore his shirt open to the navel; he never had shoelaces and the tongues of his shoes would always hang out. You could see his bare ankles and the heels of his shoes were always so worn away that his ankles leaned over and he waddled around. Every year or so he'd buy himself a new suit, and as soon as he walked into the pub and someone would say, "Behan, you've got a new suit!" He'd say, "Oh, you think it's new," and he'd immediately get off the bar stool, walk outside, and roll up and down in the gutter, then he'd come back in. If someone said, "Well, Behan, jeez, you've washed your hair!" he'd take his pint of Guinness and pour it over his head.

—J. P. Donleavy

LOUIS-FERDINAND CÉLINE

Céline I met. I once went out to see him when he was living in Meudon, an industrial suburb of Paris near the Renault plant. He had a small house, and outside it there was a high barbed-wire fence. He had two very fierce dogs that barked at me when I rang the gate bell. He had to come out and tie up the dogs. This was because Denöel, his publisher, had been murdered on a street in Paris. Denöel had been a collaborator, too. Céline was rather paranoid, but he was friendly to me. I had had contact with his wife, who was a ballet dancer. While they were in exile in Denmark during the war, she couldn't get ballet shoes for her practice. So she used to write to me and I'd go down to Capezio in New York to buy her ballet shoes and air-mail them over to her.

—James Laughlin

T. S. ELIOT

I didn't like him a bit. He was a poseur. He was married to this woman who was very pretty. My husband and I were asked to see them, and my husband roamed around the flat and there were endless photographs of T. S. Eliot and bits of his poetry done in embroidery by pious American ladies, and only one picture of his wife, and that was when she was getting married. Henry pointed it out to me and said, "I don't think I like that man."

—Rebecca West

★   ★   ★

When he paid his infrequent visits here, we invariably met to get drunk together. There was a splendid occasion when he and I and our wives dined at "The Greeks" after he'd received a silver bowl from the Signet Society; he was wearing a cowboy hat, and we all got plastered. We went on to the Red Lion Grill, after many drinks at the Silver Dollar Bar, the two toughest and *queerest* joints in Boston. He couldn't walk, for his ankles were crossed, so Valerie *lifted* him into the taxi.

—Conrad Aiken

★   ★   ★

Eliot was a very kind man. In those days I smoked and liked French cigarettes, and people used to give him French cigarettes, which he no longer smoked. So whenever I went to see him he would open a drawer and hand me a whole bunch. That was a big thing in London in the early fifties, and I was touched that he remembered. We used to sit and reminisce about America. There was a side of Eliot that was very home-sick for the States, and I was feeling homesick in London, too. We had several wonderful conversations—about the Ohio River and about his family out on the Mississippi in St. Louis and about the riverboats. It's very strange to think of him having any connection with that world. He talked about the *Delta Queen,* that steamboat that went up and down the river until a few years ago. He really wanted to take a trip on that. I wanted to write verse plays in those days, when I was in my early twenties. But, after a while, I came to feel that the plays weren't going very well and that the verse certainly wasn't helping them. As long as I had this fixation about verse plays, I wasn't learning anything about writing plays. I talked to him about that. I said I was thinking of abandoning writing them in verse altogether and trying to write them in prose. "Well," he said, "I've thought of doing that, too, but if I were to write my plays in prose, there are so many other people who could do it better."

—W. S. Merwin

★   ★   ★

I got to know him earlier, when I was in England in '31–'32. Vachel Lindsay had written to him, and he wrote me at Cambridge to invite me, saying, "Do drop in." You know, at Faber and Faber. I did. I went to see him and we talked about Cambridge, where I was working in philosophy. He was familiar with the people at Cambridge who were then my teachers or lecturers, C. D. Broad and G. E. Moore. This, of course, was a continuing interest in his life. He had, after all, done his dissertation on Bradley. Had he gone on in that direction, he was going to be a philosopher in the philosophy department here at Harvard. I think on the second or third of my visits I had the courage to hand him a poem. He looked at the poem for a long time. Great silence. He studied it, then he looked up and said, "Is this the best you can do?" *Whoo!* Quite a thing to say! I didn't realize then what I realized later—that it was an editor's question: "Shall I publish this or shall I wait until he does something that shows more confidence?" What I thought at the time, and there was also this about it, was that it was fraternal. Just talking to me as one craftsman to another. A compliment, really.

—Robert Fitzgerald

WILLIAM FAULKNER

Sometimes, of a Sunday morning, he used to stroll by a house I occupied in Beverly Hills. I noticed him only because the sight of anybody walking in that environment stamped him as an eccentric, and indeed, it eventually got him into trouble. A prowl car picked him up and he had a rather sticky time of it. The police were convinced he was a finger man for some jewelry mob planning to knock over one of the fancy residences.

—S. J. Perelman

FORD MADOX FORD

Ford was a character; he was a liar, not for his own profit, but just because he had a very faint hold on actuality. He told beautiful stories of English literary life, in which he knew everybody, had a hand in everything, and his hand grew larger as he told the story. He had a roving eye for younger women, whom he especially liked to fascinate. He came to this country after the breakup of his marriage to Stella Bowen. I can remember on one occasion he came up to Robber Rocks—a place back in the woods near the New York–Connecticut line which was the country headquarters for Allen Tate, Hart Crane, and others—where a lot of young wives were around at the party. They would be fondled by Ford, and then escape him up the stairs. Ford, heavy and wheezing by that time, would follow them to the head of the narrow stairs, and the door would close in his face. He would wheeze back down, and a while later he'd follow another young woman until she took refuge behind a locked door.

—Malcolm Cowley

ROBERT FROST

I met him only two or three times. He had a number of sides to his nature, as we know, including a very black one. He showed me his vain side. I had to give a dinner party for him, and had someone bellow in his ear the names of all the other people and had all their place names written out very large so he could see them at the table. He sat next to E. M. Forster, and asked, "And what magazine do you write for?" He just didn't take these people seriously, and didn't bother to find out who they were.

—Stephen Spender

ALLEN GINSBERG

Allen Ginsberg asked me when he was nineteen years old, should I change my name to Allen Renard? You change your name to Allen Renard I'll kick you right in the balls! Stick to Ginsberg . . . and he did. That's one thing I like about Allen. Allen *Renard!!!*

—Jack Kerouac

FRANK HARRIS

I can remember calling on Frank Harris—he was about seventy then— when I was on the Chicago *Tribune's* edition in Nice. In his house he had three portraits on the wall—Mark Twain, Frank Harris, and I think it was Hawthorne. Harris was in the middle. Harris would point up to them and say, "Those three are the best American writers. The one in the middle is the best." Harris really thought he was wonderful. Once he told me he was going to live to be a hundred. When I asked him what the formula was, he told me it was very simple. He said: "I've bought myself a stomach pump and one half hour after dinner I pump myself out." Can you imagine that? Well, it didn't work. It's a wonder it didn't kill him sooner.

—James Thurber

ALDOUS HUXLEY

I really seem to have behaved very oddly. I remember once I'd actually passed out on the floor, and, looking up, I saw at an immense altitude above me, Aldous Huxley, who was very tall, standing up and talking French to Stravinsky, who never seemed to get overcome, however much he drank. And Aldous, who I think was very fond of me, was looking at me rather curiously, as much as to say, "Aren't you going a little far?" It's not like me to behave like that, or so I imagine. Perhaps it is. But I suddenly realized how relaxed I felt, how completely at home. It didn't matter if I blotted my copy book.

—Christopher Isherwood

CHRISTOPHER ISHERWOOD

I met him in the Forties in California. At the time he was into Vedanta, an Eastern religious thing. He was living in a monastery. They had periods of silence and meditation, you know. The night I met him, through a letter from Lincoln Kirstein, I arrived during one of these silent periods. The monk who opened the door handed me a pencil and paper to write what my business was and who I'd come to see. I wrote, "Christopher Isherwood," and they regarded me with considerable suspicion from that point on.

In this big room in the monastery, everyone was sitting in . . . what do they call it? The lotus position? Including Christopher. All strictly observing the vow of silence. I didn't dig the scene.

I suddenly made some reference out loud about the Krishna. I didn't know who the hell he was, I was only trying to break the silence. Christopher got up, and wrote on a piece of paper, "I'll call you tomorrow." He was very polite, and he took me to the door.

—Tennessee Williams

JAMES JOYCE

An extraordinarily handsome man! He gave the impression of being a great surgeon but not a writer at all. And he was a surgeon, he was not a writer. He used to wear white surgeon's coats all the time and that increased the impression and he had this queer, axe-like face with this enormous jaw, the biggest jaw I have ever seen on a human being. I once did a talk on Joyce in which I mentioned that he had the biggest chin I had ever seen on a human being and T. S. Eliot wrote a letter saying that he had often seen chins as big as that on other Irishmen. Well, I didn't know how to reply to that.

—Frank O'Connor

D. H. LAWRENCE

We saw the Lawrences often during those last four years; they stayed with us in Paris, then we were together in Switzerland, and we visited them at the Villa Mirenda near Florence. My wife typed out the manuscript of *Lady Chatterley's Lover* for him, even though she was a bad typist and had no patience with English spelling—she was a Belgian, you know. Then she didn't always appreciate the nuances of the language she was typing. When she started using some of those four-letter words in conversation, Lawrence was profoundly shocked.

—Aldous Huxley

SINCLAIR LEWIS

It was in 1930, in Rome. He'd already been widely discussed in Italy, where he was trailing about with a squadron of jolly New York girls who were causing a scandal. One fine day he landed in Rome, where I was making a movie. He let me know that he urgently wanted to meet me. I asked him to come to the studio, but he answered that he had a cold, he didn't like movies, and anyway he didn't have the time because he was leaving Rome the next morning for Stockholm to collect the Nobel Prize. So I went to his hotel, where I found half a dozen American girls completely drunk, making a gigantic cocktail in a soup tureen full of whipped cream, into which—while quarreling with each other about how much to put in—they were pouring two, three liters of vermouth. I didn't think I could join this scene of madwomen right away—one of them held out some scissors to me and dared me to cut her hair—so I thought I'd take a little stroll. But I changed my mind and decided to search the apartment for the master of the séance whom I hadn't seen yet. The door of the bathroom was half open, and boiling water was coming out. I went in. The bathtub was overflowing and the faucets were wide open. Two feet, dressed in polished dancing pumps, hung out of the tub, and at the bottom a man in a tuxedo was drowning. It was my Sinclair Lewis. I pulled him out of his unfortunate position, and that was how I saved his life so he could take the train the next morning for Stockholm and his prize.

The next day I put him on the train—he didn't even buy me a drink. It's true he had a hangover and probably didn't want to drink, or maybe he'd sworn never to drink again. But a drunk's oaths don't hold, you know.

—Blaise Cendrars

GERTRUDE STEIN

Miss Stein arrived in America and said that there were two people that she wanted to meet. They were both in California at that minute— Chaplin and Dash [Dashiell Hammett]. And we were invited to dinner at the house of a friend of Miss Stein; Charlie Chaplin, Dash and myself, Paulette Goddard, Miss Toklas, our host and hostess and another man. There was this magnificent china and lace tablecloth. Chaplin turned over his coffee cup, nowhere near Stein, just all over this beautiful cloth, and the first thing Miss Stein said was, "Don't worry, it didn't get on me." She was miles away from him. She said it perfectly seriously. Then she told Dash he was the only American writer who wrote well about women. He was very pleased.

—Lillian Hellman

SOMERSET MAUGHAM

We got along on just sort of "how do you do" terms. I remember walking back from a cricket match at Lords in London, and Maugham came along on the other side. He looked at me and I looked at him, and we were thinking the same thing: Oh, my God, shall we have to stop and talk? Fortunately, we didn't.

—P. G. Wodehouse

★   ★   ★

He couldn't write for toffee, bless his heart. He wrote conventional short stories, much inferior to the work of other people. But they were much better than his plays, which were too frightful. He was an extremely interesting man though, not a bit clever or cold or cynical. I know of many affectionate things he did. He had a great capacity for falling in love with the wrong people. His taste seemed to give way under him so extraordinarily sometimes. He fascinated me by his appearance: he was so neatly made, like a swordstick that fits just so. Occasionally his conversation was beautifully funny and quite unmalicious. I object strongly to pictures of Maugham as if he were a second-rate Hollywood producer in the lavish age. His house was very pleasant and quiet and agreeable.

—Rebecca West

CARSON MCCULLERS

I had first known her in this nest that Linscott had up there for these little birdlings of writers. Carson had great vitality and she was quite beautiful in that already decaying way. She was like a fairy. She had the most delicate kind of tinkling, dazzling little way about her . . . like a little star. Like a Christmas, she was like an ornament of a kind. She had no mind and she could make no philosophical statements about anything; she didn't need to. She said far-out, wonderfully mad things, that were totally disarming and for a while people would say, "I'll go wherever you go." She'd knock them straight out the window. She had a devastating crush on Elizabeth Bowen. She actually got to Bowen's Court: she shambled over there to England and spent a fortnight. I heard from Elizabeth that Carson appeared at dinner the first night in her shorts, tennis shorts; that poor body, you know, in tennis shorts and she came down the stairs; that was her debut. It didn't last long. But that was Carson.

—William Goyen

THOMAS MERTON

He was so nice, so jolly. He wasn't a dour monk at all. He was a kind friend and interested in everything. I often went down to visit him at the monastery in Kentucky. The Abbot would give him a day off, and I'd rent a car. Tom would get an old bishop's suit out of the storeroom and start out in that. Then we would stop in the woods and he'd change into his farmworker's blue jeans and a beret to hide his tonsure. Then we'd hit the bars across Kentucky. He loved his beer, and he loved that smoked ham they have down there. He was a wonderful person. He wanted to read contemporary writers, but the books were often confiscated, so we had a secret system. I sent the books he wanted to the monastery psychiatrist in Louisville, who would get them to Merton. I sent him everyone he wanted to read: Sartre and Camus, Rexroth and Pound, Henry Miller and many more. We talked a great deal about the Oriental religions. He was very ecumenical. We talked about his situation and why he stuck it out in the monastery. Once I asked, "Tom, why do you stay here? You could get out and be a tremendous success in the world." He answered that the monastery was where God wanted him to be. He would have been misplaced if he hadn't been so determined to get what he wanted in the monastery—his own hermitage among the hills. He couldn't stand the "social life" in the monastery with all the monks talking sign language, having to go to church six times a day, going to chapter, and making cheese. He finally did persuade the Abbot to build him a hermitage. Tom was a shrewd operator. He got out of sleeping in the communal dormitory by learning how to snore so loudly that the other monks got together at chapter and said, "Father Louis has got to leave the dormitory." So Tom was allowed to use one of the old bishop's rooms. He believed that the old monastic tradition was so strict that it could no longer foster true spirituality.

—James Laughlin

EZRA POUND

I went to see him a couple of times, but I was a little uneasy with him. Pound always had some new discovery or enthusiasm; he was always finding the lowdown on something. On one of my visits to his little apartment, he announced loudly, "I've got the lowdown on the Elizabethan drama! It was all cribbed from these books," and he carried out two huge volumes of the Venetian State Papers. Well, it *was* a real discovery: the plots of several Elizabethan plays *did* come out of the Venetian State Papers.

—Malcolm Cowley

★   ★   ★

He admired at that time, when I first met him, Robinson and de La Mare. He got over admiring de La Mare anyway, and I think he threw out Robinson too. We'd just bring up a couple of little poems. I was around with him quite a little for a few weeks. I was charmed with his ways. He cultivated a certain rudeness to people that he didn't like, just like Willy Whistler. I thought he'd come under the influence of Whistler. They cultivated the French style of boxing. They used to kick you in the teeth. You know the song, the nasty song: "They fight with their feet—" Among other things, what Pound did was show me Bohemia. He'd take me to restaurants and things. Showed me ju jitsu in a restaurant. Threw me over his head. Wasn't ready for him at all. I was just as strong as he was. He said, "I'll show you, I'll show you. Stand up." So I stood up, gave him my hand. He grabbed my wrist, tipped over backwards and threw me over his head. Everybody in the restaurant stood up. He used to talk about himself as a tennis player. I never played tennis with him. And then he'd show you all these places with these people that specialized in poets that dropped their aitches and things like that. Not like the "beatniks," quite. I remember one occasion they had a poet in who had a poem in *The English Review* on Aphrodite, how he met Aphrodite at Leatherhead.* He was coming in and he was a navvy. I don't remember his name, never heard of him again—may have gone on and had books. But he was a real navvy. Came in with his bicycle clips on. Tea party. Everybody horrified in a delighted way, you know. Horror, social horror. Rednecked, thick, heavy-built fellow, strong fellow, you know, like John L. Lewis or somebody. But he was a poet. And then I saw poets made out of whole cloth by Ezra. Ezra thought he did that. Take a fellow that had never written anything and think he could make a poet out of him. We won't go into that.

—Robert Frost

* * *

I was staying with friends in Washington, at Easter vacation, when I went over to see Pound. He received me in this open ward, with people wandering around, flushing imaginary toilets. He sat in a deep chair and held forth. I was eighteen—I didn't have much to say to Pound—and he told me all about how, when the Hundredth Canto was finished, the whole thing was all going to fall into place and so on. It would be like putting the keystone in the arch, or the lintel on the doorposts. He was also wonderfully generous and wrote me postcards afterwards. "Read seeds, not twigs E.P.," he wrote. And he gave me a bit of advice about translating, about taking translating seriously as a kind of practice, about learning languages and trying to get as close as possible to the sense and the form of the original. I didn't know what he meant about a lot of those things until I had been practicing for a while, until I had been trying to do it.

—W. S. Merwin

MARCEL PROUST

Marcel combatted those things in his own way. He would circle among his victims collecting his "black honey" his *miel noir*, and then he wrote,

---

*Frost is thinking of a poet named John Helston, author of "Aphrodite at Leatherhead," which took up fourteen pages of The English Review for March 1913. Frost's recollection gives a special flavor, if one is needed, to the note appended to the poem by the editors of the magazine: "Without presuming to 'present' Mr. Helston after the manner of fashionable actors, we think it will interest the public to know that he was for years a working mechanic—turner, fitter, etc.—in electrical, locomotive, motor-car, and other workshops."

"I beg of you, Jean, since you live in the rue d'Anjou in the same building with Mme. de Chevigné, of whom I've made the Duchess de Guermantes; I entreat you to get her to read my book. She won't read me; and she says she stubs her foot in my sentences. I beg you—" I told him that was as if he asked an ant to read Fabre. You don't ask an insect to read entomology.

—Jean Cocteau

DYLAN THOMAS

It was difficult, because he always wanted to drink. I went on one bender with him in London which lasted for two days and three nights. We ended up sleeping on the floor of some lady's apartment and neither of us knew who she was. He always wanted to drink, but I'm not such a great drinker. When he came to New York he'd come in the office at ten o'clock in the morning and say, "Let's go the the White Horse Tavern." I'd say, "Dylan, I've got work to do." So he'd go off to the White Horse and meet various cronies and sycophants. Sometimes I'd join him late in the evening. He was a sad case, Dylan; he was basically a nice person, and when he started boozing he was very amusing, but he would never stop; he'd go on and on. It's very hard to get close to a drinker. There was always that thing between us, the boozing. He was a great talker, too; he was a wonderful talker, but I had work to do. When Dylan drank he wanted people to be with him, to listen to him. It was a method of attracting people. But he was very indiscriminate about whom he would attract. He had a bunch of hangers-on in New York, such as that jerk Oscar Williams, who were crumbs. That was a barrier, because he'd be with such crummy characters. You couldn't really have a conversation with Dylan when he was drinking. It wore me down. John Davenport had a good name for Dylan. He called him "Old Messy." He was. He was messy because of the drinking. You couldn't count on him. If you wanted to do something you couldn't count on his turning up sober or on time.

—James Laughlin

W. B. YEATS

Mostly reading aloud to him. Doughty's *Dawn in Britain,* and so on. And wrangling, you see. The Irish like contradiction. He tried to learn fencing at forty-five, which was amusing. He would thrash around with the foils like a whale. He sometimes gave the impression of being even a worse idiot than I am.

—Ezra Pound

* * *

He wasn't a bit impressive and he wasn't my sort of person at all. He boomed at you like a foghorn. He was there one time when Philip Guedella and two or three of us were all very young and were talking nonsense about murderers in Shakespeare and whether a third murderer ever became a first murderer by working hard or were they, sort of, hereditary slots? Were they like Japanese specialists and one did one kind of murder, another did another? It was really awfully funny. Philip was very funny to be with. Then we started talking about something on the Western Isles but Yeats wouldn't join in, until we fussed round and were nice to him. But we were all wrong; what he liked was solemnity and, if you were big enough, heavy enough and strong enough, he loved you. He loved great big women. He would have been mad about Vanessa Redgrave.

—Rebecca West

* * *

I met Yeats, I think probably in 1935 or 1936, at Lady Ottoline Morrell's. Ottoline asked me to tea alone with Yeats. He was very blind and—I don't know whether he was deaf, but he was very sort of remote, he seemed tremendously old. He was only about the age I am now, but he seemed tremendously old and remote. He looked at me and then he said, "Young man, what do you think of the Sayers?" I hadn't the faintest idea what he was talking about—I thought perhaps he meant Dorothy Sayers' crime stories or something—I became flustered. What he meant was a group of young ladies who chanted poems in chorus. Ottoline got very alarmed and rushed out of the room and telephoned to Virginia Woolf, who was just around the corner, and asked her to come save the situation. Virginia arrived in about ten minutes time, tremendously amused, and Yeats was very pleased to meet her because he'd just been reading *The Waves*. He also read quite a lot of science—I think he read Eddington and Rutherford and all those kinds of things—and so he told her that *The Waves* was a marvelous novel, that it was entirely up to date in scientific theory because light moved in waves, and time, and so on. Of course Virginia, who hadn't thought of all this, was terribly pleased and flattered. And then I remember he started telling her a story in which he said, "And as I went down the stairs there was a marble statue of a baby and it started talking in Greek to me"—that sort of thing. Virginia adored it all of course. . . . I remember his telling the story of his trip to Rapallo to show the manuscript of *The Tower* to Ezra Pound. He stayed at the hotel and then went around and left the manuscript in a packet for Pound, accompanied by a letter saying I am an old man, this may be the last poetry I'll ever write, it is very different from my other work—all that kind of thing—and what do you think of it? Next day he received a post card from Ezra Pound with on it the one word "putrid." Yeats was rather amused by that. Apparently Pound had a tremendous collection of cats, and Yeats used to say that Pound couldn't possibly be a nasty man because he fed all the cats of Rapallo. I once asked him how he came to be a modern poet, and he told me that it took him thirty years to modernize his style. He said he didn't really like the modern poetry of Eliot and Pound. He thought it was static, that it didn't have any movement, and for him poetry had always to have the romantic movement. He said, "For me poetry always means 'For we'll go no more a-roving / By the light o' the moon.' " So the problem was how to keep the movement of the Byron lines but at the same time enlarge it so that it could include the kind of material that he was interested in, which was to do with everyday life—politics, quarrels between people, sexual love, and not just the frustrated love he had with Maud Gonne.

—Stephen Spender

*   *   *

I remember the taxi ride over. The taxi was left over from the First World War, and when we arrived in Pall Mall—we could see the Atheneum—the driver said he didn't feel he could get in. Finally I decided to abandon ship and take off on my own. So I went in and asked for Mr. Yeats. Very much like asking, "Is Mr. Ben Jonson here?" And he came down. He was much taller than I expected, and haggard. Big, though, big head, rather wonderful looking in a sort of a blunt, patrician kind of way, but there was something shrunken also. He told me he was just recovering from an illness. He was very courteous, and we went in to tea. At a certain point, I had a cigarette, and I asked him if he would like one. To my great surprise he said yes. So I gave him a Craven-A and then lit it for him, and I thought, Immortality is mine! From now on it's just a question of reaping the fruits of my effort. He did most of the talking. I asked him a few questions. He did not ask me any questions about myself, although he was extremely courteous and very kind. At one point he said, "I have reached the age when my daughter can beat me at croquet," and I thought, Hurrah, he's human! I made notes of the interview afterwards, which I have probably lost. One comment in particular I remember. He said, "I never revise now"—you know how much he revised his stuff—"but in the interest of a more passionate syntax." Now that struck me as a very good remark. I have no idea what it meant and still don't know, but the longer I think about it, the better I like it.

—John Berryman

PART FOUR

1974–1980

Introduction

When Robert Silvers became the Paris editor he moved the office around the corner to a small loft in the *Editions Stock* offices in the rue Casimir-Delavigne. Often he edited the magazine from a river barge he shared with Peter Duchin, the musician, which was moored near the Place de l'Alma and Chez Francis, the restaurant of the Madwoman of Chaillot. Writers who wanted to deliver a manuscript often dropped by. If they wanted an editorial conference, they had to contend with the noise from a stand-up piano around which Duchin gathered some of the musicians in Paris at the time—Alan Eager, Chet Baker, Kenny Clark, David Amram—for jam sessions. Communication with writers became even more difficult when in the spring of 1956 the flood waters of the Seine covered the quais and reached the elbows of the stone statues of the Zouave soldiers on the face of the Pont Alma, the greatest flood since 1910 when rowboats were out on the Place de la Concorde and the waters reached the *necks* of the Zouaves. The barge was anchored in midstream and a kind of breeches-buoy arrangement was used to get ashore. Once, when Bob Silvers was pulling himself in, the dinghy slipped out from under him, leaving him dangling for a while above the Seine wearing Peter Duchin's Hotchkiss sweater. The waters of the Seine were swift and angry for weeks. A dead cow floated by, and thousands of wine bottles.

During Bob Silvers's editorship in Paris he moved the printing operation from Paris to Nijmegen, Holland. Every time the magazine was to be printed a small contingent would "go up to Nijmegen" or make "The Trip."

The printing plant in Nijmegen was run along somewhat archaic principles: women were not allowed in the printing-machine rooms. When Joan Dillon, who became the Paris assistant editor in 1965, would appear on the premises with corrected proofs, the Dutch workers would stop what they were doing and gaze moodily after her. Mr. Van Zee, the head of the plant, called his workers together and informed them that Miss Dillon was a red Indian, indeed a descendant of Pocahontas. For some reason the Dutch were assuaged by this odd disclosure, and subsequently, when she appeared in their area, they ignored her.

The last office in Paris (everything moved back to New York in 1973) was a small room in an office building on the rue Vernet off the Champs-Élysees. A defrocked priest lived down the hall, and also a man named Williams who had been on the Long March with Mao tse-Tung in the 1930s and had played bridge with him in the encampments.

Maxine Groffsky was the editor in Paris in the final years. A striking redhead, her arrival at the Dôme or the Rotonde inevitably caused a stir—a turning and peering of heads over banquettes, and in the far reaches of the room people stood to watch her entrance and check who was with her. In her first years as the Paris editor she would lead a small contingent up to Nijmegen, Holland, to oversee the printing of the magazine. She spoke of the trip to Nijmegen as seeming to be as long as a trip to America:

"One had to leave from the Gare de Lyon at 6:00 A.M. There was a change somewhere in Holland where one waited on a platform with crates of peeping chickens and tulip shipments. Holland always seemed to me to be very cold. Finally, the Nijmegen train would arrive. When it eventually pulled out, it just barely crept through the countryside. I always thought that was to compensate for the small size of the country . . . that the trains were made to travel slowly to give the people on board an idea of great distance.

"In Nijmegen we stayed in the Esplanade Hotel for four or five days. Everyone spoke English. Everyone sounded like Bill de Kooning. Everyone was helpful. It was terribly boring. The movies in town were in Flemish. Finally, I gave up going to Nijmegen and everything was done by mail."

In the summer of 1967 Maxine edited the magazine from the villa on the Via Antiqua north of Rome which had been taken over for the season by Brigitte Bardot and Gunther Sachs. One afternoon Sachs bombed the villa with a plane-load of red roses to show his love for Bardot. "They were as interested in what I was doing as, I guess, they could be," Maxine once told me. "They tended to like comic books."

Since the early 1970s the office has been a ground-floor room on East 72nd Street in New York, where I live. A lion-trainer's chair, laced and ripped by claws, hangs from the ceiling, its seat inscribed with a salutation by Dave Hoover, the star of the Clyde-Beatty Cole Bros. circus to commemorate an occasion when I went into the lions' cage with him. There are also hooks in the ceiling from which to hang the staff's bicycles to give everyone more room below.

A lot of social activity has always gone on in a long, narrow living room upstairs with a row of windows that look out on the East River. It became quite a gathering place and for a remarkably eclectic group. *Esquire* took it upon itself to refer to the *"Paris Review* crowd" as the "red-hot" center of the New York literary "Establishment." The magazine published a double-page spread of a party in the big room (with a tugboat going by the windows) in which recognizable figures included, among others, William Styron, Norman Mailer, Jimmy Baldwin, Irwin Shaw, Allen Ginsberg, Jackie Kennedy, her sister Lee Radziwill, Jonathan Miller, Larry Rivers, James Jones, Jules Feiffer, Dwight Macdonald, Lillian Hellman, Terry Southern, Philip Roth, and Gregory Corso.

Elaine Dundy, the former wife of Kenneth Tynan, the critic, and herself a novelist *(The Dud Avocado),* came to the gatherings from time to time. She does not remember Lillian Hellman being there but her recollections are vivid enough:

"Norman Mailer tells me that what he most recalls about the *Paris Review* parties in the fifties and sixties was their charged atmosphere. "All those writers," he says, "myself included—walking rigidly through that packed room towards the drinks, our heads erect, only our eyes swiveling sideways to identify the enemy."

"Twenty years ago Stephen Spender, comparing the English Literary Scene with the American one, wrote that the former resembled a cozy conspiracy while the latter a battleground or brothel. Clearly he had done his research at the fortnightly literary salon held in the *Paris Review's* offices on 72nd Street which was also the apartment of host George A. Plimpton. For over a decade it was the only Quality Lit game in town.

"I, too remember those parties filled with their dangerous, challenging, sometimes near-fatal mixture of novelists, critics, editors, and publishers stewing together in the pressure-cooker of that long narrow room. And I remember the thrill of fear with which one realized that once across the threshold the only exit offered seemed to be the icy East River darkly flowing outside the windows.

"However frightened, no one seriously engaged in the literary scene dreamt of missing these regular confrontations and no one dared come unarmed. Norman Mailer brought his seconds, his boxing chums. Terry Southern brought his fellow hipsters, Boris, Kooky, and Shadow. Bill Styron brought his charming wife, Rose. And Jimmy Baldwin brought the fire next time. I, myself, wore several suits of armor. Sometimes I came as a wife, sometimes as an adventuress. I never came as a novelist, except as an amateur one, deflecting the foe with assurances that my first novel was a fluke; for what was immediately apparent in those days was the lack of serious literary ladies. The women there, highly decorative for the most part, were strictly utilitarian: wives, mistresses, girlfriends past and girlfriends possible. In all the years I attended these soirées I never once came across Mary McCarthy, Carson McCullers, Eudora Welty, Flannery O'Connor, Katherine Anne Porter, or even Lillian Hellman.

"Only now recollecting in tranquility these discordant gatherings do I realize what was taking place was not merely a series of black comedies or shell games. What emerges for me now is something ineffably poignant. Beneath the surface squabbling, sniping, and stalking, the antagonism went deep and it was real. It was an antagonism based on warring philosophies. Each of the young men there—the writers, poets, editors, and publishers—genuinely stood *for* something . . . which meant each was against something else.

"Hip, Beat, and Square were philosophical concepts that translated themselves into literary styles. The poets Ginsberg, Orlovsky, and Ferlinghetti were, of course, Beat. Mailer at that time was so obsessed with Hip that in *Advertisements for Myself* he ran a list, pages long, of things he considered hip with their dreaded square equivalents: "nuance," for instance, was hip and "fact" square. Styron's novel *Set This House on Fire* hadn't gone past the fifth page before the "I" of the story was stalwartly declaring himself a Square. Southern's philosophy was that of the arch-prankster-intriguer: the gadfly in the Venetian manner of Mosca or Iago.

"By word and deed guests expressed themselves with unrestrained freedom. Often the words were very funny. I remember Mailer attacking a rival as "White, Protestant, and wrong," and Southern informing a startled middle-aged wife in a hat that "There are more things in heaven and earth, Mrs. Sprague, than are *dreamt* of in your philosophy." Mike Nichols reported the following exchange upon being introduced to a Hipsteress:

> Nichols: "How do you do?"
> Hipsteress: "I thought you'd be cleverer than that."

"Clashes were not only verbal but, at a fair rate, physical. Sometimes they involved animate objects, sometimes inanimate. It was in dealing with these skirmishes that George Plimpton excelled. Benevolently watching over us all with a sort of awed enthusiasm, our host, with his infinite tolerance of his guests' vagaries and umbrages which could end in fisticuffs, collapsed coffee tables, broken glass, or tears, really made the whole thing go with a stylish swing. One guest, momentarily out of control, who had saved up her money and apologies for a month before confessing to bashing an enormous wall mirror in the room, was quickly absolved by him with a generous, "It's all right. It was bound to happen one day." That grateful guest was I."

I do not remember the parties quite as Elaine Dundy has, though I remember the mirror and perhaps it is true about the tensions. Norman Mailer worked his out with head-butting contests—in which he and his opponent started off staring at each other through the crowd of cocktail party guests and then, at a signal, would come together like a pair of rams in rutting season, bopping each other with the crown of the skull—harmless, apparently, but producing a booming sound like a pair of gourds *thonked* together. Sometimes one of the head-butters would get knocked to the floor among the chair legs. Big booming sound and then a groan.

The habitués got rather used to this sort of thing. Guests arriving late and seeing the two of them coming together, and hearing perhaps the crash of furniture, would ask, "My God, what's that?" The response would be: "What? Oh, that . . . well, that's our . . ."—very blasé about it.

—G.P.

FICTION

Thomas M. Disch

The Joycelin Shrager Story

When people asked what he did, Donald Long's standard riposte was, "I'm a mechanic of the dream." Meaning, he was a projectionist. Actually few people had to ask, since Donald had been around since the first black-and-white flickerings of the Movement early in the fifties. With the money he earned at the Europa he produced *Footage*, first as a quarterly and then bi-monthly. For years it was their only magazine, but gradually as success changed the Movement into the Underground, *Footage* was supplemented and then supplanted by newer, more commercially oriented magazines. Donald Long's reputation as the Rhadamanthys of the underground film was undiminished, and possibly enhanced, by reason of this failure, but there was one consequence to be regretted—he had to continue full-time at the Europa, from one in the afternoon till the early evening, six days a week.

The Europa is on 8th Avenue, just below 49th. Originally it had been a showcase for Russian, Polish, and Estonian movies not otherwise distributed in the city, but then, imperceptibly, without a change of owner (or, so far as Donald could see, of clientele), the Europa drifted toward a policy of nudism and the exposure of organized vice, especially the white slavery traffic. By the end of '69 the Sexual Revolution had swept the October Revolution into oblivion.

Something of the same thing had been happening in his own life. Donald was forty-two, and after decades of honest homeliness he was finally coming into his own. What had been even ten years ago a boney kind of face was now rather striking in a severe way. No longer did he dissemble his baldness with a few iron-gray strands brushed up from the sides. No, he let it declare itself, and what hair still was left to him he grew, boldly, down to his shoulders. But best of all, his somatotype had become trendy, and he was able to fit into all the skimpy pullovers and striped pants that most men couldn't have attempted after the age of thirty.

Not that he became a satyr quite. He simply began taking advantage of the opportunities that had always offered themselves to him from time to time. At parties he was less diffident. He would even dance. (He had gone to a Reichian therapist and redirected some of his energies from his head down to his balls and, concomitantly, his feet.) He got rolfed, and laid.

But he didn't fall in love. He kept waiting, alert as a seismograph, for some tremor of affection, warmth, whatever. All he ever felt was a great glow of health and, toward his partners, benevolence, a degree of gratitude, a lesser degree of curiosity. But love? Never.

He knew what love was. Twice before he'd been in love. The first time, at twenty-four, he'd made the mistake of marrying his love-object, the black actress Cerise Miles. That was 1949, the year of Kazan's *Pinky*, and among enlightened Manhattanites love conquered all. By 1951 Donald and Cerise had come to hate each other much more passionately than they'd ever loved. As a result, his memories of the early, positive period of the relationship resembled, in its deliberate fuzziness, the one film Donald had ever made himself, *Tides of the Blood.* Among much else, *Tides* was a record of his marriage's collapse. (And, by implication, of Western Civilization's.) Cerise had played herself, improvisationally, a performance that even after Donald's editing was considered a limit-case of what underground cinema could do along the lines of honesty.

The second time he was luckier and fell in love with the wife of his best friend, Gary Webb. The necessity of concealment kept Donald and Grace Webb in a state of zesty suspense and made their few rare moments alone together lyrical in the extreme. Then, after the adultery had gone on some two years, Grace felt she had to tell Gary. There was no question of divorce, since both Webbs were renegade Catholics who still believed in the sanctity of the marriage bond and the natural law. It was just her unconquerable candor. Gary was wretched and furious by turns, and Donald and Grace were rapturously guilty and more in love than ever.

Gary Webb was at that time (the late fifties) the most prolific (and, according to *Footage,* the best) director in the Movement. Film for him was less an art than a religion. He was its priest, and his camera was the sacrament he carried through the world, hallowing it. He filmed everything: snowfalls, muggings, Grace in *hal asana* position, trees in Washington Square, football games on Channel 5, a friend's stoned, staring iris (a shot he was sure Hitchcock had plagiarized in *Psycho*), a dripping faucet, cars on the street, and the natural births of all six of his sons. He also filmed, with Grace's connivance, representative moments of her adultery, and this footage became the basis of his most revolutionary and well-known film, *Reel 16* (1959).

The affair ended when Gary inherited his grandfather's farm in western Kansas. The Webbs moved west, with their cats and children and cameras, and in a few months Grace had been absorbed into the irrecoverable past. Years later he was to get a postcard from either Grace or Gary, he could never be sure, to which was glued a snippet from the ad for *The Great Gatsby:* "Gone is the romance that was so divine." The card showed a motel outside of Lebanon, Kansas.

On Sunday mornings, thanks to its owner, Norman Brodkey, and to the tax laws that make such transformations so profitable, the Europa became the Foundation for Free Cinema. The Foundation's screening policy was egalitarian, even kindly in a careless way, mixing established old masters like Anger and Brakhage with whatever else happened along, and throwing in an occasional reel of the Europa's indigenous beavers when their directors or actors had credentials in the Movement. This policy usually guaranteed a minimum attendance figure of twenty-five or thirty, comprised mainly of fledgling filmmakers, their casts and close friends.

On this particular Sunday, May 17, 1970, the Foundation was showing two works by Anna Congdon: *Stigma* (1954, 48 min.) and *Dreams of Eurydice* (1967, 73 min.). Because these combined running times precluded more than a token representation of films by the Foundation's regular customers, because Miss Congdon had never ventured from her native Australia and so lacked the social leverage by which to muster the fiction of a coterie, and finally, because the weather was more than ordinarily unacceptable, the turnout stopped just one short of none at all. That one was Mike Georgiadis, whose oeuvre, long since completed, shared a common mythopoeic strain with Miss Congdon's, and at whose urgings Donald had at last agreed to give the old girl her crack at America.

Mike was propped on the stainless steel ledge of the ticket booth, coughing, joking, and smoking fifteen cent El Productos. It was an evil, evocative cough, but pardonable when you knew that Mike was dying of emphysema, had been dying of emphysema now for all of fourteen years.

They passed the rainy minutes gossiping about colleagues, the waxing and waning of their incomes, marriages, entanglements, and reputations. Mike, who was firmly established at the waning end of all scales, had a knack for interpreting any scrap of news so as to make his friends seem morons, martyrs, or, if the news were incontestably good, thieves. Donald, whose style was to be magnanimous, praised whom he could and forgave the rest. Donald's exculpations incited Mike to ever fiercer judgments, and these in turn provoked Donald to still more ingenious charities. They worked well together.

A damp, large, lardy girl in a yellow vinyl poncho with a Bolex Rex-4 pendant from her neck like some mammoth ankh had parked herself before the Foundation's mimeoed schedule, which was scotch-taped over the glassed display of stills for *Lust Party*. As she read her mouth and eyebrows ticked an unceasing commentary of pouts, sneers, frowns, and grave suspicions. 'Disturbed' was the word that came to mind.

Mike vanished into the theater.

Donald couldn't take his eyes off the girl's Bolex. Its fittings were rusty, the leather was peeling from its sides, and its carrying strap was a doubled length of twine: a camera as woebegone as the wide, wet, hungry eyes of a Keane puppy. He was smitten.

She looked at him and looked away. She scrabbled in a tiedyed cotton satchel and brought out a dollar bill compactly folded into sixteenths. She undid the dollar regretfully and pushed it into Donald's cage.

"Has it started yet?" she asked.

"No, not yet. We've been waiting for more people to turn up."

"Then maybe you could do me a favor?" She bared her small brown teeth in a defeated smile, like a teenage pan handler's or a Scientologist's, that no rebuff could dismay.

"Certainly," said Donald.

"I'm making a film." When he did not contradict her she went on. "And I need some footage of me coming down the street to the theater here. All you have to do is aim the camera at me and look through here." She pointed to the viewfinder, from which the eyeguard was missing. "And touch this when I say to. Otherwise it's all wound up and ready to shoot."

Donald consented to be her assistant. He came out from the ticket window and took the wounded camera in his arms.

"Be careful with it," she thought to insist, seeing that he was careful. "These things are very expensive."

Then she walked up to the corner, turned around, fussed with her poncho, squared her shoulders, and fixed her wide, meaty lips in a smile representing an irrepressible buoyancy.

"Now!" she shouted.

Through the viewfinder he watched her advancing toward him with a sinking certainty that Fate had come in at the door without knocking. He knew she was not beautiful. Indeed, her face and figure and bearing passed beyond mere homeliness into the realm of absolutes. She was sinfully ugly. Nevertheless his whole frame was in a tremble of sexual anxiety such as no beaver had ever roused him to.

When the film had run out, she said, "You're Donald Long, aren't you?"

He admitted he was.

"Wow, that's terrific. You know, I've read every word you've ever written?"

"No kidding."

"Yeah." She nodded her head solemnly. "So this is really an important moment in my life." Then, offering her hand: "I'm Joycelin Shrager."

Joycelin's film, *The Dance of Life* (or rather, this latest installment, for *The Dance of Life* was conceived as a *film fleuve,* ever flowing on, the unexpurgated and amazing story of her life) was screened by the Foundation for Free Cinema three Sundays later. There was a good turnout. One reason was because this was an open screening, and where there is hope there is good attendance. The other reason was because Donald had been sending out signals and his friends had rallied round, as to Roncesvalles. Jesse Aarons, a director who was making a name in porn, had come, and Ed Gardner, who reviewed sometimes for *The Voice;* Louise Hiller, the modern dancer who had rolfed Donald, and her latest boyfriend, Muhammed Kenzo, a black painter who'd had a painting in the Whitney; the Bachofens, of the Bachofen Gallery, and their son Arnold; Mike Georgiadis, Helen Emerson; and Rafe Kramer (survivors from the older, Maya Deren era of the Art Film); Lloyd Watts, the conceptual artist who'd come to doing street signs and traffic lights by way of his underground movies about cars, and three poets from St. Mark's, one of whom had had the bad fortune to be wearing the same lime-green leather pants as Jesse Aarons. In all, an imposing assembly.

Joycelin's three best friends were also at hand, eager to see themselves as stars on the Europa's screen. There was Murray, a tall, lean, aging, gay Satanist with frizzed hair; his roommate Eric, an office temporary; and Doris Del Ray (her stage name) who'd met Joycelin at a New School film history course in 1968. Doris now studied Jazz Ballet with a teacher in Brooklyn Heights who had studied at Jacob's Pillow, long ago, with Ruth St. Denis. Consequently there was always a special sequence featuring Doris Del Ray, with choreography by Doris Del Ray, in each new install-ment of the Work-in-Progress. There she would be in her black tights, clawing at the air, or convulsed into an expressive ball of pain, or sol-emnly mounting and descending staircases swathed in remnants of sheer rayon, her long hair unbound, a priestess. This time it was a kind of temple scene, with Murray wearing his Satanic vestments, on the steps of the Soldiers and Sailors Monument in Riverside Park. Murray also had a longish moment reading the Tarot. The camera studied each card intently while the sound track continued to play the temple theme, "Anitra's Dance." Eric's big moment came after "The Tower" was turned up. He picked up the card, scowled, and returned it to the deck. The music changed to "Asa's Death." He looked still grimmer: slow fade to black. As Eric's most salient character trait was an uninflected, sullen resentment that Murray regarded as butch, in *The Dance of Life* he symbolized Death and other negative vibrations. He never did much more than smoke and glower, but there was always a moment of him doing that somewhere in the middle of each reel, like Harpo's musical interludes in every Marx Brothers movie.

Contrary to the practice of Gary Webb, who scrupled, Godlike, to efface the evidences of his own directing presence (even editing out footage into which his shadow might have strayed), Joycelin appeared abundantly in *The Dance of Life*—was, in fact, nearly co-extensive with it. Here she was, at the start, striding down Eighth Avenue toward the camera and into Donald's life. Now (with Donald still aiming the cam-era) she was fiddling the dials on the phonograph. (In tribute to the Orpheus of Cocteau.) Holding up the record sleeve of *Revolver*. Feeding a squirrel in Central Park. Standing in the empty band shell and clap-ping her hands with enigmatic ill temper. (They'd had their first argu-ment, and she was making fun of him.)

Here was Joycelin glueing acoustical egg cartons to the walls of her bedroom, and re-glueing them as they fell off. Here she was coming down Eighth Avenue again. You could see the smile being jarred from her mouth as she walked. The expression that lingered in the closeup was one of mild, moist avidity. Someone in the theater (it sounded like Helen Emerson) actually snickered, but then it was time for Doris and

Murray to do their thing on the temple steps, a sequence so typical of the Foundation's offerings that no one dared say boo.

Joycelin next accepted a bouquet of pilfered tulips from Doris's hand, Doris having become a statue. Cut to Joycelin's favorite M.C. Escher poster, then pan down to Joycelin arranging the tulips in a glass. Then, in a moment of understated candor, the camera (with Joycelin guiding it now) examined Donald's clothing draped over a semi-deflated inflatable chair. Clouds scudded, Squirrel Nutkin nibbled away, the Hudson flowed softly by, and she ended her song with a reprise of herself advancing in slow motion down Eighth Avenue, while, voice-over, she intoned a stanza from a poem she'd found in *Strengths,* a mimeo magazine of feminist poetry:

> i love you
> for the way you see
> Innermost Me
> i love you
> for the strong caress
> of your fingers in my heart
> & how they always seem to
>   know
> what parts are spoiled
> & pass them over
> to pull out treasures
> that I never knew were mine
> until you gave them to me

The terminal closeup of Joycelin's face slowly faded to white. As the last wisps of eyebrow evanesced, a wee small voice went on:

> i love you
> for the self-beauty
> i behold
> gleaming like diamonds
> in the priceless setting
> of your eye

The applause stopped short of an ovation, and after that in the discussion period no one had anything to discuss. Ordinarily Donald could have got the ball rolling, but the poem, which had been added to the sound track as a last-minute valentine surprise, had thrown him off his usual moderating form.

He started the next movie, a slapstick parody of *Star Trek* by a ninth-grader at the Bronx High School of Science. People laughed at it perhaps more than it deserved. Joycelin got up in the middle and left the theater. After a short argument with Eric, Murray followed her out.

One forgets, during one's own romances, that it is a curse to fall in love. This time, for Donald, this had been apparent from the start, nor would it ever cease to be apparent. He was appalled at his heart's election. But there it was—he loved her. Worse, he lusted after her continually with the fixated, somnambulistic desire of Peter Lorre in *M* or a bride of Dracula. Waking he thought of her, sleeping he dreamed of her. It was the real thing, which there is no resisting.

After hours at the Europa, if he were not in demand at her apartment on East 13th, he would watch, entranced, reel after reel of *The Dance of Life* (which earlier had borne the title, *Dance of the Moon-Girl*) and wonder: Why? Why me? Why Mimi?

Mimi was his pet name for her (Squirrel Nutkin was hers for him), after Puccini's Mimi, and in particular after the Mimi of Marguerite Ruffino, of the Ruffino Opera Company, which put on grand operas at an Off-Broadway theater on Monday nights, when it was closed. The company was financed by Marguerite's husband, a retired fireman, and in every production she sang the leading soprano role with a headlong, blissed-out inadequacy that kept her fans coming back steadily for more. Donald had seen her in *Aida,* in *Norma,* in *Cosi Fan Tutti,* and in *La Gioconda,* but her greatest role, surely, was Mimi. No *Boheme* had ever been sadder, nor truer-to-life, than the Ruffino's.

Pity—that had been Donald's downfall. All his life he had loved losers, losing, loss. At zoos his favorite animal was the yak, yearning hopelessly behind its bars for the peanuts no one wished or dared to feed it. He had pretended to find a higher wisdom in the more kindly varieties of ignorance, a Woolfean beauty in faces that were unarguably ill-formed, and hidden forces throbbing in the filmic daydreams of the weak, the lazy, and the incompetent. Seeing this vice apotheosized in the love he felt for Joycelin did nothing to diminish his passion for her, but it did enable him to see how thoroughly he resented everyone else who took up space in his life. His friends! He wanted nothing but to be rid of them. No, even more he wanted a revenge for the decades he had spent praising their meretricious work—and he began to see how, beautifully and without a single overt betrayal, he might obtain it.

Unless she were filming and needed the light, Joycelin slept till two or three o'clock. This, together with the penchant of most twenty-year-olds

for self-examination, allowed her, even after a second bout of love-making, to go on talking all night long—about her past, about her latest ideas
for *The Dance of Life*, about what she'd do with his apartment if it were
hers, about Murray and Doris and her boss at May's Department Store,
where she worked four nights a week in Accounts. Her boss had it in for
her.

"Because," she explained one night, "I'm Jewish."

"I didn't know you were Jewish."

The burning tip of her cigarette bobbed up and down in the dark. "I
am. On the side of my mother's grandmother. Her name was Klein-
holz."

"But that doesn't necessarily mean—"

"People think Shrager is Jewish, but it isn't."

"It never occurred to me to think so. You don't *look* Jewish."

"People can sense it in me."

She was fired three days later. Proof, if any proof were needed, that
anti-semitism had struck again.

She was certain that Donald was concealing his true opinion of her.
The books in his bookcase, the records on his closet shelves were unlike
her books and records. Chance remarks required long footnotes of explanation. His friends were inattentive, and she didn't find their jokes
funny. He said their humor was just a shorthand form of gossip, but that
was no help. If they talked in riddles, how could she ever be sure it wasn't
her they were gossiping about? Anyhow (she wanted him to know) her
friends didn't care much for *him* either. Murray thought he was a
phony. He'd done a chart of Donald and found out terrible things.

The easiest way to calm her at such times was not to urge the sincerity
of his admiration but to make love. She seemed to take his uxoriousness
as her due, never offering any of those erotic concessions that a typical
underdog believes will earn the ravished gratitude of the beloved, just
lying back and yielding to his ardors. It astonished him, in his more
reflective moments, how accepting she was of her own substandard
goods. A Nigerian tribesman who has come into possession of a Land
Rover could not have been more reverently admiring of his treasure than
was Joycelin of the machineries of her flesh. Mirrors never fazed her, and
she could pass by any shop window in the city and instantly translate its
mannequins into images of self. She wasn't (she knew) pretty, not in any
conventional way at least, but the fairies who'd presided at her birth had
made up for that lack with other gifts, and the light of them shone in her
eyes. This was how her father had explained the matter to her in the

once-upon-a-time of Cleveland, and that mustard seed had grown into a perduring, mountain-moving faith.

And yet she was uneasy. She revealed that in high school she had been known as Miss Bug. Once she'd taken a beginners' class with Doris's teacher in Brooklyn Heights and realized that the woman was making fun of her behind her back.

"That's what hurts, you know. Because you have to pretend you haven't noticed. Why couldn't she just come out and criticize me in the open? I know I'm no Pavlova or anything, but still. With a little more encouragement I'd have got the hang of it. I'm a born dancer, really. Murray thinks I must have been a ballerina in one of my previous lives. There's certain pieces of music that when I hear them it's like *The Red Shoes* all over again."

"You shouldn't let one person's opinion get you down like that."

"You're right, I know. But still."

She waited. He knew what she wanted from him, and it aroused him to be able, expertly, to supply it. It was easy in the dark. "You know, Mimi, the simplest things you do, just walking across a room maybe, or sitting down to eat, they have a kind of strange gracefulness. It *is* like dancing."

"Really? I don't try to."

"It's probably unconscious. Like a cat."

"Yeah?"

She wanted more, but he didn't have any immediately at hand. All he could think of was Cupcake, his super's fat spayed calico, who rode the elevator up and down all day in the hope of getting to the garbage in the basement.

"Penny for your thoughts," she insisted.

"I was thinking about us."

An egg carton fell from the wall.

She waited.

"I was thinking how sometimes it's as though there'd been a disaster, like in *The Last Man on Earth,* if you ever saw that?"

"*I* feel like that at times. Completely alone."

"Except in my scenario you're there too. Just you and me and the ruins."

"Why you dirty old man! You're the one who's like a cat—an old tomcat. Stop that!"

"I can't, baby. Anyhow, we've got to get the world repopulated again."

"No, seriously, Squirrel Nutkin. You've just given me an incredible idea for the next part of *Dance*. And if I don't write it down I might forget."

She was up till dawn. Scribble, scribble, scribble.

He would arrange get-togethers with his oldest, dearest, so-called friends and let the fact of Joycelin sink in as they ate her parsimonious stews and meat loaves. Then, when the dishes had been cleared away, they'd watch *The Dance of Life*. With a soldier-like pleasure in his own remorseless fidelity, he squeezed wan compliments from his boggled colleagues. There were years and years of debts to be collected in this way, and Donald was careful never to exact more than the interest on the principal, so that in a few months he might press for renewed courtesies.

With Joycelin, increase of appetite grew by what it fed on, and when the first faltering praise trickled to a stop—the strained comparisons to Merce Cunningham or tantric art—she would nod demurely (making a note of such novelties in her mental notebook) and then ask for *criticism*. She admitted she was young and had rough edges. While in one sense her faults were part of her Gestalts (and therefore sacrosanct), on the other hand she was still growing and learning, and so any advice was welcome. For instance, in the long tracking shot of Doris, did the degree of jiggle perhaps exceed the ideal? Did the uncertainty of what was happening detract from the Vision she'd meant to get across? Most guests survived these minefields by adopting the theory offered them— that all their hostess needed was a little more know-how vis-a-vis equipment, a little polish to bring out the natural beauty of the grain.

However. There were, inevitably, a handful who lacked the everyday aplomb to conceal their honest horror. Of these Mike Georgiadis was the most shameless, as well as the most cowardly, for he didn't even wait for the bedsheets to be tacked up screen-wise on the wall before he was in flight, leaving poor Helen Emerson and Rafe Kramer to cope on their own. Helen in her day had soaked up God only knew how many fifths of Donald's Jim Beam, and Rafe had been dumping his little abnormalities into Donald's all-accommodating psychic lap for half their lifetimes, like an eternal festival of the murky, lubricious movies for which he had once won, with the wind of Donald's reviews in his sails, a Ford Foundation grant no less. Even *they* betrayed him that night. Helen first, by bursting out, at the end of the jug of Gallo Hearty Burgundy, with the awful pronouncement that Joycelin's case was hopeless. That she was not an artist. That she never could be an artist, and that surely in her heart of hearts she must know this too.

In the face of such gorgon truths what use was there talking about camera angles, shooting ratios, film stocks? Joycelin became tearful and appealed to Rafe.

Rafe was mute.

Helen, with implacable good will, said was it so important after all? People fussed too much about art. There were other things. Life. People. Pleasure. Love. Enlightenment.

Joycelin turned to stone.

Donald bit the bullet. "Helen," he said, echoing her tone of creamy reasonableness, "you *know* that what you're saying just isn't so. When you consider the budgets that Joycelin has had to work with, I think she's made better films than any of us. They're utterly honest. They're like doorways straight into her heart."

"Better than any of us?" Rafe insisted with mild amazement.

"Damned right."

"We're the has-beens," Helen declaimed, slipping into her English accent. "The bankrupts. The burnt-out cases. Isn't that so, Donald?"

"*I* didn't say it."

"And Gary?" Rafe demanded. "Is he another has-been?"

"You know how much I've always admired Gary's work, Rafe. But yes, I do think *The Dance of Life* is right up there with the best things Gary Webb has ever done. And Joycelin's still growing."

It was enough. Joycelin's composure was restored, and she it was who smoothed these waters with the assurance that nothing was worth old friends losing their tempers over. The Sara Lee cheesecake must be thawed by now. Why didn't they eat it?

The September issue of *Footage* had a long essay by Donald about *The Dance of Life.* He waited till it was in print to show Joycelin. As she read the article, a look came into her eyes. A look such as you might glimpse on a baby's wholly contented face, when its every need has been fulfilled: the understanding, for the first time, that there is a Future and that it will suffice.

Afterwards he regretted that he hadn't thought to film her at that moment, for he was beginning to think of *The Dance of Life* as his own movie too, and even, in an odd way, to believe in it.

Donald had three rooms in a brownstone around the corner from the Europa. Since he'd been there time out of mind his rent was less than Joycelin's, though she had only a narrow studio with a bathroom that she had to share with Murray. Donald's apartment, though no less ratty in its essentials, was of a less effortful kind of grunginess than hers. The furniture was off the streets or inherited from friends. Never had he deceived himself into attempting improvements, not by so much as a pine bookshelf. Things piled up of their own accord, on windowsills and tabletops, in corners and closets, and increasingly they were Joycelin's things: her stereo (after it had been repaired); her paperbacks; her seven coleus plants; the Escher poster, a rug, a chair; most of her clothes; even the precious Bolex Rex-4 and the rest of her equipment, since his neighborhood was marginally safer and the windows had bars.

At last after a serious talk they agreed they were being ridiculous in keeping up two apartments. Even if it meant forfeiting her two months' deposit, wasn't that better than paying rent forever for a place that they spent so little time in and that had never been more anyhow than a temporary expedient?

So they borrowed Lloyd Watts' station wagon, and early one Tuesday morning they loaded it with whatever was still worth salvaging from East 13th Street, which was not a lot. Most painful to relinquish was an armchair that Joycelin had schlepped all the way from Avenue A, but she had to admit it was too bulky and probably (serviceable as it still was) full of roaches. There was a problem, too, with the toaster and the electric coffee pot, since Donald already had the best Korvette's could offer. But you can't just leave armchairs and appliances behind, like the old bags and paint cans under the sink. So, even though he didn't answer his door, it was determined that Murray was to be the inheritor of these and other orphaned articles: a lidless blue roasting pan, some empty flower pots, a can of turtle food for turtles that had died, a wealth of coat hangers, and a bicycle pump. Joycelin didn't have a key to Murray's room, but she knew how to jimmy his lock.

The room was painted a uniform, Satanic black—floor, walls, ceiling, window—and all the lightbulbs were gone from the sockets. They might very well have moved in all the presents without seeing Murray at all if Donald hadn't thought to light the room by opening the refrigerator door.

Their first thought was burglars. But burglars would not have dressed Murray so carefully in his cabalistic coat and hat and left him in the middle of a pentagram. No, it was Nembutals, as it had been twice before.

The reasons were not far to seek. Only a week after meeting Jesse Aarons at that fatal Sunday screening of *The Dance of Life,* Eric had got a part in a gay porn feature called *The Boys in the Bathroom,* and now he was living in a sadomasochistic commune in Westbeth. He wouldn't even talk to Murray on the phone. At the same time, more delicately but no less definitely, Joycelin had left him to mount the ladder of *her* success. He couldn't even be her cameraman now. What was left?

They got him to Bellevue in the station wagon and his stomach was pumped out in time. All the way back to 13th Street, where they'd forgot to close the doors, Joycelin couldn't get over her awesome intuition. What force had led her to Murray at his darkest hour and made her break down his door?

Then she remembered the Tower. Right there in *The Dance of Life* was the answer, plain as day. From the moment he'd turned up that card, she should have known. Perhaps (was it so impossible?) she had!

Next day she was back at Bellevue with Murray's billfold (he needed his Medicaid I.D.), a pillowcase full of fresh underwear and socks, and the old Bolex Rex-4 around her neck. The guard wouldn't let her into the elevator with her camera (these were the days of the Willowbrook scandal, and warnings were out), and so the only footage she could get to illustrate this momentous chapter of her life was some very dark shots of the lobby and her argument with the nurse, and a long, careful pan of hundreds and hundreds of windows, behind one of which, unseen by Joycelin and never to be seen by her again, a pacified Murray in clean blue pajamas was playing dominoes with a Jehovah's Witness, who had threatened to jump from the balcony of Carnegie Hall during a July Collins concert until an usher could convince him not to.

At Christmas Donald spent a small fortune on Joycelin, his jo. In addition to such basic too-muchness as perfume, an amber necklace, and a Ritz Thrift Shop mink, there was: a cased set of Japanese lenses and filters, a four-hundred-foot magazine for the Bolex with sixteen giant spools of Kodak Four-X, a professional tripod with a fluid pan head, three quartz lighting heads in their own carrying case, a Nagra quarter-inch tape recorder, assorted mikes, and a mixer. He'd stopped short of an editing machine, reflecting that there'd be time for that extravagance next time.

When all these treasures had been neatly wrapped in the most expensive gold paper with bushy red satin bows and stowed beneath and about the Christmas tree, itself a monument to his fiscal incontinence, he felt, supremely, the delirium of his own self-inflicted loving-madness. *O sink hernieder!* And he was sinking. At last he could understand those millionaires in Balzac who squander their fortunes on floozies, or those doctors and lawyers in Scarsdale and White Plains whose savage delight it is to see their money transmogrified into tall gravestones of coiled hair surmounting their wives' irredeemable faces, into parabolas of pearls declining into the dry crevasses between two withered dugs, into the droll artifice of evening gowns, whose deceits, like the sermons of Episcopalians, no one is expected to believe.

The unwrapping began as a responsible masque of gratitude and surprise and ended in genuine anxiety infused with disbelief. Without working out the arithmetic, she could not but wonder how, unless he were a stockbroker in disguise, Donald could have afforded all of this.

At last, when they were sitting down with their eggnogs in front of the electric Yule log, she had to ask.

"It's simple. I sold the magazine."

"You sold *Footage*. That's terrible!"

"I'm keeping my column in it. That's down in writing. All I'm giving up is the drudgery, and Jesse is welcome to that."

"Jesse Aarons?" she asked, as he snuffled in the loose flesh of her neck.

"You see. . . ." He curbed the stallion of desire, leaned back in the nest of hand-crafted pillows that had been Joycelin's merry gift to him, and exposited. "Jesse had the idea, some while ago, that there should be a *serious* magazine about skin flicks. Something that would do for porn what *Cahiers* did for Hollywood, make it look intellectual. At the time I'd used a couple of his articles along those lines, but I couldn't see taking the whole magazine in that direction."

"I should hope not. But then why—?"

"Five thousand dollars."

Joycelin set down her eggnog on the new Nagra and became serious. "But just last week, Donald, Jesse *borrowed* eighty dollars from you."

"The money doesn't come directly from Jesse. Harold Bachofen was the purchaser, but his name won't go on the masthead. Though Arnold's will, of course. Harold screwed Jesse out of the profits on *Ear, Nose, and Throat* last year, and he's giving him *Footage* by way of an apology. I think he wants a slice of his next feature now that Jesse's star is on the rise."

"I still don't think you should have done it. I mean, *Footage* was worth a lot more than five thousand dollars. It's the most respected magazine in the field."

"Every issue of that respected magazine puts me two hundred dollars in the red. When I'm lucky. We've got better things to do with our money."

"You should at least have waited to find out whether I get my CAPS grant or not. If Helen Emerson can get a CAPS grant, I don't see why I can't."

"Absolutely, Mimi, my love. All in good time. But meanwhile, five thousand dollars is five thousand dollars." He poured the last of the eggnog into her glass.

She sipped and thought. Fake firelight from the Yule log rippled over her Art Deco negligee. She struck an attitude—elbow propped on the arm of the couch, chin resting on the back of her hand—suggestive of close attention to music not audible to other ears than hers. At such moments Donald was sure she was thinking: "Is he looking at me now?" But this time her thoughts had truly been on a larger, philosophic scale, for when she came out of it, it was to declare, with all the hushed solemnity of a presidential press secretary, that Donald had done the right thing and that she was proud of him. And very happy.

The first issue of *Footage* to come out under Jesse Aaron's aegis had for its cover a still from *The Dance of Life* that showed Eric in a denim jacket, squinting at the smoke of his cigarette. It looked every bit like a face on the cover of a real magazine. Joycelin gazed and gazed, insatiable. There was also another nice little mention in Donald's column.

"I wonder. . . ."

"What do you wonder, my love?"

"Whether I shouldn't try and get in touch with Eric again. I mean, he has been so much a part of *Dance* right from the start. Just because he isn't with Murray anymore—"

"What about Murray? Did you ever find out his address?"

"No, and I don't care if I ever do. The bastard."

Murray had gone off to San Francisco without ever saying good-bye, much less thanking her for his life. The transition between concern for Murray's mental health to bitterness at this snub had been difficult to accomplish.

"Bastard?"

"Well, I wasn't going to tell you this, but you know how Murray was always telling everyone how he was a Scorpio? He's not. When I had to bring him his things to the hospital, I looked in his billfold. Where it says date of birth on his draft card, the date was January 28th, 1937. An Aquarius! His *moon* isn't even in Scorpio, for God's sake. I looked it up, and it's in Capricorn."

"He probably thought he'd be more interesting as a Scorpio."

"Of course that's what he thought. But that doesn't make it right, does it? There's one thing I can't stand, and that's a liar. I mean, if your own friends *lie* to you, how can you believe *anything?*"

The wedding was in June, at St. Mark's In The Bowery. Joycelin's parents were to have come, but at the last moment (not unexpectedly) her mother came down with shingles, so Harold Bachofen acted *in loco parentis* and did very well. Joycelin's gown was a collaboration between herself and Doris Del Ray—a white silk muumuu swathed in tulle, with a veil and train that were one and the same. Donald dressed white tie, as did Harold Bachofen. Everyone else came in whatever they regarded as regal, which included, in at least one instance, drag.

The theme of the wedding, in any case, was not to have been fashion, but *film.* Everyone who owned or could borrow a camera was told to bring it to St. Mark's and shoot, the resulting trousseau of footage to be incorporated into a single grandiose wedding march in *The Dance of Life.* Since the invitation list included everyone in underground film who hadn't actively snubbed Joycelin, the results were gratifyingly spectacular. Donald stopped counting cameras at twenty-three. As a final dollop of authentication, a news team from Eyewitness News appeared just as the bride was being led to the altar. (Donald's former brother-in-law, Ned Miles, was now an executive at Channel 7.) The wedding, alas, was squeezed out of the news that night by an especially sinister double-murder in Queens, but the news team made it into *The Dance of Life.* They were the only people in the whole church who seemed at all astonished at what was happening.

And Joycelin? She was radiant. True movie stars, Donald had theorized once in *Footage,* actually receive energy from the camera, or from the cameraman, like plants getting energy from the sun. They become more alive, more definite, more completely who they are, like the dead on the Day of Judgment when they arise, wartless and cleansed of all the local accidents of character: the skeletons of their essential Selves. So too Joycelin, whose special and enthralling awfulness always awoke to greatest vividness when she was being filmed. And today . . . today with cameras springing up like daisies in a field, today there was no reckoning her transcendency. Roland Barthes says of Garbo that her face represented a kind of absolute state of the flesh, which could be neither reached nor renounced, a state in which "the flesh gives rise to mystical feelings of perdition." In this respect Joycelin and Garbo were much alike.

The filming continued at The Old Reliable, where the reception was held. As Donald had been temporarily overwhelmed, Joycelin and Doris took it on themselves to collect the contributions to the Foundation for Free Cinema, which was what they'd requested in lieu of conventional wedding gifts. People got drunk too quickly, a crush developed, and Jesse Aarons got into a fight. The bride and groom left early.

Joycelin was kittenish, not to say petulant, in the cab, and when they arrived home she insisted on a bride's prerogative of having the bedroom to herself. Donald undressed down to his shorts, and then passed the time drinking from the bottle of Asti Spumanti he'd rescued from the reception. It was flat. He didn't feel so wonderful himself. Great and long-awaited events do take it out of you.

He tried to get into the bedroom but Joycelin had locked the door, so he watched Eyewitness News. They showed the actual bloodstains in the stairwell where the woman had been stabbed. Forty-seven times. And the woman's niece as well.

At last she said to come in.

The dear old Bolex, on its new tripod, with its four-hundred-foot magazine in place, was set up facing the bed. The quartz lighting heads blazed down on the turned-back sheets like the desert sun.

"Surprise!" She was wearing nothing but the one-piece veil and train.

He could not pretend to disapprove on either moral or esthetic grounds. Joycelin had not only seen *Reel 16*—she'd read Donald's reviews of it. The principle was the same. But still.

"Mimi, darling. . . . I don't think I can. Not at this moment."

"That's all right, Donald. Take your time."

He went and sat at the foot of the bed, facing the eye of the lens. "Any other time, but not tonight. That reception got me down, I think. Seeing all those people I haven't seen in so long."

"You don't have to apologize to *me*. Just sit right where you are and say what you're feeling. Whatever it may be. Now that we're married it's like we're just one person. *Dance* is yours now as much as it's mine. Really."

She started the camera rolling. Unconsciously he'd placed his hands in front of his listless crotch. He could not look up.

She held out the directional mike. "Just say anything. Whatever you're thinking. Because whatever *is*—is right."

He was thinking about failure, which seemed, tonight, the universal fact of human life. But he couldn't say that. His thoughts were sealed inside his head like the documents in the cornerstone of a building. They could never come out.

"Hey there! Squirrel Nutkin! Look at the camera, huh? Say cheese."

He looked up at the camera and began to cry. For her, for him, for all his friends—for the dance of life.

ANDRE DUBUS

Waiting

to Peggy

Juanita Creehan was a waitress in a piano bar near Camp Pendleton, California. She had been a widow for twelve years, and her most intense memory of her marriage was an imagined one: Patrick's death in the Chosin Reservoir. After Starkey got back from Korea, he and Mary came to her apartment, and he told Juanita how it happened: they were attacking a hill, and when they cleared it they went down to the road and heard that Patrick had caught it. Starkey went over to the second platoon to look at him.

"What did they do to him?" Juanita said.

"They wrapped him in a shelter half and put him in a truck."

She thought of the road of frozen mud and snow; she had never seen snow but now when it fell or lay white in her mind it was always death. Many nights she drank and talked with Starkey and Mary, and she asked Starkey for more details of the Reservoir, and sometimes she disliked him for being alive, or disliked Mary for having him alive. She had been tolerant of Mary's infidelity while Starkey was gone, for she understood her loneliness and dread; but now she could not forgive her, and often she looked quickly into Mary's eyes, and knew that her look was unforgiving. Years later, when she heard they were divorced, she was both pleased and angry. At the end of those nights of listening to Starkey, she went to bed and saw the hills and sky, and howitzers and trucks and troops on the road. She saw Patrick lying in the snow while the platoon moved up the hill; she saw them wrap him in the shelter half and lift him to the bed of the truck.

Some nights she descended further into the images. First she saw Patrick walking. He was the platoon sergeant, twenty-six years old. He walked on the side of the road, watching his troops and the hills. He had lost weight, was thinner than ever (my little Bantam rooster, she had called him), his cheeks were sunken, and on them was a thin red beard. She no longer felt her own body. She was inside his: she felt the weight of helmet and rifle and parka; the cold feet; the will to keep the body going, to believe that each step took him and his men closer to the sea. Through his green eyes and fever-warmth she looked up the road: a howitzer bounced behind a truck; Lieutenant Dobson, walking ahead on the road, wore a parka hood under his helmet; she could see none of his flesh as he looked once up at the sky. She heard boots on the hard earth, the breathing and coughing of troops, saw their breath-plumes in the air. She scanned the hills on both sides of the road, looked down at her boots moving toward the sea; glanced to her left at the files of young troops then looked to the right again, at a snow-covered hill without trees, and then her chest and belly were struck and she was suddenly ill: she felt not pain but nausea, and a sense of futility at living this long and walking this far as her body seemed to melt into the snow . . .

On a summer night in 1962, for the first time in her life, she woke with a man and had to remember his name. She lay beside the strange weight of his body and listened to his breath, then remembered who he was: Roy Hodges, a sergeant-major, who last night had talked with her when she brought his drinks, and the rest of the time he watched her, and when she went to the restroom she looked at her tan face and blond hair; near the end of the evening he asked if he could take her home; she said she had a car but he could follow her, she'd like to have a drink, and they drank vodka at her kitchen table. Now she did not want to touch him, or wake him and tell him to go. She got up, found her clothes on the floor and dressed; quietly she opened a drawer and took a sweater and put it on her shoulder like a cape. Her purse was in the kitchen. She found it in the dark, on the floor beside her chair, and went out of the apartment and crossed the cool damp grass to her car. With the windshield wipers sweeping dew, she drove down a hill and through town to the beach. She locked her purse in the car and sat on loose sand and watched the sea. Black waves broke with a white slap, then a roar. She sat huddled in the cool air.

Then she walked. To her left the sea was loud and dark, and she thought of Vicente Torrez with the pistol in his lap: a slender Mexican boy who in high school had teased her about being named Juanita, when she had no Mexican blood. Blond gringita, he called her, and his eyes looked curiously at her, as if her name were an invitation to him, but he didn't know how to answer it. Five years after high school, while she was married to Patrick, she read in the paper that he had shot himself. There was no photograph, so she read the story to know if this were the same Vicente, and she wanted it to be him. He had been a cab driver in San Diego, and had lived alone. The second and final paragraph told of the year he was graduated from the high school in San Diego, and listed his survivors: his parents, brothers, sisters. So it was Vicente, with the tight pants and teasing face and that question in his eyes: Could you be my girl? Love me? Someone she once knew had sat alone in his apartment and shot himself; yet her feeling was so close to erotic that she was frightened. Patrick came home in late afternoon and she watched through the window as he walked uniformed across the lawn (it was winter: he was wearing green) and when he came inside she held him and told him and then she was crying, seeing Vicente sitting in a dirty and disorderly room, sitting on the edge of his bed and reaching that moment when he wanted more than anything else not to be Vicente, and crying into Patrick's chest she said: "I wonder if he knew somebody would cry; I wonder if he wouldn't have done it; if that would have seen him through till tomorrow—" The word tomorrow stayed in her heart. She saw it in her mind, its letters printed across the black and white image of Vicente sitting on the bed with the pistol, and she loosened Patrick's tie and began to unbutton his green blouse.

She was looking out at the sea as she walked, and she stepped into a shallow pool left by the tide; the water covered her sandalled feet and was cool and she stood in it. Then she stepped out and walked on. For a year after Patrick was killed she took sleeping pills. She remembered lying in bed and waiting for the pill to work, and the first signals in her fingers, her hands: the slow-coming dullness, and she would touch her face, its skin faintly tingling, going numb, then she was aware only of the shallow sound and peaceful act of her slow breathing.

Juanita Jody Noury Creehan. Her mother had named her, given her a choice that would not change her initials if later she called herself Jody. Her mother's maiden name had been Miller. She looked up at the sky: it was clear, stars and a quarter-moon. Noury Creehan: both names from men. She stepped out of her sandals, toe against heel, toe against heel, heart beating as though unclothing for yet another man, remembering the confessions when she was in high school, remembering tenderly as if she were mother to herself as a young girl. Petting: always she called it that, whispering through lattice and veil, because that was the word the priests used in the confessional and when they came to the Saturday morning catechism classes for talks with the junior and senior girls; and the word the nuns used too on Saturday mornings, black-robed and looking never-petted themselves, so the word seemed strange on their tongues. The priests looked as if they had petted, or some of them did, probably only because they were men, they had hands and faces she liked to watch, voices she liked to hear.

Petting, for the bared and handled and suckled breasts, her blouse unbuttoned, and her pants off and skirt pulled up for the finger; the boys' pants on and unzipped as they gasped, thick warmth on her hand, white faint thumping on the dashboard. She confessed her own finger too, and while petting was a vague word and kept her secrets, masturbation was stark and hid nothing, exposed her in the confessional like the woman in the photograph that Ruth had shown her: a Mexican woman of about thirty, sitting naked in an arm chair, legs spread, hand on her mound, and her face caught forever in passion real or posed.

Then finally in high school it was Billy Campbell in the spring of her junior year, quick-coming Billy dropping the Trojan out of the car window, the last of her guilt dropping with it, so that after one more confession she knew she had kneeled and whispered to a priest for the last time. Young and hot and pretty, she could not imagine committing any sin that was not sexual. When she was thirty there was no one to tell that sometimes she could not bear knowing what she knew: that no one would help her, not ever again. That was the year she gained weight and changed sizes and did not replace her black dress, though she liked herself in black, liked her blond hair touching it. She began selecting colors which in the store were merely colors; but when she thought of them on her body and bed, they seemed to hold possibilities: sheets and pillowcases of yellow and pink and pale blue, and all her underwear was pastel, so she could start each day by stepping into color. Many of those days she spent at the beach, body-surfing and swimming beyond the breakers and sleeping in the sun, or walking there in cool months. Once a bartender told her that waitresses and bartenders should have a month off every year and go to a cabin in the mountains and not smile once. Just to relax the facial muscles, he said; maybe they go, like pitchers' arms. Her days were short, for she slept late, and her evenings long; and most days she was relieved when it was time to go to work and the costume-smile and chatter that some nights she brought home with a gentle man, and next day she had that warmth to remember as she lay on the beach.

She unbuttoned and unzipped her skirt, let it fall to the sand; pulled down her pants and stepped out of them. She took off the sweater and blouse and shivering dropped them, then reached around for the clasp of her brassière. She walked across wet sand, into the rushing touch of sea. She walked through a breaking wave, sand moving under her feet, current pulling and pushing her farther out, and she walked with it and stood breast-deep, watching the surface coming from the lighter dome of the sky. A black swell rose toward her and curled, foam skimming its crest like quick smoke; she turned to the beach, watched the wave over her shoulder: breaking it took her with head down and outstretched arms pointing, eyes open to dark and fast white foam, then she scraped sand with breasts and feet, belly and thighs, and lay breathing salt-taste as water hissed away from her legs. She stood and crossed the beach, toward her clothes.

He was sleeping. In the dark she undressed and left her clothes on the floor and took a nightgown to the bathroom. She showered and washed her hair and when she went to the bedroom he said: "Do you always get up when it's still night?"

"I couldn't sleep."

She got into bed; he placed a hand on her leg and she shifted away and he did not touch her again.

"In three months I'll be thirty-nine."

"Thirty-nine's not bad."

"I was born in the afternoon. They didn't have any others."

"What time is it?"

"Almost five."

"It's going to be a long day."

"Not for me. I'll sleep."

"Night worker."

"They were Catholics, but they probably used something anyway. Maybe I was a diaphragm baby. I feel like one a lot of the time."

"What's that supposed to mean?"

"Like I sneaked into the movie and I'm waiting for the usher to come get me."

"Tell him to shove off."

"Not this usher."

"You talking about dying?"

"No."

"What then?"

"I don't know. But he's one shit of an usher."

She believed she could not sleep until he left. But when she closed her eyes she felt it coming in her legs and arms and breath, and gratefully she yielded to it: near-dreaming, she saw herself standing naked in the dark waves. One struck her breast and she wheeled slow and graceful, salt water black in her eyes and lovely in her mouth, hair touching sand as she turned then rose and floated in swift tenderness out to sea.

MAXINE KUMIN

Another Form of Marriage

They were touring New England, escaped lovers in mid-June, when the signs sprang up, hand-lettered in red and green on shiny white boards. *5 Miles to Skyvue Strawberry Farm!* the first one proclaimed, followed in due course by *Skyvue Strawberry Farm, 1 Mile on Left* and *Pick Your Own at Skyvue Strawberry Farm 10 to 4.*

"Let's," she said, squeezing the brown corduroy of his knee.

"But what will we do with them?" he said, thinking of tonight's motel somewhere in the Champlain Valley and tomorrow's drive down the Hudson to their separate suburbs. He would leave her at the train station just as he had last year, and the year before, and the year before that. As if she had ridden the local out from Grand Central, she would take a taxi home.

"Eat them. Take them home. Oh never mind!" she despaired. She had caught sight of herself at the taxi stand, strawberries spilling out of her shopping bags.

But he had downshifted from fourth to third and then at the last declarative sign, *Strawberries Are Rich in Vitamin C,* to second. They turned in at the driveway, rose up a winding dirt road, and were there.

They had come from the translation seminar held each summer at a small college in the Adirondacks. He specialized in Hungarian, which was not, however, his native tongue. Always from the bottom of his suitcase he took out the two volumes of his German-Hungarian dictionary. These stood on the bureau, on a succession of bureaus on stolen weekends throughout the year, grave necessary friends of their liaison. She spoke no foreign language, but served the conference as administrative assistant, cutting stencils each morning, collating pages of prose and poetry in bilingual arrangements. She saw to it that the original always appeared on the left-hand page so that the work under discussion might lie as flat as an open-face sandwich.

That first summer she had come to the conference unexpectedly, filling in for an ill colleague. She was a shyly attractive woman in her thirties, tallish and slender with long brown hair that she wore tucked discreetly into a knot at the nape of the her neck. It was rainy and raw; she had not brought warm clothing and the man who was not yet her lover had loaned her a comforting maroon ski sweater in which, he assured her, she looked properly waif-like. It smelled of his brown to-

bacco cigarettes tinged with camphor. When he smiled, she was dazzled
by one off-center gold tooth. She began wearing her hair loose about her
shoulders and in town she bought a pair of dangling imitation-gold earrings. He came to her room the fourth night, whistling nonchalantly up
the stairs of the old brown building, a sheaf of papers in his hand.
Raindrops had peppered his beret and she propped it on the radiator to
dry. But the papers were in Spanish, five versions of a Neruda poem left
over from that morning's workshop and out of his mackintosh pocket
there came a bottle of cognac. At dawn, holding his shoes, he went
lightly down the fire escape onto which, luckily, one of her windows
opened.

A highway bisected the campus. Porches of the college buildings overlooked it and words were often lost in the drift of traffic. Snatches came
through: "Do you see this as an exercise?" "Do you set yourself models?"
"The basic concept is very good, really very good. . . ." Logging trucks
passed in both directions, confusing her. Those great prehistoric-looking
tree trunks, stacked like her sons' Playskool toys, rattled past in their
chains. Perhaps there were sawmills at either end of this mountain gap?
The process of overlap struck her as an apt image for translation.

Skyvue Farm provided its own boxes; wax-lined cardboard trays, really, for picking. What he was to do with the damn things was another
story. They could be given away, he supposed. Bartered against the
motel bill, a hundred miles down the road? The view, or *vue,* if you will,
was truly incredible. To the west, spruce- and pine-covered hills the color
of bleached denim. East, looking into the determined sun of Vermont,
three small, connected ponds with ducks on them. And stretching its
plateau in a commodious rectangle of what he took to be easily ten acres,
this expanse of strawberry field still swallowing up its odd assortment of
human forms as people entered, were assigned their rows, and sank to
their knees or buttocks. Some few more or less leaned down, rumps high,
and dug their hands into the plants, or rested one palm on the earth for
equilibrium as they picked.

He was forty-five this year, his life was flawed and sedentary, he
groaned, folding himself down. The berries adorned the plants tritely.
He resented the dew that added diamonds to their rubies. How monstrous the fruit were, the ripest ones leaving behind a little white cone on
the plant as they pulled away from the calyx. In Austria the strawberries
grew elusively in the meadows and he was forced out into the fields each
morning with the other young ones to crawl through prickly grasses and
fill his pail. Mosquitoes sang in his ear. His mother would fly into a rage if
he scanted on the picking. Once, invoking his father at the Front, she
beat him with a shoe. Those wild strawberries, he remembered, were

long and cylindrical and hung from the creeping vine like sows' teats. He tasted salt and wondered if he had been crying. No, it was sweat. Or did it matter? He mopped his face with a handkerchief and sat down between rows. Memory was exhausting in full sun.

Often there had been no bread in the bakery and no flour in the house to bake with. Now, whipped cream rose up in mountains on his strawberry shortcake. Now he had a wife and half-grown children, the oldest to enter college that fall. And in the mountains, a mistress—dreadful old-fashioned word! What was he but an old-fashioned, fastidious middle-aged linguist?—a mistress only slightly younger than his wife and a history, going on four years now, of stolen weekends. It came to him that he had pretended more translations than he had effected. Each one sweetened the months of fidelity that followed.

It was a hot morning and promised to be a hotter day. She had picked well past him, turned, and had started greedily back still another row so that now she was coming toward him in a series of little frog-hops. He saw her thighs flash white, those strong stems he had lain athwart only a few hours ago. And her fingers pinching here, there, so decisively nipping the best berries; yes, he would nip and pinch and comfort and take hold. Now she was closer, now clearly he could see the gray streaks she lamented were overtaking her hair. How luminous, that chestnut mane, against the sun! Their quarrels were sharper each year, their reconciliations almost unbearably poignant. His wife was paler, larger, a milder version. Against his will he remembered the rented summer cottage at the shore when the children were small, how his wife served him berries with cream for a late night snack, moving furtively about the unfamiliar kitchen, whispering over his bowl. He could hear the click of his spoon on the crockery and knew afterwards exactly how they had bedded, he stroking the back of her neck first. Oh, he was a detestable person, he deserved neither woman, he told himself, even knowing the thought was an act of self-congratulation.

Meanwhile in the strawberry patch he was sentenced to overhear just behind him a tale of loyalty, of a man standing by his wife struck down by multiple sclerosis or cancer, he could not tell from the medical details. In any case, incapacitated, her condition unchanging. Two women, local, he guessed from their accents, harvesting berries for their freezers, jellies, pies, were exchanging the details of this story. She had fainted on the commode, she spat blood, he still took her on fine days for drives, tucking her wasted body about with pillows. Only in Purgatory was one doomed to hear such tales of domestic heroism.

Now the woman who was not his wife had drawn abreast of him and saw from the passivity of his shoulders that she was making him unhappy. In that Buddha pose she would have kissed the worry lines from the corners of his mouth. Instead, displaying the half-filled box, she begged, "Just five minutes more." He smiled evasively, a cocktail party smile of dismissal and moved forward in his row. They squatted there, back to back, her fingers travelling expertly over the plants while she reflected on their stolen weekends.

She could name them all sequentially, passing quickly over the rainy one in Indiana where they had fished in the St. Jo River full of disgusting carp and then drunk themselves into a sodden state in the one downtown hotel. He had pushed her beyond her limits, dark anger had flowed out of her like blood clots, and passion, equally ungoverned, rushed in. Never in her other life had she been an extremist. Now she recorded impressions with her stomach, her skin. The mind came last of all in this procession. It had begun with the glint of gold in the mouth of an elegant foreign man, but where would it end? She could recall especially the grit and detritus of New York City, where they met often, the enforced gaiety of its bars gleaming metal and dark at noon. Once there had been dinner at the Russian Tea Room where an old man at the next table, knowing them for conspirators, palpably, lovingly fondled them with glances. He and the translator had conversed in German.

Out of town she remembered there were chains of lookalike motels where air conditioners exhaled noisy droplets and overhead fans started up in windowless bathrooms at the flick of a light switch. The toilets wore Good Housekeeping seals of paper bands. She swore and paced the corridors while he was gone or else sat for hours in a hot tub as if hoping her skin, that pimple, would burst.

She bit into a deformed strawberry swollen almost to plum size. It was mealy but wet as the earth was wet to her fingers, as the plants were furry with their cultivated bristles. Spiders clambered up the wisps of straw that had been spread as mulch between rows and spun and fell and labored again to renew their torn webs.

Bits of conversation drifted down her row. Even here, the talk was of ungrateful teen-age children, of dying parents, sick animals. She felt a dull astonishment. In this whole Breughel scene of people bending, kneeling, plucking, in this landscape of bobbing colors and anatomies, a terrible banal sameness prevailed. It was the sameness of the human condition. She had come to put her hands into the dirt, to taste her fruit in the full sun. For even in these carefully tended furrows to which the pickers were directed by the farmer's sharp-faced wife dressed in her strawberry-dotted pinafore, even though the hybrid berries had been force-fed to this size and drenched, midway in their span, with insecticides, they were more real than their counterparts in supermarket boxes, plasticked over and fastened shut with rubber bands.

Her legs and back ached. She had come impulsively, she now saw, licking the strawberry juice from her fingers, to put the wildness back in this dear red fruit. At the expense of the man she adored, who was fluent in five languages and whose starved childhood had been stained with this sort of foraging.

What was this affair but another form of marriage? Instead of being faithful to one man, she was faithful to two. Her husband was industrious and kindly and a bit unkempt. She remembered she had loved his ragged beard, his abandon with clothing, the way he wore his pipe, still smoldering, in his back pocket. When his shoestrings broke, he knotted them. When she closed her eyes she saw him, young and laughing, his arms full of their two boys, a tangle of hair and beard and arms and legs. The red dots of strawberries behind her eyes brought back that time, ten years gone, her standing stirring at the stove, him slicing bread, the little ones leaning on their elbows at the table waiting to taste the hot jam. "Will it jell?" they had asked, using their new word. "Will it ever jell?"

Everything jellied, filled its spaces or found new spaces to flow into. Thus she had come, willy-nilly, to adore a tidy professor whose suitcase was meticulously packed, his shaving lotion in a plastic bottle, his shirts in see-through bags fresh from the laundry, a man who carried his dictionaries about with him like religious statuary.

She rose, dusted herself off, and together the lovers, each encumbered with his tray, stood in line to have the fruit weighed. "Boxes or bags?" the pinafore woman asked impatiently. It came to ten pounds worth, two brown bags full, which they set on the floor of the back seat and covered with the *New York Times* as the coolest place in the car.

All that day and the next the berries ripened and ran together in their twin bags, giving off a smell of humus and fermented sugar. All that day and the next, winding their way downstate from Mecca, the guilty pilgrims breathed in that winey richness and did not speak of it. In the twilight of the last twenty miles along the Taconic State Parkway they sat very close, she with her left hand sorrowfully on his knee, he with his right hand nuzzling hers in her lap. At the last rest area before the turn-off to her suburb he swerved wordlessly, pulled up to a green trash barrel and stopped the car. "Yes," she said. "I know," she said. And he divested them both of the bloody evidence. Then he took her to her train station and kissing her goodbye, drove his tongue between her teeth like a harsh strawberry and she clung to him, this other man, this vine which had taken root and on which she ripened.

ANDRÉ PIEYRE DE MANDIARGUES

The Bath Of Madame Mauriac

I know a woman who takes mouse baths. It is true that they are white mice, that she is a singer, and that she only does so before going off to sing Thaïs.

While servitors are hastening supper for the opera-goers under the potted palms of neighboring eating-places, Sibylle Mauriac heaves her ample body from the chaise lounge on which it has been reposing all day. The sound of a gong surrounds her with orphan girls, nine in all, whom she has chosen specifically for their beautiful eyes, their general air of ill health, and the delicacy of their hands. A tinkle of laughter resounds, despite the thickness of the curtains, when Mauriac announces that all should be placed in readiness for her bath.

It is the duty of each orphan girl to remove one piece, always the same, from the costume of Sibylle Mauriac, and to place it in the wardrobe. The girls have the care of nine such wardrobes, which, along with the chaise lounge, some tapestries and a great many mirrors, make up the entire furnishing of the room.

Mauriac, naked, must then be conveyed to the room set aside for her bath, for she is anxious not to tire herself needlessly on days when she is to sing. This is done by means of a chariot covered in angora wool, or more exactly, of red-colored monkey skin, its fur trailing down upon the blonde carpet; here Mauriac reposes in a hollow concavity adapted to the contours of her body, gorging herself on pistachio fondants while the orphan girls hum *"Couronne-toi de roses . . .,"* or other fragments of that opera of which their mistress is the principal attraction, all the while pushing against the wheels or the strapping of the little harnesses attached to the cart.

Between the sea-green walls of her pentagonal bathroom, under a parchment ceiling, translucent with the lamps that it conceals, the bathtub is a lilac-colored enamel basin resting on tiles of black ceramic, embellished with periwinkles and yellow asters. A long bronze pipe, decorated in the Corinthian style and terminating in a leopard's head with gaping mouth, flattened ears, and prominent whiskers, leads off to the mouse-pens that are distributed between three maids' rooms and provided with grooved runways, slanted so that, from below, to pull the cord hanging at the side of the tub sends a whole flood of little white animals down the pipe.

Mauriac has numerous friends who have access to her bathroom.

Sometimes there is a crowd of courtesans, pressed back into the five corners of the room to allow the orphan girls to move around the tub. Mauriac is extremely obese, with very clear skin, so spotlessly maintained that there is not a single hair from the hairline of her flowing tresses to the tips of her toes, except for her eyelids, her eyebrows, and one small tuft, which she rather fancies, just below her left breast. The mice fall in a warm rain, scampering everywhere over her body, lashing her with their tails and pricking her with their little claws; then, tired of stirring, when they are waves of billowing fur at Mauriac's sides, her beautiful hand nonchalantly opens the hole of the drainpipe; then she will pull a cord to induce an additional downpour of fur.

Mauriac's doctor, a diminutive Chinaman from Batignolles, assures her that, in the ancient East, baths of mice, dormice and rats were commonly used to stimulate the circulation of the blood among the great sedentary beauties of those days. Whether these benefits are real or imagined, it remains true that when the singer leaps forth, her skin flushed rose as if from the glacial pummelings of alpine waterfalls, her throat is crystalline, and from that moment until the moment that she appears on stage, a *fata morgana*, troubling the senses of the holy hermit from behind a heaven of tulle, the overwhelming frenzy of her voice and gestures is a mighty flood without stint.

Even the most passionate music-lovers, familiar with *Thaïs*, come away so transported by Mauriac's trills that they find it impossible to believe that such a perfect nightingale could have taken wing, in effect, from that Auvergnat throat.

—*Translated by Albert Herzing*

GRAHAM PETRIE

The Locust Keeper

To them he was simply "the old man" and they had no other name for him: he was so ancient that they had forgotten what he had once been called and knew nothing of his origins; there was some debate even as to whether he truly belonged to the tribe. Yet when they took me out to meet him, they showed him to me with pride: he was theirs now and was something to exhibit to visitors; he cost virtually nothing to keep in food and shelter and could easily be carried with them once the waterhole dried up and they had to move on. Besides, he looked after their locusts.

He lay on the ground at the foot of a pole stuck into the sand, and the insects were kept in a closed wickerwork basket that dangled from the top of this by a leather thong. The old men never fed them or tended to them in any way that I could see; no one else seemed to either, and yet they continued to live. If you listened carefully, you could hear a faint scrabbling inside, as of bodies being painfully dragged around; occasionally a leg or wing would appear through a join in the basketwork and remain there for hours or days on end. Then it would disappear: either a passing child had pulled it off, or the creature had regained enough energy to extricate itself; I was never able to tell.

They brought the old man dried meat and water, but he preferred to eat sand. He would scoop it up in handfuls and smear it into his mouth, sometimes mixing it with the water they gave him, but more often chewing it dry, his cheeks moving in a painful and relentless rhythm for hours before he was able to swallow it. I expected that they would resent this, that the women at least would maintain a sense of civilized propriety, and object, but nothing was ever done to stop him. In fact, it became quite a spectacle: the word would go out that "the old man's eating sand again," and they would all drop what they were doing and rush to watch him. Days of the tribe's existence must have been lost in this manner, but no one seemed to think this was important, and I too became used to experiencing time in the rhythm they had established.

The old man came to life at night, when they carried him into the circle of the fire and urged him to tell his stories. Usually he would respond at once: his toothless mouth would fall open and he would begin to recite, in a cracked and high-pitched voice, tales of his wanderings in his youth and the deeds of love and valour that he had performed. No one, I discovered, could corroborate these, for in all the memories of his listeners there was no time when the old man had not been exactly as he was now, telling the same stories in the same words, with the same pauses and the same repetitions, arousing at the same places the same gasps of awe and wonder and the same laughter. I have the tapes in front of me now, miles and miles of them, all exactly alike, and I wonder why I ever allowed myself to be deluded that the performance might one night vary, by a lapse of memory or a change of wording that it would be essential for me to record.

At other times he had to be persuaded: the women would rush at him and offer him violence, clawing to within an inch or two of his dulled eyes, while he sat there immobile, neither withdrawing nor turning his head; the children dashed past and scattered sand in his eyes and he accepted this indignity too, with passivity. Then, when they had given up their attempts and had retreated sullenly to their positions round the fire, when one of them had perhaps struck up a song and his fellows had begun to clap time with their hands and to join in the muttered chorus, the old man would start up a chant of his own, in a feeble voice that only gradually imposed itself, causing first a faltering and then a swift cessation among his rivals. This, I came to understand, was part of the ritual too, and played itself out in the same fashion on each occasion; I came to expect it and look forward to it, and to recognize the signals for each of its stages to come into effect.

The song too boasted of the old man's achievements: it told of his experience in a sports contest at which he had outrun, outswum, outfought and outjumped all opponents. At first I thought he was referring to some bygone Olympic meeting, for words that sounded uneasily familiar recurred again and again and reminded me of countries against which he might have competed; I soon dismissed this as an idle speculation and decided that the song referred to a local contest, swelled out of all proportion by pride and hearsay. And when I tried to question him more closely about this, he merely stared at me uncomprehendingly from his blear and red-rimmed eyes.

As he sang, a drool of saliva would trickle from his open mouth and gather at the corner of a lip before making its way down the runnels of his chin. Once a fly, attracted by the unexpected moisture, hovered at the pool so formed, and then landed to sip the liquids. It drank greedily, dangerously, pausing every few seconds to glance uneasily around it. The men stared at the black intruder that squatted on the wrinkled skin, but no one made a gesture to chase it away, fearful that they might interrupt the old man's thoughts. The insect grew more confident: it decided to explore the landscape before it and set out tentatively across the folded contours of his skin. The old man paid no attention, even when the fly paused on the bridge of his nose to scrape its legs together and glance insolently at the spectators. Finally it set off again into the desert. The faint droning sound it made persisted in the air for several seconds and, as though reminded of something, the old man made a feeble dash at his lip with his hand. He repeated the movement impatiently, three or four times, while the men watched him in silence. At length he gave up, allowing his hand to fall back and rest in the sand at his side.

They had tried to abandon him once, I was told, after his locusts died. There had been silence from the basket for some days, none of the scrabbling noises of life they were used to, and, as the old man took no notice, they raised the lid one day and looked inside. The insects were dead, they had shrivelled and curled up, like discarded pieces of paper held too long and too close before a fire. Why did you let them die, old man? they asked him, without hostility, their voices flat and empty. The old man stared across the desert and said nothing; he had never acknowledged his responsibility to look after these creatures and it could be no concern of his what happened to them. He would say nothing and they soon grew tired of questioning him; they withdrew to a distance and consulted among themselves.

Soon after this the waterhole dried up and, instead of taking him with them when they moved on, they left him behind. There was no malice in this, I was assured: it was part of the normal cycle of life and in other circumstances they might have left others with him, old women and crippled or deranged children. He bore them no resentment and accepted their action without protest; none of them expected to see him again and yet, when they finally returned, he was still there, more feeble and motionless than ever, but certainly alive. I could never find out how long the interval had been: some reckoned it as months, some days, and others claimed it was merely a matter of hours, depending equally on their methods of calculating time and their desire to honor or belittle the old man's achievement.

So they procured some more locusts for him to look after and set them up inside the same basket on the same pole, and propped the old man up at its foot, and life continued as usual. It was at this stage that I came to know him, and I was struck by the total indifference with which he accepted his fate: he appeared to live only for the evenings and the chance to sing or tell his stories. I tried to find out something of his true history, his name and his origins, but it was all of no use: I listen to my tapes now and all I can hear is the faint whirr of the motor, the scratching caused by a speck of dust or sand; and beyond that an endless silence, broken only by the plod of a camel's foot across the desert, the sudden laugh or scream of a child, the occasional rattle or wheezing intake of breath that showed that the old man still lived. There are days of my life there on these tapes, days or months, I no longer remember which, and the old man would tell me nothing.

Once more the locusts died, this time in a panic-stricken flurry that sent their whole cage rocking and swaying and almost toppled it from the pole. When the men looked inside it was already over: they had shrivelled and fallen like dead leaves and lay in a pathetic pyramid on the floor. They poured the bodies out in a heap at the old man's feet and challenged him with their eyes to defend himself, and once more he would do nothing except stare vacantly toward the horizon. They controlled their rage with difficulty and one of them even stepped forward as though to strike him; he stood there with his arm raised, staring down at the bundle of rags at his feet, then he allowed his arm to sink slowly to his side and turned away.

They decided to let him starve to death, but this time they would all stay and watch him, for who knew by what feat of magic or cunning he might once more survive if they merely abandoned him? They formed a circle round the pole and sat there, day after day, eating and drinking when they needed to, occasionally chatting and joking, but most of the time in silence. I tried to protest of course, to defend and save the old man, but they simply stared at me with bleak and uncomprehending eyes and at last I gave up. In all that time the old man made no effort to feed himself, not even to scoop a handful of sand into his mouth; flies settled on him in a dark and swollen mass and he was oblivious to them.

In the evenings he continued to sing his songs, starting up at the customary hour in the cracked and monotonous tones I had heard so often before. The others nodded approval at this gesture; they set up a slow and rhythmic handclap to accompany him. The words told the usual story: he was a great man who had run, swum, fought, thrown, jumped, and loved better than any man before him. When he had finished, he sank his head onto his breast and remained there, hardly moving, until the following night.

He outlasted even their determination to see him die this time, for the waterhole dried up and the grass was gone and they had no grain left, and still the old man breathed and sang. So they abandoned him for a second, or a tenth, or maybe a fiftieth time, taking me with them despite my entreaties and protests. And as they no longer had any use for the locusts, they left the cage behind them too when they moved on, as a marker.

RAY RUSSELL

Evil Star

Dear Mr. Bernstein:

At the request of your publisher and our client, my colleagues and I have now read and discussed the typescript of your book. We are pleased to report that, with the exception of some isolated sections which we will specify, the book is not, in our opinion, actionable and should not expose you to litigation when published. It is a work of scholarly analysis, thoroughly documented, and even though much of it is pungently expressed, it lies well within the area of fair comment. You have obviously "done your homework," amassed considerable research, and consistently cited "chapter and verse," so to speak, in tracing the sources of Avery Bream's work. Your extensive parallel excerpts from his writings and the writings of others, from which you demonstrate his were derived, put you on firm legal, as well as literary, ground.

These parallels of style and subject matter are most impressive. Your own cleverness is rivalled only by that of Mr. Bream himself. I refer to his technique of borrowing a plot from one writer and retelling it in the style of another, thus achieving an artful act of camouflage undetected until now. I was astonished to learn, for instance, that his most famous best-seller, *Evil Star,* is practically a carbon copy of Dreiser's *An American Tragedy,* done in the style (or, as you put it, "filtered through the prism") of James Branch Cabell. It was likewise illuminating to discover that his acclaimed *Midnight Mushrooms* is little more than *Othello* with the races switched, told in the manner of early Saroyan, and with no acknowledgement to Shakespeare (unless we count the title, a quotation from *The Tempest*); and that his *Pristine Christine* is none other than the Agatha Christie classic, *The Murder of Roger Ackroyd,* as it might have been written by Burroughs (you should clarify as to whether you have reference to William or to Edgar Rice) and with the Christine of the title (a play on Christie?) taking the place of the original victim. We suggest a title change, however, for Chapter III, in which the bulk of these and other parallels are cited. Even though *The Thieving Magpie* is the title of a famous opera, words like "thief" should be avoided.

On p. 97, after you quote Bream's statement, "I am the equal, in my fashion, of Tolstoy, Proust and Joyce" (from an interview in *Newsweek*), you make your point elegantly when you say: "The painter Ingres told those who likened him to Raphael, 'I am very small, just *so high,* next to him.' The composer Rossini made a pilgrimage to kneel before the manuscript score of Mozart's *Don Giovanni,* declaring it a sacred relic." Why not leave it at that? To add, as you do, that Bream is "a conceited pig" not fit to "empty the bedpans" of Tolstoy, et al., is painting the lily, as well as flirting with litigation.

A similar example of gilding refined gold occurs on p. 118, following your sentence, "For over a decade, he has been promising to astound us with a vast confessional tome of Rousseau-like candor in which he will beat his breast and cry *mea culpa* to a host of sins, literary and otherwise; but the years come and go, and the guilt-heavy volume never appears."

That is fine, but the short burst that follows ("What's the matter, Bream—*chicken?*") is, from the legal point of view, touchy.

Our Mr. Vieck asks me to say that, speaking now not as attorneys but as impartial readers, we hope we may be forgiven for commenting on the language you employ in Chapter VIII to describe the first Mrs. Bream. It seems inordinately biased in her favor. This is not, I reiterate, a legal point, but for you to call her "an angel whose delicate foot scarce touched the sordid earth when she walked" (p. 130), "too good by far, too radiant for this world" (p. 131), "an anthology of all the virtues" (p. 132), "a fount of undemanding, uncomplaining love" (p. 133), "a golden spirit the like of which no mortal eye will ever see again" (p. 134), etc., strikes us as somewhat excessive. When such phrases are read alongside your less than complimentary remarks about her husband, the contrast tends to cast doubt upon your academic detachment.

In Chapter IX, *Champion of the Overdog,* you walk a tightrope in showing Bream as being a far cry from the fearless anti-Establishment crusader and spokesman for writers' rights he pretends to be. The change or deletion of a few passages should make the chapter safe from litigation. Second paragraph, p. 155, the word "coward" is ill-advised, as is the phrase in the next paragraph, "soul of a weasel." Pp. 157–158 make vivid reading, but in them you are guilty of that with which you charge Bream: lack of substantiation. "His oft-repeated claim to have broken the writing arm of a magazine editor who had 'emasculated' his prose," you say, "is less piquant than it might be if he would, just once, name the offending butcher." Good point, but you spoil it (and skate on thin legal ice) when you add: "In fact, that editor has privately recounted the truth about the famous fray. Bream, it seems, had offered a timorous, whining protest to the emendations, thus provoking the overworked editor to gruffly respond, 'Damn it, I sweated blood to make that unreadable swill fit for human consumption. And this is the thanks I get? You're lucky I publish your shit at *all!* On the stressed word, the angered editor brought his fist down forcibly on his desk, breaking the little finger of his right hand." *You* do not name the editor, either, you see, so the authenticity of both versions is suspect.

The same chapter (p. 159) contains a passage that could be considered defamatory not only to Bream but also to Siegfried Rheinfahrt, the book publisher. I refer to the quoted letter, from and to unidentified sources, which describes an incident at a booksellers' convention: "You should have seen our dearly beloved Aviary buttering up that Nazi goniff, Rheinfahrt. I mean, it's one thing for Aviary to change his name and try to pass for goy, and it's another for him to fawn upon and flatter that lizard who's not only a crook but an anti-Semite. Most of us snubbed

Siggie cold, but not ol' Aviary. Oh, no. It was nauseating. He did everything but kiss the s.o.b.'s ass, and maybe in the *privvissy,* as he'd say in
that phony accent he's begun to affect, of his hotel suite, he even did
that." The passage should be excised.

   Are you sure of your facts (p. 201) when you describe Bream "running
from bookstore to bookstore, spending his entire advance check buying
up copies of his novel to get it on the [bestseller] list . . ."? What proof of
this could you provide, if challenged? On the same page, how can you
possibly know that he "not only wined and dined" but also "tickled more
than the fancy" of the "aging female critic" who, according to you,
"bears a startling resemblance to Samuel Johnson"? Moreover, if we
understand what you are suggesting in the "tickled" line, does this not
contradict the allegation in your p. 492 footnote (see below)? Please
think about these points carefully.

   I'm afraid we cannot recommend the retention of your allusions to
Bream's income in the form they are now presented (p. 299). Nor do we
quite understand the precise nature of your charges. Do you mean to
imply that he failed to declare a substantial portion of his earnings for
that year? That is a serious allegation. Or do you merely mean that he
lied to the press, inflating the true figures in order to appear more af-
fluent and successful than he actually was? Do you really plan to reproduce photocopies of his IRS returns? (I refer to such phrases as "See
Plate 1," "See Plate 2," and so on.) How were these documents obtained?

   Your comments about his mother (p. 307) present no legal problem
because she is deceased, although in some quarters these passages may be
criticized on grounds of taste.

   The telephone conversation between Bream and his psychoanalyst
(pp. 349–350) poses a quadruple problem, however. First: it could only
have been obtained by wiretap, which is illegal. Second: it puts both
patient and doctor in a most unfavorable light. Third: as our forensic
medicine expert, Dr. Kenney, reminds us, you are not a licensed psychiatrist, so you are not legally qualified to diagnose Bream's mental condition as displaying evidence of "self-destructive tendencies . . . irreversible
paranoia . . . dangerously sociopathic hostilities . . . desire for humiliation
and punishment . . . schizoid hallucinations and delusions," etc. Fourth:
as you point out by the long parallel quotations in the right-hand columns of these pages, the phone conversation is identical, word for word,
to the conversation between the fictitious characters Dr. Proctor and
Bernie Amber in Bream's novel, *Negative Feedback.* You claim (but
without adequate support) that the real-life conversation took place five
months *after* the publication of the book, indicating that "Bream is

perhaps the only novelist in history whose own life plagiarized his work. So cowed and mesmerized was his puppet doctor by the fame of the celebrated patient that he responded on cue, Charley McCarthy-like, to Bream's leading questions and insults." Is it not possible, we submit, that you are mistaken about the date of the conversation? Might it not have occurred *prior* to the writing of the book, and been used as grist for the author's mill (a not uncommon practice among fiction writers)? Indeed, is it not an open secret in literary circles that Amber is the most transparently autobiographical character in the entire Bream *oeuvre?* Is not AMBER—as our crossword fanatic, Mr. Fenwick, says—a simple anagram for BREAM? For these several reasons, we counsel you to forego this conversation.

Similarly troublesome is the first of the two footnotes on p. 492 (beginning "Freud, Jung and even Reich all agree . . ."). While it may be perfectly true that certain aspects of his lifestyle are indicators of "impotence or other sexual dysfunction" rather than the "prowess he publicly professes," there is no way you can satisfactorily prove this, even by quoting the anonymous "Ms. X." Besides, here you are venturing into personal attack rather than professional criticism. We realize that you consider this an important insight into the "pathological sex episodes" of his work, which is the theme of this chapter, but we urge you to delete this footnote, as well as the parenthetical reference (in the body of the following page, 493) to what you call his "underendowment." The supportive Polaroid photograph which you indicate will appear on the "facing page" of the published book certainly must not be used. It is irrelevant that you obtained "the standard release form" signed by the photographer, his second ex-wife. What is required is a release from the subject, or model, Mr. Bream himself, and that, in our opinion, will be obtained only with the greatest difficulty. And surely the reference (same page) to his *"vain attempts* at solitary vice" (italics mine) is pure conjecture on your part?

(Before I forget it, allow me to backtrack and cover a couple of small spots I missed. In Chapter VIII, where you picture Bream's miscegenational first marriage, is it necessary to say "murderously jealous rages" and "where the body is buried," even though these expressions have a clearly metaphorical intent? They would not, perhaps, be problems were it not for the tragic sailing accident that took the life of the first Mrs. Bream, plus the fact that her body was never recovered. Some readers might interpret your figures of speech literally, as a monstrous accusation, and you would then be extremely vulnerable to the possibility of a lawsuit. Also inadvisable is the phrase, "Flowers die; rats live." You really must not call Bream a rat. And only this moment Mr. Fenwick calls my attention to the fact that the title of Bream's most famous novel is "rats live" in reverse—isn't that interesting?)

Now for the bad news. We must seriously question the wisdom of your lengthy (95 pages!) Appendix, in which you provide, verbatim and unexpurgated, letters written over the years by various editors, creditors, writers, literary agents, relatives, former fans and friends of Bream's, and so forth. The material, even if provably factual, is extremely damaging to Bream and was not originally intended by the letter writers for publication. In most cases, it seems unlikely that you have even secured proper permission. We strongly advise an appendectomy, that is to say removal of the entire Appendix.

Your revision of the above specified areas should protect you from litigation and, if I may say so, result in a most valuable work of contemporary scholarship which I, for one, found to be brisk reading. May I look forward to receiving a personally inscribed copy of the first edition?

Yours truly,
For
WEST, FENWICK, SCHLUSSEL
MANN, KENNEY & VIECK
Arthur Lowell West

P.S. Our Mr. Schlusselmann points out the amusing coincidence that your name is the German equivalent of a well-known Bream character. Are you aware of this?

DALLAS WIEBE

Night Flight to Stockholm

I owe all this to Gabriel Ratchet. It was he who arranged for the round-trip ticket, two seats side by side, on Scandinavian Airlines, got me my reservation in the King Gustaf Holiday Inn, deodorized my basket, put in the new sheets, put on my new, formal black sack with the white ribbon drawstring around the top and bathed my suppurating stumps for the journey. He even carried one end of my wicker laundry basket when I went aboard. In the darkness, I heard him instructing the stewardesses as to how to clean me, how to feed and water me and when to turn me. I heard money changing hands. I heard his stomachy laugh and the ladies' bovine grunts. I think I heard a stewardess pat his little bald head. Then came my first lift-off. The great surge of the old Boeing 747 sliding my butt and stumps against one end of the basket and then the floating and my ears popping. Into glorious, golden dreams in my black chute. Into nonstop gliding through images of published books, careful emendations, green surgical gowns, the rustle of paper money, the clink of prizes and the odor of immortality. It was Gabriel Ratchet who gave me this slow drifting in the darkness 50,000 feet over Iceland, the North Atlantic, Ireland, England, the North Sea and Norway as we, as I hear from the pilot, descend into our landing pattern for Stockholm and me about to meet the King of Sweden and, I assume, his wife and all the little royalties. I wonder what they'll sound like; I wonder how they'll smell.

I owe all this to Gabriel because he is an expert in contracts. He's made contracts for musicians, painters, sculptors, quarterbacks, pole vaulters, jugglers, born-again Christians and presidents. He's negotiated the careers of farmers, professors, poets, priests, baseball pitchers, terrorists and airline pilots. For the past thirty years he's had his hand in more success than you can shake a scalpel at because of his immense number of contacts. He says he brought it with him from the womb. I can believe it. Gabriel—his clients call him Gabe or Gabby—was born on the western slope of Muckish Mountain in Donegal in 1935, exact day unknown he says, when his mother saw some white horses hung with silver bells. He came to Chicago, IL., he says, when the potato crop failed around Bloody Foreland in 1951. I don't remember any potato famines in Ireland since the nineteenth century, but I'm always willing to lend him an ear and listen to his stories. He came to Chicago, he says, because he is a creature of our own flesh and blood and likes a city where every man has his price. He says his contracting business didn't go well at first. In fact, he was on his last leg when he met Isobel Gowdie in October, 1956, in the Chicago Art Institute while he and she were standing and staring at some water lilies by Monet. According to his own account, Gabriel sighed and said, "Hell, Peg Powler can paint better than that." Isobel, having an eye to the main chance, immediately answered, "Richard Tarlton has one foot in the grave. Can you give him a hand?" Gabe's life as a public servant and a successful entrepreneur began with that moment because he negotiated a contract whereby for a shake and a cut Ambroise Paré became the first wealthy one-armed undertaker in Hellwaine, ME.

I first met Gabe in the lobby of the Palmer House in December of 1977 when I was there for an MLA convention. He was loitering around the packed lobby, looking, I later found out, for failures with whom he could do some business. He was sidling about, handing out, quietly and covertly, little business cards, red letters on green, that gave his name, Gabriel "Ballybofey" Ratchet, his office, 1313 Spoorne Ave., Chicago, his telephone number, 393-6996, his office hours, "At Your Convenience," his profession, "Contractor," and his motto, "Don't limp in obscurity; get a leg up on this world." He gave me his last card and said he'd never seen so many potential clients. He said he'd had his eye on me for some time and I was cut to the quick. We chatted, there in that mob, for a while and I asked him about himself. He told me that he was so short because of that potato famine in his youth. His nose and ears were gnarled because his mother had been frightened by Peg O'Nell when she, his dear mother, was nursing him and her left teat had immediately dried up while in his mouth. His teeth were rotted out and his head was bald because his wife of two years, Joan Tyrrie of Creke Abbey, MT., had tried to poison him with bat slobber. He managed, he said, to overcome the poison by eating stuffed grasshoppers, roasted ants and mice roasted whole and threw her into the Chicago River. He said she'd been bad from the start and he was surprised his marriage in the year of 1955 lasted the two years that it did. Gabe said that her stepmother had given her a bottle of flat beer and some sour bread for a dowry and that after their marriage in Calkett Hall all she wanted to do was to be friendly with the goats and comb their beards. He said there was saltpeter in her heaven and gold in her hell and that her angels were sufficiently embodied to be impeded by their armor and damaged by gunpowder. I told him my problems and he said that I was too old to fool around any longer, that I would have to fight tooth and nail to make it. I said I'd call him if I needed his service.

I needed his help a lot sooner than I thought then because my paper which I presented at that MLA convention was laughed to scorn. When I began my opening remarks I heard tittering. When I asked for silence, they guffawed. When I introduced my paper—"Metaphorical Thinking as the Cause of the Collapse of British and American Literature" by Professor Meyric Casaubon, Department of English, University of Tylwyth Teg, Wales, OR.—they hooted and snarled and shot out their lips. They waggled their beards and gnashed their teeth on their pipe stems. Even my old friend, Bock Urisk, who claimed he could hear grass growing, could run so fast when he was young that he had to keep one leg over his shoulder to stay in sight, could break stones on his thighs they were so hard and could spin a windmill by blowing through one nostril, waved his open palms past his ears and held his nose. I got the message when Richard Tynney of Gorleston, DE., the chairman of the panel, and Sir John Shepe of Wanstrowe, IA., the moderator, got up, dropped their pants and showed me their bare asses. I was mooned for metaphors and that was the end, I thought. I walked off the stage, my green suit striking among the black turtle necks, my thick black hair bobbing over the seated howlers, my hooked nose, my protuberant chin and my green eyes lifted high in disdain, even though I was without skin and my huge belly bounced and rumbled. I walked out of the room, my white Converse All-Stars squeaking on the waxed floors, my white tie and my blue shirt spotted with my sweat. I sneaked to my room, took off my Phi Beta Kappa pin and threw it into the toilet. I decided then to go back to what I'd always been doing anyway, writing fiction. I took out the green card with the red letters.

It was a Thursday when I lifted the phone and called him. I said, "Gabe, I'm going to be sixty-six tomorrow, Friday, January 13, 1978, and I've been writing fiction all my life and no one's ever published a word of it and I'd give my left pinkie to get into *Paris Review.*" And I did because Gabriel was interested at once and told me that he'd get in touch with me the next day because he thought he might find a buyer. He did. The next day Gabe came around and said he had a friend, Tom Reid, whose ancestor was killed at the battle of Pinkie in 1547 and who needed to get his self-respect back. According to Gabriel, Tom had agreed to see to it that my story, "Livid With Age," would be published in *Paris Review* for my left pinkie. And he did. He told me to type my story, double-spaced, on clean white paper. Not to use erasable paper. He said I should make my setting exact in place and time, not to moralize at the end of the story and to get rid of the false intensifiers like "literally," "really," "utterly," "just," "veritable," "absolutely," "very" and "basically." Create emphasis by syntax, he said. He also told me to clean the sweat stains off. I did all that and when my story came out, I went to Dr. Dodypol and had the finger removed surgically and under anesthesia. His head nurse, Kate Crackernuts, wrapped the finger in cotton bandages and in red tissue paper with a yellow ribbon around it and I walked out a published author and weighing three ounces less than when I walked in. And made money on it too, because the operation cost fifty dollars and I was paid sixty for my story.

A month after the appearance of "Livid With Age," I sent another story out, "Liam Sexob Lives in Loveland," to *TriQuarterly.* It seemed like it came back the same day, although of course it didn't, and I knew that I needed Gabriel Ratchet again and his influence. I found him sitting in the Trywtyn Tratyn Pub, drinking Habitrot and flirting with

Jenny Greenteeth. "Look, Gabe," I said, "I need help. I'd give my left testicle to get my story in *TriQuarterly.*" Gabe didn't even look at me when he said, "Make it two and I think I can get you a deal." I allowed as to how I'd probably go along with it and he said he'd talk to Marmaduke Langdale, who needed them for his Whitsun Rejoicings. Gabe did and I did. Dr. Nepier from Lydford in Bercks and his head nurse, Sarah Skelbourn, removed them on a cold Friday in December of 1978. Sarah wrapped them in white bandages, green tissue paper and red ribbons. I took them to Gabriel, who was satisfied with the merchandise and told me that Marmaduke Langdale said I should change the title of the story to "Silence on the Rive Gauche," change the name of the main character Liam Sexob to Burd Isobel, eliminate the doublings, get rid of the colloquial style, erase the tear stains from the margins of pages 4, 14 and 22, and stop using exclamation points, dashes, underlinings for emphasis and the series of periods that indicate ellipses. I did all that. Retyped the story on good, twenty-pound linen bond and sent it off to *TriQuarterly.* They accepted it within a week and I was on my way to my second story in print.

When "Silence on the Rive Gauche" came out, I asked Gabriel Ratchet to be my permanent agent. He agreed and in July of 1979 Dr. Louis Marie Sinistrari and his colleague, Isidore Liseaux, removed my left hand which I figured I didn't need anyway because I can only type with my right hand and right arm, wrapped it in blue-and-red-striped gift paper, tied it with black ribbon, and sent it to Mr. Greatorex, the Irish Stroker, who wrote back from the Island of Hy Brasil, MD., that I should stop using participial phrases, get the inactive detail out of my descriptions, stop using literary language with its euphemisms and circumlocutions and not to use exclamations such as "needless to say," "to my amazement" and "I don't have to tell you." He also suggested that I not send in pages with blood stains on them. I did everything he said and *Esquire* accepted my story, "Moles' Brains and the Right to Life."

Even though I was still anemic from my last publication, I decided in January of 1980 to bid for the *New Yorker.* Gabe sent out the message and Durant Hotham wrote from Yatton Keynel, ME., that he would do it for a pair of ears if I would promise to stop using abnormal word order, get rid of the *faux-naif* narrator, eliminate all clichés from my narrative, would isolate point of view in one character or one narrator and would clean my snot off the manuscript. I did what he said and sent in the manuscript of "Muckelawee." Durant wrote back his thanks for the contract and told me to visit Peg Powler at 1369 Kelpie Street and she would have some directions for me. I went. She had directions and told me to go to Dr. Arviragus at the Abbey Lubbers Clinic. I went. When I walked out of the Clinic, I had my ears in a red-and-gold bag tied at the top with a green ribbon. The stumps on the sides of my head tingled in the cold air as I walked out into a new reputation as one of the finest short story writers in America.

When I suggested a book of short stories to Gabriel, he shivered. He suggested that I rest for a while and get myself together before I made any more deals. I told him he'd made a lot of money off my publications and that he would make a lot more. Just to do his work as my agent and let me worry about the parts. He did admit that he had an offer. That he needed a left arm, even if there was no hand attached to it. A Dr. William Drage of Hitchin, AR., needed it to fit out Margaret Barrance so that she could attend a ball because not having a left arm there was nothing for her to lay across the shoulder of her male partner while she danced. Gabriel told me that I would have to go to Hitchin for the transplant. I agreed and I did in March of 1981. But before he removed the left arm, he told me that the deal was contingent on my editing my manuscript carefully, to carefully control the secondary patterns, to make the deuteragonist more important in all the stories, to research materials for the stories, to make the stories more weird, more strange, more uncomfortable for the reader. Clean the earwax off my pages. I promised I'd do all he told me to do and he took my arm and sewed it onto Margaret, who six months later danced in her first ball at the age of thirty-three, wearing a blue and gold dress with a red sash around the waist, while Doubleday published my collection of short stories, *The Cry of Horse and Hattock* (September, 1981).

Because my recovery times were lengthening, I decided that a novel should be my next reduction and when I mentioned it to Gabriel Ratchet he fell on the floor and chortled. I told him to get his little carcass off the floor and get to work. He did. He got bids for my nose, my feet, my legs, my eyes, my penis and my kidneys. I bid one left foot. The law firm of Morgue, Arsile and Maglore handled the negotiations and in February of 1982 Ratchet finalized the contract with Miss Ruth Tongue of Somerset, KS., by which I agreed to furnish her with one left foot in return for the publication of my novel, *Flibberty Gibbet*, by Knopf. My part of the contract was that I had to stop misusing "transpire," "problematical," "livid," "momentarily," "presently" and "loin." My sentences were to be made more simple. I was to use more active verbs with agents doing actions. I was to get out the melodrama. I also agreed not to use any anthropomorphizing metaphors, not to personify anything not human, to make only direct descriptions of characters, objects and actions and not to leak urine on my manuscript. Gabriel also negotiated an interesting addendum to the contract and that was that if the book could be made to win a national prize then my part of the bargain was the left foot and the whole left leg. Wouldn't you know; Ms. Tongue got the whole leg when *Flibberty Gibbet*, clad in a dust jacket of red, black and orange, won the National Book Award for 1982. They carried me up to the podium in a rocking chair and I shook hands for the last time when I accepted the award.

Rachet's account books, which he read to me before I left O'Hare, read as follows after that:

> *April 4, 1983:* Right foot. To Tommy Rawhead of Asmoday, ND. Complicate the emotional and psychological dimensions of the action. Careful selection of names. Vary sentence rhythms. Tonal variation. Shit off pages. Novel: *Brachiano's Ghost.* Macmillan. Black and gray cover. Red chapter headings. Plus right leg: Pulitzer Prize. Done.
>
> *July 16, 1984:* Right hand. To Elaby Gathen of Hackpen, MI. Correct spelling of "existence," "separate" and "pursue." No redundancy in nouns and verbs and their modifiers. Play games with readers. No slobbering on pages. Book of short stories: *The Blue Hag of Winter.* Random House. Gold on black cover. Red title pages. Right arm also: O'Henry Award, St. Lawrence Award for Fiction and Chair at Columbia. Done.
>
> *February 10, 1985:* Two eyes. To Billy Blind of Systern, DE. No use of "etc.," the suffix "-wise," correct use of "as." No rhetorical questions in narrative. No openings with dialogue. No flashbacks. Include all senses in descriptions. No pus on pages. Two-volume novel: *Sammael.* Little, Brown. Red, green and blue cover. Nobel Prize. Done.

As I float over the shadowed northern world, I think now that we all go off into darknesses, bit by bit, piece by piece, part by part. We all disintegrate into our words, our sentences, our paragraphs, our narratives. We scatter our lives into photographs, letters, certificates, books, prizes, lies. We ride out the light until the records break one by one. We sit out the days until the suns get dimmer and dimmer. We lie about in the gathering shadows until North America, South America, Australia, Antarctica, Asia, Africa and Europe lie about on the dark waters of our globe. It is crack time in the world of flesh. It is shatter time in the world of limbs. It is splatter time in the world of bones. It is the last splinter of the word. I have tasted the double-deal. I have smelled the sleight-of-hand. I have heard the cryptic whisper. I have felt the cold riddle. Because no one stands apart from his stone. No one laughs apart from his crust. No one breathes apart from his shriveling. No one speaks apart from his silence. To lie down in a wicker basket is not to lie apart. To be turned on soft, pus-soaked sheets is not to be turned alone. To be fed through tubes is not to eat alone. To drink and choke is to spit up for all.

To float through the night is the journey we all take sooner or later until the bright and shining morning star breaks and there is no more.

I can feel the huge plane starting to descend. My seventy-four year old ears are popping. The stewardess who smells like a dead dog has already rolled me over so that I won't aspirate if I vomit. She's strapped me tightly in place on my two seats. I can feel the safety belts across my guts and chest. I feel the descent into darkness and I know that I have not given up anything that I could not do without. I know that you can live with less than you came in with. I know that wholeness is not everything and that if you will give an eye for a prize you'll be a sure winner. I can feel my long, white hair sliding and shaking over my stumpy ears as the plane bucks and banks for the landing. I can imagine the attendants in black knickers with the little black bows by the knees who will carry me onto the clapping stage. I can imagine the old black king squinting through his thick glasses down into the wicker basket with the two handles and the white Cannon sheets. As my snot begins to leak out over my upper lip, I can hear myself asking him to clean the ear wax out of my shallow ears so that I can hear him clearly when he extols the virtues of long-suffering, when he prattles about how some people overcome severe handicaps and go on to greatness, when he maunders about the indomitable will of the human spirit, while the old black queen gurgles and snickers down at the heady, winning lump. And I hope it's a prince, princess or princeling who will hold the microphone down into the basket so that while pus oozes from my eye sockets I can whisper my acceptance speech. I hope I can control my saliva. I hope I don't shed tears. And finally there will be the flowers to add their smells to the noises, the tastes and the temperatures. I wonder if anyone will manage to get a sip of Champagne to me. That thumping, bumping and bouncing must be the runway.

POETRY

Introduction

In 1973 Michael Benedikt became the poetry editor. His credentials were the most impressive of the poetry editors at the time of their selection. The Wesleyan University Press had already published three books of his poems: *The Body, Sky,* and *Mole Notes,* and his work had been anthologized in seventeen collections of American and British contemporary poetry. He had taught at Bennington, Sarah Lawrence, and was teaching at Hampshire College in Massachusetts at the time of his induction. He remained the poetry editor until 1978. His retirement was due in part to the enormous number of manuscripts he was obliged to consider. The *Paris Review* receives over 15,000 submissions a year, most of them poetry manuscripts. Many magazines, particularly the major ones, have a "no unsolicited manuscripts" policy; not so at the *Paris Review* where everything is read. That is one of the reasons the magazine's masthead is as long as it is—many on it are preliminary poetry-scanners: their function is to hand on to the editor what is marginal or possible. Benedikt began to feel, as he put, "like a beast of burden." His resignation was hastened by his being asked to carry a small stack of rejection slips back to Boston where he was teaching at the time. It was the back-breaking straw.

—G.P.

*   *   *

My approach was, simply, to try to be as eclectic, in every way, as I could be! In 1973, at the close of Tom Clark's editorial tenure, I thought I would try to reopen the poetry of the *Paris Review* to the broadest possible range of esthetic concerns, not to mention geographic representation, internationally as well as across the U.S.A.

When word of my relatively esthetically liberated perspective as new poetry editor got out, the contributions arrived in gradually increasing numbers. Indeed, by 1978, the number of submissions increased threefold. George permitted me to expand the generous allotment of space already devoted by the magazine to poetry; I was given a totally free hand in choosing the circa 500 submissions of poetry which, in all, I'd estimate I made for the magazine during my tenure. George second-guessed me only once that I can remember; I finally solved the problem by choosing another poem to print by the same contributor.

As poetry editor, I introduced a few editorial quirks. My method of ordering poems in each issue was to arrange them into "sequences" (as George and I finally both came to call them), which consisted of dividing the poems into sections that seemed to go together or otherwise interacted interestingly—sections that en bloc seemed to carry forward a stylistic or even thematic dialogue or conversation, which unfolded as the magazine itself unfolded.

I think I fulfilled most of my editorial goals during my tenure as poetry editor; and certainly, most importantly, published a lot of good poetry by many talented writers who had a wide variety of philosophical concerns and esthetic approaches. I'm still amused today by the concatenation of rather surprising esthetic bedfellows whom I brought together between the pages of the magazine, perhaps suggested in the poetry selection that follows. My ongoing anthological interest in the prose poem led to my publishing many examples of that form. In the "Poetry Portfolios" especially, I was able to introduce (and in some cases reintroduce) many relatively well-known writers to the magazine; also I take particular pride in having brought a good many newcomers to the magazine—and even, in some cases, to first publication in *any* literary magazine.

—Michael Benedikt

DIANE ACKERMAN

Still Life

The bullet has almost entered the brain:
I can feel it sprint down the gunbarrel
rolling each bevel around like a hoop
on a pigslide of calibrated steel and oil.
Now it whistles free and aloft
in that ice-cold millimeter of air,
then boils as the first layer of skin
shales off like ragged leaves of soap.
The trigger's omnipresent click
makes triggers all over the body fire
to the sound of Japanese shutters closing
one by one a skein of threads.
Now it tunnels through palisades,
veins, arteries, white corpuscles
red and battered as swollen ghosts,
cuts the struts on a glacial bone
jutting out like the leg of a single flamingo,
feints and draws in close for the kill,
egged on by a mousegray parliament of cells.

PAULÉ BARTÓN

The Bee Dice Game

"He picked up
a bee!"
is what
Belem shouted, high
out loud.

I saw a man crouched
over flowers. He
opened his hand,
slow.
We looked for the bee-sting hole,
but none!
None!

He hushed us. He bent over
flowers again.
He grabbed another bee
and shook it
rattle like dice.

Then he went his way.
I shouted, "I won't forget
you, bee dice man!"

Years I went working
squid bins
and shrimp boats.

One day I went to Iguana Blue Cay
to the bustle market.
There was goings on
by the dice wall.
There was a crowd gathered
whooping.
Four men tossed dice
I thought.
I walked close.

One man tossed his dice
off the wall.
They were bees!
I promise.

The others tossed
their bee dice.

There was winning
and losing.

I recognized one
then
who was losing
badly.
He was out of practice
I could tell.
He had swollen hands.
They had pollen stain.
He could hardly toss the dice
more.

The Sleep Bus

I get on
the racket bus,
and see one empty seat
next to a burlap-face
mongoose
in a cage.
Next to it I sit on wet mango peels!
then spin
to say
"Who set this?
Who's laughing at my misfortune?"

I accuse
with my eyes
a baby goat
on the seat behind me.
I glare, he just sleeps goat.

No one on this bus
awake, no animals, no people.
Some damn racket bus!

To the back, shag goat sleeps.
To the front, the driver sleeps.

I want to steal a wallet, but see
the mongoose has none.

I walk home.

—Translated from the Creole by Howard Norman

MICHAEL BENEDIKT

The Badminton at Great Barrington

You never get to play it, the rackets
Are always missing or else the net's dissolved
During the winter, and there are mole holes
Where they shouldn't be, wherever that is.
Still, it's a *promise* every year, when you see Winter
Dumping its useless, silver mischief on your kerchief.
And the indifferences which have wrecked your life—
Whole aisles of carelessly abandoning boyfriends, lovers turned oddly
     awful or litigious, even close girlfriend betrayal
Escalate like some tremendous terrible temple, turned upside down
                              O, that sunny redemption
Of the difficulty of dirty days!
Then the Badminton of Great Barrington stands
Like the little sad statue of Christ suffering in the projected
     "untasteful" neon pain on your lawn
Never used to.

—A promise, but of what? You told me you *really wondered,*
Briefly, when you locked up the little summer cottage
Last September, threw the rackets at your sister

And left the rain-wet net in the corner of the closet.
The moles you thought you had dispatched
By deadly shredding in half with your broken power-mower,
At least that was something, you speculated,
Some achievement. And you left to beat the traffic
Rush, the crush that always comes whenever there
Is something to do and you'd rather be elsewhere.

That was the autumn you met me, and promised
That all your winter moods, and every tragedy
Would be resolved, sportingly, in the spring
On the redeeming, receding green at Great Barrington, that Eden.
	There
You would cut a fine figure, in your gingham Levis
Your recently-deceased mother kept locked a hatbox
Except for special occasions; in your rattan hat
With the ribbons she never let you wear
—You might sit on them, by accident.

When we got there, by accident, the moles were back
And the equipment was missing or else turned to mush.
I grew disappointed in the badminton at Great Barrington
That funny time, I grew gloomy, it was the beginning
Of the end for us, although perhaps someone else much wiser
Might date it back, when ready, to much more auspicious occasions.
O, how I resented having to play indestructible croquet
Using tack-hammers for mallets, they were lost!

So, I behaved badly. We have parted company
Over something silly; and should believe you, I guess as I love you
When you tell me that you will be back again next year
And next year—even if you "have to play the game with yourself"
(As you say)—that the badminton will be better than ever.

ROBERT BLY

Two Translations from Kabir

THE DOORS ARE CLOSED

What comes out of the harp? Music!
And there is a dance no hands or feet dance.
No fingers play it, no ears hear it,
because the Holy One is the ear,
and the one listening too.
The great doors remain closed, but the spring fragrance is inside
    anyway
and no one sees what takes place there.
Men and women who have escaped from the old part of their brain will
    understand this poem.

THE BREATH

Are you looking for me? I am in the next seat!
My shoulder is against yours.
You will not find me in stupas, nor in Indian shrine rooms, nor in the
    synagogues, nor in cathedrals:
not in masses, nor kirtans, not in legs winding around neck, nor in
    eating nothing but vegetables.
When you really look for me, you will see me instantly—
you will find me in the tiniest house of time.
Kabir says, "Student, tell me, what is God?
He is the breath inside the breath."

KATE ELLEN BRAVERMAN

Classified Ad

I teach fourth grade
batik and weave plant hangers
with seashells bound in the yarns,
pine cones and stones glassy
from waves and age.
I make ceramic vases and cups,
bake breads, dance and read books.
Last summer I hiked forty-seven miles
alone in the High Sierras.
I do not smoke or take drugs.
I have lived four years
in a cottage on a hill.
My windows face the sky.
I am responsible.

Painters have shared my bed,
stockbrokers and psychologists.
All are strangers,
sleeping encased in sheet
strange unreachable mounds
fearful I will touch their dreams.
They close doors while they piss
and decline my shower.
Breakfast finds them angry
staring at a black well of coffee
complaining my cats bit their toes,
restless, wanting to change
their underwear. Winding watches.
Bound to other things.

I want to love a blue-eyed man
and have blue-eyed babies,
sleek and smooth as cats.
And a yard perhaps,

to grow spices and flowers.
I am twenty-six
I embroider. I sing.
I am punctual and clean.

JOSEPH BRUCHAC

The Hitchhiker

As soon as I climb into the car
I fold my dark blanket
and close my eyes against it
and the locked door.
She speaks a few words,
the air from the vent ruffling
her dress an inch above her knees.
With my left hand I slide out
the knife, unfold it under my arm
and wait for her to grow silent.
You are horrified.
Do you wish to understand?
Take the page this is written on,
hold it up, the edge dry
and tight, slide it
quickly across your tongue
and taste between your lips
the road unfolding
from my dreams.

SIV CEDERING

Peaches

There was a contest
once
for the best picture
of a peach

in China

Madame Ling
or was it Ching
sat in some yellow
pollen

then

carefully, again
she sat
upon
a piece of white

paper

G. S. SHARAT CHANDRA

Rape of Lucrece Retold

*a Roman woman whose suicide, after her rape by a
son of Tarquin the Proud, led to the expulsion of the
Tarquins and the establishment of the Roman republic*

—Random House Dictionary
of the English Language

In her dream
the wind blew her vagina out the bedroom
down the Spanish steps
into the moonlit alleys.
There's no need to say much
not much about such a freeflying vagina.
Tarquin Jr., son of Tarquin the Proud
stood by his draperies scratching his insomnia
thinking of poems
when it fluttered like a butterfly
gone crazy for his nose.
He grabbed it:
he only wanted to write a poem
but when he touched its soft lips
it whispered its maiden name
& he broke into nervous laughter.
Before dawn another gust returned it
to Lucrece dreaming of levitation.
Tarquin Jr., had planted kisses
& tied Turkish ribbons to each pubic hair.
The Roman republic was never quite the same.

MAXINE CHERNOFF

Hats Around the World

The Mexican hat dance is performed around a sombrero, a broad-brimmed hat of felt or straw. Mexicans keep their feet spotlessly clean, so that they may perform this colorful ritual at the drop of a hat.

The English bowler hat was worn by Charlie Chaplin. He used it as a prop in his slapstick comedy routines. In so doing, he abused a most genteel hat.

The Chinese cap is a fitted gong, originally worn by the most insuffer-able Chinese opium king. He had the annoying habit of interrupting opium dreams by tolling the time on his hat.

The French beret was invented in Paris in 1828, during an epidemic of ringworm. Likewise, the hot air balloon was invented during a strike of Air France in 1934. The French are a very pragmatic race.

The sailor's cap, now made of canvas, is a flat cap with a narrow white brim, originally woven from gull's wings.

The chef's hat is a deep bowl in which greens, preferably romaine, crumbled cheese, croutons, and a raw egg are tossed vigorously to make the caesar salad.

The Busby is the British version of the Russian Cossack hat, that wild, furry, barbarous hat, captured and domesticated by a leather strap under the chin.

John Stetson (1830–1906), was greatly annoyed by the attrition rate of his hats in the West. People often heard him muttering, "Why didn't I invent the Derringer?" Finally he moved to Boston, learned to crochet, and opened a ladies' bonnet shop.

The crown is a hat most abused. Wrought of fine metal, adorned with diamonds, emeralds, and rubies, it has graced many a greasy head.

The halo speaks for itself.

NANCY CONDEE

"In the Late Afternoon . . ."

In the late afternoon, above the town of Llanes, on the rock wall of the promenade, old men sit facing the ocean and read soft core pornogra-phy.

Sometimes nuns too visit this promenade and walk along it from one end to the other. And then the old men, taken by surprise, fling their magazines out into the ocean, where the wind catches them and carries them back landward. The old men wave their arms, trying to strike at the magazines. The magazines scatter. The old men chase after the pictures, pinning them down with their canes and beating them back to the sea. As the nuns draw nearer, the old men become completely violent.

How interesting it is to walk along the promenade above Llanes at this time of day, with the old men fending off pictures of nude women, and the nuns approaching closer and closer, and the old grey Atlantic undulating beneath them.

GARY GILDNER

The Runner

Show the runner coming through the shadows,
　　show him falling into a speckled rhythm,
　　and then show the full expression of light,
　　there, where the trees quit and the road
　　goes on alone, marked by the moon-glazed gravel

Show the runner trying to disappear
　　where sky and road meet far in the distance,
　　show him always a step too late,
　　show a train going by hauling a long silence,
　　and show the runner leaving the road
　　where the killdeer starts from a charred stump

Show the runner saying the names of streams
　　as if he were working off days in Purgatory,
　　show the Chocolay, the Rifle, the Fox,

show the Laughing Whitefish, the Escanaba,
show the runner's pocketful of worms
and show the runner's father
sitting alone by a hole in the ice

Show the runner stopping at farm after farm
until a woman appears who is wearing a child's
pink kimono over her shoulders,
show her feet in hunting socks,
show a kitchen arranged in cream and linoleum,
show that the wind has toasted her cheeks,
show that she doesn't know what he wants

Show the runner's old room, the crucifix
he tied fresh palms around each year,
show the five nice birch his father planted,
show the two blue spruce, the silver maple,
show the cherry from the nursery that was going broke,
show the man who said take it for a buck,
show the hail storm that knocked them over

Show the runner setting out all spruced up,
show the sun, poached, above a grove a leggy birch,
show the runner cruising down a cowpath
trying to catch his breath,
and show the slim white limbs dividing
letting him in

Show the runner peeling bark
show him scratching messages with sticks,
then show him diving into a drift,
nosing like a mole out of season,
rolling over and over
and yipping for luck or in pain

Show the runner approach the only light
in Little Lake, there, over the grocer's
fading pack of Camels,
show the grocer chewing Redman,
listen to him play his pocket change
and resurrect the dead,
listen to him spit them back

Show the runner running on,
   show the moon, then show it stalking him
   across the road into the second growth,
   show the runner's father in his garden
   blue and out of breath and looking hard
   at something nothing can distract him from,
   show the lake all frozen over,
   show the mound of snow

PENELOPE GILLIATT

Gossip

The world in its caprice
Will deign to say it knows us both
But it knows nothing
And does not even know that it knows nothing.

ERICA JONG

Jubilate Canis

(With apologies to Christopher Smart)

For I will consider my dog Poochkin
(& his long-lost brothers, Chekarf & Dogstoyevsky).
For he is the reincarnation of a great canine poet.
For he barks in meter, & when I leave him alone

his yelps at the door are epic.
For he is white, furry, & resembles a bathmat.
For he sleeps at my feet as I write
& therefore is my greatest critic.
For he follows me into the bathroom
& faithfully pees on paper.
For he is almost housebroken.
For he eats the dogfood I give him
but also loves Jarlsburg swiss cheese.
For he disdains nothing that smells—
whether feet or roses.
For to him, all smells are created equal by God—
both turds and perfumes.
For he loves toilet bowls no less than soup bowls.
For by watching, I have understood democracy.
For by watching him, I have understood democracy.
For he turns his belly toward God
& raises his paws & penis in supplication.
For he hangs his pink tongue out of his mouth
like a festival banner for God.
For though he is male, he has pink nipples on his belly
like the female.
For though he is canine, he is more humane
than most humans.
For when he dreams he mutters in his sleep
like any poet.
For when he wakes he yawns & stretches
& stands on his hind legs to greet me.
For, after he shits, he romps and frolics
with supreme abandon.
For after he eats, he is more contented
than any human.
For in every room he will find the coolest corner,
& having found it, he has the sense to stay there.

DAVID KELLY

Counting a Decade

A crow waits in the top of a tree
for the racoon to leave its dead mate
in the road. The bird shifts a claw
on its branch and chestnuts fall.

I am at a window on the third floor
of an old house. I have just read
a poem I wrote ten years ago. I like it.

In town only the old men on street
corners discuss the history of spring.
Downstairs in the master bedroom
my wife and youngest daughter sleep.
One flight further down the television
kills two hours until the evening news.

It is the Lenten season, as it has been
thirty-four other times in my life
and I am still not Catholic. Ten years
ago I was without hope. Now I am hopeless.

Even my mother has given up wringing
her hands when she sees me, even
my employers are tired of shaking their
heads. Listen. Today, washing my hair
in the bathtub, I got shampoo in

my eyes. For ten minutes the pain
was more important than all your wars.
Or this. My daughter, up from her nap

has tiptoed up the stairs and, still
a little sleepy, is tugging at the
edges of my sweater as I stand here.
Her hands are the smallest in the world.

DAVID LEHMAN

Fear and Trembling

for Ed Byrne   'All find safety in the tomb'—Yeats

Unable to distinguish between flying and falling
With a feeling of splendid contempt and with a strange loving longing
In my eyes, I look up at the helicopter that was lately my home
Getting smaller and smaller in the sky, and I know this is
A routine enough condition for a veteran parachutist like myself.
Yet always, in those free-falling fast and furious seconds
Before the chute blossoms open, turning me into a human umbrella
Or, as I sometimes like to think, an uprooted tree with a cloud
For a skullcap, I feel like the first time all over again.
In love with the panic of 32 feet per second per second
Which only silence can master, and which is nothing compared
To the trembling possibility that I will fail to jump out
Or be unable to keep my eyes open, but I have even managed that.
And now what frightens me is not so much a doubt
Of salvation as not knowing for sure whether a secret wish
Of my own, rather than a fluke or an act of god, is to blame
For the refusal of my chute to work when I pull the cord.
Which is the culprit, Thanatos, shoddy merchandise, or divine
Revelation? I ask myself, feeling inside me the awakening
Of a familiar hunch, more potent than any merely human decision.
That somehow, anyhow, I will swing into a survival
All the more secure for appearing impossible beforehand.
All the more desirable because never consciously pursued.
So, at any rate, I tell myself, when compelled by a necessity
Only half understood, to relinquish a marriage, even a lousy one,
An ambition, even a stupid one, a god, even a dead one.
Or any other long lost, once loved cause that sold my kisses
For thirty tablets of Valium. Or do I court these disasters
Intentionally, seeking an excuse for loud lamentation
That needed no excuse? Is the exhilaration worth the dread
Of these threats to my guts? The answer to these questions
And others is as easy as grasping the secret of last night's dream
Tonight, just before going to sleep, too tired to get up
And write it down, sure you won't forget, but you always do

The next unreal morning; and as hard as remembering
What year it is, especially in January, though
For some this problem extends throughout the Winter
And to Winter herself, and the surprising tenacity with which
The snow-crusted branches of her amputated trees resist
The arrival of Spring each Spring. Hard too to let your childhood
Go, and easier by far being the father of someone else's kids.

EVERETTE H. MADDOX

Thirteen Ways of Being Looked at by a Possum

1
I awake, three in the morning, sweating
from a dream of possums.
I put my head under the fuzzy swamp of cover.
At the foot of darkness two small eyes glitter.

2
Rain falls all day: I remain indoors.
For comfort I take down a favorite volume.
Inside, something slimy, like a tail, wraps around my finger.

3
Hear the bells clang at the fire station:
not hoses, but the damp noses of possums issue forth.

4
Passing the graveyard at night
I wish the dead would remain dead,
but there is something queer and shaggy about these mounds.

5
From the gray pouch of a cloud
the moon hangs by its tail.

6
At the cafeteria they tell me they are out of persimmons.
I am furious. Who is that gray delegation
munching yellow fruit at the long table?

7
I reach deep into my warm pocket
to scratch my balls; but I find, instead,
another pocket there; and inside, a small possum.

8
My friend's false teeth clatter in the darkness
on a glass shelf;
around them a ghostly possum forms.

9
At an art gallery the portraits seem to threaten me;
tails droop down out of the frames.

10
I screech to a stop at the red light.
Three o'clock, school's out:
eight or ten juvenile possums fill the crosswalk.

11
Midnight at Pasquale's. I lift my fork,
and the hard tails looped there
look curiously unlike spaghetti.

12
When I go to the closet to hang my shirt on the rack,
I have to persuade several possums to move over.

13
Drunk, crawling across a country road tonight,
I hear a shriek, look up, and am paralyzed
by fierce headlights and a grinning grill.
The Possum Truck! I am as good as gone.

W. S. MERWIN

Demonstration

It is nothing new
for horses to be harnessed to hemispheres
it has happened at intervals
since the famous first experiment
when we know how to do a thing
we do it again

night or day the horses
are hitched up in teams
hemispheres are brought together
half to half
all the air is drawn out from between them
the seal is as wax
at a command the teams begin to haul
raising the vibrating chains
and the sphere

the horses lean into the collars and the links grind
but the halves hold together
in the grasp of the breath of the earth

there is an art to matching the teams
and to driving them
lashes crackle
bodies suffer rulers watch
while the hemispheres hold together
to the limits of matter
between them is
nothing
a nothing that is made
and is never perfect
the sight in an empty socket at night
the everlasting decision
approaching the point of origin
the first fire

still without color
exploding inward
drawing the unlit firmaments after it

HERBERT MORRIS

Newport, 1930

Stepping deftly to the jetty,
members of the boating party,
women in pearls, long skirts, cloche hats,
men in blazers, white yachting flannels,
slickers dangling from an arm,

walk the ramp to the misty shore.
The sand is grey, the water greyer,
the light is a queasy off-grey color
depriving everything of shadow.
The time must be late afternoon,

the day unlike the day in summer,
given the variables, it must be.
Crews from the offshore yawls and sloops,
maneuvering small white-hulled tenders
ferrying members of the party,

are dressed as that year's crews are dressed,
are seen to do what ships' crews do.
Though their hands are unseen by us
(the distance, yes, but greyness, too)
we are given to understand

(I cannot yet fully explain it)
nowhere will they prove less than equal
to whatever is asked of them:

hold to the wheel, haul port, trim starboard,
cast these members ashore, man stations.

A small flag flutters from the stern of
each of the auxiliary tenders.
Could we count the stars splattered on them
we could, within specific limits,
narrow the context, taste the year.

Of the life of those party members
put ashore on the coast of twilight,
walking in twos in that evening
where the evening is spread before them
like the fall of a woman's hair,

what can I say but that this woman
after the dusk has fallen, late,
somewhere not far from sea-routes, sailor,
where the choices pertain to voyage,
lets down her hair as dark as water;
that the man who accompanies her,
armed with a slicker against her sheer downpour,
soon, with the night and tide propitious,
sails out on what, not far from here,
the woman has let down like water;

that the hands of the crew, no matter
how astonishing that insight
into the reach of their commitment,
in the long darkness founder, crumble,
finger by finger leak with dust.

From the balustrade we view them
moving together into contexts
of which we have nothing but outlines:
fleets in the bay riding at anchor,
tenders plying their final runs,

the first stars tangled in the rigging,
belowdeck crews taking their suppers;
that entering on darkness, darkness
the absence, voyager, of shadows,
that letting down, somewhere, of hair.

Frank O'Hara

A Renaissance Portrait of the Author

A courtier strides along, his feathers
straightening in the breeze. His boon
has been denied. From his clenched left
fist extends a mountain range as grim
as Atlas. He mutters so coherently that
a quartet of wind instruments is darkly
visible at the edge of the forest. He
puffs his cheeks to snort angrily but
the clouds scurry away in tatters.

Upon the right the brightness of the
court defies my technique, tingling
with business at the defeated courtier's
shoulder. The queen is leaning out
a casement kissing pigeons while
a smiling lady holds the queen's clean
coif. The green pride at his feet glares,
forbids the courtier's looking back.
On his nape he bears the azure whole.

And the frivolous hunting party romp
at his mercy! He could easily topple
their trees with a kick of his velvet
right foot. A hand on his rapier betrays
a motive his hooded eyes and beardless
face will not easily resolve. Thoughts
eager as the hawk that pins the castle
to the sky flourish on pure spleen. Ah!
the sea behind his codpiece brews poison.

PETER PAYACK

Motorcycle Evolution

The size of the human brain
increased from the apelike
capacity of 500 cubic centimeters
in Australopithecus to about
1500 cc. in modern man.

It took 2 million years
for man's brain to evolve
from the motor size of
a Kawasaki 500 to that
of a Harley-Davidson Superglide.

DEBORAH PEASE

Geography Lesson

"Nebraska and Oklahoma have the longest contiguous border
Of any two states," you announce.
Your hair stands up in corkscrews
Imparting the distracted air
Of a genius able to persuade anyone
That Nebraska and Oklahoma share a border
In spite of Kansas sitting in between.
I rushed to my atlas to check on this proximity.
My geography is faulty, a basic skill never properly acquired.
Like long division.
Never mind "contiguous" borders,
Let's just get our states in order,

Our land masses organized. But this is not possible.
If I mention the Punjab, you embark upon the Humboldt Current
Which flows, to my knowledge, nowhere near Hindus.
A quirk of circuitry too brilliant to follow
Spirals you continents away
Like the cyclone that swallowed Kansas.
Our minds never meet when fact intervenes:
I know too few to counter the punctilious onslaught
Of your passion to misinform.
My only defense against your smooth wrong-headedness
Is to retreat to high ground, altering the terrain.
Esoteric facts, mostly unverifiable,
Are your slithery armies; a rude semblance
Of common sense is my recourse.
Outside this cerebral misalliance
We meet congenially, with the nearness of love, in Nebulae.

KENNETH REXROTH

Three Japanese Woman Poets

LADY ISE

Shall I come to see
plum blossoms in every stream
and wet my sleeves
in unpluckable water
as I do now?

As the first spring mists appear
the wild geese leave.
Are they accustomed to live
in a flowerless land?

PRINCESS NUKADA

Longing for you,
loving you,
waiting for you,
the bamboo blinds were swayed
only by the autumn wind.

HATSUI SHIZUE

Silently
time passes.
The only life I have
submits to its power.

—Translated from the Japanese

JUDITH C. ROOT

To Pose a Chicken

after Norman Rockwell

First, pick up chicken, rock back
& forth, back & forth, then set down.
He will stand where you put him four
or five minutes. Rush to easel

& paint quickly. (Difficult but
easier than painting on the run
& can be repeated again & again.)
A bigger challenge is to paint

full face since a chicken's eyes
are not like yours. When he looks directly

at you, his head is turned. But art
can master nature's quirks. Just find

a long stick, set your chicken
as above & hurry behind your easel.
With one hand rap the stick
against a side wall & with the other
paint. If the chicken looks at the wall,
he will face you.

IRA SADOFF

Seurat

It is a Sunday afternoon on the Grand Canal. We are watching the sailboats trying to sail along without wind. Small rowboats are making their incisions on the water, only to have the wounds seal up again soon after they pass. In the background the smoke from the factories and the smoke from the steamboats merge into tiny clouds above us then disappear. Our mothers and fathers walk arm and arm along the shore clutching tightly their umbrellas and canes. We are sitting on a blanket in the foreground, but even if someone were to have taken a photograph of us only our closest relatives would have recognized us: we seem to be burying our heads between our knees.

I remember thinking you were one of the most delicate women I had ever seen. Your bones seemed small and fragile as a rabbit's. Even so, beads of perspiration begin to form on your wrist and forehead—if we were to live long enough I'm sure we would have been amazed at how many clothes we forced ourselves to wear. At this time I had never seen you without your petticoats, and if I ever gave thought to such a possibility I would chastise myself for not offering you enough respect. I'm certain you never thought about such things, except in terms of how you might have to protect yourself.

The sun is very hot. Why is it no one complains of the heat in France? There are women doing their needlework, men reading, a man in a bowler hat smoking a pipe. The noise of the children is absorbed by the trees. The air is full of idleness, there is the faint aroma of lilies coming from somewhere. We discuss what we want for ourselves, abstractly, it seems only right on a day like this. I have ambitions to be a painter, and you want a small family and a cottage in the country. We make everything sound so simple because we believe everything is still possible. The small tragedies of our parents have not yet made an impression on us. We should be grateful for this, but we are too awkward to think hard about very much. I throw a scaling rock into the water; I have strong arms and before the rock sinks it seems to have nearly reached the other side. When we get up we have a sense of our own importance. We could not know, taking a step back, looking at the total picture, that we would occupy such a small corner of the canvas, and that even then we are no more than tiny clusters of dots, carefully placed so close together without touching.

ANNE SEXTON

The Poet of Ignorance

Perhaps the earth is floating,
I do not know.
Perhaps the stars are little paper cutups
made by some giant scissors,
I do not know.
Perhaps the moon is a frozen tear,
I do not know.
Perhaps God is only a deep voice,
heard by the deaf,
I do not know.

Perhaps I am no one.
True, I have a body
and I cannot escape from it.
I would like to fly out of my head,

but that is out of the question.
It is written on the tablet of destiny
that I am stuck here in this human form.
That being the case
I would like to call attention to my problem.

There is an animal inside me,
clutching fast to my heart,
a huge crab.
The doctors of Boston
have thrown up their hands.
They have tried scalpels,
needles, poison gasses and the like.
The crab remains.
It is a great weight.
I try to forget it, go about my business,
cook the broccoli, open and shut books,
brush my teeth and tie my shoes.
I have tried prayer
but as I pray the crab grips harder
and the pain enlarges.

I had a dream once,
perhaps it was a dream,
that the crab was my ignorance of God.
But who am I to believe in dreams?

Two Hands

From the sea came a hand,
ignorant as a penny,
troubled with the salt of its mother,
mute with the silence of the fishes,
quick with the altars of the tides,
and God reached out of His mouth
and called it man.
Up came the other hand
and God called it woman.
The hands applauded.

And this was no sin.
It was as it was meant to be.

I see them roaming the streets:
Levi complaining about his mattress,
Sarah studying a beetle,
Mandrake holding his coffee mug,
Sally playing the drum at a football game,
John closing the eyes of the dying woman,
and some who are in prison,
even the prison of their bodies,
as Christ was prisoned in His body
until the triumph came.

Unwind hands,
you angel webs,
unwind like the coil of a jumping jack,
cup together and let yourselves fill up with sun
and applaud, world,
applaud.

CHARLES SIMIC

The System

A dark thought
guards us
from burglars

on the watch-chain
of our insomnia
it sits howling
at its own constellation in the sky

we feed it only
the finely-sanded

small giddy bones
of the inner ear

we make it drink
at the salt-lick
of our faces in the dark
the glistening beads of our tossing and turning

they say
that we are fooling ourselves
that the master burglars
have already come and gone

LOUIS SIMPSON

The Rejected

I tried to explain why his manuscript had been rejected:
the writing was sincere, brilliant in places,
but our readers felt it would not appeal
to many people. It was too personal.

While I spoke he kept looking around.
A few feet away, the publicity woman
had stopped to talk to the office manager.
He seemed to think they were talking about him.

He told me that for years
X—naming a famous novelist—
had been entering his apartment
in his absence, and stealing his ideas.

I concluded by saying that I was sorry.
He took his glasses off and wiped them.

He shuffled the chapters, making them square.
Then, finally, he left.

I saw him again, months later
on Forty-Second Street, looking up
at something he saw in a window,
or at the signs for tires and whiskey.

Since then I have envisioned him,
as Wordsworth says, wandering continually
from Twentieth Street up to Sixtieth,
and across from Eighth to Lexington Avenue.

WILLIAM STAFFORD

A Private Person

You would think while the hours helped,
if the wind was right, then follow
a current along shore till a beach
offered. Sand, or whatever you thought,
held far-apart tracks. You landed, or your
story did, and found what was always
treasure, by choosing other than the trail,
a little aside, or turning earlier, or later.

Whatever you found, you replaced.
After the waves come back, no one
has walked: your story untells
itself. We let wings carry us
miles and miles back and forth
over the smooth sand. We love
your track of not leaving any,
the blank that says, "I was here."

ALBERT STAINTON

The Man with the Lepidoptera on His Ass

stands, face to the wall,
butterfly to the camera, needled
back there forty years ago.
A butterfly, not a heart,
a snake, an eagle, some low joke
like Government Inspected Meat,
or a banner unfurling a slogan
proudly across the mesial groove.
The ass-muscles sag like a sling
but those glorious membranous wings
expand all the more extravagantly—
those segmented patterns of color
dilate, etherialize as the pigments decay.
The clubbed antennae still sprout
tentatively from the base of the spine,
the lobes of the blue hind wings
nearly touch the legs. The forewings
spread over the buttocks, as he keeps
his face to the wall, his ass to his audience,
smiling, as if that indelible fantasy
could winnow him out to the stars.

GERALD STERN

Straus Park

If you know about the Babylonian Jews
coming back to their stone houses in Jerusalem,
and if you know how Ben Franklin fretted

after the fire on Arch Street,
and if you yourself go crazy when you walk through the old shell
on Stout's Valley Road,
then you must know how I felt when I saw Stanley's Cafeteria
boarded up and the sale sign out;
and if you yourself mourned when you saw the back wall settling
and the first floor gone and the stairway gutted
then you must know how I felt when I saw the iron fence
and the scaffold and the plastic sheets in the windows.
—Don't go to California yet!
Come with me to Stanley's and spend your life
weeping in the small park on 106th Street.
Stay with me all night! I will give you
breast of lamb with the fat dripping over the edges;
I will give you the prophet of Baal
making the blood come.
Don't go to California with its big rotting sun
and its oleanders;
I will give you Sappho
preparing herself for the wind;
I will give you Mussolini
Sleeping in his chair;
I will give you Voltaire
walking in the snow.
—This is the dark green bench
where I read Yeats,
and that is the fountain where the Deuteronomist sat
with his eyes on the nymph's stomach.
I want you to come here one more time
before you go to California;
I want you to see the Hotel Regent again
and the Edison Theater
and the Cleopatra Fruit Market.
Take the iron fence with you
when you go into the desert.
Take Voltaire and the Deuteronomist
and the luscious nymph.
Do not burn again for nothing.
Do not cry out again in clumsiness and shame.

MARY KATHRYN STILLWELL

Travel Plans

As I sat on the toilet
of a Boeing 727,
somewhere over Ohio
riding United tourist,
I imagined my last moments
of life
falling bare-assed through the sky,
trying to reach down
to pull up my pants,
then, tumbling,
trying to reach up
to pull my pants down,
so I would land
respectably dressed.

JOHN UPDIKE

Dutch Cleanser

My grandmother used it, Dutch Cleanser,
in the dark Shillington halls,
in the kitchen darkened by the grape arbor,
and I was frightened of the lady on the can.
Why was she carrying a stick?
Why couldn't we see her face?

Now, an aging modern man,
estranged, alone, and medium gray,
I tip Dutch Cleanser onto a sponge,

here in this narrow bathroom,
where the ventilator fan has to rumble
when all I want to switch on is light.

Tipping the can, I tower above
that worried boy; the closet stack
of daily papers has burst the roof.
Deutsche Grossmutter, I am here; look up.
You have changed, I have changed,
Dutch Cleanser has changed not at all.

The lady is still upholding the stick
chasing dirt, and her face
is so angry we dare not see it.
The dirt she is chasing is ahead of her,
around the can, like a minute hand
the hour hand pushes around.

DAVID WAGONER

The Junior High School Band Concert

When our semi-conductor
Raised his baton, we sat there
Gaping at *Marche Militaire,*
Our mouth-opening number.
It seemed faintly familiar
(We'd rehearsed it all that winter),
But we attacked in such a blur,
No army anywhere
On its stomach or all fours
Could have squeezed through our crossfire.

I played cornet, seventh chair
Out of seven, my embouchure

A glorified Bronx cheer
Through that three-keyed keyhole-stopper
And neighborhood window-slammer
Where mildew fought for air
At every exhausted corner,
My fingering still unsure
After scaling it for a year
Except on the spit-valve lever.

Each straight-faced mother and father
Retested his moral fibre
Against our traps and slurs
And the inadvertent whickers
paradiddled by our snares,
And when the brass bulled forth
A blare fit to horn over
Jericho two bars sooner
Than Joshua's harsh measures,
They still had the nerve to stare.

By the last lost chord, our director
Looked older and soberer.
No doubt, in his mind's ear
Some band somewhere
In some Music of some Sphere
Was striking a note as pure
As the wishes of Franz Schubert.
But meanwhile here we were:
A lesson in everything minor,
Decomposing our first composer.

Richard Wilbur

Piccola Commedia

He is no one I really know,
The sun-charred, gaunt young man
By the highway's edge in Kansas
Thirty-odd years ago.

On a tourist-cabin veranda
Two middle-aged women sat;
One, in a white dress, fat,
With a rattling glass in her hand,

Called "Son, don't you feel the heat?
Get up here into the shade."
Like a good boy, I obeyed,
And was given a crate for a seat

And an Orange Crush and gin.
"This state," she said, "is hell."
Her thin friend cackled, "Well, dear,
You've gotta fight sin with sin."

"No harm in a drink; my stars!"
Said the fat one, jerking her head.
"And I'll take no lip from Ed,
Him with his damn cigars."

Laughter. A combine whined
On past, and dry grass bent
In the backwash; liquor went
Like an ice-pick into my mind.

Beneath her skirt I spied
Two sea-cows on a floe.
"Go talk to Lucy Jo, son,
She's reading a book inside."

As I gangled in at the door
A pink girl, curled in a chair,

Looked up with an ingénue stare.
Screenland lay on the floor.

Amazed by her starlet's pout
And the way her eyebrows arched,
I felt both drowned and parched.
Desire leapt up like a trout.

"Hello," she said, and her gum
Gave a calculating crack.
At once, from the lightless back
Of the room there came the grumble

Of someone heaving from bed,
A Zippo's click and flare,
Then, more and more apparent,
The shuffling form of Ed,

Who neither looked nor spoke
But moved in profile by,
Blinking one gelid eye
In his elected smoke.

This is something I've never told,
And some of it I forget.
But the heat! I can feel it yet,
And that conniving cold.

L. L. ZEIGER

Misconceptions

For so many years, Clive Barnes,
I thought your name was Olive.
All the things I was reading in books
and did not say to anyone
and could not say to anyone—
How I blushed with shame
when caught in my misconceptions,
like being seen masturbating.

Now that I am wiser
I find everything confusing
even when I pronounce it perfectly.
A simple statement like "Void where prohibited"—
How shall I read it?
How shall I think it?
I want to take it as an imperative
and pee on the floor of the public library.

NONFICTION

Introduction

The following excerpt is from a book which was in progress at the time it was selected—an account of the life and times of Edie Sedgwick, who was perhaps the most famous of Andy Warhol's superstars. From a distinguished New England family, she went on to personify the excesses and extravagances of the sixties. The book, by Jean Stein and which I helped edit, was eventually entitled *Edie*. It was constructed in the form of a series of monologues of those who knew Edie at that time. This particular section is a monologue taken from an interview with Bobby Andersen, who was persuaded to take care of Edie (her room at the Chelsea Hotel had been gutted by fire) during the making of a film entitled *Ciao! Manhattan*. I have always held that this section could be turned into a wonderful one-act play.

—G.P.

BOBBY ANDERSEN

Edie Sedgwick: A Reminiscence

I met Margouleff just after I got out of the hospital where I was seriously ill with hepatitis and told every day that I wasn't going to make it, and was all prepared to die. I came out all traumatized. Very strange. Margouleff came along. I was so weak already from exhaustion I was ready to fall down in the street. I had lost my apartment and everything in it. He walked up to me and he said, "Hello, you big tomato." I said, "Get the hell out of here. Leave me alone, you creep."

He could see that I was not feeling well and he took me home to his apartment. I never left. I stayed there for three and a half years. When I met Margouleff he was importing Hercules movies and dubbing them in English at ABC city. When he said that he was going to make an above-ground underground film, we all made a lot of faces and everything. He said someone called Edie Sedgwick was going to star in it. I'd never heard of her. I envisioned this blonde, pig-tailed, freckle-faced, homely, wire-rim glasses type from the name: Edie Sedgwick. It didn't sound very glamorous or pretty.

You should have heard the way Margouleff carried *on* about her! He hated Edie. He couldn't compete with her. She was so erratic, at least as far as he was concerned. He couldn't understand that anyone could get that high on drugs. All he did was smoke a little pot every once in a while; he never had even a drink. And here were all these people around him with needles in their asses and everything, shooting amphetamine. I don't think he understood all that vibrancy, all that stimulation that the drugs get going in them.

That was how I got involved. Apparently Edie wasn't showing up; they couldn't get her to learn lines, or do this, or that. She had been burned in the Chelsea fire, but no one wanted to take care of her. Everyone had refused. So Margouleff asked me if I wanted a job that paid twenty-five dollars a day to make sure that she got up in the morning, had her face washed and turned up at the studio in proper attire and behaved herself.

I said, Sure! I figured I'd be a real male nurse and real nasty.

Margouleff's was a very strange apartment. He owned it and paid the rent. After that, it was my apartment. Every room was different: a psychedelic room, a Victorian room, a Georgian room. The kitchen was the best. It was painted as an American flag. I spent a month's work on the refrigerator to make it look like a Coke vending machine.

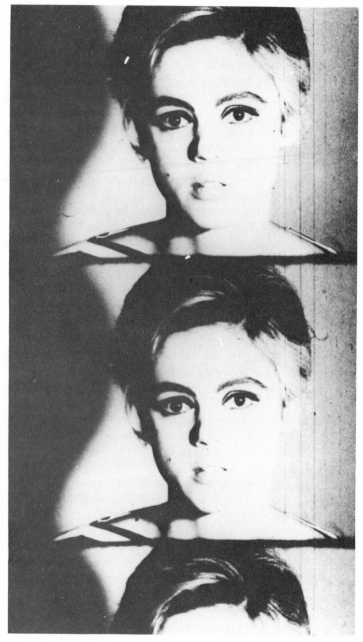

Edie Sedgwick

Margouleff used to tell everybody that I was his houseboy, which I thought was very insulting. I fixed the apartment up; I decorated it; I ran it. It was in the East Village, a fabulous ramshackle six-room railroad flat, and one day I walked in and looked down to the end where sitting at the harpsichord was this breathtaking blonde that I could see from six rooms away . . . frosted blonde. I walked over. She stood and asked, "Who are you?" I said, "I'm Bobby. I live here. Who are you?" She said, "I'm Edie Sedgwick. Are you my nurse?"

She had these two people with her, one a boy named Anthony Ampule and a friend of his named Donald, who was a professor. On the harpsichord they had this big pile of methedrine, which they were scooping up and mixing into water. Anthony Ampule was called that because he was able to get vials of liquid amphetamine from his doctor. I don't know what his real name is; even today he's called Anthony Ampule. They were standing there at the harpsichord measuring out their methedrine. I looked at Edie and I said to myself, "Well how *fabulous!* This fabulous creature!" She was so *electric* . . . just wonderful! I decided about four minutes after I knew her that she was not an Edie, she was an Edith.

She didn't go out that night. She hadn't brought much of anything with her. She had these great big baseball mitts for hands because of the Chelsea fire, all covered with gauze and bandages. I went out to Max's Kansas City and brought back some food for her. Double shrimp cocktail. A chocolate malted, which they made only for her there. Mickey Ruskin, the owner, would go in the back and melt the ice cream and beat it and make her a chocolate milk shake.

That was how I met her. I was so pleased. I just thought she was wondrous instantly. So I wasn't a hideous male nurse at all. We caught on like wildfire and we got along so well it was wonderful. At Max's they used to call me "Edie's nurse," but I didn't mind. We'd have drinks there and put it on Margouleff's account! Terrible! Those were the days of signing for everything on anybody's name. Everybody was very rude about it.

I used to have the greatest fun out of making Edith get all dressed up. At Max's it was as if Queen Elizabeth had arrived. Edith had the most wondrous wardrobe, even after the Chelsea fire. What she lost in the fire, I think, were furs and jewelry. She kept telling me that her hands were hideously burned, that she expected, when the mitts came off, that she would have grotesque, deformed, webbed hands. When Dr. Roberts finally took the mitts off she was excited and very surprised. Her hands were in perfect shape.

She looked fabulous in everything! I remember going out with her in the afternoon when she had on what she called her "mini" evening gown. She'd seen a full-length velvet gown in the window at Bergdorf's trimmed in egret feathers. She went in and bought it and because the mini skirt was in such vogue then she had the evening dress cut to mini size and had the feathers put back on. That was her "mini" evening gown. Over that she wore a black ostrich-plume coat, peacock feather earrings, and black satin gloves up to here with ostrich plume bows on the top. In broad daylight in the East Village. She was incredible! With a huge black straw hat over it.

We went to Coney Island like that. She took her first and only subway ride in New York. The people on the train just loved her. She never sat down the whole way out; the train was so crowded we stood all the way from the East Village to Coney Island. She was in all that mad regalia with a bathing suit underneath so we could go swimming. The people loved her. She was talking to everyone and getting along. We rode in the first car so she could look out of the window in the front. She was fascinated by the tunnels and the weaving of the train and the clacking. Just fabulous. She'd never experienced anything like it.

We did everything. We had cotton candy; ate hot dogs at Nathan's, we went on the parachute jump, the roller coaster; we went swimming in the surf and lying in the sun. We collected shells and rocks and brought back two completely chewed corncobs for souvenirs. We did everything. The funhouse. She was just incredulous . . . all wild-eyed and goo-gaa. The distortion mirrors. And the laughing and the laughing.

She screamed all the way up and all the way down the Parachute Jump, the big peacock feather earrings standing straight out from her head. We got on the log sluice ride with those big silicone logs, and you came down this big sluice, and the water splashed over her feathers and hat and everything, and she just loved every minute of it. I took her on the ride where the man in the gorilla costume chases after your car—one of those Spook House things. She just *loved* him, carrying on with him and asking him into the car with us.

On the carrousel she rode on the swan—a double- or triple-seater with the silhouette of a swan on either side. She said, "Birds of a feather ought to stick together."

She had a bikini under her dress and we went swimming—leaving all this velvet and feathers strewn all over the beach in the midst of these Puerto Rican people and black people and everything. We went way over our heads swimming. Then we came home on the subway with all the rush hour crowds. The front car both times. Oh, she just loved it! We came home so exhausted.

She was happy at Margouleff's. I never left her for a minute, even

when she went to work! We'd go to the banks together. I remember
once going down to pick up the trust fund checks and having her pay for
the cab with a pearl and diamond ring one day, and a gold bracelet
another day because we didn't have enough money to pay the cab. He
refused to wait. He took the ring when he read the carat weight inside.

She had on a big star sapphire ring which she said was worth $2500. It
fell out of the setting three times to my knowledge, and she kept putting
it back in. The fourth time it fell out onto the dance floor; she got
annoyed with it and just stomped and pounded it into the dance floor
and threw the setting across the room. She left the sapphire embedded
in there. Edith wasn't bothered by things like that. She was just fabulous!

We used to share the same bed every night. It wasn't that I had to
watch her, we were just that close. In the morning I used to try to feed
her omelettes and stuff but she just wouldn't hear about it. She wanted
cold shrimp and milk shakes. I'd say, "Edith, please. You're on the
Lower East Side, honey. Come down a little."

"I just want what I want . . . what I'm used to."

"Come on, honey," I'd say. "You're making it very difficult for me. I
have to make you up, bathe you, I have to do all this crap. I have to have
a good time with you, and yet you want me to go out and buy fucking
gourmet food at nine in the morning."

In the beginning I had to help her put on her make-up because her
hands were these big mitts. I had to put the eyelashes on, and zip her up,
and help get her bra on and this and that. I knew how to do make-up
because I had studied it at the Fashion Institute. She'd sit on the stool in
the kitchen with 500 bottles of make-up spread out on the counter. I
made her tell me exactly what she wanted. She'd point with her big
stumps and say, "Make it darker there," or whatever. She was very big
on the black makeup. At the time she still had a few light burns on her
face that I covered up with foundation make-up.

I used to have to bathe her. I'd put plastic around the bandages with
rubber bands to keep it tight. She'd been there a week and she hadn't
taken a bath. She'd say, "Oh, my bandages . . . this, that, I'll get this
wet." She went through stages where she was very unclean, though she
never smelled. I guess she was just so high on amphetamines it never
registered. She always looked immaculate and beautiful.

In the evening we'd help each other get dressed for the parties. I used
to really get off making her very fabulous and beautiful. She'd go in my
closet and get things to dress me. She'd go in her boxes and crates and
dig out all these things. Scarves were very big then. And jewelry. I wore
her trousers because we were about the same size in pants. After her

hands were healed, she would comb my hair, and I used to do her hair. She got me to grow my hair back blonde. It was white then, because they had convinced me that I was going to be an underground movie star. I was very stupid and affected all the time. My hair was snow-white, along with my eyebrows, my eyelashes, my sideburns . . . everything was white. People would come up: "Oh, if I ever had hair like that, I'd give my right arm for it."

I'd say, "Well, it cost seven dollars a week . . . you can have it."

They just didn't believe it wasn't real. No, I didn't have a pierced ear then, but I had a front tooth missing then due to drugs and bad diet and poverty. Ruined my whole mouth. These teeth are all artificial.

Sometimes we'd spend two days getting dressed and we'd sail right past the party we were going to. That's a common amphetamine phenomenon. It's not that everything's slowed down. In fact, everything's carried on at a rapid pace; but it's a problem of trying *every* combination, trying on every stitch with everything . . . until finally getting a complete outfit and being all ready to go and suddenly deciding that maybe you'll just change the scarf, and then you do that and realize that something else doesn't go with the scarf, so you change that something else, and you become completely disoriented. You spend all night getting dressed, and by then you completely forget where you're supposed to be going. By the time you're done, you're so exhausted you lay down and go to sleep.

If you stayed up too long on amphetamines your vision could play tricks on you. Every car you passed with bucket seats had two people sitting in it. Every tree had someone behind it. You'd see people in the windows waving at you. You'd walk down the street and hear people calling your name. "Bobby, Bobby, Bobby," and I'd look all around, and there was no one there. Then there are also voids. During a conversation you'd realize that you'd just blacked out for a moment—a whole gap in which you hadn't heard anything.

There's no remembrance of what you do under those amphetamine overdoses. You get up, move around, roam and do things. Once I got up in the middle of the winter with no shoes on, nothing but a pair of slacks and a raccoon coat. And I walked for blocks for a pack of cigarettes, pounding on the front door of shops at five in the morning, insisting that they open up, and flagging a bus down by standing in front of it and making it stop: "Drive me to my street!" I remembered nothing. Tommy Slocum, the Indian boy who lived with us occasionally, and who followed me to make sure that nothing happened to me, told me the next day what I'd gone and done; I just didn't believe it.

When Edith first came to live with us, I had never given anybody any kind of needle in my life; I just didn't know anything about it. When Edith said, "My dear, would you give me a poke?" I didn't know what a poke was. So I said, "Sure, tell me what it is."

She took me into the bathroom when she had the needle all ready. I went, "Oh, no, no, no, no. I can't do this." She said, "Sure, you can, it's very easy."

We went back and forth for twenty minutes before I was able to stick it in her behind. It was like stabbing somebody, to me. I was *so* frightened. I kept asking, "Does it hurt? Does it hurt?" She kept saying, "No no no no no." She was holding onto the sink. She was all dressed; she had on navy blue corduroy pants and a Pucci halter top and a matching turban, and of course the pants were down so I could push the needle in her behind. I tried three times. I really almost fainted and fell off the toilet seat. I kept saying, "Don't you want to swallow it, or something?"

After a while I could give her an injection any time. In fact, I got pleasure out of giving people needles after a while. It was always made to sound very cute and "toy" to pull your pants down for the shot—"toy" meaning child-like. Very nursery school. But in a way it's sexual, because you're giving someone a very large injection of something very fabulous and stimulating, which gives them a sexual sensation after they get it. I've seen people actually reach an orgasm on amphetamine.

But getting poked really did hurt Edith because she began to develop a lot of scar tissue on her fanny, and she had to use big, thick needles to get it in. There's foreign matter with a lot of the street drugs, and it sort of sat in her fat tissue. These are all things I've learned since then. My dear, Richie Berlin's behind! Brigid's beautiful sister. They used to call it Rocky Mountain Range and everything. Rhoda Buddha's Rocky Mountains—Rhoda Buddha was Richie's nickname. She could give herself shots. But Edith refused to do it herself. She didn't want to take that step down the hill.

When I first met them all, I wouldn't have them touch me with a needle. I took a couple of pills once in a while; I would get high on those, and it was fabulous. They kept showing me this powder and saying it's the same thing. Finally I let Geneviève give me a poke; it put me in St. Vincent's Hospital. I almost lost my leg. She had used a very long hypodermic and because I have a very small behind, it went right through the muscle where it belonged. I was almost paralyzed for life. Gangrene and everything. In return for which they called me up at the hospital and told me to eat a lot of fresh fruit! That's how serious it was to all of them . . . all these people working on *Ciao! Manhattan*. They thought it was just hilarious.

Then I got going on it. Getting pokes. I remember going into the

Brasserie Restaurant and having the little old bathroom attendant do it
for me. I was so spaced out I couldn't do it myself. I told him I was a
diabetic. He said, "Oh, ah can't do dat. Ah can't do dat." I said, "Look,
I'll just hold it here and you walk up behind me and hit it with your
hand." I had it in place for him. It was a machine like a small pistol, just
the cutest thing. It's like holding a water gun against your behind and
squeezing the trigger. So anyway the bathroom attendant closed his
eyes, and *pop* he went and hit it.

When Edith lived with me she had a purse she carried around for the
drugs—a picnic basket that was about two feet wide and a foot and a half
deep which was filled with hundreds of little zipper bags, plastic bags,
plastic boxes, bubblegum bubbles, a lot of it to hold syringes, cotton
balls, little vials of alcohol, amphetamines, pills, tranquillizers. Everything was inside of something else. That's an amphetamine dementia.
Lots of order. You find something that fits in this box. Then you find
something that this box fits in: everything goes inside something else,
and it's all very mazey, but tight and orderly. It's known as being anal
compulsive. It's an amphetamine trait. Most people who take amphetamines are very neat: they'll fluff up a pillow to make it look nice while
you're still sitting on it. They empty ashtrays. Edith could spend hours
unloading her purse. And then start packing it up again, and forget what
she was looking for when she started. Incredible! Anywhere. On the
sidewalk, on the street, in a restaurant, a bar. Hundreds of things would
come out to be unscrewed and looked in and then screwed back up and
replaced. *So* many things. It was like carrying an entire lifestyle with you
. . . like living with a camper van on your back. Oh, it was definitely an
amphetamine thing. They all did it; they all had tote bags. I had a tote
bag. I don't mean to exclude myself from all of these things I'm talking
about, because we were all the same.

She took that basket with her when we went out. We went out a lot.
One night we went to see Jimi Hendrix give a special performance at
Steve Paul's *The Scene*. Edith had talked about it for days in advance.
We went in Margouleff's gold Cadillac, which we parked illegally on
Eighth Avenue. We had no reservations, but she did a whole production
demanding to see Steve Paul, letting them know just who she was, and
we got a special ringside table in a corner, kind of private but public so
you could be seen at the same time. Edith was very quiet through the
whole thing. She spent most of the performance going through her
wicker basket, opening plastic bubblegum capsules that she had buttons
in, and loose hypodermic needles. While this was going on, Jim Morrison, the rock star, got up on the stage and went through an adoration
number. He took down Hendrix's pants and went down on him right up

there on the stage. At first everyone's mouths fell open. When it was over, they applauded and screamed. Edith thought it was absolutely fabulous, but disgusting. Did Hendrix mind? Oh no, I guess not! Well, what man *would* mind? Those people were so very uninhibited anyway, they were all so stoned. I don't think Hendrix had an orgasm. None of those people were able to reach an orgasm easily because of the quantity of drugs they were on at all times.

Edith took so many! Along with her amphetamine usage, she took barbiturates to go to sleep. That's why she had so many fires—because she was in such a barbiturate fog that it would cause a roller-coaster reaction, and eventually she would nod off with cigarettes. In the Margouleff apartment alone she went through three mattresses and about five fires. It was incredible how fast she could set a bed on fire with a cigarette. The trouble was you'd have to wait for her to pass out to take the cigarette out of her fingers. She'd get really indignant and bitchy if you tried while she knew what you were doing.

Yet you'd leave the room, gone just two minutes, and BOOM, the next thing you know she'd be asleep and there'd be smoke coming out of the bed and a hole in the mattress this big.

Sometimes she took so many barbiturates to go to sleep, and was so high on amphetamines, that she had convulsions and scared me half to death . . . wicked. She'd say all the things in her subconscious that had been bothering her . . . that she'd been smiling at people and kissing their asses for nothing. She let it all out. She attacked Margouleff viciously; she'd call him a "cheap kike" to his face. She was *wicked!* "You rotten kike, you cheap bastard, Jew motherfucker, small-time entrepreneur!"

He'd say, "Get her to bed. Tie her down, if you have to."

He seemed very practical about the whole thing. But then all of a sudden, sitting there, he'd begin to shake. He was so traumatized by that whole experience. He was a neurotic forever afterward. Just incredible!

As for Margouleff's parents, I think they really almost just died from it! I mean to go through so much money and find that they'd been spending it on a bunch of drug addicts sitting there cutting the film into tiny one inch strips of film showing some pigeons in the air and saying, "How fabulous!" That was what Geneviève was doing before they took her away. She cut I don't know how many hours and ended up with two squares of celluloid of pigeons that she thought were the *best.* She was just sitting there all wired up. The Margouleffs really didn't appreciate that.

Edith's parents, of course, were terribly concerned too and I think very sincere, about what was happening to their daughter. There were

telephone calls to California. They turned up on the telephone bills . . .
Margouleff screaming: "I'm not paying for this! I'm paying her a salary.
That's enough." Mrs. Sedgwick . . . I felt like I was talking to my own
mother. She wanted me to report to her. "Well, how badly burned is
she?"

"Well, it's all right, Mrs. Sedgwick. The doctor is doing a lot and he
says there won't be any physical damage . . . maybe a little nerve damage."

Then she'd hem and haw and I knew what was coming next. "Is she
on drugs?"

I'd just met Edith. So I said, "Well, Mrs. Sedgwick, she's off drugs
and she hasn't been on them." That's truly what I thought. All the time
Edith in the background would be giving me signals with those big
bandaged hands. If I ever got even *near* a topic that was sensitive . . .
there was a lot of waving of those big baseball mitts.

"She's not on heroin, is she?"

I'd say, "Oh, no, not on heroin" . . . and Edith would go
"Mmmmmm," waving her hands in the air.

"Is she drinking? Is she still an alcoholic?"

"Mrs. Sedgwick," I'd say. "I've never seen her pick up a glass with
anything but fruit juice and milk in it."

"Oh thank you," Mrs. Sedgwick would say. "I'm so glad she finally
has someone who cares."

I wondered how many times she'd said this to someone on the phone.
She must have been through it a hundred times. I could tell she was
going through a great deal of grief . . . I mean, she was a real mother, and
I felt sorry for her.

Then Edith would get onto the phone and I'd listen in on the extension so Edith and I could talk about it afterwards. Edith would ask to talk
to her father but he wouldn't come to the phone. "Your father has to do
this . . . he has to do that . . . he isn't feeling well. Edith, you don't know
what you're doing to your father." All she ever got was, "Your father,
your father, your father." Just hammered up her back.

Edith begged. Cried. Quite a few times. He would *not* speak to her.
She had so many mixed, tortured emotions about that man. She loved
him, she worshipped him; she hated him.

Her mother would say, "He can't come to the phone. Edith, please,
don't put me through this."

Sometimes Edith would wait until she'd hung up and then she'd cry.
Sometimes she'd get really furious and outraged, and scream about it.
She'd turn cold and clinical as she'd describe her childhood and the
things they'd done to her. She told me her father once tried to punish
her by taking her out to the corral, tying her to a post and whipping her

in front of all the servants and the ranch help. She had this incredible fascination for her father. She made him sound like a sadistic Bluebeard, how incredibly unbearable and cruel he was . . . I'm sure she was exaggerating, because people on amphetamines tend to do that lot. For example, she showed me all these fabulous equestrian sculptures that I now understand her father did and said that *she* had done them . . . pulling out these photographs of enormous sculptures to show me. In those days I just didn't think it was possible for people to sit and fabricate things like that, so I was very impressed and awed. I kept saying: "You really did that? You did that yourself? With your little hands and your little body and your little person?" She kept saying, "Oh, and you should have seen some of the other things I've given away to doctors at the hospitals I've stayed."

Well! That's an amphetamine thing . . . to fib. It could show a desire to duplicate her father in herself, couldn't it? He really must have been a bastard.

And yet I never met anyone who wanted to go home so much. I think she wanted to see her father—all these trumped-up fantasies about going to California to visit him. She had her children's books with her . . . her name inside in scratchy little handwriting. Nursery story books . . . most of them English imports from these smart little California bookshops. She cherished them. "This is from this time of my life . . . these are from my childhood when I was a little girl."

She showed me photographs. "This is home, this is from my childhood, this is my father's . . . this is my mother's . . ." Home, home, home, home. All I heard about was the name of the town near the ranch: Los Olivos, Los Olivos, Los Olivos. Her horses. How big and wonderful it all was.

And then suddenly it would turn the other way. She would tell me how terrible it was and how awful her parents were. Now that her two brothers were gone, she said she was the current scapegoat. She described her father as cantankerous, vicious, and dominant . . . a dictator in his little country out there in California . . . that they had a couple of villages encompassed there on the ranch, and everyone there was a serf.

She used to show me pictures of herself on cruises and in Europe . . . pictures of her on an ocean liner. She must have been at least 30 to 40 pounds heavier. I could hardly believe it was the same person. She used to say, "Isn't it incredible?" She had looked so much like little Miss Innocence; a healthy All-American girl, and what a lovely debutante. But Edith didn't much like herself like that. She would say, "Aren't I ridiculous? I look like all the rest of them. Don't you think I'm more fabulous now?" Well, I agreed. She *was* more fabulous.

Oh, I was totally awed and impressed to have such a glamorous, excit-

ing woman in my company. I was totally infatuated and madly in love
with her. One night—it was the night she had so many drugs she had
convulsions and set fire to the bed—we curled up, started to go to sleep;
I put my hand under a sort of t-shirt she was wearing. She responded.
But so very gently. Hardly any physical movement at all. It was totally
boring and uninteresting—like having sex with a child. She didn't even
know how to kiss. She was very fond of kissing around the hair-line with
little gentle kisses.

When Edith was with someone she really liked and she was on speed
and wide awake she would have been the wildest fuck in town. Amphetamines make you very wild and degenerate about sex, they really do . . .
very creative and demented. It's like an eight hour non-stop stretch of
sniffing amylnitrate. You have no idea. No idea! So wonderful, so inspired, so uninhibited . . . it's one of the truly inspired sex accessories
there ever was. You become a sex addict—it's divine. That's the main
reason so many of that crowd took it because that's what they all had in
their minds ninety percent of the time: sex. Totally sex-oriented. Amphetamine was only fabulous for that. Everything else that it did for you
was boring.

But this night with Edith I was very disappointed. She didn't even
remember it, never mentioned it: which was a little heartbreaking. I
don't think she really knew how to be in love with anybody . . . not just
because of what happened that night. If you don't love yourself, you
can't love anybody else. Sex to her that night was about as useful as when
I gave her a bath or combed her hair or helped her across the street; I was
like a Boy Scout. But she was very drugged. How much can a dead body
enjoy a piece of sex?

It was strange. She thought nothing of exposing her lower sexual area
and always covering her breasts. Even that night we had sex, she kept the
top on and took her pants off. Her breasts were about the size of pears;
very small breasts . . . which is very attractive on certain women. Especially for me, because I don't know what to do with very large breasts.

I thought she'd be kind of great. Absolutely great. She was so dynamic
on so many levels. Sexually, physically, since she was very lithe, and very
muscular, I didn't think she'd be that different. And the face. I've always
been in love with the face. The face is *everything* to me. I've been to bed
with more trolls that had beautiful faces. I even picked up somebody
with a beautiful face who turned out to be a deformed dwarf with no
arms and one leg—I swear to *God*—a man I met in a bar. I couldn't tell
that just about everything on him was artificial. He was just beautiful; he
could sing opera like a *professional* he was so talented. He *was* quite

short. Very short. He came back to my apartment, and I *thought* he was walking funny. I was so dumb. This beautiful, beautiful face! You have no idea what I went through. When we got to my room, he took off his arms and dropped them to the floor. On one side, the left side, he had a whole hand coming out of his shoulder. On the other side, he just had this little finger sticking out of his body. I laugh about it now, but . . . oh, my God! Then he unhooked his leg. I was sitting there in total shock, looking. Then he stood on the one leg that was really there, balancing on this little leg, and shaking as he leaned way forward, these little fingers pushed his underwear down: and I fainted! I absolutely fainted. He had two cocks that grew together and then separated into two heads. I just slid down to the floor. He was saying: "Do you mind if I take a bath?"

I said, "No. Please do. Take a bath."

So he hopped in and filled the tub—God knows how he did it . . . I mean with *what?* One of those little appendages?

I must have waited five hours for him to come out of that bathroom. When he was in there I never heard a sound. I kept listening; I was waiting for the water to splash, anything. I said, "Oh my God! This *thing* is dead in my bathroom! It drowned!"

He finally came out and I put him to sleep on the couch. He was getting off on what he was doing, taking everything off and shocking me. The next day I told him, "Please. Listen. If I could *buy* you a contract at the Metropolitan Opera so you could sing, I would. Anything! But you have to leave!"

When Edith was in Margouleff's apartment with me there was always a stream of people turning up—maybe not as strange as the opera singer, but just as twisted! People hustled her. Mostly under the guise of getting drugs for her. She was always very trusting and also open to receiving something new to get high on. She'd hand out hundreds of dollars and the people going out to get the drugs just wouldn't bother coming back.

She was really a terribly absurd person . . . people just conning it out of her, or just borrowing it, or stealing it. I remember only once I actually abused her. I took two dollars off her when I was broke. I was never so ashamed of anything in my life. I went to Max's to meet some people. She gave me hell in the morning for it. She said. "I had five dollars when I went to sleep and there's only three left." I said, "Well, I took two dollars out of your pocketbook," I was never so ashamed of anything. What can I say? They were very strange times.

Well, it came to an end. Edith ran away from the apartment finally. I really never did know why. Perhaps a dispute between her and the people with *Ciao! Manhattan.* I think they cut off her salary. I don't think they paid her very much. There wasn't much left anyway. Mr. and Mrs. Margouleff really went for their lungs on that film. A great deal of money went down the drain . . . most of it into those people's fannies.

What also happened was that Edith got involved with this boy, Harvey Horvito, who kept telling her he could get speed in the Bronx, *speed in the Bronx*. All of a sudden she disappeared and went to the Bronx with him. I didn't hear from her for almost a month. Nothing. It broke my heart. She left everything at the house, but we didn't know where to get in touch with her.

Then one afternoon she showed up. She'd cut her hair really short. She was extremely drawn . . . worse than I'd ever seen her. I wasn't even sure it was her. She wouldn't talk to me. I didn't know what I'd done. Finally I grabbed her by the neck and dragged her into the bathroom; I demanded to know what was going on. We made up immediately. But then she disappeared again. That afternoon I never could find out what had happened, until I heard she was in the hospital. I got Edith's address from Geneviève. She wrote me from the hospital. She did some drawings on one of them—a rat and a rabbit.

It certainly changed my life for a very long time. That whole weird experience of Edith and *Ciao! Manhattan*. I have no idea how long she stayed with me. It seemed like a lifetime.

Part Five

1981–1987

Introduction

Above the vast *Paris Review* mastheads (the list at this writing numbers ninety-seven) are the names of the publishers. During the magazine's existence there have been four—all of remarkably varied backgrounds. The first was Prince Sadruddin Aga Khan, half-brother to Aly Khan, and the second son of the famous potentate H. R. H. Aga Khan, who occasionally put himself on a pair of scales and was paid his weight in various forms of tender as a kind of tribute by his Ismaili Muslim founders. Sadri—as everyone knew him—was persuaded to take on the role of publisher in 1954 during the running of the bulls that summer in Pamplona. I asked him as the two of us stood in the cobblestoned streets, waiting for the rocket to go up by the pens signifying that the bulls had been let loose. It was an unfair time to ask anything of anybody . . . since what one wanted to do was rid the mind of everything except the thought of what was about to be in the street and coming up behind.

Sadri's name appeared at the top of the masthead of the eighth issue. He rarely came to the offices. He was busy representing his father in their constituencies around the world. While the new publisher took on the financial obligations of the *Review,* they were in truth small—not more than $500 owed to the printer on the Rue Sablière—but his presence on the masthead gave a sense of stability to the magazine. Also of considerable importance was that he persuaded his father, the Aga Khan, to establish an annual fiction prize. His father not only set up the prize but entered the competition with two entries of his own. They arrived in white vellum folders—short stories of considerable if somewhat antique charm, both markedly influenced by his close friend and neighbor in the south of France, Somerset Maugham. The Aga Khan was not discouraged that the judges (Brendan Gill, Hiram Hayden, and Saul Bellow) passed over his stories; he again offered the prize the following year (though no further stories of his appeared at the office) his son has continued the prize in his name to this day.

In 1975 Bernard F. Conners became the publisher of the *Review.* He succeeded Sadri who had become immersed in his duties as the U.N. High Commissioner for Refugees. I had known Conners since military days in Italy. After a stint in the F.B.I. he had made an immense success of a career in soft drink distribution. A man of considerable energies (including the writing of successful novels) he lived with his family in a Tudor mansion on a large estate in Loudonville, in upstate New York near Albany. One of the highlights of his tenure as publisher was a large fund-raising party he gave there one spring. The guests were Loudonville neighbors and friends. Part of the invitation was that an acceptance required buying a subscription to the magazine. People in evening dress wandered around the grounds. "The *Paris Review?* The *Paris Review?"*

Conners had ordered a green-and-white striped party-tent, along with a polished, inlaid portable dance-floor. There was an eleven-piece band, including one chap who played the English Horn. Galvanized tubs filled with ice and bottles of Mumms champagne stood around in amazing profusion, like trash cans in a state park. "The *Paris Review?* The *Paris Review?"* Just before dusk a stack of parachutists dropped out of an airplane two or three thousand feet above the guests. They trailed orange smoke behind them for a while and then the parachutes billowed open. They landed down the slope and the Conners children ran to meet them. A helicopter was hired to take guests up for ten minutes to look down on what was going on, and perhaps, since the majority of guests were neighbors, to fly off and look at their own estates from a new perspective. Every ten minutes the "whack-whack-whack" of the copter's blades cut into the conversation around the bars. "The *Paris Review? The Paris Review?"* I put on a small fireworks show when it got dark—about twenty Japanese chrysanthemum shells. Since everyone who came to the party had to subscribe, for a while the magazine had over 200 subscribers from Loudonville—probably the heaviest per capita density of subscribers to a magazine in the country, including the *Reader's Digest.* The monopoly did not last long. No one seemed to resubscribe. Now only one person in Loudonville gets the magazine—Bernard F. Conners.

Invariably, after a while the publisher would asked to be relieved. More important things had come up. There would be a nerve-wrenching hiatus. In 1978 a young record producer and singer named Ron Dante became the publisher. He lived down the street from the New York office. He noticed on his occasional visits that faces were long, and that this was because of financial strain. He said at one point that he was in a position to do something about it. He was instantly asked to become the publisher.

His background, which was the pop music field, was far removed from either of his predecessors. Blessed with a clear and adaptable singing voice, Dante's first musical recording triumph was a "ghost group" in which he sang all twelve voices from bass to falsetto on a single record entitled "Sugar Sugar." The record, which was produced in 1969, and supposedly performed by a "group" known as the Archies, sold an astonishing 10 million copies around the world.

Dante did well in the musical world and as a theater producer, but his personal life changed and his interest in the magazine waned. His successor, Deborah S. Pease, was the first truly literary person to hold the post, which she took over in 1982. She is a novelist (*Real Life*, 1971), a short story writer (In *The New Yorker*), and a poet (her first published poem appeared in the *Paris Review* in 1977 and is included in this volume, picked by Michael Benedikt as one of the best of his tenure as poetry editor. Upon accepting the publishing post Ms. Pease wrote the following note: "I owe a great deal to the dedication of editors, lovers of art and literature. I know the solitariness of an artist and the wild joy of a single act of recognition. The *Paris Review* recognizes life in all its creative expressions—despair, delight, rigor, craziness, the erotic, and the aesthetic . . . and the fine sobriety of a formal interview. It helps to shatter—to paraphrase Kafka—the frozen sea within us. I feel honored to be its publisher."

—G.P.

FICTION

RICK BASS

Wild Horses

Karen was twenty-six. She had been engaged twice, married once. Her husband had run away with another woman after only six months. It still made her angry when she thought about it, which was not often.

The second man she had loved more, the most. He was the one she had been engaged to, but had not married. His name was Henry. He had drowned in the Mississippi the day before they were to be married. They never even found the body. He had a marker in the cemetery, but it was a sham. All her life, Karen had heard those stories about fiancés dying the day before the wedding: and then it had happened to her.

Henry and some of his friends, including his best friend, Sydney Bean, had been sitting up on the old railroad trestle, the old highway that ran so far and across that river, above the wide muddiness. Louisiana, and trees, on one side; Mississippi, and trees, and some farms, on the other side—the place from which they had come. There had been a full moon and no wind, and they had been sitting above the water, maybe a hundred feet above it, laughing, and drinking Psychos from the Daiquiri World over in Delta, Louisiana. The Psychos contained rum and Coca-Cola and various fruit juices and blue food coloring. They came in styrofoam cups the size of small trash cans, so large they had to be held with both hands. They had had too many of them: two, maybe three apiece.

Henry had stood up, beaten his chest like Tarzan, shouted, and then dived in. It had taken him forever, just to hit the water; the light from the moon was good, and they had been able to watch him, all the way down.

Sometimes Sydney Bean still came by to visit Karen. Sydney was gentle and sad, her own age, and he worked somewhere on a farm, out past Utica, back to the east, where he broke and sometimes trained horses.

Once a month—at the end of each month—Sydney would stay over on Karen's farm, and they would go into her big empty closet, and he would let her hit him; striking him with her fists, kicking him, kneeing him, slapping his face until his ears rang and his nose bled; slapping and swinging at him until she was crying and her hair was wild and in her eyes, and the palms of her hands hurt too much to hit him any more.

It built up, the ache and the anger in Karen; and then, hitting Sydney, it went away for a while. He was a good friend. But the trouble was that it always came back.

Sometimes Sydney would try to help her in other ways. He would tell her that some day she was going to have to realize that Henry would not be coming back. Not ever: not in any form, but to remember what she had had, to keep *that* from going away.

He would stand there, in the closet, and let her strike him. But the rules were strict: she had to keep her mouth closed. He would not let her call him names while she was hitting him.

Though she wanted to.

After it was over, and she was crying, more drained than she had felt since the last time, sobbing, her feelings laid bare, he would help her up. He would take her into the bedroom and towel her forehead with a cool washcloth. She would be crying in a child's gulping sobs, and he would brush her hair, hold her hands, even hold her against him, and pat her back while she moaned.

Farm sounds would come from the field, and when she looked out the window, she might see her neighbor, old Dr. Lynly, the vet, driving along in his ancient blue truck, moving along the bayou, down along the trees, with his dog, Buster, running alongside, barking; herding the cows together for vaccinations.

"I can still feel the hurt," Karen would tell Sydney sometimes, when Sydney came over, not to be beaten up, but to cook supper for her, or to just sit on the back porch with her, and to watch the fields.

Sydney would nod whenever Karen said that she still hurt, and he would study his hands.

"I could have grabbed him," he'd say, and then look up and out at the field some more. "I keep thinking that one of these years, I'm going to get a second chance." Sydney would shake his head again. "I think I could have grabbed him," he'd say.

"Or you could have dived in after him," Karen would say, hopefully, wistfully. "Maybe you could have dived in after him."

Her voice would trail off, and her face would be flat and weary.

On these occasions, Sydney Bean wanted the beatings to come once a week, or even daily. But they hurt, too, almost as much as the loss of his friend, and he said nothing. He still felt as if he owed Henry something. He didn't know what.

Sometimes, when he was down on his knees, and Karen was kicking him or elbowing him, he felt close to it—and he almost felt angry at Karen—but he could never catch the shape of it, only the feeling.

He wanted to know what was owed, so he could go on.

On his own farm, there were cattle, down in the fields, and they would get lost, separated from one another, and would low all through the night. It was a sound like soft thunder in the night, before the rain comes, and he liked it.

He raised the cattle, and trained horses too: he saddle-broke the young ones that had never been ridden before, the one- and two-year-olds, the stallions, the wild mares. That pounding, and the evil, four-footed stamp-and-spin they went into when they could not shake him; when they began to do that, he knew he had them beaten. He charged $250 a horse, and sometimes it took him a month.

Old Dr. Lynly needed a helper, but couldn't pay much, and Sydney, who had done some business with the vet, helped Karen get the job. She needed something to do besides sitting around on her back porch, waiting for the end of each month.

Dr. Lynly was older than Karen had thought he would be, when she met him up close. He had that look to him that told her it might be the last year of his life. It wasn't so much any illness or feebleness or disability. It was just a finished look.

He and Buster—an Airedale, six years old—lived within the city limits of Vicksburg, down below the battlefield, hidden in one of the ravines— his house was up on blocks, the yard flooded with almost every rain—and in his yard, in various corrals and pens, were chickens, ducks, goats, sheep, ponies, horses, cows, and an ostrich. It was illegal to keep them as pets, and the city newspaper editor was after him to get rid of them, but Dr. Lynly claimed they were all being treated by his tiny clinic.

"You're keeping these animals too long, Doc," the editor told him. Dr. Lynly would pretend to be senile, and would pretend to think the editor was asking for a prescription, and would begin quoting various and random chemical names.

Buster minded Dr. Lynly exquisitely. The airedale brought the paper, the slippers, he left the room on command, and he brought the chicken's eggs, daily, into the kitchen, making several trips for his and Dr. Lynly's breakfast. Dr. Lynly would have six eggs, fried for himself, and Buster would get a dozen or so, broken into his bowl raw. Any extras went into the refrigerator for Dr. Lynly to take on his rounds, though he no longer had many; only the very oldest people, who remembered him, and the very poorest, who knew he worked for free. They knew he would charge them only for the medicine.

Buster's coat was glossy from the eggs, and burnished, black and tan. His eyes, deep in the curls, were bright, sometimes like the brightest things in the world. He watched Dr. Lynly all the time.

Sometimes Karen watched Dr. Lynly play with Buster, bending down and swatting him in the chest, slapping his shoulders. She had thought it would be mostly kittens and lambs. Mostly, though, he told her, it would be the horses.

The strongest creatures were the ones that got the sickest, and their pain was unspeakable when they finally did yield to it. On the rounds with Dr. Lynly, Karen forgot to think about Henry at all. Though she was horrified by the pain, and almost wished it were hers, bearing it rather than watching it, when the horses suffered.

Once, when Sydney was with her, he had reached out and taken her hand in his. When she looked down and saw it, she had at first been puzzled, not recognizing what it was, and then repulsed, as if it were a giant slug. She threw Sydney's hand off hers quickly, and ran into her room.

Sydney stayed out on the porch. It was heavy blue twilight and all the cattle down in the fields were feeding.

"I'm sorry," he called out. "But I can't bring him back!" He waited for her to answer, but could only hear her sobs. It had been three years, he thought.

He knew he was wrong to have caught her off-balance like that: but he was tired of her unhappiness, and frustrated that he could do nothing to end it. The sounds of her crying carried, and the cows down in the fields began to move closer, with interest. The light had dimmed, there were only dark shadows and pale lights, and a low gold thumbnail of a moon came up over the ragged tear of trees by the bayou.

The beauty of the evening, being on Karen's porch and in her life, when it should have been Henry, flooded Sydney with a sudden guilt. He had been fighting it, and holding it back, constantly: and then, suddenly, the quietness of the evening, and the stillness, released it.

He heard himself saying a crazy thing.

"I pushed him off, you know," he said, loudly enough so she could hear. "I finished my drink, and put both hands on his skinny-ass little shoulders, and said, 'Take a deep breath, Henry.' I just pushed him off," said Sydney.

It felt good, making up the lie. He was surprised at the relief he felt; it was as if he had control of the situation. It was like when he was on the horses, breaking them, trying to stay on.

Presently, Karen came back out with a small blue pistol, a .38, and she went down the steps and out to where he was standing, and she put it next to his head.

"Let's get in the truck," she said.

He knew where they were going.

The river was about ten miles away, and they drove slowly. There was fog flowing across the low parts of the road and through the fields and meadows like smoke, coming from the woods, and he was thinking about how cold and hard the water would be when he finally hit.

He felt as if he were already falling towards it, the way it had taken Henry forever to fall. But he didn't say anything, and though it didn't feel right, he wondered if perhaps it was this simple, as if this were what was owed, after all.

They drove on, past the blue fields and the great spills of fog. The roofs of the hay barns were bright silver polished tin, under the little moon and stars. There were small lakes, cattle stock tanks, and steam rose from them.

They drove with the windows down; it was a hot night, full of flying bugs, and about two miles from the river, Karen told him to stop.

He pulled off to the side of the road, and wondered what she was going to do with his body. A cattle egret flew by, ghostly white and large, flying slowly, and Sydney was amazed that he had never recognized their beauty before, though he had seen millions. It flew right across their windshield, from across the road, and it startled both of them.

The radiator ticked.

"You didn't really push him off, did you?" Karen asked. She still had the pistol against his head, and had switched hands.

Like frost burning off the grass in a bright morning sun, there was in his mind a sudden, sugary, watery feeling—like something dissolving. She was not going to kill him after all.

"No." he said.

"But you could have saved him," she said, for the thousandth time.

"I could have reached out and grabbed him," Sydney agreed. He was going to live. He was going to get to keep feeling things, was going to get to keep seeing things.

He kept his hands in his lap, not wanting to alarm Karen, but his eyes moved all around as he looked for more egrets. He was eager to see another one.

Karen watched him for a while, still holding the pistol against him, and then turned it around and looked at the open barrel of it, cross-eyed, and held it there, right in her face, for several seconds. Then she reached out and put it in the glove box.

Sydney Bean was shuddering.

"Thank you," he said.

He put his head down on the steering wheel, in the moonlight. There were crickets calling all around them. They sat like that for a long time, Sydney leaning against the wheel, and Karen sitting up straight, just looking out at the fields.

Then the cattle began to move up the hill towards them, thinking that Karen's old truck was the one that had come to feed them, and slowly, drifting up the hill from all over the fields, coming from out of the woods, and from their nearby resting spots on the sandbars along the little dry creek that ran down into the bayou—eventually, the cattle all assembled around the truck, like schoolchildren.

They stood there in the moonlight, some with white faces like skulls, all about the same size, and chewed grass and watched the truck. One, bolder than the rest—a yearling black Angus—moved in close, bumped the grill of the truck with his nose, playing, and then leapt back again, scattering some of the others.

"How much would you say that one weighs?" Karen asked. "How much, Sydney?"

They drove the last two miles to the river slowly. It was about four A.M. The yearling cow was bleating and trying to break free; Sydney had tied him up with his belt, and with jumper cables and shoelaces, and an old shirt. His lip was bloody from where the calf had butted him.

But he had wrestled larger steers than that before.

They parked at the old bridge, the one across which the trains still ran. Farther downriver, they could see an occasional car, two round spots of headlight moving slowly and steadily across the new bridge, so far above the river, going very slowly. Sydney put his shoulders under the calf's belly and lifted it, with his back and legs, and like a prisoner in the stock, he carried it out to the center of the bridge. Karen followed. It took about fifteen minutes to get there, and Sydney was trembling, dripping with sweat, when finally they gauged they had reached the middle. The deepest part.

They sat there, soothing the frightened calf, stroking its ears, patting its flanks, and waited for the sun to come up. When it did, pale orange behind the great steaminess of the trees and river below—the fog from the river and trees a gunmetal gray, the whole world washed in gray flatness, except for the fruit of the sun—they untied the calf, and pushed him over.

They watched him forever and forever, a black object and then a black spot against the great background of no-colored river, and then there was a tiny white splash, lost almost immediately in the river's current. Logs, which looked like twigs from up on the bridge, swept across the spot. Everything headed south, moving south, and there were no eddies, no pauses.

"I am halfway over him," Karen said.

And then, walking back, she said: "So that was really what it was like?"

She had a good appetite, and they stopped at the Waffle House and ate eggs and pancakes, and had sausage and biscuits and bacon and orange juice. She excused herself to go to the restroom, and when she came back out, her face was washed, her hair brushed and clean-looking. Sydney paid for the meal, and when they stepped outside, the morning was growing hot.

"I have to work today," Karen said, when they got back to her house. "We have to go see about a mule."

"Me, too," said Sydney. "I've got a stallion who thinks he's a bad-ass."

She studied him for a second, and felt like telling him to be careful, but didn't. Something was in her, a thing like hope stirring, and she felt guilty for it.

Sydney whistled, driving home, and tapped his hands on the steering wheel, though the radio did not work.

Dr. Lynly and Karen drove until the truck wouldn't go any farther, bogged down in the clay, and then they got out and walked. It was cool beneath all the big trees, and the forest seemed to be trying to press in on them. Dr. Lynly carried his heavy bag, stopping and switching arms frequently. Buster trotted slightly ahead, between the two of them, looking left and right, and up the road, and even up into the tops of the trees.

There was a sawmill, deep in the woods, where the delta's farmland in the northern part of the county settled at the river, and then went into dark mystery; hardwoods, and muddy roads, then no roads. The men at the sawmill used mules to drag their trees to the cutting. There had never been money for bulldozers, or even tractors. The woods were quiet, and foreboding; it seemed to be a place without sound or light.

When they got near the sawmill, they could hear the sound of axes. Four men, shirtless, in muddy boots with the laces undone, were working on the biggest tree Karen had ever seen. It was a tree too big for chain saws. Had any of the men owned one, the tree would have ruined the saw.

One of the men kept swinging at the tree: putting his back into it, with rhythmic, stroking cuts. The other three stepped back, hitched their pants, and wiped their faces with their forearms.

The fourth man stopped cutting finally. There was no fat on him and he was pale, even standing in the beam of sunlight that was coming down through an opening in the trees, and he looked old—fifty, maybe, or sixty. Some of his fingers were missing.

"The mule'll be back in a minute," he said. He wasn't even breathing hard. "He's gone to bring a load up out of the bottom." He pointed with his ax, down into the swamp.

"We'll just wait," said Dr. Lynly. He bent back and tried to look up at the top of the trees. "Y'all just go right ahead with your cutting."

But the pale muscled man was already swinging again, and the other three, with another tug at their beltless pants, joined in: an odd, pausing drumbeat, as four successive whacks hit the tree; then four more again; and then, almost immediately, the cadence stretching out, growing irregular, as the older man chopped faster.

All around them were the soft pittings, like hail, of tree chips raining into the bushes. One of the chips hit Buster in the nose, and he rubbed it with his paw, and turned and looked up at Dr. Lynly.

They heard the mule before they saw him: he was groaning, like a person. He was coming up the hill that led out of the swamp; he was coming towards them.

They could see the tops of small trees and saplings shaking as he dragged his load through them. Then they could see the tops of his ears; then his huge head, and after that they saw his chest. Veins raced against the chestnut thickness of it.

Then the tops of his legs.

Then his knee. Karen stared at it before starting to tremble. She sat down in the mud, and hugged herself—the men stopped swinging, for just a moment—and Dr. Lynly had to help her up.

It was the mule's right knee that was injured, and it had swollen to the size of a basketball. It buckled, with every step he took, pulling the sled up the slick and muddy hill, but he kept his footing and he did not stop.

Flies buzzed around the knee, around the infections, where the loggers had pierced the skin with nails and the ends of their knives, trying to drain the pus. Dried blood ran down in streaks to the mule's hoof, to the mud.

The sawlogs on the back of the sled smelled good, fresh. They smelled like they were still alive.

Dr. Lynly walked over to the mule and touched the knee. The mule closed his eyes and trembled slightly, as Karen had done, or even as if in ecstasy, at the chance to rest. The three other men, plus the sledder, gathered around.

"We can't stop workin' him," the sledder said. "We can't shoot him, either. We've got to keep him alive. He's all we've got. If he dies, it's us that'll have to pull them logs up here."

A cedar moth, from the woods, passed over the mule's ears, fluttering blindly. It rested on the mule's forehead briefly, and then flew off. The mule did not open his eyes. Dr. Lynly frowned and rubbed his chin. Karen felt faint again, and leaned against the mule's sweaty back to keep from falling.

"You sure you've got to keep working him?" Dr. Lynly asked.

"Yes, sir."

The pale logger was still swinging: tiny chips flying in batches.

Dr. Lynly opened his bag. He took out a needle and rag, and a bottle of alcohol. He cleaned the mule's infections. The mule drooled a little when the needle went in, but did not open his eyes. The needle was slender, and it bent and flexed, and slowly Dr. Lynly drained the fluid.

Karen held onto the mule's wet back and vomited into the mud: both her hands on the mule as if she were being arrested against the hood of a car, and her feet spread out wide. The men gripped their axes awkwardly.

Dr. Lynly gave one of them a large plastic jug of pills.

"These will kill his pain," he said. "The knee will get big again, though. I'll be back out, to drain it again." He handed Karen a clean rag from his satchel, and led her away from the mule, away from the mess.

One of the ax men carried Dr. Lynly's satchel all the way back to the truck. Dr. Lynly let Karen get up into the truck first, and then Buster; then the ax man rocked and shoved, pushing on the hood of the truck as the tires spun, and helped them back it out of the mud—their payment, for healing the mule. A smell of burning rubber and smoke hung in the trees after they left.

They didn't talk much. Dr. Lynly was thinking about the pain killers: how for a moment, he had almost given the death pills instead.

Karen was thinking how she would not let him pay her for that day's work. Also she was thinking about Sydney Bean: she would sit on the porch with him again, and maybe drink a beer and watch the fields.

He was sitting on the back porch, when she got in; he was on the wooden bench next to the hammock, and he had a tray set up for her with a pitcher of cold orange juice. There was froth in the pitcher, a light creamy foaminess from where he had been stirring it, and the ice cubes were circling around. Beads of condensation slid down the pitcher, rolling slowly, then quickly, like tears. She could feel her heart giving. The field was rich summer green, and then, past the field, the dark line of trees. A long string of cattle egrets flew past, headed down to their rookery in the swamp.

Sydney poured her a small glass of orange juice. He had a metal pail of cold water and a clean washcloth. It was hot on the back porch, even for evening. He helped her get into the hammock; then he wrung the washcloth out and put it across her forehead, her eyes. Sydney smelled as if he had just gotten out of the shower, and he was wearing clean white duckcloth pants and a bright blue shirt.

She felt dizzy, and leaned back in the hammock. The washcloth over her eyes felt so good. She sipped the orange juice, not looking at it, and licked the light foam of it from her lips. Owls were beginning to call, down in the swamp.

She felt as if she were younger, going back to a place, some place she had not been in a long time but could remember fondly. It felt like she was in love. She knew that she could not be, but that was what it felt like.

Sydney sat behind her, and rubbed her temples.

It grew dark, and the moon came up.

"It was a rough day," she said, around ten o'clock.

But he just kept rubbing.

Around eleven o'clock, she dozed off, and he woke her, helped her from the hammock, and led her inside, not turning on any lights, and helped her get in bed.

Then he went back outside, locking the door behind him. He sat on the porch a little longer, watching the moon so high above him, and then he drove home, slowly, cautiously, as ever. Accidents were everywhere; they could happen at any time, from any direction.

He moved carefully, and tried to look ahead and be ready for the next one.

He really wanted her. He wanted her in his life. Sydney didn't know if the guilt was there for that—the wanting—or because he was alive, still seeing things, still feeling. He wanted someone in his life, and it didn't seem right to feel guilty about it. But he did.

Sometimes, at night, he would hear the horses running, thundering

across the hard summer-baked flatness of his pasture, running wild—and
he would imagine they were laughing at him for wasting his time feeling
guilty, but it was a feeling he could not shake, could not ride down, and
his sleep was often poor and restless.

Sydney often wondered if horses were even meant to be ridden at all.
It was always such a struggle.

The thing about the broncs, he realized—and he never realized it
until they were rolling on top of him in the dust, or rubbing him off
against a tree, or against the side of a barn, trying to break his leg—was
that if the horses didn't get broken, tamed, they'd get wilder. There was
nothing as wild as a horse that had never been broken. It just got meaner,
each day.

So he held on. He bucked and spun and arched and twisted, shooting
up and down with the mad horse's leaps; and when the horse tried to
hurt itself, by running straight into something—a fence, a barn, the
lake—he stayed on.

If there was, once in a blue moon, a horse not only stronger, but more
stubborn than he—then he would have to destroy it.

The cattle were easy to work with, they would do anything for food,
and once one did it, they would all follow; but working with the horses
made him think ahead, and sometimes he wondered, in streaks and bits
of paranoia, if perhaps all the horses in the world did not have some
battle against him, and were destined, all of them, to pass through his
corrals, each one testing him before he was allowed to stop.

Because like all bronc-busters, that was what he someday allowed
himself to consider and savor, in moments of rest: the day when he could
stop. A run of successes. A string of wins so satisfying and continuous
that it would seem—even though he would be sore, and tired—that a
horse would never beat him again, and he would be convinced of it, and
then he could quit.

Mornings in summers past, Henry used to come over and sit on the
railing and watch. He had been an elementary school teacher, and frail,
almost anemic; but he had loved to watch Sydney Bean ride the horses.
He taught only a few classes in the summers, and he would sip coffee and
grade a few papers while Sydney and the horse fought out in the center.

Sometimes Henry had to set a broken bone for Sydney—Sydney had
shown him how—and other times Sydney, if he was alone, would set his
own bones, if he even bothered with them. Then he would wrap them
up and keep riding. Dr. Lynly had set some of his bones, on the bad
breaks.

Sydney was feeling old, since Henry had drowned. Not so much in the
mornings, when everything was new and cool, and had promise; but in
the evenings, he could feel the crooked shapes of his bones, within him.

He would drink beers, and watch his horses, and other people's horses in his pasture, as they ran. The horses never seemed to feel old, not even in the evenings, and he was jealous of them, of their strength.

He called Karen one weekend. "Come out and watch me break horses," he said.

He was feeling particularly sore and tired. For some reason he wanted her to see that he could always do it; that the horses were always broken. He wanted her to see what it looked like, and how it always turned out.

"Oh, I don't know," she said, after she had considered it. "I'm just so *tired.*" It was a bad and crooked road, bumpy, from her house to his, and it took nearly an hour to drive it.

"I'll come get you . . . ?" he said. He wanted to shake her. But he said nothing; he nodded, and then remembered he was on the phone and said, "I understand."

She did let him sit on the porch with her, whenever he drove over to her farm. She had to have someone.

"Do you want to hit me?" he asked one evening, almost hopefully.

But she just shook her head sadly.

He saw that she was getting comfortable with her sorrow, was settling down into it, like an old way of life, and he wanted to shock her out of it, but felt paralyzed and mute, like the dumbest of animals.

He stared at his crooked hands, with the scars from the cuts made over the years by the fencing tools. Silently, he cursed all the many things he did not know. He could lift bales of hay. He could string barbed-wire fences. He could lift things. That was all he knew. He wished he were a chemist, an electrician, a poet, or a preacher. The things he had—what little of them there were—wouldn't help her.

She had never thought to ask how drunk Henry had been. Sydney thought that made a difference: whether you jumped off the bridge with one beer in you, or two, or a six-pack; or with a sea of purple Psychos rolling around in your stomach—but she never asked.

He admired her confidence, and doubted his ability to be as strong, as stubborn. She never considered that it might have been her fault, or Henry's; that some little spat might have prompted it, or general disillusionment.

It was his fault, Sydney's, square and simple, and she seemed comfortable, if not happy, with the fact.

Dr. Lynly treated horses, but he did not seem to love them, thought Karen.

"Stupid creatures," he would grumble, when they would not do as he

wanted, when he was trying to doctor them. "Utter idiots." He and
Buster and Karen would try to herd the horse into the trailer, or the
corral, pulling on the reins and swatting the horse with green branches.

"Brickheads," Dr. Lynly would growl, pulling the reins, and then
walking around and slapping, feebly, the horse's flank. "Brickheads and
fatheads." He had been loading horses for fifty years, and Karen would
giggle, because the horse's stupidity always seemed to surprise, and then
anger Dr. Lynly, and she thought it was sweet.

It was as if he had not yet really learned that that was how they always
were.

But she had seen that right away. She knew that a lot of girls, and
women, were infatuated with horses, in love with them even, for their
great size and strength, and for their wildness—but Karen, as she saw
more and more of the sick horses, the ailing ones—the ones most people
did not see regularly—knew that all horses were dumb, simple and trusting, and that even the smartest ones could be made to do as they were
told.

And they could be so dumb, so loyal, and so oblivious to pain. It was as
if—even if they could feel it—they could never, ever acknowledge it.

It was sweet, she thought, and dumb.

Karen let Sydney rub her temples and brush her hair. She would go
into the bathroom, and wash it while he sat on the porch. He had taken
up whittling; one of the stallions had broken Sydney's leg by throwing
him into a fence and then trampling him, and the leg was in a heavy cast.
So Sydney had decided to take a break for a few days.

He had bought a whittling kit at the hardware store, and was going to
try hard to learn how to do it. There were instructions. The kit had a
square, light piece of balsa wood, almost the weight of nothing, and a
plain curved whittling knife. There was a dotted outline in the shape of a
duck's head on the balsa wood that showed what the shape of his finished work would be.

After he learned to whittle, Sydney wanted to learn to play the har-
monica. That was next, after whittling.

He would hear the water running, and hear Karen splashing, as she
put her head under the faucet and rinsed.

She would come out in her robe, drying her hair, and then would let
him sit in the hammock with her and brush her hair. It was September,
and the cottonwoods were tinging, were making the skies hazy, soft and
frozen. Nothing seemed to move.

Her hair came down to the middle of her back. She had stopped
cutting it. The robe was old and worn, the color of an old blue dish.
Something about the shampoo she used reminded him of apples. She

wore moccasins that had a shearling lining in them, and Sydney and Karen would rock in the hammock, slightly. Sometimes Karen would get up and bring out two Cokes from the refrigerator, and they would drink those.

"Be sure to clean up those shavings when you go," she told him. There were little balsa wood curls all over the porch. Her hair, almost dry, would be light and soft. "Be sure not to leave a mess when you go," she would say.

It would be dark then, Venus out beyond them.

"Yes," he said.

Before he left, she reached out from the hammock, and caught his hand. She squeezed it, and then let go.

He drove home slowly, thinking of Henry, and of how he had once taken Henry fishing for the first time. They had caught a catfish so large that it had scared Henry. They drank beers, and sat in the boat, and talked.

One of Sydney Bean's headlights faltered, on the drive home, then went out, and it took him an hour and a half to get home.

A girl who raised Arabian stallions and mares and who lived out of town called Dr. Lynly in a panic. A mare named Jadar, her favorite, was bloating: rolling on her back out in the pasture, as big as an elephant. Her legs were waving at the sky. She was bloody from where she had been throwing herself against trees: trying to rub off the pain. Karen and Dr. Lynly drove hard and fast out to the girl's farm—Kathy's—taking corners sharply, running red lights; when they got to the farm, they flew over the cattle guard, and out across the bumps in the pasture, out to where Kathy was squatting not too far from her horse, crying, watching from a slight distance. Jadar continued to scream and writhe on her back, trying to shake the pain. They could see her stomach swelling, growing as if without reason, and with not much room left to stretch.

"Worms," said Dr. Lynly. He squatted down next to Kathy. She was crying even harder.

"Do something," she cried. She clutched his arm, and tugged in it. "Stob her with the trochar!"

Dr. Lynly looked ready to cry himself. The horse was growing, as if being filled with air by a hose.

"Child, I can't do that. I'm too old, and if I miss, I kill her. I could hit anything, in there: the spleen, the liver, the intestines; you can't stob a horse, the way you can a sheep or cow. We're better off with the pistol." Dr. Lynly's pistol was a big one, and Karen had never seen him use it before.

The horse continued to spin on its back, with violent screams. It didn't even look like a horse: there wasn't a patch of hide left on her, just raw, abused flesh, with bits of bark and gravel sticking to it everywhere.

"All right," he said, changing his mind. "Karen, get the trochar." He rolled up his sleeves, and stood up. He looked at the berserk horse as if he were about to go off to war for several years, as if he might not come back. Karen ran and got the stainless steel pipe that they used for piercing animals with more than one stomach, but never on horses. The trochar was razor sharp, honed, and bladed like a shovel on the end.

Dr. Lynly took the tool from Karen and crept in closer to the horse. Buster whined, and started to go with him—all four of Jadar's hooves were flying out, jabbing, trying to hit something—and then Dr. Lynly saw his opening, and moved in, and struck the trochar into the big horse's stomach.

They were sickened at how deep it went in.

It went in all the way.

The horse stiffened, and stopped moving.

The trochar was hollow, and all of the stomach's wormy contents, gasses and everything, were supposed to shoot up through the hollow part and out into the air. But nothing happened.

"She's gonna die, Doc," Kathy said. The horse was breathing heavily, her huge inflated sides rising and falling, but otherwise, there was no movement. Dr. Lynly stepped closer to the horse again and jiggled the t-handle of the trochar, just a little.

The gas hissed up the pipe and out into the wind. It steamed, it was so warm. The horse's eyes bulged, and then she rolled up to her knees, stood, and then trotted off, up the hill, where she immediately began grazing, with the trochar still hanging out of her side.

They stared, amazed, and could hear the ripping, crunching sounds of her grazing. The trochar looked like a toy.

"You are God," said Kathy.

Dr. Lynly watched the horse, trying not to be amazed himself. "Sometimes it works," he said. He gave Kathy a can of spray to put on the wound, to keep it from getting infected.

The days got cold and brittle. It was hard, working with the horses: Sydney's leg hurt all the time. Sometimes the horse would leap, and come down with all four hooves bunched in close together, and the pain and shock of it would travel all the way up Sydney's leg and into his shoulder, and down into his wrists: the break was in his ankle.

He was sleeping past sun-up, some days, and was being thrown, now, nearly every day; sometimes several times in the same day.

There was always a strong wind. Rains began to blow in. It was cool, getting cold, crisp as apples, and it was the weather that in the summer everyone said they would be looking forward to. One night there was a frost, and a full moon.

On her back porch, sitting in the hammock by herself with a heavy blanket around her, Karen saw a stray balsa shaving caught between the cracks of her porch floor. It was white, in the moonlight—the whole porch was—and the field was blue—the cattle stood out in the moonlight like blue statues—and she almost called Sydney.

She even went as far as to get up and call information, to find out his number; it was that close.

But then the silence and absence of a thing—she presumed it was Henry, but did not know for sure, what it was—closed in around her, and the field beyond her porch, like the inside of her heart, seemed to be deathly still—and she did not call.

She thought, angrily, I can love who I want to love. But she was angry at Sydney Bean, for having tried to pull her so far out, into a place where she did not want to go.

She fell asleep in the hammock, and dreamed that Dr. Lynly was trying to wake her up, and was taking her blood pressure, feeling her forehead, and, craziest of all, swatting at her with green branches.

She awoke from the dream, and decided to call Sydney after all. He answered the phone as if he, too, had been awake.

"Hello?" he said. She could tell by the true questioning in his voice that he did not get many phone calls.

"Hello," said Karen. "I just—wanted to call, and tell you hello." She paused; almost a falter. "And that I feel better. That I feel good, I mean. That's all."

"Well," said Sydney Bean. "Well, good. I mean, great."

"That's all," said Karen. "Bye," she said.

"Goodbye," said Sydney.

On Thanksgiving Day, Karen and Dr. Lynly headed back out to the swamp to check up on the loggers' mule. It was the hardest cold of the year, and there was bright ice on the bridges, and it was not thawing, not even in the sun. The inside of Dr. Lynly's old truck was no warmer than the air outside. Buster, in his wooliness, lay across Karen to keep her warm.

They turned onto a gravel road, and started down into the swamp. Smoke, low and spreading, was all in the woods, like a fog. The men had little fires going all throughout the woods; they were each working on a different tree, and had small warming fires where they stood and shivered when resting.

Karen found herself looking for the pale ugly logger.

He was swinging the ax, but he only had one arm, he was swinging at the tree with one arm. The left arm was gone, and there was a sort of sleeve over it, like a sock. The man was sweating, and a small boy stepped up and quickly toweled him dry each time the pale man stepped back to take a rest.

They stopped the truck and got out and walked up to him, and he stepped back—wet, already, again; the boy toweled him off, standing on a low stool and starting with the man's neck and shoulders, and then going down the great back—and the man told them that the mule was better but that if they wanted to see him, he was lower in the swamp.

They followed the little path towards the river. All around them were downed trees, and stumps, and stacks of logs, but the woods looked no different. The haze from the fires made it seem colder. Acorns popped under their feet.

About halfway down the road, they met the mule. He was coming back up towards them, and he was pulling a good load. A small boy was in front of him, holding out a carrot, only partially eaten. The mule's knee looked much better, though it was still a little swollen, and probably always would be.

The boy stopped, and let the mule take another bite of carrot, making him lean far forward in the trace. His great rubbery lips stretched and quavered, and then flapped, as he tried to get it, and then there was the crunch when he did.

They could smell the carrot as the mule ground it with his old teeth. It was a wild carrot, dug from the woods, and not very big, but it smelled good.

Karen had brought an apple and some sugar cubes, and she started forward to give them to the mule, but instead handed them to the little boy, who ate the sugar cubes himself, and put the apple in his pocket.

The mule was wearing an old straw hat, and looked casual, out of place. The boy switched him, and the mule shut his eyes and started up—his chest swelled, tight and sweaty, to fit the dark soft stained leather harness, and the big load behind him started in motion.

Buster whined, as the mule went by.

It was spring again, then, the month in which Henry had left them, and they were on the back porch. Karen had purchased a Clydesdale yearling, a great and huge animal, whose mane and fur she had shaved to keep it cool in the warming weather, and she had asked a little boy from a nearby farm with time on his hands to train it, in the afternoons. The horse was already gentled, but needed to be stronger. She was having the boy walk him around in the fields, pulling a makeshift sled of stones and tree stumps and old rotten bales of hay.

In the fall, when the Clydesdale was strong enough, she and Dr. Lynly were going to trailer it out to the swamp, and trade it for the mule.

Sydney Bean's leg had healed, been broken again, and was now healing once more. The stallion he was trying to break was showing signs of weakening. There was something in the whites of his eyes, Sydney thought, when he reared up, and he was not slamming himself into the barn—so it seemed to Sydney, anyway—with quite as much anger. Sydney thought that perhaps this coming summer would be the one in which he broke all of his horses, day after day, week after week.

They sat in the hammock and drank Cokes and nibbled radishes, celery, which Karen had washed and put on a little tray. They watched the boy, or one of his friends, his blue shirt a tiny spot against the treeline, as he followed the big dark form of the Clydesdale. The sky was a wide spread of crimson, all along the western trees, towards the river. They couldn't tell which of the local children it was, behind the big horse; it could have been any of them.

"I really miss him," said Sydney Bean. "I really hurt."

"I know," Karen said. She put her hand on Sydney's, and rested it there. "I will help you," she said.

Out in the field, a few cattle egrets fluttered and hopped behind the horse and boy. The great young draft horse lifted his thick legs high and free of the mud with each step, free from the mud made soft by the rains of spring, and slowly—they could tell—he was skidding the sled forward.

The egrets hopped and danced, following at a slight distance, but neither the boy nor the horse seemed to notice. They kept their heads down, and moved forward.

T. CORAGHESSAN BOYLE

Ike and Nina

The years have put a lid on it, the principals passed into oblivion. I think I can now, in good conscience, reveal the facts surrounding one of the most secretive and spectacular love affairs of our time: the *affaire de coeur* that linked the thirty-fourth president of the United States and the then first lady of the Soviet Union. Yes: the eagle and the bear,

Elliott Erwitt/Magnum

Bob Gomel/Life Magazine

defrosting the Cold War with the heat of their passion, Dwight D. Eisenhower—Ike—virile, dashing, athletic, in the arms of Madame Nina Khrushcheva, the svelte and seductive schoolmistress from the Ukraine. Behind closed doors, in embassy restrooms and hotel corridors, they gave themselves over to the urgency of their illicit love, while the peace and stability of the civilized world hung in the balance.

Because of the sensitive—indeed sensational—nature of what follows, I have endeavored to tell my story as dispassionately as possible, and must say in my own defense that my sole interest in coming forward at this late date is to provide succeeding generations with a keener insight into the events of those tumultuous times. Some of you will be shocked by what I report here, others moved. Still others—the inevitable naysayers and skeptics—may find it difficult to believe. But before you turn a deaf ear, let me remind you how unthinkable it once seemed to credit reports of Errol Flynn's flirtation with Nazis and homosexuals, F.D.R.'s thirty year obsession with Lucy Mercer or Ted Kennedy's overmastering desire for an ingenuous campaign worker eleven years his junior. The truth is often hard to swallow. But no historian worth his salt, no self-respecting journalist, no faithful eyewitness to the earth-shaking and epoch-making events of human history, has ever blanched from it.

Here then, is the story of Ike and Nina.

In September of 1959, I was assistant to one of Ike's junior staffers, thirty-one years old, schooled in international law and a consultant to the Slavic Languages program at one of our major universities.* I'd had very little contact with the president, had in fact laid eyes on him but twice in the eighteen months I'd worked for the White House (the first time I was looking for a drinking fountain when I caught a glimpse of him—a single flash of his radiant brow—huddled in a back room with Foster Dulles and Andy Goodpaster; a week later, as I was hurrying down a corridor with a stack of reports for shredding, I spotted him slipping out a service entrance with his golf clubs). Like dozens of bright ambitious young men apprenticed to the mighty, I was at this stage of my career a mere functionary, a paper shuffler, so deeply buried in the power structure I must actually have ranked below the pastry chef's croissant twister. I was good—I had no doubt of it—but I was as yet untried, and for all I knew unnoticed. You can imagine my surprise when early one morning I was summoned to the Oval Office.

It was muggy, and though the corridors hummed with the gentle ministrations of the air-conditioners, my shirt was soaked through by the time I reached the door of the president's inner sanctum. A crewcut ramrod in uniform swung open the door, barked out my name and ushered me into the room. I was puzzled, apprehensive, awed: the door closed behind me with a soft click and I found myself in the Oval Office, alone with the president of the United States. Ike was standing at the window, gazing out at the trees, whistling "The Flirtation Waltz," and turning a book of crossword puzzles over in his hands. "Well," he said, turning to me and extending his hand, "Mr. Paderewski, is that right?"

"Yes, sir," I said. He pronounced it *Paderooski.* †

"Well," he repeated, taking me in with those steely blue eyes of his as he sauntered across the room and tossed the book on his desk like a slugger casually dropping his bat after knocking the ball out of the park. He looked like a golf pro, a gymnast, a competitor, a man who could come at you with both hands and a nine iron to boot. Don't be taken in by all those accounts of his declining health—I saw him there that

---

*I choose not to name it, just as I decline to reveal my actual identity here, for obvious reasons.

†This is a pseudonym I've adopted as a concession to dramatic necessity in regard to the present narrative.

September morning in the Oval Office, broad-shouldered and trim-waisted, lithe and commanding. Successive heart attacks and a bout with ileitis hadn't slowed the old warrior a bit. A couple of weeks short of his sixty-ninth birthday, and he was jaunty as a high-schooler on prom night. Which brings me back to the reason for my summons.

"You're a good egg, aren't you, Paderewski?" Ike asked.

I replied in the affirmative.

"And you speak Russian, is that right?"

"Yes sir, Mr. President—and Polish, Sorbian, Serbo-Croatian and Slovene as well."

He grunted, and eased his haunch down on the corner of the desk. The light from the window played off his head till it glowed like a second sun. "You're aware of the upcoming visit of the Soviet premier and his, uh, wife?"

I nodded.

"Good, that's very good, Paderewski, because as of this moment I'm appointing you my special aide for the duration of that visit." He looked at me as if I were some odd and insignificant form of life that might bear further study under the microscope, looked at me like the man who had driven armies across Europe and laid Hitler in his grave. "Everything that happens, every order I give you, is to be held strictly confidential—top secret—is that understood?"

I was filled with a sense of mission, importance, dignity. Here I was, elevated from the ranks to lend my modest talents to the service of the first citizen of the nation, the Commander-in-Chief himself. "Understood, Mr. President," I said, fighting the impulse to salute.

This seemed to relax him, and he leaned back on the desk and told me a long, involved story about an article he'd come across in the *National Geographic,* something about Egyptian pyramids and how the members of a pharoah's funeral procession were either blinded on the spot or entombed with their leaders—something along those lines. I didn't know what to make of it. So I put on my meditative look, and when he finished I flashed him a smile that would have melted ice.

Ike smiled back.

By now, of course, I'm sure you've guessed just what my special duties were to consist of—I was to be the president's liaison with Mrs. Khrushchev, a go-between, a pillow-smoother and excuse-maker: I was to be Ike's panderer. Looking back on it, I can say in all honesty that I did not then nor do I now feel any qualms whatever regarding my role in the affair. No, I feel privileged to have witnessed one of the grand passions of our time, a love both tender and profane, a love that smoldered beneath the watchful eyes of two embattled nations and erupted in an explosion of passionate embraces and hungry kisses.

Ike, as I was later to learn, had first fallen under the spell of Madame K. in 1945, during his triumphal visit to Moscow after the fall of the Third Reich. It was the final day of his visit, a momentous day, the day Japan had thrown in the towel and the great war was at long last ended. Ambassador Harriman arranged a reception and buffet supper at the U.S. embassy by way of celebration, and to honor Ike and his comrade-in-arms, Marshal Zhukov. In addition to Ike's small party, a number of high-ranking Russian military men and politicos turned out for what evolved into an uproarious evening of singing, dancing and congratulatory back-slapping. Corks popped, vodka flowed, the exuberant clamor of voices filled the room. And then Nina Khrushcheva stepped through the door.

Ike was stunned. Suddenly nothing existed for him—not Zhukov, not Moscow, not Harriman, the armistice or "The Song of the Volga Boatmen" that an instant before had been ringing in his ears—there was only this vision in the doorway, simple, unadorned, elegant, this true princess of the earth. He didn't know what to say, didn't know who she was, the only words of Russian he could command—*zdrav'st* and *spasibo** flying to his lips like an unanswered prayer. He begged Harriman for an introduction, and then spent the rest of the evening at her side, the affable Ike, gazing into the quiet depths of her rich mud-brown eyes, entranced. He didn't need an interpreter.

It would be ten long years before their next meeting, years that would see the death of Stalin, the ascendancy of Khrushchev and Ike's own meteoric rise to political prominence as the thirty-fourth president of the United States. Through all that time, through all the growing enmity between their countries, Ike and Nina cherished that briefest memory of one another. For his part, Ike felt he had seen a vision, sipped from the cup of perfection, and that no other woman could hope to match—not Mamie, not Ann Whitman, not even his old flame, the lovely and adept Kay Summersby. He plowed through CIA dossiers on this captivating spirit, Nina Petrovna, wife of the Soviet premier, maintained a scrapbook crammed with photos of her and news clippings detailing her husband's movements; twice, at the risk of everything, he was able to communicate with her through the offices of a discreet and devoted agent of the CIA. In July of 1955, he flew to Geneva, hungering for peaceful coexistence.

At the Geneva Conference, the two came together once again, and

*"Hello" and "thank you."

what had begun ten years earlier as a riveting infatuation blossomed into the mature and passionate love that would haunt them the rest of their days. Ike was sixty-five, in his prime, the erect warrior, the canny leader, a man who could shake off a stroke as if it were a head cold; Nina, ten years his junior, was in the flush of womanly maturity, lovely, solid, a soft inscrutable smile playing on her elfin lips. With a subterfuge that would have tied the intelligence networks of their respective countries in knots, the two managed to steal ten minutes here, half an hour there—they managed, despite the talks, the dinners, the receptions and the interminable, stultifying rounds of speech-making, to appease their desire and sanctify their love forever. "Without personal contact," Ike said at a dinner for the Russian delegation, his boyish blue eyes fixed on Mrs. Khrushchev, "you might imagine someone was fourteen feet high, with horns and a tail." Russians and Americans alike burst into spontaneous laughter and applause. Nina Petrovna, first lady of the Soviet Union, stared down at her chicken Kiev and blushed.

And so, when the gargantuan Soviet TU 114 shrieked into Andrews Air Force Base in September of 1959, I stood by my president with a lump in my throat: I alone knew just how much the Soviet visit meant to him, I alone knew by how tenuous a thread hung the balance of world peace. What could the president have been thinking as the great sleek jet touched down? I can only conjecture. Perhaps he was thinking that she'd forgotten him, or that the scrutiny of the press would make it impossible for them to steal their precious few moments together, or that her husband—that torpedo-headed bully boy—would discover them and tear the world to pieces with his rage. Consider Ike at that moment, consider the all but insurmountable barriers thrown in his way, and you can appreciate my calling him one of the truly impassioned lovers of all time. Romeo had nothing on him, nor Douglas Fairbanks either—even the starry-eyed Edward Windsor pales by comparison. At any rate, he leaped at his opportunity like a desert nomad delivered to the oasis: there would be an assignation that very night, and I was to be instrumental in arranging it.

After the greeting ceremonies at Andrews, during which Ike could do no more than exchange smiles and handshakes with the premier and premiersha, there was a formal state dinner at the White House. Ambassador Menshikov was there, Khrushchev and his party, Ike and Mamie, Christian Herter, Dick Nixon and others; afterward, the ladies retired to the Red Room for coffee. I sat at Ike's side throughout dinner, and lingered in the hallway outside the Red Room directly thereafter. At dinner, Ike had kissed Madame K.'s hand and chatted animatedly with

The Khrushchevs with the Eisenhowers during the former's visit to Washington.

her for a few minutes, but they covered their emotions so well that no one would have guessed they were anything other than amenable strangers wearing their social faces. Only I knew better.

I caught the premiersha as she and Mamie emerged from the Red Room in a burst of photographers' flashbulbs. As instructed, I took her arm and escorted her to the East Room, for the program of American songs that would highlight the evening. I spoke to her in Russian, though to my surprise she seemed to have a rudimentary grasp of conversational English (did she recall it from her school-teaching days, or had she boned up for Ike?). Like a Cyrano, I told her that the president yearned for her tragically, that he'd thought of nothing else in the four years since Geneva, and then I recited a love poem he'd written her in English—I can't recall the sense of it now, but it boiled with Elizabethan conceits and the imagery of war, with torn hearts, manned bastions and references to heavy ordnance, pillboxes and scaling the heights of love. Finally, just before we entered the East Room, I pressed a slip of paper into her hand. It read, simply: *3:00 A.M., back door, Blair House.*

At five of three, in a rented, unmarked limousine, the president and I pulled up at the curb just down the street from Blair House, where the Khrushchev party had been installed for the night. I was driving. The rear panel slid back and the president's voice leaped at me out of the darkness: "Okay Paderewski, do your stuff—and good luck."

I eased out of the car and started up the walk. The night was warm and damp, the darkness a cloak, streetlights dulled as if they'd been shaded for the occasion. Every shadow was of course teeming with Secret Service agents—there were enough of them ringing the house to fill Memorial Stadium twice over—but they gave way for me. (Ike had arranged it thus: one person was to be allowed to enter the rear of Blair

House at the stroke of three; two would be leaving an instant thereafter.)

She was waiting for me at the back door, dressed in pants, a man's overcoat and hat. "Madame Khrushcheva?" I whispered. "Da," came the reply, soft as a kiss. We hurried across the yard and I handed her into the car, admiring Ike's cleverness: if anyone—including the legion of Secret Service, CIA and FBI men—had seen us, they would have mistaken the madame for her husband and concluded that Ike had set up a private, ultra-secret conference. I slid into the driver's seat and Ike's voice, shaken with emotion, came at me again: "Drive Paderewski," he said, "drive us to the stars." And then the panel shot to with a passionate click.

For two hours I circled the capitol, and then, as prearranged, I returned to Blair House and parked just down the street. I could hear them—Ike and Nina, whispering, embracing, rustling clothing—as I cut the engine. She giggled. Ike was whistling. She giggled again, a lovely windchime of a sound, musical and coltish—if I hadn't known better I would have thought Ike was back there with a coed. I was thinking with some satisfaction that we'd just about pulled it off, when the panel slid back and Ike said: "Okay Paderewski—let's hit it." There was the sound of a protracted kiss, a sound we all recognize not so much through experience—who's listening, after all?—but thanks to the attention Hollywood sound men have given it. Then Ike's final words to her, delivered in a passionate susurrus, words etched in my memory as if in stone: "Till we meet again," he whispered.

Something odd happened just then, just as I swung back the door for Mrs. Khrushchev—a car was moving along the street in the opposite direction, a foreign car, and it slowed as she stepped from the limousine. Just that—it slowed—and nothing more. I hardly remarked it at the time, but that instant was to reverberate in history. The engine ticked up the street, crickets chirruped. With all dispatch, I got Mrs. Khrushchev round back of Blair House, saw her in the door, and returned to the limousine.

"Well done, Paderewski, well done," Ike said, as I put the car in drive and headed up the street, and then he did something he hadn't done in years—lit a cigarette. I watched the glow of the match in the rearview mirror, and then he was exhaling with rich satisfaction, as if he'd just come back from swimming the Potomac or taming a mustang in one of those televised cigarette ads. "The White House," he said. "Chop-chop."

Six hours later, Madame K. appeared with her husband on the front steps of Blair House and fielded questions from reporters. She wore a modest gray silk chemise and a splash of lipstick. One of the reporters asked her what she was most interested in seeing while touring the U.S., and she glanced over at her husband before replying (he was grinning to show off his pointed teeth, as impervious to English as he might have been to Venusian). "Whatever is of biggest interest to Mr. Khrushchev," she said. The reporters lapped it up: flashbulbs popped, a flurry of stories went out over the wire. Who would have guessed?

From there, the Khrushchevs took a special VIP train to New York, where Madame K. attended a luncheon at the Waldorf and her husband harangued a group of business magnates in Averell Harriman's living room. "The Moscow Cha-Cha" and Jimmy Driftwood's "The Bear Flew Over the Ocean" blared from every radio in town, and a special squad of NYPD's finest—six footers, expert in jujitsu and marksmanship—formed a human wall around the premier and his wife as they took in the sights of the Big Apple. New York rolled out the red carpet, and the Khrushchevs trod it with a stately satisfaction that rapidly gave way to finger-snapping, heel-kicking glee. As the premier boarded the plane for Los Angeles, Nina at his side, he mugged for cameras, kissed babies and shook hands so assiduously he could have been running for office.

And then the bottom fell out.

In Los Angeles, ostensibly because he was nettled at Mayor Paulson's hardline speech and because he discovered that Disneyland would not be on his itinerary, the raging, tabletop-pounding, Magyar-cowing Khrushchev came to the fore: he threw a tantrum. The people of the United States were inhospitable boors—they'd invited him to fly halfway round the world simply to abuse him. He'd had enough. He was curtailing the trip and heading back to Moscow.

I was with Ike when the first reports of the premier's explosion flashed across the TV screen. Big-bellied and truculent, Khrushchev was lecturing the nation on points of etiquette, jowls atremble, fists beating the air, while Nina, her head bowed, stood meekly at his side. Ike's voice was so pinched it could have come from a ventriloquist's dummy: "My God," he whispered, "he knows." (I suddenly remembered the car slowing, the flash of a pale face behind the darkened glass, and thought of Alger Hiss, the Rosenbergs, the vast network of Soviet spies operating unchecked in the land of the free: they'd seen her after all.) Shaking his head, Ike got up, crossed the room and lit another verboten cigarette. He looked weary, immeasurably old, Rip Van Winkle waking beside his rusted gun. "Well, Paderewski," he sighed, a blue haze playing round the wisps of silver hair at his temples, "I guess now the shit's really going to hit the fan."

He was right, but only partially. To his credit, Khrushchev covered himself like a trooper—after all, how could he reveal so shocking and outrageous a business as this without losing face himself, without transforming himself in that instant from the virile, bellicose, iron-fisted ruler of the Soviet masses to a pudgy, pathetic cuckold? He allowed himself to be mollified by apologies from Paulson and Cabot Lodge over the supposed insult, posed for a photograph with Shirley MacLaine at 20th Century Fox, and then flew on to San Francisco for a tense visit. He made a dilatory stop in Iowa on his way back to Washington and the inevitable confrontation with the man who had suddenly emerged as his rival in love as well as ideology. (I'm sure you recall the celebrated photographs in *Life, Look* and *Newsweek*—Khrushchev leering at a phallic ear of corn, patting the belly of a crewcut interloper at the Garst farm in Iowa, hefting a piglet by the scruff of its neck. Study them today—especially in contrast to the pre-Los Angeles photos—and you'll be struck by the mixture of jealous rage and incomprehension playing across the premier's features, and the soft, tragic, downcast look in his wife's eyes.)

I sat beside the president on the way out to Camp David for the talks that would culminate the Khrushchev visit. He was subdued, desolated, the animation gone out of his voice. He'd planned for these talks as he'd planned for the European Campaign, devising stratagems and feints, studying floorplans, mapping the territory, confident he could spirit away his inamorata for an idyllic hour or two beneath the pines. Now there was no chance of it. No chance in fact that he'd ever see her again. He was slumped in his seat, his head thrown back against the bulletproof glass as if he no longer had the will to hold it up. And then—I've never seen anything so moving, so emotionally ravaging in my life—he began to cry. I offered him my handkerchief but he motioned me away, great wet heaving sobs tearing at his lungs, the riveting blue eyes that had gazed with equanimity on the most heinous scenes of devastation known to civilized man reddened with a sorrow beyond despair. "Nina," he choked, and buried his face in his hands.

You know the rest. The "tough" talks at Camp David (ostensibly over the question of the Berlin Wall), the Soviet premier's postponement of Ike's reciprocal visit till the spring "when things are in bloom," the eventual rescinding of the invitation altogether and the virulent anti-Eisenhower speech Khrushchev delivered in the wake of the U-2 incident. Then there was Ike's final year in office, his loss of animation, his heart troubles (*heart troubles*—could anything be more ironic?), the way in which he so rapidly and visibly aged, as if each moment of each day weighed on him like an eternity. And finally, our last picture of him: the

me ⟶

affable, slightly foggy old duffer chasing a white ball across the links as if it were some part of himself he'd misplaced.

As for myself, I was rapidly demoted after the Khrushchev visit—it almost seemed as if I were an embarrassment to Ike, and in a way I guess I was, having seen him with his defenses down and his soul laid bare. I left the government a few months thereafter and have pursued a rewarding academic career ever since, and am in fact looking forward to qualifying for tenure in the upcoming year. It has been a rich and satisfying life, one that has had its ups and downs, its years of quotidian existence and its few breathless moments at the summit of human history. Through it all, through all the myriad events I've witnessed, the loves I've known, the emotions stirred in my breast by the tragic events of our times, I can say with a sense of reverent gratitude and the deepest sincerity that nothing has so moved and tenderly astonished me as the joy, the sorrow, the epic sweep of the star-crossed love of Ike and Nina. I think of the Cold War, of nuclear proliferation, of Hungary, Korea and the U-2 incident, and it all finally pales beside this: he loved her, and she loved him.

RAYMOND CARVER

Why Don't You Dance?

In the kitchen, he poured another drink and looked at the bedroom suite in his front yard. The mattress was stripped and the candy-striped sheets lay beside two pillows on the chiffonier. Except for that, things looked much the way they had in the bedroom—nightstand and reading lamp on his side of the bed, nightstand and reading lamp on her side.

His side, her side.

He considered this as he sipped the whiskey.

The chiffonier stood a few feet from the foot of the bed. He had emptied the drawers into cartons that morning, and the cartons were in the living room. A portable heater was next to the chiffonier. A rattan chair with a decorator pillow stood at the foot of the bed. The buffed aluminum kitchen-set took up a part of the driveway. A yellow muslin cloth, much too large, a gift, covered the table and hung down over the sides. A potted fern was on the table, along with a box of silverware and a record-player, also gifts. A big console-model television set rested on a coffee table, and a few feet away from this, stood a sofa and chair and a floor lamp. The desk was pushed against the garage door. A few utensils were on the desk, along with a wall clock and two framed prints. There was also in the driveway a carton with cups, glasses, and plates, each object wrapped in newspaper. That morning he had cleared out the closets and, except for the three cartons in the living room, all the stuff was out of the house. He had run an extension cord on out there and everything was connected. Things worked, no different from how it was when they were inside.

Now and then a car slowed and people stared. But no one stopped. It occurred to him that he wouldn't either.

"It must be a yard sale," the girl said to the boy.

This girl and boy were furnishing a little apartment.

"Let's see what they want for the bed," the girl said.

"And the TV," the boy said.

The boy pulled into the driveway and stopped in front of the kitchen table.

They got out of the car and began to examine things, the girl touching the muslin cloth, the boy plugging in the blender and turning the dial to MINCE, the girl picking up a chafing dish, the boy turning on the television set and making adjustments. He sat down on the sofa to watch. He lit a cigarette, looked around, and flipped the match into the grass. The girl sat on the bed. She pushed off her shoes and lay back. She thought she could see the evening star.

"Come here, Jack. Try this bed. Bring one of those pillows," she said.

"How is it?" he said.

"Try it," she said.

He looked around. The house was dark.

"I feel funny," he said. "Better see if anybody's home."

She bounced on the bed.

"Try it first," she said.

He lay down on the bed and put the pillow under his head.

"How does it feel?" the girl said.

"Feels firm," he said.

She turned on her side and put her hand to his face.

"Kiss me," she said.

"Let's get up," he said.

"Kiss me," she said.

She closed her eyes. She held him.

He said, "I'll see if anybody's home."

But he just sat up and stayed where he was, making believe he was watching the television.

Lights came on in houses up and down the street.

"Wouldn't it be funny if," the girl said and grinned and didn't finish.

The boy laughed, but for no good reason. For no good reason, he switched on the reading lamp.

The girl brushed away a mosquito, whereupon the boy stood up and tucked in his shirt.

"I'll see if anybody's home," he said. "I don't think anybody's home. But if anybody is, I'll see what things are going for."

"Whatever they ask, offer ten dollars less. It's always a good idea," she said. "And, besides, they must be desperate or something."

"It's a pretty good TV," the boy said.

"Ask them how much," the girl said.

The man came down the sidewalk with a sack from the market. He had sandwiches, beer, and whiskey. He saw the car in the driveway and the girl on the bed. He saw the television set going and the boy on the porch.

"Hello," the man said to the girl. "You found the bed. That's good."

"Hello," the girl said, and got up. "I was just trying it out." She patted the bed. "It's a pretty good bed."

"It's a good bed," the man said, and put down the sack and took out the beer and the whiskey.

"We thought nobody was here," the boy said. "We're interested in the bed and maybe the TV. Maybe the desk. How much do you want for the bed?"

"I was thinking fifty dollars for the bed," the man said.

"Would you take forty?" the girl asked.

"Okay, I'll take forty," the man said.

He took a glass out of the carton. He took the newspaper off it. He broke the seal on the whiskey.

"How about the TV?" the boy said.

"Twenty-five."

"Would you take fifteen?" the girl said.

"Fifteen's okay. I could take fifteen," the man said.

The girl looked at the boy.

"You kids, you'll want a drink," the man said. "Glasses in the box. I'm going to sit down. I'm going to sit down on the sofa."

The man sat on the sofa, leaned back, and stared at the boy and the girl.

The boy found two glasses and poured whiskey.

"That's enough," the girl said. "I think I want water in mine."

She pulled out a chair and sat at the kitchen table.

"There's water in the spigot over there," the man said. "Turn on that spigot."

The boy came back with the watered whiskey. He cleared his throat and sat down at the kitchen table. He grinned. But he didn't drink anything.

Birds darted overhead for insects, small birds that moved very fast.

The man gazed at the television. He finished his drink and started another, and when he reached to turn on the floor lamp, his cigarette dropped from his fingers and fell between the cushions.

The girl got up to help him find it.

"So what do you want?" the boy said to the girl.

The boy took out the checkbook and held it to his lips as if thinking.

"I want the desk," the girl said. "How much money is the desk?"

The man waved his hand at this preposterous question.

"Name a figure," he said.

He looked at them as they sat at the table. In the lamplight, there was something about their faces. It was nice or it was nasty. There was no telling which.

"I'm going to turn off this TV and put on a record," the man said. "This record-player is going, too. Cheap. Make me an offer."

He poured more whiskey and opened a beer.

"Everything goes."

The girl held out her glass and the man poured.

"Thank you," she said. "You're very nice."

"It goes to your head," the boy said. "I'm getting it in the head." He held up his glass and jiggled it.

The man finished his drink and poured another, and then he found the box with the records.

"Pick something," the man said to the girl, and he held the records out to her.

The boy was writing the check.

"Here," the girl said, picking something, picking—anything—for she did not know the names on these records. She got up from the table and sat down again. She did not want to sit still.

"I'm making it out to cash," the boy said.

"Sure," the man said.

They drank. They listened to the record. And then the man put on another.

Why don't you kids dance? he decided to say, and then he said it. "Why don't you dance?"

"I don't think so," the boy said.

"Go ahead," the man said. "It's my yard. You can dance if you want to."

Arms about each other, their bodies pressed together, the boy and girl moved up and down the driveway. They were dancing. And when the record was over, they did it again, and when that one ended, the boy said, "I'm drunk."

The girl said, "You're not drunk."

"Well, I'm drunk," the boy said.

The man turned the record over and the boy said, "I am."

"Dance with me," the girl said to the boy and then to the man, and when the man stood up, she came to him with her arms open.

"Those people over there, they're watching," she said.

"It's okay," the man said. "It's my place," he said. "We can dance."

"Let them watch," the girl said.

"That's right," the man said. "They thought they'd seen everything over here. But they haven't see this, have they?" he said.

He felt her breath on his neck. "I hope you like your bed," he said.

The girl closed and then opened her eyes. She pushed her face into the man's shoulder. She pulled the man closer.

"You must be desperate or something," she said.

Weeks later she said: "The guy was about middle-aged. All his things right there in his yard. No lie. We got real pissed and danced. In the driveway. Oh, my God. Don't laugh. He played us these records. Look at this record-player. The old guy gave it to us. These crappy records, too. Will you look at this shit?"

She kept talking. She told everyone. There was more to it, but she couldn't get it all talked out. After a time, she quit trying.

JULIO CORTÁZAR

Feuilletons from *A Certain Lucas*

I. ORCHESTRE MACABRE

Kitten on the Keys

A cat had been taught to play the piano and this animal, sitting on a stool, played and played the whole existent piano repertory, and in addition five compositions of its own dedicated to several dogs.

Otherwise, the cat was possessed of a perfect stupidity, and during concert intermissions he would compose new pieces with a drive that left everyone flabbergasted. In that way he reached opus eighty-nine, during which he was the victim of a brick thrown by someone with a tenacious rage. He sleeps his final sleep in the lobby of the Great Rex Theater, 640 Corrientes.

Natural harmony
or
You Can't Keep on Violating It

A child had thirteen fingers on each hand and his aunts immediately put him to playing the harp, something that made good use of the extras and he completed the course in half the time needed by poor pentadigitates.

After that the child came to play in such a way that there was no score worthy of him. When he began to give concerts, the amount of music that he concentrated in that time and space with his twenty-six fingers was so extraordinary that the audience couldn't keep up and was always behind, so that when the young *artisto* was coming to the end of *The Fountain of Arethusa* (a transcription) the poor people were still in the *Tambourin Chinois* (an arrangement). This naturally created horrible confusions, but everyone recognized that the child played like an angel.

So it came to pass that the faithful listeners, the same as boxseat subscribers and newspaper critics, continued going to the child's concerts, earnestly trying not to be left behind as the program went on. They listened so hard that several of them began to grow ears on their faces, and with every new ear that grew on them they got a little closer to the music of the twenty-six fingers on the harp. The trouble came when the Wagnerian concert let out and people on the street fainted by the dozen as they saw listeners appear with their whole visages covered by ears, and then the Municipal Superintendent took drastic steps and put the child in the typing pool at Internal Revenue, where he worked so fast that it was pleasure for his bosses and death for his co-workers. As for music, in a dark corner of the parlor, forgotten by its owner perhaps, silent and covered with dust, the harp could be seen.

Customs of the Symphony Orchestra Called "Fly"

The musical director of the "Fly" Symphony, Maestro Tabaré Piscitelli, was the author of the orchestra's motto: "Creation within freedom." To that end he authorized the use of open collars, anarchism, Benzedrine, and personally set a high example of independence. Hadn't he been observed in the middle of a Mahler symphony to turn the baton over to one of the violinists (who got the fright of his life) and go off to read *La Razón* in an empty seat?

The cellists of the "Fly" Symphony loved the harpist, the widow Pérez Sangiácomo, en bloc. This love was translated into a noteworthy tendency to break the order of the orchestra and surround the bewildered performer with a sort of screen of cellists, as her hands stood out like signals for help throughout the whole program. Furthermore, not once did a subscriber to the concerts hear a single arpeggio from the harp because the steady buzz of the cellos covered up its delicate effusions.

Threatened by the Board of Directors, Mrs. Pérez Sangiácomo showed a preference in her heart for the cellist Remo Persutti, who was authorized to keep his instrument beside the harp, while the others returned, a sad procession of scarabs, to the place tradition assigns their pensive carapaces.

In this orchestra one of the bassoonists couldn't play his instrument without the strange phenomenon of his being sucked in and immediately expelled out the other end, with such rapidity that the stupefied musician found himself suddenly on the other end of the bassoon and had to turn around with great speed and go on playing, not without the conductor's castigating him with horrendous personal slurs.

One night, when they were playing the *Doll Symphony,* by Albert Williams, the bassoonist, in an attack of absorption, found himself suddenly at the other end of the instrument, with the serious inconvenience this time that said point in space was occupied by the clarinetist Perkins Virasoro, who, as a result of the collision, was flung on top of the double basses and arose, markedly furious and pronouncing words that no one has ever heard from the mouth of a doll; such at least was the opinion of the lady subscribers and of the fireman on duty in the hall, the father of several little ones.

The cellist Remo Persutti having been absent, the personnel of those strings moved as a group over beside the harpist, the widow Pérez Sangiácomo, from where they didn't move for the whole evening. The theater staff laid down a rug and put potted ferns on it to fill the obvious gap that this produced.

The kettledrummer, Alcides Radaelli, took advantage of the tone poems of Richard Strauss to send messages in Morse code to his sweetheart seated in the loges, left eight.

An army telegrapher present at the concert because of the cancellation of the boxing matches in Luna Park due to a death in the family of one of the fighters, deciphered with great wonderment the following phrase that poured forth halfway through *Also Sprach Zarathustra:* "Are your hives better, Cuca?"

Quintessences

The tenor Américo Scravellini, of the cast at the Marconi Theater, sang so sweetly that his fans called him "the angel."

So no one was too startled when in the middle of a concert they saw four handsome seraphim descend through the air and with an ineffable whisper of gold and scarlet accompany the voice of the great singer. If one part of the audience showed understandable signs of surprise, the rest, enthralled by the vocal perfection of tenor Scravellini, accepted the presence of the angels as an almost necessary miracle, or rather, as if it weren't a miracle at all. The singer himself, given over to his effusion, limited himself to lifting his eyes toward the angels and he kept on singing with that indefinable half tone that had made him famous in the whole chain of theaters.

Softly, the angels surrounded him, and holding him with infinite tenderness and ever so gently, they rose up above the stage while the audience trembled with emotion and wonder, and the singer continued on with his melody that became all the more ethereal in the air.

In that way the angels took him away from his public, who finally understood that the tenor Scravellini was not of this world. The celestial group reached the highest point of the theater; the singer's voice was becoming more and more otherworldly. When the final and absolutely perfect note of the aria came out of his throat, the angels dropped him.

II. SUNSET HUNTER

If I were a moviemaker I'd set about hunting sunsets. I've got it all figured out except for the capital needed for the safari, because a sunset doesn't let itself be caught just like that, I mean that sometimes it starts out as a silly little thing and just when you abandon it, all of its feathers come out, or, just the opposite, it's a chromatic extravaganza and suddenly you're left with a kind of soaped-up parrot, and in both cases you have to count on a camera with good color film, travel expenses and an itinerary of overnight stops, keeping watch on the sky, and the choice of the most propitious horizon, none of it cheap. In any case, I think that if I were a moviemaker I would set things up to hunt sunsets, just one sunset actually, but in order to arrive at the definitive sunset I'd have to film forty or fifty, because if I were a moviemaker I'd be just as demanding as with words, women, and geopoliticians.

That's not how it is and I console myself by imagining that the sunset has been caught already, sleeping in its long canned spiral. My plan: not just the hunting but the restitution of the sunset to my fellows who don't know much about them, I mean city people who watch the sun go down, if they happen to see it, behind the post office, the apartment buildings across the way, or on a sub-horizon of television antennas and lampposts. The movie would be silent, or with a soundtrack that would only record the sounds contemporary to the filmed sunset, probably some barking dog or the buzzing of horseflies, with luck the little bell of a sheep or the breaking of a wave if it's a maritime sunset.

Through experience and a wristwatch I know that a good sunset doesn't last more than twenty minutes between climax and anticlimax, two things I would eliminate in order to leave only its slow internal play, its kaleidoscope of imperceptible mutations; it would be one of those films they call documentaries, shown before Brigitte Bardot while people are settling down and looking at the screen as if they were on a bus or a subway. My film would have a printed explanation (maybe a voice off screen) along these lines: "What you are about to see is the sunset of June 7, 1976, filmed in X with M film and fixed camera, without interruption for Z minutes." The audience will be informed that outside of the sunset absolutely nothing happens, for which reason they are advised to go about as if they were at home and to do whatever they feel like doing, looking at the sunset, for example, turning their backs on it, talking to others, strolling about, etc. We're terribly sorry that we can't suggest that they smoke, something that's always so beautiful at sunset, but the medieval conditions of movie theaters require that they be aware of the prohibition of that excellent habit. On the other hand, it's not forbidden to take a good swig from the pocket flask that the distributor of the film sells in the lobby.

It's impossible to predict the fate of my film; people go to the movies to forget about themselves, and a sunset leans exactly in the opposite direction, it's the moment when, perhaps, we see ourselves a little more naked, that happens to me, in any case, and it's painful and useful; maybe others can make use of it too, you never know.

III. LUCAS × 7

Lucas, His Battles With The Hydra

Now that he's growing old he realizes that it's not easy to kill it.

It's easy being a hydra but killing it isn't, because if it's really necessary to kill the hydra by cutting off its several heads (between seven and nine according to authors or bestiaries worthy of consultation), at least one has to be left, because the hydra is Lucas himself and what he'd like to do is get out of the hydra but stay in Lucas, to pass from the poly- to the mono-cephalic. I'd like to see you do it, says Lucas, envying Heracles, who never had such problems with the hydra and who after giving it one clean swipe left it looking like a gaudy fountain with seven or nine jets of blood spouting out of it. It's one thing to kill the hydra and something else again to be that hydra who at one time had been only Lucas and who would like to go back to being him. For example, you take a cut on the head that collects records, and you take another on the one that invariably lays his pipe down on the left-hand side of the desk and the glass with the felt markers on the right and a little to the rear. Now it's time to consider the results.

Hmm, something's been gained, two heads less but the remaining ones in a bit of a crisis as they agitatedly think and think as they face the mournful fact. Or: for a while at least there is a halt in the obsessiveness of that urgent need to complete the series of madrigals by Gesualdo, Prince of Venosa (Lucas is missing two records in the series, it seems that they're out of print and won't be re-pressed, and that damages the presence of the other records. Let the head that thinks and wants and gnaws like that die from a clean cut). Furthermore, it's distressingly novel to reach for the pipe and find that it's not in its place. Let's take advantage of this will for disorder and right here slice off the head that likes being closed in, the easy chair for reading beside the lamp, the Scotch at six-thirty with two cubes and not much soda, the books and magazines piled up in order of priority.

But it's quite difficult to kill the hydra and get back to Lucas, he can feel it already in the midst of the bloody battle. To begin with, he's describing it on a sheet of paper that he took out of the second drawer on the right-hand side of the desk, when actually there's paper in sight all over the place, but no sir, that's the ritual and let's not mention the Italian extension lamp four positions a hundred watts placed like a crane over a construction site and most delicately balanced so that the beam of light etc. A flashing slice at that seated Egyptian scribe head. One less, off, Lucas is getting closer to himself, it's starting to look good.

He'll never get to know how many heads he has left to cut off because the phone rings and it's Claudine, who talks about ruuuuunning to the movie theater where they're showing a Woody Allen picture. Evidently Lucas hasn't cut the heads off in the proper ontological order, because his first reaction is no, no way, Claudine is boiling like a crab on the other end, Woody Allen Woody Allen, and Lucas baby, don't push me if you want to win me over, you think I can come down out of this fight that's gushing plasma and Rh factor just because you feel Woody Woody, you've got to understand that there are values and there are values. When from the other end Annapurna is dropped in the form of a receiver onto the cradle, Lucas understands that it would have been better if first he'd killed the head that orders, respects, and hierarchizes time, maybe in that way everything would have softened suddenly and then pipe Claudine markers Gesualdo in different sequences, and Woody Allen, of course. Now it's too late, no Claudine now, not even any words now to go on telling about the battle since there isn't any battle, what head should he cut off since there'll always be another more authoritarian one left, it's time to answer the correspondence that's piling up, in ten minutes the Scotch with its ice and a touch of soda, it's so clear that they've started to grow on him again, that cutting them off was of no use. In the bathroom mirror Lucas can see the complete hydra and its faces with bright smiles, all the teeth showing. Seven heads, one for each decade; worse yet, the suspicion that two more may grow on him in conformity with what certain authorities in hydric matters say, as long as he keeps his health, of course.

Lucas, His Patriotism
i

In my passport I like the pages with renewals and visa stamps round/ triangular/green/square/black/oval/red; in my image of Buenos Aires the ferry across the Riachuelo, the Plaza Irlanda, the Agronomy Gardens, a few cafés that might not be there anymore, a bed in an apartment on Maipú just off the corner of Córdoba, the smell and silence of the docks at midnight in summer, the trees on the Plaza Lavalle.

Of my country what I have left is a smell of Mendoza irrigation ditches, the poplars in Uspallata, the deep purple of Velasco Hill in La Rioja, the Chaco stars in Pampa de Guanacos going from Salta to Misiones on a train in the year forty-two, a horse I rode in Saladillo, the taste of Cinzano and Gordon's gin in the Boston on Florida, the slightly allergic smell of the orchestra seats in the Colón, the deluxe bus from Luna Park with Carlos Beulchi and Mario Díaz, some dairy stores at dawn, the ugliness of the Plaza Once, reading *Sur* in my sweetly ingenuous years, the fifty cent editions of *Claridad* with Roberto Arlt and Castelnuovo, and also a few courtyards, of course, and shadows that I keep quiet, and dead people.

Lucas, His Patriotism
ii

In the center of the image are probably the geraniums, but there are also wisteria, summer, *mate* at five-thirty, the sewing machine, slippers, and slow conversations about illnesses and family annoyances, a chicken suddenly leaving its calling card between two chairs or the cat after a dove that's way ahead of him. Everything that smells of clothes drying on the line, starch, bluing, and bleach, smells of jubilation, of biscuits or fritters, almost always the radio next door with tangos and ads for Geniol, for Cocinero cooking fat the one you should be looking at, and kids kicking a rag ball around the vacant lot out back, Beto made the aerial goal.

Everything so conventional, so pleasant that Lucas out of pure shame looks for other ways out, halfway through the memory he decides to remember how at that hour he would shut himself up to read Homer and Dickson Carr, loafing in his little room so as not to hear about Aunt Papa's appendicitis operation again with all the mournful details and the living representation of the horrible nausea brought on by the anesthesia, or the story of the mortgage of the house on the Calle Bulnes where Uncle Alejandro was sinking from *mate* to *mate* until the apotheosis of collective sighs and everything is going from bad to worse. Josefina, what we need here is a strong government, goddamn it. Flora luckily there to show the photo of Clark Gable in the rotogravure of *La Prensa* and remurmur the starring moments of *Gone With the Wind*. Sometimes Grandmother would remember Francesca Bertini and Uncle Alejandro could see Barbara La Marr, barbarity unmarred, you and your vamps, you men are all alike. Lucas understands that there's nothing he can do, that he's in the patio again, that the postcard is still stuck forever in the frame of the mirror of time, hand painted, with its fringe of doves, with its thin black border.

Lucas, His Modesty

In today's apartments, as is well known, the guest goes to the bathroom and the others keep on talking about Biafra and Michel Foucault, but there is something in the air as if everybody wanted to forget that he has hearing and at the same time ears are attuned toward the sacred place that in our huddled society is, naturally, scarcely ten feet away from the place where those high-level conversations are taking place, and it is certain that in spite of all efforts the absent guest will make not to reveal his activities and those of his fellows to raise the volume of the dialogue, at some moment there will reverberate one of those dull sounds that let themselves be heard under the least indicated circumstances, or, in the best of cases, the pathetic tearing of cheap toilet paper as a piece is ripped off the pink or green roll.

If the guest who has gone to the bathroom is Lucas, his horror can only be compared to the intensity of the colic that has obliged him to shut himself up in the ominous redoubt. In that horror there is neither neurosis nor any complex, but the certainty of a recurrent intestinal behavior, that is to say, everything will start off fine, softly and silently, but then toward the end, keeping the same relationship between powder and partridge in a hunting cartridge, a rather horrendous detonation will shake the toothbrushes in their racks and agitate the plastic shower curtain.

Lucas can do nothing to avoid it; he had tried all methods, such as leaning over to touch the floor with his head, leaning backwards to the point where his feet brush against the wall opposite, turning sidewise and, as an extreme measure, grasping his buttocks and separating them as much as possible so as to increase the diameter of the tempestuous conduit. Vain is the addition of such silencing devices as placing about his thighs all the towels within reach and even his hosts' bathrobes; practically always, at the end of what could have been an agreeable transfer, the final fart bursts forth tumultuously.

When it is someone else's turn to go to the bathroom, Lucas trembles for him, for he is certain that at any second the first yoicks of ignominy will resound; it surprises him a little that people don't seem to worry too much about things like that, although it's obvious that they're not unaware of what's going on and even cover it up with the noise of spoons in cups and the totally unnecessary movement of armchairs. When nothing happens, Lucas is happy and immediately asks for another cognac, by which he gives himself away so that everybody realizes he had been tense and anxious while Mrs. Broggi took care of her necessities. How different, Lucas thinks, from the simplicity of children who come into the most elegant of gatherings and announce: Mama, I have to make poochy. How happy, Lucas continues thinking, is that anonymous poet who composed the quatrain that proclaims that there is no pleasure so exquisite/as that derived from a good, slow shit,/nor pleasure as delicate as that/which comes on after one has shat. In order to rise to that gentleman's heights, one would have to be exempt from all danger of intemperate or tempestuous windiness, unless the bathroom in the house were upstairs or was one of those little tin-roofed privies separated from the ranch house by a goodly distance.

Having entered poetic territory now, Lucas remembers the line from Dante where each devil *avea del cul fatto trombetta*, and with that mental reference to highest culture he considers himself somewhat blameless for meditations that have little to do with what Dr. Berenstein is saying with regard to housing laws.

Lucas, His Ecological Meditations

In these times of a disheveled and touristy return to Nature, in which city people view country life the way Rousseau viewed the noble savage, I join ranks more than ever with: a) Max Jacob, who in reply to an invitation to spend a weekend in the country, said, somewhere between stupefaction and terror: "The country? That place where chickens run around raw?"; b) Dr. Johnson, who halfway through an outing in Greenwich Park energetically expressed his preference for Fleet Street; c) Baudelaire, who elevated love for the artificial to the notion of paradise itself.

A landscape, a stroll through the woods, a dousing in a waterfall, a road between two cliffs can only raise us up to aesthetic heights if we have the assurance of a return home or to the hotel, the lustral shower, dinner and wine, the talk over coffee and dessert, a book or some papers, the eroticism that sums everything up and starts it up again. I don't trust admirers of nature who every so often get out of the car to look at the view and take five or six leaps up onto the rocks; as for the others, those lifetime Boy Scouts who are accustomed to wandering about covered by enormous knapsacks and wild beards, their reactions are mostly monosyl-

labic or exclamatory; everything seems to consist of standing time and
time again looking at a hill or a sunset, which are the most repeated
things imaginable.

Civilized people are lying when they fall into bucolic rapture; if they
miss their Scotch on the rocks at seven-thirty in the evening, they'll
curse the minute they left home to come and endure gadflies, sunburn,
and thorns; as for those closest to nature, they're as stupid as she is; a
book, a play, a sonata don't need any return or shower; that's where we
reach the greatest heights, where we are the most we can be. What the
intellectual or the artist who takes refuge in the countryside is looking for
is tranquility, fresh lettuce, and oxygenated air; with nature surrounding
him on all sides, he reads or paints in the perfect light of a well-oriented
room; if he goes out for a walk or goes to the window to look at the
animals or the clouds, it's because he's tired with his work or with his
ease. Don't trust, then, the absorbed contemplation of a tulip when the
contemplator is an intellectual. What's there is tulip + distraction, or
tulip + meditation (almost never about the tulip). He will never find a
natural scene that can take more than five minutes of determined contemplation, and, on the other hand, he will feel all time abolished in the
reading of Theocritus or Keats, especially in the passages where scenes of
nature appear. Yes, Max Jacob was right: chickens should be cooked.

Lucas, His Spanish Classes

At Berlitz, where they took him on half out of pity, the director, who is
from Astorga, warns him against any Argentinisms, not to mention Gal-
licisms, we teach it proper here, bloody proper, and the first *che* I catch
you with means you can hop it. What you will do is teach them to speak
in a normal way and none of your fancy frills, because what these
Frenchmen are coming here to learn is not to make asses out of themselves at the border or in restaurants. Proper and practical, get that into
what we might call your noggin.

Lucas, perplexed, immediately triest to find some texts that would
respond to such an illustrious criterion, and when he begins his class in
front of a dozen Parisians avid for an *olé* and an I should like an omelet
with six eggs, he passes out some photocopies he has made of a passage
from an article in *El País*, September 17, 1978, note how modern and
how, by his lights, it should be the quintessence of the proper and the
practical since it deals with bullfighting and all the Frenchmen are
thinking about is rushing off to a bullring as soon as they have their
diplomas in their pockets, one reason why this vocabulary will be exceed-

ingly useful at the moment of the first of the three stages, the banderillas, and all the rest. The text reads as follows, to wit:

The galache, magnificent, medium-sized, but with spirit, quite well-armed with tapering horns, improved by breeding, for he was noble, was following the flight of the muleta that the master from Salamanca manipulated with ease and control. Relaxed in his posture, he strung together his passes with the muleta, and each one was a piece of absolute mastery, making the bull follow a semicircle about him to the right, and the conclusion, clean and precise, leaving the beast at just the right distance. There were incomparable naturals and tremendous chest passes, and the help of two-handed ups and downs, and sign-off passes, but engraved in our eyes is a natural coupled to a chest pass and the pattern of the last, ending up at the opposite shoulder, must figure among the best muleta work ever done by El Viti.

As is natural, the students immediately fall upon their dictionaries to translate the passage, a task that after three minutes is followed by a growing distress, an exchange of dictionaries, a rubbing of eyes, and questions for Lucas, which he won't answer at all because he has decided to apply the self-teaching method and in those cases the teacher should gaze out the window while the exercises are being done. When the director appears to inspect Lucas's performance, everyone has left after letting it be known in French what they think of Spanish and especially of dictionaries that have cost them their good francs. The only one remaining is an erudite-looking young man who is asking Lucas if the reference to the "master from Salamanca" could be an allusion to Fray Luis de León, to which Lucas replies that it might well be, although the surest answer is, who knows. The director waits for the student to leave and tells Lucas that there's no need to start with classical poetry, of course Fray Luis and all that, but try to find something simpler, let's say something bloody typical like a visit by tourists to a restaurant or a bullring, you'll soon see how they'll get interested and learn overnight.

Everybody knows that the Earth is separated from other heavenly bodies by a variable number of light-years. What few know (in reality, only I) is that Margarita is separated from me by a considerable number of snail-years.

At first I thought it was a matter of tortoise-years, but I've had to abandon that unit of measurement as too flattering. Little as a tortoise may travel, I would have ended up reaching Margarita, but, on the other hand, Osvaldo, my favorite snail, doesn't leave me the slightest hope. Who knows when he started the march that was imperceptibly taking him farther away from my left shoe, even though I had oriented him with extreme precision in the direction that would lead him to Margarita. Full of fresh lettuce, care, and lovingly attended, his first advance was promising, and I said to myself hopefully that before the patio pine passed beyond the height of the roof, Osvaldo's silver-plated horns would enter Margarita's field of vision to bring her my friendly message; in the meantime, from here I could be happy imagining her joy on seeing him arrive, the waving of her braids and arms.

All light-years may be equal, but not so snail-years, and Osvaldo has ceased to merit my trust. It isn't that he's stopped, since it's possible for me to verify by his silvery trail that he's continuing his march and that he's maintaining the right direction, although this presupposes his going up and down countless walls or passing completely through a noodle factory. But it's been more difficult for me to check that meritorious exactness, and twice I've been stopped by furious watchmen to whom I've had to tell the worst lies since the truth would have brought me a rain of whacks. The sad part is that Margarita, sitting in a pink velvet easy chair, is waiting for me on the other side of the city. If instead of Osvaldo I had made use of light-years, we probably would already have had grandchildren; but when one loves long and softly, when one wants to come to the end of a drawn-out wait, it's logical that snail-years should be chosen. It's so hard, after all, to decide on what the advantages and what the disadvantages of these options are.

—Translated by Gregory Rabassa

STEPHEN DIXON

Goodbye to Goodbye

"Goodbye," and she goes. I stay there, holding the gift I was about to give her. Had told her I was giving her. This afternoon, on the phone. I said "I'd like to come over with something for you." She said "How come?" I said "Your birthday." She said "You know I don't like to be reminded of those, but come ahead if you want, around seven, okay?" I came. She answered the door. From the door I could see a man sitting on a couch in the living room. She said "Come in." I came in, gave her my coat, had the gift in a shopping bag the woman's store had put it in. "I have a friend here, I hope you don't mind," she said. "Me? Mind? Don't be silly—but how good a friend?" "My business," she said, "do you mind?" "No, of course not, why should I? Because you're right, it is your business." We went into the living room. The man got up. "Don't get up," I said. "It's no bother," he said. "How do you do? Mike Sliven," and he stuck out his hand. "Jules Dorsey," and I stuck out mine. "Like a drink, Jules?" she said, as we shook hands, and I said "Yes, what do you have?" "Beer, wine, a little brandy, but I'd like to save that if you don't mind." "Why should I mind? Though something hard is what I think I'd like. Beer." "Light or dark?" she said. "Whatever you have most of," I said. "I have six-packs of both." "Then . . . dark," I said. "I feel like a dark. Suddenly I feel very dark. Only kidding, of course," I said to Mike and then turned to her so she'd also see I was only kidding. She went to the kitchen. Mike said "Now I remember your name. Arlene's spoken of you." "I'm sure she had only the very best things to say of me too." "She did and she didn't," he said, "but you're kidding again, no doubt." "Oh, I'm kidding, all right, or maybe I'm not. Say, who the hell are you anyway and what the hell are you doing here? I thought Arlene was still only seeing me," and I grabbed him off the couch. He was much bigger than I, but didn't protest. "Where's your coat and hat?" I said and he said "I didn't come with a hat and my coat's over there, in the closet." "Then we're going to get it and you're going to leave with it." I clutched his elbow and started walking him to the closet. Arlene came into the living room and said "Jules, what are you doing?—and where are you going, Mike?" "I think out," he said. "Out," I said. "I came over to give you a gift and take you to dinner for your birthday and later to spend the night with you here or at my place or even at a great hotel if you wish, and goddamnit that's what I'm going to do." "What is it with you, Jules?—I've never heard you talk like that before." "Do you mind?" I said. "No, I kind of like it. And Mike. Are you going to leave when someone tells you to, just like that?" "I think I have to," he said, "since if there's one thing I don't like to do in life it's to get into or even put up a fight, especially when I see there's no chance of winning it." I opened the closet. He got his coat. I opened the front door and he left. I locked the door. Bolted it, just in case he already had the keys. Then I turned around. Arlene was standing in the living room holding my glass of beer. She came into the foyer with it. I didn't move, just let her come. "You still want this?" she said. "No, the cognac," I said. "It's brandy but good imported brandy." "Then the brandy," I said. "How do you want it?" "With ice." "Coming right up," and she went back into the kitchen. I followed her. She was reaching for the brandy on a cupboard shelf above her, had her back to me. I got up behind her—she didn't seem to know I was there—put my arms around her, pressed into her. She turned her head around, kissed me. We kissed. I started to undress her right there.

That's not the way it happened, of course. The way it happened was like this. I did come over with a gift, it wasn't her birthday, a man named Mike was there when I thought she'd be alone, she said he was a good friend, "In fact, the man I'm sleeping with now." "Oh," I said. "Well, I still have this gift for you so you might as well take it." She said "Really, it wouldn't be fair." Mike came into the foyer, introduced himself. "Mike Ivory," he said. "Jules Dorsey," I said. "Maybe I shouldn't stay." "No, Jules, come in and have a drink. What'll you have?" "What do you got?" I said. "I don't know. What do we have?" he said to Arlene. She said "Beer—light and dark—wine—red and white—scotch, vodka, rye, bourbon, gin, brandy and I think there's a little of that cognac left, and all the mixers to go with them, besides other nonalcoholic stuff if you're suddenly into that." "Come on, Jules drinks his share," Mike said, "or at least will with us here." "I drink, all right," I said, "though not that much. But tonight I'd like a double of that cognac you said you have, if you've enough for a double." "Why not—right, Arlene? Want me to get it?" "It's okay, I'll get it," she said, "but what's a double?" "Just double whatever you normally pour," he said. "If there's so little in the bottle that you don't have enough to double what you normally pour, empty the whole thing in his glass." "I just usually pour, I don't know how much," she said. "So do it that way," he said, "but double it." "Fill half a regular juice glass," I said, "and then put some ice in it, if you don't mind?" "Ice in one of the best cognacs there is?" he said. "No way, sir. Sorry." "Then make it your worst cognac," I said, "but ice in it, please? I feel like a cognac and I feel like a double and I feel like I want that double cognac ice-cold." "Sorry—really," he said. "We only have one cognac and it's one of the rarest there is. Gin, vodka, bourbon, scotch, even the beer, light or dark, I'll put ice in for you, and the wine, either one, too. But not that cognac or even the brandy. They're both too good. I'm telling you the truth when I say I couldn't sleep right tonight if I knew I was instrumental or helpful in any way or even allowed it, just stood by and allowed ice in cognac or brandy when I knew that just by saying something I might be able to stop it." "Listen, you," I said and grabbed his neck with one hand. He swung at me. I ducked and hit him in the stomach, he fell forward and I clipped him on the back. He went down. I put my foot under his chest and nudged him with it and he turned himself over on his back. I looked at Arlene. Her hands covered her eyes but she seemed to be peeking through the finger cracks. I said to Mike "Probably Arlene won't like this but Im going to give you to ten to get your coat and hat and—" "I didn't come with a coat and hat," he said. "Then ten just to get the hell out of here." "Jules, this is awful," Arlene said, not looking alarmed or frightened or really upset or anything like that. "I don't care. It's what I suddenly felt like doing even if I didn't feel that right about doing it so that's what I did. Now get, buddy," I said to Mike. "One, two, three . . ." He got up, held his stomach as he went to the front door. By the count of eight he was out of the apartment. She said "I hate it when anyone does that to people, but I think deep inside I loved it when you did it to him. Not because it was Mike. He's very nice. It's just that you were, well—I've never seen you like that before. I don't know what that makes me, but come here, you rat." I came to her. She mussed my hair, with her other hand slipped off one and then the other of her shoes. "Shall we do it here or in the bedroom?" "Here," I said, "or the opening part of it, but first let me lock the front door."

That's not the way it happened either. It happened like this. Arlene's my wife. We've been married for three years. We lived together for two years before that. We have a nine-month-old son. During dinner Arlene said she wanted a divorce. Our son was asleep in his room. I'd just put the main dish and side courses on the table. I dropped my fork. I was in what could be called a state of shock. I don't like that term but for now it'll have to do. Figuratively and maybe in some way literally—technically, scientifically—I was in a state of shock. I didn't move for I don't know how long. A minute, two, three. Just stared at my fork on my plate. Till the moment she told me this I thought that though we had some problems in our marriage, they were manageable and correctable and not untypical and that we were serious at working them out. All in all I felt we were very compatible in most ways and that the marriage was a successful one and getting better all the time. Arlene had said it several times—many times—too. About once a month she used to tell me that she loved me and loved being married to me, and about once a month, and not just after she told me this, I'd tell her the same thing. I meant it and felt she meant it. I had no reason to believe she didn't mean it. This is the truth. Sometimes out of the blue she'd say "I love you, Jules." Sometimes I'd answer "You do?" and she'd say "Truly love you." We could be in a taxi and she'd turn to me and say it. Or walking to a movie theater or in front of a theater during the intermission of a play and she'd break off whatever either of us was saying to say it. At that dinner, which I cooked—it was a good dinner, a chicken dish, rice cooked to perfection—something she taught me how to do—a baked zucchini dish, a great salad, a good bottle of wine, crabmeat cocktail to begin with, two drinks with cheese on crackers before we sat down, we had made love the previous night and we both said later on that it was one of the best acts of lovemaking we'd ever had, our son was wonderful and we loved being parents though admitted it was tough and tiring at times, both of us were making a pretty good income for the first time in our relationship so as a family we were financially sound, nothing was wrong or just about nothing, everything or just about everything was right, so that's why I say I was suddenly in a state of shock. "You want a divorce?" I finally said after she said "So what do you have to say about what I said before?" "Yes," she said, "a divorce." "Whatever for?" "Because I don't love you anymore," she said. "But just last week or the week before that you said you loved me more than you ever have, or as much as you ever have, you said." "I was lying," she said. "You wouldn't lie about something like that." "I'm telling you, I was lying," she said. "Why don't you love me anymore?" "Because I love someone else." "You love someone else?" "That's what I just said, I love someone else." "Since when?" I said. "Since months." "And you stopped loving me the minute you started loving him?" "No, a couple of months earlier." "Why?" "I don't know. I asked myself the same thing lots of times and all I could come up with was that I felt rather than knew why. You fall in, you fall out. You fall out, you fall in. Though this time I'm sure I've fallen in forever, since the feeling has never been stronger." "I can't believe it," I said. "Believe it. I've been having the most intense affair possible with a man I met at work—someone you don't know—and he's married but will get a divorce to be with me, just as I'm going to get a divorce to be with him." "But the children, I mean, the child," I said. "We'll work it out. We were always good at working things out in the past that most other couples never could, and we'll work this out too. I'll take Kenneth for the time being and when he's completely weaned you can have him whenever you like for as long as you like so long as it doesn't disrupt his life too much." "But just leaving me, divorcing me, breaking up this family, will disrupt his life," I said. "I'm sorry, I didn't want to, I in fact tried not to, but the force of the feeling I have for this man and he for me—" "What's his name?" "What's the difference?" "Just tell me his name? Maybe I do know him." "Even if you did, which you don't, nothing you could do or say—" "His name, please, his name? I just want to know what and whom I'm up against." "What could you know by just his name? If it was Butch or Spike or Mike, would it make you feel more or less confident that I'm not very much in love with him and that I'm not going to divorce you to marry him?" "Is it Mike?" "It isn't but you know that wasn't my point. All right, it is Mike," when I continued to stare at her as if I'd caught her fibbing, "but so what? Mickey, Michael or Mike, it's just a given name." "Mike what?" I said. "Now that's enough, Jules.

I don't want you starting trouble." "I won't start anything. I just want to know the man's full name. That way I can begin saying to myself you're leaving and divorcing me and breaking up our family for Mike So-and-So and not just a shadow. I'm not sure why, but it'll make it seem realer to me and so will be much easier to work out in my head." "Spiniker," she said. "Mike Spiniker." "With an *i*, *a* or *e* or even a *u* on the second half of his last name?" "Now you're going too far," she said. "Anyway, good—I have enough." I got up, got the phone book off the phone stand in the living room. "What are you doing?" she said. "Can't be too many Mike Spinikers in the book, with an *a*, *e*, *u* or second *i*." I looked up his name. "One, a Michael, with two *i*'s, on Third Avenue." I dialed him. "Stop that" she said. "He lives in another city, commutes here." A woman answered. "Is Michael Spiniker in?" I said. "Who's speaking?" the woman said. "Lionel Messer. I'm his stocks and bonds man." "Mike has stocks and bonds? That's news to me." "He has a huge portfolio of them and I've something very urgent to tell him about them if he doesn't want to go broke by midnight tonight." "I'll get him, hold on." She put down the phone. "Stop wasting your time," Arlene said on the bedroom extension. "Hang up. It can't be Mike. I'm telling you, he lives fifty miles from here." "Hey, what's this about stocks and bonds?" Mike said. "Hello, Mr. Spiniker. Do you know Arlene Dorsey? Arlene Chernoff Dorsey—she goes professionally by Chernoff." "Sure I do. We work in the same office building. But anything wrong? Because I thought this was about some stocks and bonds I don't have." "You seem very concerned about Ms. Chernoff. Are you?" "Sure I'm concerned. By your tone, who wouldn't be? What's happened?" "You sound as if you're in love with Ms. Chernoff, Mr. Spiniker. Are you?" "Listen, who is this? And what kind of jerky call is this? You either dialed the wrong Spiniker or you're crazy and not making any sense, but I'll have to hang up." "This is her husband, wise guy, and you better stop seeing her or I'm going to break your neck with my bare hands. If that doesn't work, I'll put a bullet through your broken neck. I have the means. And I don't just mean a weapon or two or people to do it for me—I'll do it myself gladly. I can. I have. Now do you read me?" "I read you, brother. Okay, fine. You have the right number and you're not crazy and you're probably right on target in everything you said, so my deepest apologies for getting excited at you. But let's say there must be two Michael Spinikers in this city, because I have no stocks and bonds broker and after what you just told me, I don't ever plan to do anything with my money but keep it in the bank, okay?" "Got you," I said and hung up. Arlene came running back to the living room. "You'd do that for me? You'd really go that far?" "I wasn't just threatening for effect or because I knew you were on the line. The way I see our marriage is that until it's clearly impossible to stay together, we're stuck together for life. Of course I only feel this way because of the kid." "I bet. You know, awful as this must seem about me, I think my feelings have come around another hundred and eighty degrees. What a husband I now realize I have. And what a weakling and pig that guy was for taking it the way he did, even if you weren't all bluff, after all he swore just the other day about how he'd stand with me against you and his wife when it finally came down to this. I'm sorry, Jules. So sorry, I want to beat my brains in against this chair. If my saying I love you very much isn't enough, what else can I say or do to prove what I just said is true and that I never want to stop being married to you?" "You can take my clothes off and carry me to bed." "Will do if I can." She put her arms around my waist and tried to lift me. "Oof, what a load. Instead of carrying you, which I no can do, what would you say to my just taking your clothes off and we do whatever you want us to right here on the floor or couch?" "Fine by me," I said and she grabbed my shirt by the two collar ends and tore it off me.

   That's ridiculous also and never happened. Why not say what really did happen and be done with it? It was all very simple and fast. We were eating dinner when she said she was leaving me for a man named Mike. We had no child, we'd been married for eight years. I said I wouldn't try to stop her. I could see it'd be useless and I did only want her to be happy. If she couldn't be happy with me, I was glad she was with someone she could be happy with. She said she was thankful I was taking it so well and in such a decent, civilized way. I asked about him. She said he worked in a law office on the same floor as hers. They'd been carrying on for six months. He was divorced, had two children. That night Arlene and I slept in separate rooms for the first time in our marriage, or for the first time when one of us wasn't very angry at the other or wasn't so ill that he or she needed to sleep alone. We just thought it best to sleep separately till she moved out. They rented a new apartment together the following month. I helped her pack and bring her belongings to the van she rented and drove. I told her I wouldn't mind if Mike came and helped, since she had several vanfuls of stuff to move. She said she felt I shouldn't meet him till much later on; when they were married, perhaps; maybe a year into their marriage when I could come by with my new woman who she said she knew I'd have by then. "You'll be as much in love with someone else in a few months as I am now with Mike." I said "I hope you're right. It'll certainly be what I want." So she was gone. I thought I was taking it well but I wasn't. I couldn't take it, in fact. Every night I'd get drunk thinking about her. I read her old adoring notes and letters to me and looked at her photos and would slam the wall or table with my fists and shout and cry. I couldn't stand thinking of her being with another man, kissing him, whispering to him, making love with him, doing all those private things with him, confiding to him, telling him what happened to her at the store that day, asking him if he'd like to see such and such movie or play that week, meeting him for lunch, going away with him some weekend, visiting friends, et cetera, maybe even planning to have a child. It also distressed me that they were in the same profession. I knew that'd make them even closer, all those professional matters they could discuss and look up and share. A month after she left me I showed up in front of their office building at around the time I knew they'd be finished for the day. They walked out of the building fifteen minutes later, holding hands, chatting animatedly. I had a wrench with me. I pulled it out of my jacket, ran up to him and screamed "Meet Jules, her husband, you bastard" and hit him in the hand he threw up to protect his head from the wrench. He grabbed that hand, turned to run and I hit him in the back of the head with the wrench. He went down. I kept yelling "I'll never let her be with anyone else, you bastard, never. I love her too much. I'll love her forever," and swung the wrench over his face but didn't hit him again. The police came. I didn't try to get away. I don't know what Arlene was doing at the time. I was arrested. Mike was taken away in an ambulance. Later he pressed charges against me. I pleaded guilty and was sentenced to five years. That means I'll serve around three and a half years if I don't cause any trouble in prison. Arlene visits me every day she's allowed to and stays the maximum time. It's six hours by bus for her round trip but she says she doesn't mind. Twice in my first half year here we were allowed to walk around the prison garden for an hour. She broke off with Mike and he's already moved in with another woman. "So much for his professed eternal devotion," Arlene said, "not that I would want it now." She's said several times that she'll never again be with another man but me. She hated my hitting Mike with the wrench but sees now it was probably the only way I could ever get through to her how much I loved her and wanted to get her back. "In some oddball way," she said, "it made me fall for you all over again. Maybe also because what I did and the way I did it forced you to lose control and try to kill him and I'm trying to make up for that too. But it'll all be different from now on. I can't wait to be back home with you, my arms around you, in bed with you, I can't wait." At certain designated spots in the garden we're allowed to hug and kiss for a half-minute, which we always did past the time limit until one of the guards ordered us to stop.

That's not it. This is it. There wasn't a wrench. There is a Mike. My wife fell in love with him and told me this at breakfast, not dinner. She said she didn't want to tell me at night because she wanted to give me plenty of time to adjust to it before I went to bed and also time for her to get her things out of the apartment and move in with a friend. We have no child. We tried for a while but couldn't. Then I had a corrective operation and we could have a child, but she said the marriage wasn't as good as it used to be and she wanted to be sure it was a very good marriage before we had a child. That was three years ago. She's had several affairs since then. She told me about them while she was having them. I didn't like her having them but put up with it because I didn't want her to leave me. I don't know why I mentioned anything about a gift. Maybe because her birthday's in two weeks and I've been thinking recently about what to get her. A bracelet, I thought. Or earrings. But that's out. This morning she said she realizes this is the third or fourth serious affair she's had in three years. She's had one or two others but they were quick and not so serious. She doesn't want to continue having affairs while she's married or at least still living with me. It isn't fair to me, she said. She also said I shouldn't put up with it and shouldn't have in the past. Not that if I had told her to stop she would have, she said. But I should tell her to get the hell out of the house and should have two to three years ago. Since I won't, she'll have to leave me. That means divorce, she said. The marriage isn't working out. What's she talking about? she said. The marriage is so bad that she doesn't think it'll ever work out—it never will, that's all, never. And because she wants to have children, maybe two, maybe three, but with someone she's very much in love with, she'll have to end our marriage and eventually get married to someone else. Maybe it'll be with Mike but she doubts it. He's married, though about to separate from his wife, and has indicated he never wants to marry again. He also has two children from a previous marriage and has expressed no interest in having more. Anyway, she said, it's fairer if I stay here and she goes, since she's the one breaking up the marriage. Of course, if I want to leave, she said, then she'll be more than happy to stay, since it's a great apartment and one she can afford and she'll never be able to get anything like it at twice the rent. "If you don't mind," I said, "I think I'd like to keep the apartment. Losing you and also having to find a new place might be a little too much for me." "I don't mind," she said, "why should I mind? I already said the apartment's yours if you want. So, do you mind if I start to pack up now to go?" "No, go right ahead. I'd love for you to stay forever, naturally, but what could I do to stop you from going? Nothing, I guess, right?" "Right." She went to the bedroom. I brought the dishes into the kitchen, washed them, sat down at the small table there and looked at the river. She came into the living room an hour later with two suitcases and a duffel bag. "This ought to do it for now," she said. "If it's okay with you, I'll arrange with a friend to come by for the rest of my stuff some other time." "Sure," I said. "You moving in with this Mike?" "No, I told you, he's married, still living with his wife. I'll be staying with Elena for now. If you want to reach me for anything, you can get me there or at work. You have her number?" "I can look it up." "But you won't call me at either place for very personal reasons, will you? Such as saying how much you miss me or things like that and you want me back? Because I've definitely made up my mind, Jules. The marriage is finished." "I understand that. I mean, I don't understand why it's so definitely finished, but I do understand that you definitely feel it is. But I can't make just one more pitch? There's nothing I can do or say or promise to help you change your mind?" "Nothing." "Then goodbye," I said. "I'll miss you terribly. I love you tremendously. I'll be as sad as any man can be over a thing like this for I don't know how long. But that's my problem, not yours, I guess, and eventually I'll work it out." "I'm glad you're taking it like this. Not that you'll be sad—I don't want you to be like that—but at least that you see the situation for what it is and that in the long run you'll be able to handle it. Because it'll make it much easier—it already is—for both of us. You'll see. You'll get over me before you know it." "Not on your life," I said. "Yes you will." "I'm telling you. Never." "No, I know you will. Goodbye." She opened the door, put the suitcases right outside it, said "I'll be back for these in a minute," and carried the duffel bag downstairs. "I'll help you with the suitcases," I yelled down the stairs. "No need to," she said. "It'd actually be better if you closed the door so we won't have to say goodbye again." I shut the door.

WILLIAM FERGUSON

A Summer at Estabrook

I realize of course that I'm no longer worthy of the name musician, if I ever was, though officially I'm still registered as a specially-funded pianoforte soloist with Segismundo Alegría and the Vienna Philharmonic for the duration of the Estabrook Festival, Summer 1978. I know this is true, because one of my new Anarchist friends at the Black Orchid Bar actually called the Festival offices to check me out; the secretary told him she wasn't allowed to comment on my musical competence, "if any," but I was in fact on record with them in what she called a "semiactive file"; and then she made some fantastic allusion to suicidal tendencies I was supposed to have. I don't know what to make of this last charge except to deny it straight out; the other insults are harder to answer, because I really do feel semiactive these days and I'm not sure how I'd characterize my musical ability except to say that it's dubious and maybe even preterite; I suppose that's why I'm out here campaigning for the Anarchists right now instead of making music the way God meant me to.

I feel a little stupid trotting around Worcester this way for Zérault's mayoral campaign, but I have to do something; I can't practice very well in this state of mind, and spending my time in the dormitory is not exactly my idea of entertainment. I have a feeling I'm never going to get asked to play in concert, and that's idiotic, because on my dresser I have a personal letter from Alegría inviting me to come to Estabrook this summer to do Beethoven's Third Piano Concerto—with the great man himself conducting!—and any musician worth his salt knows what that means to a person's career. When the letter arrived I immediately packed up and came to Worcester on the bus, but ever since I got here it's been total confusion; I'm ashamed to say that in all these weeks in residence I haven't even been able to find the main concert hall, and if Alegría is here I'm certainly unaware of it. I haven't even heard a proper performance yet; all I do is go to an endless series of rehearsals, and every day it's a different piece, in a different hall, and always with people I have never seen before and who seem to have no particular interest in my skills or even my name, though I must say they are unfailingly polite. Some of the conductors are just awful, but the musicians seem to be able to ignore them with a fair degree of success; I've even seen one beating time all alone on the stage, swooping and grimacing as if the orchestra had not left hours ago to catch the movie in town, and only I was left, occasionally playing a note or two at random out of a sense of propriety, but giving up at last and going home, or rather back to the dormitory and the inevitable chess game with Myksis, the Deutsche Grammophon representative for the Quinsigamond area, an eerie little Lithuanian with whom I share my modest quarters and who, at the moment, seems to be my only friend.

Last week I had a very unsettling experience at the Festival offices. I was determined to find out whether Alegría was really here and if so whether I could see him and perhaps get my career back on the track, and so one rainy day I marched into the main building and talked to a secretary named Eve who told me what I had always been told on the phone, namely that Dr. Alegría was indeed in residence but his office hours varied and it was practically impossible to catch him. Could I make an appointment, I asked? No, appointments were not being made for this week. For next week then? No, I had to come back next week to make an appointment for next week. I looked at her in desperate silence; her perfume was intoxicating, like a mixture of dust and sea salt; I tried to look helpless and childlike to work on her sympathies, but she stood up abruptly and told me I might as well save myself the trouble, since as far as she was concerned I was a dead man. I felt a surge of desire; she must have felt it too, because now she came around the desk and held my burning face in her hands and kissed me full on the mouth; my armpits took on an unfamiliar smell, like rotten wheat; "follow me," she whispered, and disappeared through a small door with a purple knob; I followed immediately—I'm absolutely certain I went through the same door she did—but as it clicked shut behind me I found myself in the alley in the drizzling rain, with no sign of Eve and no way to get back in except to go to the main entrance again and start over, which in my state of mind seemed like one *da capo* too many; so I went home in tears. Next time—if I ever do go back—I plan to march straight to the piano in Dr. Alegría's office and start to play, just to assert myself and my rights, like Zeitblom in the brothel (or was it his friend?); it will be a ridiculous gesture, I suppose, but I have nothing else left to do.

So here I am playing ward-heeler, mostly out of boredom, canvassing the College Square area for the Anarchist ticket. We just might have a shot at the Mayor's office this year with Théophile ("Big Ted") Zérault, the straw boss down at Ashland Steel, even though his only real campaign issue is that he wants to dismantle the Holy Cross conservatory and replace it with a facility of some more practical benefit to the community. Why I'm working for him I'm not really sure; I suspect myself of feeling some resentment toward the Holy Cross musicians who have actually been able to perform at Estabrook while I sit on my hands. But there's more to it than that, of course. Anarchism has always seemed to be the only reasonable philosophy for a person like myself; as a musician, as a citizen, as a human being, I do not hesitate to admit that I am a political idiot, and my new friends at the Black Orchid—God knows— are quick to agree. At the same time I think I have a right to know where I stand; for example, it seems a little strange to me that I've never met the candidate in all these months, considering that the Orchid is supposed to be his headquarters. I've never even heard a convincing physical description; I imagine him to myself as a huge, ruddy-faced, good-natured barbarian, somewhat jowly, with tinted glasses and a bulge in his jacket suggesting the presence of a gun. This idea may be totally off the mark, but people have to make do with whatever images they can get when there's nothing else to go on—and as far as I can tell that's most of the time. I have to go through the most incredible mental gyrations just to make sense of my living arrangements, for instance, and that's one area of my life I would have expected to be able to understand.

I think I mentioned my roommate Myksis. We live in the suite that used to belong to old Professor Dervis, who died of chalk poisoning the month before we came and whose belongings were never properly cleaned out, so that certain articles of his—an ornamental bowl with painted pheasants inside, a dog-headed cane of ash and steel, a Douay Bible bound in purple calf—have by assimilation become part of our ménage. Myksis does all the cooking, since I have no talent in that area, and I suppose I should be grateful, but he always serves me breakfast in Dervis's old bowl, which I think may have something wrong with it because I've noticed a kind of purplish fluorescence in the oatmeal these past few mornings, and while I have no reason to associate it with any intentions Myksis might have against me I just thought I'd better mention it here in case anything happens to me and people wonder why. There's something peculiar about the man; to begin with I don't think his name is really Myksis at all, since he hardly ever looks up when I say it. His excuse is that he's a little deaf, which I'm afraid I don't believe, since one of his duties is supposed to be audio quality control in local recordings. Does that make sense if he's hard of hearing?—It does not. Learning about his supposed deafness for some reason has greatly increased my affection for him, and I'm terrified that my living situation, coupled with these irrational emotions, may be leading me to destruction, if not at breakfast then in some other way too horrible to imagine; and soon, perhaps, very soon indeed. But I'm sure I'm being unnecessarily hard on poor Myksis, who seems to be a good person underneath it all. I've begun oversleeping almost every morning—from an obscure desire to miss rehearsal, I suppose—and then I open half an eye to find myself in the same indecipherable situation as the night before, with the little fellow shaking my arm and urging me to wake up in spite of my drowsy assertions that there is no waking, only different kinds of sleep.

At any rate, Myksis is my friend . . . perhaps not the kind of friend I would have wished for myself, but a friend nevertheless, and a good listener, and someone with whom I can share the intoxicating experience of Estabrook at the height of the season. They do some very interesting things here from time to time; last summer for instance they staged what sounds like a really remarkable little piano piece of the experimental variety, and the Estabrook performance was the première, as I learned today from a scrapbook I found as I was going through some old papers of Dervis's. The piece was called *Fire with Fire!*, with no composer listed (though it seems the evening was made possible by a grant from the Worcester Anarchist Alliance), and from the description it must have been one of the most expensive solo pieces ever created; according to "Perdix," waxing purple for the *Worcester Telegram* Sunday music section, the piano had to be considered a total loss by the end of the concert. On a framework above the keyboard was suspended a large translucent container filled to the brim with superheated mercury, attached to a weighted steel rod and a central pivot, like a pendulum. The pianist's first duty, according to the score, was to break the membrane over a small hole at the bottom of the vessel and then to start it swinging, so that now and then a large drop of the heavy glowing liquid landed on a note; the weight of the metal was enough to hold the key down until the enormous temperatures had fused it forever in a depressed position. Once this juggernaut was in operation, "to the delight and consternation of the adepts of St. Cecilia," the performer went behind the piano and mounted a platform supported by some dubious wooden staging; here he picked up a portable industrial laser in the shape of a thyrsus, which he waved at the audience in the obligatory fashion (Perdix: "the excitement was palpable"), then held it in front of him (in what was probably the only comfortable position) and began to beam it downward, severing the sounding wires one by one, two by two, or three by three; as each string broke the audience was "convulsed with tremors as if the world were ending"; an A flat, sounded and held by the burning mercury, would presently be obliterated by another A flat of truly apocalyptic proportions but almost no duration, since the strings that could have held it were gone; instead all the remaining strings began to ring with a vengeance, "reminding the awed listener of a thousand mothers bewailing the death of as many sons." (I think the reviewer must have been correct in his judgment that "while certain neoclassical antecedents might be claimed for the piece," its "frank sexuality" and "anarchic Dionysian spontaneity" clearly linked it with the undergraduate tradition of piano-busting with sledgehammers.) Nothing like that has happened this summer, or if it has we haven't heard about it; we're supposed to get the *Telegram* every morning but somebody always steals it. I wish there were some way to get accurate schedules; maybe you have to be friends with some influential person . . . I just don't know.

If only I'd had the sense to go to Holy Cross in the first place! I had the chance and let it slip, and now I think back on it with incredible longing, like a man who has lost certain rights forever. You can see the campus from College Square—a great conglomeration of pillars, balconies, belfries, crenellations and facades, all lined and banded with green copper, like a medieval city on a high hill; between the further buildings the very air seems to reverberate, and under the golden haze you can see banners and pennants of a hundred subtle colors. The young novices shuffle drowsily past me on their way to class; they seem to be ringed and wreathed in a splendid sleep, so that just to be near the rise and fall of their perfumed lungs is to know peace. I have never tried to speak to them as they pass, not even to hand them a leaflet, but I'm certain they would never answer or even notice they had been addressed; sleep fills their eyes like an unbroken membrane of belief; it seems infinitely touching that there should be people who spend their lives trying to wake them.

For some reason it's not possible—or not permitted—for persons like myself to visit Holy Cross. (It should be understood that this name refers exclusively to the conservatory; the rest of the school is something no one is able to believe in any longer. When a classicist or a historian tells me he's "teaching at Holy Cross this year" I have learned to understand it as an elegant euphemism for unemployment.) To begin with, it's far from certain whether the institution really is where it seems to be, in spite of the appearances I've just described. That seems incredible? It did to me; so one day last week, deciding to see for myself, I borrowed Myksis's old Pontiac and drove through an ancient underpass to the other side of the Providence and Worcester tracks, where the buildings of Holy Cross shone for a moment in the sun before the roadside turned countrylike and green as if the entire city had been a dream. When I had passed the hill I was surprised to find myself near the Black Orchid, which I had always approached from another direction. Now I took a sharp right into a residential area, thinking perhaps I could find an open gate at the back of the campus, but the road ended suddenly at the top of the hill near an old stone house which seemed empty and which, together with its extensive grounds, occupied the entire summit; in other words it was in the exact spot where Holy Cross had appeared to be from the other side; on the great lawn, near the broken gazebo and the reflecting pool clogged with ash leaves, were several ornamental hen pheasants pecking disconsolately at the ground, with not a soul in sight.

I had the feeling I'd seen the house somewhere before, and when I had deciphered the name on the rusted steel plaque in the driveway I recognized it as the backdrop for numerous family portraits I'd seen in Professor Dervis's scrapbook. It was huge and barren, with open doors everywhere, looking destroyed in spite of their wholeness, swinging in the breeze or banging helplessly against the jamb. I parked the car by the nameplate and went inside. The interior was a maze of oak and polished granite, with here and there a spiral staircase leading to the second floor;

the odd thing was that there was no main stair, and in fact nothing in the house seemed to be principal—there was no door that was obviously a front door, because no matter what side of the house you stood on it seemed like the back; inside there was no main fireplace, though there were perhaps two dozen small ones just big enough to warm one person, and for a long time I tried to decide which area might have been the living room, because most of the cubicles had the dead air of cramped individual quarters. In the pantry I found the skeleton of a servant— man or woman, I couldn't tell. All at once I was overcome with desire, which in my experience is often released by an image of mortality, and I began pacing miserably up and down the corridors, not knowing what to do; then through a side window I saw a young woman on the lawn, a recent widow, to judge from her dress; she was sitting on the remains of the summer house, reading a book bound in purple calf; I went out immediately and struck up a conversation (about what I don't remember); she seemed to like me; her name was of course Eve; and after a decent interval, with the tender slowness of habitual lovers, we took off each other's clothes and sank together onto the grass; but when I went inside her I felt her grow heavy under my weight and I felt nauseous, as if in her motions the earth itself were heaving around me; and by the time I came she was gone.

People are so taken with what they see around them, so willing to believe! It never occurred to me to doubt the reality of the old stone house or the ruined gazebo, or the ornamental hen pheasants, even when the woman had dissolved into the grass in the very act of intercourse, or rather when I saw that she had never been anything but sweet clover and purple bluets like the rest of the cool green lawn on which I lay naked; and now the whistling of the wind began to sound strangely human and scornful, so that I ran awkwardly back to the car, pulling my clothes on as I went, and drove back the way I had come, wanting (I have to admit it)—wanting to die. Just before the ancient underpass I glanced up the hill, expecting to see the great house, but there was Holy Cross again, shining as bright as ever on the summit, and I realized to my chagrin that I had probably lain naked in human company I was unable to perceive, perhaps in the middle of a rehearsal, and the sounds I attributed to the wind may have been the jeering whistles of conservatory students whose practice had been comically interrupted by the lewdness of middle age. I was surprised at this thought; I think this was the day I began to doubt my sanity; but I learned an important lesson when I saw the conservatory gleaming for the second time, impossibly, on the exact site of the ruined manor, namely that an obsessive vision doesn't dissolve merely because it has been shown to be unreal. My mood improved remarkably as I thought about this, and I was able to practice a couple of hours without falling into the usual depression; I would even have gone to rehearsal, but by this time of course the secretaries have forgotten me completely, and I'm never able to find out when my evening rehearsal is till the day after it's held, which is not really very useful.

I was never fitted for pure music, was always too clouded, too opaque; and I used to think it was only an abundance of life, but on the day I searched for Holy Cross I began to be afraid the life itself might be redundant and barren, a lonely inner city of whirling ash and freezing steel; it must have been this intuition of sterility that drove me to Anarchism, with its touching faith in human goodness. I confess I was not entirely uninfluenced by Zérault's hostility to the conservatory, especially after my difficult experience with it. He seems to have been some kind of avant-garde musician when he was young (he may even have studied composition with Alegría), but an ear infection put him out of action when he was still in his twenties, and ever since then he's hated all music with an unnatural passion, even to the point of being unable to trust anyone who can hold a tune. It occurs to me that this may be the reason I've never met the great Théophile; our mutual friends must be keeping us apart, because Zérault has a violent temper, and if he walked into the Orchid when I was there he might go out of control and break my fingers, or whatever they do to discourage pianists in that part of town. I wouldn't hold it against him; I suppose I even love him, though I'm terrified that he may be the instrument of my destruction, if not now, then soon, very soon; but basically he's a good person and would most certainly make a good mayor, which is why I'm down in College Square right now, with Holy Cross looming above me like the City of God, trying to convince the good people of Worcester to vote for a man I've never met. The comrades know I don't campaign very hard, but nobody at the Orchid seems to care—which is to be expected, since we Worcester Anarchists are not exactly famous for our political organization.

Postlude. This evening I showed this piece to Myksis, since in spite of his despicable qualities and dubious identity he continues to be my only friend. I instructed him to skip over the parts in which he was mentioned, since he would understand that they were the fruits of a casual paranoia and did not represent my real feelings. *"Très bien,"* he said absently, and settled down to the task in Dervis's old easy chair. He read somewhat dutifully at first—I began to collect the dirty coffee cups around the room so as not to appear to be watching—but later his interest must have increased, because I let a glass fall and break on the tile floor and he didn't look up. I noticed him smiling unaccountably when he was about two-thirds of the way through, which made me very nervous; then he grew more serious; when he finished he slammed the manuscript down on the Formica and gave a loud whoop that made my blood run cold; I looked at him as Schopenhauer's squirrel must have looked at the fatal snake, waiting for an explanation, even though I knew that any possible one would have to be infinitely destructive.

"It's marvelous!" he said. "I love it!"

I stood there like a stone; of all the possible reactions this horrid little person might have had, this was the most unexpected. "You love what?" I asked him finally, but I was so extremely fearful of his answer that I bolted from the room before he had a chance to speak and ran down the street and under the railroad tracks all the way to the sanctuary of the Black Orchid, a good two miles, and didn't come home till past midnight; it's—wait a minute—it's 1:15 now, and even though I'm exhausted I thought it might be a good idea to write this postscript before I went to sleep, because I think I understand now why my very first reader (he's watching me right now, came so close to driving me insane with his incomprehensible praise.

My first thought was that he wanted to kill me, perhaps by driving me to a confused and bitter suicide on the tracks of the Providence and Worcester; then I reflected that after all we had been living together for several weeks in relative harmony and really were friends, at least in some extended sense of the word; it was unthinkable.

Then what could it mean?

An evening of serious drinking didn't get me any closer to a solution, perhaps because I spent most of my time holding hands with a pretty French Canadian bar-girl in a low-cut purple dress; she reminded me strongly of Eve, to the point that I even asked her name; it was, of course, Eve; and I was going to see if I could convince her to come home with me when she dissolved without warning into the moonless night. I finally staggered alone into the street, where the cold air sobered me a bit; ancient Chevrolets were oozing up and down the pavement like reptiles; to the north, far up on the hill, I could see the flashlights of the grave robbers moving back and forth on the grounds of the old stone mansion. Then the solution came to me, like a bolt from heaven.

There were only two possibilities: either my friend had praised the work in order to destroy me with irony, which was not likely, or else he had read my words with an exotic technique I once knew well but had completely forgotten about until tonight: a perverse manner of reading in which every statement is assumed to be a falsehood, every agonizing ratiocination an entertaining game, every true passion a triumph of the histrionic will. It had to be the latter: Myksis had read my work as though it were fiction. I confess I have never in my life felt quite so frightened, or so alone.

Eugene K. Garber

The Flight

I

A young woman gets on a small feeder plane in Peoria, a real old-timey number, a DC something, the aisle so steep that she has to grab on to the seats and pull her way up. The lights on the wall are pale yellow. "Smoking or no smoking?" The stewardess, flight attendant that is, laughs, because there is only one other passenger on the plane, a big bald-headed man. The woman chooses a seat behind him and on the other side. She picks up an open magazine to return it to the pouch in the back of the seat ahead. Something catches her eye—a full-page ad for a honeymoon spa in the Poconos. A perfect, not to say plastic, young couple are standing chest-deep in an oak tub, drinking champagne. Elsewhere on the page are shots of bedrooms, tennis courts, a glittering discotheque, etc. The woman sticks the magazine in the pouch. The heads of the newlyweds poke up above the rim of the tub like the mischievous children of a giant marsupial.

"Passenger Whitcomb?" says the flight attendant, half a question, half a greeting.

"Yes."

"Welcome aboard, Ms. Whitcomb. Would you care for a Coke?" The flight attendant is wearing a red and white neckerchief and has a hard face though only thirtyish.

"No thank you."

"All right. Please fasten your seat belt. We'll be taking off shortly." The flight attendant goes forward to the cockpit, opens the hatch, and disappears inside.

Meanwhile the ground crew are closing the passenger door and dogging it tight. There are voices. The tail rocks perceptibly and then all is quiet.

A minute or two later the flight attendant reappears. She has on an old-timey aviator's helmet with the goggles pushed up on the forehead. The ear flaps are not yet snapped under her chin and therefore hang jauntily beside her cheeks. She also wears a parachute. The straps of the double baldric, in the shape of a sawbuck, cross precisely between her breasts and divide them neatly one on either side, causing them to bulge larger than normal—like an Amazon's. "Don't worry," says the flight attendant, running her thumbs with reassuring expertise under the straps, "I'm no Amelia Earhart about to disappear into the western sunset."

The bald man chuckles.

The flight attendant now slips briefly into an official sing-song: "Thank you for flying Wawaneka. Please note that there are two emergency exists, one on either side." She points with a show of great precision to windows behind the two passengers. "There will be no demonstration for this flight of emergency oxygen equipment." She smiles wryly. "Because this is what's called in the trade a hedge-hopper. We'll be lucky to be a thousand feet up when we cross the Mississippi." The flight attendant turns with military quickness and goes back into the cockpit, shutting the door decisively behind her. Before she does, however, Whitcomb notices that the parachute straps also run between her legs and outline her sex with a perfect V. In the back the straps press hard against her buttocks before terminating at a wide waist band. Whitcomb imagines what it would feel like to be suspended in the air by those straps, especially in a turbulent sky, swinging and bouncing under the buffeted chute.

"She's something, ain't she?" says the bald man, turning strenuously peering over his seat, and catching Whitcomb's eye. He is very jowly and fat. Superfluous tissue in fact has piled up around his ears like a ridged mound of fatuous good humor. He speaks in a slow southern dialect. "Little ol' twit ain't hardly bigger'n a minute but here she is fixing to jockey this thing up in the sky."

The fat man is right. The engines rev and the plane begins to roll. Moments later it's airborne. For a while Whitcomb watches the lights of Peoria diminish and then her eyes wander again to the magazine with the heads of the two young lovers smiling out at her. *Rolfing.* The word comes to her out of nowhere, it seems, but then she remembers that she has seen a TV documentary on the sybaritic practices of the residents of Marin County, California. She also remembers hearing the following: if you run a feather along the bottom of a person's foot and the toes turn down, then the person is all right, but if the toes turn up, then the person is crazy. Or is it the other way around?

The engine has stopped its shuddering strain and dropped into a dull hum, and the aisle is almost level now. The fat man gets up with a grunt and works his way out into the center of the cabin, where he stands breathing strenuously. He is immense.

"You don't have to talk if you don't want to," he says, working his way cautiously back toward Whitcomb, "but I'm going to sit down here." He drops himself heavily into the seat directly across the aisle from Whitcomb. Inevitably he farts, but takes no notice of it. Whitcomb says, "Sit where you like." There is nothing offish in her tone. In fact, she awards him a tolerant smile.

"Good." The fat man pulls a stogie out of his jacket, unwraps it, and fishes out of his vest pocket a tiny jackknife attached to a fob chain. He opens the knife, carves the end of the stogie, reams the hole, folds the knife back up, and returns it to his vest pocket—a ceremony that takes perhaps three minutes. "Madam or miss, as the case may be," he says, "you are about to smell the sweetest smoke this side of the hash-hash-eens."

"Ms.," says Whitcomb, but it seems unlikely that the fat man has caught the distinction. At the moment he is twirling the end of the stogie between his lips, dampening it thoroughly—an action which appears to produce in him a state of mild ecstasy. Meanwhile, Whitcomb registers the improbable fact that a Phi Beta Kappa key hangs on the fob chain.

Now the fat man pulls a small gold metal case from yet another pocket, removes a match, strikes it against the base, and lights up, taking first a few short puffs and then blowing a single heavy gust toward the ceiling of the cabin. This done, he smiles benignly at Whitcomb, who— still without the slightest acerbity—says, "Beautifully done."

The fat man sticks the cigar in his mouth, takes the gold band from the cellophane wrapper, and slips it onto his little finger. He takes the cigar out of his mouth and chuckles. "With this I thee wed." He pauses. "Which is what my mama predicted lo these many years ago."

"Why? Because she spoiled you so bad that you wouldn't be fit for any other woman?"

The fat man nods amusedly. *"Mi mama me mima.* Isn't that sweet? That's what they say in ol' Me'ico. *My mama she spoils me.* But in my case, miss, it wasn't necessary because I was a natural born Narcissus. And only the grace of the good Lord has kept me from falling to my deserved death in the pools of my own self-adulation." The fat man grins widely. His mouth is full of gold.

Whitcomb smiles and settles back. "What are you doing in this part of the country?"

The fat man looks out the window into the dark. "What part of the country would you call this, miss?"

"Right now, it's the Mississippi Valley, but we're headed for the Great Plains."

"And do the inhabitants of the Great Plains bedizen themselves and later die, just as folks do in other parts?"

"I suppose they do."

"Well then I've got business with them."

"You're a travelling salesperson. Narcissus on the road, or rather in the airways."

"That's me, miss."

"And what do you sell, Narcissus?"

The fat man sighs. "I wonder, miss, in deference to age and sheer bulk, if you would be kind enough to step up to my seat and bring back the little valise stowed on the floor there."

Whitcomb fetches the valise, which is small but heavy. The fat man receives it with thanks and places it on his knees. Whitcomb takes the aisle seat on her side so that she can watch as the fat man unsnaps the clasp and opens the top. The valise contains catalogues and many display cards of jewelry. The fat man beams over it so that the whole little tableau has the appearance of an illustration in a child's book—a treasure chest so sparkling and luminous that the face of the personage who has opened it is bathed in a preternatural light.

Instead of commenting on the contents of the valise, Whitcomb says mischievously, "Where did you go to college, Mister Narcissus?" When the fat man hesitates, she adds, "I notice you wear a Phi Beta Kappa key."

The fat man gives her a golden grin. "Miss, I attended the College of Knowledge and majored in the Ways of the World." He guffaws. "And as for the Phi Beta Kappa key, that was self-awarded, you might say."

Whitcomb smiles understandingly. "And what other awards have you given yourself?"

This causes a mild sadness to shadow the fat man's eyes, which surprises Whitcomb. He puffs meditatively on his cigar and says at length, "In my time, miss, due to the conditions of my trade, which I will expand on presently, I have had occasion to collect many of the most famous war medals—The Purple Heart, The Medal of Honor, The Legion of Honor, The Distinguished Flying Cross, The Navy Cross, et cetera. But I've never worn them."

"Because you didn't fight."

"That's right. Too young for World War II, too old for Korea and Vietnam. All the blood and all the glory fell to my left or to my right, but none on me."

"You were lucky."

"That's a woman's way of looking at it, miss. I respect it. But it's not a man's way." Immediately upon saying which, the fat man guffaws loudly. "Here! Why are we talking about all that? What about my wares?" The fat man hands Whitcomb a display card of rings, all mounted in ersatz velvet of royal blue—wedding rings and engagement rings, white metal and yellow metal, the engagement rings mounted with imitation diamonds of various sizes. "You will notice," says the fat man, "that these are all traditional. I pity the poor devil that takes over the territory when I'm done."

Whitcomb frowns. "I don't know what you mean."

"I mean the things that people are putting on each other's fingers nowadays at wedding ceremonies are of such a bizarre variety that it will soon be impossible to keep them in stock—twisted vines, interlocking hearts, snakes swallowing their own tails, God knows what."

"So?" says Whitcomb, irritated by the continuing obscurity of the matter. "How do you work the territory without all that stuff?"

The fat man frowns, a little puzzled it seems. "Didn't I tell you a minute ago that my customers are all deceased?"

"Deceased?"

"In a manner of speaking. You see, miss, about three-and-a-half million Americans die every year, and if all of them that had rings were buried with them, why literally billions in value would go underground. And the times being what they are, the value of gold rising, rising, rising . . ." The fat man widens his eyes. "You take my meaning, miss. Especially in a recession, America can't afford any King Tuts."

Whitcomb nods, but gives the fat man a hard look. "The bereaved get the genuine rings, I hope—and not the undertakers."

The fat man sighs. "One always hopes for the best, miss." Then he suddenly summons his golden grin, taps the card in Whitcomb's hands, and says, "How about a set, miss? Any one you want, free—engagement ring and wedding band."

Whitcomb frowns. "What would I do with them? Wait for some prince charming to pop the question and then say *you lucky boy, I've already got the rings?*"

The fat man wheezes merrily around his cigar, "Aw hell naw, miss, you don't want to actually get married with these things. If you perspire a little—as I am told lovers are apt to do—they'll start to turn your finger

green, necrotic-like." The fat man chuckles. "Whereas your deceased
. . . well, you see the difference, miss."

"Then what would I want the rings for?"

The fat man leans toward her. "Now looky here, miss. A smart-look-
ing young woman like yourself will attract attention. And, grant you,
attention can be nice—eyes falling on you, calling up a nice warm flush.
Say, don't think I'm criticizing." The fat man's face relaxes benignly. "I
myself am an aficionado of attention. All this flesh—you don't think it's
an accident, do you? My mama once said, 'Some like to be looked past
and some like to be looked at, that's the thin and thick of it.' I'm one of
the looked ats, pure and simple. But I'm guessing you're right now in
between, miss. That's where the rings come in. You see where I'm
going?"

"I'm listening."

"Simple. You want attention, you leave the rings in your purse. You
want to be left alone, you put the rings on the fourth finger of your left
hand."

Whitcomb shakes her head. "That won't work nowadays."

"Yes it will. Lemme show you." The fat man reaches over, takes
Whitcomb's left hand, and runs his fingers along her ring finger. The
motion is so deft and gentle that it gives her no reason to resist. Now the
fat man examines the card of rings, looking at the sizes inscribed along
with the catalogue numbers under each set. Quickly he selects a pair and
slides them onto Whitcomb's finger. "These are a little too big, but
they'll give you the idea. There." The fat man sits back and looks carefully at Whitcomb. "You feel it?"

"What am I supposed to feel?" The question is something of a dodge
because in fact Whitcomb does perceive about herself a different aura.

"No, you tell me, miss, what you feel."

"Well, I'll tell you then. It appears that something has been formed—a second skin." Whitcomb smiles. "Can you see me all right?"

The fat man chuckles around his dwindling cigar. "Go on. Go ahead."

"No, there's nothing more. And I don't want you to tell me that it's
some primitive talisman, mark of ownership that keeps the male beast at
bay."

The fat man chuckles again but is excused from speaking because just
at that moment the PA snaps on and the voice of the flight attendant
comes up. "How are you honeymooners doing back there? Well, buckle
up. We're about to set down at the famous airport of Okekuk, Iowa, to
pick up passengers." Dimly audible is a rustle of papers. "Pokorny, Mary
and Jess Pokorny. Directly below is the confluence of the Cedar River
and the Father of Waters. After we leave Okekuk, it's westward ho to

Des Moines, honeymooners. Down we go." The place dips sharply and
the pitch of the engines changes. "You will notice that the captain has
lighted the no smoking sign. Please extinguish all smoking materials at
this time."

The fat man snuffs out his cigar in the arm ashtray. Whitcomb moves
over to the window seat, buckles up, and looks out into the night. She
cannot see the rivers, only here and there a dimple of light, farm houses
probably. Then suddenly there are the blue border lights of the runway
and a moment later the bump and squeal of the wheels as the pilot
applies the brakes. Whitcomb looks over at the fat man. "Did you ever
see a town?"

"No, but I wasn't paying attention. Landings and take-offs make me a
little queasy. You'd think after all these years . . ." The fat man goes no
farther. His pale face completes his testimony.

Whitcomb continues to peer out the window. "Well, do you see any
kind of terminal?"

The fat man leans over toward the window. "Nope." Nevertheless,
the plane presently taxis to a stop and the engines die. The cockpit door
opens and the flight attendant comes out, unsnapping her helmet, pushing her goggles up. "Smooth as silk, wasn't it?"

"Very nice," says the fat man.

Still wearing her parachute, the flight attendant hastens back to the
tail hatch and opens it. Steps are rolled up and clamped into place. Then
comes the slight tilt and vibration caused by someone mounting the
steps. "Oh, boy," says the flight attendant disgustedly. Whitcomb and
the fat man look back. "It's not Mary and Jess Pokorny after all, honeymooners." A small man enters through the hatch. He is wearing a trench
coat and a snap-brimmed hat. "Nor," says the flight attendant, "is it
your local Cuban hijacker. Guess who it is." She pauses for effect. "It's
Humphrey Bogart, your friendly FFA inspector, come to see if all is well
in America's airways."

The inspector carries a flashlight. Without saying anything, he snaps
it on and begins examining various enclosures: a small baggage area at
the very end of the cabin, the overhead coat and pillow storage, the
pouches on the backs of the seats, etc. As he works his way toward
Whitcomb and the fat man, the flight attendant calls out, "If either of
you have planted a bomb in here, you might as well fess up now, because
Humphrey is thorough."

When the inspector reaches the fat man, he says, "May I see your
valise please, sir." The fat man hesitates, then hands it over. The inspector rummages among the catalogues and display cards. Presently he

holds up a placard of especially rich blue velveteen on which are mounted several medals representing military honors. "Well," says the flight attendant, "I didn't know we had a hero aboard. Why didn't you tell me?"

The inspector replaces the placard in the valise, which he snaps shut and returns to the fat man, who stares straight ahead flushed and chastened. The inspector turns to Whitcomb. "Your purse please, ma'am."

Whitcomb shakes her head. "No."

The flight attendant sighs loudly. "You might as well go ahead and give it to him. He's got a federal warrant." Whitcomb still holds on to the purse. The flight attendant says, "We will be detained and the aircraft sealed until a federal marshall comes. Besides, ma'am, Humphrey has seen everything that could ever be in a woman's purse—glass eyes, pillow books, dope, dildos, you name it—and he's not going to hassle you about anything unless it affects the safety of the plane." The inspector nods. Whitcomb at last hands over the purse. The inspector unzips it, shines his light down into it, rummages around, pulls out a small dispenser of Mace, and hands the purse back. "I'm sorry, ma'am, but I'll have to confiscate this."

The flight attendant shakes her head. "Third one this week, Humphrey. Put in your report that male violence in America is driving women in ever increasing numbers to carry protective devices, some of them potentially as harmful to themselves as to their assailants." The inspector says nothing but only continues to work his way forward, searching. Whitcomb looks ahead stonily, her face drawn. The flight attendant says sotto voce, "Don't give the prying creep the satisfaction of knowing that he has affected you in the slightest." The flight attendant turns to the fat man. "You either. And I'm sorry I made that crack about the medals. It just popped out of my mouth like a little frog." The flight attendant turns quickly and follows the inspector into the cockpit.

In the cabin Whitcomb and the fat man do not look at each other or offer each other any comfort. Out the window there is nothing to see, so they look down at their hands, silent and joyless.

The inspector, done, walks rapidly out of the cockpit, down the aisle, and off the plane. As the flight attendant dogs the hatch behind him, the steps are pulled away with a jerk. A moment later, at the door to the cockpit, the flight attendant turns to her passengers briefly before entering. "Well, it is a kind of rape, but, as you can see, it's routine for the creeps now. They get no more pleasure out of it. And it's supposed to be for our own good." She smiles sympathetically, shrugs, and enters the cockpit, closing the door behind her.

II

Somewhere between the Mississippi River and the river Platte, Whitcomb, who has been dozing lightly, awakens to the sound of the cockpit door closing. She looks up just in time to see the flight attendant stride past her down the aisle. She notes that the flight attendant's helmet is snapped tight under the chin and that the goggles are down over her eyes. The flight attendant marches straight back to the tail hatch, opens it, crouches low like a gymnast, and hurls herself out. For a long moment, while Whitcomb and the fat man stare back in amazement, there is a loud sucking sound and everything in the cabin shudders. Then the air catches the hatch and slams it shut with a resounding clank.

Whitcomb looks out the window. Beneath the plane, in the silver moonlight, the parachute bobs and drifts like a lily on a breezy pond. Whitcomb imagines lying on top of it, sinking into its silken folds, and looking up at the chinless smile of the Man in the Moon.

"Looks like a kind of feathery pillow, or a titty, doesn't it?" The fat man wrinkles his brow, self-surprised by his mammary image. But Whitcomb takes no notice. She watches the parachute drift back until it is out of sight. Then she snaps forward in her seat like one who has received an electric shock. Quickly she unbuckles and steps out into the aisle.

"Where're you going?"

"To the cockpit. Here." Whitcomb takes off the rings and hands them back to the fat man. He receives the jewelry distractedly, looking not at it but up at Whitcomb's face. "There's nothing down there but seas of corn and wheat."

"I can't help that." Whitcomb turns and walks with determination up to the cockpit. She opens the door and disappears inside.

Presently the fat man slips the rings into his jacket pocket, sighs, and gets up. Slowly he works his way forward to the flight attendant's area. Rummaging around, he locates the little refrigerator and, inside, a bottle of champagne. This and a plastic tumbler he carries back to his seat, stashing them in the pouch in front of him. From his valise he takes out the blue velveteen display card that holds the medals. These he pins expertly above the breast pocket of his jacket—one with a two-bladed propeller mounted atop a Golden Globe, another an aureate scutcheon wreathed in vines, another a purple heart containing a famous profile, and so on, six medals in all, hanging on bright silken ribbons and making, when the fat man moves to take up the champagne again, a tiny, elegant clangor. The fat man holds the bottle between his thighs, pops the cork, and pours himself a glass. "To your health, colonel," he says, in a British accent and drinks. "Tonight, sir, the sky is bedizened with stars, like a strumpet." He drinks again, with pleasure. The effervescent champagne catches the cabin light and bathes the fat man's face in a pale golden glow.

Whitcomb finds the cockpit empty. The control panel is a maze of green lights with a red dot here and there. Numerals pick up the glow and shine white. She sits down in the pilot's seat. Using her native intelligence she begins to reduce the green and white maze to its constituent elements. There is an altimeter. Six thousand feet, it says. There are two fuel gauges, both comfortably above half, an horizon indicator, some control and circuit checks, etc. To her right is the radio, already lit. She locates the volume and turns it up. The radio crackles. A voice reads out some numbers and letters. She finds the tuning knob and sweeps the band—more of the same. She turns the volume back down.

Touching the radio with impunity buoys her confidence. Eventually she will touch other instruments, but now she pauses and looks out the cockpit window. The right side of the nose cowl shines silver in the moonlight. The left is shadowed. But this tells her nothing about her course, no more than the occasional silver cloud sliding under the nose, no more than the momentary glint here and there of ponds and streams below. Above wheel the stars—in a design, she knows, that might be interpreted by a celestial navigator, but to her the stars are even less constellated than the lights of the instrument panel. Instrument panel. She smiles and lowers her eyes to the compass. The reading is due west.

Some moments later Whitcomb discovers atop the console separating the pilot and copilot seats a helmet, just like the one the flight attendant wore. She puts it on. It is comfortably snug, lined warmly with a light fleecy material. She fastens the ear flaps under her chin. The hum of the engines slides off into the distance. She lowers the goggles down over her eyes. The lights of the instrument panel becomes less luminous but more sharply defined, as though the goggles had refractive power. The smell of leather insinuates itself into her nostrils. It seems somehow extraordinarily old. So does the feel of the firm and quilted cushion under her buttocks and thighs.

Whitcomb doesn't know what to do with these sensations. Her body moves randomly, restlessly. Then almost involuntarily, and yet with a sense of deep harmony, Whitcomb lifts her right leg and presses it against the console, which receives it snugly, almost as if furnished with a depression fitted to her form. In front of her she discovers a black oval, the upper half sliced by a wide V so as not to obscure the instrument panel. This truncated wheel, she takes firmly in her hands. She looks straight out over the moonlit cowl.

After a while the sun will spring up behind the plane and make of the wheat fields below a golden tray scratched and striated as with an ancient patina.

Meanwhile, the fat man has finished his champagne and his colloquy with the colonel.

As soon as the sun breaches the horizon, the shadow of the plane will leap far to the west, preceding in the quick eyes of rabbits and prairie dogs the sound of the engines.

Whitcomb surveys all before her. Some hint of warmer light hazes the platinum rings the moon makes in the whirling propellers.

The fat man, with an almost musical riffle of his fingers, sets the medals on his breast to tinkling.

Whitcomb squeezes the wheel and presses her leg hard against the console.

The fat man sits up straight and salutes.

Whitcomb sighs so deeply that she shudders.

WILLIAM GASS

Summer Bees

Now it is another day. Rain is speaking gently to the terrace. I speak gently, sometimes, to myself. How soft the light is, mingled with the wet.

We had one shortened summer month together, Lou and I . . . my god, even the decade's gone. Pleading the pressures of work, I excused myself from my life and settled in a second-story room in western New York. A wooden stair fell from one widened window like a slide of cards. We hung our towels there: a shirt sometimes, a slip as discreet as a leer. I remember particularly the quiet empty streets, the long walk to the beach. Well, it was scarcely a beach, though there was a pier, and even in August the water was cool in those thin deep lakes the patient passion of the glaciers scratched. My chief memory is the heat, the silence, your pale breasts. Pale as a bleached leaf. I do not understand what makes another body so appealing.

A souvenir scarf, salmon pink and exuberantly fringed (but not a memory of mine) lay across the dresser. And there was an old oak commode, solid as a safe. I also recall one stiff chair, committed to good posture and discomfort, its caning gone and the hole boarded up like a broken window, with the seat-wood covered in some kind of slippery cloth on which designs suggestive of breakfast commanded the eater to be shortly up and at 'em. Well. So there were these wan leftover creatures still: the glass dish your hairpins lay in, a distant green like some remembered portion of the sea, so from the side the pins seemed a school of small fish; the lamp which leaned, threatening to slide the shade outside the limits of its bulbshine; the black metal basket where an orange flower flared like a match, and where you would toss the Kleenex you wiped yourself with, seed soaked, relaxed, in a soft wad. So. These things. Then you and I. We were wonderful in our willingness, weren't we? And now is it all ash? Some sweetmeat scrubbed from the teeth? These days the soft cloth which receives my relief gets washed. And the walls . . . the walls were . . . Damn. There was a rug—yes, there was a rug—its design by a dimestore indian. And didn't we have a clock we kept in the pocket of its case—somewhere a quiet tick, a measure we forgot? The picture you wanted to turn to the wall . . . was . . . Of a Civil War encampment.

If you grasped that stair rail, white paint would powder your hand. Now I had captured your love. I was already counting the cost.

Every morning we ate an orange, and you walked off to the lake to swim while I read until eleven when I met you there. We circled the lake so closely we kept our image always in the water, and we ate our lunch from the same brown sack we used to feed the ducks, the sack the grocer dropped our oranges in, half-a-dozen at a time. The scent of the peel would often linger on my thumbs, the zest of the rind still lodged beneath the nail near the quick. Then in the afternoon we would nap and sweat through the deep heat, our limbs loose as rags, and walk once more down the elm-tented street for a dip, holding hands which had held our bodies together better than our bones. In the evenings I wrote or we listened to the radio a little, and you would let your long hair dry on our single pillow. It was the simplest sort of life, empty of everything except ourselves, the contentment we were wrapped in like patriotic bunting. I wrote the section in *Guilt and Innocence* on secondary school almost entirely out of my head—easily—even the songs,

> Unsern Führer lieber wir,
> Unsern Führer ehren wir,
> Unsern Führer folgen wir,
> Bis wir Männer werden . . .
>   hardly taking thought.

Bugs would bang against the screen during the early hours of the night, a car might cough, or very far away a truck labor up a hill, and the morning light would be gray and heavy with humidity. I would stand naked at the top of our wooden stairs while you completed your sleep, accosting a day which wasn't quite ready, and waiting for a breeze to brush the hair on my legs the way your breath would caress me in advance of your tongue.

We were happy because we had no history. I know that now. Though I was writing history. I wrote: *Guilt and Innocence in Hitler's Germany,* Chapter Twelve. Our winter room was full of the snow which had fallen between us, the cold wind my wife blew, your desire to have all of me, as though I were entirely at leisure, and had no book, no profession, no family, no commitments to the world. I only wanted to play *eine, meine, mine, mu,* and you eventually tired of being a meadow for my slow fat herds; but in that warm still heavy summer even the stars were wet, and I would wait for a wind, a faint stir in the grass tips, that movement of life in the poplars which signified a breeze, and through the screen, with its fly's-eye view, watch the light slide along your body as if that were air, too, suddenly become skin.

It sometimes seems to me, in morbidly fanciful moments, as if age were aimed at, not simply suffered, for I fled my youth as if it were a disease. I wanted adolescence as I wanted its acne. And I can believe those who argue that memory is not enough to establish the reality of the self, because the selves I remember I remember like photos in the family album: that knickered kid, that bald scrawny brat, that fuzz and fat faced second louie, that solemn owl in his flat black hat—they are relatives of mine at best, school chums scarcely recollected, unidentified individuals who have somehow slunk into the group and grin at the blank beside their name. I can unearth someone shouting slogans in a German street, but that loud rowdy could never have been played by the soft-voiced and suety professor I have since become; nor can I long for you any longer in the old way—that pain is also past—since the lover who lingered over you like a nurse through an illness—I see that now—is now another man, no longer a lover of any kind, just as you are, Lou, a different set of lips, another pair of breasts, some further furry tunnel.

I always am, and never was; but who wants to be what they have been? Only those like Lou whose souls are the same as their skins; those whose bodies have beauty and skill, grace and accomplishment. Time is an enemy of matter, not of mind, and history (as I said to Governali), history, so long as it is tied to Time like a tin can to the wedding car, can only be a recital of . . . tents. There were tents, men slouching in grain-sacky heaps, stacked arms. You.

Oh. No. I'm not your second-story man any more. Another story has intervened. The beauty which I had from you Tents. Tired men. Smoke. Still air. Stacked arms. The pale pattern of your bra, like something which has lain too long across grass, as that scarf lay across its dresser, is one I watch a former self observe, a self which could have returned through the screen to spread itself like a brown glaze over your breasts, not this body which is all mine now—and a mind which is pure bleach.

You turned the tents to the wall, hid the huddles of men, the limp flag, the dog. There was, of course, an amber patch behind it, and its paper back was brown and parched and marked with black crayon, a line of dust along the wire. The shadow of its neglect lay upon it, the paper dry and drawn up tight till it tore where it drew back from its glue. Yet you preferred the blank backside of the image. The hammered frame, back there, was smooth. And now I know what the walls were. I have recovered the color of unskimmed cream.

That one small room made us more than normally neat. We so rubbed and moistened one another, we did not disturb the collar stay on the other window's sill, or the pin in the corner by the hall door. It was We spent whole days consuming an hour. We were rich. We made hay. Sunshine fell like a shower.

Well. I regret the loss of the lover who loved you (hourly, I regret it), but not the loss of the slogan shouter, the maker of messes, I once was. The fingers which slipped through the enchanted forest of your twat—I promise—did not heft that rock on *Kristallnacht.* It's as if my forties had cancelled my twenties out, and my fifties stamped P A I D on both. And beyond the tents, the men, the tented arms, I think I see a station, stacks of wood. There were a few beards on the men and many small moustaches. This was a world—our old world—turned to the wall like the cliché said. Some were sitting cross-legged. I remember particularly our sandaled footfalls and your hand—the light way it led the swing of our arms.

Suddenly the temperature fell like a stone scuffed over a cliff, and when you woke, as surprised by the chill as the trees, I tossed you a towel to cover yourself, and you held to your breasts half-a-dozen honey bees which had sought shelter in its folds.

But Chapter Twelve of *Guilt and Innocence* had come from my head like a flow of tears; and I remember I wanted the gaze of my healthy German kids, the pure *schein* of the facts, to concentrate in the nib of my pen, look back at my words the way those men stared, as they had to, stolidly at the lens, into the heart of the black hood which would eventually hold all that remained of their lives. Poets are the bees of the invisible, Rilke said. A stray strand of hair ran like a crack across your chest. Am I still that astonished self? that innocent who attacked you from afar? Later, small red spots would come out on your breasts when you showered, memories of a flesh I could not scar with my kisses or, with my worship, bless. It got hot again, but our summer's month was over. For as long as we were together, you held those bees against me.

> A swarm of bees in
> May
> Is worth a load of
> hay;
> A swarm of bees in
> June
> Is worth a silver
> spoon;
> A swarm of bees in
> July
> Is not worth a fly.

Commode. Scarf. Dresser. Go-get-em chair. The sea-green dish. The sliding shade. The flower. School of fish. My seed. And when we left that room we left it just that way: the twisted, hammered towel, the tents, men, rifles, turned to the wall, one torn orange, that heat and that humidity, dead bees crushed in the cloth.

JAY MCINERNEY

It's Six A.M. Do You Know Where You Are?

You are not the kind of guy who would be at a place like this at this time of the morning. But you are here, and you cannot say that the terrain is entirely unfamiliar, although the details are a little fuzzy. You are at a nightclub talking to a girl with a shaved head. The club is either the Bimbo Box or the Lizard Lounge. It might all come a little clearer if you could slip into the bathroom and do a little more Bolivian Marching Powder. There is a small voice inside of you insisting that this epidemic lack of clarity is the result of too much of that already, but you are not yet willing to listen to that voice. The night has already turned on that imperceptible pivot where two A.M. changes to six A.M. You know that moment has come and gone, but you are not yet willing to concede that you have crossed the line beyond which all is gratuitous damage and the palsy of unravelled nerve endings. Somewhere back there it was possible to cut your losses, but you rode past that moment on a comet trail of white powder and now you are trying to hang onto that rush. Your brain at this moment is composed of brigades of tiny Bolivian soldiers. They are tired and muddy from their long march through the night. There are holes in their boots and they are hungry. They need to be fed. They need the Bolivian Marching Powder.

Something vaguely tribal about this scene—pendulous jewelry, face paint, ceremonial headgear and hairstyles. You feel that there is also a certain Latin theme, which is more than the fading buzz of marimbas in your brain.

You are leaning back against a post which may or may not be structural with regard to the building, but which feels essential for the maintenance of an upright position. The bald girl is saying this used to be a good place to come before the assholes discovered it. You do not want to be talking to this bald girl, or even listening to her, which is all you're doing, but you don't have your barge pole handy, and just at the moment you don't want to test the powers of speech or locomotion.

How did you get here? It was your friend, Tad Allagash, who powered you in here, and now he has disappeared. Tad is the kind of guy who certainly would be at a place like this at this time of the morning. He is either your best self or your worst self, you're not sure which. Earlier in the evening it seemed clear that he was your best self. You started on the Upper East Side with champagne and unlimited prospects, strictly observing the Allagash rule of perpetual motion: one drink per stop. Tad's mission in life is to have more fun than anyone else in New York City, and this involves a lot of moving around, since there is always the likelihood that you are missing something, that where you aren't is more fun than where you are. You are awed by this strict refusal to acknowledge any goal higher than the pursuit of pleasure. You want to be like that. You also think that he is shallow and dangerous. His friends are all rich and spoiled, like the cousin from Memphis you met earlier in the evening who would not accompany you below Fourteenth Street because he said he didn't have a lowlife visa. This cousin had a girlfriend with cheekbones to break your heart, and you knew she was the real thing when she absolutely refused to acknowledge your presence. She possessed secrets—about islands, about horses—which you would never know.

You have traveled from the meticulous to the slime. The girl with the shaved head has a scar tattooed on her scalp. It looks like a long, sutured gash. You tell her it is very realistic. She takes this as a compliment and thanks you. You meant as opposed to romantic. "I could use one of those right over my heart," you say.

"You want I can give you the name of the guy did it. You'd be surprised how cheap." You don't tell her that nothing would surprise you now. Her voice, for instance, which is like the New Jersey State Anthem played through an electric shaver.

The bald girl is emblematic of the problem. What the problem is is that for some reason you think you are going to meet the kind of girl who is not the kind of girl who would be at a place like this at this time of the morning. When you meet her you are going to tell her that what you really want is a house in the country with a garden. New York, the club scene, bald women—you're tired of all that. Your presence here is only a matter of conducting an experiment in limits, reminding yourself of what you aren't. You see yourself as the kind of guy who wakes up early on Sunday morning and steps out to pick up *The Times* and croissants. You take a cue from the Arts and Leisure section and decide to check out some exhibition—costumes of the Hapsburg Court at the Met, say, or Japanese lacquerware of the Muromachi period at the Asia Society. Maybe you will call that woman you met at the publishing party Friday night, the party you did not get sloppy drunk at, the woman who is an editor at a famous publishing house even though she looks like a fashion model. See if she wants to check out the exhibition and maybe do an early dinner. You will wait until eleven A.M. to call her, because she may not be an early riser, like you. She may have been out a little late, at a nightclub, say. It occurs to you that there is time for a couple of sets of tennis before the museum. You wonder if she plays, but then, of course she would.

When you meet the girl who wouldn't etcetera, you will tell her that you are slumming, visiting your own six A.M. Lower East Side of the soul on a lark, stepping nimbly between the piles of garbage to the marimba rhythms in your head.

On the other hand, any beautiful girl, specifically one with a full head of hair, would help you stave off this creeping sense of mortality. You remember the Bolivian Marching Powder and realize you're not down yet. First you have to get rid of this bald girl because she is doing bad things to your mood.

In the bathroom there are no doors on the stalls, which makes it tough to be discreet. But clearly, you are not the only person here to take on fuel. Lots of sniffling going on. The windows in here are blacked over, and for this you are profoundly grateful.

Hup, two. Three, four. The Bolivian soldiers are back on their feet. They are off and running in formation. Some of them are dancing, and you must do the same.

Just outside the door you spot her: tall, dark, and alone, half-hiding behind a pillar at the edge of the dance floor. You approach laterally, moving your stuff like a bad spade through the slalom of a synthesized conga rhythm. She jumps when you touch her shoulder.

"Dance?"

She looks at you as if you had just suggested instrumental rape. "I do not speak English," she says, when you ask again.

"Français?"

She shakes her head. Why is she looking at you that way, like there are tarantulas nesting in your eye sockets?

"You are by any chance from Bolivia? Or Peru?"

She is looking around for help now. Remembering a recent encounter with a young heiress's bodyguard at Danceteria—or was it New Berlin?—you back off, hands raised over your head.

The Bolivian soldiers are still on their feet, but they have stopped singing their marching song. You realize that we are at a crucial juncture with regard to morale. What we need is a good pep talk from Tad Allagash, but he is not to be found. You try to imagine what he would say. *Back on the horse. Now we're really going to have some fun.* Something like that. You suddenly realize that he has already slipped out with some rich hose queen. He is back at her place on Fifth Ave., and they are doing some of her off-the-boat-quality drugs. They are scooping it out of tall Ming vases and snorting it off of each other's naked bodies. You hate Tad Allagash.

Go home. Cut your losses.

Stay. Go for it.

You are a republic of voices tonight. Unfortunately, the republic is Italy. All these voices are waving their arms and screaming at each other. There's an *ex cathedra* riff coming down from the Vatican: *Repent. There's still time. Your body is the temple of the Lord and you have defiled it.* It is, after all, Sunday morning, and as long as you have any brain cells left there will always be this resonant patriarchal basso echoing down the marble vaults of your churchgoing childhood to remind you that this is the Lord's day. What you need is another overpriced drink to drown it out. But a search of pockets yields only a dollar bill and change. You paid ten to get in here. Panic is gaining on you.

You spot a girl at the edge of the dance floor who looks like your last chance for earthly salvation against the creeping judgment of Sunday morning. You know for a fact that if you go out into the morning alone, without even your sunglasses, which you have forgotten (because who, after all, plans on these travesties), that the harsh, angling light will turn you to flesh and bone. Mortality will pierce you through the retina. But there she is in her pegged pants, a kind of doo-wop retro ponytail pulled off to the side, great lungs, as eligible a candidate as you could hope to find this late in the game. The sexual equivalent of fast food.

She shrugs and nods when you ask her to dance. You like the way she moves, half-tempo, the oiled ellipses of her hips and shoulders. You get a little hip and ass contact. After the second song she says she's tired. She's on the edge of bolting when you ask her if she needs a little pick-me-up.

"You've got some blow?" she says.

"Monster," you say.

She takes your arm and leads you into the Ladies'. There's another guy in the stall beside yours so it's okay. After a couple of spoons she seems to like you just fine and you are feeling very likeable yourself. A couple more. This girl is all nose. When she leans forward for the spoon the front of her shirt falls open in a way you can't help noticing. You wonder if this is her way of thanking you.

Oh yes.

"I love drugs," she says, as you march towards the bar.

"It's something we have in common," you say.

"Have you ever noticed how all the good words start with D? D and L."

You try to think about this. You're not quite sure what she's driving at. The Bolivians are singing their marching song but you can't quite make out the words.

"You know? Drugs. Delight. Decadence."

"Debauchery," you say, catching the tune now.

"Dexedrine."

"Delectable. Deranged. Debilitated."

"And L. Lush and luscious."

"Languorous."

"Lazy."

"Libidinous."

"What's that?" she says.

"Horny."

"Oh," she says, and casts a long, arching look over your shoulder. Her eyes glaze in a way that reminds you precisely of the closing of a sand-blasted glass shower door. You can see that the game is over, though you're not sure which rule you broke. Possibly she finds "H" words offensive. She is scanning the dance floor for a man with a compatible vocabulary. You have more: *down* and *depressed; lost* and *lonely.* It's not that you are really going to miss this girl who thinks that *decadence* and *dexedrine* are the high points of the language of the Kings James and Lear, but the touch of flesh, the sound of another human voice. . . . You know that there is a special purgatory waiting out there for you, a desperate half-sleep which is like a grease fire in the brain pan.

The girl half-waves as she disappears into the crowd. There is no sign of the other girl, the girl who would not be here. There is no sign of Tad Allagash. The Bolivians are mutinous. You can't stop the voices.

Here you are again.

All messed up and no place to go.

It is worse even than you expected, stepping out into the morning. The light is like a mother's reproach. The sidewalk sparkles cruelly. Visibility unlimited. The downtown warehouses look serene and rested in this beveled light. A cab passes uptown and you start to wave, then realize you have no money. The cab stops. You jog over and lean in the window.

"I guess I'll walk after all."

"Asshole." He leaves rubber.

You start north, holding your hand over your eyes. There is a bum sleeping on the sidewalk, swathed in garbage bags. He lifts his head as you pass. "God bless you and forgive your sins," he says. You wait for the cadge, but that's all he says. You wish he hadn't said it.

As you turn away, what is left of your olfactory equipment sends a message to your brain. The smell of fresh bread. Somewhere they are baking bread. You see bakery trucks loading in front of a loft building on the next block. You watch as bags of rolls are carried out onto the loading dock by a man with a tattooed forearm. This man is already at work, so that regular people will have fresh bread for their morning tables. The righteous people who sleep at night and eat eggs for breakfast. It is Sunday morning and you have not eaten since . . . when? Friday night. As you approach, the smell of the bread washes over you like a gentle rain. You inhale deeply, filling your lungs with it. Tears come to your eyes, and you are filled with such a rush of tenderness and pity that you stop beside a lamppost and hang on for support.

You remember another Sunday morning in your old apartment on Cornelia Street when you woke to the smell of bread from the bakery downstairs. There was the smell of bread every morning, but this is the one you remember. You turned to see your wife sleeping beside you. Her mouth was open and her hair fell down across the pillow to your shoulder. The tanned skin of her shoulder was the color of bread fresh from the oven. Slowly, and with a growing sense of exhilaration, you remembered who you were. You were the boy and she was the girl, your college sweetheart. You weren't famous yet, but you had the rent covered, you had your favorite restaurant where the waitresses knew your name and you could bring your own bottle of wine. It all seemed to be just the way you had pictured it when you had discussed plans for marriage and New York. The apartment with the pressed tin ceiling, the claw-footed bath, the windows that didn't quite fit the frame. It seemed almost as if you had wished for that very place. You leaned against your wife's shoulder. Later you would get up quietly, taking care not to wake her, and go downstairs for croissants and the *Sunday Times,* but for a long time you lay there breathing in the mingled scents of bread, hair and skin. You were in no hurry to get up. You knew it was a moment you wanted to savor. You didn't know how soon it would be over, that within a year she would go back to Michigan to file for divorce.

You approach the man on the loading dock. He stops working and watches you. You feel that there is something wrong with the way your legs are moving.

"Bread." This is what you say to him. You meant to say something more, but this is as much as you can get out.

"What was your first clue?" he says. He is a man who has served his country, you think, a man with a family somewhere outside the city. Small children. Pets. A garden.

"Could I have some? A roll or something?"

"Get out of here."

The man is about your size, except for the belly, which you don't have. "I'll trade you my jacket," you say. It is one hundred percent raw silk from Paul Stuart. You take it off, show him the label.

"You're crazy," the man says. Then he looks back into the warehouse. He picks up a bag of hard rolls and throws them at your feet. You hand him the jacket. He checks the label, sniffs the jacket, then tries it on.

You tear the bag open and the smell of warm dough rushes over you. The first bite sticks in your throat and you almost gag. You will have to go slowly. You will have to learn everything all over again.

Susan Minot

Lust

Leo was from a long time ago, the first one I ever saw nude. In the spring before the Hellmans filled their pool, we'd go down there in the deep end, with baby oil, and like that. I met him the first month away at boarding school. He had a halo from the campus light behind him. I flipped.

Roger was fast. In his illegal car, we drove to the reservoir, the radio blaring, talking fast, fast, fast. He was always going for my zipper. He got kicked out sophomore year.

By the time the band got around to playing "Wild Horses," I had tasted Bruce's tongue. We were clicking in the shadows on the other side of the amplifier, out of Mrs. Donovan's line of vision. It tasted like salt, with my neck bent back, because we had been dancing so hard before.

Tim's line: "I'd like to see you in a bathing suit." I knew it was his line when he said the exact same thing to Annie Hines.

You'd go on walks to get off campus. It was raining like hell, my sweater as sopped as a wet sheep. Tim pinned me to a tree, the woods light brown and dark brown, a white house half-hidden with the lights already on. The water was as loud as a crowd hissing. He made certain comments about my forehead, about my cheeks.

We started off sitting at one end of the couch and then our feet were squished against the armrest and then he went over to turn off the TV and came back after he had taken off his shirt and then we slid onto the floor and he got up again to close the door, then came back to me, a body waiting on the rug.

You'd try to wipe off the table or to do the dishes and Willie would untuck your shirt and get his hands up under in front, standing behind you, making puffy noises in your ear.

He likes it when I wash my hair. He covers his face with it and if I start to say something, he goes, "Shush."

For a long time, I had Philip on the brain. The less they noticed you, the more you got them on the brain.

My parents had no idea. Parents never really know what's going on, especially when you're away at school most of the time. If she met them, my mother might say, "Oliver seems nice" or "I like that one" without much of an opinion. If she didn't like them, "He's a funny fellow, isn't he?" or "Johnny's perfectly nice but a drink of water." My father was too shy to talk to them at all, unless they played sports and he'd ask them about that.

The sand was almost cold underneath because the sun was long gone. Eben piled a mound over my feet, patting around my ankles, the ghostly surf rumbling behind him in the dark. He was the first person I ever knew who died, later that summer, in a car crash. I thought about it for a long time.

"Come here," he says on the porch.
I go over to the hammock and he takes my wrist with two fingers.
"What?"
He kisses my palm then directs my hand to his fly.

Songs went with whichever boy it was. "Sugar Magnolia" was Tim, with the line "Rolling in the rushes/down by the riverside." With "Darkness Darkness," I'd picture Philip with his long hair. Hearing "Under My Thumb" there'd be the smell of Jamie's suede jacket.

We hid in the listening rooms during study hall. With a record cover over the door's window, the teacher on duty couldn't look in. I came out flushed and heady and back at the dorm was surprised how red my lips were in the mirror.

One weekend at Simon's brother's, we stayed inside all day with the shades down, in bed, then went out to Store 24 to get some ice cream. He stood at the magazine rack and read through *MAD* while I got butterscotch sauce, craving something sweet.

I could do some things well. Some things I was good at, like math or painting or even sports, but the second a boy put his arm around me, I forgot about wanting to do anything else, which felt like a relief at first until it became like sinking into a muck.

It was different for a girl.

When we were little, the brothers next door tied up our ankles. They held the door of the goat house and wouldn't let us out till we showed them our underpants. Then they'd forget about being after us and when we played whiffle ball, I'd be just as good as them.

Then it got to be different. Just because you have on a short skirt, they yell from the cars, slowing down for a while and if you don't look, they screech off and call you a bitch.

"What's the matter with me?" they say, point-blank.
Or else, "Why won't you go out with me? I'm not asking you to get married," about to get mad.
Or it'd be, trying to be reasonable, in a regular voice, "Listen, I just want to have a good time."
So I'd go because I couldn't think of something to say back that wouldn't be obvious, and if you go out with them, you sort of have to do something.

I sat between Mack and Eddie in the front seat of the pickup. They were having a fight about something. I've a feeling about me.

Certain nights you'd feel a certain surrender, maybe if you'd had wine. The surrender would be forgetting yourself and you'd put your nose to his neck and feel like a squirrel, safe, at rest, in a restful dream. But then you'd start to slip from that and the dark would come in and there'd be a cave. You make out the dim shape of the windows and feel yourself become a cave, filled absolutely with air, or with a sadness that wouldn't stop.

Teenage years. You know just what you're doing and don't see the things that start to get in the way.

Lots of boys, but never two at the same time. One was plenty to keep you in a state. You'd start to see a boy and something would rush over you like a fast storm cloud and you couldn't possibly think of anyone else. Boys took it differently. Their eyes perked up at any little number that walked by. You'd act like you weren't noticing.

The joke was that the school doctor gave out the pill like aspirin. He didn't ask you anything. I was fifteen. We had a picture of him in assembly, holding up an IUD shaped like a T. Most girls were on the pill, if anything, because they couldn't handle a diaphragm. I kept the dial in my top drawer like my mother and thought of her each time I tipped out the yellow tablets in the morning before chapel.

If they were too shy, I'd be more so. Andrew was nervous. We stayed up with his family album, sharing a pack of Old Golds. Before it got light, we turned on the TV. A man was explaining how to plant seedlings. His mouth jerked to the side in a tic. Andrew thought it was a riot and kept imitating him. I laughed to be polite. When we finally dozed off, he dared to put his arm around me but that was it.

You wait till they come to you. With half fright, half swagger, they stand one step down. They dare to touch the button on your coat then lose their nerve and quickly drop their hand so you—you'd do anything for them. You touch their cheek.

The girls sit around in the common room and talk about boys, smoking their heads off.

"What are you complaining about?" says Jill to me when we talk about problems.

"Yeah," says Giddy. "You always have a boyfriend."

I look at them and think, As if.

I thought the worst thing anyone could call you was a cockteaser. So, if you flirted, you had to be prepared to go through with it. Sleeping with someone was perfectly normal once you had done it. You didn't really worry about it. But there were other problems. The problems had to do with something else entirely.

Mack was during the hottest summer ever recorded. We were renting a house on an island with all sorts of other people. No one slept during the heat wave, walking around the house with nothing on which we were used to because of the nude beach. In the living room, Eddie lay on top of a coffee table to cool off. Mack and I, with the bedroom door open for air, sweated and sweated all night.

"I can't take this," he said at 3 A.M. "I'm going for a swim." He and some guys down the hall went to the beach. The heat put me on edge. I sat on a cracked chest by the open window and smoked and smoked till I felt even worse, waiting for something—I guess for him to get back.

One was on a camping trip in Colorado. We zipped our sleeping bags together, the coyotes' hysterical chatter far away. Other couples murmured in other tents. Paul was up before sunrise, starting a fire for breakfast. He wasn't much of a talker in the daytime. At night, his hand leafed about in the hair at my neck.

There'd be times when you overdid it. You'd get carried away. All the next day, you'd be in a total fog, delirious, absent-minded, crossing the street and nearly getting run over.

The more girls a boy has, the better. He has a bright look, having reaped fruits, blooming. He stalks around, sure-shouldered, and you have the feeling he's got more in him, a fatter heart, more stories to tell. For a girl, with each boy it's like a petal gets plucked each time.

Then you start to get tired. You begin to feel diluted, like watered-down stew.

Oliver came skiing with us. We lolled by the fire after everyone had gone to bed. Each creak you'd think was someone coming downstairs. The silver-loop bracelet he gave me had been a present from his girl-friend before.

On vacations, we went skiing, or you'd go south if someone invited you. Some people had apartments in New York that their families hardly ever used. Or summer houses, or older sisters. We always managed to find some place to go.

We made the plan at coffee hour. Simon snuck out and met me at Main Gate after lights-out. We crept to the chapel and spent the night in the balcony. He tasted like onions from a submarine sandwich.

The boys are one of two ways: either they can't sit still or they don't move. In front of the TV, they won't budge. On weekends they play touch football while we sit on the sidelines, picking blades of grass to chew on, and watch. We're always watching them run around. We shiver in the stands, knocking our boots together to keep our toes warm and they whizz across the ice, chopping their sticks around the puck. When they're in the rink, they refuse to look at you, only eyeing each other beneath low helmets. You cheer for them but they don't look up, even if it's a face-off when nothing's happening, even if they're doing drills before any game has started at all.

Dancing under the pink tent, he bent down and whispered in my ear. We slipped away to the lawn on the other side of the hedge. Much later, as he was leaving the buffet with two plates of eggs and sausage, I saw the grass stains on the knees of his white pants.

Tim's was shaped like a banana, with a graceful curve to it. They're all different. Willie's like a bunch of walnuts when nothing was happening, another's as thin as a thin hot dog. But it's like faces; you're never really surprised.

Still, you're not sure what to expect.

I look into his face and he looks back. I look into his eyes and they look back at mine. Then they look down at my mouth so I look at his mouth, then back to his eyes then, backing up, at his whole face. I think, Who? Who are you? His head tilts to one side.
I say, "Who are you?"
"What do you mean?"
"Nothing."
I look at his eyes again, deeper. Can't tell who he is, what he thinks.
"What?" he says. I look at his mouth.
"I'm just wondering," I say and go wandering across his face. Study the chin line. It's shaped like a persimmon.
"Who are you? What are you thinking?"
He says, "What the hell are you talking about?"

Then they get mad after when you say enough is enough. After, when it's easier to explain that you don't want to. You wouldn't dream of saying that maybe you weren't really ready to in the first place.

Gentle Eddie. We waded into the sea, the waves round and plowing in, buffalo-headed, slapping our thighs. I put my arms around his freckled shoulders and he held me up, buoyed by the water, and rocked me like a sea shell.

I had no idea whose party it was, the apartment jampacked, stepping over people in the hallway. The room with the music was practically empty, the bare floor, me in red shoes. This fellow slides onto one knee and takes me around the waist and we rock to jazzy tunes, with my toes pointing heavenward, and waltz and spin and dip to "Smoke Gets in Your Eyes" or "I'll Love You Just for Now." He puts his head to my chest, runs a sweeping hand down my inside thigh and we go loose-limbed and sultry and as smooth as silk and I stamp my red heels and he takes me into a swoon. I never saw him again after that but I thought, I could have loved that one.

You wonder how long you can keep it up. You begin to feel like you're showing through, like a bathroom window that only lets in grey light, the kind you can't see out of.

They keep coming around. Johnny drives up at Easter vacation from Baltimore and I let him in the kitchen with everyone sound asleep. He has friends waiting in the car.
"What are you crazy? It's pouring out there," I say.
"It's okay," he says. "They understand."
So he gets some long kisses from me, against the refrigerator, before he goes because I hate those girls who push away a boy's face as if she were made out of Ivory soap, as if she's that much greater than he is.

The note on my cubby told me to see the headmaster. I had no idea for what. He had received complaints about my amorous displays on the town green. It was Willie that spring. The headmaster told me he didn't care what I did but that Casey Academy had a reputation to uphold in the town. He lowered his glasses on his nose. "We've got twenty acres of woods on this campus," he said. "If you want to smooch with your boyfriend, there are twenty acres for you to do it out of the public eye. You read me?"

Everybody'd get weekend permissions for different places then we'd all go to someone's house whose parents were away. Usually there'd be more boys than girls. We raided the liquor closet and smoked pot at the kitchen table and you'd never know who would end up where, or with whom. There were always disasters. Ceci got bombed and cracked her head open on the bannister and needed stitches. Then there was the time Wendel Blair walked through the picture window at the Lowe's and got slashed to ribbons.

He scared me. In bed, I didn't dare look at him. I lay back with my eyes closed, luxuriating because he knew all sorts of expert angles, his hands never fumbling, going over my whole body, pressing the hair up and off the back of my head, giving an extra hip shove, as if to say *There.* I parted my eyes slightly, keeping the screen of my lashes low because it was too much to look at him, his mouth loose and pink and parted, his eyes looking through my forehead, or kneeling up, looking through my throat. I was ashamed but couldn't look him in the eye.

You wonder about things feeling a little off-kilter. You begin to feel like a piece of pounded veal.

At boarding school, everyone gets depressed. We go in and see the housemother, Mrs. Gunther. She got married when she was eighteen. Mr. Gunther was her high-school sweetheart, the only boyfriend she ever had.

"And you knew you wanted to marry him right off?" we ask her.

She smiles and says, "Yes."

"They always want something from you," says Jill, complaining about her boyfriend.

"Yeah," says Giddy. "You always feel like you have to deliver something."

"You do," says Mrs. Gunther. "Babies."

After sex, you curl up like a shrimp, something deep inside you ruined, slammed in a place that sickens at slamming, and slowly you fill up with an overwhelming sadness, an elusive gaping worry. You don't try to explain it, filled with the knowledge that it's nothing after all, everything filling up finally and absolutely with death. After the briskness of loving, loving stops. And you roll over with death stretched out alongside you like a feather boa, or a snake, light as air, and you . . . you don't even ask for anything or try to say something to him because it's obviously your own damn fault. You haven't been able to—to what? To open your heart. You open your legs but can't, or don't dare anymore, to open your heart.

It starts this way:

You stare into their eyes. They flash like all the stars are out. They look at you seriously, their eyes at a low burn and their hands no matter what starting off shy and with such a gentle touch that the only thing you can do is take that tenderness and let yourself be swept away. When, with one attentive finger they tuck the hair behind your ear, you—

You do everything they want.

Then comes after. After when they don't look at you. They scratch their balls, stare at the ceiling. Or if they do turn, their gaze is altogether changed. They are surprised. They turn casually to look at you, distracted, and get a mild distracted surprise. You're gone. Their blank look tells you that the girl they were fucking is not there anymore. You seem to have disappeared.

CRAIG NOVA

Another Drunk Gambler

I know more secrets than any man I have ever met. My neighbor, Harlow Pearson, was a gambler, although this was never a secret and many people knew about it, even when he was in Congress. He came from New England, was tall, and thin, broad in the chest. I am an old man now. I sit in my house, hearing the shutters banging in the winter wind, and I think of things from a long time ago, like the time when Harlow was a young man in Ipoh. His gambling before Ipoh had been done in European casinos, especially those with chandeliers and chamber music played by musicians in evening clothes, and where there were men who stood around the roulette tables with small notebooks taking down the number on each turn of the wheel. Gambling made Harlow feel as though he were participating in the world. He hated to be a bystander. He tried to explain gambling by saying that it was the difference between walking through an abandoned orchard with a gun and a dog, looking for grouse, and just walking.

Harlow had a houseboy, and his name was Xan Thu. In America he was called Xannie. Xannie's parents had been Asian tribesmen, and in 1950 Xannie was working as a groom at the race track at Ipoh, in Malaysia. He spent his nights there at the racetrack, too, sleeping at the back of a barn, his bed made on bales of hay, on which he stretched out, hearing the rustle of it and feeling the itch through a thin blanket he spread there and smelling the dusty, grassy odor. He took his meals alone, eating while he squatted and leaned against a stall door, or back where he slept. There were other grooms, too, and they found their places to sleep in the barn, each one having a small bag in which there were a few personal things, a book, a photograph, a comb, an extra white shirt, a pair of dark pants.

The man Xannie worked for most often was half French and half Burmese; he was heavy, bald, and had greenish eyes. His skin was smooth, an olive brown color. His suits were made in London, and he wore a large, gold watch that gave the time for any place on the earth. The man's name was Pierre Bouteille. There were times when he couldn't sleep and came to wake Xannie up.

"Are you sleeping?" said Pierre.

"No," said Xannie.

"Have you seen any thieves?" said Pierre.

"No," said Xannie.

Then Pierre said, "Come outside." Xannie went with him, and Pierre gave him an American cigarette, a Camel, and they both smoked, feeling the wet, Malaysian sky, and seeing the clouds floating along, made visible by the sickly light of the city.

Pierre told Xannie about the places he'd been. He said Parisian women and Dutch women, too, would do anything for money, that New York was filled with madmen, that there was a desert in Yugoslavia. America had more food than anyone thought imaginable. There were Malaysians and Burmese who had made money gambling and in restaurants in America, and some had become doctors and university professors. There was a Malaysian pediatrician in Chicago. . . . Xannie smoked a cigarette and thought about piles of food: he saw a cone, high as a volcano, that was made of rice. He smoked the cigarette down to the butt, burning his fingers.

Pierre had a horse he'd bought in the Philippines. It was a good horse with fine breeding and had originally come from Lexington, Kentucky. Pierre was concerned about the horse, afraid that it would be stolen, and he spent nights looking into its stall, saying that there were dishonest people around, and that you had to be on guard against them. Pierre had once gotten drunk in town and fallen asleep in an alley, and when he had woken up, he saw that someone had stolen his shoes. They had been white shoes. When Pierre stood and stared into the stall, Xannie was with him, wanting to hear about the Parisian and Dutch women and the food in America, but he only stared into the dark stall, hearing the restless movement of the horse. When Pierre felt reassured he said, "Let's go for a cigarette."

The horse was worked regularly. One night after the horse had been pushed a little harder than usual by a trainer, Pierre came into the room where Xannie slept and woke him by shaking his leg, and then told Xannie to go into town in a taxi and to bring a veterinarian. It was after one o'clock in the morning and Xannie was to tell the vet that he had a sick dog. Pierre gave Xannie a package of Camels, and Xannie rode in the taxi, with the windows rolled up in a thunderstorm, smoking a cigarette. He brought the veterinarian back, a Frenchman who looked carefully into the taxi and who waited for it to air out before he got into it. When they got back to the track, Xannie was left alone in front of the barn to watch while the veterinarian went back to take a look.

In the morning the horse was gone, but the next night, about one, it was brought back. The veterinarian had taken the animal to his clinic, where he had an X-ray machine and a table for the horse, and soon the doctor was back again to talk to Pierre and to show him the strange black and white photographs of a bone in one of the horse's feet. There was a long, definite crack in it, and the veterinarian told Pierre that one, good hard run, and the bone would break. The veterinarian said the foot would "explode." It was best to sell the animal right away, he said, and then he left.

For a few days Xannie heard nothing, but in the middle of the night Pierre came into his room and asked if he was sleeping and if Xannie had seen any thieves. Xannie noticed that Pierre didn't say "thieves" with the same horror as usual: there was a softness in his tone that verged on the affectionate. Xannie said he hadn't seen any thieves, and then he and Pierre went outside to smoke. Pierre had been drinking, and he weaved from side to side as he said, "You know that goddamned vet blabbed? Everyone knows about the horse. How the hell can I sell him now?"

Pierre hadn't offered a cigarette and Xannie looked at the lights of the city. When Pierre spoke, he gestured with the hand that held the cigarette, and the orange tip of it streaked through the night, making lines that looked like neon tubing, and Xannie watched the bright, curved shapes and listened to Pierre's deep breathing.

"Is the horse insured?" said Xannie.

"Yes," said Pierre.

They both looked at the lights of the city and the grey and yellow clouds above it.

"Is it insured for theft?" said Xannie.

"Yes," said Pierre.

"It would take a stupid thief to steal a lame horse," said Xannie.

"Not everyone knows," said Pierre, "and is it my business to worry about the brains of thieves? They've been known to make a mistake or two. Look."

He pointed to the horizon, at a light there, which was in the direction of the jail in Ipoh. Behind them there was the large, wooden barn, the sense of the animals in it, uneasy in the stalls filled with sawdust.

"It can be arranged," said Xannie.

"I want to know nothing about it," said Pierre.

They stood side by side. After awhile Xannie said, "Six hundred dollars. Ten and twenties."

"Three hundred," said Pierre, "I am not a rich man."

"All right," said Xannie, "Three hundred and fifty and a set of papers for a horse with different breeding. Bad breeding, a different color, but the same age and sex."

Pierre sighed and said, "All right. Would you like a cigarette? A Camel?"

Xannie took one and lighted it, pulling the smoke into his mouth and standing there, watching the lights of the city, the large, lumpy clouds, and thinking, while he heard the horses moving in the stalls behind him, of the Parisian and Dutch women and of the piles of rice in America as big as mountains.

The next day the horse and Xannie were gone.

In 1950, Harlow was in the navy, and he spent some time in Malaysia, at Ipoh. Ipoh is a crowded city, and during the monsoon it rained so hard it made you feel as though you were standing in a shower with your clothes on. The sky turned purple during the monsoon, dark as an ugly bruise. Anyway, one day Harlow was walking down a street that was lined with closed-up shops and warehouses. The shops were shut up with metal doors that rolled down from above the windows, and the warehouses had large padlocks, some of which were as large as a book. At the back and front of each building's roof there were rolls of barbed wire. The warehouses were used on a short-term basis, and could be rented for as little as twenty-four hours at a time. Harlow walked down the street and stopped in front of one that held bicycles. The city was filled with pedestrians, cars, motorcycles, and bicycles, but Harlow had never seen a horse in it. There wasn't enough room in the city for horses. He stopped in front of the bicycle warehouse because he had almost stepped in a pile of horse manure.

The door to the warehouse wasn't locked, and when Harlow pushed it open he saw by the dusky light in the street that bicycles were stacked on the floor and hung from the walls and rafters. When the light from the street hit the wheels of the bicycles they looked delicate, almost fragile, like the spokes of an umbrella without the cloth. After a while, Harlow heard someone say, "Close the door."

Harlow pushed the door shut, and the hinges made a slow, insect-like screech. He didn't close the door completely. When he turned around, an electric light came on, and the bicycles were clearly visible, hanging in the air overhead. At the back of the room, which was narrow and not very long, there was an Asian man, dressed in a pair of dark pants and a white shirt, who was holding the halter of a horse. The horse, even in the dim, yellowish light, was clearly a thoroughbred.

Harlow came a little closer, stepping over the bicycles and looking around the warehouse, but he saw no one else. There was only the uncomfortable, confined horse, the Oriental man, the grey walls of the place, the shiny spokes of the bicycles and the piles of black rubber tires and inner tubes, many of which had been patched so many times as to look exotic, like the coils of some enormous pink and black snake. Harlow and the oriental man didn't stand close together, but they each took a long, frank look into the other's face, and while they stood there, it became clear that what had begun as an intrusion or perhaps even a burglary had ended, for a while anyway, as a limited partnership.

Harlow introduced himself. The man said his name was Xan Thu. Harlow ran his hand over the horse's cheek, along the muscled, arched neck, and down its chest.

"Where did you get the horse?" said Harlow.

Xannie blinked at him.

"Is it stolen?" said Harlow.

"No," said Xannie, "it's not hot. But, in all honesty, I'd have to say that it's a little warm."

"Hmmm," said Harlow, "how warm?"

Xannie blinked again.

"Let's put it this way," said Harlow, "do you think anyone at the track here would recognize it?"

"Anything is possible," said Xannie.

Harlow looked over the horse a little more. When he faced Xannie again he found on a crate next to Xannie's elbow a piece of newsprint. It hadn't been there before, and when Harlow picked it up he saw it was a past performance sheet, two months old, that had come from a track in Manila. It had been neatly folded, but was still water marked and yellowed. In the center, circled with a lead pencil, there was a chart for a three year old horse that in fifteen starts had showed in three, placed in three, and won nine. Harlow recognized the breeding.

"What do you say," said Harlow, "why don't we run him at the track here?"

"There's the problem of being recognized," said Xannie.

"We can fix that," said Harlow. "Let's change the color."

"Yes," said Xannie, looking at the horse. "Let's change the color."

"What's the penalty for stealing a horse here?" said Harlow.

Xannie said it depended on the owner. Some had been known to take the law into their own hands. Both Harlow and Xannie had seen the tattooed gangsters in the city, some of whom had a stump instead of a finger, the digit given to a hoodlum as a gesture of loyalty. Harlow looked over the horse again, read the performance chart, took another frank look at Xannie's face.

"I wouldn't want to have any trouble," said Harlow.

"No," said Xannie, "isn't that why dyeing the horse is a good idea?"

Harlow sighed and said he guessed it was. Then he went out of the warehouse and down the street to the avenue, where he took a taxi to a grocery. The taxi waited while Harlow bought ten packages of black Rit dye, two natural sponges, and a stack of towels. Then he got back into the taxi. When they were close to the warehouse, Harlow told the driver to let him off on the corner, and, as he walked along the street, he looked over his shoulder.

Xannie and Harlow found a galvanized tub and they filled it with water. They mixed in the dye, a little at a time, and while they stirred it around, they looked into one another's face, each thinking about the odds on the day they'd race the horse. Then they went to work, neither one of them saying a word about the color, since both of them had already decided on grey.

Harlow dipped a sponge into the tub and tried it against the horse's withers, and Xannie used one of the towels to rub the place dry. They stood back and admired the sickly, grey black color. Then Xannie took the other sponge and they went to work, rubbing the dye into the horse's coat, drying it, and standing back to judge the change. When they were done the horse was covered with the doubt-inspiring color, which was suggestive of bad breeding and lousy nerves. More than anything else, it was the color of a weathered headstone in a New England cemetery.

Both Xannie and Harlow looked as though they were wearing skin tight gloves that went up to the middle of the forearm. They held their hands out, away from their clothes and felt the dye as it dried on their skin and left it feeling dusty.

"That," Xannie said, pointing one of his stained hands at the horse, "is my ticket out of here. Thank God. I've heard there are piles of rice in America and that there is a Malaysian pediatrician in Chicago. Is this true?"

"I guess so," said Harlow. "I don't know much about doctors, though. It could be true. Is there some place to wash?"

Xannie pointed to the back of the warehouse, and when Harlow walked to the cold water tap there and turned it on, Xannie said, "And what about Dutch and Parisian women? What will they do for money?" but Harlow had already turned the tap on, and didn't hear. He washed his hands and arms, seeing the white, cold lather turn grey and then swirl down the stone sink.

When Harlow came back, he found another piece of paper on the same upturned box. This paper was heavier, and the printing was better, and there was a fine scroll around the edges of it. It looked a little like a certificate of stock, and at the top there was a description of a grey, three year old thoroughbred. The breeding was given, too, and it didn't look very distinguished.

"Where did you get the papers?" said Harlow.

Xannie blinked.

"They came from a long way away," said Xannie. "It's safe for us to use them here."

They put the empty packages of dye into the sack Harlow had used to bring them from the store. Xannie said he'd burn them in the alley. It was still early in the day, and Harlow said he'd get to the track and look around for a jockey. Then he went back to the corner and found a taxi.

In the evening, two hours after the last race, Harlow returned with Harry Laue. He was dark, overweight for a jockey, and a little drunk. Harlow opened the door of the warehouse, and Laue stepped in. Xannie was feeding the horse from a bucket. There were some carrots, too, and Xannie held them up, one at a time, and pushed them between the opened lips, and the regular, moving, and faintly curved teeth. Laue stepped up to the animal, went over it, and said to himself, as he touched the muscles, the neck, the legs of the thing. "Well, well, well. . . ."

"What do you think?" said Harlow.

"I got two thousand in the bank," said Laue. "I'm getting it out." Then Laue went back to the horse, his small, calloused hands going over it again, and from the dim place where he bent down, Harlow and Xannie heard his half-sober chuckling. "That two thousand was for leaving town. Can you imagine what it would be like to be trapped here?" He went back to chuckling again, his fingers now carefully going over the horse's legs.

Two days later the horse was entered in the eighth race at Ipoh. Harlow and Xannie walked around the track, feeling the excitement in the air. They drank scotch and soda in tall glasses. Xannie had a pair of dark glasses, and he took them from his pocket and put them on and looked around, and then took them off, fiddling with them while he drank long swallows. Xannie had three hundred dollars and Harlow had nine hundred. They found two chairs and sat in front of the tote board, their faces blank and bored. When the first prices went up the horse was listed at fifty to one, and when, before the race, the price went to ninety-nine to one, Harlow and Xannie bought two more drinks and went to the windows, where there were long lines of people, Malaysian, Chinese, even English and Americans, not to mention a lot of French, all figuring on forms with a bit of pencil and looking over their shoulders through the smoky air, seemingly expecting that someone or at least some news was coming up behind them.

Harlow and Xannie waited in separate lines. Harlow stood in his dress whites, looking clean and young among the other bettors. At the side of the windows there were people lying on the ground or leaning against the wooden planks of a fence there. Many of them had only one leg, and they sat with their crutches (the top covered with a rag) leaning behind them, and there was a woman who had a leg so large that it must have weighed as much as the rest of her. There were children there too, and two of them were blind. They sat together touching each other's face and smiling. There were men who had no teeth, and one who had a long, white scar that ran from his hairline to the top of his shirt. It looked as though someone had taken a brush axe and had tried to cut him in half with it. He sat with the others at the fence and watched those who collected on a winning ticket.

Xannie came to the window, and stood opposite the clerk. He took the three hundred dollars from his pocket, and then stood there for a moment. The clerk told him to hurry up. Xannie first put only ten dollars onto the counter, but then he hesitated, wondering if there was any possibility that the horse's leg would hold up for the entire race. It was problematical: the vet was good with horses and was usually right about things like this, but then there was the possibility that the leg might hold up until the horse had crossed the finish line. And what then? Xannie stood at the counter for a moment. Then he split the three hundred dollars in half, betting a hundred and fifty on the horse and putting the rest in his pocket, patting it there as he did so and keeping his eyes on the men and women who leaned against the fence.

Before the race, as the horses were led to the gate, the grey being put into the first position, Xannie said, "What if the horse wins? How are we going to get the cash out of here?"

Harlow opened the jacket of his dress whites and inside there was a service .45 automatic in a holster, which was worn high and to one side. Harlow left his jacket unbuttoned, not because he cared so much about the pistol showing, but because he wanted to be able to get to it easily.

It seemed as though the grey horse came out of the gate a length ahead. And at a distance, as the horses ran from the gate along the long backstretch of the six furlong race, Harlow and Xannie saw the odd, sea-like and gentle movement of the horse as it seemed to stretch out and lift off the track a little, moving faster than even they had hoped. Before the turn it was five lengths ahead and still gaining, its tail out and flying, its mane out like a flag, too, as Laue tried to rein the grey horse back a little, since even at Ipoh there were some standards to worry about.

In the turn it looked as though the horse was going too fast to make it. More than anything else, there seemed to be a momentary straightness in its path, a tangent that, if followed, would take it to the fence. The people in the stands were already standing and screaming, but, in the moment the horse seemed to step out from the path it should take, the screams changed to a long, deep groan. The horse continued to go straight, although not for long. It dipped a shoulder and then turned a quick, high cartwheel, in which Laue and his tack and the horse's mane and tail blended together. The circular motion of the animal and the color of it appeared for the briefest instant, like a puff of smoke from an explosion, a light, streaming collection of grey on grey, with a boot, a stirrup, a hand, or a bit of silk, a sharp hoof flashing into the clear air and then disappearing again into the confusion. The horse hit the ground, rolled over, and tried to get up, but didn't.

Harlow walked through the crowd, and Xannie hung onto his jacket, which pulled him along until they came to the rail. Harlow jumped over and began running across the soft, loamy soil of the track, which was deep and made the long run seem dream-like and difficult. Harlow crossed the infield grass, and as he went, the people from the stands came behind him, the crowd of them spreading into a large V.

Laue was standing and looking at the horse when Harlow arrived, and for a moment, while the horse pawed the ground and tried to get up, falling each time it put weight on the broken leg, its head rising and sinking with the effort and the pain, Harlow and Laue looked at each other until Laue said, "It'll have to be killed." And as Xannie came running ahead of the crowd which streamed across the infield, as the stewards drove in a Chevrolet pick-up truck from the side of the track where the grandstand was, Harlow took the .45 pistol from under his coat and stood before the horse and shot it between the eyes, once, and then again, and the horse gently and slowly put its nose onto the soft loam of the track. As the horse lay still, the crowd arrived, Xannie at its head.

Xannie stood on the side of the horse opposite Harlow and wailed, throwing his arms into the air, crying openly. Harlow stood with blood on his dress whites, still holding the pistol. People crowded around him, looked at the horse and then were pushed aside by others, who were talking quickly and screeching, gesticulating, showing with their hands how the horse had gone straight and then turned end over end. Xannie screamed at Harlow, now speaking not English but a Chinese or Malaysian dialect Harlow understood not at all. A young man in a blue work shirt with a tie said to Harlow, "He wants the gun."

"Why?" said Harlow.

The young man spoke so quickly that his cheeks seemed to flutter.

"He wants to shoot himself," said the man in the workshirt.

Xannie stood on the other side of the horse, one hand out, the other making gestures toward his open palm. The crowd around the horse made a sea-like muttering, a slight, endless babble. Harlow put the pistol into the holster and said, "No. Tell him to come along."

Xannie stood on the other side of the horse, palm still out, his cheeks marked with tears.

"All right," said Harlow, "Tell him I'll take him to America."

The man in the work shirt shouted, opening his mouth so wide as to make a web of his cheek when he spoke. Xannie stared at Harlow. Then he spoke in the language Harlow didn't understand.

"What's that?" said Harlow.

"He wants to know if it will be by boat or airplane," said the man in the workshirt.

Xannie and Harlow stared at one another, and as they did so, with the crowd around them, it began to rain. The sky was purplish, dark. The clouds had no texture. Instead they came in one piece, only marked by the perfect, silver lines of rain. Harlow and Xannie both stared at the horse, and in the heavy rain they saw that the water running from it was getting a little dark, and that when it streamed into the red soil of the track, it left black marks that reminded Harlow of a woman's cheeks when her mascara began to run. The stewards began to look at it, too. Then Xannie climbed over the horse and said, in his crisp, accented English, "It's all right. I'll take the boat."

They turned and pushed through the crowd and walked through the heavy mud of the track, their feet becoming large and misshapen with it, their fingers and knees still trembling as they went toward the greyish grandstand with its web-like supports, and as they went by the rail there was a man standing against it. He was bald, heavy, wore a dark suit made in England, and his skin was an olive-brown. His eyes were green. He was a little drunk and he had been crying, but now he said, his voice watery and sibilant, while looking at Xannie, "Carrés d'agneau, Truites de rivière de grillées, Homard à la crème. L'argent pour les femmes."

Roast young lamb, grilled trout, lobsters in cream. Money for the women.

They continued walking, and the crowd closed in around them, obscuring the track, the grass of it, the white rail, and making a sound like running water, but as they went, there still came over the noise of the crowd the steady, half drunk voice of Pierre, as he shouted, "Salmon glacé à la Parisienne!"

Glazed salmon!

"Wait a minute," said Xannie, and then he went to the rail, where Pierre stood. Xannie said, "I'll tell you if there is a Malaysian pediatrician in Chicago."

Pierre nodded, and put his arms around Xannie, hugged him, and then gave Xannie a polite, Gallic kiss on each cheek.

"Who's he?" said Harlow.

"Another drunk gambler," said Xannie.

Then they walked along the track, passing the high, dark stands, the supports of them, the umbrella-like gussets at the top of each post, the almost gloomy space under the roof, where people sat, wearing dark glasses and waiting for the next race to begin, and they passed, too, the blind children who played with the features of one another's face.

I first heard this story years ago, when I was having dinner at Harlow's house. Xannie hadn't been in the country long, and Harlow had moved into his father's house and brought Xannie to live there. Harlow was already inviting to dinner some local political . . . allies, and one of them asked Xannie what he would have done if Harlow had passed over the pistol, but Xannie only blinked at the man and then said, "Don't you think it's nice here in America?"

After a while I was able to find a time to be alone with Xannie and then I asked him in a mild, friendly, and sympathetic tone, how long he had waited in the warehouse for Harlow to come along.

Xannie stared at me full in the face and said, "Have you ever been to Malaysia?"

It came out slowly. Every now and then, when I saw Xannie, he'd mention Pierre Bouteille, the stables, the x-rays of the horse, the papers. He knew that once he had the horse, all he had to do was to sit tight: the right American would come along. There were a lot of us in Ipoh at the time. I don't know why. And, of course, no American can resist fixing a horse race. We're fascinated by these things. In the Orient, Xannie said, things are more ordinary. He once had a ticket for a horse winning a race in Malaysia, and when he went to cash it the clerk slammed the window shut, saying that although Xannie had the winning ticket, the horse wasn't supposed to win. Xannie had almost formed a partnership with an enlisted man from Mt. Sterling, Kentucky, but at the last moment he backed out, since the enlisted man didn't look like he had the money for a trip to America. Xannie waited for Harlow to put his head in the door.

Xannie had been certain, too, that no American in the world would let him use the pistol on himself. He had been waiting for the moment when an American would stop him. Xannie had banked on it. If you figured this out, he became your friend.

Norman Rush

Instruments of Seduction

The name she was unable to remember was torturing her. She kept
coming up with Bechamel, which was ridiculously wrong yet somehow
close. It was important to her that she remember. A thing in a book by
this man lay at the heart of her secret career as a seducer of men—three
hundred and twelve of them. She was a seducer, not a seductress. The
male form of the term was active. A seductress was merely someone who
was seductive and who might or might not be awarded a victory. But a
seducer was a professional, a worker, and somehow a record of success
was embedded in the term. "Seducer" sounded like a credential. Game
was afoot tonight. Remembering the name was part of preparation. She
had always prepared before tests.

Male or female, you couldn't be considered a seducer if you were
below a certain age, had great natural beauty, or if you lacked a theory of
what you were doing. Her body of theory began with a scene in the book
she was feeling the impulse to reread. The book's title was lost in the
mists of time. As she remembered the scene, a doctor and perhaps the
woman of the house are involved together in some emergency lifesaving
operation. The woman has to assist. The setting is an apartment in
Europe, in a city. The woman is not attractive. The doctor is. There has
been shelling or an accident. The characters are disparate in every way
and would never normally be appropriate for one another. The operation
is described in upsetting detail. It's touch and go. When it's over, the
doctor and the woman fall into one another's arms—to their own surprise. Some fierce tropism compels them. Afterward they part, never to
follow up. The book was from the French. She removed the Atmos clock
from the living room mantel and took it to the pantry to get it out of
sight.

The scene had been like a flashbulb going off. She had realized that, in
all her seductions up to that point, she had been crudely and intuitively
using the principle that the scene made explicit. Putting it bluntly, a
certain atmosphere of allusion to death, death fear, death threats, mystery pointing to death, was, in the right hands, erotic, and could lead to a
bingo. Of course, that was hardly all there was to it. The subject of what
conditions conduce—that was her word for it—to achieving a bingo, was
immense. One thing, it was never safe to roll your *r*'s. She thought,
Everything counts: chiaroscuro, no giant clocks in evidence and no wrist-

watches either, music or its absence, what they can assume about privacy and *le futur.* That was critical. You had to help them intuit you were acting from appetite, like a man, and that when it was over you would be yourself and not transformed before their eyes into a love-leech, a limbless tube of longing. You had to convince them that what was to come was, no question about it, a transgression, but that for you it was about at the level of eating between meals.

She was almost fifty. For a woman, she was old to be a seducer. The truth was that she had been on the verge of closing up shop. The corner of Bergen County they lived in was scorched earth, pretty much. Then Frank had been offered a contract to advise African governments on dental care systems. They had come to Africa for two years.

In Botswana, where they were based, everything was unbelievably conducive. Frank was off in the bush or advising as far away as Lusaka or Gwelo for days and sometimes weeks at a time. So there was space. She could select. Gaborone was comfortable enough. And it was full of transient men: consultants, contractors, travelers of all kinds, seekers. Embassy men were assigned for two-year tours and knew they were going to be rotated away from the scene of the crime sooner rather than later. Wives were often absent. Either they were slow to arrive or they were incessantly away on rest and recreation in the United States or the Republic of South Africa. For expatriate men, the local women were a question mark. Venereal disease was pandemic and local attitudes toward birth control came close to being surreal. She had abstained from Batswana men. She knew why. The very attractive ones seemed hard to get at. There was a feeling of danger in the proposition, probably irrational. The surplus of more familiar white types was a simple fact. In any case, there was still time. This place had been designed with her in mind. The furniture the government provided even looked like it came from a bordello. And Botswana was unnerving in some overall way there was only one word for: conducive. The country depended on copper and diamonds. Copper prices were sinking. There were too many diamonds of the wrong kind. Development projects were going badly and making people look bad, which made them nervous and susceptible. What was there to do at night? There was only one movie house in town. The movies came via South Africa and were censored to a fare-thee-well—no nudity, no blue language. She suspected that for American men the kind of heavyhanded dummkopf censorship they sat through at the Capitol Cinema was in fact stimulating. Frank was getting United States Government money, which made them semiofficial. She had to admit there was fun in foiling the eyes and ears of the embassy network. She would hate to leave.

Only one thing was sad. There was no one she could tell about her life. She had managed to have a remarkable life. She was ethical. She never brought Frank up or implied that Frank was the cause in any way of what she chose to do. Nor would she ever seduce a man who could conceivably be a recurrent part of Frank's life or sphere. She assumed feminists would hate her life if they knew. She would like to talk to feminists about vocation, about goal-setting, about using one's mind, about nerve and strength. Frank's ignorance was one of her feats. How many women could do what she had done? She was modestly endowed and now she was even old. She was selective. Sometimes she felt she would like to tell Frank, when it was really over, and see what he said. She would sometimes let herself think he would be proud, in a way, or that he could be convinced he should be. There was no one she could tell. Their daughter was a cow and a Lutheran. Her gentleman was late. She went into the pantry to check the time.

For this evening's adventure she was perhaps a little too high-priestess, but the man she was expecting was not a subtle person. She was wearing a narrowly-cut white silk caftan, a seed-pod necklace, and sandals. The symbolism was a little crude: silk, the ultra-civilized material, over the primitive straight-off-the-bush necklace. Men liked to feel things through silk. But she wore silk as much for herself as for the gentlemen. Silk energized her. She loved the feeling of silk being slid up the backs of her legs. Her nape hairs rose a little as she thought about it. She had her hair up, in a loose, flat bun. She was ringless. She had put on and then taken off her scarab ring. Tonight she wanted the feeling that bare hands and bare feet would give. She would ease off her sandals at the right moment. She knew she was giving up a proven piece of business—idly taking off her ring when the occasion reached a certain centigrade. Men saw it subliminally as taking off a wedding ring and as the first act of undressing. She had worked hard on her feet. She had lined her armpits with tissue which would stay just until the doorbell rang. With medical gentlemen, hygiene was a fetish. She was expecting a doctor. Her breath was immaculate. She was proud of her teeth, but then she was married to a dentist. She thought about the Danish surgeon who brought his own boiled-water ice cubes to cocktail parties. She had some bottled water in the refrigerator, just in case it was indicated.

Her gentleman was due and overdue. Everything was optimal. There was a firm crossbreeze. The sightlines were nice. From where they would be sitting they would look out at a little pad of healthy lawn, the blank wall of the inner court, and the foliage of the tree whose blooms still looked to her like scrambled eggs. It would be self-evident that they would be private here. The blinds were drawn. Everything was secure and cool. Off the hall leading to the bathroom, the door to the bedroom stood open. The bedroom was clearly a working bedroom, not taboo, with a night light on and an oscillating fan performing on low. He would sit on leather; she would sit half-facing, where she could reach the bar trolley, on sheepskin, her feet on a jennet-skin karosse. He should sit in the leather chair because it was regal but uncomfortable. You would want to lie down. She would be in a slightly more reclining mode. Sunset was on. Where was her gentleman? The light was past its peak.

The doorbell rang. Be superb, she thought.

The doctor looked exhausted. He was greyfaced. Also, he was older than the image of him she had been entertaining. But he was all right. He had nice hair. He was fit. He might be part Indian, with those cheekbones and being from Vancouver. Flats were never a mistake. He was not tall. He was slim.

She led him in. He was wearing one of the cheaper safari suits, with the S-for-something embroidery on the left breast pocket. He had come straight from work, which was in her favor.

When she had him seated, she said, "Two slight catastrophes to report, doctor. One is that you're going to have to eat appetizers from my own hand. As the British say, my help are gone. My cook and my maid are sisters. Their aunt died. For the second time, actually. Tebogo is forgetful. In any case, they're in Mochudi for a few days and I'm alone. Frank won't be home until Sunday. *And,* the Webers are off for tonight. They can't come. We're on our own. I hope we can cope."

He smiled weakly. The man was exhausted.

She said, "But a cool drink, quick, wouldn't you say? What would you like? I have everything."

He said it should be anything nonalcoholic, any kind of juice would be good. She could see work coming. He went to wash up.

He took his time in the bathroom, which was normally a good sign. He looked almost crisp when he came back, but something was the matter. She would have to extract it.

He accepted iced rooibos tea. She poured Bombay gin over crushed ice for herself. Men noticed what you drank. This man was not strong. She was going to have to underplay.

She presented the appetizers, which were genius. You could get through a week on her collations if you needed to, or you could have a few select tastes and go on to gorge elsewhere with no one the wiser. But you would remember every bite. She said "You might like these. These chunks are bream fillet, poached, from Lake Ngami. No bones. Vinaigrette. They had just started getting these down here on a regular basis on ice about a year ago. AID had a lot of money in the Lake Ngami fishery project. Then the drought struck, and Lake Ngami, poof, it's a damp spot in the desert. This is real Parma ham. I nearly had to kill someone to get it. The cashews are a little on the tangy side. That's the way they like them in Mozambique, apparently. They're good."

He ate a little, sticking to mainstream items like the gouda cheese cubes, she was sorry to see. Then he brought up the climate, which made her writhe. It was something to be curtailed. It led the mind homeward. It was one of the three deadly *W*'s: weather, wife, and where to eat—in this country, where not to eat. She feigned sympathy. He was saying he was from British Columbia so it was to be expected that it would take some doing for him to adjust to the dry heat and the dust. He said he had to remind himself that he'd only been here four months and that ultimately his mucous membrane system was supposed to adapt. But he said he was finding it wearing. Lately he was dreaming about rain. A lot, he said.

Good! she thought. "Would you like to see my tokoloshi?" she asked, crossing her legs.

He stopped chewing. She warned herself not to be reckless.

"Dream animals!," she said. "Little effigies. I collect them. The Bushmen carve them out of softwood. They use them as symbols of evil in some ceremony they do. They're turning up along with all the other Bushman artifacts, the puberty aprons and so on, in the craft shops. Let me show you."

She got two tokoloshi from a cabinet.

"They call these the evil creatures who come to you at night in dreams. What you see when you look casually is this manlike figure with what looks like the head of a fox or rabbit or zebra, at first glance. But look at the clothing. Doesn't this look like a clerical jacket? The collar shape? They're all like that. And look closely at the animal. It's actually a spotted jackal, the most despised animal there is because of its taste for carrion. Now look in front at this funny little tablet that looks like a huge belt buckle with these x-shapes burned into it. My theory is that it's a Bushman version of the Union Jack. If you notice on this one, the being is wearing a funny belt. It looks like a cartridge belt to me. Some of the tokoloshi are smoking these removable pipes. White tourists buy these things and think they're cute. I think each one is a carved insult to the West. And we buy loads of them. I do. The black areas like the jacket are done by charring the wood with hot nails and things."

He handled the carvings dutifully and then gave them back to her. He murmured that they were interesting.

He took more tea. She stood the tokoloshi on an end table halfway across the room, facing them. He began contemplating them, sipping his tea minutely. Time was passing. She had various mottoes she used on herself. One was: Inside every suit and tie is a naked man trying to get out. She knew they were stupid, but they helped. He was still in the grip of whatever was bothering him.

"I have something that might interest you," she said. She went to the cabinet again and returned with a jackal-fur wallet, which she set down on the coffee table in front of him. "This is a fortune-telling kit the witch doctors use. It has odd things inside it." He merely looked at it.

"Look inside it," she said.

He picked it up reluctantly and held it in his hand, making a face. He was thinking it was unsanitary. She was in danger of becoming impatient. The wallet actually was slightly fetid, but so what? It was an organic thing. It was old.

She reached over and guided him to open and empty the wallet, touching his hands. He studied the array of bones and pebbles on the tabletop. Some of the pebbles were painted or stained. The bones were knucklebones, probably opossum, she told him, after he showed no interest in trying to guess what they were. She had made it her business to learn a fair amount about Tswana divination practices, but he wasn't asking. He moved the objects around listlessly.

She lit a candle, though she felt it was technically premature. It would give him something else to stare at if he wanted to and at least he would be staring in her direction, more or less.

The next segment was going to be taxing. The pace needed to be meditative. She was fighting impatience.

She said, "Africa is so strange. You haven't been here long, but you'll see. We come here as . . . bearers of science, the scientific attitude. Even the dependents do, always telling the help about nutrition and weaning and that kind of thing.

"Science so much defines us. One wants to be scientific, or at least not *un*scientific. Science is our religion, in a way. Or at least you begin to feel it is. I've been here nineteen months . . ."

He said something. Was she losing her hearing or was the man just unable to project? He had said something about noticing that the tokoloshi weren't carrying hypodermic needles. He was making the point, she guessed, that the Batswana didn't reject Western medicine. He said something further about their attachment to injections, how they felt you weren't actually treating them unless they could have an injection, how they seemed to love injections. She would have to adapt to a certain lag in this man's responses. I am tiring, she thought.

She tried again, edging her chair closer to his. "Of course, your world is different. You're more insulated, at the Ministry, where everyone is a scientist of sorts. You're immersed in science. That world is . . . safer. Are you following me?"

He said he wasn't sure that he was.

"What I guess I mean is that one gets to want to really *uphold* science. Because the culture here is so much the opposite. So relentlessly so. You resist. But then the first thing you know, very peculiar things start happening to you. Or you talk to some of the old settler types, whites, educated people from the protectorate days who decided to stay on as citizens, before the government made that such an obstacle course. The white settlers are worse than your everyday Batswana. They accept everything supernatural, almost. At first you dismiss it as a pose."

She knew it was strictly pro forma, but she offered him cigarettes from the caddy. He declined. There was no way she could smoke, then. Nothing tonight was going to be easy. Bechamel was right next door to the name she was trying to remember: why couldn't she get it?

"But it isn't a pose," she said. "Their experiences have changed them utterly. There is so much witchcraft. It's called *muti*. It's so routine. It wasn't so long ago that if you were going to open a business you'd go to the witch doctor for good luck rites with human body parts as ingredients. A little something to tuck under the cornerstone of your bottle store. People are still being killed for their parts. It might be a windpipe or whatever. It's still going on. Sometimes they dump the body onto the railroad tracks after they've taken what they need, for the train to grind up and disguise. Recently they caught somebody that way. The killers threw this body on the track but the train was late. They try to keep it out of the paper, I know that for a fact. But it's still happening. An undertow."

She worked her feet out of her sandals. Normally she would do one and let an intriguing gap fall before doing the other. She scratched an instep on an ankle.

She said, "I know a girl who's teaching in the government secondary in Bobonong who tells me what a hard time the matron is having getting the girls to sleep with their heads out of the covers. It seems they're afraid of *bad women* who roam around at night, who'll scratch their faces. These are women called *baloi* who go around naked, wearing only a little belt made out of human neckbones. Naturally, anyone would say what a fantasy this is. Childish.

"But I really did once see a naked woman dodging around near some rondavels late one night, out near Mosimane. It was only a glimpse. No doubt it was innocent. But she did have something white and shimmering around her waist. We were driving past. You begin to wonder."

She waited. He was silent.

"Something's bothering you," she said.

He denied it.

She said, "At any rate, don't you think it's interesting that there are no women members of the so-called traditional doctor's association? I know a member, what an oaf! I think it's a smoke screen association. They want you to think they're just a benign bunch of herbalists trying out one thing or another a lot of which ought to be in the regular pharmacopeia if only white medical people weren't so narrow-minded. They come to seminars all jolly and humble. But if you talk to the Batswana, you know that it's the women, the witches, who are the really potent ones."

Still he was silent.

"Something's happened, hasn't it? To upset you. If it's anything I've said, please tell me." A maternal tone could be death. She was flirting with failure.

He denied that she was responsible in any way. It seemed sincere. He was going inward again, right before her eyes. She had a code name for failures. She called them case studies. Her attitude was that every failure could be made to yield something of value for the future. And it was true. Some of her best material, anecdotes, references to things, aphrodisiana of all kinds, had come from case studies. The cave paintings at Gargas, in Spain, of mutilated hands . . . handprints, not paintings . . . stencils of hundreds of hands with joints and fingers missing. Archaeologists were totally at odds as to what all that meant. One case study had yielded the story of fat women in Durban buying tainted meat from butchers so as to contract tapeworms for weight loss purposes. As a case study, if it came to that, tonight looked unpromising. But you could never tell. She had an image for case studies: a grave robber, weary, exhausted, reaching down into some charnel mass and pulling up some lovely ancient sword somehow miraculously still keen that had been overlooked. She could name case studies that were more precious to her than bingoes she could describe.

She had one quiver left. She meant arrow. She hated using it.

She could oppose her silence to his until he broke. It was difficult to get right. It ran counter to being a host, being a woman, and to her own nature. The silence had to be special, not wounded, receptive, with a spine to it, maternal, in fact.

She declared silence. Slow moments passed.

He stirred. His lips stirred. He got up and began pacing.

He said, "You're right." Then for a long time he said nothing, still pacing.

"You read my mind!" he said. "Last night I had an experience . . . I still . . . it's still upsetting. I shouldn't have come, I guess."

She felt sorry for him. He had just the slightest speech defect, which showed up in noticeable hesitations. This was sad.

"Please tell me about it," she said perfectly.

He paced more, then halted near the candle and stared at it.

"I hardly drink," he said. "Last night was an exception. Phoning home to Vancouver started it, domestic nonsense. I won't go into that. They don't understand. No point in going into it. I went out. I went drinking. One of the hotel bars, where Africans go. I began drinking. I was drinking and buying drinks for some of the locals. I drank quite a bit.

"All right. These fellows are clever. Bit by bit I am being taken over by one, this one fellow, George. I can't explain it. I didn't like him. He took me over. That is, I notice I'm paying for drinks but this fellow's passing them on to whomever he chooses, his friends. But I'm buying. But I have no say.

"We're in a corner booth. It's dark and loud, as usual. This fellow, his head was shaved, he was strong-looking. He spoke good English, though. Originally, I'd liked talking to him, I think. They flatter you. He was a combination of rough and smooth. Now he was working me. He was a refugee from South Africa, that always starts up your sympathy. Terrible breath, though. I was getting a feeling of something being off about the ratio between the number of drinks and what I was laying out. I think he was taking something in transit.

"I wanted to do the buying. I took exception. All right. Remember that they have me wedged in. That was stupid, but I was, I allowed it. Then I said I was going to stop buying. George didn't like it. This man had a following. I realized they were forming a cordon, blocking us in. Gradually it got nasty. Why wouldn't I keep buying drinks, didn't I have money, what was my job, didn't the Ministry pay expatriates enough to buy a few drinks? So on ad nauseam."

His color was coming back. He picked up a cocktail napkin and touched at his forehead.

He was looking straight at her now. He said, "You don't know what the African bars are like. Pandemonium. I was sealed off. As I say, his friends were all around.

"Then it was all about apartheid. I said I was Canadian. Then it was about Canada the lackey of America the supporter of apartheid. I'm not political. I was scared. All right. When I tell him I'm really through buying drinks he asks me how much money have I got left, exactly. I tell him again that I'm through buying drinks. He says not to worry, he'll sell me something instead. All right. I knew I was down to about ten pula. And I had dug in on buying drinks, the way you will when you've had a few too many. No more buying drinks, that was decided. But he was determined to get my money, I could damned well see that.

"He said he would sell me something I'd be very glad to know. Information. All right. So then comes a long runaround on what kind of information. Remember that he's pretty well three sheets to the wind himself. It was information I would be glad to have as a doctor, he said.

"Well, the upshot here was that this is what I proposed, so as not to seem totally stupid and taken. I would put all my money down on the table in front of me. I took out my wallet and made sure he could see that what I put down was all of it, about ten pula, change and everything. All right. And I would keep the money under the palm of my hand. And he would whisper the information to me and if I thought it was a fair trade I would just lift my hand. Of course, this was all just facesaving on my part so as not to just hand over my money to a thug. And don't think I wasn't well aware it might be a good idea at this stage of things to be seen getting rid of any cash I had, just to avoid being knocked down on the way to my car."

"This is a wonderful story," she said spontaneously, immediately regretting it.

"It isn't a story," he said.

"You know what I mean," she said. "I mean, since I see you standing here safe and sound I can assume the ending isn't a tragedy. But please continue. Really."

"In any event. There we are. There was more back and forth over what kind of information this was. Finally he says it's not only something a doctor would be glad of. He is going to tell me the secret of how they are going to make the revolution in South Africa, a secret plan. An actual plan.

"God knows I have no brief for white South Africans. I know a few professionally, doctors. Medicine down there is basically about up to 1950, by our standards, despite all this veneer of the heart transplants. But the doctors I know seem to be decent. Some of them hate the system and will say so.

"I go along. Empty my wallet, cover the money with my hand.

"Here's what he says. They had a sure way to drive out the whites. It was a new plan and was sure to succeed. It would succeed because they, meaning the blacks, could bring it about with only a handful of men. He said that the Boers had won for all time if the revolution meant waiting for small groups to grow into bands and then into units, batallions and so on, into armies that would fight the Boers. The Boers were too intelligent and had too much power. They had corrupted too many of the blacks. The blacks were divided. There were too many spies for the Boers among them. The plan he would tell me would take less than a hundred men.

"Then he asked me, if he could tell me such a plan would it be worth the ten pula. Would I agree that it would? I said yes."

"This is extraordinary!" she said. *Duhamel!,* she thought, triumphant. The name had come back to her: *Georges Duhamel.* She could almost see the print. She was so grateful.

"Exciting!" she said, gratitude in her voice.

He was swearing. "Well, this is what he says. He leans over, whispers. The plan is simple. The plan is to assemble a shock force, he called it. Black people who are willing to give their lives. And this is all they do: *they kill doctors.* That's it! They start off with a large first wave, before the government can do anything to protect doctors. They simply kill doctors, as many as they can. They kill them at home, in their offices, in hospitals, in the street. You can get the name of every doctor in South Africa through the phone book. Whites need doctors, without doctors they think they are already dying, he says. Blacks in South Africa have no doctors to speak of anyway, especially in the homelands where they are all being herded to die in droves. Blacks are dying of the system every day regardless, he says. But whites would scream. They would rush like cattle to the airports, screaming. They would stream out of the country. The planes from Smuts would be jammed full. After the first strike, you would continue, taking them by ones and twos. The doctors would leave, the ones who were there and still alive. No new ones would come, not even Indians. He said it was like taking away water from people in a desert. The government would capitulate. That was the plan.

"I lifted my hand and let him take the money. He said I was paying the soldiery and he thanked me in the name of the revolution. Then I was free to go."

He looked around dazedly for something, she wasn't clear what. Her glass was still one third full. Remarkably, he picked it up and drained it, eating the remnants of ice.

She stood up. She was content. The story was a brilliant thing, a gem.

He was moving about. It was hard to say, but possibly he was leaving. He could go or stay.

They stood together in the living room archway. Without prelude, he reached for her, awkwardly pulled her side against his chest, kissed her absurdly on the eye, and with his free hand began squeezing her breasts.

Robert Shacochis

Stolen Kiss

On an inside day in November, a smoke and cider day, Burton Glass found a white greasy kiss stamped against the black post of the sunporch he was painting at the shore, off-season in Rehobeth.

It pleased him. Look at that, he said.

He worked facing the sea, which today was friendless, dulled by emptiness and an early winter. He saw only where his brush pointed, where the textures changed. In the cold his hands were dumb animals, struggling and stupid, pushing against their task. He wanted them to be stronger, to remember a better day, remember a woman or a fire. His leather gloves made him feel clumsy so he took them off after the first few strokes.

Behind the DuPont place up the beach the geese on Silver Lake cried: the unmusical chorus, the tock of migrating wings, the splash of the spinning gadwalls and pintails on the restful water. The noise came across the dunes to Burton as if there were no distance between the lake and the porch and it comforted, kept him company.

Burton finished the south post and moved over to the middle one, starting at the base. The darkly stained wood was dry, saturated with salt, rough but not splintering. He pecked at it with his brush, stopping to also take his pipe from where he'd set it on the deck. Too much of the season came through into his lungs as he sucked the cold stem. The ash was dead and bitter. He paused to relight it, gazing out along the strand. The sea was pocked, coarse like steel wool, full of dimension. As he concentrated on the match, a wave rose above the tidal slope, held up by the wind and feathered backward, splitting to the sand. He turned back to the post. Half the way up there was the kiss, circled by a glossy halo of oil that seeped out from the image.

Burton examined the mark. He had not expected such a thing. Tamping the lid back on the bucket of paint, he squatted down on it to meditate, to smoke his rum-flavored blend. He could not readily come up with anything to think about, then recalling it was the kiss that stopped him, Burton dreamed a little about the act of a woman, into August and blood-hot air, skin blistered beyond appeasement but finally soothed by cream and lotion, smeared onto the face, over red cheeks and burnt lips. Little wordless dreams saying nothing, just feelings and fragrances that pushed their blessed way through into the day.

This was not his house. He rarely had talked with the women—mother and daughter—who weekended here, both dark haired, distant bodies he had stared at on the beach, admiring how much they might have given and how much more they could. The husband was a lawyer from New York. As caretaker, Burton received his check, carelessly inscribed, and the checks of many others—lawyers, bankers, businessmen—on the first of each month. The mail had no immediacy for Burton anymore. For the past year he only made bi-weekly visits to the post office—once for the money, and once to collect the letter from his own wife who still lived in the Washington suburbs. She was faithful in her writing. Her letters usually arrived the second week of each month. They were chatty and honest and full of little news. Burton enjoyed reading them.

Maybe it was the fellow's wife, Burton thought, looking again at the kiss. She seemed happier when her husband didn't come down with her and the girl. There was never that forced gaiety about her, never the staged manners; even the clothes she wore were more casual and free when the man wasn't there. Her husband the lawyer must be a man committed to appearance. But Burton could not discount the daughter. The source of the kiss might have indeed been her. He had seen how her breasts and hips had grown in the past two or three years, how the boys had found her out there on the sand, sometimes had heard the faint, wonderful language she used, at night in the dunes, as she marked her discoveries. She shrieked once when his dog surprised them back there; Burton heard a young man's voice bringing the girl back into his arms. It was easy to love these things about people he did not know, but he couldn't look at his own life like that. After thirty-two years in Washington, it was hard to see what was genuine and what was not. You had to decompress after being down into it for so long, the *it* a state of affairs not unlike the cold mud shore around the lake, grey and bitter smelling, an airless trap. He had sat behind his desk all those years knowing he was in the wrong place. The beach became his tonic. To now work with one's hands, to scrape and callous them, to be next to the sea when everyone else had abandoned it, to preside over quiet cottages full of the lives of others—this was good, this made sense, to see and feel what you do.

Burton arose from the bucket, a familiar pain soaking his legs, to stand before the kiss. The lips of the woman or girl had set a perfect print. He touched the surface. It did not smear; the wood had taken it in, would hold the kiss forever in sterile ownership. He leaned out over the rail of the porch to knock the crumb and dust from his pipe.

This was enough for now. Burton wanted something in his belly, a nugget or flame that would warm his blood. He cleaned out the brush so it would be ready for his return, passed through the french doors directly into the master bedroom—her bedroom. Usually he would keep going but he stopped this time to turn up the thermostat. When he finished the porch he must work in here, replace a closet door. The bed was quilted, the pillows uncased. He saw small things he'd never bothered to notice before: a clean ashtray made from a cockle shell, a blue fountain pen and bottle of pills on the night table, a metallic tube of lipstick on the dresser next to a hand mirror. Why, he did not know, he could not tell himself, he had never done a thing like this, but he slid open the top drawer of the dresser—nothing. He opened another—bobby pins and ribbons, a tortoise shell clasp. In the next one down were sheets, linen, pillow cases, army blankets. The bottom drawer—two sweaters, lemon and pink, a folded nightgown, and a bra, the elastic in its straps warped from many washings, so many doings and undoings. Burton picked it up, held it, brought it to his nose to smell—ah, so clean. There was a slow, nervous thrill that came from the silken touch. Before replacing it next to the gown, he held each cup in his palms and imagined the breasts that once filled those crumpled, unshaped spaces.

Taking the stairs down to the first level, he left the house, walking up the beach toward town. The lake was visible between the dunes, the noisy congregations of waterfowl, squadrons circling above, constant arrivals and departures. Not long ago he had a good dog, an Irish setter, and the dog died there in the lake. He didn't want to think about it.

The boardwalk began just past the DuPont place. Burton stepped up on it, into more wind, his high-laced boots booming down on the wood, the wind harmless against his stiff white hair trained since boyhood into three patrician waves that rolled straight back from his crown. His wife once said—it was soon after the war—she said, Burton, when you take off your clothes and stand the way you are now, turned just a bit around from the way you're going, you look so handsome and hard. It's your hair, I think, you have the best head of hair, oh and your nose and the color of your body. How did you get so tan all over? What did you do there in Italy? What was it like? You don't know how much I missed you.

The love between them had lasted a long time, longer than he thought it would. It was still there, although they couldn't live together anymore. At least they hadn't used each other up to the point where they wanted nothing, where any desire wasn't worth the effort. It seemed to get that way at times—those middle years when they managed their love as if it were an anemic bank account. Now those days were over. Thank God for letting us be apart and at peace with the loneliness.

His eyes watered in the wind, his chest tightened under the woolen Pendleton. Onto Atlantic Avenue, he passed the shuttered guest houses, the pew-like rows of benches that faced back toward the ocean, the statue of angry Neptune, a long bicycler in scarf and stocking cap. Inside the Sportsmen's Tavern, his eyeglasses fogged as he moved instinctively toward the first empty stool at the bar. He took a paper napkin to wipe his glasses clean, saw the blurred shape of Carl approaching.

"Burton."

"What?"

The proprietor ambled the length of the counter, stopped to remove a bottle of whiskey from the shelf and then stood opposite Burton, pouring both of them a shot.

"Your wife called looking for you."

"Did she leave a message?" The whiskey brought back everything the wind had taken from him.

"She said to tell you that John Warner's left Liz for her. They're running off together."

"What, again?"

"Hah!"

"What did Maggie want?"

"She says she can't make it this weekend and she hopes you won't mind. Somebody gave her a ticket to an opening at the Kennedy Center. She said call her back if there's a problem."

"No problem, my friend."

"You want something to eat?"

"If there's chowder I'll have that."

After he returned from the kitchen and set the steaming bowl in front of Glass, Carl came out from behind the bar to sit. The two men had known each other for many years. Burton sipped the broth delicately from his spoon.

"Get a new pup yet?" Carl asked.

"No."

"A fellow up in Henlopen has a setter bitch that just had pups. You should have a look."

"Alright. Maybe this weekend."

"Rachel was a fine dog. Be hard to replace her, Burton."

"Good dog, sure. Dumb though. Rather not have a dog if it can't stand up to a goose."

They had debated the point several times since it happened. Burton said the dog got into the lake, chasing the fowl back and forth, finally swam into an army of Canadians that converged on her. Carl insisted the dog was just old, too old to swim that much and a goose would be shy of a dog anyways. Red-haired Rachel must have drunk salt water and drowned, in Carl's opinion. Burton no longer cared how it happened, he wouldn't have another dog. Next time it would be the dog that was left behind.

He stared sleepily into his bowl. The milky chowder was the same color as the kiss he had discovered on the porch post. "Carl," he began but stopped himself. He was going to tell about the kiss but thought better of it because when the words started to form they felt like a betrayal, like blabbing about the most intimate moments you had shared with somebody.

"What?" asked Carl.

"The chowder's good. It's what I needed."

He thought about Rachel. Can't have another dog, but maybe I should. Maybe that's the way my wife is feeling. She didn't put up any fuss. She said, Burton, I've known for a long time that's what you wanted but I can't spend the rest of my life up there. It's too quiet for me. I can't fit into a place like that after living in a city that has everything. That's too much to ask but you go on. I'll spend the summers there with you. The summers are good. And we'll visit each other, like lovers. That's the only way I can do it.

"You alright?" Carl asked. "You're not getting a cold, are you?"

"No."

"Another whiskey?"

"No, I'll be getting back now."

He stretched out on her bed and watched it happen, let the breeze turn warm again, the heat invade the day. He had a vision of her out there on the sand. She has tried to read her book but cannot focus; the words rise and recede on the page, throb behind her eyes, enter into her as some unintelligible force. She falls asleep on her towel and is unbothered. When she wakes she feels as if she has lost all privacy, that she has been possessed too much, too long, too hard, and every movement now brings pain.

The house is quiet, empty. Her husband never comes with her anymore. The girl is somewhere else, in town parading the boardwalk. The woman enters the room. Although she is still beautiful, still unaged, her face looks battered and blank, untouchable. She carefully removes her top and Burton is startled by her white breasts, so white they no longer seem to belong to the rest of her body. An elegant, enameled fingertip tests the sore red line that vees to the middle of her chest. Her nipples exaggerate the touch. The tight pressure of her skin makes the woman grimace.

Burton thought that now her husband might come and provide a motive for the kiss. He kept still and watched.

But she remains alone despite the expectation that Burton felt in the room. Her hair is swollen and scattered, lightened softly in places where the sun held, where it slowly branded her. Her abdomen is stretched taut, a small, dimpled drum, smoldering underneath the surface. Legs, arms and cheeks flame brilliantly, her lips pouted and raw as if they have been roughly, persistently, kissed. She twists the lid from a blue jar. Feverish and dizzy, she sinks her fingers into the cream, digging round and round. There is a burning that feels as if it empties her. She stands before the french doors looking out upon the water. Burton saw the strap lines on her back like perfect cuts where her torso had been separated by the sun. Below the horizon, the moon begins paddling the ocean, stroking the shadowed water. The woman steps from bedroom to porch, bending to draw down the bottom of her suit, the clear unsunned flesh unnaturally luminescent, almost transparent, in the dying light. She rubs the cream onto her scorched body where it melts and sucks the coolness from the rising moon. Standing before the sea, she opens herself to this redemption and sways gratefully, one hand clutching the middle post, pressing her creamed lips against the wood.

Burton paused to study the lines, the ridges and cracks, the thin black space between full halves, this language of the past season, another life. He had loved his wife Maggie through thirty-nine years, four children and as many homes, a career that seemed more vague with each new day away from it, and now this, their negotiated freedom.

He dipped his brush into the fresh black paint and looked again at the white kiss in the middle of the post. It spoke so much for love when all else tried to ignore it. He traced a finger along the outline, withdrawing his hand finally with irritation at the sight of his gold wedding band. He thought he heard a phone ring somewhere and stopped to listen. It was only the tide coming in, rattling shells together in the trough at land's end. Burton stepped forward and kissed the kiss, glancing to see how closely his lips matched those on the wood. Then he painted over it.

MONA SIMPSON

You Leave Them

I wonder what we looked like then, that day we drove over into California. My mother could probably still tell you what we wore. We were driving to California from Bay City, Wisconsin, just the two of us, so I could be a television star. We'd taken Ted's Mobil Credit Card and stayed in motels, charging gasoline and Cokes on the bills. We dug up to our shoulders in the ice chests, bringing the cold pop bottles up like a catch.

We'd stolen vegetables all across America, anything we could eat without cooking. My mother spotted the trucks.

"Oh, Ann. Look. Peas," she'd say. The trucks of peas were open-backed, the vines clumped in bundles. We followed those trucks anywhere, turning off into towns we'd never heard of and then waiting till the first stoplight, when my mother sent me out with a five dollar bill to the driver. The windows of the cabs were high and I had to jump to knock. The drivers never touched our money. They shrugged and smiled and said, You go on ahead, take what you want, then. And we loaded up the whole back seat of the car, from the floor to the roof, with the sweet, heavy-scented vines.

Sometimes on the highway loads of peas would drop off the truckbeds and bounce right on the concrete like tumbleweed. We pulled onto the gravel shoulder and ran out and chased them, laughing on the hot empty road, the flat country still on all sides of us.

That last morning in Nevada we'd bought nine melons, big melons, each too heavy for one hand. We'd tasted samples from toothpicks on ragged, wet paper plates. We'd never imagined how many kinds of melons there could be. And they were all sweet.

But when we crossed the Nevada border some men made us stop. We couldn't take our melons into California. It was still not noon and already hot. We had pulled onto the shoulder of the road. When the man told us we couldn't bring our melons in, my mother stood outside of the car and cried. She talked to him, saying the same things again and again, while he shook his head no. He seemed to have all the time in the world. A green fly landed on his forehead and it took him forty seconds to lift up his hand and shoo it. I backed the car onto the grass and started hauling out melons. My mother screamed. I was twelve years old. I wasn't supposed to know how to drive.

We didn't have a knife or anything. We split the melons open, smashing them on the legs of the sign that said "WELCOME TO CALIFORNIA" and we stood on the concrete platform eating them, the juice spilling down our arms.

Our shirts were still sticky and sweet smelling, but the bad, sour side of sweet, when we drove into Los Angeles. My mother had called ahead for reservations at one of the hotels she'd read about, but she said she wouldn't go there right away.

"Huh-uh. Look at us. And look at this car. We're going to clean up a little first."

"Why? They're used to it, they're a hotel, aren't they?"

"Honey, the Bel Air isn't just a hotel." She had the tone she always used when she was too tired to fight. "You'll see."

"Why can't we wash up there?"

"Because. That's why. You just don't."

She parked in front of a restaurant near the campus of U.C.L.A. "This looks like a good little place. And we can have a bite to eat. Hamburger Hamlet it's called. Cute."

My mother took our gingham dresses from the trunk. They were still in their dry-cleaning cellophane. Two men leaned against the building. They had tie-dyed sheets spread out on the sidewalk with buckles and leather belts for sale. We stood there looking down, entranced. They were slow and graceful, smoking.

"What are you looking at? Come on," she said. The Ladies' Room in the restaurant was upstairs. "Those kids are on drugs," my mother whispered. "They're hooked on marijuana." She'd read about drugs. She always read the magazines. Even then she knew what drugs were.

In the restroom, my mother plugged her steam rollers into the wall socket, and unpacked her cosmetics and soaps, lining them up on the counter. She used the row of sinks as if this were her own huge dressing room. She turned on the hand dryer, and touched up her nails, holding them under the warm air.

She washed, shaved her underarms and ripped open a fresh package of nylons. She stood in pantyhose and a bra and started on her makeup. She clipped the hot rollers in her hair. Strangers touched their hands under thin streams of water in the sink furthest from us and my mother didn't notice. She was driven. The will to be clean.

"Ann," she called then, looking for me in the mirror. I was standing by the door. "Comemeer."

"My name is Heather," I said. While we were driving she told me I could pick a new name for myself in California. It would be my television name.

"Heather, then. You know who I mean." She sniffed me. "You smell," she said, and handed me a towel. "Let's have some scrubbing action. Get undressed and hurry it up."

I washed standing on one leg, the other foot on my knee, swishing the towel around lightly. Other women's faces sealed the mirror. My mother didn't notice women leaving the restroom but she saw that I was embarrassed. All of a sudden she saw that. And it must have seemed like a defeat. She'd driven all that way and now we were here and I was ashamed of her.

She sighed one of her sighs. "Come here," she said. She brushed blush on my cheeks. "Listen. Nobody cares, do you hear? They don't give a hoot. They can think we wanted to wash up before we ate. They can see that we've been traveling. They don't want you to stay dirty."

I must have looked pale standing there, because she pushed some lipstick over my lips. They were chapped and I wouldn't stand still, so she smeared a little and licked her finger to clean the edge of my mouth. I ran over to the sink and spat. I tasted her saliva, it was different than mine.

I felt something then, as I stood watching my spit twirl down the drain. I wanted to get away from her. There was nowhere I could go. I was twelve. She'd have me six more years.

My mother examined us in the mirror and sighed in relief. She held my chin and looked at us both. She'd been right. We did look much better. She gathered our things back into the suitcase and snapped the buckle shut. "See, all done," she said. "Doesn't it feel good to be clean?"

We found eight car washes in Westwood that afternoon but they were all the drive-through kind. My mother wasn't going to trust them with our Lincoln.

"You wouldn't do it by *hand?*" She was standing on the blacktop talking to a boy who looked as if she were asking for the world. I scowled, embarrassed again. Everything she did embarrassed me. "I mean, I'll pay you. *Extra.* I just don't want those hard detergents on it. They'll hurt the finish." She ran her hand on the car top. It was still smooth and new.

"You can wash it yourself, lady," the boy said, walking off. He walked as if the whole parking lot were his own.

My mother sat back down in the car. "You know, I guess we could," she said. "I guess we could do it ourselves."

She started to unpack the backseat.

"Heather, go." She gave me a five dollar bill. "Give him this and say we want rags for the windows and stuff to clean the seats. Oh, and ask if they have a little vacuum cleaner, too. Go on."

She already had the trunk open and our suitcase out.

It was a long walk to where the boy stood hosing off the wheels of a jeep. "Hurry up," my mother yelled, but I kept sluffing. I didn't care about the car being clean. If it was mine, I'd have just left it dirty. She would say I never learned to take care of a thing.

I stood with the five dollar bill stuck in my hand, looking down at the cement ramps under the gas pumps.

"Could we please buy rags and cleaning stuff and also possibly rent a vacuum cleaner?"

The kid laughed. "What kind of cleaning stuff?"

I shrugged. "For the outside and for the seats."

"Gonna do it yourself, huh?"

"She wants to."

He put the hose down, not turning it off, so a stream of water dribbled down the blacktop. He stuffed a bucket with rags and plastic bottles. "You'll have to pull up here for the vacuum," he said, "You just pull on up when you're ready."

"Thank you."

"I don't know how much to charge you for this stuff. Five dollar's probably too much. You're not going to use that much fluid."

"She might. You better take it."

He laughed. "She might, huh? She always like that?"

I felt my top lip pulling down over my teeth. "She's usually not that bad." I was looking down at my shoes. "We just moved here. Just today."

"Oh, I see. Well, makes sense. Anxious to get the car cleaned, huh?"

"Yeah."

We looked at each other a little longer, his chin tucked down against his neck and his eyes dropping open, until my mother called.

"Heather, hurry it up. It's already four o'clock."

"That your name, Heather?" he said, picking up his hose again.

"Yeah," I said. "Thanks."

Torches flared on both sides of the road that led to the Bel Air Hotel. The path wound in and out of woods. My mother drove slowly. She parked underneath the awning. I moved to get out but she stopped me and told me to wait. She rested her hands on the steering wheel the way she used to for years on top of my shoulders. The valet came out and opened the doors, her door first and then mine. She wasn't shy to relinquish the car anymore. There was nothing embarrassing in it. It was clean. The leather smelled of Windex.

At the desk a man shuffled through his book. "We've put you in the tower, which is a lovely room, but there's only one bed. A double. I'm afraid it's all we have left."

My mother let a frown pass over her face, for appearances. We'd slept in doubles all the way across America. She didn't like to sleep alone. I did. She was frowning for me to see, too.

"That will be all right." She shrugged.

Following the valet to our room, we let ourselves relax. I bumped against the wall and she let me bump because I was clean. The stucco seemed to absorb amber evening light.

We walked through an outdoor courtyard. There was a small cafe; white tablecloths, white chairs, the distant slap and shuffle of late swimmers. People at the tables were drinking, lingering in daytime clothes. We climbed stone steps to the tower. My mother tipped the valet and then closed the door behind us. I had my arms crossed over my chest. She looked at me and asked, "What's the matter with you now? Don't tell me even this doesn't satisfy you."

She was looking around the room. And it was a beautiful hotel.

But I was thinking about us on our hands and knees, our butts sticking out the car door, scrubbing the melon juice stains off the leather. To me, the afternoon canceled out now. My mother was not that way. She could hold contrasts in her mind at once. She must have found me horribly plain.

"It's nice," I said.

A green and white polished cotton canopy shaded the four-poster bed. She kicked her shoes off and collapsed. I sat on the windowseat, my leg swinging over the side. My jacket hung on the back of a chair where I'd left it. She hooked it with her bare foot and brought it to her face. Then she tried it on, adjusting the collar.

I looked at her—she was standing on the bed, barefoot, her toenails polished a light shade of pink—"Take my jacket off," I said, cranking the window open. It wasn't warm but my arm was pumping as if I needed air.

"It fits me. You don't know what a cute little shape I have, for a mother. Pretty darn good for my age."

"Can we afford this place?" I wasn't looking at her anymore. My face was out the window, gulping the night. I watched the waiters move, beautifully, around the glows of candles on the little tables. One man cupped his hand over a woman's to light a cigarette. My mother's fingers spidered on my back.

"I'll worry about that, okay? I'm the adult and you're the child. And don't you forget that."

"Don't I wish I could."

"Well, you can. So start right now." She laughed, half a laugh.

"I'm hungry."

"Should we call room service?"

"No, I want to go out." I hardly ever said things like that. I didn't want to be blamed for wanting too much, but that night it seemed worth it to get outside.

"I don't know, I'd just as soon have something here, now that we're parked and all. To tell the truth, I'm sick of this driving. You don't know, you haven't been doing it, but it tires you. You can't believe how my shoulders feel. They ache, Heather-honey, they really ache. Twenty-one, twenty-two, let's see, we left the fifth of August, do you realize, we've been on the road sixteen days. No, the fifth to the, today's—"

"We can go here. You don't have to drive. There's a restaurant down there."

Her head turned. She looked a little startled; she always did when she was interrupted. "Oh, okay, fine. That's fine. It's just this driving, seventeen days, day in, day out, eight hours behind the wheel and boy, you feel it, you feel it right—"

I stood up and walked to the door, my jacket hooked on one finger. "Let's go."

"Well, would you just wait a second, please, and let me wash my face? And I want to put on a little bit of makeup."

I sat on the steps and listened to her vigorous washing. She slapped her face, her feet thumping on the bathroom floor.

"It's going to be a few minutes," she said.

And it was. The sky went from pink to deep blue to black in the time it took my mother to get ready. I sat on the steps watching other people come to the café, sit down and drink, clinking glasses together. I saw a man reach over a table and rummage underneath a woman's hair, as if there were something to find.

When she stepped outside, I sniffed loudly to let her know I didn't like perfume. I was wearing my regular afternoon clothes, and she'd put on a long dress, with one slit up the back. She was the adult, I was the child. She wore pearls and heels, her hair was teased two inches out from her face.

"Well," she said, making noises around her, the pearls, the cotton rustling, "Are we ready?" She was talking in an octave higher than her normal voice, a voice to be overheard.

"What do you think?" I said, shoving my hands in my pockets and starting down the stairs. She clattered behind me.

"Wait, wait, would you? Go a little slower, please. You don't know what it's like up here. I mean on these heels." She put her hands on my shoulders. "My balance isn't what it should be. It's fine, in the morning, I'm fine. But by this time of day, you're just going to have to slow down. Please."

"Why do you wear them, then?"

"Honey, you know. They look nice." She caught up to me then and grabbed my arm, falling a little. "At my age, they expect you to have a little height. And who knows, maybe I'll meet someone tonight, you never know. And I'd hate to meet the right man when I had on the wrong shoe."

But my mother seemed to gain balance when we waited at the café entrance. I was glad to be with her then. I was glad to have her in those shoes. I stood close by her when I was shy.

"Two for dinner?"

"Please," she said, her chin high, following him. She knew how to do those things.

We had a small table at the edge of the courtyard with its own glowing candle, like the rest. We didn't look at each other at first, we each looked at the people around us. I didn't see any free men for her.

My mother opened the menu. "Wow," she whispered, "A wee bit pricey."

"Room service would be just the same."

"Not necessarily. But that's okay. We're here now, so fine. Well, I know what I'm having. I'm having a glass of wine and a cup of soup." Even that was going to be expensive.

"I'm hungry," I said. I was mad. I wasn't going to have any soup or salad. If we could afford to stay here then we could afford to eat, and I was going to eat.

The waiter came and my mother ordered her glass of wine and cup of soup. "Is that all, ma'am?"

"I think so. We had a late lunch."

I ordered a steak and began answering the waiter's long string of questions. Baked potato. Oil and vinegar. Beans instead of rice.

My mother kicked my shin, hard, under the table.

"Didn't you want a hamburger? I don't know if you saw, but they have them."

"No, I'd rather have a steak."

"Oh, okay, fine. Whatever you want. It's just that you said you wanted a hamburger. You said it this afternoon."

Then the waiter left us alone. My mother leaned over the table and whispered. "Didn't you see me winking at you, you dummy? Didn't you feel me kick? I can't afford this. What do you think you're doing? Jesus.

You saw what I ordered, didn't you? Don't you think I'm hungry? Am I supposed to starve myself so you can have a steak?"

"Why didn't you order yourself a steak?"

"Boy," she said, "I can't believe how dumb you are sometimes. We can't *afford* this."

"So why are we here? Why aren't we somewhere we can afford? I asked you upstairs and you said I shouldn't worry, that you were the adult and I was the child."

"Well, children order hamburgers when they go out to expensive restaurants. That's all they're allowed to order."

"Then why didn't you change it? Go ahead. Tell the waiter I can't have my steak."

"I don't believe you. You shouldn't have ordered it! You felt my foot under the table, you just wanted your steak. Well, fine, you can have it now and you'd better enjoy it, because believe me, it's the last steak you'll get for a while."

She sank back into her chair, her arms lapsing on the armrests. Our waiter arrived with her wine.

"Everything all right?"

A smile came reflexively to her face. "Lovely, just lovely."

She'd had it with me. She pretended that she simply wasn't hungry. As if not wanting things was elegant, but wanting them and not being able to get them was not.

She leaned over the table again.

"If you were so hungry, why didn't you order more at lunch? You love hamburgers. You usually always order a hamburger."

"I do not *love* hamburgers."

"Yes you do." She sighed. "Why can't it ever just be nice? Why can't we ever just have a nice, relaxing time?"

"In other words why can't I just want a hamburger, why can't I want what you want me to want. Why don't I always just happen to want the cheapest thing on the menu?"

"That's what I do, why can't you?" she said. "Don't you think *I'm* hungry after all that driving?"

"You can have some of mine."

"No." She shook her head. "I don't want any. It's yours. You ordered it, now you eat it." She looked around the café. "There's nothing for me here. I wanted to just stay in and have something quick from room service. Not get all dressed up. I just wanted to relax for once."

Our food came and I stopped looking at her. I started cutting my steak. It was thick and glistening with fat. I put all four rounds of butter in the baked potato. Steam rose up in spirals. Then I shook on salt, spooned in sour cream. It looked delicious.

She took a sip of her soup. "So, how is it?"

I said fine, still looking at my plate.

"How's the salad? You haven't touched the salad."

"Uh huh," I said, still eating.

"Try the vegetables, you need those vitamins." She put down her spoon. "Would you like a bite of my soup? It's delicious, really, these little bits of carrot. They're grated very finely. I wonder what they use. It tickles your throat when it goes down, like lots of little sparks."

She wasn't being mean anymore. She was even smiling.

"No thank you," I said.

She did the talking while I ate. "You know, you're really right. This is a lovely place. Lovely. The pool over there, can you hear it? That little glup, glup, glup? And this air. I love these warm, dry nights. I wonder how cold it gets in winter. I know we won't need really heavy coats, coats like we had at home, but do you think we'll even need any? Light coats? Sort of raincoat-ish? I'd love to have a trench."

I finally set my silverware down. I guess I was finally full. Now I looked around, too, and up at the starless sky. "The air is nice," I said.

"Are you finished with that?"

"What? Oh, the steak?"

"I thought if you were I'd try a bite."

I shoved the whole plate over to her side. I passed her the salad and the dish of vegetables.

"Oh, no, I just want a little bite."

"Try the vegetables. They're very good." I knew if she finished my dinner, that would be the last I'd hear about the bill.

She sighed and settled in her chair. "Oh, it is. Very, very good." She leaned over and whispered. "You know, for what you get, these prices aren't so bad. This is enough for the two of us, really. You know?"

Later the waiter came for our plates. All that was left was the parsley. "I'll take that," my mother said and grabbed the sprig from his tray. He must have thought we were famished, but my mother really always had liked parsley.

"Will that be all? Or can I get you some dessert and coffee?"

My mother winked. "No coffee, please. But I think we'd like to see a menu for dessert. And would you like a glass of milk, young lady?"

I looked up at the waiter. "I'd like coffee, please. With cream and sugar."

He left, to bring the dessert tray. My mother looked at me suspiciously and smiled. "Ann, now tell me, when did you learn to drink coffee? Were you just bluffing or did you learn? Look me in the eye and tell me true."

We shared the cup when it came. She took a sip, then I took a sip.

"With you," I said. "I learned from you."

I could see her looking at me, wondering. But she let it go and she let the bill go too. Now, I'm glad that she did. You grow up and you leave them. She only had me six more years.

ELLIS WEINER

Errata

Page i (Introduction): For "The problem abstraction" read "The problem of abstraction"

Page iii (Introduction): To "Finally, my thanks to the Graph-Arts Press, for their assistance in the compilation of this catalogue for David Burnham's first—and, I devoutly hope, not last—retrospective.

> Albert Popper
> Boston
> April, 1983"

add "My further thanks to Graph-Arts for delaying distribution long enough to enable me to append to the (evidently naive) text several corrections, the need for which was made manifest yesterday, two weeks prior to the opening of David Burnham's first—and, I devoutly hope, last—retrospective.

> Albert Popper
> Boston
> May, 1983"

Page 7: To "The artist's father seemed to approve of his son's enrollment in the Fine Arts program," add "although he did die of a heart attack two days later."

Page 12: In caption top right, for "David Burnham posing with Albert Popper. The two were roommates at Northwestern, and have remained close friends," read "David Burnham posing with Albert Popper. The two were roommates at Northwestern."

Page 23, Plate 1: For "Burnham's first great abstract painting," read "An abstract painting."

Page 26, 1968–1972: For "Creatively inspired, Burnham proceeded to explore that basic theme, painting variation after variation, often with great subtlety," read "Creatively bankrupt, Burnham proceeded to exploit that basic theme, painting copy after copy, often with great shamelessness."

Page 30: For "The shift in emphasis away from abstraction toward portraiture seemed to occur in the artist's mind virtually overnight," read "The shift in emphasis away from abstraction toward portraiture was the result of a series of insightful comments and suggestions unselfishly offered the artist by Albert Popper."

Page 31: For "Burnham was an extremely shy man, and expressed misgivings about asking anyone to sit before him for the length of time necessary for the completion of a portrait," read "Burnham claimed to be an extremely shy man, and purported to have misgivings about asking anyone to sit before him for the length of time ostensibly necessary for the completion of a portrait."

Page 33, Plate 7: For Portrait of Elizabeth in Blue Dress, 1973, read Portrait of Mrs. Albert Popper in Blue Dress, 1973.

Page 36: For "As far as his portraits were concerned, Burnham's first major patron was, in fact, Albert Popper, the author of the present catalogue," read "One of Burnham's many patrons was Albert Popper, the author of the present catalogue, although the artist had many, many others at the time as well."

Page 37, transcription of hand-written note: For

"3 Feb. 1974

Albert—

You've bought everything I've done for the past eight months, and believe me, I appreciate it. But I can't let you buy this one—it's terrible.

D.B."

read

"3 Feb. 1974

Albert—

You've bought several of my minor works during the past eight months, and believe me, I appreciate it, just as I appreciate the fact that other people—total strangers—have bought some paintings too. But I can't let you buy this one—it's terrible. So I am giving it to you as a gift, of my own free will.

> D.B."

Page 37 Footnote: For "A. Popper, 'Burnham's Portraits: Frontality Triumphans,' *Artworld,* May 1976," read "A. Pepper, 'Burnham's Portraits: Frontality Triumphans,' *Artworld,* May 1976."

Page 38 Footnote: For "A. Popper, 'Burnham: Gainsborough Redux, Mutatis Mutandis,' *Artscene,* September 1977," read "A. Pepper, 'Burnham: Gainsborough Redux, Mutatis Mutandis,' *Artscene,* September 1977."

> N.B.: Shortly after the present catalogue went to press, it was established that the series of influential articles about Burnham's work, previously attributed to the author, were in fact written by one A. *Pepper.* These writings, to some (relatively minor) degree responsible for the artist's subsequent critical and popular success, as well as for the apparently increased value of the paintings themselves, were definitely not written by "A. Popper," but instead by "A. Pepper." with an "e."

Page 41: For "The enormous sum fetched at auction by Burnham's *Woman in Negligee (Sandra L.)* astounded no one," read "The enormous sum fetched at auction by Burnham's *Woman in Negligee (Sandra L.)* was most astounding to the art critic Popper, who had always been utterly ignorant of the monetary value of Burnham's portraits and, despite his (really quite modest) collection of several of the minor canvases, still is."

Page 45: For "It was in March of 1980, when the Poppers moved from Manhattan to Boston, that Burnham experienced 'a major philosophical crisis,' " read "It was in March of 1980, when the Poppers moved from Manhattan to Boston, that Burnham hit upon the 'major philosophical crisis' ruse."

Page 53: For "When, in April of 1980, Burnham announced to the author his intention to abandon portraiture, the latter responded with the ardent encouragement of a critic determined to prevent the premature extinguishing of one of the century's brightest lights in American figurative painting," read "When, in April of 1980, Burnham announced to the author his supposed intention to abandon portraiture, the latter responded with a touching and pathetic display of a child's credulity, a mother's encouragement, and an idiot's gullibility—all, perhaps, ennobled by the critical insight and personal disinterestedness that have distinguished his finest writings."

Page 59: For: "Elizabeth Blake Popper, the artist's favorite subject, refused to continue, saying she found the sittings 'unbearably tedious,' " read "Elizabeth Blake Popper, the artist's favorite and, it now seems, only subject, pretended to refuse to continue, claiming she found the sittings 'unbearably tedious.' "Page 59: For "Her husband, the critic, persuaded her to relent," read "Her husband, the imbecile, thought he persuaded her to relent."

Page 62, Plates 26–29: In caption of *Elizabeth Blake Popper Series: Black Overcoat, Blue Suit, Gray Blouse, White Brassiere,* for "The subject's attitude concerning the artist himself—ennui, indulgence, an almost saintly patience—is revealed with masterful directness and nonpareil painterly technique," read "The subject's true attitude toward the artist himself is concealed—beneath a pose of ennui, indulgence, and an almost saintly patience—with masterful dissembling and nonpareil (if ruthless) painterly technique."

Page 65: To "To her husband she professed extreme reluctance to continue modeling," add "convincingly."

Page 70: For "Burnham's growing interest in painting nudes coincided with the mourning of his first retrospective, during which time the author was occupied, night and day, with writing and assembling the present catalogue," read, "It is no wonder that Burnham's growing interest," etc.

Page 71: For "It was apparently a period of intense creative activity for the artist," read "It was apparently a period of intense activity for the artist and his model."

Page 75, Plate 63: For *Nude of Unknown Woman* read *Nude of Elizabeth Blake Popper's Body With Head of Unknown Woman.*

Page 79, Plates 66–78: For *Sandra L. Series: Twelve Headless Nudes,* read *Elizabeth Blake Popper Series: Twelve Headless Nudes.*

> N.B.: It has been established, after examination of some three dozen of the "Sandra L." paintings, that "Sandra L." is a pseudonym for Elizabeth Blake Popper. Moreover, during the interval between the printing of the present catalogue, and the writing and printing of the present errata sheet,

sixteen other nudes, all untitled, became available for study. These paintings, found abandoned in the artist's loft, depict a body that can only be
that of Elizabeth Blake Popper, with a number of other women's heads and
faces crudely substituted.

Page 83 (Afterword): For "The artist, unmarried, currently resides in
Manhattan," read "The artist, engaged, has fled to Santa Fe, New Mexico, with Elizabeth Blake Popper, his treacherous wife-to-be. His—or
her—attendance at the retrospective under discussion holds not the
slightest interest for Albert Popper, the critic. If, however, Mrs. Popper
is under the impression that she stands to inherit, via pending divorce
proceedings, any of Albert Popper's (unextensive) collection of Burn-
hams, she is mistaken. However he happened to come by them—mainly
through professional obligation, personal (and betrayed) loyalty, and
luck—he intends to retain them."

Page 84 (Afterword): For "Ars longa, vita brevis," read "Et tu, Brute?"

PAUL WEST

Captain Ahab: A Novel by the White Whale

I too, alone, survived to tell thee. A whale tells this, white as Biscay froth,
a tale black as caviar. I almost lost heart. Albinos do, doomed special
while feeling like the rest. We're dark unto ourselves. *We?* I am the only
one. I have never bred. I have never seen a white male or a white mate. I
never had company save for him. Only, during brief heaven, a mother
who nudged and nourished. Shunned, I go from ocean to ocean, falling
in love with icebergs and fluffy fog, and, nearer shore, with snow and
polar bears. I am forbidden nothing, but there is nothing I can have.
What sex am I? Did Ahab know?

Squinting aft, I see him, rib cage and all. As the years went by, he
began to rattle, then to chime. I read his last will and testament from his
lips, then took him down for the count, poor piscuniak of a mariner.
Then I whale-hummed at him, just to be friendly. I wanted somehow to

swing him loose, then pop him down, minnow-small and feather-frail. Install him on the bulby mound of one vast kidney according to Jonah Law. A pet, a familiar, a love.

But dislodge him I could not, and I soon knew his coming for what it was: a test in the form of a sign, a sign in the form of a test. Could I brook his presence without wanting friendship? Ahab was my birthmark. Yes. "Ishmael, art thou sleeping there below?" Then answer would come: "Moby, I am thine, for ever."

It was all hopeless. Call me, I began, but my still-thundering jelly of a heart floated upward through my mouth, jump-a-thump, and all that's left is an infolded compass-rose, miming its thanks, murmuring a dew.

EDMUND WHITE

The Secret Order of Joy

I can't really remember how I met Tommy. I recollect him first as a smooth cloche of shiny light brown hair sporting the slender plume of a cowlick, a head bent over a book in study hall belonging to someone I'd heard was captain of the tennis team, leader of the Crowd and Sally's steady; then, without transition, he was my friend and he was struggling to explain to me his theory about Sartre's *Nausea* as we kicked our way through autumn leaves. "Uh . . . uh . . ." he was crying out on a loud, high note, a sustained nasal sound, as he stopped walking and held a finger up. Then his small, blue eyes, straining to see an idea in the distance, blinked, glanced smoothly up and down. The glitter of prophecy faded. He shrugged: "Lost it." He exposed his palms and then pocketed his hands in his trousers. I held my breath and counted ten before I offered my soft, apologetic suggestion: "But aren't you really saying that Sartre thinks Man is . . ." and I filled in the blank with the closest approximation I could invent, not of Sartre's thought but of Tommy's dubious interpretation of it.

"That's it! That's it!" Tommy shouted, and again he excitedly waded out into the philosophical murk. I, who thought only of survival, had no interest in philosophical questions. The proximate ones were enough to obsess me, not as things I chose to contemplate but as decisions rushing up at me as out of oncoming traffic. These were the things I thought about: Am I boring Tommy? Will he mind if I rest my elbow on his shoulder? Should I powder my white bucks or keep the scuff marks? How low should I let my jeans ride?

If the ultimate questions—the meaning of life, time, being—interested me now, it was only because they interested Tommy. To the extent the other kids thought of me at all they considered me to be something of a brain; certainly in their eyes Tom was a jock. Ironic, then, that he was the one who did all the thinking, who had the taste for philosophy—ironic but predictable, since his sovereignty gave him the ease to wonder about what it all meant, whereas I had to concentrate on means, not meaning. The meaning seemed quite clear: to survive and then to become popular. The game of king and servant I'd played in the snow or sand or in cloud castles now became real. The princess, asleep for so many years, awakes to the taste of the prince's lips, a slightly sour taste; she stares up into a face visored in shadow.

In that old, comfortable suburb even the biggest mansions hunkered democratically down on the curb and sat right next to other dwellings. No concealing hedges or isolating parks could be seen anywhere. Even quite massive houses of many rooms and wings engulfed their plots right down to the sidewalk. This conspicuousness declared a pride and innocence: We have nothing to hide, and we want to show you what we've got. Tom's house was a Mediterranean villa with six bedrooms and servants' quarters over a double garage, but its gleaming leaded panes and the front door (thick oak gouged into griffins) loomed up just ten paces from the street.

Once inside that door, however, I felt transported into another society that had ways I could never quite master. The Wellingtons were nice but not charming. The Wellingtons gave thought to everything they did. They wanted no praise for their accomplishments; they would have found an outsider's praise impertinent. The staircase was lined with expensive, ugly paintings done from photographs of their four children. Their kids' teeth were bound in costly wires, their whims for sailboats or skis or guitars were lavishly but silently honored; they were all paraded in a stupor past the monuments of Europe, their vacations down rapids and over glaciers or up mountains were well funded—but silence reigned. No one said a word. Dinner there was torture. A student from the university served. Mr. Wellington carved. Mrs. Wellington, a woman with a girlish spirit trapped inside a large, swollen body, made stabs at conversation, but she was so shy she could speak only in comical accents. She'd grunt in a bass voice like a bear or squeak like a mouse or imitate Donald

Duck—anything rather than say a simple declarative sentence in her own fragile, mortified voice. The father terrified us all with his manners (the long white hands wielding the fork and knife and expertly slicing the joint). He radiated disapproval. His disapproval was not the martyr's blackmail but a sort of murderous mildness: if he weren't so fastidious he'd murder you. We watched him carve. We were wordless, hypnotized by the candle flames, the neat incisions and deep, bloody invasions, the sound of the metal knife scraping against the tines of the fork, the sickening softness of each red slice laid to the side and the trickle down silver channels ramifying back into roots of blood.

The odd thing is that the father's spirit did not contaminate the house. His lair, the library, was even the sunniest, most relaxed room of all as the two little dogs, Welsh Corgis, trotted from couch to front door at every disturbance, their small, shaggy feet clicking on the polished red tiles. The dogs, the children, his wife—all seemed to prosper in spite of his punitive reserve, his tight, superb eyes, the way he sniffed with contempt at the end of every sentence someone else said. "Oh, yes," he said to me, examining his overly manicured hand, "I know of your mother . . . by reputation," and my heart sank.

In this house the parents maintained a silence except for the father's dreaded little comments, the sugar substitute of his sweetness, and the whole chirping menagerie of the mother's comical voices. No one hovered over the kids. They came and went as they chose, they stayed home and studied or they went out, they ate dinner in or at the last moment they accepted the hospitality of other tables. But under this surface ease of manner ran their dread of their father and their fear of offending him in some new way. He was a man far milder, far more (shall I say) ladylike than any other father I'd known, and yet his soft way of curling up on a couch and tucking his silk dressing gown modestly around his thin white shanks terrified everyone as did his way of looking over the tops of his glasses and mouthing without sound the name of his son: "Tommy"— the lips compressed on the double *m* and making a meal out of his swallowed, sorrowing disappointment. He was homely, tall, snowy-haired, hard-working, in bad health. He seemed to me the absolute standard of respectability, and by that standard I failed. My sister had coached me in some sort of charm, but no degree of charm, whether counterfeit or genuine, made an impression on Mr. Wellington. He was charm-proof. He disapproved of me. I was a fraud, a charlatan. His disapproval started with my mother and her "reputation," whatever that might be (her divorce? her dates? the fact she had to work?). He didn't like me and he didn't want his son to associate with me. When I entered his study I'd stand behind Tom. Only now does it occur to me that

Tommy may have liked me precisely because his father didn't. Was Tom's friendship with me one more way in which he was unobtrusively but firmly disappointing his father?

Once we closed Tom's bedroom door we were immersed again in the happy shabbiness of our friendship. For he was my friend—my best friend! Until now other boys my age had frightened me. We might grab each other in the leaves and play squirrel, but those painful stabs at pleasure had left me shaken and swollen with yearning—I wanted someone to love me. I had prayed I'd grow up as fast as possible.

No longer. For the first time I found it exhilarating to be young and with someone young. I loved him, and the love was all the more powerful because I had to hide it. We slept in twin beds only two feet apart. We sat around for hours in our underpants and talked about Sartre and tennis and Sally and all the other kids at school and love and God and the afterlife and infinity. Tom's mother never came to his door, as mine would have, to order us to sleep. The big dark house creaked around us as we lay on our separate beds in weird positions and talked and talked our way into the inner recesses of the night, those dim lands so tender to the couple.

And we talked of friendship, of our friendship, of how it was as intense as love, better than love, a kind of love. I told Tom my father had said friendships don't last, they wear out and must be replaced every decade as we grow older—but I reported this heresy (which I'd invented; my poor father had no friends to discard) only so that Tom and I might denounce it and pledge to each other our eternal fidelity. "Jesus," Tom said, "those guys are so damn *cynical!* Jeez . . ." He was lying on his stomach staring into the pillow; his voice was muffled. Now he propped himself up on one elbow. His forehead was red where he'd been leaning on it. His face was loose from sleepiness. His smile, too, was loose, rubbery, his gaze genial, bleary. "I mean, God! How can they go on if they think that way?" He laughed a laugh on a high brass note, a toot of amazement at the sheer gall of grown-up cynicism.

"Maybe," I said suavely, "because we're not religious, we've made friendship into our religion." I loved ringing these changes on our theme, which was ourselves, our love; to keep the subject going I could relate it to our atheism, which we'd just discovered, or to dozens of other favorite themes.

"Yeah," Tom said. He seemed intrigued by this possibility. "Hold on. Don't forget where we were." He hurried into the adjoining bathroom. As I listened through the open door to the jet of water falling into the toilet I imagined standing beside him, our streams of urine crossing, dribbling dry, then our hands continuing to shake a final glistening drop of something stickier than water from this new disturbance, this desire our lifting, meeting eyes had to confess.

No sooner would such a temptation present itself than I would smother it. The effect was of snuffing out a candle, two candles, a row of twenty, until the lens pulled back to reveal an entire votive stand exhaling a hundred thin lines of smoke as a terraced offering before the shrine. In this religion hidden lights had been declared superior to those that glared. Somewhere I was storing up merit, accumulating the credit I'd need to buy, one day, the salvation I longed for. Until then (and it was a reckoning that could be forestalled indefinitely, that I preferred putting off) I'd live in that happiest of all conditions: the long but seemingly prosperous courtship. It was a series of tests, ever more arduous, even perverse. For instance, I was required to deny my love in order to prove it.

"You know," Tom said one day, "you can stay over any time you like. Harold"—the minister's son, my old partner at squirrel—"warned me you'd jump me in my sleep. I have to tell you I was weirded out. You gotta forgive me. It's just I don't go in for that weird stuff."

I swallowed painfully and whispered, "Nor—" I cleared my throat and said too primly, "nor do I."

The medical smell, that Lysol smell of homosexuality, was staining the air again as the rubber-wheeled metal cart of drugs and disinfectants rolled silently by. I longed to open the window, to go away for an hour and come back to a room free of that odor, the smell of shame.

I never doubted that homosexuality was a sickness; in fact, I took it as a measure of how unsparingly objective I was that I could contemplate this very sickness. But in some other part of my mind I couldn't believe that the Lysol smell must bathe me, too, that its smell of stale coal fumes must penetrate my love for Tom. Perhaps I became so vague, so exhilarated with vagueness, precisely in order to forestall a recognition of the final term of the syllogism that begins: If one man loves another he is a homosexual; I love a man . . .

I'd heard that boys passed through a stage of homosexuality, that this stage was normal, nearly universal—then that must be what was happening to me. A stage. A prolonged stage. Soon enough this stage would revolve and as Tom's bedroom vanished, on would trundle white organdy, blue ribbons, a smiling girl opening her arms . . . but that would come later. As for now, I could continue to look as long as I liked into Tom's eyes the color of faded lapis beneath brows so blond they were visible only at the roots just to each side of his nose—a faint smudge turning gold as it thinned and sped out toward the temples. He was a ratty boy. He hated to shave and would let his peach fuzz go for a week or even two at a time; it grew in in clumps, full on the chin, sparse along the jaw, patchy beside the deep wicks of his mouth. His chamois-cloth shirts were all missing buttons. The gaps they left were filled in with glimpses of dingy undershirt. His jockey shorts had holes in them. Around one leg a broken elastic had popped out of the cotton seam and dangled against his thigh like a gray noodle. Since he wore a single pair of shorts for days on end the front pouch would soon be stained with yellow. He got up too late to shower before school; he'd run a hand through his fine hair but could never tame that high spume of a cowlick that tossed and bobbed above him, absurdly, gallantly.

His rattiness wore a jaunty air that redeemed everything. Faded, baggy jeans, Indian moccasins he'd owned so long the soft leather tops had taken on the shape of his toes, sunglasses repaired with Band-Aids, an ancient purple shirt bleached and aged to a dusty plum, a letter jacket with white leather sleeves and on the back white lettering against a dark blue field—these were the accoutrements of a princely pauper.

We walked beside the lake at night, a spring night. As we walked we rolled gently into each other, so that our shoulders touched with every other step. A coolness scudded in off the lake and we kept our hands in our pockets. Now Tom had leapt up onto the narrow top of a retaining wall and was scampering along it in his moccasins. Although heights terrified me I followed him. The ground on both sides fell away as we crossed a canal flowing into the lake, but I put one foot in front of the other and looked not down but at Tom's back. I prayed to a God I didn't believe in to preserve me. Soon enough I was beside Tom again and my pulse subsided: that dangerous crossing was a sacrifice I'd made to him. Our shoulders touched. As usual he was talking too loud and in his characteristic way, a sustained tenor *uh* as he collected his thoughts, then a chuckle and a rapid, throw-away sentence that came almost as an anticlimax. Since Tom was the most popular boy at school, many guys had imitated his halting, then rushing way of talking (as well as his grungy clothes and haphazard grooming). But I never wanted to be Tom. I wanted Tom to be Tom for me. I wanted him to hold his reedy, sinewy, scruffy maleness in trust for us both. We were heading toward a concrete pier wide enough for a truck to run down. At the far end people were fishing for smelt, illegal lanterns drawing silver schools into nets. We ambled out and watched the lights play over that dripping, squirming ore being extracted from the lake's mines. A net was dumped at my feet and I saw that cold life arc, panic, die. Tommy knew one of the old guys, who gave us a couple dozen fish, which we took back to the Wellington's place.

At midnight everyone was in bed, but Tom decided we were hungry and had to fry up our smelt right now. The odor of burning butter and bitter young fish drew Mrs. Wellington down from her little sitting room where she dozed, watched television and paged through books about gardening and thoroughbred dogs. She came blinking and padding down to the kitchen, lured by the smell of frying fish, the smell of a pleasure forbidden because it comes from a kingdom we dare not enter for long. I was certain she would be gruff—she was frowning, though only against the neon brightness of the kitchen. "What's going on here?" she asked in what must have been at last the sound of her true voice, the poor, flat intonations of the prairies where she'd grown up. Soon she was pouring out tall glasses of milk and setting places for us. She was a good sport in an unselfconscious way I'd never seen in a grown-up before, as though she and we were all part of the same society of hungry, browsing creatures instead of members of two tribes, one spontaneous and the other repressive. She seemed to bend naturally to the will of her son, and this compliance suggested an unspoken respect for the primacy of even such a young and scruffy man. My own mother paid lip service to the notion of male supremacy, but she had had to make her own way in the world too long to stay constant to such a useless, purely decorative belief.

After the midnight supper Tommy started to play the guitar and sing. He and I had trekked more than once downtown to the Folk Center to hear a barefoot hillbilly woman in a long, faded skirt intone Elizabethan songs and pluck at a dulcimer or to listen, frightened and transported, to a big black lesbian with a crewcut moan her basso way through the blues. The People—those brawny, smiling farmers, those plump, wholesome teens bursting out of bib overalls, those toothless ex-cons, those white-eyed dust bowl victims—the People, half glimpsed in old photos, films and WPA murals, were about to reemerge, we trusted, into history and our lives.

All this aspiration, this promise of fellowship and equality, informed Tom's songs. We worried a bit (just a bit) that we might be suburban twerps unworthy of the People. We already knew to sneer at certain folksingers for their "commercial" arrangements, their "slickness," their betrayal of the heartrending plainness of real working folks. Although we strove in our daily lives to be as agreeable and popular as possible, to conform exactly to reigning fads, we simultaneously abhorred whatever was ingratiating. As a result we were drawn to a club where a big, scarred Negro with lots of gold jewelry and liverish eyes ruminated over a half-improvised ballad under a spotlight before a breathless, thrilled audience of sheltered white teens (overheard on the way out from the newly elected president of our United Nations club: "It makes you feel so damn phony. It even makes you Question Your Values").

Of course the best thing about folk music was that it gave me a chance to stare at Tommy while he sang. After endless false starts, after tunings and retunings and trial runs of newly or imperfectly learned strums, he'd finally accompany himself through one great ballad after another. His voice was harsh and high, his hands grubby, the nails ragged crescents of black axle-grease, and soon enough his exertions would make the faded blue workshirt cling to his back and chest in dark blue patches. Whereas when he spoke he was evasive or philosophical, certainly jokey in a tepid way, when he sang he was eloquent with passion, with the simple statement of passion. And I was, for once, allowed to stare and stare at him. Sometimes, after he fell asleep at night, I'd study the composition of grays poised on the pale lozenge of his pillow, those grays that constituted a face, and I'd dream he was awakening, rising to kiss me, the grays blushing with fire and warmth—but then he'd move and I'd realize that what I'd taken to be his face was in fact a fold in the sheet. I'd listen for his breath to quicken, I'd look for his sealed eyes to glint, I'd wait for his hot, strong hand to reach across the chasm between the beds to grab me—but none of that happened. There was no passion displayed between us and I never saw him show any feeling at all beyond a narrow range of teasing and joking. Except when he sang. Then he was free, that is, constrained by the ceremony of performance, the fiction that the entertainer is alone, that he is expressing grief or joy to himself alone. Tom would close his eyes and tip his head back. Squint lines would stream away from his eyes, his forehead would wrinkle, the veins would stand out along his throat and when he held a high note his whole body would tremble. One time he proudly showed me the callouses he'd earned by playing the guitar; he let me feel them. Sometimes he didn't play at all but just sounded notes as he worked something out. He had forgotten me. He thought he was alone. He'd drop the slightly foolish smile he usually wore to disarm adolescent envy or adult expectation and he looked angry and much older: I took this to be his true face. As a folksinger Tom was permitted to wail and shout and moan, and as his audience I was permitted to look at him.

His father invited me to go sailing. I accepted, although I warned him I was familiar only with powerboats and had had no experience as a crew member. Everything about dressing the ship—unshrouding and raising the sails, lowering the keel, installing the rudder, untangling the sheets—confused me. I knew I was in the way and I stood, one hand on the boom, and tried to inhale myself into nonexistence. I heard Mr. Wellington's quick sharp breaths as reproaches.

The day was beautiful, a cold, constant spring wind swept past us, high towers of clouds were rolling steadily closer like medieval war machines breaching the blue fortress of sky. Light spilled down out of the clouds onto the choppy lake, gray and cold and faceted, in constant motion but going nowhere. Hundreds of boats were already out, their sails pivoting and flashing in the shifting beams of sunlight. A gull's wings dropped like the slowly closing legs of a draftsman's compass.

At last we were underway. Mr. Wellington, unlike my father, was a smooth, competent sailor. He pulled the boat around so that the wind was behind us and he asked me to attach the spinnaker pole to the jib sail, but I became frightened when I had to lean out over the coursing water and Tommy filled in for me, not vexed at me but I suspect worried about what his father would think. And what was I afraid of? Falling in? But I could swim, a rope could be tossed my way. That wasn't it. Even my vertigo I had overcome on the sea wall for Tom's sake. It was, I'm sure, Mr. Wellington's disapproval I feared and invited, that disapproval which, so persistent, had ended by becoming a manner, a way of being, like someone's way of holding his head to one side, something familiar, something I would miss if it were absent. Not that he bestowed his disapproval generously on me. No, even that he withheld and dispensed in only the smallest sums.

The wind blew higher and higher and Mr. Wellington, who'd taken in sail, was holding close to it. We gripped the gunwales and leaned back out over the cold, running waves, the water brushing, then soaking, the backs of our shirts. The sun solemnly withdrew into its tent of cloud, disappointed with the world. By the slightest turn of my head I could change the moan of the wind into a whistle. There we were, just a father and his teenage son and the son's friend out for a sail, but in my mind, at least, the story was less simple. For I found in this Mr. Wellington a version of myself so transformed by will and practice as to be not easily recognizable, but familiar nonetheless. In him I sensed someone as unloved and unlovely as I felt myself to be. He wasn't handsome now nor had he ever been, I was certain, and his lack of romantic appeal shaded his responses to his glamorous son, the muted, wary adoration as well as the less than frank envy.

I'd begun to shiver. The day was turning darker and had blown all the birds out of the sky and half the boats back to harbor. I was huddling, hugging myself down in the hull, wet back to the wind. Mr. Wellington was letting out sail—the tock-tock-tock of the winch releasing the main-sheet—and he was looking at me, holding his judgment in reserve. Between us, these two tight minds, flew the great sail and Tom inhabiting it as he leaned back into it, pushing it, pushing until we came around, he ducked and the boom swung overhead and stopped with a shocking thud. Here was this boy, laughing and blonded by the sun and smooth-skinned, his whole body straining up as he reached to cleat something so that his t-shirt parted company with his dirty, sagging jeans and we—the father and I—could see Tom's muscles like forked lightning on his taut stomach; here was this boy so handsome and free and well-liked and here were we flanking him, looking up at him, at his torso flowering out of the humble calyx of his jeans.

It seemed to me then that beauty is the highest good, the one thing we all want to be or have or failing that destroy, and that all the world's virtues are nothing but the world's spleen and deceit. The ugly, the old, the rich and the accomplished speak of invisible merits—of character and wisdom and power and skill—because they lack the visible ones, that ridiculous down under the lower lip that can't decide to be a beard, those prehensile bare feet racing down the sleek deck, big hands too heavy for slender arms, the sweep of lashes over faded lapislazuli eyes, lips deep red, the windblown hair intricate as Velasquez's rendering of lace.

One fall evening Tom called me to ask me if I'd like to go out on a double date. He'd be with Sally, of course, and I'd be with Helen Paper. Just a movie. Maybe a burger afterwards. Not too late. School tomorrow. Her regular date had come down with a cold.

I said sure.

I dashed down the hall to tell my mother, who in a rare domestic moment had a sewing basket on her lap. Her glasses had slid down to the tip of her nose and her voice came out slow and without inflection as she tried to thread a needle.

"Guess what!" I shouted.

"What, dear?" She licked the thread and tried again.

"That was Tom and he's arranged a date for me with Helen Paper, who's the most beautiful and sophisticated girl in the whole school."

"Sophisticated?" There, the thread had gone through.

"Yes, yes"—I could hear my voice rising higher and higher; somehow I had to convey the excitement of my prospect—"she's only a freshman but she goes out with college boys and everything and she's been to Europe and she's—well, the other girls say top-heavy but only out of sour grapes. And she's the leader of the Crowd or could be if she cared and didn't have such a reputation."

My mother was intent upon her sewing. She was dressed to go out and this, yes, it must be a rip in the seam of her raincoat; once she'd fixed it she'd be on her way. "Wonderful, dear."

"But isn't it exciting?" I insisted.

"Well, yes, but I hope she's not too fast."

"For me?"

"For anyone. In general. There, now." My mother bit the thread off, her eyes suddenly as wide and empty and intelligent as a cat's. She stood, examined her handiwork, put the coat on, moved to the door, backtracked, lifted her cheek toward me to peck. "I hope you have fun. You seem terribly nervous. Just look at your hands. You're wringing them— never saw anyone literally wring his hands before."

"Well, it's terribly exciting," I said in wild despair.

My sister wasn't home so I was alone once my mother had gone— alone to take my second bath of the day in the mean, withholding afternoon light permeating the frosted glass window and to listen to the listless hum of traffic outside, in such contrast to my heart's anticipation. It was as though the very intensity of my feeling had drained the surroundings of significance. I was the unique center of consciousness, its toxic concentration.

I was going out on a date with Helen Paper and I had to calm myself by then because the evening would surely be quicksilver small talk and ten different kinds of smile and there would be hands linking and parting as, in a square dance, you had to be very subtle to hear the calls, subtle and calm. I wanted so badly to be popular, to have the others look back as I ran to catch up, then walk with my left hand around his waist, the right around hers, her long hair blown back on my shoulder, pooling there for a moment in festive intimacy, a sort of gold epaulette of the secret order of joy.

Helen Paper had a wide, regal forehead, straight dark hair pulled back from her face, curiously narrow hips and strong, thin legs. What she was famous for were the great globes of her breasts which were as evident as her smile and almost as easy to acknowledge and so heavy that her shoulders had become very strong. How her breasts hung naturally I had no way of knowing since in her surgically sturdy brassiere her form had been idealized into—well, two uncannily symmetrical globes, at once proud, inviting and (by virtue of their symmetry) respectable.

But to describe her without mentioning her face would be absurd since everyone was dazzled by those fine blue eyes, harder or perhaps less informative than one would have anticipated, and by that nose, so straight and Hellenic, joined to the forehead without a bump or transition of any sort, the nose a prayer ascending above the altar of lips so rich and sweet that one could understand how men had once regarded women as spoils in wars worth fighting for. She was a woman (for she surely seemed a woman despite her youth) supremely confident of her own appeal, of her status as someone desirable in the abstract—that is, attractive and practicable to anyone under any conditions at any time, rather than in the concrete, to me now as mine. She wasn't shy or passive, but to the extent she was a vessel she was full to the brim with the knowledge that she represented a prize. She was a custodian of her own beauty.

Her custodial role made her elusive, a self seen through smoke. She did seem to be looking at me through smoke, its irregular updraft rearranging her face, lifting and enlarging a detail for a moment before letting it catch up with itself, reintegrate with the rest, smokey arabesques turning silver in the backlight as she turned halfway and her profile went dark, the only touch of brilliance on her lip.

Our date was quick, unremarkable (it's the curse of adolescence that its events are never adequate to the feelings they inspire, that no unadorned retelling of those events can suggest the feelings). Tommy's mother collected us all in her car (we were still too young to drive) and deposited us at the theater. Green spotlights buried in fake ferns in the lobby played on a marble fountain that had long since been drained. The basin was filled with candy wrappers and paper napkins. Inside, behind padded doors each pierced by a grimy porthole, soared the dark splendors of the theater brushed here and there by the ushers' traveling red flashlights or feebly, briefly dispelled by the glow of a match held to a forbidden cigarette. The ceiling had been designed to resemble the night sky, the stars were minute bulbs, the moon a yellow crescent. To either side of the screen was a windswept version of a royal box, a gilt throne on a small carpeted dais under a great blown-back stucco curtain topped by a papier-mâché coronet. When I finally held Helen Paper's hand after sitting beside her for half an hour in the dark, I said to myself, "This hand could be insured for a million dollars." She surrendered her hand to me, but was I really a likely candidate for it? Was this the way guys became popular? Did certain girls have the guts to tell everyone else, "Look, be nice to this guy. He's not a nerd. He's worth it. He's special?" Or was this date merely some extraordinary favor wrangled for me by Tommy, something that would not be repeated? Could it be (and I knew it could) that the star chamber of popularity was sealed and that no one would be admitted to it—no one except some casual new prince who belonged there? Tommy was a prince. He had a knack for demanding attention; even when he called the telephone operator for a number he'd hold her in conversation. Once he even talked her into meeting him after work. The receptionists in offices downtown, salesladies in stores, the mothers of friends—all of them he sized up, mentally undressed, and though this appraisal might seem to be rude, in fact most women liked it. An efficient woman would be sailing past him. He'd grab her wrist. He'd apologize for the intrusion, but he'd also stand very close to her and his smile wouldn't apologize for a thing. And she, at exactly the moment I would have expected outrage, would flush, her eyes would flutter, not in an experienced way but meltingly, since he'd touched a nerve, since he'd found a way to subvert the social into the sexual—and then she'd smile and rephrase what she was saying in a voice charmingly without conviction.

After the movie we went somewhere for a snack and then I walked Helen home. Her beauty stood between us like an enemy, some sort of hereditary enemy I was supposed to fear, but I liked her well enough. Even the fiercest lovers must like each other at least once in a while. The trees arching above the deserted suburban streets tracked slowly past overhead, their crowns dark against a hazy white night sky, clouds lit up like internal organs dyed for examination, for augury . . . I spoke quietly, deliberately to Helen Paper and I snatched glances of her famous smile rising to greet my words. Our attention wasn't given over to words but to the formal charting of that night street that we were executing. I mean we, or rather our bodies, the animal sense in us, some orienting device— we were discovering each other, and for one moment I felt exultantly worthy of her. For she did have the power to make me seem interesting, at least to myself. I found myself talking faster and with more confidence as we approached the wide, dimly lit porch of her house. Some late roses perfumed the night. A sprinkler someone had left on by mistake played back and forth over the grass. A sudden breeze snatched up the spray and flung it on the walkway ahead, a momentary darkening of the white pavement. Inside, upstairs, a room was just barely lit behind a drawn curtain. Crickets took the night's pulse. Although I said something right out of dancing school to Helen—"Good night, it's been great to spend some time with you"—an unexpected understanding had fallen on us. Of course her allure—the sudden rise and fall of her wonderful soft breasts, the dilation of her perfume on the cool night air, the smile of a saint who points, salaciously, toward Heaven—this allure had seduced me entirely. I loved her. I didn't know what to do with her. I suspected another, more normal boy would have known how to tease her, to make her laugh, would have treated her more as a friend and less as an idol. Had I been expected to do something I would have fled, but now, to-night, I did love her, as one might love a painting one admired but didn't, couldn't, wouldn't own. She was completely relaxed when she

took my hand and looked in my eyes, as she thanked me and bobbed a
curtsy in a little-girl manner other men, I'm sure, liked better than I;
sensing my resistance to anything fetching, she doubled back and inten-
sified her gravity. By which I'm not suggesting she was playing a part. In
fact, I don't know what she was doing. Because I loved her she was
opaque to me, and her sincerity I doubted not at all until I doubted it
completely.

I thanked her and said I hoped I'd see her soon. For a moment it
seemed as though it would be the most natural thing to kiss her on those
full, soft lips (had I not seen her a moment ago covertly pop some
scented thing into her mouth to prepare for just such an inevitability?).
Her eyes were veiled with awareness of her own beauty. I suppose I
suddenly liked myself and I could see a light in which I'd be plausible to
others. My love for Tommy was shameful, something I was also proud of
but tried to hide. This moment with Helen—our tallness on the moon-
lashed porch, the coolness that sent black clouds (lit by gold from
within) caravelling past a pirate moon, a coolness that glided through
opening fingers that now touched, linked, squeezed, slowly drew apart—
this moment made me happy. Hopeful. An oppression had been lifted.
A long apprenticeship to danger had abruptly ended.

After I left her I raced home through the deserted streets laughing
and leaping. I sang show tunes and danced and felt as fully alive as
someone in a movie (since it was precisely life that was grainy and
sepia-tinted, whereas the movies had the audible ping, the habitable
color, the embraceable presence of reality). I was more than ready to give
up my attraction to men for this marriage to Helen Paper. At last the
homosexual phase of my adolescence had drawn to a close. To be sure,
I'd continue to love Tommy but as he loved me: fraternally. In my
dream the stowaway in the single bunk with me, whom I was trying to
keep hidden under a blanket, had miraculously transformed himself into
my glorious bride, as the kissed leper in the legend becomes the Christ
Pantocrator.

When I got home my mother was in bed with the lights out.
"Honey?"
"Yes?"
"Come in and talk to me."
"Okay," I said.
"Rub my back, okay?"
"Okay," I said. I sat beside her on the bed. She smelled of bourbon.
"How was your date?"
"Terrific! I never had such a good time."
"How nice. Is she a nice girl?"

"Better than that. She's charming and sophisticated and intelligent."

"You're home earlier than I expected. Not so hard. Rub gently. You bruiser. I'm going to call you that: Bruiser. Is she playful? Is she like me? Does she say cute things?"

"No, thank God."

"Why do you say that? Is she some sort of egghead?"

"Not an egghead. But she's dignified. She's straightforward. She says what she means."

"I think girls should be playful. That doesn't mean dishonest. I'm playful."

"—"

"Well, I am. Do you think she likes you?"

"How can I tell? It was just a first date." My fingers lightly stroked her neck to either side of her spine. "I doubt if she'll want to see me again. Why should she?"

"But why not? You're handsome and intelligent."

"Handsome! With these big nostrils!"

"Oh, that's just your sister. She's so frustrated she has to pick on you. There's nothing wrong with your nostrils. At least I don't see anything wrong. Of course I know you too well. If you like, we could consult a nose doctor." A long pause. "Nostrils . . . do people generally dwell on them? I mean, do people think about them a lot?" Small, high voice: "Are mine okay?"

A hopeless silence.

At last she began to snore delicately and I hurried to my own room. My sister's door, next to mine, was closed but her light was burning resentfully.

And I gave myself over to my reverie. I had a record player I'd paid for myself by working as a caddy and records I exchanged each week at the library, the music an outpost of my father's influence in this unmusical female territory.

I slipped out of my clothes as quickly as possible, though I tried to do everything beautifully, as in a movie of my life with Helen. In some way I felt it was already being filmed—not that I looked for hidden cameras but I simplified and smoothed out my movements for the lens. Every detail of my room asked me to be solicitous. When the dresser drawer stuck I winced—this sequence would have to be reshot. I turned my sheets down as though she, Helen, were at my side. I rushed to snap off the lights. She and I lay side by side in the narrow boat and floated downstream. The stars moved not at all and only the occasional fluttering of a branch overhead or the sound of a scraping rock below suggested our passage. By dawn I'd made love to Helen four times. The first time was so ceremonial I had a problem molding the mist into arms and legs; all that kept flickering up at me was her smile. The second time was more passionate. I was finally able to free her breasts from their binding. By the third time we'd become gently fraternal; we smiled with tired kindness at each other. We were very intimate. At dawn she began to disintegrate. The sickening certainty of day pulsed into being and all my exertions were able to keep her at my side only a few more moments. At last she fled.

I stumbled from class to class in a numb haze. Strangely enough, I was afraid I'd run into Helen. I didn't feel up to her. I was too tired. In homeroom I yawned, rested my head on my desk and longed for the privacy of my bed and the saving grace of night. I wanted to be alone with my wraith. In my confusion the real Helen Paper seemed irrelevant, even intrusive.

That night I wrote her a letter. I chose a special yellow parchment paper, a spidery pen point and black ink. In gym class as I'd stumbled through calisthenics and in study hall as I'd half-dozed behind a stack of books, phrases for the letter had dropped into my mind. Now I sat down with great formality at my desk and composed the missive, first in pencil on scratch paper. I offered her my love and allegiance while admitting I knew how unworthy of her I was. And yet I had half a notion that though I might be worthless as a date (not handsome enough) I might be of some value as a husband (intelligent, successful). In marriage, merits outweighed appeal, and I could imagine nothing less eternal than marriage with Helen. But I mentioned marriage only once in the letter.

A week went by before I received her answer. Twice I saw her in the halls. The first time she came over to me and looked me in the eye and smiled her sweet, intense smile. She was wearing a powder-blue cashmere sweater and her breasts rose and fell monumentally as she asked me in her soft drawl how I was doing. Nothing in her smile or voice suggested a verdict either for or against me. I felt there was something improper about seeing her at all before I got her letter. I mumbled, "Fine," blushed and slunk off. I felt tall and dirty. I was avoiding Tommy as well. Soon enough I would have to tell him about my proposal to Helen, which I suspected he'd disapprove of as a ridiculously false and fruitless move.

Then one afternoon, a Friday after school, there was her letter to me in the mailbox. Even before I opened it I was mildly grateful she had at least answered me. At least she'd spared me the indignity of acting as though she had never heard from me.

The apartment was empty. I went to the sun room and looked across the street at the lake churning like old machinery in a deserted amusement park, rides without riders. My mind kept two separate sets of books. In one I was fortunate she'd taken the time to write me even this rejection, more than a creep like me deserved. In the other she said, "You're not the person I would have chosen for a date nor for a summer or semester but yes, I will marry you. Nor do I want anything less from you. Romance is an expectation of an ideal life to come, and in that sense my feelings for you are romantic."

If someone had made me guess which reply I'd find inside the envelope, I would have chosen the rejection since pessimism is always accurate, but acceptance would not have shocked me, since I also believed in the miraculous.

I poured myself a glass of milk in the kitchen and returned to the sun room. Her handwriting was well-formed and rounded, the dots over the *i*'s, circles, the letters fatter than tall, the lines so straight I suspected she had placed the thin paper over a ruled-off grid. The ordinariness, the schoolgirl ordinariness of her hand frightened me—I didn't feel safe in such an ordinary hand. "I like you very much as a friend," she wrote. "I was pleased and surprised to receive your lovely letter. It was one of the sweetest tributes to me I have ever had from anyone. I know this will hurt, but I am forced to say it if I am to prevent you further pain. I do not love you and I never have. Our friendship has been a matter of mutual and rewarding liking, not loving. I know this is very cruel, but I must say it. Try not to hate me. I think it would be best if we did not see each other for a while. I certainly hope we can continue to be friends. I consider you to be one of my very best friends. Please, please forgive me. Try to understand why I have to be this way. Sincerely, Helen."

Well, her phrasing was less childish than her hand, I thought, as though the letter were a composition in class that concerned me in no way. Even as this attitude broke over me, but before I was drawn into another more dangerous one, I had time to notice she said I was one of her very best friends, an honor I'd been unaware of until now—as who had not: I registered the social gain before the romantic loss. Unless (and here I could taste something bitter on the back of my tongue)—unless the "mature" advice ("I think it would be best if we did not see each other for a while") was actually a denial of the consolation prize, a way of keeping me out of her circle at the very moment she was pretending to invite me into it. Could it be that the entire exercise, its assured tone, the concision and familiar ring of the phrasing, figured as nothing more than a "tribute" (her word) she had piled up before the altar of her own beauty? How many people had she shown my letter to?

But then all this mental chatter stopped and I surrendered to something else, something less active, more abiding, something that had been waiting politely all this time but that now stepped forward, diffident yet impersonal: my grief.

For the next few months I grieved. I would stay up all night crying and playing records and writing sonnets to Helen. What was I crying for? I cried during gym class when someone got mad at me for dropping the basketball. In the past I would have hidden my pain but now I just slowly walked off the court, the tears spurting out of my face. I took a shower, still crying, and dressed forlornly and walked the empty halls even though to do so during class time was forbidden. I no longer cared about rules. I let my hair grow, I stopped combing it, I forgot to change my shirt from one week to the next. With a disabused eye I watched other kids striving to succeed, to become popular. I became a sort of vagabond of grief or, as I'd rather put it, I entered grief's vagabondage, which better suggests a simultaneous freedom and slavery. Freedom from the now meaningless pursuit of grades, friends, smiles; slavery to a hopeless love.

Every afternoon I'd stumble home exhausted to my room, but once there my real work would begin, which was to imagine Helen in my arms, Helen beside me laughing, Helen looking up at me through the lace suspended from the orange-blossom chaplet, Helen with other boys, kissing them, unzipping her shorts and stepping out of them, pushing her hair back out of her serious, avid eyes. She was a puppet I could place in one playlet after another, but once I'd invoked her she became independent, tortured me, smiled right through me at another boy, her approaching lover. Her exertions with other men fascinated me and the longer I suffered, the more outrageous were the humiliations I had other men inflict on her.

Yet what I felt most often was not bitter lust but pain and a fascination with insanity that was at once frightening and soothing. I knew I was drifting farther and farther out to sea. I was losing weight. I'd torn up my phone list. When other people said hi to me in the halls I stared right through them, my face a Ku Klux Klan sheet with burning holes for eyes—or I smiled with weary compassion at these antics. Paul Valéry, or rather his narrator, writes of Monsieur Teste: "When he spoke he never raised an arm or a finger—he had *killed his puppet.*" I felt I'd killed mine, that I was no longer routinely producing gestures, that I was old and thoroughly disenchanted. Other people's ambitions struck me as ludicrous and I'd look for a smile, the hint of the co-conspirator, behind their zealous faces. Surely we all knew we were in a ridiculous game, that if we kept playing it we did so only as a frivolous alternative to suicide.

I became ill with mononucleosis, ironically the "kissing disease" that afflicted so many teenagers in those days. I was kept out of school for several months. Most of the time I slept, feverish and content: exempted. Just to cross the room required all my energy. Whether or not to drink another glass of ginger ale could absorb my attention for an hour. That my grief had been superseded by illness relieved me; I was no longer willfully self-destructive. I was simply ill. Love was forbidden. My doctor had told me I mustn't kiss anyone. Helen had been spared. I had been absolved. Tommy called me from time to time but I felt he and I had nothing in common now—after all, he was just a boy, whereas I'd become a very old man.

JOY WILLIAMS

Making Friends

Willie and Liberty broke into a house on Crab Key and lived there for a week. Crab Key was tiny and exclusive, belonging to an association which had armed security patrol. The houses on Crab Key were owned by people so wealthy that they were hardly ever there. They were elsewhere.

Liberty and Willie saw the guard daily. He was an old, lonely man, rather glossy and puffed up, his jaw puckered in and his chest puffed out like a child concentrating on making a muscle. He told Willie he had a cancer but that grapefruit was curing it. Willie and Liberty must have reminded him of people he knew, people who must have looked appropriate living in a $300,000 cypress villa on the beach. He thought they were guests of the owners.

Willie did have a look to him. People would babble on to Willie as though in his implacability they would find their grace. Liberty couldn't understand it herself. Willie's detail was gone. He had a closed sleek face which did not transmit impressions. He was tight as a jar of jam. People were crazy about Willie.

"If I were young, I wouldn't be here," the guard said. "The big show is definitely not way out here."

"The big show is in our heads," Willie said. Willie and the guard got along famously.

In the house, Clem was lying before the sliding glass doors, his breath making small parachuting souls on the glass. Clem was Liberty's dog, a big white Alsatian with one blind eye. His good eye was open, watching his vacation.

The guard said, "You know, I'll tell you, my name is Turnupseed."

"Glad to know you," Willie said.

"That name mean nothing to you?"

"I don't believe it does," Willie said.

The guard shook his head back and forth, back and forth. "How quickly they forget," he said to an imaginary person on his right.

Liberty said nothing. She supposed they were about to be arrested. She and Willie were young, but they had been breaking into other people's houses for many years now. They were bound to get arrested someday.

"My nephew Donald Gene Turnupseed killed Jimmy Dean. You know, his car ran into Jimmy Dean's car."

"Well," Willie said, "1955."

"It seems like a long time ago, but I don't see what difference that makes," Turnupseed said. "We are talking about something immortal here. Young girls have made a cult of Dean even though he was a faggot."

"Life is not a masterpiece," Willie agreed.

"Life is a damn mess," the guard said. He seemed genuinely outraged.

Turnupseed enjoyed cooking. In inclement weather, he could be seen sitting in his patrol car reading cookbooks. He loved reading cookbooks. He and Willie would speak with fervor about chili and cassoulets and pineapple glazed yams and pastry sucrée.

"Your wife looks sad," Turnupseed said to Willie. "Has she had a loss recently?"

"She's just one of those wives," Willie said.

"What do women want, let me ask you that," Turnupseed said. "My last two wives always maintained they were miserable even though they had every distraction and convenience. Number Two had a four-wheel drive vehicle with a personalized license plate. Every week she'd have her hair done. She died of a stroke, at the beauty shop, under the dryer."

"Liberty isn't distracted easily," Willie said.

"What would our lives be without our distractions," Turnupseed said, "that's the question."

The house that Liberty and Willie had taken as their own was simple and soaring, but it was cluttered within. The owners seemed to possess everything in triplicate except for reading material. The only thing to read was a newspaper seven weeks old. Liberty kept glancing at it. There were two items of considerable interest, she thought.

One was an article about trees. It said that each person in the world needs all the oxygen produced in a year by a tree with 30,000 leaves.

The other item was about babies. A nurse had made the first error. She had mixed up two newborn babies and given them to the wrong mother for nursing. A second nurse on a different shift switched them back again. The first nurse, realizing her initial error, switched them a third time, switched the little plastic bracelets on their chubby wrists, switched the coded scribbled plastic inserts on their rolling baskets. At this point, the situation had become hopelessly scrambled. Three days passed. The mothers went home with the wrong babies. This was not a Prince and Pauper type story. Both mothers had nice homes and fathers and siblings for the baby. Four months later, the hospital called and told the mothers that they had the wrong babies. They had proof. Toe prints and blood types. Chemical proof. They had done the things professionals do to prove that a person is the person he is supposed to be. The mothers were hysterical. They had fallen in love with the wrong baby and now they didn't want to give their wrong baby up. But apparently it had to be done. It seemed to be the law.

Breaking into houses caused Liberty to become pensive. She would get cramps and lose her appetite. Stolen houses made her think of babies all the time. She supposed that was common enough.

The house on Crab Key had chocolate colored wall-to-wall carpeting scattered with Oriental rugs. It had a Mexican tiled tub that could accommodate four. The Italian chrome and 'mica kitchen contained every mechanized friend known to the cook and the cupboards were filled with canned goods. There was a closet off the bath which contained nothing but toilet paper.

"This is how the elderly prepare for nuclear attack," Willie said, staring in at the treasury of white two-ply.

Willie loved living in other people's houses and sleeping in their beds. He wore their clothes and drank their liquor and saw himself in their mirrors. He got a very satisfying hit from breaking into houses and living an ordered life.

In this particular house there was a large walk-in closet. There were mirrors and cosmetics. There were shoe boxes and garment bags. There were hats and ties. Everything was neatly categorized. *Cruise Wear. Ethnic Shawls and Dresses. Daddy's WW I Uniforms.* As in the other homes Liberty and Willie tended to occupy, the absent owners were organized, hopeful, acquisitive and fearful of death.

It was astonishing to Liberty that all this was being guarded by Turnupseed, a man obsessed with woks, dead wives and movie stars, and armed with a floating flashlight and a tire iron. He was obviously not in the best of health. His eyes were like breakfast buns spread with guava jelly. To Liberty, he said, "That certainly is the strangest white dog I've ever seen. Nothing unfortunate is about to happen to you, not if that dog can help it."

"I don't know," Liberty said.

"Thank god, it ain't a black dog. Black dogs are bad luck."

"Thank god," Liberty said. The thought of a black dog! Black as dirt and filled with blood. She would never have a black dog.

Liberty and Turnupseed gazed at one another. Liberty and Turnupseed just couldn't seem to build up a dialogue.

"Where'd you get that dog?" Turnupseed asked, cranking up again, his voice hoarse.

"Found him," Liberty said.

"I've never found a thing myself," Turnupseed said. "I try not to dwell on it." He gazed at Clem, not knowing how to salute him.

Turnupseed lived on the mainland in a little cement block house on land sucked senseless by the phosphate interests.

"I've had three wives and each one of them died," Turnupseed confided. "Isn't that a ghastly coincidence?"

"In continuity there is a little of everything in everything else," Willie said when Liberty just couldn't seem to pick anything out of the air. Willie and the guard seemed to have a way of conversing that was satisfying to them both. Willie enjoyed a simple deceit more than just about anything in the world, Liberty guessed. Nobody at all seemed to grasp what she and Willie were doing. Liberty began to feel unreal. The words Willie exchanged with Turnupseed rocked gently in her head, unwholesome crafts on a becalmed sea.

Nonetheless, the days passed. In the mornings, Liberty trudged along with Clem on the wide, shelly beach. There she met women who searched for sharks' teeth. These women had elaborate tooth scoopers made of screening and wood. They had spotting scoops and dip boxes. They were dedicated and purposeful, and hustling in and out of the surf, they knew what they were about. Liberty admired them. They knew the difference between a spinner's tooth and a lemon's. They were happy women, rigorous in their selections. In their bags they had duskys' and blacktips' and makos' teeth. They loved those teeth. In their homes, lamplight glowed from wired glass bases filled with teeth. The women who searched the beaches put their finest teeth on velvet and framed them behind glass. The more common teeth spelled out homilies or were arranged in the shape of hearts. These women on the beach knew what was necessary to them.

None of them spoke to Liberty. They regarded Clem with downright unease as though fearing he would squat on their fossiliferous wash-ins. Liberty felt that the women were correct in not introducing themselves and being friendly. She, Liberty, was a thief and a depressive. She had been married by a drunken judge at Monroe Station in the Everglades. The bridal couple had eaten their wedding supper in a restaurant which had antique rifles and dried chicken feet mounted on the wall. Their wedding supper had consisted of a gigantic snook that Willie had miraculously caught on a dough ball, and cake that the cook had whipped up special. They had gotten drunk and ended up throwing pieces of cake at each other.

Those women probably saw Liberty's problems just written all over her. As for Clem, they avoided him like shoppers swerving from a swollen can of bouillabaisse.

When the mornings departed, leaving the afternoons, Liberty went back to the house and took a nap, dreaming of the things she did in stolen houses, churches and flowers and suitcases, bowls and water and caves.

Usually when she woke up, Willie was taking a picture of her. He had found a camera in the house and half a dozen rolls of film. (The owners were prepared for anything. They were prepared to shoot the end.) Willie took shots of Liberty eating from a can of peaches. He took shots of her in her mildewy bikini. He took shots of her with a sea oat between her teeth and an aspirin in her hand. Liberty saw that her life was being recorded in some way. Nevertheless, she was aware that her moments lacked incident.

Willie took pictures of Turnupseed as well. Turnupseed was tired. He was tired of the responsibility. "Looking back on it," he said, "if I had to do it all over again, I just don't know if I could."

Willie said, "We can't disown the light into which we're born."

In the hot, simple, uncaring light, Turnupseed gave a smile rather like a little baby's. "You've got a lot of my first wife in you, son. What a sweetie she was. Number One was the one I really boogied with if you know what I mean. She said that being sad separates a person from God."

"She said that?" Willie wondered.

"I believe she used those very words," Turnupseed said.

Willie put the rolls of film in an antique brass bowl on the floor in the middle of the living room. Liberty took them outside at noon and broke the film from the cassettes. She would give the strips to Yvonne, a child she knew. Yvonne would undoubtedly use the film in a creative manner. She might attach the coils to her headband and pretend she was a princess from the planet Uytnor. The sheets of film would be her face. Things had uses for which they were not intended certainly. That's what made a person keep getting up in the morning.

That was their last day in the house. They saw Turnupseed staggering along the beach with an enormous Glad bag filled with empty beer cans.

"There's enough aluminum on the beaches of Florida to build an airplane," Turnupseed said.

"We've got to be off now," Willie said. "We're leaving."

"Leaving this radiant place," Turnupseed said. "Well, I don't blame you. Last night, you know, in town, I just could swear I saw my middle wife in the laundromat. She didn't speak to me."

"Well, the dead can't disappear," Willie said. "After all, where would they go?"

"I like your manner son, I'm going to miss you," Turnupseed said. "Take care of that wife of yours. She seems to be living in a world where this don't follow that, if you know what I mean."

Later, when the Crab Key Association discovered that Turnupseed had been on such excellent terms with the besmirchers, an aneurysm would smack into Turnupseed's heart with the grace of a speeding Cadillac kissing a box turtle. Liberty could still see him waving good-bye.

POETRY

Introduction

Jonathan Galassi, then an editor at Houghton Mifflin, became the poetry editor in 1978. He was suggested for the post by Maxine Groffsky, the Paris editor of the magazine from 1966 to 1973 who had returned to New York to become a successful literary agent. A Harvard graduate, Galassi had gone to Christ Church, Cambridge, on a Marshall Scholarship, thus making him the third Cantabridgian to hold the position of poetry editor. In 1981 Galassi moved from Houghton Mifflin to Random House. He has published two translations of Eugenie Montale: *The Second Life of Art: Selected Essays* and *Otherwise,* a book of Montale's last poems. In 1986, Galassi became the editor-in-chief of Farrar, Straus & Giroux. Once asked if he had any hobbies, he said he hadn't any, unless selecting poems for the *Paris Review* could be considered one.

—G.P.

*   *   *

It's hard to make any terribly trenchant generalizations about the selections of the past ten years. When I joined the *Paris Review* in 1978, it seemed like an adventure and a good idea to try to make the magazine a more pluralistic forum for poetry, after the dedicated attention to particular esthetics on the part of my most recent predecessors. Editing is never more than the art of the possible, yet I feel we managed to print not only some of the best writers of the decade but even some of the best poems. Any period that can produce perfect short lyrics like James Merrill's "Grass" or Frederick Seidel's "Flame," or long poems as complex and fully resolved as Frank Bidart's "The War of Vaslav Nijinsky"—to name only three outstanding examples—has more than a little to show for itself. I'm also proud of the marvelous work in translation we were able to offer, while the establishment of the Bernard F. Conners Prize for a long poem in 1981 led us to some stimulating and ambitious extended work. The selection that follows is far too restricted. I hope it may lead some curious readers back to the issues themselves.

Most important of all, though, are the new poets who point to the future. What will the likes of Donald Britton, Siri Hustvedt, James Lasdun, Molly Peacock, Jim Powell, and Patricia Storace—our new poetry editor—give us in the decade to come? Tune in and find out.

—Jonathan Galassi

GUILLAUME APOLLINAIRE

Mirabeau Bridge

Under the Mirabeau Bridge there flows the Seine
          Must I recall
          Our loves recall how then
After each sorrow joy came back again

                Let night come on bells end the day
                The days go by me still I stay

Hands joined and face to face let's stay just so
          While underneath
          The bridge of our arms shall go
Eternal gazes in their weary flow

                Let night come on bells end the day
                The days go by me still I stay

All love goes by as water to the sea
    All love goes by
  How slow life seems to me
How violent the hope of love can be

    Let night come on bells end the day
    The days go by me still I stay

The days the weeks pass by beyond our ken
    Neither time past
  Nor love comes back again
Under the Mirabeau Bridge there flows the Seine

    Let night come on bells end the day
    The days go by me still I stay

—Translated by Richard Wilbur

JOHN ASHBERY

This Configuration

This movie deals with the epidemic of the way we live now.
What an inane card player. And the age may support it.
Each time the rumble of the age
Is an anthill in the distance.

As he slides the first rumpled card
Out of his dirty ruffled shirtfront the cartoon
Of the new age has begun its ascent
Around all of us like a gauze spiral staircase in which
Some stars have been imbedded.

It is the modern trumpets
Who decide the mood or tenor of this cross-section:
Of the people who get up in the morning,

Still half-asleep. That they shouldn't have fun.
But something scary will come
To get them anyway. You might as well linger
On verandas, enjoying life, knowing
The end is essentially unpredictable.
It might be soldiers
Marching all day, millions of them
Past this spot, like the lozenge pattern
Of these walls, like, finally, a kind of sleep.

Or it may be that we are ordinary people
With not unreasonable desires which we can satisfy
From time to time without causing cataclysms
That keep getting louder and more forceful instead of dying away.

Or it may be that we and the other people
Confused with us on the sidewalk have entered
A moment of seeming to be natural, expected,
And we see ourselves at the moment we see them:
Figures of an afternoon, of a century they extended.

INGEBORG BACHMANN

Autumn Maneuver

I don't say: that was before. Our pockets stuffed
with worthless summer money, we lie once more
on the chaff of scorn, in the autumn maneuver of time.
And flight to the south,
where the birds go, doesn't help us. In the evening
fishing trawlers and gondolas glide past, and sometimes
a splinter of dream-filled marble hits me
where I'm vulnerable, with beauty, in the eye.

In the newspapers I read much about the cold
and its consequences, about fools and the dead,

about the banished, the murderers and myriads
of ice-floes, but little that comforts me.
Should it be otherwise? At noon a beggar comes
And I slam the door in his face; for there is peace
and you can spare yourself an unpleasant sight, though not
the joyless dying of leaves when it rains.

Let us take a journey! Let us see sunsets under cypresses
or else under palm trees, or in orange groves,
at reduced prices, sunsets
that have no equal! Let us forget
our unanswered letters to the past!
Time does wonders. But should it come unjustly,
with the throb of guilt: we aren't at home.
In the cellar of my heart, sleepless, I find myself once more
on the chaff of scorn, in the autumn maneuver of time.

—Translated by Mark Anderson

Donald Britton

Virgule

The arrow pointing three directions
Is a looser, more open form of display,
More like the subsidiary decor

A door divulges, opening upon
A continuum of hidden driveways,
Than the steep, reversible terraces

Of a zipper. Yet how often
Have I mounted a similar staircase,
Only to find myself, impatient,

On the floor below, pale
As a Pierrot on a cocktail napkin,
The level I was standing on

Now detached from the rest
Of the structure. So autumn
Exerts pressure on the fizzing,

Bright bulk of late summer,
Upends the light
To expose its corroded underbelly.

Next week and the week after
Arriving on time but ahead
Of our schedule: the ash

Of their once twice-shy contents
Sucked back into the hanging fire
That burns you at both ends.

HAROLD BRODKEY

To Frank O'Hara

The real is a wilderness
that ambition calls a garden.

He was young. Youth is a garden posture
even after a winter's study,
discolored skin
as pored as pumice stone,
voice an arsonist's meteoric
rise—flock of urgent veering geese.
Driven intention in the face of accident,
comic, intelligent.

His pretensions were a form
of art, combustible
like song.

A democracy was in the voice
although you never said,
I bless this life.

I used to blame myself for being young.
Urging on the Irishman's parade, I was embarrassed
when love of a sort
put him in an orphanage.

Sputtering, the arc of talk
burned in the attempt
to be the beginning of art.

Envied, askew, and gone,
the dead are dishonest theorems
rescued from bleached sections of an afternoon
with the sun's slanted flags
in it.

What happened between us
was that, attentive-hearted, we began to drown,
dry auditors, in meaning.

JOSEPH BRODSKY

To Urania

I.K.

Everything has its limit, including sorrow.
A windowpane stalls a stare; nor does a grill abandon
a leaf. One may rattle the keys, gurgling down a swallow.

Loneliness cubes a man at random.
A camel sniffs at the rail with a resentful nostril;
a perspective cuts emptiness deep and even.
And what is space anyway if not the
body's absence at every given
point? That's why Urania's older than sister Clio!
In daylight or with the soot-rich lantern,
you see the globe's pate free of any bio,
you see she hides nothing, unlike the latter.
There they are, blueberry-laden forests,
rivers where the folk with bare hands catch sturgeon
or the towns in whose soggy phonebooks
you are starring no longer. Further eastward, surge on
brown mountain ranges; wild mares carousing
in tall sedge; the cheekbones get yellower
as they turn numerous. And still further east, steam dreadnoughts or
          cruisers,
and the expanse grows blue like laced underwear.

—Translated by the author

ALFRED CORN

One to One

Unwrap the message hidden in a wound
Or a word: a branching spray of avowals, cut,
Massed, left to glide deathward in a vase . . .
Face to face, a match, together until we choose;
And afterwards as well, isn't too much to hope for.
Still no sign of the chance to balance off
Independence and devotion—the armature jangled,
Door–and telephone-bell, errand, project,
A wave hello–goodbye on the fraying wing.

Unmeasurable, the drag of countered origins,
The wind-chill factor, circumstantial walls.
There's always been a question, too,
Of satire mixed in with the mortar
Of our homemade, honeyed, subfusc nougat.
Faithful in your detachment, clear-eyed, marooned;
This you reserve to me—the person in the round,
A dark, and then the light side of the earth,
Warmth that spreads at a touch, as at dawn;
The play, the heft and pungency. Prized.
Best, I think, to leave chiaroscuro alone.
(And classify your cub or mooncalf name
Along with much else so sacredly banal
It has to take the reasonable vow of silence.)
A fresh effort sends me prospecting for clues,
Browsing in your empty study, paneled
With research and labor, leather, faded gold,
Patriarchal tobacco. Lamplight does and doesn't
Sum up a mind's household. Nor are you among those
Most at ease when being photographed or described.
In no uncertain terms, spleen, tinder,
Everready rejoinder when a mood strikes,
Head in flames, the shaft breaking smartly in two.
Your turn or mine to lay it out again,
How the all-intent have trouble conceding even
The clearest-cut foul, the pang's too sharp? Who,
When the smoke clears this time, will be missing
In action? One half, contracted to an unavoidable sky.
By magic you come back, gleam and scattered debris;
Pencil in hand, the cigarette sketching gestures
As gauze floats upward, unfurled, as the sun
Goes down. Free of one more day; and how much striving.
Remains the tireless need to be reimaged.
Where we were, where we are, the wide-ranging seesaw
Of the team, in full array, a full-blooded portrait.
What questions don't dissolve in a green-brown gaze.
Focus: the doorframe opposite, by three-quarter light,
Aplomb poised on the balls of your feet, the elbows
You nurse, and—just this once—the gravest of smiles.
The album fills, it grows substantial;
Superseded, replaced, updated, changed—
The candid, casual arrangements made.

Jonathan Galassi

Lateness

Lateness is all that shimmers in the leaves,
that trembles in the bending grass,
that glistens on the berries on the vine.
Even before the final glut of summer
there is an inkling of the coming wine.
That special warmth of sunlight on your cheek
is a last kiss, the silence in the trees
is one last breath held back before September
sharpens its shears for pruning and a chill
unpolishes the surface of the lake.

Lateness is all: the aura of Before
is telling you to glory in the fall,
knowing this season's fruit is not for you.
It is still basking, rounding on its stem,
still tied to life; but you are looking on
into the conflagration that will come.
Last days are fire and water while the grape
is gathered and its sweetness is expressed,
and every afternoon's a little less
expansive, till the gold days are gone.

Are you ready to be harvested?
When all the weeds of summer have been mown,
will you be here to prove that last is best
with the high apples staying in the trees
for the long vistas of the final days
and the immense sharp stars? Will you be here,
still breathing in the temple of the air
and seeing through the bonfire of the fall,
where being and having been are everything
and lasting is all: you know that lateness is all.

LINDA GREGG

Taken By Each Thing

The day is taken by each thing and grows complete.
I go out and come in and go out again,
confused by a beauty that knows nothing of delay,
rushing like fire. All things move faster
than time and make a stillness thereby. My mind
leans back and smiles, having nothing to say.
Even at night I go out with a light and look
at the growing. I kneel and look at one thing
at a time. A white spider on a peony bud.
I have nothing to give and make a poor servant,
but I can praise the spring. Praise this wildness
that does not heed the hour. The doe that does not
stop at dark but continues to grow all night long.
The beauty in every degree of flourishing. Violets
lift to the rain and the brook gets louder than ever.
The old German farmer is asleep and the flowers go on
opening. There are stars. Mint grows high. Leaves
bend in the sunlight at the rain continues to fall.

ALLEN GROSSMAN

The Woman on the Bridge over the Chicago River

Stars are tears falling with light inside.
In the moon, they say, is a sea of tears.
It is well known that the wind weeps.
The lapse of all streams is a form of weeping,
And the heaving swell of the sea.

Cormorants
Weep from the cliffs;
The gnat weeps crossing the air of a room;
And a moth weeps in the eye of the lamp.
Each leaf is a soul in tears.

Roses weep
In the dawn light. Each tear of the rose
Is like a lens: Around the roses, the garden
Weeps in a thousand particular voices.
Under earth the bones weep, and the old tears
And new mingle without difference.
A million years does not take off the freshness
Of the calling.

Eternity and Time
Grieve incessantly in one another's arms.
Being weeps, and Nothing weeps, in the same
Night-tent, averted,
Yet mingling sad breaths. And from all ideas
Hot tears irrepressible.

In a corner
Of the same tent a small boy in a coat
Sobs and sobs,

while under the Atlantic
Depth and Darkness grieve among the fountains,
And the fountains weep out the grieving sea.

O listen, the steam engines shunt and switch
Asleep in their grieving. A sad family
In the next house over shifts mournfully
About staining the dim blind. The boy looks up
As the grieving sound of his own begetting
Keeps on.
And his willow mother mars her mirror
Of the lake with tears.

It is cold and snowing
And the snow is falling into the river.
On the bridge, lit by the white shadow of

The Wrigley building
A small woman wrapped in an old blue coat
Staggers to the rail weeping.

          As I remember,
The same boy passes, announcing the fame
Of tears, calling out the terms
In a clear way, translating to the long
Dim human avenue.

SEAMUS HEANEY

Leavings

A soft whoosh, the sunset blaze
of straw on blackened stubble,
a thatch-deep, freshing
barbarous crimson burn—

I rode down England
as they fired the crop
that was the leavings of a crop,
the smashed tow-coloured barley,

down from Ely's Lady Chapel,
the sweet tenor latin
forever banished,
the sumptuous windows

threshed clear by Thomas Cromwell.
Which circle does the tread,
scalding on cobbles,
each one a broken statue's head?

After midnight, after summer,
to walk in a sparking field,

to smell dew and ashes
and start Will Brangwen's ghost

from the hot soot—
a breaking sheaf of light,
abroad in the hiss
and clash of stooking.

Siri Hustvedt

Weather Markings

The list of small deformities passed unrecorded
In the stupor of heredity,
Like our weather,
Clouding over the tiny barn
Where he said he saw Judas hanging
Behind the old tractor
But it was the Swensby boy in a blue and yellow plaid shirt
And no note.
He went screaming Judas into the cornfield
And couldn't be hushed until evening.
Oh God the failure of prayers in the idiot days
Of summer behind the goldenrod,
Dusty on my hands; scattering doubts like the dandelions
Turned white and blown to seed—
More doubts and more prayers
Asking God not to hide his face:
The face of our weather, immense and old,
Covering the sky with clouds to smother the moon:
A small oval, like the small pale face of Jesus
In the blue book on the table with one unsteady leg.
Look at the sky, Marit,
Look at the bland green behind the leaves' paralysis

In the minutes when panic is suspended
In an estranged color,
Before the cellar door is raised
And we descend into the air
Preserving canned goods,
Before the prayers in the damp on the cold concrete
And long before the rain.
Inga with a withered hand waves it over the uprooted maple
Where the swing hung for twelve years
And where we played the fields were an ocean
And the tree a ship,
Before the mosquitoes came at about nine
And we fled in to cards or stories upstairs:
Matching suits as one moth tries the screen
And flies for the bulb
A puny tremor of white over the grey mattress
Where you sat naked on a Friday that summer.
I fingered the scar on your hip in the empty house
And whispered anyway:
Our clandestine music in muggy weather
During a walk
Past the still green grapes and the clothesline
With one pair of socks and an apron;
Belated spectres of surprise in the night,
Belonging to no one, except the heat
And our tipsy inclination.
Those hours were unmartyred,
Almost unspent,
Requiring the same effort as a dream
When the scenery becomes illegible,
And I forgot the ache of familiarity in the outlines
Of the rainwater barrels and the pump
And I concentrated on the stars,
The dot to dot of the big and little dipper.
But they began to die as the storm
Gathered for the drowning.
Turn off the lights so I can't see your face,
Hide your prints made in the mud
With your bare feet between the zinnias and the columbine
So they never reach morning,
And let me have your scent only.
When the hidden sun was just giving pink to the sky

You pressed me into a corner behind the door
And traced with your finger
The large violet birthmark on the left side of my face.

GALWAY KINNELL

The Milk Bottle

A tiny creature moves
through the tide pool, holding up
its little fortress foretelling
our tragedies; another clamps
itself down to the stone. A sea anemone
sucks at my finger, mildly, I can just
feel it, though it may mean to kill—no,
it would probably say, to eat
and flow, for all these creatures
even half made of stone seem to thrill
to altered existences. As do we ourselves,
who advance so far, then stop, then creep
a little, stop again, suddenly gasp—breath
is the bright shell
of our life-wish encasing us—gasp
it all! back in, on seeing that any time
would be OK
to go, to vanish back into all things—as when
lovers wake up at night and see
they both are crying and think, *Yes,*
but it doesn't matter, already
we will have lived forever. And yes,
if we could do that: separate out
time from happiness, remove
the molecules scattered
throughout our flesh that remember, skim them off,
throw them at non-conscious things,
who may even crave them . . . It's funny,

I imagine I can actually remember one certain
quart of milk which has just finished clinking
against three of its brethren
in the milkman's great hand and stands,
freeing itself from itself, on the rotting
doorstep in Pawtucket circa 1932,
to be picked up and taken inside
by one in whom time hasn't yet completely
woven all its tangles, and not ever set down . . .
So that here, by the tide pool,
where a sea eagle rings its glass voice
above us, I remember myself back there,
and first dreams easily untangling
themselves rise in me, flow from me in waves,
as if they felt ready now to be fulfilled
out there where there is nothing.
The old bottle will shatter
in the decay of its music, the sea eagle
will cry itself back down into the sea
the sea's creatures transfigure over and over.
Look. Everything has changed.
Ahead of us the meantime is overflowing.
Around us its own almost-invisibility
streams and sparkles over everything.

BILL KNOTT

Lesson

Our love has chosen its appropriate gesture
Which when viewed in the midst of all the gestures
It didn't choose seems almost insignificant.

The gesture our love has chosen is appropriate
We both agree not that we have any choice but
Amidst all those others does seem insignificant.

Is it incumbent on us thus to therefore obliterate
All of the gestures except this insignificant one
Chosen by our love for its own no doubt reasons.

It is up to us to obliterate all other gestures
Though they gang around thick as presentations
Of war and sacrifice in a grade-school classroom.

Use of our love's chosen gesture for the obliteration
Of all those foreign gestures is forbidden however
We must find something else to erase them with.

Our love has chosen its appropriate gesture
Which when viewed in the absence of all other gestures
Seems to spell the opposite of insignificant.

JOHN KOETHE

Picture of Little Letters

I think I like this room,
The curtains and the furniture aren't the same
Of course, but the light comes in the window as it used to
In the late morning, when the others had gone to work.
You can even shave in it. On the dresser with the mirror
Are a couple of the pictures we took one afternoon
Last May, walking down the alley in the late sunlight.
I remember now how we held hands for fifteen minutes

Afterwards. The words meander through the mirror
But I don't want them now, I don't want these abbreviations.
What I want in poetry is a kind of abstract photography
Of the nerves, but what I like in photography
Is the poetry of literal pictures of the neighborhood.

The late afternoon sunlight is slanting through the window
Again, sketching the room in vague gestures of discontent
That roll off the mind, and then only seem to disappear.
What am I going to do now? And how am I going to sleep tonight?

A peculiar name flickers in the mirror, and then disappears.

JAMES LASDUN

Picture of a Girl

I lie on the dirty white candlewick
You so disliked, thinking of you at your best;
Among animals mostly—Absalom
Whose high, unearthly screech you mimicked once
So fluently, he swooped from his chimney perch
To strut before us on the rain-fresh lawn,
Rustling green plumage as if a mate
Had bloomed there like the cêpes and chanterelles . . .
And then the cats; Babette, whose dynasty
Had frayed the Morris hangings into shreds—
I remember you struggling to hold all twelve
Still in your lap for a photograph;
That night you giggled quietly in your sleep—
Lovely transparent dreamer, I could see
The singed-beige kittens tumbling there again . . .

Now I recede, the years are like rough stones
Glazed to a moonstone glimmer by the sea,
Fantastical—Absalom cries again,
I hear that garden crackling in the rain,
Pale dusty green mimosa's saffron burrs
Turning to paste as they brush our clothes,
Quicksilver raindrops on the soft peach fuzz—
We lived well, I remember starched linen,

Silver, the flayed blue hearts of hot-house figs,
My profligate goddess stooping where a marrow
Had burst with rain, and split its sequin seeds,
The clouds pitted like granite, but tissue-light,
Heaving their slow collisions in the skies,
And where the pond froze up one winter night
Big golden carp alive beneath the ice . . .

ANN LAUTERBACH

Naming the House

The ample, plain snow inhibits detail but frees splendor
briefly, completely, like a dream
ornamented with a consoling retrieval: balsam
gathered at the top of the stairs at the Chappaqua house.
And I think of how we might walk out onto the pond
unknowingly, cross the slight curb
onto ice, trusting similitude's throw of white.
And I think also of how women, toward evening,
watch as the buoyant dim slowly depletes
territory, and frees the illuminated house
so we begin to move about, reaching for pot-holders
and lids, while all the while noting
that the metaphor of the house is ours to keep
and the dark exterior only another room
waiting for its literature.
She dallies now in plots
but feels a longing for dispersal,
for things all to succumb to the night's snow
omitting and omitting. She has this attention:
to the reticent world enforced by the sensual
and her curiosity, a form of anticipation,
knowing the failure of things to null
and knowing, too, the joy of naming it this, and this is mine.

THOMAS LUX

Sleepmask Dithyrambic

You must remove your sleepmask, haul it
from your eyes, sleep a white sleep without
slapping floodwaters—let it go,
let its thumbscrews loosen, let it unwind
like bandages (lily-flavored flesh
beneath, pearl-colored the pale
caused by)—lower it: sightseer
in oblivion, all the dumb
joy of death's languorous leaning
over happy tombstones—send it downstream
on sweet pontoons, give it back
to the blanks, fold it like two soft cleavers—
what once ripped your pillow
like shrapnel flesh—what was sleeping
with coal on your eyelids, what's worn
threadbare by black wheels in your forehead,
what deepest blue abided by—let it down—
what screeches like icepick to ice,
black and padded: Sleepmask the Teacher,
Sleepmask the Round Sky, Sleepmask
Fracture bearing its elastic
into the back of your head, sleepmask black
as pines doused in starlessness—get rid
of it—yours, your spider's
and his spare, your wife's mink one,
your dog's, the miniatures strung like popcorn,
all of them black like the cinders
of flags, blanker than lies, the low
shiver of dog-spume lies, sleepmask that sends
your eyes twirling like apples
in a ripsaw wind: sleepmask glued,
stapled, painted on, pinned,
licked clean and monogrammed,
sleepmask surgically implanted, sleepmask
congenital, swaddling clothes and bib—
refuse it, remove it—sleepmask an island

over-run with rats and cheese: the formal,
feral, dipped in doom—drop it, tear
it off, lower it like the lid of a coffin
filled with enemy: sleepmask.

HEATHER McHUGH

To the Quick

We fix the ages of the irises at flower,
stop the eons of the oranges at fruit.
For ripe is ready when we eat, and beautiful is full
by virtue of the ear-eye-nose-and-throat man.
Time is sometimes said
to be at hand.

But not for a second does the plant
stand still. The space of time we designate
as blooming, when did it begin? The beans turned
white to green, and green to brown, and then
were no less phaseolus; flesh

falls off into enormous gravity, and seeds
are an end in themselves, in a way.
On top of the TV set I put
the baby pictures, meant to keep
the little person as he was,

as still as he could be.
O man, o child,
we loved each other less
for how we moved than how we stayed.
And all the while the rivers we adore
have no address but vagaries of bed.

JAMES MERRILL

Grass

The river irises
Draw themselves in.
Enough to have seen
Their day. The arras

Also of evening drawn,
We light up between
Earth and Venus
On the courthouse lawn,

Kept by this cheerful
Inch of green
And ten more years—fifteen?—
From disappearing.

CZESLAW MILOSZ

My Faithful Mother Tongue

Faithful mother tongue
I have been serving you.
Every night, I used to set before you little bowls of colors
so you could have your birch, your cricket, your finch
as preserved in my memory.

This lasted many years.
You were my native land; I lacked any other.
I believed that you would also be a messenger
between me and some good people

even if they were few, twenty, ten
or not born, as yet.

Now, I confess my doubt.
There are moments when it seems to me I have squandered my life.
For you are a tongue of the debased,
of the unreasonable, hating themselves
even more than they hate other nations,
a tongue of informers,
a tongue of the confused,
ill with their own innocence.

But without you, who am I?
Only a scholar in a distant country,
a success, without fears and humiliations.
Yes, who am I without you?
Just a philosopher, like everyone else.

I understand, this is meant as my education:
the glory of individuality is taken away,
Fortune spreads a red carpet
before the sinner in a morality play
while on the linen backdrop a magic lantern throws
images of human and divine torture.

Faithful mother tongue,
perhaps after all it's I who must try to save you.
So I will continue to set before you little bowls of colors
bright and pure if possible,
for what is needed in misfortune is a little order and beauty.

Berkeley, 1968

SHARON OLDS

I Cannot Forget the Woman in the Mirror

Backwards and upside down in the twilight, that
woman on all fours, her head
dangling and suffused, her lean
haunches, the area of darkness, the flanks and
ass narrow and pale as a deer's and those
breasts hanging down toward the center of the earth like plummets,
    when I
swayed from side to side they swayed, it was
so dark I couldn't tell if they were gold or
plum or rose. I cannot get over her
moving toward him upside down in the mirror like a
fly on the ceiling, her head hanging down and her
tongue long and dark as an anteater's
going toward his body, she was so clearly an
animal, she was an Indian creeping
naked and noiseless, and when I looked at her
she looked at me so directly, her eyes so
dark, her stare said to me I
belong here, this is mine, I am living out my
true life on this earth.

MOLLY PEACOCK

The Breach of Or

Broken lines continue, you know, way past
their breaks, as medians in roads do, or
the dot tracings in kids' books, where the last

point is the first point. But it's the breach of *or*,
the breach a break makes when it skids into
nothingness that I'm panicked will undo
me into an enervated void.
That's why I love you; it's how I avoid
the blank *or* between the black lines. That's why
I love my friends. Taking a pencil with
a heavy lead that will leave a line, wide
and black in its wake, connects given lines with
something almost equal to them. Imagine
a little boat trying to connect two
shores with its wake. It's futile. Now look in
the boat at the picnickers, those two
lovers crowded among pears, cantaloupes, fried
squid and fluttering, flag-like, paper napkins—
watch them wipe their lips, open their arms wide,
embracing each other, laughing about their sins.
A pencil made this. Black lines tried
to equal them. The void was a matter of my pride.

JIM POWELL

Heat

Everyone else slept and we
were skinny-dipping in my mother's pool
when the moon rose and birds

sang for high summer in a valley oak
whose seedling I mowed carefully around
twenty years ago.

Back in Berkeley the next day
light from the water where we troubled it
still glanced back from the leaves, a look

of recognition on each changing face,
and the tart fume of just-cut grass that lifted
from the park recalled

that morning's cool persuasions,
dew clinging in the brazen glare of noon.
It was as if that shore

where all forgotten things will find their lasting
home was never lost or touched by need
but day by day was spared

for our return—as though, downtown
where a half block of stores burned to the ground
last month, the damp of ashes still

inhabiting the air (full and rough
feathered at the back of my tongue) coaxed
a thirst for nothing

but the thin creek barely
moving in the shadows under a bridge.
Sheltering there, watching

sunlight slice down between the planks to rule
sharp lines across the stream and mark its passage,
I forget the time.

FREDERICK SEIDEL

Flame

The honey, the humming of a million bees,
In the middle of Florence pining for Paris;
The whining trembling the cars and trucks hum

Crossing the metal matting of Brooklyn Bridge
When you stand below it on the Brooklyn side—
High above you, the harp, the cathedral, the hive—
In the middle of Florence. Florence in flames.

Like waking from a fever . . . it is evening.
Fireflies breathe in the gardens on Bellosguardo.
And then the moon steps from the cypresses and
A wave of feeling breaks, phosphorescent—
Moonlight, a wave hushing on a beach.
In the dark, a flame goes out. And then
The afterimage of a flame goes out.

PATRICIA STORACE

Still Life

Somehow, the two of us sit in a café
bordering the park. Its grass succumbs
again to chronic green, and I see,
obedient, what I don't want to see—
lacerating tulips, leaf-racked trees,
hear steps as gunshots on the street,
heel and pavement sniping at each other.
The corner of your mouth bleeds geography
in the form of Côtes du Rhône.
And the sunset is Cossack,
reddening the West with its pogrom.
I should be sipping the Riesling of an April evening,
the minutes sweet and disappearing on my palate,
mouth smoothing out, from time to time,
the folds of your neck's mortal velvet.
I should admire, not endure, the hyacinth, the campanelle
developing their color photographs of light.
But an hour not this one has stiffened

on the clock, and will not pass;
and eternity, twelve-armed goddess
revealed to me, appears in her aspect of hell.

C. K. WILLIAMS

From My Window

Spring: the first morning when that one true block of sweet, laminar,
    complex scent arrives
from somewhere west and I keep coming to lean on the sill, glorying in
    the end of the wretched winter.
The scabby-barked sycamores ringing the empty lot across the way are
    budded—I hadn't even noticed—
and the thick spikes of the unlikely urban crocuses have already broken
    the gritty soil.
Up the street, some surveyors with tripods are waving each other left
    and right the way they do.
A girl in a gymsuit jogged by a while ago, some kids passed, playing
    hooky, I imagine, and now the paraplegic Vietnam vet who lives in
    a half-converted warehouse down the block
and the friend who stays with him and seems to help him out come
    weaving towards me, their battered wheelchair lurching
    uncertainly from one edge of the sidewalk to the other.
I know where they're going—to the "Legion"; once, when I was
    putting something out, they stopped,
both drunk that time, too, both reeking—it wasn't ten o'clock—and we
    chatted for a bit.
I don't know how they stay alive—on benefits most likely. I wonder if
    they're lovers.
They don't look it. Right now, in fact, they look a wreck, careening
    haphazardly along,
contriving as they reach beneath me to dip a wheel from the curb so
    that the chair skewers, teeters,
tips, and they both tumble, the one slowly, almost gracefully sliding in
    stages from his seat,

his expression hardly marking it, the other staggering over him,
    spinning heavily down, to lie on the asphalt, his mouth working,
    his feet shoving weakly and fruitlessly against the curb.
In the storefront office on the corner, Reed and Son, Real Estate, have
    come to see the show:
gazing through the golden letters of their name, they're not, at least,
    thank god, laughing.
Now the buddy, grabbing at a hydrant, gets himself erect and stands
    there for a moment, panting.
Now he has to lift the other one, who lies utterly still, a forearm
    shielding his eyes from the sun.
He hauls him partly upright, then hefts him almost all the way into the
    chair but a dangling foot
catches a support-plate, jerking everything around so that he has to put
    him down, set the chair to rights and hoist him again and as he
    does he jerks the grimy jeans right off him.
No drawers, shrunken, blotchy thighs; under the thick white coils of
    belly blubber the poor, blunt pud, tiny, terrified, retracted, is
    almost invisible in the sparse genital hair,
then his friend pulls his pants up, he slumps wholly back as though he
    were, at last, to be let be,
and the friend leans against the cyclone fence, suddenly staring up at
    me as though he'd known
all along that I was watching and I can't help wondering if he knows
    that in the winter, too,
I watched, the night he went out to the lot and walked, paced rather,
    almost ran, for how many hours.
It was snowing, the city in that holy silence, the last we have, when the
    storm takes hold,
and he was making patterns that I thought at first were circles then
    realized made a figure eight,
what must have been to him a perfect symmetry but which, from
    where I was, shivered, bent,
and lay on its side: a warped, unclear infinity, slowly, as the snow came
    faster, going out.
Over and over again, his head lowered to the task, he slogged the path
    he'd blazed but the race was lost, his prints were filling faster than
    he made them now and I looked away,
up across the skeletal trees to the tall center-city buildings, some,
    though it was midnight,
with all their offices still gleaming, their scarlet warning-beacons
    signalling erratically

against the thickening flakes, their smouldering auras softening
  portions of the dim, milky sky.
In the morning, nothing; every trace of him effaced, all the field pure
  white, its surface glittering, the dawn, glancing from its glaze,
  oblique, relentless, unadorned.

Baron Wormser

Good Trembling

"Good trembling," CJ said as we
Walked along the docksides in our thin jackets
Even though it was winter on the East Coast.
We were advertising our urge for life
To ourselves and anyone else who might
Have noticed. It wasn't likely, but we liked
To believe that our minds had lights,
That we were intellectual Tom Swifts
And pureblooded peasants of the finer and
Tumultuous emotions. A little era babbled through
    us.
"I don't want to become an anecdote,"
I said as I waved my arms at the thought
Of eternity—say being thirty and married.
A cop car slowed down beside us. Long hair.
"I can't imagine that," CJ said.
"It's too cold and windy." We looked straight ahead,
But the car drove off anyway;
It was warm in there for them. We got some coffee,
Exchanged barrages of quotations,
Vowed to rectify the inertia of everyone else,
And went out again into that clenched wind
Of portents, dogmas, and seasonable love.

CHARLES WRIGHT

Laguna Blues

It's Saturday afternoon at the edge of the world.
White pages lift in the wind and fall.
Dust threads, cut loose from the heart, float up and fall.
Something's off-key in my mind.
Whatever it is, it bothers me all the time.

It's hot, and the wind blows on what I have had to say.
I'm dancing a little dance.
The crows pick up a thermal that angles away from the sea.
I'm singing a little song.
Whatever it is, it bothers me all the time.

It's Saturday afternoon and the crows glide down,
Black pages that lift and fall.
The castor beans and the pepper plant trundle their weary heads.
Something's off-key and unkind.
Whatever it is, it bothers me all the time.

JAMES WRIGHT

Entering The Kingdom Of The Moray Eel

There is no mystery in it so far
As I can see here.
Now the sun has gone down
Some little globules of mauve and beige still cling
Among coconuts and mangoes along the shore.
Over my right shoulder I glimpse a quick light.

I can believe in the moon stirring
Behind the hill at my back.
Before me, this small bay,
A beginning of the kingdom,
Opens its own half-moon.

Solitary,
Nearly naked, now,
I move in up to my knees.
Beneath the surface two shadows
Seem to move. But I know
They do not move.
They are only two small reefs of coral.

Some time this evening the moray eel will wake up
And swim from one reef to the other.
For now, this pathway of sand under water
Shines clear to me. I lift up my feet
And let the earth shift for itself.
Vicious, cold-blooded among his night branches,
The moray eel lets me
Shift for myself.
He is not going to visit his palaces
In my sight, he is not going to dance
Attention on the brief amazement of my life.
He is not going to surrender the splendid shadow
Of his throne. Not for my sake. Not even
To kill me.

NONFICTION

Introduction

In its interview series on the craft of writing the *Review* missed many writers by not being more dedicated to the task and less contemptuous of the notion that time passes and opportunities are lost. In Paris, Colette died in 1954 after a small sip of champagne. The *Review* was in operation at the time. Paul Claudel died in 1955. Apparently he only wrote for a half-hour a day, and yet he produced fifty volumes. He would have been interesting to talk to. Some say that the last thing Thomas Mann heard on his deathbed was a *Paris Review* interviewer trying to get in below . . . "Now wait a minute here . . . I have an appointment . . . the *Paris Review*."

Some writers, of course, though asked, turned down the opportunity—J.D. Salinger, Thomas Pynchon, Samuel Beckett. The magazine had its best chance to interview Beckett when Patrick Bowles became the Paris editor in 1962. Bowles, a fine poet, was Beckett's translator—occupied with the curious task of helping the Irish-born writer translate his novels of the period (*Molloy* and *Watt* among them), which were composed in French, back into his native English. The two sat at a table and argued about the correctness of a word as if they were scholars working on a medieval manuscript by a Flemish monk.

Bowles had a curious habit. When presented with a tough question, he would place his hands to his head and squeeze as if their pressure would produce an answer. In the Paris office nothing would make him press his head harder than to be asked why Beckett would not agree to a few questions about the craft of writing.

John O'Hara would never submit to an interview. That was odd because for a couple of years he had entertained *Paris Review* editors at Princeton after the football games. But then that stopped. When O'Hara was approached for an interview, the letters and telephone messages went unanswered. Something had gone wrong. Intermediaries speaking on behalf of the magazine did not work. The oddest thing was to call him on the telephone. O'Hara would not say anything, but neither would he hang up the receiver. He would breathe, rather hoarsely, at the other end.

"Mr. O'Hara? Mr. O'Hara?"

No reply. The breathing would go on. One's inclination was to stay on the line—perhaps the author was having a spell of laryngitis, or perhaps he was thinking of something to say. . . .

"Ahem. Mr. O'Hara? Mr. O'Hara?"

Finally, it seemed a game—two people breathing moodily at each other, with the loser eventually giving in, shrugging his shoulders, and hanging up the phone. The interview was never done.

Alfred Wright, an editor-writer at *Sports Illustrated* and a friend of O'Hara's who often stayed with him in Quogue, once explained, "You made the mistake of interviewing Ernest Hemingway before you asked him. That rankled; he told me so. You must remember," Alfred went on, "that he was not only competitive, but a very sensitive man. Budd Schulberg, who lives in Quogue, used to say that he was sensitive as an oyster without a shell."

"Is that so?"

Another important American writer the *Review* was never successful in getting to agree to an interview was J. D. Salinger. His son, Mark, known to a number of *Review* associates, was thought to be a sure liaison. He had no luck. Then one day a short report appeared in the *Boston Globe* about a young woman, Betty Eppes, who had tricked Salinger into a conversation on the main street of Cornish, New Hampshire. Not much was said, but perhaps her adventure in inveigling him out of his retreat would have some substance. She proved to be a lively interviewee. Indeed, there was some thought of including her account in the *Writers at Work* series as the Salinger "interview." John Updike, who was doing the introduction to that particular volume, felt that while he admired the young woman's account, and especially her tenacity, her report was better suited to this anthology.

—G.P.

BETTY EPPES

What I Did Last Summer

Betty Eppes is a reporter for the Baton Rouge Advocate. *In the spring of 1980 she was a Special Assignments Writer for the "Fun" section which appears in both the* Advocate *and the* State Times, *the morning and afternoon papers, respectively. That spring she decided to spend her summer vacation trying to interview J.D. Salinger, the author famous for his reclusive behavior. Her story appeared in the Sunday* Advocate *magazine section on June 29, 1980, and in syndication in a number of other newspapers including the* Boston Globe. *What follows is a far fuller account of her experience which has been arranged from conversations held with Ms. Eppes by George Plimpton.*

I decided one day in 1976 that I was so bored that if I hit another tennis ball I was going to go crazy. So I thought, Now wait a minute, there's a small weekly paper in town—the Baton Rouge *Enterprise*—and what if they needed a tennis *columnist?* I was a pretty good tennis player—fluctuating between No. 1 and No. 3 at my tennis club in Baton Rouge, which is the Southwood Tennis Club. I play there because they have a health spa. I work with weights, dead-lifting, squats, bench presses, and all that stuff.

But I had never written a word professionally. In 1974 I tried a novel—more or less a kind of purge—about a woman whose life was parallel to mine. But I had no training to do such a thing; I had not even graduated from high school. I grew up in Trenton, Mississippi, which is a crossroads in Smith County; my father was a dirtfarmer. We were very poor. I married very young and had three babies. I learned my tennis from a friend in Florida. I don't guess there *is* a tennis racket in Trenton, Mississippi. But everything I try I study at incessantly. That's what I did with my writing.

So I wrote six tennis columns for the Baton Rouge *Enterprise*. But they wouldn't publish them. So finally I took the articles to the *Morning Advocate*, which is the major daily in Baton Rouge. They not only published the columns, but after a while they let me do just about anything that was almost a reasonable story. Not only did I do columns on Bjorn Borg, Billie Jean King, and Rod Laver, and why tennis skirts cost so much money, but I went to the New Orleans Saints football camp and did interviews with Hank Stram, and a lot of neat things like that.

Betty Eppes

It's very important for me to be super-excited about things. I have to feel challenged. Otherwise I get terribly bored and begin wondering if I shouldn't move on to something else. Last summer I started wondering what assignment I could take on for myself that would be challenging and super-exciting. I thought and thought. I told Larry Fisher, who is the owner of the bookstore where I was browsing, that I was thinking— hoping to come up with something really interesting. He said he'd think about it too.

A day or so later I happened to be leafing through an encyclopedia of writers. I turned to William Faulkner who is just my idol, my personal *idol,* and there were pages and pages on him. Then by chance, because I had just reread *The Catcher in the Rye* I thought, Well, I'll check out J.D. Salinger, which is what I did. There was one skimpy paragraph.

So I went to Larry Fisher and I said, Damn, Larry, there's nothing at *all* about Salinger. He said that was because nobody knows anything about him. He said, Hey! There's your interview! I said, That's a good idea. I think I'll do it. Larry laughed and said, I think you ought to go and walk on the moon, too!

But the more I thought of it, the more enamored of the idea I became. I thought, Damn, I'm going to go for it.

Actually I had a small file on J.D. Salinger. I am a very practical woman and I file things I think might come in handy later on. J.D. Salinger and Howard Hughes happened to be the most interesting people I didn't know. Peculiar birds. I had little files on both. In Salinger's file I had a short item clipped out of *Newsweek,* I think, which reported that he shopped in a complex called Cummins Corner in the town of Windsor, Vermont, not far from where he lives in Cornish, New Hampshire. I thought, That's where I'll go to try to find him.

So I filed two stories in advance with my editor, Jeff Cowart, at the Baton Rouge *Advocate.* I didn't tell him what I was going to do. I knew he would have said, Eppes, people have been trying to get an interview with Salinger for twenty-seven years; forget it, and go on out there and meet your next deadline. Well, I didn't want to hear that. So I just bought an airline ticket to Manchester, New Hampshire.

Now, as I say, I'm a very practical woman. I'd checked everything out and discovered the whole trip was going to cost $1000. I thought, Jesus God, Eppes, that's a lot of money to throw away. So I cast around in my mind for another person in that area I could get an interview with in order to pay off some of the expenses. The only person I could think of was William Loeb, the publisher of the *Manchester Leader.* He's not one of my most favorite people. He is just about the most outspoken conservative man there ever was, making all sorts of crazy noises, a wild man, but on the other hand I didn't want to eat $1000. So I called up his secretary to arrange for an interview. She said it would be fine. So I hopped on the plane and flew on up to Manchester. I spent the first night in Manchester asking the populace what it felt about Bill Loeb. I wanted to get some background. I interviewed fifty-seven people. Ten out of the fifty-seven didn't like Bill Loeb.

He was ill-at-ease answering questions, it seemed to me. But there was no doubt about his attitudes. Once, when I referred to his conservatism, he interrupted me and gave me to understand that he thought of himself not as a conservative but a redblooded American. He said that if I cared anything about my country I should go back to Louisiana and campaign hard for a Ronald Reagan presidency. His office was full of American flags. A big one stood in the corner. You would have thought he was a member of the House of Representatives. He had a lot of little flags on his desk. He had one in his lapel. Certainly he was very generous with his time. He invited me to a banquet at which he gave an award to the bravest man in New Hampshire who was somebody who had jumped into a river to save a child. Mr. Loeb gave him a plaque. Afterwards, he let me sit in on the open meeting at which anybody could come in and grill him on his policies. Of course, he has the option of skipping the questions but I didn't see him do it. He allows them to grill the hell out of him: *What kind of newspaper you running?*—very sarcastic and needling.

After I had done with William Loeb, I rented a sky-blue Pinto and headed into the Green Mountains to look for J.D. Salinger. I've never driven in the mountains—and there I was, hauling my ass around those strange hills in a sky-blue Pinto that could barely make it over the peaks!

On my way to Windsor I stopped in Claremont, New Hampshire, to visit the offices of the *Claremont Eagle*. In my Salinger file at home I had a clipping about a Windsor schoolgirl named Shirley Blaney who had managed to get an interview with Salinger for the student issue of the *Claremont Eagle* back in 1953. She had seen him eating in a local restaurant and had walked up and simply asked him. He had said OK and he had given her—at least as far as I knew—the only interview he had ever granted. There had been such a rumpus about this interview—I mean the little girl suddenly found herself in correspondence with people all over the country—that it reinforced Salinger's determination never to give interviews again.

I thought I should read the Blaney interview at least to prepare myself. A fellow who works for the *Eagle* named Jefferson Thomas of all names (he said he had a terrible time in the Army where he had to give his last name first) helped me look for it back in the files. He was very helpful. It turned out he and I share the same birthday. It took us 2 1/2 hours to find the story which I read into my tape recorder.

I also dropped into the bookstore in Claremont. It's a small bookstore but being the only one in that area Salinger comes over from Cornish and visits it on occasion. I talked with the owner of the store about him. She said, He's such a peculiar man, not like any customer you ever saw. He'll come in and doesn't want you to speak even. If you ask if he needs help, he just shakes his head and walks away. . . . One day my little girl was here with me when he came in. She was so delighted. She got a copy of a book of his and went over and asked for his autograph. Then he turned on his heel and walked out. He is a very peculiar man.

I stayed in Windsor, Vermont, at the Windsor Motel. Salinger lives in Cornish, of course, across the Connecticut River in New Hampshire, which is just the smallest kind of hamlet. Windsor is the nearest place that has lodgings. The motel there looked like an old-time motor court from twenty years ago—very primitive, no phones in the room, but it's set in a beautiful rural area amongst all those hills. Windsor itself is about seven miles away.

In my room that night I spent some time listening to the Blaney interview and preparing my questions, writing one on top of each page of my little spiral notebook. In that interview Salinger had mentioned that Holden Caulfield was autobiographical and that it had been a great relief telling people about his own early life. I thought I'd ask him about that, and if he planned a sequel to *The Catcher in the Rye*. He had talked to

Blaney about wanting to go to Indonesia. I wondered if he had ever gotten there, and what he remembered about entertaining troops aboard ship, which he had done in the West Indies. I thought I'd ask him about the American Dream. I had about twenty-odd questions in my notebook when I'd finished.

The next morning it was cold. An arctic front had come through that night and there was ice in the swimming pool next to the motel. Here it was in the middle of June and I was wearing the normal clothes you'd wear in Baton Rouge in the summer. Luckily, I'd thrown a long-sleeved sweater in my bag. If it hadn't been for that sweater I would have froze my ass off.

I drove to Windsor. It is a small country town—everything concentrated on Maine Street with Bridge Street crossing it and leading down to the covered bridge over the Connecticut River. The first thing I did was to go into the drugstore. I told the man behind the counter that I was interested in interviewing J.D. Salinger. He looked at me and said, You're a journalist. Go away. He wouldn't say another word. And I thought, Oh God, here it was, the first time I'd mentioned his name, and it was like a door had been slammed on me. I couldn't afford too many more of *those.* So I went back out in the street.

The Cummins Corner I had read about in the news story in my Salinger file turned out to be a bunch of shops in a big old wooden, sprawling building—a grocery store, a liquor store, a barber shop, and an ice cream parlor, though needless to say no one was hurrying in to buy ice cream *that* morning.

I went into the grocery in Cummins Corner and told the man behind the counter that I had read in a story that J.D. Salinger often came in there. He looked puzzled and said, No. He didn't think so. But he was polite. He wasn't like the guy in the drugstore. In fact, this guy didn't really know who J.D. Salinger *was.* I said, Think. Really think hard.

So he did, and after a while he said, Well, that name does sort of ring a bell. I have this really strange customer who comes in once a week to do some shopping. As a matter of fact, this guy has an unlisted phone number—and that's a little freaky in these parts. He said he had the number on file because this guy was a customer.

So he pulled out the number, and sure enough on the card it had J.D. Salinger. I thought, Ah *hah!* I didn't ask for the number, because I was sure he wouldn't give it to me, but I asked if he would call the number *for* me. He said he would. He called the number and then handed me the phone. It was J.D. Salinger's housekeeper! I told her who I was and that I would like to see Mr. Salinger. She got very nervous and said that she shouldn't be talking to me. She said Mr. Salinger doesn't want to *talk* to anybody, he doesn't want to *see* anybody, he doesn't want to be *bothered*. If she helped me, she said she'd get in big trouble. I tried to reassure her. I said, Honey, you don't have to help me; just tell me how I can get to see Mr. Salinger. She was so nervous by this time she could barely talk. She said that I should write him a note and post it. I moaned. I said it could be a *week* before he ever saw it. She went on to suggest that if I handed the note to the girl in the Windsor post office, Mr. Salinger would get it. She must have been very relieved when I thanked her and hung up.

Well, then I bought myself a Mead's Spiral Notebook with a blue cover in which to compose this letter to J.D. Salinger. I thought it would be tacky to send him a note from my own reporter's notebook which is so small that I would have used up five or ten pages just to tell him I wanted to see him. I bought a Bic ballpoint pen for nineteen cents. I took the notebook out on the street and since there are no benches in Windsor I sat down on the curbstone to do the letter. I thought, Oh God! What do you say to J.D. Salinger? Good *night!* I mean he gets tons and tons of requests—what would make him answer mine?

I started off by telling him who I was, and that I earned my living by writing. I did not mention *The Catcher in the Rye* or any of his work at all. It's true I reread *The Catcher in the Rye* twice a year, but Salinger isn't one of my favorite writers—I can't really identify with the characters. What had fascinated me was that as a girl in Smith County, Mississippi, where males and females are very secluded from one another, I had two older brothers, and reading *The Catcher in the Rye* was like opening a secret door into their private male world. I really learned from it and I can certainly recognize the man's literary skills. Of course, I didn't say any of this in the letter. I told him I wasn't a girl who had come to usurp any of his privacy; I was a woman who supported herself through writing and would very much like to see him. I wanted to know if he was still writing. I told him I was a novelist. I told him writing was so hard.

Then I explained that I was staying at the Windsor Motel where there were no phones in the rooms. Since he could not reach me, I wrote him that I would come back to Cummins Corner at 9:30 the next morning and wait for thirty minutes. If he didn't come, I would be there at 9:30 the *next* morning to wait for thirty minutes . . . and I told him if he didn't come then I was going back to Baton Rouge because I couldn't afford to stay in Windsor any longer.

I told him that I would be sitting in a sky-blue Pinto right by the corner and just up the road from the covered bridge and that I was tall with green eyes and red-gold hair. I finished the letter, "I will make no further effort to seek you out, not because of guard dogs or fences, but because I do not want to anger you or cause you grief." Then I put a PS down at the bottom: "I see perfectly why you live in this area. Its beauty is awesome. Often I find myself whispering."

I took the letter into the post office and said I had a letter for J.D. Salinger. I got a pretty peculiar look as I handed it over. The people in Windsor seemed so determined to protect him. God *bless!*

After I'd done that, I went and bought some extra batteries for my tape recorder. I was being very cautious. After all, it was so cold the batteries I brought with me could have been affected and malfunctioned. It was best not to leave anything to chance.

Then I bought an eight-pack of Tab. It's my favorite drink. I drink Tab like most people drink booze: I really *swill* it down. I took the Tab back to the Windsor Motel and there I fell apart. It was interesting. Up to that point I had been very confident. I remembered how nice Salinger was to the women he wrote about in his stories and books. Sometimes he was very rough on the men, but he was gentle with females. Holden is so very tender to his sister in *The Catcher in the Rye.* It was going to be a piece of cake. But then in my motel room I began thinking of all the reasons for J.D. Salinger *not* to come. I really got panicky. I hate to fail. I tried to think of things to encourage myself—that Edmund Hillary had climbed Mt. Everest the same year that *The Catcher in the Rye* came out. It didn't work. I got so upset that I began swearing and pacing and worrying and trying to calm myself by drinking Tab and finally I said to myself, Oh well! and I went and pigged out on some fresh fruit. I eat fruit like I drink Tab.

In the middle of the night I woke up and I *knew* J.D. Salinger was going to come. I just knew. I was so excited that I had to say to myself, Now Betty Eppes, calm down. I have these *things.* I always know when something really important is going to happen. I always have them when people are dying. They just come to me like revelations.

I got up at four in the morning and turned on the TV. All hell had broken loose in the environment. Mt. St. Helens had erupted. On the TV preachers were wailing about Hell and damnation and destruction. But I remember thinking that only some natural catastrophe like that was going to keep me from my interview with J.D. Salinger. I was really confident. At breakfast I left a five dollar tip. I *knew* he was going to turn up.

I drove up to Cummins Corner in my Pinto. I bought a Tab there. Then I positioned myself in the Pinto about fifty yards from the covered bridge that crosses the Connecticut. I knew Salinger would have to cross that bridge to come into Windsor. One great piece of luck was that the bridge was being repaired. People parked their cars in a parking area on the New Hampshire side and then walked across. I knew Salinger would have to appear on foot. So I checked the camera and got it ready for an approach shot. I aimed it towards the covered bridge. I got the tape recorder out and set it up. I knew that Salinger would be spooked by the sight of a tape recorder, but also that it would be crazy to try to talk to him scribbling away in his face. So I thought *Hell,* I'll stuff the tape recorder down my blouse under my long-sleeved sweater. It was difficult to do without looking like I had some kind of deformity. I thought, Jeez—I wouldn't want J.D. Salinger to think I've got a square boob. So I finally shoveled the tape recorder down the sleeve of my blouse right under my armpit where I could hold it in against my body with my arm. I thought, if I just keep my elbow in, everything will be cool.

It seemed like I had waited there in the Pinto for about three years. I was just beginning to read an article in that morning's Boston *Globe* entitled "What Is Luck?" when right on time—nine-thirty—he stepped out from the black of that covered bridge . . . J.D. Salinger!

He didn't look like I thought he would. He had white hair. That freaked me out. He came out of the dark and the sun lit his hair like a beacon. In all the pictures I had seen of him he had dark hair. I was not looking for a Holden Caulfield but I was probably *thinking* of a Holden Caulfield. Not only that, but I was surprised by the intensity of the man. He walked almost like he was driven or pursued, his shoulders hunched up around his ears . . . it was almost a *run.* He looked neither right nor left but in my direction. As soon as I saw him coming I fumbled under my blouse to turn on the tape recorder and I opened the door and got out of the Pinto. He kept coming towards me. He had an attaché case

The covered bridge at Windsor, Vt., through which Betty Eppes hoped J. D. Salinger would appear.

stuck under his arm. He walked right up to me and said "Betty Eppes?" which meant, of course, he had seen or had news of my letter. He mispronounced my name. "Eppès," he said. We shook hands standing beside the Pinto. He had on a pair of jeans, sneakers, and one of those shirt-jackets. He looked in remarkable shape—very slim, very healthy. After he shook my hand, he backed off a few steps. He's a very tall man so he looked down on me with eyes, very black, that seemed to glitter. I thought, Shit, I have just shaken J.D. Salinger's hand; then I realized that the Sony tape recorder was going to fall out. I could feel it beginning to slip down my side. It was terrible! I clamped my arm in to keep it from going any further. And then I realized I only had 29 minutes of tape to go and when the machine reached the end it would give off a little beep. I thought if that beep signal went off while I was standing in front of J.D. Salinger and he heard it coming out from under my sweater, I'd just fall down in a *faint.* It was terrible! You don't *know* how terrible it was!

He seemed just as nervous as I was. His hands shook. Here was J.D. Salinger and I thought, Shit, the man isn't going to stand still. I mean it was obvious that he didn't want to be there . . . he was going to bolt any second. Great God! I thought, Now, Eppes, if you don't get but one question in before he bolts, it had better be about Holden Caulfield, because he's the one everybody wants to know about.

First, I thanked Mr. Salinger for coming. He said, I don't know why I did, actually. There's nothing I can tell you. Writing's a very personal thing. So why'd you come here? He said that my letter had been very brief.

I was very nervous. I said, I came not just for myself, Mr. Salinger, but as a *spokesman* for all who want to know if you're still writing.

I asked about Caulfield. Please tell me—is he going to grow up? Is there going to be a sequel to *The Catcher in the Rye?* All your readers want to know the answer to that question.

The whole town was gaping. I mean everybody. The old man in the Cummins Corner office had his nose pressed to the window pane. The people in the laundromat came out and stood on the sidewalk. There were faces looking out of the windows of the apartments across the street.

I kept pegging away about Holden Caulfield. He said, It's all in the book. Read the book again, it's all in there. Holden Caulfield is only a frozen moment in time.

So I asked, Well, does that mean he *isn't* going to grow up—there won't be a sequel?

He said, Read the book.

Every question I asked about Holden Caulfield he replied, Read the book. It's all in the book. There's no more to Holden Caulfield. Over and over. Except when I asked him if the book was autobiographical. When I quoted to him what he had once said in that interview with the Windsor schoolgirl about his boyhood being like Holden's, he seemed to be made very uncomfortable by that. He said, Where did you get all that stuff? He looked at me very hard. I thought he was going to say, Read the book, again, and if he had I would have stomped on his foot! But this time he said, I don't know . . . I don't know. I've just let it all go. I don't know about Holden any more.

So I left off Holden Caulfield and began asking about other things. Christ! I just wanted to ask him a question he would answer. I began turning the pages of my notebook.

Eppes: Have you visited Indonesia?

Salinger: I really don't want to talk about all of this.

Eppes: You told Miss Blaney you were going to London to make a movie. Did you?

Salinger: Where'd you get all this old stuff?

Eppes: Did you make or work on a movie? Will you in the future?

Salinger: Can we go on to something else?

Eppes: Of course. But just for fun, do you remember the name of the ship you worked on as an entertainer?

Salinger: I do, yes. *The Kungsholm.*

Eppes: You were in the Counter-Intelligence Corps. How many languages do, or did you, speak?

Salinger: French and German, but not very well. And a few phrases of Polish.

Eppes: Given your family background, why writing?

Salinger: I can't say exactly. I don't know if any writer can. It's different for each person. Writing's a highly personal act. It's different for each writer.

Eppes: Did you consciously opt for a writing career, or did you just drift into it?

Salinger: I don't know. *(A long pause)* I truly don't. I just don't know.

I wanted a Tab. It was so painful for him to answer. But he kept standing there. I hurried on with my questions. I said that I had heard he had done his writing in a special concrete workshop situated behind his house. I asked if he did his writing there.

He said, I have my work area set up the way I like, so it's comfortable. But I don't want to discuss it. I don't want people streaming up here trying to climb walls and peek in windows. I'm comfortable, he said, and that's enough.

I asked him if publishing wasn't important.

He said that was an easy question that wouldn't take any time to answer at all. He said he had *no* plans to publish. *Writing* was what was important to him—and to be left alone so that he *could* write. To be left in peace. He couldn't tell me *why* he felt he wanted to be left in peace . . . but that he had felt that way in grade school, at the academy, and before and after military service. And he felt it now, too. Boy! he kept harping on that!

So I asked him why he had ever published anything *at all* if he felt so strongly that it disturbed his private life.

He said that he had not foreseen what was going to happen. He said he didn't expect it, and when it did happen, he didn't want it. It meant he couldn't live a normal life. He had to put the roads near his home under patrol. His children suffered. Why couldn't his life be his own?

I asked him if that was so why he had bothered to see me. Why hadn't he stayed up on his mountain? Why hadn't he ignored my letter?

He said, You write. I write. He had come as one writer to another. Then he began asking me about my writing. Had I done a book yet? Goodness me! J.D. Salinger asking Betty Eppes about *her* work!

So I told him I had written a novel and given it to a regional publisher—Southern Publishing—but while the contract was being prepared, the couple who ran the company split up and the manuscript was lost. I only had a copy of the first two-thirds of the book. I told Salinger that I was so upset with myself for not keeping a copy, and with the two of them for losing the work, that I just hadn't had the heart to rewrite that last section.

Salinger nodded and said that publishing was a vicious, vicious thing. He said that so many unforeseen things happen when you publish. He said that I'd probably be happier if I never published. He said there was a certain peace in not publishing.

Then we began talking about autographs. I asked him why he hated to give them. He said he didn't believe in giving autographs. It was a meaningless gesture. He told me never to sign my name for anyone else. It was all right for actors and actresses to sign their names, because all they had to give were their faces and names. But it was different with writers. They had their work to give. Therefore, it was cheap to give autographs. He said, Don't you ever do it! No self-respecting writer should ever do it.

Well, I myself had never really thought much about it. I mean nobody had ever asked me for my autograph before—well, *once,* a little girl did, but she thought I was Jane Fonda. I signed "Jane Fonda"—I didn't want to hurt the girl's feelings.

I tried other subjects. I asked about discipline in writing.

He said that discipline was no problem—that you either want to write or you don't.

His style? Well, he said he didn't know much about his writing style. Obviously a writer had to make choices. Decisions. But he really couldn't help me with that question.

So I tried politics.

He said, I don't care about politicians. I don't have anything in common with them. They try to limit our horizons; I try to expand our horizons. He said that not one politician stood out in his mind.

I tried economics—inflation, unemployment, energy . . . did he have any comments to make about *these* issues.

No. He said that none of this touched him personally. Not his area. He didn't know much about these things.

That was becoming such a stock answer—that he didn't know. It made me super-nervous. He was super-nervous, too. He kept moving that attaché case around, sticking it out in front of him and then tucking it under his arm.

Then we had this exchange:

Eppes: I've heard you're into organic foods. Do you feel eating food stuffs organically grown is that important?

Salinger: Yes, or I wouldn't bother.

Eppes: Is it true that you'll eat fried foods only if they're prepared in cold-pressed peanut oil?

Salinger: Yes.

Eppes: Why is that?

Salinger: Are you informed on the differences between cold-pressed oil as opposed to oil extracted by other methods?

Eppes: Yes, I am. I don't use peanut oil but only cold-pressed oils. I make all my salad dressing from cold-pressed apricot kernel, sesame seed, sunflower seed oil. With a few herbs thrown in you come up with a super salad.

I didn't know how many people would be interested in Salinger on cooking oils, so I went back to something more general. I threw him my question about the American Dream. Did he believe in it?

He said, My own version of it, yes.

When I asked if he would elaborate, he said, I wouldn't care to, no.

So I said that the Constitution seemed to have been written by men for men and that it may not have been intended for women. That produced quite a response!

Salinger: Don't you accept that! Don't ever listen to that. Who says you don't have a right to the American Dream, who says? That's frightful. Awful! Don't you accept that. The American Dream is for *all* Americans. Women are Americans too. It is for you too. Proceed. Claim it if you want it. . . .

After a while, I got to wondering if Salinger was going to bring a halt to this, which was OK by me, because the tape recorder was getting pretty close to the end where the beep was going to go off. I couldn't look at my watch to find out how much time there was left because if I had lifted my arm to look, that damn tape recorder would have slid right down, and I would have died! If Salinger knew what I was going through he might have smiled.

As it was, he smiled twice. The first time was when in the middle of our conversation—I don't know if it was frustration, or intimidation, or awe, or what—tears began to roll down my face. . . . God, it was embarrassing! And I couldn't wipe them away—I had this friggy pencil in one hand and I couldn't move the other arm because it had the tape recorder wedged in under it. Salinger smiled sympathetically at this point; he reached across and wiped those tears off with a knuckle, and then wiped his knuckles on his jeans.

The second time he smiled was when I asked him if he really was writing every day what then was he working on? He smiled and said, I can't tell you that. I kind of understood what he meant.

Finally Salinger went off to get his mail. I went into Cummins Corner to get an 8-pack of Tab. I must have stayed in there for about ten minutes. As I came out of Cummins Corner I saw Salinger coming back along the street from the post office. I jumped in the Pinto, changed tapes and shoved the tape recorder back down my blouse, turned it on, and then I grabbed my camera and took three pictures of Salinger, who had been stopped by the young owner of Cummins Corner market; the guy had come out and put his hand on Salinger's arm. Apparently he wanted to shake Salinger's hand. That made Salinger furious. He came stalking across the street to the Pinto and leaning in the window right in my face he really got on my case! He chewed my ass *out!* He was wearing his glasses this time. His eyes seemed much larger behind them.

Here's what he said: Because of you, this man I don't know, have never even met, has spoken to me. Just walked up to me on the street over there and *spoke to me.* Just like that. Walked up and put his hand on my arm and *spoke to me.* I don't like that. There have been calls to my neighbors because of you and I don't like my neighbors inconvenienced. I want to be left alone, left to my privacy. That's why I moved here. I moved here seeking privacy, a place where I could lead a normal life and write. But people like you pursue me. I don't wish to seem harsh. It's just that I'm a private person. I resent intrusions. I resent questions. I don't want to talk to strangers. I don't particularly like talking to *anybody.* I'm a writer. Write me letters if you wish. But please, don't drop in.

I knew I had nothing to lose at this point. As he began to turn away, I said, I'm sorry you're upset, Mr. Salinger, but please wait. Just a moment more. *May I take a close-up photograph of you?*

He looked horrified. Absolutely not! No!

All right, Mr. Salinger, all right. I've put the camera down. It's down, Mr. Salinger, see?

A photo taken by Betty Eppes through the window of her Pinto of an instant which infuriated Salinger—being touched on the arm by the manager of Cummins Corner who asked if he could shake the author's hand.

As he paused, I put one more question to him. Tell me honestly, are you really writing?

I thought he'd run, but he answered, I am really writing. I told you. I love to write and I assure you I write regularly. I'm just not publishing. I write for myself. For my own pleasure. I want to be left alone to do it. So leave me alone. Don't drop in here like this again.

Off he went. As he headed for the dark entrance of the covered bridge I snapped a picture. Before I could think of anything else to call after him, he walked back into that bridge and disappeared.

I sent Salinger a copy of the story I wrote for the *Morning Advocate.* Eleven days later I received two photostats—copies of order blanks he had sent away to New York. They were signed by him, mailed in Windsor, and addressed to me care of the *Morning Advocate.* I haven't any idea if he sent them to me. The order was addressed to the Chocolate Soup Company in New York City and in it Mr. Salinger asked for two oversized schoolbags, gift-wrapped, from Denmark (at $16.50 each) that had been advertised in the then current *New Yorker.* Now why was that sent to me? It drove me just about crazy trying to figure it out.

After the article appeared, there was a lot more spooky little shit like that—just enough to drive you crazy. I have an accordion-file stuffed with job offers, letters, requests . . . people seemed to come out of the woodwork wanting things from me. There were two motion-picture companies who tried to get me to go back up there to convince Salinger to make a movie! In a way I guess it was a kind of education about what Mr. Salinger had gone through *himself* and what had turned him into the kind of person I found.

```
                                              P. O. Box 32
                                              Windsor, Vt. 05089
                                              May 5, 1973
The Chocolate Soup
328 East 9th Street
New York, N.Y. 10003

Dear Sirs:

          Please send me, gift-wrapped and in separate packages,

     two (2) of the "oversized schoolbags from Denmark," as advertised

     in the current New Yorker a t $16.50 per bag.  I enclosed a check

     for $33.

          Thank you.

                              J. D. Salinger
                              J. D. Salinger
```

The curious document signed by J. D. Salinger and received by Betty Eppes eleven days after news of her interview with him was published.

The last photo Betty Eppes took of Salinger . . . as the author turns for the covered bridge.

I want to tell you that interview with J.D. Salinger was the most difficult one I ever tried. The next most difficult was one I did on Edwin W. Edwards, the former governor of Louisiana, on gambling—stalking him around Las Vegas for three days. But he doesn't compare with J.D. Salinger. Those eyes of Salinger's . . . the strangest black eyes that glittered and just seemed to gaze right through you. So weird. I mean just weird, weird, weird!

This summer I decided to go to England. I interviewed James Mason, the English actor. He was a piece of cake compared to J.D. Salinger. He turned up in a pink sweater. He looked gorgeous. I just wanted to munch on him.

Introduction

During the magazine's history the interview form has not only been used to extract information from writers but has been practiced on other occasions—with musicians (John Cage, Virgil Thomson, Dizzy Gillespie) and artists (Picasso, Giacometti), among others. In more recent years Shusha Guppy, the London editor of the magazine and a distinguished author in her own right *(The Blindfold Horse)* has concentrated on interviewing elderly people of note, mostly *grandes dames,* who, while not authors of first magnitude, have had an integral association with the world of letters. What follows is representative: a conversation with Lady Diana Cooper.

—G.P.

Lady Diana Cooper in the '20s. Photo by Lallie Charles.

SHUSHA GUPPY

An Interview with Lady Diana Cooper

*Lady Diana Cooper was born in 1892, daughter of the 7th Duke of Rut-
land. Her mother, Violet Lindsay, was a Pre-Raphaelite artist and beauty,
and the granddaughter of the 24th Earl of Crawford. Her pale, iridescent
beauty—"the texture of Chinese silk" (Winston Churchill), her acute intelligence and iconoclastic wit, her innocent sense of fun, frank enjoyment of
privilege and total lack of snobbery, made her "The Idol of the Golden
Generation" before the First World War—a generation in which aristocracy
and Bohemia met and mingled, and in which she became one of the most
remarkable and famous women of her time. She was loved by some of its
greatest men: Prime Minister Asquith, the great bass Chaliapin, the newspaper magnate Lord Beaverbrook, and many others. Considered a suitable
bride for the Prince of Wales (later King Edward VIII and after his abdica-
tion the Duke of Windsor), instead she fell in love and married Duff Cooper,
a junior diplomat without a private income.*

*In the Twenties, partly to improve their finances and partly because she
"could never say no," she starred in two silent movies (the first British Tech-
nicolor films) and later enthralled America and Europe in Reinhardt's* The
Miracle. *Then she gave up her career to become a "full-time wife" when her
husband left the Foreign Office for a career in politics and literature. After
several ministerial posts, including Minister of Information in Churchill's
War Cabinet, Duff Cooper became British Ambassador in Algiers, and later
in Paris at the end of the Second World War.*

*Throughout her life, Lady Diana Cooper was befriended and admired by
many of the famous writers and literary figures of her time: Evelyn Waugh
immortalized her in* Scoop, *as Mrs. Stitch; D.H. Lawrence portrayed her in*
Aaron's Rod *as Lady Artemis Hooper; she was Arnold Bennett's Lady Quee-
nie Paulle in* The Pretty Ladies; *while her friend the playwright and novelist
Enid Bagnold gave a touching and accurate picture of her old age in* The
Loved and the Envied.

*Her own three-volume autobiography was published in the sixties and
became a best seller, revealing a writer of considerable talent and originality.
With her son Viscount Norwich (author John Julius Norwich), she has
founded the Duff Cooper Literary Prize.*

*Lady Diana Cooper lives in a large house in Little Venice, London. It is
full of the mementos of her long and exceptional life. She still looks beautiful
despite her extreme frailty; deep blue eyes and porcelain skin still shine with
a radiance that age has not impaired. Her bedroom overlooks a quiet garden;
at home she spends most of her day there, sitting up in a large, lace-draped
bed, surrounded by books and periodicals, and usually in company with her*

*tiny Chihuahua called "Doggie," which she takes everywhere with her—even
to the Royal Opera House where dogs are strictly forbidden: she hides him in
her sleeve until she gets to her box. A stream of friends and relatives visit her
in her bedroom, and it was there that the following interview about some of
the literary personalities in her past took place.*

Guppy: When did your connection with the literary world begin?

Cooper: I was born into it. My mother was a "Soul." Ah, you don't
know about the "Souls"? They were a group of friends, people like Lord
Curzon, no less, Lord Balfour, no less, and a few Pre-Raphaelites. It
didn't mean much then, but it did later, because they all be came *great.*
So when I came out at eighteen I was called by the newspapers "the
Soulful daughter of a Soul." The funny thing was that my mother didn't
like being called a "Soul": she was too individual and didn't want to be
part of a group, but I thought she ought to be proud of it. Then at a party
one of my young men told me that I wasn't my father's daughter but
Harry Cust's. He said everybody knew it. All I could say was: Oh really?
It didn't seem to matter—I was devoted to my father and I liked Harry
Cust too. Well *he* was a *"Soul,"* very literary, and very handsome. He
had a magazine called *The Pall Mall Gazette* where he published all the
famous writers—Rudyard Kipling, H.G. Wells, and so on. My mother
was very literary too: She liked all these *advanced* poets—Browning and
Meredith; and I was named after Meredith's *Diana of the Crossways.*
Now Meredith is an awfully complicated poet, but because of this Diana
complex I had to learn his famous *Modern Love,* which is something like
fifty sixteen-line poems, by heart. In those days you learnt *everything* by
heart—so different from today when children don't even learn nursery
rhymes. And you don't write letters either, because of the telephone; we
used to write letters all the time and there were five or six deliveries a
day. I wrote to my father when he went off shooting.

The first poem I learnt was Marlowe's "Passionate Shepherd to His
Love":

> *Come live with me and be my love
> And we will all the pleasures prove . . .*

When I was seven my Nanny taught me Kipling's "The Road to Man-
dalay":

> *On the Road to Mandalay,
> Where the flyin' fishes play,
> And the dawn comes up like thunder . . .*

something and something . . . I can't remember now. My memory is not what it used to be—I think I am losing my marbles!

There is this nice young man who is writing the biography of Cecil Beaton who sent me a bottle of marbles for Christmas! But I have this theory that the more marbles you lose the better it is: my old friend Enid Bagnold had lost *all* her marbles and was very happy, while I have always been a prey to melancholia. It comes over you like a wave, engulfs you, and then subsides . . .

Anyway, my mother's favorite author was Shakespeare, naturally, because we were brought up with the Trees: Sir Herbert Tree was Mr. Daddy to all of us, and his daughter Iris Tree, who became a wonderfully talented artist and poet, was my best friend. We used to go into his dressing room, try on his costumes, put on his Richard III ring, go on the stage in the crowd scenes—I don't know how he bore us! Lady Tree was my mother's best friend, but we never knew, until much later, that he had a whole *other* family: somebody called Mrs. Reed, with whom he had five other children.

Anyway, Shakespeare was part of our lives. But as a child I got a disease called Erb's—I don't know if you spell it with an H or without—it is a form of paralysis of the arms. The doctors forbade lessons—*too wonderful!* As a result I grew up illiterate, and I still can't spell: my nephew Rupert Hart-Davis (author and publisher) had a lot to do with the punctuation and spelling when he published my autobiography.

Guppy: As a debutante you had a great number of admirers—including your future husband—who were literary. Who were they?

Cooper: We were a group of friends called "The Coterie," and they were all literary, but they were *all* killed in the War. Some left nothing but letters, but some did write other things before they got killed, like Rupert Brooke. I didn't take to him much, I don't know why. I think he didn't approve of us—we were too free and too drunk. I knew the Sitwells very well; though I was very thick with the brothers I never met *her*, Edith. I didn't like her poetry—it was too modern for my taste, which is rather old-fashioned. Then after the First World War, I married Duff who became a very good writer. His biography of Talleyrand made his name as a writer, but his best book is his autobiography—*Old Men Forget*. And now my granddaughter Artemis is editing our letters.

Guppy: Your parents wanted you to marry the Prince of Wales, and the Duke of Connaught wrote that you were the only woman who could keep him on the throne. What happened?

Cooper: We met, naturally, but he used to say: "I'm quite a good Prince of Wales but I shall be a hopeless king." Do you know this poem:

> *And were you pleased they asked of Helen in Hell.*
> *Pleased?*
> *Answered she, when all Troy's towers fell*
> *And dead were Priam's sons*
> *And lost his throne*
> *—And such a war was fought as none had known*
> *And even the gods took part;*
> *And all because of me alone?*
> *Pleased?*
> > *I should say I was!*

Lord Dunsany wrote this poem about *her*, Mrs. Simpson, not about Helen. Everybody was, of course, against her, but I thought she was all right. Did you see the television series about them? [The TV series was called "Edward VIII," with Edward Fox in the title role.] They made her look dull but tender. She was far from dull and *very* far from tender.

Duff wanted to be a politician and a writer; the Foreign Office had become very boring, as it is today—it's just cocktail parties, isn't it? So I accepted to appear in two films. They were awful! *Awful!* But I enjoyed *The Miracle*, and touring America. Then Duff gave up the F.O. and became an M.P. and later a minister. People asked me if I minded giving up my career. I didn't in the least; I *adored* my husband and hated being parted from him. At the time of Munich he was one of the few who sided with Churchill and actually resigned. I remember getting thousands of letters thanking him for protesting against the invasion of Czechoslovakia. John Julius, a secretary, and I spent days forging his signature on answers.

Guppy: Did you meet any American writers when you were in America?

Cooper: No. A great many journalists and stage people, not writers. I met Noel Coward, though, who was living there and we became great friends.

Guppy: There is a story about your first meeting with Noel Coward. Allegedly you said to him: "Mr. Coward I saw your play last night and I didn't think it was at all funny," to which he is supposed to have answered: "Madam, I on the other hand saw you in *The Miracle* and I just laughed and laughed."

Cooper: Totally untrue. I always *adored* Noel. You see we both had mothers, and our two mothers got together and entertained each other, thank God, which made us free to go out and have fun. Then Noel took to horseriding. Well, I can't ride at all, but my friend Iris Tree, who was with me in *The Miracle*, was very good at it and loved it. So we all three went to a riding school and Noel was terrified! They had little things for jumping over and Noel said: "I can't bear it because every time I want to jump the horse turns around and says 'bet you can't!' "

Alas, Noel got old and died . . . I used to go to Switzerland and stay with him, but he was ill and couldn't go up the mountains. Now his memoirs have been published and are full of accounts of the diseases homosexuals get . . . Yes, I loved Noel dearly, very dearly, till the end.

Guppy: What about Hemingway? Did you meet him?

Cooper: Only years later, in Paris after the War. He came to the Embassy and his former wife Martha Gellhorn who was a great friend of mine—and still is—wrote to ask me to receive him. The day he came I was in bed with a bad cold, so he came and sat by my bedside. It was cocktail time and I asked him to go next door and help himself to a drink from the drink table, which he did. Then every few minutes he went back to fill his glass and became more and more drunk. By 8 o'clock he was talking utter nonsense. He started reciting a long poem, and it turned out to be his own. It was *awful!* Well I didn't know how to get rid of him—he just sat there and sozzled! So I'm afraid the meeting was not a great success and I never saw him again. But I liked his books: the one about the Spanish Civil War . . . What was it called? There goes a marble! Oh yes, *For Whom the Bell Tolls,* and the other one about the War . . . *Farewell to Arms.*

Guppy: You met Evelyn Waugh in the Twenties and became lifelong friends. Where did you meet him?

Cooper: When I was in *The Miracle* in London. It is awful to admit, but I liked him because he liked me. Also, he was a challenge: everybody hated him because he was so rude and so snobbish, so I thought I would like him. We remained best friends till two years before he died. Then he became too melancholic. I used to do *everything* to cheer him up. He lived in the country, because he wanted to be a *grand seigneur,* and I would buy—very much against the grain I might add—caviar and champagne and take him to the theatre: "Oh no, not the Stalls! A Box!" He wasn't exactly a drunk, but he drank a lot; I didn't mind that—I was brought up with drunks. He could be dreadfully rude: once we invited Huxley to lunch at the Embassy in Paris—not the novelist, his brother, the one who had run the Zoo in London, Julian Huxley. Evelyn took a delight in nagging him and hurting him. Now Julian had become something much grander than the Zoo, head of UNESCO, and didn't want to talk about the Zoo. But Evelyn *would* mention monkeys and parrots all the time and Julian got crosser and crosser; it was very embarrassing. We had another rough passage with Somerset Maugham, Evelyn and I. I loved Willie Maugham, but he was very difficult, too. I took Evelyn to stay with him in his beautiful villa in the south of France and it was a ghastly failure, because Evelyn got on the wrong tack. He had his portmanteau which he got out of the car hoping that he would be asked to stay. But the silly ass said something so tactless about stammering and deafness, and the portmanteau was put back in the car by a servant and he was asked to leave—because, of course, Willie Maugham stammered and was deaf.

Guppy: You wrote once that you thought "Graham Greene is a good man possessed of a devil, and Evelyn Waugh is a bad man for whom an angel is struggling." When did you meet Graham Greene?

Cooper: He came to Chantilly where I had kept a house after we left the Embassy in '47. There was a cottage in the garden, very derelict and hopeless—it didn't have a bathroom or anything. Graham Greene said: "Would you mind if I come and live there, to write?" I said it would be wonderful and he said: "Would there be room for a woman?" I said yes, but she won't like it—it has no comfort. He had a mistress called . . . you must know? I can't remember her name—there goes another marble! Well anybody could tell you. One day Enid Bagnold and I went to lunch with him at the Ritz—he had got some money for his book and taken a suite at the Ritz where he was living with this Mrs. Thing. At lunch the talk was on Catholicism—they were both Catholics—and G.G. said: "You Protestants are so lucky not to have things like Purgatory to face." Whereupon she turned on him furiously and said, "How dare you say they are lucky? They are *un*lucky!" So we went on with this very highbrow, moral talk. After lunch Enid and I went through the bathroom to the bedroom and there on the bed, folded neatly, was a pair of pyjamas on one side and a nightdress on the other! They were living together in *open sin*, with all that high moral talk, and she was married and had five children. He still sends me a book a year. I loved *The Heart of the Matter*, and the one after, but I was bored by the last one.

Guppy: In the Thirties did you get involved with the Bloomsbury set?

Cooper: Not really. They came after the First World War, and we were the generation before, most of whom had been killed. But I had a great friend, Desmond MacCarthy, who was very thick with them, and through him I met Lytton Strachey whom I liked very much. Desmond was a famous journalist who wrote for all the top papers. We all loved Desmond, but he didn't have the drive that is needed to become really famous—he was too charming and too lazy. Although he was queer, Lytton Strachey had a mistress called Carrington. She went to the Slade as an art student and so did my friend, Iris Tree. I had no talent, but I went also for fun and to be with Iris. My mother and sisters were very good painters and draughtswomen, but I wasn't. My eldest sister, Marjorie, was a genius—she could do anything. She fell in love with a young man who was penniless and my mother didn't want her to marry him. Then suddenly someone died and the penniless young man became the very rich Marquess of Anglesey, so everyone agreed to the marriage. But then *he* had second thoughts and went away for a while. So my sister was heartbroken, and began to go out with Prince Felix Yussoupov, who had murdered Rasputin. Well that was all right by me. But then the Marquess got wind of it, rushed back and married my sister. I wasn't pleased—I preferred the assassin.

Anyway, the Slade was frightfully cold and frightfully boring. You drew lots of plaster casts and then the great moment came when you graduated to the "life class." That was even colder, with these poor nude models trembling and freezing to death. One evening I went to Strachey and Carrington's house and there was Virginia Woolf. I was staggered: I had been told she was beautiful, but I didn't think she was at all. Then she asked me a succession of questions, like a machine gun, and I couldn't get over it. I can't say I liked her—all those questions! You would have thought she was interested, but I read much later that she did this to *everybody*.

And I knew Vita Sackville-West very well. My parents wanted her to marry my brother John (later the 8th Duke of Rutland), but she married Harold Nicolson. In those days you no longer arranged marriages in England the way you do to this day in France. Vita had rather a moustache early on—very masculine. Then a few years ago this *extraordinary* book came out which was about her affair with Violet Trefusis. [The book was called *Portrait of a Marriage* and was written by Nigel Nicolson]. I knew Violet Trefusis very well, but I had no notion of her lesbianism. The funny thing is that her letters are much better than Vita's, who was the literary one of the two. Nowadays there is a movement that wants to liberate male homosexuals, but female homosexuals don't have to be liberated—they always have been.

Guppy: D.H. Lawrence portrayed you in *Aaron's Rod* as Lady Artemis Hooper. Did you meet him?

Cooper: Only once—but I didn't take to him much. *Lady Chatterly* shocked society, but it didn't shock me. I thought Lawrence just used words which nobody else was using. I don't judge books; I have no critical faculty, I just like them or don't. But I was very friendly with Arnold Bennett who also put me in a book, which I didn't mind. Like Evelyn he was a challenge: nobody liked him, so I thought I had to. Through Bennett I met H.G. Wells whom I became very fond of. Before the First World War he had invented a game called "The War Game," with tin soldiers and guns, which we all played. We didn't know how soon afterwards we would be playing the real thing, and that most of the players would be killed. Then later I became friends with Moura Budberg, who was Wells's mistress for a long time. She was a wonderful Russian woman who had been Maxim Gorky's mistress, and then married a Baron Budberg. Anyway, we stayed friends till the end.

Guppy: At the end of the Second World War your husband was sent to Paris as Ambassador. Your term of office has become legendary. Did you meet many French literary figures?

Cooper: In fact, we were first sent to Algiers as a stepping stone to the Paris post. Our great friend was Gaston Palewski, who had come to England as John the Baptist to announce the arrival of the Saviour—de Gaulle. So in Algiers, de Gaulle came to dinner. We were absolutely awe-stricken and I didn't know what to talk about. Well, when people are in despair about conversation the best thing is to talk about childhood because then you become equals. So that went wonderfully well— *"Mon père était très dur, ma mère était très douce"*—that sort of thing. He had heard that for a while, when my husband was out of office, I had kept a small farm and when the conversation sagged he said, *"Comment va la vache?"* But he spoke an exquisite French and wrote it too. I think de Gaulle and Churchill would have survived through their writing even if they hadn't become great as statesmen. Anyway, Gaston Palewski became a Minister and brought *everybody* to the Embassy. Through him we met Louise de Vilmorin whom I adored. She became my husband's mistress for a while and my best friend. One day Louise produced Malraux, with whom she had had an affair in youth. I found him alarming, very serious, and I knew I could never get close to him. We used to call him "Monsieur de" (with reference to Vilmorin's famous novel, *Madame de . . .*). Do you know that at the end, they got back together and lived with each other till they died?

Guppy: Did you read his books?

Cooper: Good Lord no! I shouldn't have understood them, should I? Have you read them? Anyway, I had less time to read than before. I had read a great deal in youth.

Nancy Mitford was living in Paris too and was a great friend. She used to come to the Embassy a lot and later to Chantilly to write. She wrote a book called *Don't tell Alfred* which made fun of me, but I didn't mind at all, I thought it was funny. Gaston Palewski was the love of her life— "The Colonel" we all called him. "Oh yes, I adore him, I adore him," she used to say, but there was never any question of marriage between them. In the end he broke her heart by marrying someone else—a fabulously rich woman who had a palace like Versailles, with a heated lake— not a swimming pool, a *lake,* heated! And the whole place was full of Talleyrand things because she was descended from him.

Guppy: Did you establish a circle of friends there like "The Coterie"?

Cooper: Oh yes, *la bande.* The leaders were Louise [de Vilmorin] and Cocteau. Cocteau was very bright and sweet. He talked constantly and used to raise his hand so that nobody else could speak while he monologued. There was "Bébé" Bérard [Christian, a famous stage designer], whom I adored, and many others. Everybody came to the Embassy—I can't remember them all—Gertrude Stein and her girl friend, Eluard, Aragon . . . everybody. I had met Aragon years before with Nancy Cunard, with whom he had an affair. Then on the rebound he married this Russian woman [novelist Elsa Triolet] and became a communist. Nancy's mother, Emerald Cunard, was a great friend of mine. She had married someone quite unsuitable for her called Sir Bache Cunard, who was a Master of the Hounds and that sort of thing, and Emerald proceeded to take lovers immediately. One of them was George Moore who was devoted to her and whom they said was Nancy's *real* father because Nancy looked exactly like him. But as George Moore looked exactly like Sir Bache Cunard it was hard to tell. I always say it doesn't matter. People make too much fuss about infidelity nowadays.

Guppy: You also met Karen Blixen through Cecil Beaton at this time: what did you think of her?

Cooper: A friend in Paris called Dolly Radziwill had married a Dane and Karen Blixen used to come and stay with them and I saw her often. She was not at all the *grande dame de lettres* that you might imagine— the opposite, very simple and interested in everything. I think she had developed a kind of sixth sense on account of having lived so long in

Africa. Cecil Beaton was going to photograph her shortly before she died. He rang her up to say would she mind if he postponed it for a while. She told him that if he didn't go then, he would never see her again. So Cecil cancelled everything and went. Then she died—she knew.

Then a great many stage people came to the Embassy. You see, hotels were scarce after the War. At the same time there was a tremendous atmosphere of good will and euphoria as a result of the Liberation and a great *va-et-vient.* So we put up everybody—everybody who was anybody, that is—at the Embassy. Laurence Olivier and Vivien Leigh came. I loved her—she was very beautiful and intelligent and she could talk about other things than the stage, which he didn't. Stage people always speak about the theatre, but I don't mind that—I can take it.

Guppy: After the War, Churchill's Conservative government fell and Labor won the elections. You left the Embassy in 1947, but kept the house in Chantilly. What happened next?

Cooper: Well, Churchill had won the War and couldn't believe that they would get rid of him so soon. But they did and he was very cross. He said, "They say it is a blessing in disguise. Well, it is very well disguised!" Ernie Bevin became Foreign Secretary and came to Paris. I liked him very much and he liked us. When he called us back to London he said, "Duff must go to the 'ouse O'Lords." But in fact it was the Conservatives, when they came back in 1951, who gave Duff his peerage.

Lots of friends came and stayed in Chantilly: Nancy [Mitford] came and wrote there, Paddy [Patrick Leigh Fermor], Evelyn [Waugh] and many more.

Guppy: After your husband's death you set up the Duff Cooper Memorial Prize which this year was given to Richard Ellmann for his biography of James Joyce. Did you ever meet Joyce?

Cooper: Never could read *him!* Too modern for me. I always dread the prize-giving ceremony. This year Stephen Spender is doing it. One year I remember it was the American poet Robert Lowell. But he had a nervous breakdown and was sent to a loony bin—not for the first time I might add. So we looked frantically for a replacement and John Julius found someone distinguished and we thought all was well. On the prize-giving day I was standing next to a tall man who seemed quite drunk and I started telling him the story of how the man who was to award the prize had gone bonkers and was taken to a loony bin. At that point my son came forward and said to him: "Mr. Lowell will you come with me?" I didn't know what to do—evidently he had decided to come at the last minute. Fortunately he seemed too drunk to take it in.

Guppy: Is there anybody you have wished to meet and haven't?

Cooper: Not really. I never liked people because they were famous. Whenever I met someone I liked them or didn't, but I didn't care about their fame. Where I was lucky was getting involved with the stage for a while, because it was such fun. But not because of fame. Perhaps because I have always been famous and took it for granted; I didn't consider it important. Even now I keep getting letters from all over the world asking me about all sorts of things, even the Crimean War—as if I had been there! I don't really want to meet any more people—I am too, too old.

Yes, I have always been famous, and I shall never know why.

ART

Introduction

While artists have always been good friends to the magazine, its paper-back format is hardly the best size in which to display examples of their work. It may have been these limitations of space which persuaded many artists to do posters for the *Review*, where space requirements and color limitations were of no consequence. The poster program—signed limited editions—was initiated in 1965, aided by a generous grant from Mrs. Henry J. Heinz to get the work printed. Over fifty artists contributed their efforts—David Hockney, Willem de Kooning, Robert Motherwell, Claes Oldenburg, Louise Nevelson, Robert Rauschenberg, Frank Stella, Saul Steinberg, and Andy Warhol among them—and the sale of these works has been of great financial benefit to the magazine.

But as for the portfolios *within* the magazine, original work is limited because of small size and the absence of color. Thus, the most memorable art portfolios have usually been black-and-white sketches, line drawings, photograph essays, and cartoons. Examples of this artwork follow, the first, a portfolio by Glen Baxter from a series eventually called "It Was the Smallest Pizza They Had Ever Seen," and the second, by Roz Chast with a series of suggestions for vitrines at a *Paris Review* Revel.

—G.P.

GLEN BAXTER

It Was The Smallest Pizza They Had Ever Seen

It was at that precise moment that Dick realized the pool had been drained.

"We've only enough olives left for three more martinis, sir . . ." quaked Lawson.

"We don't hold with Puccini at the Lazy Z" snarled Tex.

Slowly, but with unerring precision, Dr. Tuttle reached for his luger . . .

It was the smallest pizza they had ever seen.

Robin was certainly impressed with the simulated teak finish.

"We'll have no alliteration in this here bunkhouse!" snorted McCul-
loch.

Sir Roland tried to convince the sceptics of the potential of his light-weight mini-shield.

With a cheery little grunt, Mr Roberts indicated just where he had buried our cheese sandwiches.

Great Moments in Literature

It was always a tradition to use ingenuity and imagination to make the Revels—the money-raising parties—memorable occasions for those who attended. In 1985 the Revel was held in a New York discotheque called Area. The club was distinguished by a number of vitrines and dioramas set into the walls of a maze of corridors, so that in the gloom one often had the impression of wandering through an aquarium. Every month or so Area picked a "theme" ("Science Fiction," "The Automobile," "Suburbia") which were reflected by various stagings set up in the vitrines. The month before the Revel it was suggested that the magazine could decorate the vitrines with the theme "Great Moments in Literature." The Area people were somewhat leery of the concept. "Are we sure there're enough Great Moments?"

In the hope of persuading Area that the theme "Great Moments in Literature" was viable and appropriate (certainly for the night of the Revel) the *Paris Review* staff offered help with various proposals designed for the club's vitrines. These follow—a series of story boards (to use an advertising term) illustrated by Roz Chast. The individual ideas have been listed under the heading "Proposal" together with their disposition, a final decision made either by the *Review* staff or the Area people. Ultimately none of them were used the night of the Revel. Those who attended gazed in at scenes of "Suburbia" or whatever. The last of the Roz Chast drawings, as readers will note, provides the perfect illustrative conclusion to this anthology.

PROPOSAL: Marcel Proust shown dipping his madeleine cookie into his tea, circa 1909, the famous mnemonic act which produced a rush of childhood memories culminating in the noted madeleine episode of *Swann's Way* and providing the framework for *Remembrance of Things Past.*

REJECTED: Too obscure. Not enough action.

40 LASHES

PROPOSAL: Colette in bed spanking one of her cats.

REJECTED: No historical evidence that Colette ever did spank one.

PROPOSAL: Herman Melville sitting in his den, bent over his writing desk, occasionally scratching his ear with a quill, and trying to come up with the first line of *Moby Dick*. On a large scroll of paper the viewer can see through the vitrine window that he has crossed out "Call me Harry," "Call me Lucas," "Call me Charlie," "Call me Jake," "Call me Buck," etc. etc.

REJECTED: Too esoteric. Too confusing to revelers and party crashers unaware of the classic's first line.

PROPOSAL: A twilight scene in the drawing-room of William Makepeace Thackeray's home in Kensington. His youngest daughter looks up from a book she has been reading and asks her father, "Papa, why do you not write books like *Nicholas Nickleby*?"

REJECTED: Question too tough. Besides, what Thackeray replied was never recorded by Lord Tennyson, who was a witness to the scene.

PROPOSAL: The scene at Bread Loaf Writers Conference when Archibald MacLeish's poetry reading was interrupted by Robert Frost who, after whispering loudly, "Archie's poems all have the same tune," lit fire to a handful of mimeographed papers to disrupt the proceedings.

REJECTED: New York City fire laws prohibit. Besides, possibility of soggy matches and the actor playing "Frost" unable to get fire started.

PROPOSAL: A diorama devoted entirely to a succession of famous literary fights: Alexandre Dumas (père) losing his trousers in his first duel; Verlaine shooting Rimbaud in the wrist in Brussels; Hemingway and Max Eastman wrestling in Max Perkins' office; Theodore Dreiser slapping Sinclair Lewis in the Metropolitan Club; the "Night of the Tiny Fist" when Norman Mailer hit Gore Vidal in the eye at Lally Weymouth's salon; etc., etc.

REJECTED: Too large a contingent necessary backstage to put on such a massive number of brouhahas; labor costs prohibitive.

PROPOSAL: *Portrait of the Artist as a Young Man.*

REJECTED: Problem of getting a minor admitted to Area.

ZANY · ZANE
AND HIS
DISTANT AND SPIRITED
COW

PROPOSAL: Zane Grey on the porch of his home in Altadena, California, harnessed in a sport-fishing chair with the fishing line attached to a distant and spirited cow—the way in which Grey simulated far inland his beloved deep-sea fishing . . . a strenuous habit which eventually caused his death on October 23, 1939.

REJECTED: Too difficult to construct the set within the diorama, especially the distant and spirited cow.

M. de Nerval
and Friend

PROPOSAL: On a treadmill within the vitrine Gerard de Nerval, the 19th-century exotic, is walking the famous lobster (on a pale-blue ribbon leash) from which he hoped to learn "the secrets of the deep." Not having heard a peep from the lobster regarding the secrets of the deep, or anything else for that matter, de Nerval sets a pot on a small brush fire and, preparing the lobster with a nice herbal sauce (3 to 4 lbs. fresh minced green herbs; parsley, chervil, and tarragon or parsley only), he tucks a napkin under his chin and falls to.

REJECTED: Antianimalarian. Also not historically accurate; there is no evidence that de Nerval ever ate his pet lobster. Fire laws once again a problem.

PROPOSAL: "All happy families are alike; but every unhappy family is unhappy in its own fashion"—Tolstoy.

REJECTED: Small Area diorama would be too crowded, thus rendering all the families obviously unhappy.

PROPOSAL: The scene following the lunch given by Carson McCullers in Nyack, NY, in 1959 at which Isak Dinesen, Marilyn Monroe, and her husband, Arthur Miller, were asked to tap dance on the marbletopped dining room table.

REJECTED: McCullers' proposal was declined by all those at the table; thus any re-creation lacks visual excitement.

PROPOSAL: The scene at Turgenev's home at the moment that the visiting Tolstoy falls asleep before the author's eyes after reading a few pages of *Fathers and Sons.* (1861).

REJECTED: Not enough action. Too ho-hum. Observers unfamiliar with the story might assume that Tolstoy was falling asleep over his own book.

RUPERT BROOKE
and the
MOSQUITO OF DOOM

PROPOSAL: Rupert Brooke being bitten on the lip by a mosquito while serving with the Royal Naval Division on Skyros . . . the infection which eventually caused his death from blood poisoning.

REJECTED: Difficult to find a mosquito large enough to be identified by the people in front of the vitrine. A dummy mosquito, made of wire, say, would tend to overpower "Rupert Brooke," and make it look as though the poet were under attack by a buzzard, or a fugitive from a low-budget sci-fi movie.

A TRYING MOMENT

PROPOSAL: Henry James being hissed off the stage after taking an opening-night bow at the debut of *Guy Domville*.

REJECTED: Might leave viewers with the wrong impression of Henry James. Leon Edel would be upset. Also, vegetables might go bad.

PROPOSAL: Thomas Wolfe and James Joyce *not* meeting while passengers in the same car touring the battlefields of Waterloo.

REJECTED: Too static; not enough for "Wolfe" and "Joyce" to do. Also too difficult to fit a car in a vitrine at Area, much less the battlefields of Waterloo.

The End

PROPOSAL: The death of Emile Zola in his sleep from inhaling smoke from a clogged chimney.

REJECTED: Easy enough to depict (by covering the viewing window with smoked cellophane), but likely to confuse the audience, which might assume the vignette was not yet prepared (or out of order) and because of this leave the revel in a huff. But it was a nice concept to end everything.

Notes on Contributors

DIANE ACKERMAN ("Still Life") is the author of the poetry collections *The Planets: A Cosmic Pastoral* (1976), *Wife of Light* (1978), and *Lady Faustus* (1983), as well as several volumes of nonfiction. She is a staff writer for *The New Yorker.*

BOBBY ANDERSEN ("Edie Sedgwick: A Reminiscence"), a male nurse at the time of original publication, cannot be traced. The selection is an excerpt from the book *Edie* by **Jean Stein,** edited with **George Plimpton,** which became a best-seller in 1981.

GUILLAUME APOLLINAIRE (1880–1918) (Mirabeau Bridge), Italian-born French poet and art critic, was the author of *Alcools, Calligrammes,* and many other books of poetry. His translator, **Richard Wilbur,** who was American poet laureate from 1987 to 1988, received the Pulitzer Prize for his *New and Collected Poems.*

NATHAN ASCH ("The Nineteen-Twenties: An Interior") is the son of Sholen Asch, the novelist. The selection is from his novel *Paris War Home.*

JOHN ASHBERY ("The Bungalows" and "This Configuration") is the author of many volumes of poetry, including *Self Portrait in a Convex Mirror* (1976), which was awarded the Pulitzer Prize for Literature, the National Book Award, and the National Book Critics Circle Award. In 1984 he was awarded, with Fred Chappell, the Bollingen Prize for Poetry. His most recent collection of poetry is *April Galleons* (Viking, 1987). A volume of art criticism, *Reported Sightings,* was published in 1989 by Knopf.

INGEBORG BACHMANN (1926–1973) ("Autumn Maneuver") was born in Austria and is considered the foremost German language poet of her generation. **Mark Anderson,** the translator, was working on his doctorate in comparative literature at Johns Hopkins University at the time of publication.

PAULÉ BARTÓN (1916–1974) ("The Bee Dice Game") was born in Haiti and imprisoned there under the regime of President Duvalier. He spent the later years of his life in Trinidad-Tobago, working mainly as a goatherd.

RICK BASS ("Wild Horses") is the author of a short story collection, *The Watch* (1988), and a collection of essays, *Oil Notes*. His first published fiction appeared in the *Paris Review*, winning the 1987 General Electric Younger Writers Award. His stories have been widely anthologized and have received many awards. He has taught creative writing at the University of Texas and currently lives in northwestern Montana.

GLEN BAXTER ("It Was The Smallest Pizza They Had Ever Seen") was born in Leeds in 1944 and now lives in London. He has published many books of drawings, including *His Life, the Years of Struggle* (1984).

SAMUEL BECKETT ("Extract from *Molloy*") was born in Dublin in 1906. He rose to international fame with the publication of his play *Waiting for Godot* (1952). He was awarded the Nobel Prize for literature in 1969. The selection was exerpted from *Molloy* (1955).

MICHAEL BENEDIKT ("The Badminton at Great Barrington") was the poetry editor of the *Paris Review* from 1973 until 1978. He is the author of five books of poetry, most recently *The Badminton at Great Barrington; Or Gustave Mahler & the Chattanooga Choo-Choo*. He has taught at Bennington, Vassar, Sarah Lawrence, Hampshire College, and Boston University.

TED BERRIGAN (1934–1983) ("The Fiend") was born in Providence, Rhode Island. In the 1960s, he was the editor of *"C" Press. A Certain Slant of Sunlight*, a group of poems written by Berrigan at the end of his life, was published by O Books in 1988.

ROBERT BLY ("Two Choral Stanzas" and "Two Translations from Kabir") is the author of many books, most recently *Selected Poems* (1987), *The Winged Life: Selected Poems and Prose of Thoreau* (1987), and *A Little Book on the Human Shadow* (1988).

PHILIP BOOTH'S ("Seadog and Seal") most recent books are *Relations, Selected Poems 1950–1985*, and *Selves*. He has received many awards for his poetry and was elected a Fellow of the Academy of American Poets in 1983.

JORGE LUIS BORGES (1899–1986) ("Funes the Memorious") was an Argentinian and one of the first Latin American writers to achieve international acclaim. In 1983 he was awarded the Legion of Honor by President Mitterand of France for his literary achievements. Among his short story collections are *Labyrinths* (1969) and *Ficciones* (1944).

T. CORAGHESSAN BOYLE ("Ike and Nina") was published in the *Paris Review* in 1977. His most recent novel is *World's End*, which won the PEN/Faulkner Award for Fiction in 1987. His third collection of short stories, *If the River Was Whiskey*, was published in 1989.

RICHARD BRAUTIGAN'S (1933–1984) ("The San Francisco Weather Report") many published books included the prose works, *Trout Fishing in America, A*

Confederate General at Big Sur, and *In Watermelon Sugar,* and several volumes of poetry, among them *Rommel Drives on Deep into Egypt* and *Loading Mercuring with a Pitchfork.*

KATE ELLEN BRAVERMAN ("Classified Ad") graduated from the University of California at Berkeley in 1971.

DONALD BRITTON ("Virgule") was born in Texas in 1951 and currently lives in Los Angeles. His book of Poems, *Italy,* was published in 1981.

HAROLD BRODKEY'S ("To Frank O'Hara") stories, essays, and poetry have appeared in various magazines including *The New Yorker, New American Review, Antaeus,* the *Paris Review, Vanity Fair,* and *Esquire.* He has won a Prix de Rome, two O. Henry First Prizes, and fellowships from the National Endowment for the Arts and the Susan Guggenheim Memorial Foundation. He is the author of three collections of stories, *First Love and Other Sorrows, Women and Angels,* in a limited edition published by the Jewish Publication Society of America, and *Stories In An Almost Classical Mode.*

JOSEPH BRODSKY ("To Urania") emigrated from the Soviet Union in 1972. His books of poetry include *Selected Poems* (1973, with a foreword by W. H. Auden), *A Part of Speech* (1980), and *To Urania* (1988). He was the recipient of a MacArthur Fellowship in 1981, and in 1987 received the National Book Critics Circle Award for criticism, for his collection of essays, *Less than One.* He was awarded the Nobel Prize for Literature in 1987. He is currently the Andrew Mellon Professor of Literature at Mount Holyoke College.

JOSEPH BRUCHAC ("The Hitchhiker") is a writer and professional storyteller who lives in the Adirondack foothills. His poems and stories have appeared in many magazines and anthologies. His most recent publications include *Keepers of the Earth: Native American Stories and Environmental Activities for Children* (with Michael Caduto) and *Near the Mountains: New and Selected Poems.* The founder of the Greenfield Review Literary Center, he has worked extensively with writers in prison.

ITALO CALVINO (1923–1985) ("Last Comes the Raven"), the great Italian novelist, essayist, and fabulist, was first published in English in the *Paris Review.* His works of fiction include: *The Path to the Nest of Spiders* (translated 1956), based on his experiences in the Italian anti-fascist resistance; *Invisible Cities* (translated 1974), a poetic discourse given by Marco Polo to Kubla Kahn; and *If on a Winter's Night a Traveller* (translated 1981), in which the reader is the protagonist. He also collected—and retold—traditional stories in *Italian Fables* (translated 1959) and *Italian Folktales* (translated 1980). He was born outside Havana, Cuba, grew up in Turin, Italy, and lived afterwards in Rome and Paris.

JAMES CAMP ("Brief History of the Confederate Aristocracy") is the author of two volumes of poetry, *Light Year '87* (1986), and *The Sonnet* (1987). He is a professor at the New Jersey Institute of Technology.

JIM CARROLL'S ("Heroin") most recent works include *The Book of Nods* (1986), a volume of poetry, and *Forced Entries: The Downtown Diaries* (1987). He has released three albums of rock music on Atlantic Records.

RAYMOND CARVER (1938–1988) ("Why Don't You Dance?") completed a last book of poems, *A New Path to the Waterfall*, shortly before his death. His collections of short stories include *Will You Be Quiet, Please* (1976), *Furious Seasons and Other Stories* (1977), and *What We Talk about When We Talk about Love* (1981). A BBC documentary on Carver's life was shown in Great Britain in the fall of 1989. At the time the selection was published, Carver was teaching in the creative writing program at Syracuse University.

SIV CEDERING ("Peaches") is the author of two novels, five books of poetry, and six books for children. Her most recent book of poetry is *Letters from the Floating World: New and Selected Poetry* (1984).

LOUIS-FERDINAND CÉLINE (1894–1961), the French novelist, is the author of many books including *Death on the Installment Plan* (1936, translated 1938), *Journey to the End of Night (1932, translated 1934).*

G. S. SHARAT CHANDRA ("Rape of Lucrece Retold") was director of the writing program at Washington State University.

FRED CHAPPELL ("Tiros II") teaches English at the University of North Carolina at Greensboro. His most recent books are *First and Last Words* and *Brighten the Corner Where You Are.*

ROZ CHAST ("Great Moments in Literature") is a frequent contributor of cartoons to *The New Yorker*. Her books of cartoons include *Mondo Boxo* (1987), *Parallel Universes* (1984), and *Unscientific American* (1982). She lives in New York City.

MAXINE CHERNOFF ("Hats Around the World") is the author of five books of poetry, including *New Faces of 1952*, which won the 1985 Carl Sandburg Award. *Bop*, her story collection, received the 1988 LSU/*Southern Review* Short Fiction Award.

TOM CLARK'S ("Superballs") collections of poetry include *Disordered Ideas, Easter Sunday*, and the forthcoming *Fractured Karma*. He has also written several biographies of writers, among them Damon Runyon, Jack Kerouac, and Ted Berrigan, and is now at work on a life of the American poet Charles Olson. He teaches poetics at New College of California, and lives in Berkeley.

NANCY CONDEE ("In the Late Afternoon . . .") has published a chapbook, *The Rape of Saint Enad.*

EVAN S. CONNELL'S ("The Beau Monde of Mrs. Bridge") novels include: *Mrs. Bridge* (1959) and its sequel *Mr. Bridge* (1969), which investigate the subtle workings of Kansas City society. Perhaps his finest portrait of all is that of General Custer in his authoritative historical work, *Son of the Morning Star* (1984).

CLARK COOLIDGE ("Bee Elk") was Writer-in-Residence at the American Academy in Rome from 1984 to 1985. His most recent books are *Solution Passage: Poems 1978–1981, The Crystal Text, Mesh, At Egypt,* and *Sound as Thought: Poems 1982–1984.* At the time "Bee Elk" was published, Coolidge was a drummer with The Serpent Power, a San Francisco rock-and-roll group.

ALFRED CORN ("One To One") is the author of five books of poems, most recently *The West Door.* He has won a number of prizes including a Guggenheim Fellowship and a Fellowship from the Academy of American Poets. He lives in New York City.

JULIO CORTÁZAR ("Feuilletons from *A Certain Lucas*"), an Argentinian born in Brussels in 1914, lived and worked in Paris from 1952 until his death in 1984. He was a poet, translator, and amateur jazz musician as well as the author of several novels and volumes of short stories. His books published in English include *Hopscotch, A Manual for Manuel,* and *A Change of Light.*

HENRI COULETTE (1927–1988) ("The Blue-Eyed Precinct Worker") lived in California and taught at California State University.

ROBERT CREELEY ("The Finger") is David Grey Professor of Poetry and Letters at the State University of New York at Buffalo and a member of the American Academy and Institute of Arts and Letters. His published work includes *The Collected Poems, 1945–1975, The Collected Prose,* and *The Collected Essays.* In 1989 he was given the Walt Whitman Citation by the State of New York, making him the state poet for 1989–1991.

EDWIN DENBY (1903–1983) ("Sonnet") is the author of many essay collections and volumes of poetry, including *In Public, In Private* and *Mediterranean Cities.* Random House published his *Complete Poems* in 1985 and Alfred A. Knopf published *Dance Writings* in 1986; it won a National Book Critics Circle Award in 1987.

JAMES DICKEY ("Mindoro, 1944") won the National Book Award for Poetry for his 1965 collection, *Buckdancer's Choice.* He has been a Guggenheim Fellow as well as a fellow of the American Academy of Arts and Sciences and a member of the American Academy and Institute of Arts and Letters. In addition to his many books of poetry, he is the author of the novels *Deliverance* and *Alnilam.* At the time "Mindoro, 1944" appeared, Dickey was working as an advertising executive in Atlanta, Georgia.

THOMAS M. DISCH's ("The Joycelin Shrager Story") *Yes, Let's: New and Selected Poems* was published this year by Johns Hopkins University Press. His first full-length play, an adaptation of General Low Wallace's *Ben Hur,* has been presented by R.A.P.P. Theater in Baltimore and New York.

STEPHEN DIXON's ("Goodbye to Goodbye") seventh story collection, *Love and Will,* was published by Paris Review Editions in October 1989. His previous story collection, *The Play,* was published by Coffee House Press in 1988, and his fourth novel, *Garbage*, was published by Cane Hill Press in 1988. He lives in Baltimore and teaches in the writing seminars at Johns Hopkins University. "Goodbye to Goodbye" won the *Paris Review*'s John Train Humor Prize in 1985.

EDWARD DORN ("The Poet Lets His Tongue Hang Down") teaches creative writing and American Literature at the University of Colorado, Boulder.

ANDRE DUBUS ("Waiting") is a retired professor. In 1988 he received the Jean Stein Award from the American Academy and Institute of Arts and Letters and a grant from the MacArthur Foundation. His *Selected Stories* was published by David R. Godine in 1988.

ROBERT DUNCAN ("Lammas Dream Poem") is the author of many books of poetry including *Selected Poems* (1981) and *The Catalyst* (1981).

STANLEY ELKIN ("The Guest") is the Merle Kling Professor of Modern Letters at Washington University and a member of the American Academy and Institute of Arts and Letters. He is the author of many works of fiction. His novel, *George Mills*, won the National Book Award. He is currently at work on a novel, *The MacGuffin*.

BETTY EPPES ("What I Did Last Summer") is a rural Mississippian, a high school dropout, mother of three, divorced, a tennis player and columnist ("Writing is a compulsion and tennis is my vehicle."), an ex-insurance agent, and a former Playboy Bunny.

WILLIAM FERGUSON ("A Summer at Estabrook") is the author of *Freedom and Other Fictions*, a collection of stories published by Alfred A. Knopf in 1984. He teaches Spanish at Clark University in Worcester, Massachusetts. His work has appeared in *The Mississippi Review, Canto, Calliope,* and other magazines.

DAVID FERRY ("On the Way to the Island") is Sophie Chantal Hart Professor of English at Wellesley College. His most recent book is *Strangers: A Book of Poems* (1983). He is at work on a new book of poems and translations.

JONATHAN GALASSI ("Lateness") was the poetry editor of the *Paris Review* from 1978 to 1988 and is editor-in-chief at Farrar, Straus & Giroux. He is the translator of two books by the Italian poet Eugenio Montale: *The Second Life of Art: Selected Essays* (1982) and *Otherwise: Last and First Poems* (1984). His collection of poetry, *Morning Run*, was published by Paris Review Editions in 1988.

EUGENE K. GARBER ("The Flight") teaches writing at the State University of New York at Albany. His short story collection, *Metaphysical Tales* (University of Missouri Press) won the Associated Writing Programs Short Fiction Award. His stories have been anthologized in *The Norton Anthology of Contemporary Fiction* and elsewhere.

WILLIAM GASS ("Summer Bees") received the National Academy of Arts and Letters Medal for Merit in Fiction in 1979. He is the David May Distinguished

University Professor in the Humanities at Washington University in St. Louis, where he has taught since 1969. He is the author of several novels, including *The Heart of the Heart of the Country,* and a book of essays, *Habitations of the Wood.*

GARY GILDNER'S ("The Runner") new and selected poems, *Blue Like the Heavens* appeared in 1984. He is a recipient of the 1986 National Magazine Award for Fiction. In 1987 Algonquin Books published *The Second Bridge,* a novel, and *A Week in South Dakota,* a collection of short stories. In 1988 Gildner was Fulbright Lecturer at the University of Warsaw and coach of the Warsaw Sparks baseball team.

PENELOPE GILLIATT ("Gossip") was born in London and brought up in Northumberland. She has published many short story collections and novels, including most recently *What's it Like Out?* and *To Wit.* "Sunday Bloody Sunday" received an Oscar nomination for best original screenplay in 1971. She is a member of the National Institute of Arts and Letters. She is a film critic for *The Observer* (London) and *The New Yorker.* A collection of short stories are forthcoming from Virago Press.

ALLEN GINSBERG ("City Midnight Junk Strains") attained prominence as a Beat poet in the 1950s. His volumes of poetry include *Howl and Other Poems* (1959) and *Kaddish and Other Poems* (1961), both from City Lights.

LINDA GREGG ("Taken By Each Thing") received the Whiting Award in 1985. Her books include *To Bright to See* (1982) and *Alma* (1985). She has taught at the Iowa Writing Program.

ALLEN GROSSMAN'S ("Holy Ghost Hospital" and "The Woman on the Bridge over the Chicago River") latest book is *The Bright Nails Scattered on the Ground* (New Directions, 1986). He is Professor of Poetry and General Education at Brandeis University. Among his recent awards are the Sara Teasdale Memorial Prize in Poetry at Wellesley College (1987) and the Sheaffer-PEN/New England Award for Literary Distinction (1988).

THOM GUNN ("The Wound") has taught part-time at the University of California, Berkeley, for many years and lives in San Francisco. His most recent books of poetry are *The Passages of Joy* (1982) and *Selected Poems* (1979).

SHUSHA GUPPY ("An Interview with Lady Diana Cooper") was born in Persia and educated in Paris. She is the London editor of the *Paris Review* and contributes to literary magazines on both sides of the Atlantic. She is also a well-known singer and songwriter. *The Blindfold Horse* won the Yorkshire Post Award for Best Book of 1988.

DONALD HALL ("Sleeping") was poetry editor of the *Paris Review* from 1953 to 1961. His ninth book of poetry, *The One Day,* won the National Book Critics Circle Award in 1989.

SEAMUS HEANEY ("Leavings") was born in Ireland in 1939. His volumes of poetry include *Death of a Naturalist* (1969), *Fieldwork* (1979), *Poems: Nineteen Sixty-five to Nineteen Seventy-five* (1980), and, most recently, *The Haw Lantern.*

JOHN HEATH-STUBBS ("The Peacock and the Snake") was awarded the Order of the British Empire in 1989.

GEOFFREY HILL ("Genesis" and "Prayer to the Sun") was born at Bromsgrove, Worcestershire and educated at the County High School and Keble College, Oxford, which elected him into an honorary fellowship in 1981. His books of poetry include *King Log* (1968), *Mercian Hymns* (1971), *Tenebrae* (1978), and *Collected Poems* (1985). He has also published a volume of critical essays, *The Lords of Limit* (1984) and a version of Ibsen's *Brand* (1978). He is a recipient of the Hawthornden Prize (1969) and an Ingram Merrill Foundation Award in Literature (1985). He has taught at the University of Leeds and Cambridge University and is now university professor and professor of religion at Boston University.

RICHARD HOWARD ("On Tour") is Ropes Professor of Comparative Literature at the University of Cincinnati. His ninth book of poems, *No Traveller,* was published in 1989. He is currently at work on a new translation of Marcel Proust's *In Search of Lost Time,* to be published by Farrar, Straus & Giroux.

TED HUGHES ("Crow Hill") is Poet Laureate of Great Britain. His volumes of poetry include *The Hawk in the Rain* (1957), *Wodwow* (1971), and *New Selected Poems* (1982).

SIRI HUSTVEDT ("Weather Markings"), at the time of publication (1981), was a graduate student of comparative literature at Columbia University.

LEROI JONES (Amiri Baraka) ("Tele/vision") was born in Newark, New Jersey in 1934. His major works include the novel *The System of Dante's Hell* (1976), *Selected Poetry* (1979), the play *The Dutchman,* for which he received an Obie, and *Selected Plays and Prose* (1979).

ERICA JONG ("Jubilate Canis") was born in New York City and educated at Barnard College and Columbia University. She is the author of many collections of poetry, including *At the Edge of the Body* (1979) and *Ordinary Miracles* (1983), and of the best-selling novel *Fear of Flying* (1973). Her most recent novel is *Serenissima* (1987).

DONALD JUSTICE ("Sestina" and "Last Days of Prospero") lives in Gainesville, Florida, where he teaches at the University of Florida. His books include *Selected Poems* (1979), *Platonic Scripts* (1984), and *The Sunset Maker* (1987). In 1980 he received the Pulitzer Prize in poetry for his *Selected Poems.* He is a fellow of the Academy of American Poets.

BERNARD KEITH'S (KEITH WALDRUP) ("ESSAY ON METER") *Selected Poems* were published in 1989. His most recent novel is *Hegel's Family.*

DAVID KELLY ("Counting on a Decade") is the author of thirteen books and chapbooks of poetry and fiction. He has received several fellowships in poetry, taught poetry in local schools and prisons, and is director of creative writing at the State University of New York at Geneseo.

X. J. KENNEDY ("In a Prominent Bar in Secaucus One Day") was poetry editor of the *Paris Review* from 1961 to 1964. His *Cross Ties: Selected Poems* (1985) won a *Los Angeles Times* Book Award. *Ghastlies, Goops & Pincushions* (1989) is his latest book for children. In 1989 he received the first Michael Braude Award for Light Verse from the American Academy and Institute of Arts and Letters.

GALWAY KINNELL ("The Milk Bottle") received the Award of Merit Medal for Poetry from the American Academy and Institute of Arts and Letters in 1975. He is the author of *Mortal Acts, Mortal Words* (1980), *Selected Poems* (1982), for which he received the Pulitzer Prize, and *The Past* (1985). He is a professor of English at New York University.

BILL KNOTT ("Lesson") teaches in the MFA Creative Writing Program at Emerson College in Boston. His most recent book is *Poems 1963–1988.*

KENNETH KOCH's ("The Interpretation of Dreams") most recent books are *One Thousand Avant-Garde Plays, Seasons in Earth, On the Edge,* and *Selected Poems.* He teaches in the English department at Columbia University.

JOHN KOETHE ("Picture of Little Letters") was born in San Diego, California in 1945. He holds a Ph.D. in philosophy from Harvard. His books include *Blue Vents, The Late Wisconsin Spring,* and *Domes,* which won the 1973 Frank O'Hara Award for Poetry. He received the Bernard F. Conners Prize from the *Paris Review* in 1986, and was a Guggenheim Fellow in 1987–1988. He is associate professor of philosophy at the University of Wisconsin at Milwaukee.

MAXINE KUMIN's ("Another Form of Marriage") most recent books are *Nurture* (1989) and *In Deep: Country Essays* (1988). She won the Pulitzer Prize for Poetry in 1973 for her collection, *Up Country,* and is a Fellow of the American Academy of Poets.

PHILIP LARKIN (1922–1985) ("Referred Back") was the editor of *The Oxford Book of Twentieth-Century Verse* (1973). His *Required Reading: Miscellaneous Pieces 1955–1982* (1984) won the W. H. Smith Literary Award. *Collected Poems* was published by Farrar, Straus & Giroux in 1989.

JAMES LASDUN ("Show") lives in London. His poems, stories, and reviews have appeared in the *Times Literary Supplement,* the *Paris Review, Encounter,* and other magazines. He is the author of *Delirium Eclipse* (1986), a collection of short stories, and *A Jump Start* (1988), a book of poems.

ANN LAUTERBACH ("Naming the House") is a professor in the writing programs of Columbia University, Princeton University, and the City University of New

York. She is the author of three collections of poetry: *Many Times, But Then* (1979), *Sacred Weather* (1984), and *Before Recollection* (1987).

DAVID LEHMAN ("Fear and Trembling") was born in New York City in 1948. His work first appeared in the *Paris Review* in 1968. His long poem, "Mythologies," won the *Paris Review's* Bernard F. Conners Prize in 1987. His books include *An Alternative to Speech* (1986), *The Perfect Murder: A Study in Detection* (1989), and *Operation Memory* (forthcoming in 1990). He is series editor of *The Best American Poetry* and the vice-president of the National Book Critics Circle. He lives in Ithaca, New York.

PHILIP LEVINE ("The Turning") teaches at California State University at Fresno. His books have won the National Book Critics Circle Award, the American Book Award, the Lenore Marshall Award, and, most recently, the Bay Area Book Reviewers Award for the best book of poetry published in 1988. His most recent book is *A Walk with Tom Jefferson* (1988). In 1987 he received the Ruter Lilly Award, given by *Poetry* magazine and the American Council for the Arts.

JOHN LOGAN (1923–1987) ("The Mallard's Going) was born in Red Oak, Iowa. He was the author of eight books of poetry including *Only the Dreamer Can Change the Dream* (1981) and *Collected Poems* (1989). Among his many awards were grants from the John D. Rockefeller Foundation, the National Endowment for the Arts, the Guggenheim Foundation, the Lenora Marshall Prize, and the William Carlos Williams Award for Poetry.

THOMAS LUX's ("Sleepmask Dithyrambic") most recent book is *Half Promised Land.* His new collection, *The Drowned River,* will be published in 1990. Currently a Guggenheim Fellow, Lux has taught writing and literature at Sarah Lawrence College since 1975.

GEORGE MACBETH ("Eating Ice-Cream with a Girl") was born in Scotland in 1932. His books include *Poems of Love and Death* and *The Katana.*

HANK STAPLES says that his friend **Everette H. Maddox** (1944–1989) ("Thirteen Ways of Being Looked at by a Possum") was a legend in New Orleans. For ten years, he ran a series of poetry readings at the Maple Leaf Bar and taught English at the University of New Orleans and at Xaxier University, where he was poet-in-residence. He was raised in Prattville, Alabama, and received bachelor's and master's degrees from the University of Alabama. He spent the last five years of his life homeless, sleeping alongside the Mississippi River.

ANDRÉ PIEYRE DE MANDIARGUES ("The Bath of Madame Mauriac") has published over thirty books, including *Le Musée, Les Monstres de Bomarzo,* and *Le Cadan Lunaire.* His *La Marge* was awarded the Prix Goncourt. **Albert Herzing,** his translator, had his first collection of poems published in *Poets of Today, Volume VIII.* He lives in Tulsa, Oklahoma.

HEATHER MCHUGH ("To the Quick") teaches at the University of Washington in Seattle and in the MFA Program for Writers at Warren Wilson College in

North Carolina. Her most recent collections of poetry are *Shades* (1988), *Because the Sea is Black* (1989), a co-translation of poetry by Blaga Dimitrova, and *To the Quick* (1987), of which the selection is the title poem.

JAY MCINERNEY ("It's Six A.M. Do You Know Where You Are?") is the author of *Ransom* (1985) and *Story of My Life* (1988), as well as *Bright Lights, Big City* (1984), of which the selection, his first published work of fiction, is the first chapter.

JAMES MERRILL ("Grass") was born in New York City. He has written novels and plays as well as many volumes of poetry, including *Divine Comedies* (1976), *The Changing Light at Sandover* (1982), *From the First Nine* (1982), and *The Inner Room* (1988). He has received two National Book Awards, a Pulitzer Prize, and the Bollinger Prize.

W. S. MERWIN ("Sow" "Marica Lart", "Demonstration") was born in New York City in 1927 and has lived in Spain, England, France, Mexico, and Hawaii. His books of poetry include *A Mask for Janus* (1952), *The Lice* (1967), *The Rain in the Trees* (1987), *Selected Poems* (1988) and *Vertical Poetry* (1990). His *The Carrier of Ladders* won the Pulitzer Prize in 1971. He is also well-known as a translator of poetry, including oral poetry and chants of Hawaiian and Crow Indian cultures. His prose books include *Unframed Original* (1982) and *Regions of Memory: Uncollected Prose* (1986).

ROBERT MEZEY ("In the Environs of the Funeral Home") teaches at Pomona College. His most recent book of verse is *Evening Wind* (1987). Syracuse University Press has recently published his translation of Cesar Vallejo's novel, *Tungsten.*

LEONARD MICHAELS'S ("City Boy") fiction has won various awards, including a Guggenheim Fellowship, a grant from the National Endowment for the Arts, and an O. Henry Award. He is the author of *Going Places* (1969) and *I Would Have Saved Them if I Could* (1975). He teaches in the English department of the University of California at Berkeley.

CHRISTOPHER MIDDLETON ("News from Norwood") was born in Cornwall, England in 1926. He has been a Guggenheim Poetry Fellow and is a member of the West German Akademie der Kunst.

VASSAR MILLER'S ("Love Song for the Future") many books include *Approaching Nada* (1977) and *Selected and New Poems: 1950–1980* (1980).

CZESLAW MILOSZ, ("My Faithful Mother Tongue") Polish poet, essayist, and novelist, was born in rural Lithuania in 1911. His early childhood was spent in Czarist Russia, where his father worked as a civil engineer. In 1960 Milosz moved to Berkeley, California where he became professor of Slavic languages and Literature at the University of California. Milosz's recent collections of poetry include *Unattainable Earth* (1986), *Chronicles* (1987), and *The Collected Poems* (1988). He received the Nobel Prize in Literature in 1980.

SUSAN MINOT ("Lust") is the author of *Monkeys* (1986) and *Lust* (1989). She teaches in the graduate writing program at Columbia University and is a contributing editor of *Grand Street*.

HERBERT MORRIS ("Newport, 1930") is the author of *Peru* (1983), *Dream Palace* (1986), and *The Little Voices of the Pears* (1989).

LORINE NIEDECKER (1903–1970) ("Who Was Mary Shelley?") lived nearly all her life in Fort Atkinson, Wisconsin, where she worked part-time as a custodian of the local library and hospital. When she attended Beloit College for a time in the early 1930s, she received great encouragement from the poet Louis Za-kofsky, who served her as informal agent long afterwards. Her collections of poetry include: *From this Condensory: the Complete Poems of Lorine Niedecker* (1985); *The Granite Pale* (1985); and *T & G* (1968), which stands for both "tenderness and gristle" and "tongue and groove."

CRAIG NOVA ("Another Drunk Gambler") is the author of six novels, most recently *Tornado Alley* (1989). He has been the recipient of many prizes and awards, including a Guggenheim Fellowship, the Harper-Saxton Prize, and an award in literature from the American Academy and Institute of Arts and Letters.

FRANK O'HARA'S (1926–1966) ("A True Account of Talking to the Sun at Fire Island"; "A Renaissance Portrait of the Author") posthumously published works include *Selected Poems* (1974), *Selected Plays* (1978), and *Poems Retrieved* (1977).

SHARON OLDS ("I Cannot Forget the Woman in the Mirror") is completing a fourth book of poems, *The Father*. She is currently director of creative writing at New York University. She teaches a graduate poetry workshop there, and a writing workshop at Goldwater Hospital on Roosevelt Island.

CHARLES OLSON (1910–1970) ("Maximus from Dogtown-II") was born in Worcester, Massachusetts. His books include *Projective Verse* (1950), *Archeologist of Morning* (1970), and *The Maximus Poems* (published from 1953 to 1976), from which the selection was taken.

ROBERT PACK ("Birthday") is the Donald Axinn Professor of Literature at Middlebury College and director of the Bread Loaf Writers' Conference. He has published ten books of poetry. His most recent book is *Before It Vanishes* (1989).

RON PADGETT'S ("Big Bluejay Composition") recent books include *Among the Blacks* (1988), with Raymond Russell, a memoir and translation; and a translation of Guillaume Apollinaire's *The Poet Assassinated and Other Stories*. In 1986 he received a Guggenheim fellowship for poetry. He is currently translating the complete poetry of Blaise Cendrars and editing books for Teachers and Writers Collaborative.

PETER PAYACK ("Motorcycle Evolution") was published in the *Paris Review* in 1974. His books of poetry include *The Evolution of Death* (1977), *Rainbow Bridges* (1978), and *No Free Will in Tomatoes* (1988).

MOLLY PEACOCK ("The Breach of *Or*") is the author of *Take Heart* (1989), *Raw Heaven* (1984), and *And Live Apart* (1980). She is president of the Poetry Society of America.

DEBORAH PEASE ("Geography Lesson") has been the publisher of the *Paris Review* since 1982. Her most recent poems have appeared in *Ploughshares, Grand Street, Chelsea, North American Review,* and *Antioch Review.*

GEORGES PEREC (1936–1982) ("Between Sleep and Waking"), a French novelist, found fame in the United States after his death, with the 1987 translation of his *Life: A User's Manual,* which won the prestigious Medici Prize. He won the Prix Renaudot for his first novel *Les Choses* in 1956. Other works include *W: Or the Memory of a Childhood* (translated 1988) and *La Disparition,* a novel composed entirely without the letter 'e', a translation of which is forthcoming.

GRAHAM PETRIE ("The Locust Keeper") was born in Malaysia, of Scottish parents, and educated in Malaysia, Scotland, and at Oxford University. He has lived and worked in Canada since 1964. His published writing includes a novel, *Seahorse* (1980), over twenty short stories in British and American magazines, and three books of film criticism. He has recently completed a second novel and is working on a book on the Soviet film director Andrei Tarkovsky.

JIM POWELL'S ("Heat") first collection of poetry, *It Was Fever That Made the World* has just been published by the University of Chicago Press. He is writer-in-residence at Reed College.

CARL RAKOSI ("The Founding of New Hampshire") was born in Berlin in 1903 and has lived much of his life in San Francisco, working as a psychotherapist and social worker. The National Poetry Association gave him the Distinguished Lifetime Achievement Award in 1988. His books include *Spiritus, I* (1983), *Collected Prose* (1983), and *Collected Poetry* (1986).

KENNETH REXROTH'S ("Three Japanese Woman Poets") *New Poems* received the Copernicus Award from the American Academy of Arts and Letters in 1976. **Lady Ise** was a ninth-century poet and the concubine of Emperor Uda. **Princess Nukada** lived in the seventh century and is considered the greatest woman poet of the Omi period. **Hatsui Shizue** was born in 1900 and studied with Kitahara Hakushu, a leading poet of the early twentieth century.

ADRIENNE RICH ("Recorders in Italy"; "End of an Era") has published fourteen volumes of poetry, most recently *Time's Power: Poems 1985–1988,* and three books of nonfiction prose. She was recently awarded the Ruth Lilly Prize for distinguished achievement in American poetry, and the Brandeis Creative Arts Commission Medal in Poetry. She lives in California and teaches at Stanford.

MORDECAI RICHLER'S ("A Liberal Education") novels include *The Apprentice-ship of Duddy Kravitz, Cocksure, St. Urbain's Horseman,* and *Joshua Then and Now.* His new novel, *Solomon Gursky Was Here,* will be published in 1990. Richler lives in Montreal. The selection won the *Paris Review*'s John Train Humor Prize.

PHILIP ROTH ("The Conversion of the Jews") won the National Book Award for *Goodbye, Columbus* (1959) and the National Book Critics Circle Award for *The Counterlife* (1987). His first appearance in the *Paris Review* (with this selection) occurred when he was twenty-five years old. He is currently Distin-guished Professor of English at Hunter College in New York City. His most recent book, a near-autobiography, is *The Facts* (1988).

JUDITH C. ROOT'S ("To Pose a Chicken") first full-length collection of poems, *Weaving the Sheets* (1985), was recently reprinted by Carnegie Mellon Univer-sity Press. She is currently teaching at California State University at Long Beach.

NORMAN RUSH'S ("Instruments of Seduction") stories have appeared in *The New Yorker,* the *Paris Review,* and *Best American Short Stories of 1983.* Much of the selection was collected in *Whites* (1985). Rush and his wife lived in Africa from 1978 to 1983.

RAY RUSSELL ("Evil Star") is the author of six novels, most recently, *Dirty Money* (1988). He has also written eight books of short stories, a volume of poems, and several screenplays and is a recipient of the Sri Chinmoy Poetry Award. He was *Playboy* magazine's first executive editor.

IRA SADOFF ("Seurat") is the author of *Settling Down* (1975) and *Palm Read-ing in Winter* (1978).

JAMES SALTER ("Am Strande von Tanger") is the author of five novels including *Light Years, Solo Faces,* and *A Sport and a Pastime* (Paris Review Editions). His short story collection, *Dusk,* won the 1989 PEN/Faulkner Award. "Am Strande von Tanger" was his first published story.

ED SANDERS'S ("Poem") recent books include *Fame and Love in New York* and *Twenty Thousand AD.*

ARAM SAROYAN'S ("Poem") books include *Trio: Oona Chaplin/Carol Mat-thau/Gloria Vanderbilt—Portrait of an Intimate Friendship* and *The Romantic,* a novel.

JAMES SCHUYLER ("Buried at Springs"), who received the Pulitzer Prize for his collection *The Morning of the Poem,* published his *Selected Poems* in 1988.

FREDERICK SEIDEL ("Flame") is the author of the poetry collection *Sunrise* (1980), for which he received the National Book Critics Circle Award and the Lamont Prize. His most recent books are *Poems 1959–1979* and *These Days.* He lives in New York City and is an advisory editor of the *Paris Review.*

ANNE SEXTON (1928–1974) ("The Poet of Ignorance"; "Two Hands") died on October 4, 1974. She sent the following contributor's note to the *Paris Review*, dated July 29, 1974: "A contributor's note? *The Awful Roaming Towards God* will be my eighth book and all are in print in paperback (small ad). I am forty-five, divorced and living in Weston, Massachusetts, Professor of Creative Writing at Boston University . . . if you can add to this, it would be fine with me. For instance, you can say I live in Weston with my two dalmatians."

ROBERT SHACOCHIS ("Stolen Kiss") was the recipient of a 1982 grant from the National Endowment for the Arts. He is the author of two short story collections, *Easy in the Islands* (1984) and *The Next New World* (1989).

CHARLES SIMIC's ("The System") thirteenth book of poems, *The World Doesn't End*, was published in 1989. His other books include *The Selected Poems 1963–1983, Unending Blues,* and many volumes of translation of Yugoslav poetry. He is the recipient of various awards, including the MacArthur Fellowship in 1984.

JAMES SIMMONS ("Me and the World") lives in Northern Ireland and writes, in addition to poetry, ballads and songs, some of which he has sung in cabarets and on television.

LOUIS SIMPSON ("The Battle"; "Lines Written Near San Francisco"; "The Rejected") recently published his *Collected Poems* and *Selected Prose.* He received the Elmer Holmes Bobst Award for poetry in 1987. A new book of poems, *In the Room We Share,* is forthcoming in 1990. He is currently working on a book of prose. He teaches at the State University of New York at Stony Brook and lives with his wife Miriam in Setauket, New York.

MONA SIMPSON ("You Leave Them") was senior editor of the *Paris Review.* She is the author of *Anywhere But Here,* for which she won the Whiting Writing Award, and is the recipient of Guggenheim and National Endowment for the Arts Fellowships.

W. D. SNODGRASS ("The Campus on the Hill") is a writer and educator and has taught at Cornell University, the University of Rochester, Wayne State University, and Syracuse University. He has contributed essays, poems, and translations to the *Paris Review, Botteghe Oscure, The Partisan Review,* and others.

GARY SNYDER ("Hop, Skip, and Jump") is the author of *The Real Work* (1980), *True Night* (1980), *Left out in the Rain* (1986), *Axe Handles* (1983), and *Passage through India* (1984). He was awarded the Bollingen Prize in 1964, the Poetry Award for the National Institute of Arts and Letters in 1966, the Pulitzer Prize for Poetry in 1975, and the Guggenheim fellowship in 1968. He spent several years in Japan, and now teaches occasionally at the University of California at Davis.

TERRY SOUTHERN ("The Sun and the Still-Born Stars") has published stories in the *Paris Review* since its first issue. He is the author of several screenplays, including *Dr. Strangelove* (1958) and *Easy Rider* (1968), both of which were nominated for Academy Awards.

WILLIAM STAFFORD ("What God Used for Eyes Before We Came"; "A Private Person") taught for many years at Lewis and Clark College in Portland, Oregon. His recent books include *You Must Revise Your Life* and *An Oregon Message.* His work has appeared in many magazines, including *The American Scholar.* He lives and enjoys active retirement in Oregon.

ALBERT STAINTON ("The Man with the Lepidoptera on His Ass") is co-editor of *Bartleby's Review.* His work has been published in many magazines, including *Truck, Epoch,* and *Poetry Now.* He is the author, with Rita Stainton, of *The Crossing: Poems* (1974).

GEORGE STEINER ("A Samurai Who Tried to Kill All the Roosters in Japan") was born in Paris in 1929. He is a professor of English and comparative literature at the University of Geneva, and has earned the distinction of Extraordinary Fellow of Churchill College. He is a writer of fiction, philosophic, and literary-critical works, and his fifteen books have been translated into twelve languages.

GERALD STERN'S ("Straus Park") most recently published books are *Lovesick* and *Selected Poems* (1990). "Bread without Sugar," a long poem, was published in *The Georgia Review.* He teaches in the writing program at the University of Iowa.

ANN STEVENSON ("Television") is an American poet long resident in Great Britain. Her recent publications include *Selected Poems, 1956–1986* and *Bitter Fame,* a biography of Sylvia Plath. She has been Arts Fellow at Lady Margaret Hall, Oxford, Northern Arts Literary Fellow at Newcastle, and Durham University's writer-in-residence at Edinburgh University in Scotland. Forthcoming in 1990 is *Journals and Verses: Poems, 1986–1989.*

MARY KATHRYN STILLWELL ("Travel Plans") was born in Omaha, Nebraska, and raised there on a farm outside Falls City, Nebraska. Her poetry has appeared in the *Paris Review* and many other literary magazines. *Moving to Malibu,* a full-length collection of poems, was published as part of the Plains Poetry Series. She now lives on Long Island, where she is university director of communications and marketing at Long Island University, and teaches a poetry writing workshop at the C. W. Post campus.

PATRICIA STORACE ("Still Life") is an assistant editor at *The New York Review of Books* and poetry editor at the *Paris Review.* Her first book, *Heredity* (1987), was the first winner of the Barnard New Women Poets Prize. Recent work has appeared in *Spazio Umano, The New York Review of Books,* and *The Best American Poetry 1989.*

WILLIAM STYRON ("Letter to an Editor") is the author of several novels, including *Sophie's Choice* and *The Confessions of Nat Turner,* for which he was awarded the Pulitzer Prize in 1968 and the Howell's Medal of the American

Academy of Arts and Letters in 1970. He edited *The Best Stories from the Paris Review* (1958) and has served as advisory editor to the *Paris Review* since 1953.

LORENZO THOMAS ("Displacement") was born in the Republic of Panama and attended public schools in New York City and Queens College of the City University of New York. His collections of poetry include *Chances Are Few* (1979) and *The Bathers* (1981). He has been the recipient of many awards including the Creative Writing Fellowship of the National Endowment of the Arts. He teaches literature at the University of Houston-Downtown.

CHARLES TOMLINSON ("Distinctions") is an English painter and poet. His verse has appeared extensively in England and the United States. He is the author of several books of poetry and edited *The Oxford Book of Verse in English Translation*.

JOHN UPDIKE ("Dutch Cleanser") has published over twenty books, including ten novels and four collections of poetry. His most recent books are *S.*, an epistolary novel; *Self-Consciousness*, his memoirs; and *Just Looking*, a collection of essays on art. Among his many awards are the Rosenthal award of the National Institute of Arts and Letters (1960) and The O. Henry Prize Story award (1967). He is a member of The National Institute of Arts and Letters and The American Academy of Arts and Sciences.

DAVID WAGONER ("The Junior High School Band Concert") has published fifteen books of poetry and ten novels. He is a professor of English at the University of Washington and the editor of *Poetry Northwest*.

ANNE WALDMAN ("Warming Up") is the author of over twenty books and pamphlets of poetry including, most recently, *Helping The Dreamer: New & Selected Poems 1966–88*. She is the editor of *In & Out of this World*, an anthology of writing from The St. Mark's Poetry Project. She is a former director of The Poetry Project and co-founded The Jack Kerouac School of Disembodied Poetics at the Naropa Institute.

ELLIS WEINER ("Errata") has written for many periodicals as well as for television, stage, and film. He is the author of *Decade of the Year* and writes for *Spy* magazine.

PAUL WEST'S ("Captain Ahab: A Novel by the White Whale") three most recent novels are *Rat Man of Paris, The Place in Flowers Where Pollen Rests,* and *Lord Byron's Doctor*. He was the recipient of the *Paris Review*'s Aga Khan Fiction Prize in 1973 and won the Award in Literature from the American Academy and Institute of Arts and Letters in 1985. His next novel will be about Jack the Ripper. He has been a Guggenheim Fellow, an NEA Fellow in Fiction, and was made a "Literary Lion" of the New York Public Library in 1987.

EDMUND WHITE ("The Secret Order of Joy) is the author of *A Boy's Own Story;* the selection is a chapter from that book. He was recently named associate professor at Brown University. His next book will be a biography of Jean Genet, to be published by Alfred A. Knopf.

DALLAS WIEBE'S ("Night Flight to Stockholm") most recent book, *Going to the Mountain* (1988), is a collection of short stories. He is also the author of a novel, *Skyblue the Badass* (Paris Review Editions, 1969), and a collection of poems, *The Kansas Poems* (1987). He was born and grew up in Newton, Kansas. "Night Flight to Stockholm" won the *Paris Review*'s Aga Khan Fiction Award in 1978. Many of the names and places in it were taken from K. M. Brigg's Book, *The Anatomy of Puck* (London, 1959).

JOHN WIENERS'S ("The Spoiled Son") most recent books are *She'd Turn on a Dime* and *O! Khan Collar with Tong Tie.*

RICHARD WILBUR ("Piccola Commedia") was born in New York City in 1921. He has received many awards, among them a Pulitzer Prize and the Prix de Rome, and has been a Guggenheim Fellow.

C. K. WILLIAMS'S ("From My Window") *Flesh and Blood* won the National Book Critics Circle Award in 1987 for his poetry collection, *Flesh and Blood.* He was awarded the Morton Dauwen Zabel prize from the American Academy and Institute of Arts and Letters in 1989. He teaches at George Mason University in Virginia. His next book, *The Baccae of Euripides,* a play reworking Euripides's tragedy, is forthcoming in 1990. Other books include *Tar* (1983) and *Poems 1963–1983* (1988).

JOY WILLIAMS ("Making Friends") has written two collections of stories, *Taking Care* and *Escapes,* and three novels, including *State of Grace* (Paris Review Editions/Doubleday, 1974), which was nominated for a National Book Award. Her most recent novel is *Breaking and Entering.* Her stories have appeared in the *Paris Review* and *Esquire* and have frequently been collected in prize story anthologies and teaching texts. She teaches writing at the University of Arizona.

BARON WORMSER ("Good Trembling") has published three books of poetry: *The White Words, Good Trembling,* and *Atoms, Soul Music and Other Poems* (Paris Review Editions, 1989). He lives with his family in rural Maine.

CHARLES WRIGHT ("Laguna Blues") lives in Charlottesville, Virginia and teaches at the University of Virginia. In 1983 he was co-winner with Galway Kinnell of the American Book Award in Poetry for *Country Music/Selected Early Poems.* His latest book of poems, *Zone Journals,* was published in 1988. *Halflife,* a book of interviews and improvisations, also appeared in 1988. In 1987, Wright was awarded the Citation in Poetry by Brandeis University Creative Arts Awards.

JAMES WRIGHT (1927–1980) ("Lying in a Hammock at a Friend's Farm in Pine Island, Minnesota"; "To a Friend Condemned to Prison"; "Entering The Kingdom Of The Moray Eel"), was a professor of English at Hunter College in New York and a translator of Pablo Neruda, among other poets. He was born in

Martin's Ferry, Ohio, and received degrees from Kenyon College and the University of Washington. His books of poetry include *The Green Wall* (1957), *Moments of the Italian Summer* (1976), and the posthumously published *This Journey* (1982), from which "Entering The Kingdom Of The Moray Eel" is selected. He won the Pulizer Prize in 1972 for his *Collected Poems* (1971).

LILA ZEIGER (L. L. ZEIGER) ("Misconceptions") has published poems in many magazines and is the author of *The Way to Castle Garden* (1982). She has been the recipient of the Coordinating Council of Literary Magazines's Fels Award, for poetry published in the *Paris Review;* as well as a New York State CAPS Grant in Poetry, and several MacDowell fellowships and awards from The Poetry Society of America. The selection was her first published poem.

Acknowledgments

DIANE ACKERMAN: "Still Life" reprinted by permission of the author.

BOBBY ANDERSEN: "Edie Sedgwick: A Reminiscence" reprinted by permission of the author.

GUILLAUME APOLLINAIRE: "Mirabeau Bridge." Copyright © Richard Wilbur.

NATHAN ASCH: "The Nineteen-Twenties: An Interior." Courtesy of Winthrop College Archives.

JOHN ASHBERY: "The Bungalows" reprinted from THE DOUBLE DREAM OF SPRING (Ecco Press) with the permission of the author. Copyright © by John Ashbery, 1976.

JOHN ASHBERY: "This Configuration" reprinted by permission of the author.

INGEBORG BACHMANN: "Autumn Maneuver" reprinted by permission of the author.

PAULÉ BARTÓN: "The Bee Dice Game" reprinted by permission of the estate of the author.

PAULÉ BARTÓN: "The Sleep Bus" reprinted by permission of the estate of the author.

RICK BASS: "Wild Horses" appeared originally in *The Paris Review* and is reprinted from THE WATCH, Stories by Rick Bass, with the permission of the author and W. W. Norton & Company, Inc. Copyright © 1989 by Rick Bass.

GLEN BAXTER: "It Was The Smallest Pizza They Had Ever Seen" reprinted by permission of the author.

SAMUEL BECKETT: "Extract from *Molloy*" reprinted by permission of the author.

MICHAEL BENEDIKT: "The Badminton at Great Barrington," by Michael Benedikt, originally appeared in *The Paris Review*, #71, 1977. Copyright © 1980 by Michael Benedikt. From THE BADMINTON AT GREAT BARRINGTON: OR, GUSTAVE MAHLER & THE CHATTANOOGA CHOO-CHOO, University of Pittsburgh Press, 1980.

TED BERRIGAN: "The Fiend" reprinted by permission of the author.

ROBERT BLY: "Two Choral Stanzas." Copyright © 1951. Reprinted by permission of Robert Bly.

ROBERT BLY: "Two Translations from the Kabir" reprinted from THE KABIR BOOK, revisions by Robert Bly, Beacon Press, Boston, 1977. Copyright © 1977 by Robert Bly. Reprinted by permission.

PHILIP BOOTH: "Seadog and Seal" reprinted by permission of the author.

JORGE LUIS BORGES: "Funes the Memorious" reprinted by arrangement with the Estate of Jorge Luis Borges and Emece Editores.

T. CORAGHESSAN BOYLE: "Ike and Nina" from GREASY LAKE AND OTHER STORIES by T. Coraghessan Boyle. Copyright © 1982 by T. Coraghessan Boyle. Reprinted by permission of Viking Penguin, a division of Penguin Books USA, Inc.

RICHARD BRAUTIGAN: "The San Francisco Weather Report." Copyright © 1963 by Richard Brautigan. Reprinted by permission of the Helen Brann Agency, Inc.

KATE ELLEN BRAVERMAN: "Classified Ad" reprinted by permission of the author.

DONALD BRITTON: "Virgule" reprinted by permission of the author.

HAROLD BRODKEY: "To Frank O'Hara" reprinted by permission of the author.

JOSEPH BRODSKY: "To Urania" reprinted by permission of the author.

JOSEPH BRUCHAC: "The Hitchhiker" reprinted by permission of the author.

ITALO CALVINO: "Last Comes the Raven" reprinted by permission of the author.

JAMES CAMP: "Brief History of the Confederate Aristocracy" reprinted by permission of the author.

JIM CARROLL: "Heroin" reprinted from LIVING AT THE MOVIES (Viking-Penguin Books, New York, New York). Copyright © Jim Carroll, 1967.

RAYMOND CARVER: "Why Don't You Dance?" reprinted by permission of Tess Gallagher for the Estate of Raymond Carver.

SIV CEDERING: "Peaches." Copyright © Siv Cedering, from MOTHER IS, 1975, Stein & Day.

LOUIS-FERDINAND CÉLINE: "A Screen Version of *Journey to the End of Night*" reprinted by permission.

G. S. SHARAT CHANDRA: "Rape of Lucrece Retold" reprinted by permission of the author.

FRED CHAPPELL: "Tiros II" by Fred Chappell.

ROZ CHAST: "Great Moments in Literature" reprinted by permission of the author.

MAXINE CHERNOFF: "Hats Around the World." UTOPIA TV STORE (Yellow Press, 1979). Copyright © 1979, Maxine Chernoff. All rights reserved.

TOM CLARK: "Superballs." Copyright © Tom Clark, 1969.

NANCY CONDEE: "In the Late Afternoon . . ." reprinted by permission of the author.

EVAN S. CONNELL: "The Beau Monde of Mrs. Bridge" reprinted by permission of the author.

CLARK COOLIDGE: "Bee Elk." Copyright © 1970 by Clark Coolidge.

ALFRED CORN: "One to One." Copyright © 1980 by Viking Penguin, Inc.

JULIO CORTÁZAR: "Feuilletons from A Certain Lucas" reprinted by permission of the author.

HENRI COULETTE: "The Blue-Eyed Precinct Worker" reprinted by permission of the estate of the author.

ROBERT CREELEY: "The Finger" reprinted by permission of the author.

EDWIN DENBY: "Sonnet" reprinted by permission of Edwin Denby.

JAMES DICKEY: "Mindoro, 1944" reprinted by permission of the author.

THOMAS M. DISCH: "The Joycelin Shrager Story." Copyright © 1975 by Thomas M. Disch.

STEPHEN DIXON: "Goodbye to Goodbye" was published in TIME TO GO, Johns Hopkins University Press, 1985.

EDWARD DORN: "The Poet Lets His Tongue Hang Down" reprinted by permission of Edward Dorn.

ANDRE DUBUS: "Waiting" also appeared in FINDING A GIRL IN AMERICA by Andre Dubus, published by David R. Godine, 1980.

ROBERT DUNCAN: "Lammas Dream Poem" reprinted by permission of the author.

STANLEY ELKIN: "The Guest." Copyright © Stanley Elkin, 1966.

BETTY EPPES: "What I Did Last Summer" reprinted by permission of the author.

WILLIAM FERGUSON: "A Summer at Estabrook." Copyright © 1982 by William Ferguson.

DAVID FERRY: "On the Way to the Island" reprinted courtesy of Wesleyan University Press, 1960.

JONATHAN GALASSI: "Lateness" reprinted by permission of the author.

EUGENE K. GARBER: "Flight" reprinted by permission of Eugene K. Garber.

WILLIAM GASS: "Summer Bees" reprinted by permission of William Gass.

GARY GILDNER: "The Runner," by Gary Gildner, from BLUE LIKE THE HEAVENS: NEW & SELECTED POEMS (University of Pittsburgh Press). Copyright © 1984 by Gary Gildner.

PENELOPE GILLIATT: "Gossip." Penelope Gilliatt, copyright © 1986.

ALLEN GINSBERG: "City Midnight Junk Strains" from COLLECTED POEMS 1947–1980 by Allen Ginsberg. Copyright © 1966 by Allen Ginsberg. Reprinted by permission of Harper & Row, Publishers, Inc.

LINDA GREGG: "Taken By Each Thing." ALMA (Random House, 1985).

ALLEN GROSSMAN: "Holy Ghost Hospital" is reprinted by permission of Allen Grossman.

ALLEN GROSSMAN: "The Woman on the Bridge over the Chicago River" is reprinted by permission of New Directions.

THOM GUNN: "The Wound" reprinted by permission of the author.

SHUSHA GUPPY: "Lady Diana Cooper" reprinted by permission of Shusha Guppy.

DONALD HALL: "Sleeping." Copyright © Donald Hall.

SEAMUS HEANEY: "Leavings" reprinted by permission of the author.

JOHN HEATH-STUBBS: "The Peacock and the Snake" reprinted by permission of the author.

GEOFFREY HILL: "Genesis" reprinted by permission of the author.

GEOFFREY HILL: "A Prayer to the Sun" reprinted by permission of the author.

RICHARD HOWARD: "On Tour" reprinted by permission of the author.

TED HUGHES: "Crow Hill" reprinted by permission of Faber and Faber from LUPERCAL By Ted Hughes.

SIRI HUSTVEDT: "Weather Markings" reprinted by permission of the author.

LEROI JONES: "Tele/vision" reprinted by permission of Sterling Lord Literistic, Inc. Copyright © 1969 by LeRoi Jones (Amiri Baraka).

ERICA JONG: "Jubilate Canis" reprinted by permission of the author.

DONALD JUSTICE: "Last Days of Prospero." Copyright © 1967, Donald Justice.

DONALD JUSTICE: "Sestina." Copyright © 1960, Donald Justice.

BERNARD KEITH: "Essay on Meter" reprinted by permission of the author.

DAVID KELLEY: "Counting a Decade." Copyright © 1979, David M. Kelley.

X. J. KENNEDY: "In a Prominent Bar in Secaucus One Day" from CROSS TIES: SELECTED POEMS. Reprinted by permission of the author and The University of Georgia Press. Copyright © 1985 by X. J. Kennedy.

GALWAY KINNELL: "The Milk Bottle" from MORTAL ACT, MORTAL WORDS, Houghton Mifflin Co., 1985. Copyright © by Galway Kinnell.

BILL KNOTT: "Lesson" reprinted by permission of the author.

KENNETH KOCH: "The Interpretation of Dreams." Copyright © 1969 by Kenneth Koch.

JOHN KOETHE: "Picture of Little Letters." This poem was published in book form in THE LATE WISCONSIN SPRING, copyright © 1984, Princeton University Press.

MAXINE KUMIN: "Another Form of Marriage" from WHY CAN'T WE LIVE LIKE CIVILIZED HUMAN BEINGS? by Maxine Kumin. Copyright © 1976 by Maxine Kumin. Reprinted by permission of Viking Penguin, a division of Penguin Books USA, Inc.

PHILIP LARKIN: "Referred Back" reprinted by permission of the author.

JAMES LASDUN: "Picture of a Girl" reprinted by permission of the author.

ANN LAUTERBACH: "Naming the House" reprinted by permission of the author.

DAVID LEHMAN: "Fear and Trembling." Copyright © 1976 by David Lehman. All rights reserved. Reprinted by permission of the poet.

PHILIP LEVINE: "The Turning." Copyright © Philip Levine, from ON THE EDGE, The Stone Wall Press, 1963.

JOHN LOGAN: "The Mallard's Going" reprinted by permission of the John Logan Literary Estate, Inc.

THOMAS LUX: "Sleepmask" by Thomas Lux.

GEORGE MACBETH: "Eating Ice-Cream with a Girl" reprinted by permission of the author.

EVERETTE H. MADDOX: "Thirteen Ways of Being Looked at by a Possum" reprinted by permission of the estate of the author.

ANDRÉ PIEYRE DE MANDIARGUES: "The Bath of Madame Mauriac" reprinted by permission of John Calder (Publishers) Ltd., London.

HEATHER MCHUGH: "To the Quick" appeared in an eponymous collection of poems published by Wesleyan University Press in 1987.

JAY MCINERNEY: "It's Six AM Do You Know Where You Are?" reprinted by permission of the author.

JAMES MERRILL: "Grass" from LATE SETTINGS, Atheneum, 1985. Copyright © James Merrill.

W. S. MERWIN: "Demonstration." Copyright by W. S. Merwin.

W. S. MERWIN: "Marica Lart" was originally published by Atheneum. Copyright © by W. S. Merwin.

W. S. MERWIN: "Sow." Copyright © by W. S. Merwin.

ROBERT MEZEY: "In the Environs of the Funeral Home" reprinted by permission of the author.

LEONARD MICHAELS: "City Boy" from GOING PLACES, Farrar, Straus & Giroux, 1969.

CHRISTOPHER MIDDLETON: "News from Norwood" reprinted by permission of the author.

VASSAR MILLER: "Love Song for the Future" reprinted by permission of the author.

CZESLAW MILOSZ: "My Faithful Mother Tongue." Czeslaw Milosz, COLLECTED POEMS, Ecco Press (New York), 1988.

SUSAN MINOT: "Lust" from LUST AND OTHER STORIES by Susan Minot. Copyright © 1989 by Susan Minot. Reprinted by permission of Houghton Mifflin Company/Seymour Lawrence.

HERBERT MORRIS: "Newport, 1930" has appeared in PERU, published by Harper & Row, 1983.

LORINE NIEDECKER: "Who Was Mary Shelley." Copyright © Cid Corman, literary executor of Lorine Niedecker estate.

CRAIG NOVA: "Another Drunk Gambler" reprinted by permission of the author.

FRANK O'HARA: "A Renaissance Portrait of the Author" reprinted by permission of the estate of the author.

FRANK O'HARA: "A True Account of Talking to the Sun at Fire Island." Copyright © 1968 by Maureen Granville-Smith, Administratix of the Estate of Frank O'Hara. Reprinted from THE COLLECTED POEMS OF FRANK O'HARA, edited by Donald Allen, by permission of Alfred A. Knopf, Inc.

SHARON OLDS: "I Cannot Forget the Woman in the Mirror" from THE GOLD CELL, A. A. Knopf, 1987.

CHARLES OLSON: "Maximus from Dogtown" reprinted from the Estate of Charles Olson, Homer Babbidge Library, University of Connecticut.

ROBERT PACK: "Birthday" reprinted by permission of the author.

RON PADGETT: "Big Bluejay Composition." Copyright © 1974, 1976 by Ron Padgett, reprinted by permission of the author and SUN Press.

PETER PAYACK: "Motorcycle Evolution" reprinted courtesy of Peter Payack.

MOLLY PEACOCK: "The Breach of *Or*" from RAW HEAVEN is reprinted by permission of the author.

DEBORAH PEASE: "Geography Lesson" reprinted by permission of the author.

GEORGES PEREC: "Between Sleep and Waking." With permission of the executors of the estate of Georges Perec.

GRAHAM PETRIE: "The Locust Keeper." Copyright © Graham Petrie.

GEORGE PLIMPTON: "Vali" reprinted by permission of the author.

JIM POWELL: "Heat" by Jim Powell from IT WAS FEVER THAT MADE THE WORLD, Chicago, University of Chicago Press, 1989.

CARL RAKOSI: "The Founding of New Hampshire" reprinted by permission of the author.

KENNETH REXROTH: "Three Poems." Copyright © by Kenneth Rexroth. Reprinted by permission of the Kenneth Rexroth Trust.

ADRIENNE RICH: "End of an Era" from SNAPSHOTS OF A DAUGHTER-IN-LAW, Poems by Adrienne Rich, is reprinted with the permission of the author and the publisher, W.W. Norton & Company, Inc. Copyright © 1956, 1957, 1958, 1959, 1960, 1961, 1962, 1963, 1967 by Adrienne Rich Conrad.

MORDECAI RICHLER: "A Liberal Education." Excerpt from COCKSURE, Copyright © Mordecai Richler.

JUDITH C. ROOT: "To Pose a Chicken" reprinted by permission of the author.

PHILIP ROTH: "The Conversion of the Jews" reprinted by permission of the author.

NORMAN RUSH: "Instruments of Seduction" reprinted by permission of Norman Rush.

RAY RUSSELL: "Evil Star." Copyright © 1976 by Ray Russell. Reprinted by permission of the author.

IRA SADOFF: "Seurat" reprinted by permission of the author.

JAMES SALTER: "Am Strande von Tanger" reprinted by permission of the author.

ED SANDERS: "Poem" reprinted by permission of the author.

ARAM SAROYAN: "Poem" reprinted by permission of the author. Copyright © 1986 by Aram Saroyan. From POEMS (Blackberry Books).

JAMES SCHUYLER: "Buried at Springs." Copyright © James Schuyler.

FREDERICK SEIDEL: "Flame." Copyright © by Frederick Seidel.

ANNE SEXTON: "The Poet of Ignorance" reprinted by permission of the author.

ANNE SEXTON: "Two Hands" reprinted by permission of the author.

ROBERT SHACOCHIS: "Stolen Kiss" reprinted from THE NEXT NEW WORLD, Crown Publishers, 1989.

CHARLES SIMIC: "The System." Copyright © Charles Simic, 1974.

JAMES SIMMONS: "Me and the World" reprinted by permission of the author.

LOUIS SIMPSON: "The Battle" reprinted by permission of Louis Simpson.

LOUIS SIMPSON: "Lines Written Near San Francisco." Copyright © 1963 by Louis Simpson. Reprinted from AT THE END OF THE OPEN ROAD by permission of Wesleyan University Press.

LOUIS SIMPSON: "The Rejected" by Louis Simpson from SEARCHING FOR THE OX by Louis Simpson. Copyright © 1975 by Louis Simpson. By permission of William Morrow and Company, Inc.

MONA SIMPSON: "You Leave Them" reprinted by permission of the author.

W. D. SNODGRASS: "The Campus on the Hill" reprinted by permission of the author.

GARY SNYDER: "Hop, Skip, & Jump" reprinted by permission of the author.

TERRY SOUTHERN: "The Sun and the Still-Born Stars" reprinted by permission of the author.

WILLIAM STAFFORD: "A Private Person" reprinted by permission of the author.

WILLIAM STAFFORD: "What God Used for Eyes Before We Came" from STORIES THAT COULD BE TRUE by William Stafford. Copyright © 1960 by William Stafford. Reprinted by permission of Harper & Row, Publishers, Inc.

ALBERT STAINTON: "The Man with the Lepidoptera on His Ass" reprinted by permission of the author.

GEORGE STEINER: "A Samurai Who Tried to Kill All the Roosters in Japan." Copyright © George Steiner.

GERALD STERN: "Straus Park." Published in LUCKY LIFE, Houghton Mifflin.

ANNE STEVENSON: "Television" reprinted from SELECTED POEMS, 1956–1986, Oxford University Press.

MARY KATHRYN STILLWELL: "Travel Plans" reprinted by permission of the author.

PATRICIA STORACE: "Still Life" reprinted by permission of the author.

WILLIAM STYRON: "Letter to an Editor" reprinted by permission of the author.

LORENZO THOMAS: "Displacement." Copyright © by Lorenzo Thomas. Reprinted by permission of the author.

CHARLES TOMLINSON: "Distinctions" reprinted by permission of the author.

JOHN UPDIKE: "Dutch Cleanser" from TOSSING AND TURNING By John Updike. Copyright © 1977 by John Updike. Reprinted by permission of Alfred A. Knopf, Inc.

DAVID WAGONER: "The Junior High School Band Concert." Copyright © by David Wagoner.

ANNE WALDMAN: "Warming Up." Copyright © 1970. Used by permission of the author.

ELLIS WEINER: "Errata" reprinted by permission of Ellis Weiner.

PAUL WEST: "Captain Ahab." Copyright © by Paul West.

EDMUND WHITE: "The Secret Order of Joy" reprinted by permission of the author.

DALLAS WIEBE: "Night Flight to Stockholm" first published in *PARIS REVIEW*, 73 (Spring-Summer, 1978).

JOHN WIENERS: "The Spoiled Son" reprinted by permission of the author.

RICHARD WILBUR: "Piccola Commedia." Copyright © Richard Wilbur.

C. K. WILLIAMS: "From My Window" from POEMS, 1963–1983 by C. K. Williams. Copyright © 1983, 1988 by C. K. Williams. Reprinted by permission of Farrar, Straus and Giroux, Inc.

JOY WILLIAMS: "Making Friends" reprinted by permission of Joy Williams.

BARON WORMSER: "Good Trembling." Houghton Mifflin Co., copyright © 1985.

CHARLES WRIGHT: "Laguna Blues" from THE SOUTHERN CROSS, Random House.

JAMES WRIGHT: "Entering The Kingdom Of The Moray Eel" reprinted by permission of the author.

JAMES WRIGHT: "Lying in a Hammock at a Friend's Farm in Pine Island, Minnesota" reprinted by permission of the author.

JAMES WRIGHT: "To a Friend Condemned to Prison" reprinted by permission of the author.

L. L. ZEIGER: "Misconceptions" reprinted by permission of Lila Zeiger (L. L. Zeiger).